BASICS OF

MARKETING MANAGEMENT

THEORY AND PRACTICE

BASICS OF MARKETING MANAGEMENT

THEORY AND PRACTICE

For the Students of BBA, BBM, B.Com., MBA, MBM, M.Com., and Other Undergraduate, Postgraduate, Diploma and Technical Courses of Different Indian Universities

Dr. R.B. RUDANI

BBA, DCS, M.Com. (Management), Ph.D.(Management)

Associate Professor, Business Management
N.R. Vekaria Institute of Business Management Studies
Commerce College Campus, Bilkha Road
Junagadh, Gujarat

S Chand And Company Limited

(ISO 9001 Certified Company)

S Chand And Company Limited

(ISO 9001 Certified Company)

Head Office: D-92, Sector–2, Noida – 201301, U.P. (India), Ph. 91-120-4682700

Registered Office: A-27, 2nd Floor, Mohan Co-operative Industrial Estate, New Delhi – 110 044, Phone: 011-49731800

www.**schandpublishing.com;** e-mail: **info@schandpublishing.com**

Marketing Offices:

Chennai : Ph: 23632120; chennai@schandpublishing.com
Guwahati : Ph: 2738811, 2735640; guwahati@schandpublishing.com
Hyderabad : Ph: 40186018; hyderabad@schandpublishing.com
Jalandhar : Ph: 4645630; jalandhar@schandpublishing.com
Kolkata : Ph: 23357458, 23353914; kolkata@schandpublishing.com
Lucknow : Ph: 4003633; lucknow@schandpublishing.com
Mumbai : Ph: 25000297; mumbai@schandpublishing.com
Patna : Ph: 2260011; patna@schandpublishing.com

First Edition 2009
Revised Editions 2010, 2012
Reprint with Corrections 2014
Reprint 2019, 2021, 2022

Reprint 2024

ISBN: 978-81-219-3168-7 **Product Code:** H8MAM60MKTG10ENZX12O

PRINTED IN INDIA

By Vikas Publishing House Private Limited, Plot 20/4, Site-IV, Industrial Area Sahibabad, Ghaziabad – 201 010 and Published by S Chand And Company Limited, A-27, 2nd Floor, Mohan Co-operative Industrial Estate, New Delhi – 110 044.

PREFACE TO THE REVISED EDITION

Previous revised editions of this volume were published in 2010 and 2012. Despite of due care, some errors were still found out. During last more than a year, I checked the contents carefully in connection with the comments from students and teachers enough for revising the book thoroughly for the third time. This time, I tried seriously to remove all minor shortcomings in this revised volume. In the revised edition, new chapters have not been added, but every chapter has been checked for errors to reach the reasonable level perfection. It is my humble attempt to present the basic aspects of modern marketing in an error-free manner.

In line of syllabi of most of Indian universities and examination style, I have added in this edition chapterwise MCQs (Multiple Choice Questions) and MTQs (Matching Type Questions) to enhance versatility and utility of the book.

Despite of my sincere efforts, there is enough space for further improvement. I will be pleased if the readers will bless me with the feedback in forms of constructive suggestions. It would be my immense pleasure to incorporate their valuable suggestions in the next addition to the volume's versatility and utility.

Expecting warm response,
Thanks

Dr. R.B. Rudani

PREFACE TO THE FIRST EDITION

There has been experienced chronic a thirst for standard book in subject of marketing management. So far attempts have been made by many domestic and foreign writers and publishers in marketing area to assist students and readers to get clear idea on basics of the subject. Most books written by Indian and foreign authors are general in nature and cannot cater to specific need of teaching and learning communities, particularly at graduate level. Most students of first year BBA, B. Com., and other management courses pass their higher secondary (10+2) education in regional languages and, therefore, find it difficult to read and comprehend high profile reference books on any area of management. This is particularly true in marketing area. At undergraduate level, students and teachers need straightforward, simple, and to-the-point books. Here, the basic purpose is to impart conceptual knowledge along with actual practice of marketing. Utility of book depends on language level, contents, pattern of writing, and many other relevant aspects. Students and teachers normally prefer standard books written in a simple, lucid, and effective language. This is my sincere endeavor to meet a few expectations of teachers and students. My constant and intense interaction with management students at graduate level for more than one and half decades, and expert guidelines from learned professors of various universities have helped me to perceive students' actual needs and their problems from students' view point. I am confident that the present volume would be served as a source of reference for readers, the guide for students, and the text for teachers.

The book is intended to be used by students and teachers of business administration and commerce at graduate level. However, it can be recommended for postgraduate students of Commerce (M. Com.) and Management (MBA and other postgraduate Diploma courses). Even students of other disciplines can use the book as ready-reference to get primary idea at glance. Traders and low-profile managers can use the same to get immediate idea on any decision area of marketing.

Care has been taken to express every topic in a to-the-point manner, avoiding unnecessary description. The book has been written differently than traditional mode of writing. I am sure that students and teachers will definitely enjoy the novelty. Similarly, without compromising quality of language, the simple and effective language has been used to assist students understand every topic easily.

I have tried to materialize my rich experience as a student of management discipline right from undergraduation (the BBA) to the Ph.D., and intensive teaching experience, particularly, in the BBA discipline for more than 19 years. I have sincerely tried to minimize practical difficulties faced by the BBA and other students in Marketing subject, some of them, I had faced during my study.

A large number of reference books have been used along with rich teaching and learning experience to enrich contents of the book. I hope students, teachers, managers, and trainers will find the book as a useful source.

I am confident that my attempt will definitely fulfill the expectations of learning and teaching communities in the area. I hope that students and professors will welcome and appreciate my innovative and qualitative approach toward the textbook. I am pleased if I am obliged with valuable suggestions.

ORGANISATION OF BOOK

The book has been designed with a great care to assists readers get instant clear idea about marketing management. The volume is comprised of, in all, sixteen chapters. Each of the chapters describes meaning, characteristics, scope, important, process, and relevant fundamental aspects. At the end of every chapter, a set of review questions has been supplemented to help teachers and students. As and when needed, charts, tables, figures, etc., have used to clarify the concept.

The first chapter deals with introductory aspects, covering all basic aspects. Marketing Management Model, at the end of the chapter, is distinctive point. The second chapter contains a few important emerging issues in marketing. The third chapter briefly explains relevant issues about marketing environment and demand forecasting. While chapter four concerns with consumer behaviour and market segmentation. The chapter five to the chapter eight deal with marketing mix (marketing programme, called as 4P's). Main marketing mix elements such as product, price, promotion and place have been adequately discussed.

The 9th chapter contains useful details about marketing information and marketing research. The chapter has been written in view of the actual practice of marketing research. Rural marketing and marketing of services have been briefly discussed in the 10th and the 11th chapters respectively. The Chapter 13th describes issues related to marketing control while the chapter 14th concerns with analyzing competitors.

Case study, the 15th chapter, involves sixteen cases, particularly, prepared for management students to help them perceive marketing situation and apply theoretical knowledge for marketing decision-making. This part also contains useful guideline for teachers to handle the case and tips for the students to attempt the same.

The last 16th chapter is Project Report in Marketing field. It is the unique chapter containing important detail to help students prepare practical training report in marketing area. In many universities, at graduate level, the students have to undergo for practical training for one to three weeks and have to prepare report on the assigned topics. In most universities, training report and project report are integral part of curricula. It is treated as 100 marks practical paper in some Indian universities. This part covers a list of about 35 topics/titles for preparing project report, main contents of each of the topics, useful guidelines along with standard format to prepare a report.

The author would be pleased to receive creative feedback from student community and learned teachers of the subject. It would be my immense pleasure to incorporate valuable suggestions in the next addition to improve versatility and utility of the volume.

Expecting warm response,

Thanks

Dr. R.B. Rudani

ACKNOWLEDGEMENTS

Revision is meant for extending versatility and enhancing utility. It involves adding, removing, adjusting, improving contents, and presetting the same contents in different manner. To revise a book is also a challenge. The mission cannot be satisfactorily completed without sincere help of various people. An author can write the first edition by his own, but cannot revise the same in the same manner. Every author owes to a number of people for their contribution. Meaningful revision depends on constructive suggestions and complaints from readers – students, teachers, and others – a few words of appreciation from friends, relatives and colleagues, and warm support of family members. I feel deep sense of gratitude towards those who supported me, directly or indirectly, and played a critical role in revising this book.

Revising is based on an excessive table work at home. Peaceful, conducive, and conformable home environment is extremely essential to continue working for hours together. Family members who have provided me with a loving, supportive, and inspirational climate needed to complete this volume with other publication work on hand. My family members, my wife – Harsha, son – Krutarth, and little daughter – Dhruvi extended an immense moral and emotional support while revising the text. Particularly, my wife Harsha extended me all possible support to invest maximum time and energy in completing the revising task in time. Truly, their contribution remained significant in this edition. I deeply express thanks to my family members.

I express special gratitude to those professors and students who used the first edition of this book and blessed me with a valuable and frank feedback for improving quality, contents, and versatility of the volume. I am thankful to my beloved students whose moral support had become the base to struggle continuously for excellence.

Friends and colleagues were the bumper source of encouragement to do an excellent job. I am indebted to friends, relatives, colleagues and associates, and college authorities for extending convenience, encouragement, and assistance.

I have revised the text directly in the Microsoft Office Word Document. This is really a wonderful package that provided me with immense convenience and comfort in adding, deleting, and revising relevant topics. I used this package to draw tables and attractive diagrams. Revising without MS Office seems extremely difficult. I am truly obliged by all those who developed and improved this excellent tool for conformable writing and revising.

I have used many books on Marketing Management, Salesmanship, Consumer Behaviour, Retailing, Service Marketing, Advertising, Logistics Management, E-commerce, and many others to revise the text in a comprehensive manner. I am, especially, thankful to all those authors whose books have been used intensively to revise the contents of the text. It is not possible to refer names of all those expert writers on the field. But, I remain indebted to those eminent writers. In the same way, I meaningfully and adequately exploited the Internet sources to give the latest touch to this edition. I express gratitude to those who are related to this source of information.

Nothing is possible unless Almighty Lord inspires and enables a man to do. I, with an immense sense of devotion, thank God for extending His invisible but capable blessing and assistance which have remained instrumental to do this job. I exerted considerable degree of resiliency due to God's discriminative favour.

Last but not least, my sincere thanks go to the publisher, S. Chand & Company Pvt. Ltd., for bringing out the revised edition in time. The authority and staff must be appreciated for their positive response to publish this edition within a short duration.

Dr. R.B. Rudani

BRIEF CONTENTS

DETAILED CONTENTS

CHAPTER

1

INTRODUCTION TO MARKETING

INTRODUCTION

Marketing has been recognized as the dominant branch of business management. It is a life-giving catalyst system that contributes to excel business operations. Decisions on other branches like finance, personnel, and production depend on marketing. The design of entire business strategies is formulated in light of marketing activities. Since consumer satisfaction is accepted as business philosophy, marketing has been placed at the center of business operations. It is clear that marketing plays critical role in deciding success of business. It is marketing that can translate the business philosophy into reality.

A nation develops socially and economically when its population has powerful marketers – people who possess marketing skills and abilities. It is poor marketing ability, not poor availability of productive resources that hinders economic development. Marketing skills and abilities are keys to sell the products at profits to sellers and satisfaction to buyers. Marketing knowledge enables businessmen for identifying and estimating the unmet needs of consumers, discovering the best products that meet their expectations, and convincing them to buy those products at profits. It is not business philosophy alone, it is theory of success in any field of human activities.

There are three basic terms relating to marketing, namely, 'market,' 'marketing' and 'marketing management.' The chapter discusses key issues relating to these terms.

MARKET

The term 'market' has been derived from Latin word 'marcatus.' It means a place where business is conducted. Thus, traditionally market was considered as a place where buyers and sellers gathered to exchange their goods. In same way, it can be said as the area of operation or circle of exchange. Market consists of all the supporting things facilitating the exchange.

DEFINITIONS

Term 'market' has been defined differently by different experts of varied areas. Let's examine some definitions to understand the exact nature of the term.

1. **C. B. Memoria:** "A market is convenient meeting place for buyers and sellers to come together in order to conduct buying and selling."
2. **Duddy and Reizan:** "A market means forces of demand and supply. It also implies aggregated demand for a commodity. Further, total number of buyers (potential and actual) can also say as market."
3. **Philip Kotler:** "A market consists of all potential customers sharing a particular need or want who might be willing and able to engage in exchange to satisfy this need or want."
4. **S. A. Sherlekar:** "A market consists of the forces of demand (buyers) and supply (sellers) facilitating an exchange process between buyers and sellers."
5. **According to Economists:** A market means forces of demand and supply. It also implies aggregated demand for the commodity or total number of buyers (potential and actual) for the product.
6. We can also say: *A market consists of buyers and sellers engaged in negotiation to arrive at exchange.*
7. Further, one can say: *A market is said to exist whenever and wherever the buyers and sellers of goods and services meet in search of opportunities for adjustment of their mutual interest and transact business in an atmosphere of free and open competition.*
8. Finally, it can be said: *Market is an area of operation, mechanism, system, or circle of exchange that facilitate selling and buying activities.*

CHARACTERISTICS OF MARKET

Analysis of above stated definitions reveals following characteristics:

1. Market is a convenient meeting place.
2. It consists of two parties – buyers and sellers.
3. Buying and selling are the key activities at the market.
4. Essence of communication and negotiation.
5. Exchange is in center of market. It facilitates exchange process.
6. Market operates for mutual interests.
7. It involves forces of demand and supply.
8. Total number of buyers or aggregated demand is equated with market.
9. Market exists only when people (buyers and sellers) have needs and wants, they are willingness to satisfy them, and they are able to pay.
10. Feedback or response is essential for improvement and continuity of market operations.

In fact, market is circle of exchange. It is such a system or arrangement that facilitates exchange process. Buyers and sellers find it convenient to exchange products with money. Figure 1 shows market system.

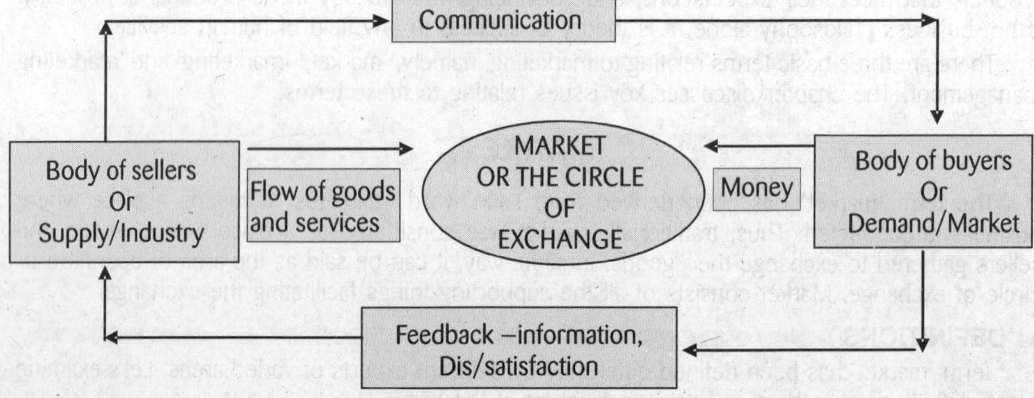

Figure 1: Exchange Circle

MARKETING

Marketing is a wide and comprehensive term. It is treated as philosophy, knowledge, or guideline to achieve business goals. It is also assumed as specific skill and ability to satisfy customers at profits. It teaches the practicing managers what they need to do in pursuit of business goals. Marketing doesn't mean only buying and selling, but it consists of a large number of activities necessarily performed for a maximum consumer satisfaction.

Advanced information technology, rapid means of transportation and communication, intense competition across the world, customer-orientated business strategies, spread of consumerism, business ethics, ecological issues, functioning of MNCs, and so forth have transformed nature and scope of modern marketing.

DEFINITIONS

Let's define the term:

1. **Philip Kotler**: "Marketing is social and managerial process by which individuals and groups obtain what they need and want through creating and exchanging product and value with others."
2. **N. C. Nair**: "Marketing is creation and delivery of a standard of living of society."
3. **William Stanton**: "Marketing is creation and delivery of a standard of living. It includes finding out what consumers want, planning and developing product or service that satisfies those wants, then determining the best way to price, promote, and to distribute that product or service."
4. **Peter F. Drucker**: "Marketing means to create customers."
5. **American Marketing Association**: "Marketing is performance of business activities that directs the flow of goods and services from producers to consumers."
6. Actually, it is knowledge comprises of concepts, principles, functions and processes. So, we can say: *Marketing is idea, thinking, guideline, or philosophy that concerns with satisfying needs and wants of society through exchange process.*
7. Marketing involves a large number of activities that direct exchange process. In this regard, we can say: *Marketing consists of all activities designed to generate and facilitate the exchange intended to satisfy human needs or wants.*

Most of the definitions emphasize that marketing concerns with facilitating an exchange. Exchange is the center of marketing. We must understand meaning of 'exchange.' Exchange means getting something by offering something of value. In other words: *Exchange is an act or a process of obtaining a desired product (goods and/or services) from someone by offering something in return,* Figure 1 *shows exchange cycle.*

CONDITIONS OF EXCHANGE

Exchange is possible if following conditions are fulfilled:

(1) There must be at least two parties – buyers and sellers.

(2) Each party has something that has value for the other party.

(3) Each party is capable of communication and delivery.

(4) Each party is free to accept or reject the exchange offer.

(5) Each party believes that it is desirable to transact with other party.

(6) Exchange is considered as on-going process. It is a process of negotiation. Exchange process ends with transaction.

CHARACTERISTICS OF MODERN MARKETING

The definitions necessarily state following characteristics of modern marketing:

1. *Marketing is the idea or philosophy that guides practicing managers.* It is an intangible knowledge. It teaches and preaches how marketing goals can be achieved more effectively.

2. *Marketing involves specific skills and abilities* to identify needs, discover products, and convince the target customers to buy the products at profits.
3. *It is the economic activity*. It consists of economic transactions. Goods and services are exchanged with money. It is commerce plus something. It is not mere supplying products to consumers.
4. *It is a facility for achieving the desired exchange*. It involves transfer of ownership. It is conducted within limit of the Law.
5. *It is a consumer-oriented philosophy*. It starts and ends with consumers. It is a medium of satisfying consumers' needs at profits. Consumer satisfaction is the prime goal of modern marketing.
6. *It emphasizes on integrated or system approach*. Modern marketing focuses on coordinated efforts to satisfy customers.
7. *It is a dynamic and competitive process*. It is based on consumers' needs and wants. It changes as per the change in consumers' attitudes and interest. Marketing activities are preformed under competitive situation.
8. *It is a social and managerial process*. It operates within society. It directly and indirectly affects social welfare. Similarly, for optimum satisfaction of consumers, elements of management are also applied. For efficient functioning of marketing department, competent managers are necessary.
9. *It deals with improving living standards of society*. Along with adequate profits, it tries to raise the standard of living of society by producing and distributing qualitative products at reasonable price.
10. *It starts before production and continues even after consumption*. Products are manufactured only after knowing needs and wants of market. In the same way, marketer should undertake after-sales actions to find out whether they have been satisfied.
11. *It focuses on target market*. It is aimed at satisfying needs and wants of a well-defined group of customers, known as the target market.
12. *It involves managing of demand*. It is undertaken in response to demand of specific customers for the product.
13. *Modern marketing stresses on long-term relationship building* with customers and other stakeholders.
14. Other characteristics: Besides main features, there are some minor characteristics, such as:
    i. It is universally applicable activity. It can be applied in every type human activity – economic, social, political, and religious.
    ii. Modern marketing involves aggressive promotional efforts to attract and convince buyers, and to face competition.
    iii. It follows the integrated efforts – all departments of organisation are responsible for marketing goals, i.e., consumer satisfaction.
    iv. It is a creative task. Marketer requires applying innovative (creative) techniques for maximum consumer satisfaction. Sometimes, it may be misleading and ambiguous.
    v. Modern marketing assumes the adequate profits. Every business unit must earn adequate profits. Satisfying customers with profit – is the principle of modern marketing.

IMPORTANCE OR ROLE OF MARKETING

As stated in the beginning of the chapter, a nation develops socially and economically when its population has powerful marketers – people who possess marketing skills and abilities. It is a poor marketing ability, not a poor availability of productive resources that hinders economic development. Marketing has a vital role to play for socio-economic development of the nation. It contributes to cultural development, too. Here, role of marketing does mean the contribution of knowledge of modern marketing science. If selling efforts are directed as per the modern marketing theory, philosophy or guideline, which benefits a nation can obtain. Marketing contributes in a number of ways for overall development of the society at large. It is obvious that nothing will happen unless someone sells something to others. Marketing positively affects production on one hand, and selling on the other hand.

Marketing skills and abilities distinguish the nation from other nations. It guides the businessmen to identify and estimate the unmet needs, discovering the best products that meet their expectations, and convincing them to buy those products at profits. Marketing knowledge makes the entire economic system meaningful and effective. This is due to the fact that the latest development in business management places marketing activities in the center of business and other braches of management are treated as supplementary to marketing management. More clearly, it can be stated that production management, personnel management, and financial management are virtually the branches of marketing management, not of business management. These branches support and facilitate marketing activities. Entire business activities have been replaced by marketing field alone. Now, only marketing management is a dominant area in business operations. Marketing is not business philosophy alone, it is the theory of success in any field of human activities.

Peter F. Ducker, a well-known writer in management field, on importance of marketing, states that it is a unique and distinguished function of business that fulfills organisational and social needs. In the same way, **Adam Smith,** the eminent economist, explains that the end of all production is consumption and nothing happens in the country until somebody sells something. The words of **Paul Mazur** are worth noted. He asserts that marketing raises standard of living of society if it performs its role adequately. Marketing become springboard of all industrial production. It should be mentioned that availability and quality of natural resources are not essential conditions for economic and social development, but how and where they are utilized, produced, and sold. Here, comes marketing.

Marketing guides the managers to find out needs and wants of specific markets and to satisfy them more effectively. When all the business activities are performed as per the modern marketing theory, almost all problems can be brought to end. This guideline should be applied at micro as well as macro levels in order to realize overall positive impact of marketing on social and economic development. Marketing leads to the righteousness in all significant aspects of economic activities. The right product can be produced and distributed to the right consumers, at the right price, at the right time, in the right way/mode, at the right place, and for the right purpose. Direct role of marketing can be explained with reference to following points:

1. Increased Consumption

Marketing activates consumption. Marketers try to offer superior products and undertake rigourous efforts to inform and convince consumers to buy. Consumption increases and the increased consumption is the fundamental condition for economic and social development. High level of consumption affects positively to production, national income, and per capita income as well.

2. Meaningful Economic Plan

When economic plan is prepared on the basis of needs of a specific group of people within given resources, the priority can be established. It establishes a balance between demand and supply. As a result, more meaningful and relevant plan can be prepared.

3. Improved Standard of Living of Society

When production and distribution are made market-oriented, costs can be reduced and quality can be improved. People can be supplied with the standard products at reasonable price. The standard of living can be raised. Every businessman at micro and macro level tries to maximize consumer satisfaction. He constantly tries for superior products. Thus, marketing encourages innovation, inventions, and modernization. It brings to society the new varieties and models that further boost living standard.

4. Promoting Competition

Marketing can promote competition and avoids the evil of monopoly. Such phenomenon has direct impact on quality and avai'ability of products at reasonable price.

5. Utilization of Untapped Resources

Need-based production results into mobilization of untapped natural resources. So, the idle/ untapped resources can be converted into useful goods and services. Marketing accelerates economic development.

6. Development of Ancillary Services

All marketers try to facilitate their consumers. They are in search of better services to provide the customers with the right products with minimum difficulties. As a result, quantity and quality of ancillary/auxiliary services like banking, transportation, insurance, warehousing, communication, and so on can automatically improve. Ancillary services are basic input in socio-economic prosperity.

7. Competent Managers and Entrepreneurs

Marketing process creates competent managers and successful entrepreneurs. They have a prime role in achieving economic excellence.

8. Development of Educational Institutes

Marketing promotes educational, professional, and technical institutes. Growth of educational and training institutes is vital or fundamental need for overall progress. It also promotes mobility of population throughout the world.

9. Supporting Government Policies

Marketing makes distribution of products effective and efficient. Goods and services are made available at every corner of the world. It removes obstacle of non-availability products. Marketing supports globalization, liberalization, and modernization policies of the governments.

10. Generation of Employment Opportunities

It increases employment opportunities. On a rough estimate, more than 70% job opportunities are generated in marketing field alone. It is a real blessing for developing and underdeveloped countries to ease unemployment problem.

11. Development of Agriculture Sector

Along with industrial development, marketing also accelerate the agricultural development. Marketing offers the latest tools, seeds, fertilizers, and techniques to agriculture sector. Similarly, a need-based production of agricultural products can revitalize entire marketing system for agro-products, and producers are directly benefited. A balanced economic development is possible.

12. The Worldwide Peace

Marketing leads to cultural development among the countries of the world. Further, it establishes interdependence among counties for satisfying their mutual needs. It improves international relations. It minimizes chances of wars between/among countries. Marketing ensures the worldwide peace.

13. Others

Apart from above points, we can also discuss role of marketing in light of some minor points:

i. It leads to price stability.

ii. It sets and improves business standards (ethics or moral principles) for benefits of people.

iii. It results into triple rewards – consumers, company, and country are benefited.
iv. It improves consumption patterns in society.
v. It is essential for growth of small scale industries (SSIs)
vi. It is a centre of business activities.
vii. It balances between production and consumption, etc.

MARKETING MANAGEMENT

Marketing is knowledge, and marketing management is systematic application of such knowledge for improving business decision-making and excelling business performance. It is the management of marketing activities and processes. It implies the application of all the fundamentals of management science, including functions, processes, principles, and theories to marketing field. More specifically, marketing management concerns with planning, organising, staffing, directing, and controlling the marketing efforts to realize marketing goals. The prime goal of marketing management is to achieve maximum consumer satisfaction within limit of given resources.

DEFINITIONS

However, following eminent authors in the fields define marketing management as under:

1. **William Stanton:** "Marketing management is a total system of business activities designed to plan, price, promote, and distribute want satisfying products, services, and ideas to target market in order to achieve organisational objectives."

   He also defines a little differently as: "Marketing management is a system of integrated business activities designed to develop strategies and plan (marketing mix) for satisfying customers' wants of selected market segments."
2. **American Marketing Association (1985):** "Marketing management is a process of planning and executing conception, pricing, promotion and distribution of ideas, goods, and services to create exchange that satisfy individual and organisational needs."
3. **Philip Kotler:** "Marketing management is the analysis, planning, implementing, and controlling of programme designed to bring desired exchange with target audience for the purpose of mutual gain. It relies heavily on the adoption and coordination of product, price, promotion, and place for achieving effective response."
4. Marketing management concerns with managing demand. In this reference, it has been defined as: *Marketing management is management of demand. It is concerns with managing level and timing of demand.*
5. In fact, marketing management is application of management science to marketing activities. It can be defined as: *An application of fundamentals of management (concepts, principles, functions, and processes) to marketing area is marketing management.*

Philip Kotler stresses on the demand management. According to him marketing management is the management of demand. He stated: "Marketing Management has the task of influencing the level and timing of demand in a way that will help the organisation achieves its objectives. Thus, marketing management is essentially the demand management."

MARKETING MANAGEMENT TASKS

A marketer has to perform various activities to achieve marketing goals. He is responsible to carry out a large number of functions of marketing department. The duties, activities, or functions performed by the marketing manager are called as marketing management tasks. He needs to look after various functions to ensure smooth functioning of marketing department. In short, marketing management tasks involve all those activities or functions necessary to be performed to achieve marketing goals. Even, decisions taken by marketing manager in relation to marketing goals also indicate marketing management tasks. Marketing management tasks can be broadly classified into two categories – general tasks and demand-related tasks.

GENERAL TASKS

General task are general in nature. They are to be performed irrespective of the demand level or demand situation. Each and every marketing manager has to perform certain tasks for whatever type and level of demand exists. In fact, general tasks have direct or indirect impact on demand level. They are also indirectly related to demand. But, such tasks are not undertaken purely on the basis of particular demand situation. General marketing management tasks may include:

1. Identifying and analysing marketing opportunities
2. Setting marketing goals and objectives
3. Designing a broad marketing programme, including general policies, rules, strategies, procedures, budgets, etc
4. Developing in detail the marketing programme/mix, including product, price, promotion, and distribution
5. Preparing and maintaining a suitable structure of organisation for marketing department
6. Maintaining good and healthy relations with parties relating to company's operations, inside and outside the organisation
7. Discharging social responsibilities
8. Exercising overall control on various activities of marketing department.

DEMAND RELATED TASKS

While general tasks are general in nature, the demand-related marketing management tasks consist of certain actions directed to influence level and timing of demand. The demand-related tasks are more relevant to study and practice of marketing management. It is clear that demand creation is the prime task of marketing manager. Virtually, marketing management can be said as the demand management, and marketing manager as the demand manager. All the decisions of marketing manager are taken with reference to type and level of demand. He has to create demand, to maintain demand and has to monitor demand level. Demand management includes taking decisions on product, price, promotion, and place for following purposes:

1. To create demand, when there is no demand for the product.
2. To promote/increase demand, when demand for the product is less than the expected level.
3. To maintain demand, when demand for the product is at the desired level.
4. To reduce demand, when demand is more than expected level, i.e., demand is more than supply.
5. To eliminate demand, when demand for certain products is not desirable for well-being of consumers and society.

It shows that the manager is found constantly engaged in managing the demand level. His duty consists of monitoring or chasing demand level. Every decision is taken to influence demand level. Therefore, marketing manager has to identify what type of demand situation is prevailing for the product, and accordingly, he should formulate marketing strategies. Thus, demand-related tasks are contingent upon different demand situations. **Philip Kotler** has identified eight types of demand situations and relative marketing management tasks. There may be more demand situations, too.

1. Negative Demand

Negative demand exists because of negative attitudes of the buyers for the product. Major segments of potential market dislike the product. They want to remain away from the product. They have a strong prejudice toward the product. The market holds a strong objection against production, distribution, and use of the product. Here, whether the product is beneficial or harmful is not the question, but for any reason, customers want to avoid the product. Even, they are ready pay price to avoid the product. This type of situation is labeled as negative demand. Examples of such demand may include, demand of non-vegetarian products for vegetarians, demand of vasectomies or family planning techniques in some castes and religions, compulsory military training for those who don't like it, transfer in awkward or disliking territories, etc.

When there is negative demand, the task of marketing management is known as **Conversion Marketing.** Conversion marketing consists of finding the reasons for negative demand and convincing the people regarding uses and benefits of products. Thus, conversion marketing involves converting negative demand into positive. The manager should put forth scientific reasons to change beliefs, attitudes, and customs of buyers. Conversion marketing involves effective advertising, capable salesmanship, and attractive publicity.

2. No Demand

Some products have no demand. No demand simply means customers are not buying the product. They are not buying because they do not know about the product, its availability, and benefits it offers, or they lack interest in the product; they are indifferent toward the product. Thus, they do not buy either because they are not aware of or because they are not interested in the product. This situation is called as no demand. Product may be useful, but customers do not perceive its benefits or usefulness. No demand situation exits when:

i. Product has no utility value. For example, Five Star Hotel in tribal area.

ii. Product has utility value, but in certain areas it is not useful. For example, boat in the desert, camel in ice-land, or electric appliances in area without facility of electricity.

iii. Unfamiliar or newly innovated product to which people do not know. For example, a completely new educational course.

iv. Costly or inaccessible product. For example, highly costly car in economically poor regions.

When there is no demand, the task of marketing management is known as **Creative Marketing** or **Stimulating Marketing.** Stimulating marketing involves finding the ways to connect the uses and benefits of the product with person's natural needs and interest. He takes aggressive promotional steps to inform and convince customers regarding benefits of the product. Exhibition, demonstration, free trial of product, free samples, and use of advertising by powerful media can help in creating demand. For a new product, this type of demand situation is natural.

3. Latent Demand

Latent demand means hidden or invisible demand. Demand exists but cannot be seen. There exits a strong needs for the product that can satisfy certain expectations of the market. But, such product is not available. Exiting products lack desirable attributes, uses, qualities, and performance. They are not capable to meet these expectations. So, people expect superior product to satisfy their expectations. This situation can be called as latent demand. Examples of the products include harmless cigarettes, highly fuel-efficient and pollution-free vehicles, exam-free education, tension-free job/work, sugarless sweets (for diabetic patients), speedy and safe journey with minimum fare, free membership of the prestigious club, painless injections, tasty pills, etc. All people want such products that can serve maximum welfare and satisfaction.

When latent demand situation exists, the task of marketing management is known as **Development Marketing.** Development marketing refers to developing products as per the expectations (expected attributes, qualities, and performance) of customers. Marketing manager has to estimate total latent demand and costs of production along with perceived value of market. If feasible, he should produce and market such products. Under the development marketing, the latent demand is converted into physical product; expectations are converted into tangible forms. But, in many cases, latent demand remains latent as expectations are too high, far away from the reality.

4. Declining or Falling Demand

Declining or falling demand is also known as *faltering demand*. When demand for goods and services, compared to the past sales volume and the current supply level, is less, and is falling continuously, is known as declining demand or falling demand. This is obvious phenomenon as product passes through different stages of its life cycle. Sooner or later, most of products experience such demand situation. This is due to change in fashion, taste, technology, customer behaviour, or innovation. Examples of products with falling demand include radio, black and white television set, certain professional courses related to IT, old model motor cycles and cars, ink pen, oily soaps, Gujarati (in Gujarat state) medium colleges in commerce stream, certain television serials, regional films, traditional dresses, and so on.

In relation to falling demand, the task of marketing management is known as **Re-marketing**. Re-marketing involves making minor or major changes in the existing product to restore demand level. Changes include improving qualities, changing attributes, and/or excelling performance. By making needed changes, downfall can be stopped, even demand can be increased. Along with product modification, marketing manager should also change pricing, promotional, and distribution strategies to stop downfall in demand and/or increase demand.

5. Full Demand

Full demand is the demand situation in which demand is adequate or at desired level. Company is satisfied with volume of sales or the level of demand and its position in market. In real practice, this situation hardly prevails. It is an ideal demand state. Full demand has two indications – one is, demand is equal to its production capacity or supply, and the second is, the company can fulfill its marketing goals.

Demand is at satisfactory level doesn't mean that manager has to do nothing. If suitable actions are not taken, such level will not continue for a longer period. The task of marketing management is known as **Maintenance Marketing**. Maintenance marketing calls for monitoring or maintaining demand. Manager has to keep watch on changing fashion, attitudes, interest, and wants of customers. As per projected changes in consumers' behaviour, required changes should be made in entire marketing programme (4'P's) to cope with the future changes in advance.

6. Irregular Demand

Irregular demand is the state of demand in which demand for the product experiences variations (ups and downs) continuously. For any reason, demand is fluctuating. There are many products, which have irregular demand. For examples, seasonal products like fan, heater, refrigerator, air conditioners, cold drinks and ice creams, and so on. Even, railways and airways reservation and demand of hotels in different seasons have irregular demand. Firecrackers, flowers, and other products used during marriage seasons have also irregular demand. Irregular demand is not advisable as the company has access capacity in slack seasons, and it cannot cope with demand during peak seasons.

Marketing management task related to irregular demand is known as **Synchromarketing**. It involves the task of balancing demand levels. Marketing manager should formulate appropriate marketing strategies to regulate or balance demand fluctuations. It may involve altering price, changing intensity of promotional efforts, matching distribution network, or even balancing supply level.

7. Overfull Demand

Overfull demand is the demand situation in which level of demand is more than firm's capacity to cope or handle. It is not possible for the company to meet demand of the product either because of short supply, or because of difficulty in distribution. In short, demand for the product is much higher than the supply. This situation occurs when:

i. There is a temporary or permanent shortage of products.

ii. There is a sudden increase in popularity and use of products.

iii. Production is restricted.

iv. Rumors or fear of scarcity, and desire for hoarding the products.

v. Wars, diseases, or natural calamities take place.

vi. Disturbance in supply or distribution occurs, etc.

There are many products which have got overfull demand. Examples of products with overfull demand are admission in medical and engineering colleges, job opportunities in developing and underdeveloped countries, petroleum products like kerosene, petrol, diesel, LPG, etc.

Note that the manager doesn't want to destroy or eliminate demand, but to reduce it. The task of marketing management is known as **Demarketing**. Here, the task to marketing manager is to reduce demand (when supply cannot be, for any reason, increased) or strengthen supply side of the products. Care should be taken to prevent adverse impact on use and popularity of the products. Demarketing involves one or more of following actions:

i. Price rise or quality reduction

ii. Improving supply side of such products

iii. Educating people to reduce use or wastage of the products

iv. Setting standards to discourage over demand

v. Restricting distribution and rationing of products

8. Unwholesome Demand

When production, distribution, and consumption of the product are not desirable for customers or society at large, demand of such products can be said as unwholesome demand. It is the state of the unhealthy demand. Here, there is demand, but product is, for any of the ways, harmful for consumers and society. The use of products has adverse effect on welfare of consumers. There are some products, which have unwholesome demand such as brawn sugar, morphine, heroine, explosive material like RDX, fatal weapons, tobacco-based products, x-rated and horror movies, erotic and exciting speech (idea or talk) leading to provocation of communal sentiments, and many other such products.

Marketing management tasks relevant to this demand situation can be called as **Counter Marketing**. Counter marketing consists of curbing or restricting production, distribution, and consumption of such products. Counter marketing tries to eliminate production and use of products. Counter marketing tasks are performed more by others (like voluntary associations, social workers, government, and other national/international organisations like the WHO, Red-cross Society, UNESCO etc.,) than the companies dealing with the products. Counter marketing involves one or more of following actions:

i. Reducing or restricting its production

ii. Imposing a complete legal ban on availability and distribution of such products

iii. Considerable price hike

iv. Educating and convincing people by effective promotional means to reduce or stop the use of the products. Increasing awareness by government, social organisations, woman's associations, etc

v. Linking severe punishment and penalties with activities related to such products

Table 1: Summary of different demand situations and relevant marketing management tasks:

No.	Demand Situations	Formal Name of Marketing Mngt. Tasks	Main Actions or Efforts
1.	**Negative Demand**	Conversion Marketing	To convert negative demand into positive
2.	**No Demand**	Creative or Stimulating Marketing	To create demand for the product
3.	**Latent Demand**	Development Marketing	To discover the product to meet latent demand
4.	**Declining or Falling Demand**	Remarketing	To change product qualities, and features to stop falling demand
5.	**Full Demand**	Maintenance Marketing	To maintain current level of demand
6.	**Irregular Demand**	Synchromarketing	To regulate demand level
7.	**Overfull Demand**	Demarketing	To reduce demand level
8.	**Unwholesome Demand**	Counter Marketing	To abolish or eliminate demand

FUNCTIONS OR SCOPE OF MARKETING MANAGEMENT

Marketing management is a powerful branch of business management. It is a wide term that covers a range of activities. The modern marketing approach – the integrated marketing – covers other branches of business management such as financial management, personnel management, and production management, too. So, indirectly, it can be said that scope of marketing management is similar to scope of the entire business management. Marketing management involves all those activities required to be performed for satisfying consumers at profits. It also involves undertaking certain socially significant activities. Following functions can be included in scope of marketing management:

1. Setting Marketing Goals

The prime task of marketing manager is to set marketing goals and objectives. Clearly and precisely defined objective can help marketing manager to direct marketing efforts effectively. The goals and objective (whether strategic and operating, or short-term and long-term) must be suitably communicated with the employees concern. As far as possible, objectives should be expressed in the quantifiable terms.

2. Selecting Target Market

Segmenting the total market and selecting the target market is a fundamental task of marketing management. Modern marketing practice is based on the target market, and not on the total market. Marketing manager cannot satisfy the needs and wants of entire market. He must concentrate his efforts only on well-defined specific groups of customers, known as the target market. All the marketing functions are directed to cater needs and wants of the target market only. Based on company's overall capacity, the target market should be selected.

3. Formulating Suitable Marketing Organisation

To implement marketing plan, a suitable organisation structure is essential. On the basis of analysis of type of products, type of market, geographical concentration of market, and many other relevant factors, appropriate organisation must be designed. Various alternative structures are available, such as product organisation, geographic organisation, functional organisation, matrix organisation, etc. Based upon requirements, the appropriate structure should be prepared and modified as per needs.

4. Maintaining Healthy Relations with other Departments

Marketing department needs cooperation from other departments of organisation, including financial department, personnel department, and production department, to satisfy customers effectively. Their support is considered to be important to satisfy consumers. Thus, for integrated efforts, marketing manager should try to establish good relations with them. Likewise, within marketing department, he must establish coordination among various personnel.

5. Establishing and Maintaining Profitable Relations with Outside Parties

Alike internal support, the external relations are also extremely necessary. Marketer, in order to carry out marketing activities effectively, must establish and maintain healthy relations with various parties, such as suppliers, service providers, government agencies, dealers, consultants, and so forth. Without their support, marketing manager cannot carry out functions successfully. Due to important role of external relations, contemporary marketing practices can be said as *relationship marketing.*

6. Marketing Research Activities

Marketing research is one of the important functions of modern marketing. Marketing research involves systematic collection, analysis, and interpretation of data on any problem related to marketing. It provides the manager with valuable information on which marketing decisions can be taken. Marketing research is essential to know adequately about consumers and market situation. It is a basic function to satisfy consumers. Marketing efforts are based on the marketing research information.

7. Sales Management

Sales management is one of the important functions of marketing management. Sales management concerns with planning, implementation, and controlling selling efforts. It performs all the activities directly related to execution of sales. Sales department carry out selling functions. Sales department formulates sales policies, ensures adequate quantity of products, maintains sales records, formulates structures for sales department, manages sales force (salesmen), and controls selling efforts.

8. Product Decisions

(Refer to marketing mix, product mix discussed later on in this chapter)

9. Pricing Decisions

(Refer to marketing mix, price mix)

10. Marketing Promotion Decisions

(Refer to marketing mix, promotion mix)

11. Distribution-related decisions

(Refer to marketing mix, place mix)

12. Exercising Effective Control on Marketing Activities

Control is essential to ensure that activities are performed as per plan. Control involves establishing standards, measuring actual performance, comparing actual performance with standards, and taking corrective actions, if needed. Control keeps the entire marketing department alert, active, and regular. Marketing manager should set up an effective controlling system to monitor marketing efforts.

MARKETING CONCEPTS OR EVOLUTION (STAGES) OF MARKETING

We know that marketing consists of deliberate and conscious efforts directed toward marketing goals. There are various guidelines or marketing philosophies that a marketer can adopt to realize marketing goals. Such guidelines or guiding philosophies are known as marketing concepts. Concepts also imply the alternative marketing approaches that guide a manager how marketing goals can be achieved. Each of the concepts varies in priority to product, customers, organisation needs, social welfare, etc. Further, each of the concepts involve following aspects:

1. Assumptions regarding customers, when they will respond positively.
2. Assumptions regarding the market structure, including competition.
3. It suggests how marketing goals can be achieved, suggesting specific marketing tasks.
4. It highlights the contemporary marketing practices or situations.
5. Each successive concept indicates the improvement over the previous one.

Philip Kotler has given five completive/alternative concepts. They include:

1. The Production Concept
2. The Product Concept
3. The Selling Concept
4. The Marketing Concept
5. The Societal Concept

These concepts may be termed as the approaches or, sometimes, the evolution stages of marketing development. When they are taken as the evolution stages, the order (sequence) from the first concept to the last concept must be maintained. First three concepts are traditional; the forth is modern concept; and the last is the latest concept. Today's marketing practices are based on combination of last three concepts. Figure 2 shows alternative concepts with key elements.

The Production Concept

Philip Kotler defines: "The production concept holds that consumers will favour those products that are widely available and low in cost. Managers of production-oriented organisations concentrate on achieving higher production efficiency and wide distribution coverage."

This is traditional approach to marketing management. It was applicable when there was no competition and market was dominated by sellers. Here, it is assumed that consumers are interested only in the products, which are cheap in price and are widely available. So, lower price and easy availability are given priority by the market. The manager with production-oriented concept must try to reduce cost by higher production efficiency, and must ensure easy availability of products by wide distribution coverage.

Elements of the production concept include:

i. Low price

ii. Easy/wide availability of product

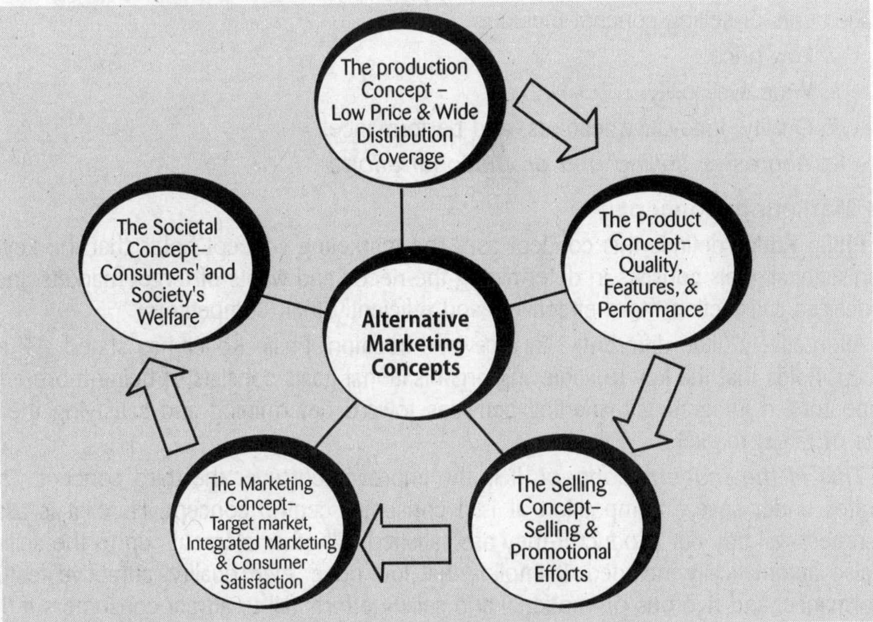

Figure 2: Five Alternative Marketing Concepts with Key Elements.

The Product Concept

Philip Kotler defines: "The product concept holds that consumers will favour those products that offer the most quality, performance, and innovative features. Managers in product-oriented organisations focus their energy on making superior products and improving them over time."

The product concept is an improvement over the production concept. Under this concept, it is assumed that consumers will favour the products, which offers higher quality, attractive features, and better performance. This concept also works under monopoly situation. Managers' duty is to concentrate on achieving quality, features, and performance of products and improving them continuously. It is improvement over the first one does mean that low price and easy availability will indirectly involve in this concept.

Elements of the selling concept include:

i. Low price.

ii. Wide availability.

iii. Better qualities, innovative features, and performance.

The Selling Concept

Philip Kotler defines the concept as: "The selling concept holds that consumers, if left alone, will ordinarily not buy enough of the organisation's products. The organisation must, therefore, undertake aggressive selling and promotional efforts."

It is an improvement over the second concept. Selling and promotional efforts are added in the former one. This concept functions under competitive market. It is assumed that consumers will not buy company's products (even products are cheap, widely available, and of better quality, features and performance) if they are not informed, convinced, or requested. Consumers like to be requested, contacted, and informed. They like to feel importance. This concept emphasizes on managers' effective promotional and selling efforts. By using one or more of promotional tools, such as advertising, sales promotion, personal selling, and publicity, the manager can inform, request, or contact consumers to make them buy the product.

Elements of selling concept include:

i. Low price.

ii. Wide availability.

iii. Quality, innovative features, and performance.

iv. Aggresive selling and promotional efforts.

The Marketing Concept

Philip Kotler defines this concept as: "The marketing concept holds that the key to achieve organisational goals consists in determining the needs and wants of target markets and delivering the desired satisfaction more effectively and efficiently than competitors."

Alternatively (little differently) in a revised addition, Philip Kotler has stated: "The marketing concept holds that the key to achieving organisational goals consists of being more effective than competitors in integrating marketing activities toward determining and satisfying the needs and wants of target markets."

This is the modern concept. It is the improvement over the third concept. This concept operates under severe competition. It is a consumer centric concept. Here, it is assumed that consumers will buy our product if they are satisfied. All other elements up to the selling concept are also automatically included. It implies that low price, high quality, attractive features, better performance, and rigorous promotional and selling efforts fail to attract consumers if they are not satisfied. Consumers can be satisfied only if the products suit their needs and wants. Marketer should first identify needs and wants of the target market, and then should design the product to satisfy these needs and wants. It clearly implies that company's efforts, of whatever nature and degree, are of no value if consumers are not satisfied. Manager's efforts include all the activities that can satisfy target market.

Elements of the marketing concept include:

i. Low price.

ii. Wide availability.

iii. Quality, features, and performance.

iv. Selling and promotional efforts.

v. Target markets (instead of total market).

vi. Integrated marketing.

vii. Emphasis on consumer satisfaction.

Key Elements or Pillars of Marketing Concept

Elements are also called pillars of the marketing concept. Marketing concept is based on four elements (over and above the individual elements of the former four concepts), such as:

1. **Consumer Orientation:** Consumer orientation means designing entire marketing programme (4'P's) in such way that maximum consumer satisfaction can be achieved. Marketing efforts are directed to satisfy consumers. Every decision is taken to satisfy needs and wants of the target consumers. Due to competition, the marker tries to satisfy customers more effectively and efficiently than the competitors.
2. **Target Market Focus:** Target market means *the well-defined specific groups of consumers whose needs and wants a company wants to satisfy*. No company, with whatever capacity and resources, can satisfy all the needs of all the consumers. Therefore, it is necessary to define and select specific groups of consumers, which can be said as target market. It is the aimed market for which product is manufactured; price is set; promotional efforts are undertaken; and distribution network is designed.

3. **Profitability:** Marketing concept emphasizes on adequate profits. Every company must earn the adequate profits with reference to amount of investment and degree of risk. But, the essential condition is that a company should earn profit along with consumer satisfaction. The matching offers satisfy consumers' needs and wants, and the desired level of profits satisfies the company.
4. **Integrated Marketing:** Costumer satisfaction is the result of integrated efforts of all the employees of various departments in the organisation. Consumer satisfaction requires the active involvement and full commitment of all the departments including production, personnel, finance, and marketing. Unless their efforts are integrated, the desired products cannot be produced and distributed to the target market. There must be high degree of cooperation and coordination among departments of organisation.

The Societal Concept

Philip Kotler describes the societal concept as: "The societal concept holds that the organisation's task is to determine the needs, wants, and interests of target markets and to deliver desired satisfaction more effectively and efficiently than competitors in a way that preserves or enhances the consumer's and society's well-being."

The societal concept is based on the following assumptions:

1. Consumers want to protect their long-term interest and welfare.
2. Consumers favour those products, which protect their interest and social welfare.
3. Therefore, management is concerned with developing products that satisfy consumers with protecting their interest.
4. Marketer needs to make the organisation consumer-oriented and society-oriented for their long-term benefits.

Societal concept is the latest marketing philosophy and guideline. Alike other former concepts, it is improvement over the marketing concept. It is argued that consumer satisfaction might not necessarily result into consumer welfare. Consumer satisfaction doesn't guarantee protection of costumers' and society's long-term interest and welfare. When consumers are offered the matching products, they are satisfied. But, sometimes, welfare of users and society are not protected. Societal concept emphasizes on satisfying needs and wants of the target market with protecting consumers' and society's long-term interest. It stresses on triple reward system, i.e., reward to company, customers, and society. Societal concept involves:

i. Low price.
ii. Wide availability.
iii. Quality, features, and performance.
iv. Selling and promotional efforts.
v. Integrated marketing
vi. Consumer satisfaction.
vii. Protection of consumers' and society's long-term interest and well-being.

So, under this concept, the duty/task of managers is to satisfy consumers in such a way that consumers' and society's well-being can be ensured. For example, a consumer wants cigarette, wine, or other alcoholic products; they are satisfied if they are offered such products. Note that use of such products doesn't protect long-term interest of consumers and society. Societal concept heavily depends upon the fair, just, and socially beneficial marketing practices.

Managerial Actions: The societal concept suggest following managerial actions:

1. Producing and distributing products as per needs and wants of the target market with precaution that the use of products doesn't adversely affect the long-term interest of consumers and society.

2. Production process should be such that have a minimum adverse effect on ecological balance. Manager should adopt such a production techniques, which prevent or minimize different type of pollutions.
3. Marketing practices should be performed within framework of the laws and legal provisions. Marketer should support in implementing legal provisions made in the very interest of consumers and society.
4. Business firms should discharge their social responsibilities.
5. Marketer should refrain from profiteering, adulteration, overcharging, hoarding, etc.
6. Marketer should not use advertising and other promotional tools that provoke eroticism, violence, communal riots and religious sentiments, and violate cultural and ethical values. The market promotion should be directed to inform, educate, and facilitate buyers.
7. In short, marketer should design the marketing programme in such a way that consumers' long-term interest and social welfare can be preserved. He should produce and distribute such products, which are beneficial for society as a whole.

Emergence of consumerism is reactive to the failure of marketing to protect consumer interest. Government of India has formulated and implemented at least 30 Laws; most of them have been revised frequently, for the protection of consumer interest. However, in real practice, we hardly find applicability of societal concept. It is more ideological than practical. The realization of societal concept in practice needs social reforms and mental revolution, not only Laws and legal provisions.

DIFFERENCE BETWEEN CONCEPTS

Difference between Selling Concept and Marketing Concept; Marketing Concept and Societal Concept

One finds significant difference among these three concepts. Proper understanding of difference among these competitive concepts helps practiceners to decide which of these concepts can be practically applied. The basic difference between the selling concept and the marketing concept, and the marketing concept and the societal concept has been briefly stated in Table 2.

Table 2: Difference between selling, marketing, and societal concepts:

Key points	Selling concept	Marketing concept	Societal concept
Objective	To maximize sales volume.	To maximize consumer satisfaction.	To maximize long-term interest and welfare of consumers and society.
Assumption	Consumer will not buy if they are left alone.	They will buy if they are satisfied.	They will buy if they are satisfied with protection of long-term interest.
Market condition	Normal competition.	Throat-cut competition.	Throat-cut competition.
Communication	Normally one-way.	Normally two-way.	Actively two-way.
Main theme	Sell what you can produce.	Produce what you can sell.	Produce what you can sell but with protecting long-term interest of consumers and society.
Nature	It is the traditional concept.	It is the modern concept.	It is the latest concept.
Scope	Scope is narrow.	Scope is wide.	Scope is wider or comprehensive.

Task of manager	To undertake the intensive selling and promotional efforts.	Find out needs and wants of the target market and satisfy them more effectively than competitors.	Find out needs and wants of target market and satisfy them in a way that consumers' and social interest and welfare are protected.
Benefits	Mostly one-way. Major benefits go to seller only.	Probably two-way. Seller and probably buyers are benefited.	Three-way benefits. Consumers, seller, and society are benefited.
Profitability	Maximum profit.	Maximum profit with maximum consumer satisfaction.	Reasonable profit with protection of consumers' interest and social welfare.
Moral justice	No scope for moral justice.	Somewhat, but no guarantee.	There is guarantee for moral justice.
Beginning of marketing process	It starts with production	It starts with market or consumers.	It stars with consumers and society
Approach followed	It follows isolated approach.	It follows integrated approach.	It follows integrated and relationship approach.
Market focus	The entire market.	The target market.	The target market and the entire society.

MARKETING MIX OR FOUR P's (4P's)

In order to satisfy needs and wants of the target market, the marketing manager has to take decisions on various marketing areas. The combination of such marketing areas is known as marketing mix. Marketing mix is also called as marketing programme. Main decisions of marketing mix involve 4P's; 4P's is made of the first letter of each decision set in marketing mix. 4P's consists of Product decisions, Price decisions, Promotional decisions, and Place decisions. However, modern marketing mix involves more than 4P's. Many experts and practitioners have included additional P's such as public relations, people, packaging, politics, etc. Additional P's show duplication of one or more of basic four P's. For example, public relations is a part of promotion mix, people are core in all marketing activities (in all P's), packaging is a part of product mix, and politics is a part of daily life behaviour of every modern manager. More than 4P's indicate duplication of any of original elements. However, 4P's concept has remained popularly unbeaten. Most of the management writers have considered marketing mix with 4P's. Even, in this book, the concept of 4P's has been strictly followed.

DEFINITIONS

Now, let us study some of definitions:

1. **Neil H. Borden:** "Marketing mix consists of a list of the important elements or ingredients that make up marketing programme and a list of forces to which manager must adjust."
2. **R. S. Dawer:** "Group of various policies used by producer to succeed in market can be said as marketing mix."
3. Thus, it can be said: *Marketing mix refers to a set of decisions related to product, price, promotion, and distribution (place) for particular market segment or target market.*
4. It consists of decision variables. Marketing strategies are formulated by adjusting (combining) these variables. Therefore, it can be defined as: *Marketing mix means a set of controllable*

variables (such as product, price, promotion, and place) that a marketer can use to influence buyers' response within given marketing environment.

5. Finally, it can be defined as: *Marketing mix consists of four tools or weapons like product, price, promotion, and place. They are used by marketing managers to protect company's interest, satisfy consumers' needs and want, and/or fight with competitors.*

ELEMENTS OF MARKETING MIX OR 4P'S

The constituents of marketing mix are said as marketing mix elements. Elements are also referred as decision variables. Marketing mix consists of mainly four elements. Each element is also referred as mix, for example, product mix, price mix, promotion mix, and place mix. Each mix contains a set of decisions. They are called as 4P's. Some writers have sited more 4P's, but other P's are not very practical and popular. Additional P's indicate duplication of one or more of basic 4P's. Here, our discussion is limited to 4P's only. Figure 3 depicts four elements of marketing mix.

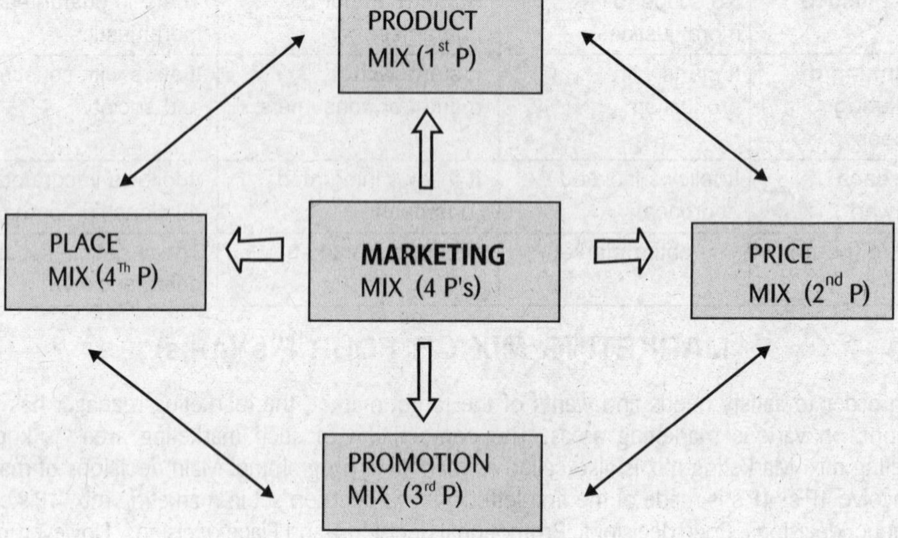

Figure 3: Elements of Marketing Mix (4Ps)

Product Mix

Product (mix) consists of various decisions relating to product. Product is the basic element of marketing mix because all other elements are required only when there is product. It is the center of all the marketing activities. Here, product includes both goods and services. Marketer can satisfy needs and wants of consumers by product. Product is the vehicle, medium, or means by which consumers can satisfy their needs. Important and long-term marketing decisions on product may be termed as product strategies. Product mix concerns with following decisions:

1. Development and introduction of new products
2. Matching the products with needs and wants of target consumers
3. Modifications (in term of qualities, features, and performance) on existing products
4. Product-related strategies including branding, packaging, labeling, colour, weight, grading, etc.
5. Product line decisions including different varieties or models, and product mix decisions including width, depth, length, and consistency
6. Product-related services like after-sales services, home delivery, guarantee, warrantee, and demonstration

7. Study of competitive (or comparative) advantages of products
8. Product life cycle, relevant strategies for each of the stages of product life cycle, and consumer adoption process

Price Mix

Price mix is another important element of marketing mix. It is considered as very critical element. Price can be defined as the economic value of product normally expressed in form of money. The price of product should be set in such a way that buyers can pay and company can earn adequate profits. In case of price-sensitive customers on one hand and the prestige-sensitive customers on the other hand, the pricing decisions become vital in marketing. Normally, pricing decisions involves:

1. Determining product development costs
2. Determining manufacturing (variable and fixed) costs the product
3. Studying pricing policies and strategies of the close competitors
4. Formulating appropriate pricing policies for the products
5. Deciding on level or margin of profits
6. Deciding on variable v/s fixed pricing, price discrimination, discounts, allowances, and seasonal effect
7. Identifying and analyzing of various relevant factors influencing pricing decisions
8. Pricing policies/strategies in different stages of product life cycle
9. Deciding on price-setting methods
10. Pricing decisions for direct and indirect distribution of products

Promotion Mix

Promotion mix deals with those activities directed to increase sales volume. It is also known as market communication. In today's marketing practices, market promotion has much vital role. Promotion mix involves all those efforts directed to increases sales of products on a continuous basis. It includes providing information to customers, inspiring them to buy, and offering incentives. Note that market promotion is concerned not only with raising sales volume, but it is also a tool for establishing long-term relations with the parties involved and is a matter of image, reputation, and goodwill for the company. Promotion mix consists of following elements or tools:

Advertising: Advertising is a popular and powerful tool of market promotion. It is a paid form of non-personal presentation and promotion of ideas, goods, and services by identified sponsor. It is a tool for mass communication. It includes following aspects:

i. Setting advertising objectives
ii. Deciding on advertising message, copy, media, schedule, agency, and budget
iii. Evaluating social aspects and advertising effectiveness
iv. Coordinating advertising efforts with other tools of market promotion

Personal Selling: It is also known as salesmanship and management relating to personal selling is sales force management. Personal selling decisions consist of followings:

i. Setting personal selling objectives
ii. Deciding on sale force size
iii. Recruitment, selection, training, transfer, and promotion of salesmen
iv. Remunerating and motivating, and controlling salesmen
v. Associating personal selling efforts with other market promotional tools

Sales Promotion: Sales promotion involves offering short-term incentives to prompt buying and increase sales. It includes temporary efforts to attract customers and induce them to buy. Most popular forms of sales promotion are free gifts, discounts, exchange offer, free home delivery, after-sales services, guarantee, warrantee, various purchase schemes, etc. Sales promotion covers following decisions:

i. Sales promotion objectives
ii. Sales promotion methods – consumer level, salesmen level, and dealer level
iii. Timing of sales promotion
iv. Assessing costs and effectiveness of sales promotion
v. Associating sales promotion efforts with other elements of market promotion

Publicity: It is a non-person stimulation of demand for the product, service, or business unit by placing commercially significant news in mass media or getting a favourable presentation on radio, television, or stage that is not paid by the sponsor. It is also a part of public relations. It includes:

i. Deciding on objectives of publicity
ii. Deciding on indirect expenses of publicity
iii. Determing types of efforts to get publicity
iv. Assessing impact of publicity on sales and reputation of company
v. Coordinating publicity with other promotional tools

Place Mix

Place mix is related to distribution of product. This element of marketing mix basically concerns with physical distribution and channel of distribution. This is the last element of marketing mix but very important as marketing goals can be achieved only if the products reach the hand of consumers conveniently. This element concerns with making the products available to the customers effectively. That means, the right products can be made available to the right consumers, in the right way, at the right time and at the right place, and in the right form. Place decisions involve:

i. Studying geographical concentration of customers
ii. Studying types of distribution channels and channel members
iii. Analyzing various relevant factors affecting channel decisions
iv. Selecting suitable channel of distribution.
v. Strategic decisions related to distribution activities
vi. Physical distribution including transportation, communication, warehousing, inventory control, insurance, banking, etc
vii. Balancing distribution costs and selling price
viii. Designing a suitable distribution network, and long-term distribution strategies
ix. Developing and adopting logistics management for effective distribution of products

Table 3 shows the summery of key decisions in each of the marketing mix elements.

Table 3: An Overview of Marketing Mix Elements

Main Marketing Mix Elements	Key Decisions in each of Marketing Mix Elements
Product Mix	• Product Mix, Product Line and Product Items • Product Qualities • Product Features • Product-related Services • Brand and Branding • Packing and Packaging • Labeling • Issues Relating to New Product Development

	• Product Life Cycle • Consumer Adoption Process
Price Mix	• Pricing Objectives • Price Setting Responsibility • Component of Selling Price • Factors Affecting Pricing Decision • Price-Setting Methods • General Pricing Policies • Issues Relating to Discount, Price Allowance and Rebate, Cash V/s • s Credit Price, Price Discrimination, etc.
(Market) Promotion	• Promotion Objectives • Promotion Budget • Decisions on Market Promotion Tools: – Advertising – Personal Selling and Sales Force – Sales Promotion – Publicity and Public Relations • Measuring Promotion's Cost v/s Contribution
Place (Distribution) Mix	• Objectives of Physical Distribution • Key Decisions of Physical Distribution: – Transportation – Warehousing – Inventory Management – Insurance – Billing and Collection, etc. • Direct v/s Indirect Distribution • Market Channel Options and Selection of Suitable Option • Channel Members' Services • Market Logistic Management

FACTORS AFFECTING TO MARKET MIX

Marketing mix is affected by a number of factors; some are internal factors while others are external factors. While deciding on marketing mix, marketing manager has to take into account all these internal and external factors. The marketing programme prepared in light of the relevant factors can best fit with needs of consumers and objectives of organisation. Each of the factors affects one or more of the marketing decisions.

Internal Factors

These factors are internal to organisation. And, hence, they are controllable. With reference to internal factors, management has relatively more freedom to decide. Note that the internal factors do not mean the company has complete control over them. They are also known as organisational factors. Marketing mix must be formulated and/or adjusted with relevant internal factors. The list of external factors is as under:

1. General and marketing objectives
2. Company's general policies, rules, and procedures
3. Management attitudes toward value, customer, social welfare, etc.
4. Availability and quality of raw materials
5. Resource ability of company

6. Organisational structure
7. Nature and types of employees
8. Personal factors related to management, etc.

External Factors

External factors are uncontrollable factors. They have tremendous effect on success of marketing programme. No company can deny the role of external factors in designing marketing mix. They are also called the environmental factors. The manager should consider these factors with care and caution. Some of the important external factors may be listed as under:

1. Demand
2. Competition
3. Suppliers and middlemen
4. Availability of infrastructure facilities, like transportation, warehousing, communication, insurance, banking, etc.
5. Consumer behaviour (all social, cultural, economic, and other factors)
6. Economic conditions and business cycle
7. Government economic policies and restrictions
8. Innovations and inventions
9. Ethical consideration and social responsibilities
10. Global economic factors, etc.

RECENT TREND IN MODERN MARKETING

Marketing has undergone drastic and dramatic changes since last two decades. But, even recently, it has been undergoing tremendous transformations. The expected changes of a few years ago have become the realities of today. Changes have been witnessed in customers, marketing thinking, and management actions. Today's customers have become more complex, more conscious, more rational, and long-term service seekers. With tremendous changes in legal and political environment across the world, borderless trading, excessive use of information technology and wide applicability of customer orientation have changed marketing philosophy and approach. In order to respond fresh opportunities and challenges emerging continuously in dynamic business environment, a company must change its thinking as well as acting patterns. Philip Kotler and others have identified following trends in contemporary marketing philosophy and practice as well. Most of such trends are equally applicable to developing countries like India:

1. More Emphasis on Quality, Value, and Customer Satisfaction

Today's customers place a greater weight to direct motivations (convenience, status, style, features, services and qualities) to buy product. Today's marketers give more emphasis on the notion, "offer more for less."

2. More Emphasis on Relationship Building and Customer Retention

Today's marketers are focusing on lifelong customers. They are shifting from transaction thinking to relationship building. Large companies create, maintain and update large customer database containing demographic, life-style, past experience, buying habits, degree of responsiveness to different stimuli, etc., and design their offerings to create, please, or delight customers who remain loyal to them. Similarly more emphasis is given to retain them throughout life. Marketers strongly believe: "Customer retention is easier than customer creation."

3. More Emphasis on Managing Business Processes and Integrated Business Functions

Today's companies are shifting their thinking from managing a set of semi independent departments, each with its own logic, to managing a set of fundamental business processes, each of which impact customer service and satisfaction. Companies are assigning cross-disciplinary personnel to manage each process. Marketing personnel are increasingly working on cross-disciplinary terms rather than only in the marketing department. This is the positive development, which broadens marketers' perspectives on business and also leads to broaden perspective of employees from other department.

4. More Emphasis on Global Thinking and Local Market Planning

As stated earlier, today's customers are global, or cosmopolitan. They exhibit international characteristics. This is due to information technology, rapid means of transportion, liberalization, and mobility of people across the world. Companies are pursuing markets beyond their boarders. They have to drop their traditions, customs, and assumptions regarding customers. They have to adapt to their offering as per the cultural prerequisites. Decisions are taken by local representatives, who are much aware of the global economic, political, legal, and social realities. Companies must think globally, but act locally. Today's marketers believe: "Act locally, but think globally."

5. More Emphasis on Strategic Alliances and Networks

A company cannot satisfy customers without help of others. It lacks adequate resources and requirements to succeed. Company needs to involve in partnering with other organisations, local as well as global partners who supply different requirements for success. Senior manager at top-level management spends an increasing amount of time for designing strategic alliance and network that create competitive advantages for the partnering firms. Merger, acquisition, and partnering are result of a strong thirst for strategic alliance and networks.

6. More Emphasis on Direct and Online Marketing

Information technology and communication revolution promise to change the nature of buying and selling. Companies follow direct channel in term hiring salesmen, setting own distribution network, designing network marketing, applying online marketing, and contracting with giant shopping/retailing malls.

People anywhere in the world can access the Internet and companies' home pages to scan offers and order goods. Via online service, they can give and get advice on products and services by chatting with other users, determine the best values, place orders, and get next-day delivery. As a result of advances in database technology, companies can do more direct marketing and rely less on wholesale and retail intermediaries. Beyond this, much company buying is now done automatically through electronic data interchange link among companies. All these trends portend a greater buying and selling efficiency.

7. More Emphasis on Services Marketing

As per general survey, about 70% people are, either directly or indirectly, involved in service marketing. Because services are intangible and perishable, variable and inseparable, they pose additional challenges compared to tangible good marketing. Marketers are increasingly developing strategies for service firms that sell insurance, software, consulting services, banking, insurance, and other services.

8. More Emphasis on High-tech Industries

Due to rapid economic growth, high-tech firms emerged, which differ from traditional firms. High-tech firms face higher risk, slower product acceptance, shorter product life cycles, and faster technological obsolescence. High-tech firms must master the art of marketing their venture to the financial community and convincing enough customers to adopt their new products.

9. More Emphasis on Ethical Marketing Behaviour

The market place is highly susceptible to abuse by those who lack scruples and are willing to prosper at the expense of others. Marketers must practice their craft with high standards. Even, governments have imposed a number of restrictions to refrain them from malpractices. Marketers are trying to sell their products by obeying and observing moral standards or business ethics.

10. Other issues

i. Craze for international standards and emphasis on quality, value and customer satisfaction. Application of TQM (even, Six Sigma) in every aspect of marketing management.
ii. Changed attitude toward competition. They compete not for maximum gains but for maximum offers to customers.
iii. Relationship marketing at both levels at internal functions of organisation and at outside with service providers, to satisfy customers.
iv. Concept of global and complex customers.
v. Marketing department is placed in the center of management. It enjoys unique and dominant status in organisation.
vi. Use of latest technology for survey and research.
vii. More emphasis on after-sales services.
viii. Entertaining value in advertising, etc.

CORE CONCEPTS OF MARKETING

Marketing is a business philosophy in which consumers are placed in center. Business activities are directed to satisfy consumers. Further, the latest marketing philosophy emphasizes on triple rewards, i.e., satisfaction to customers, profits to company, and welfare to society. Philip Kotler, the eminent writer on the subject, defines modern marketing as, "Marketing is social and managerial process by which individuals and groups obtains what they needs and wants through creating and exchanging product and value with others." Careful and detailed analysis of this definition necessarily reveals some core concepts of marketing, shown in Figure 4.

1. Needs

Existence of unmet needs is precondition to undertake marketing activities. Marketing tries to satisfy needs of consumers. Human needs are the state of felt deprivation of some basic satisfaction. *A need is the state of mind that reflects the lackness and restlessness situation.* Needs are physiological in nature. People require food, shelter, clothing, esteem, belonging, and likewise. Note that needs are not created. They are preexisted in human being. Needs create physiological tension that can be released by consuming/using products.

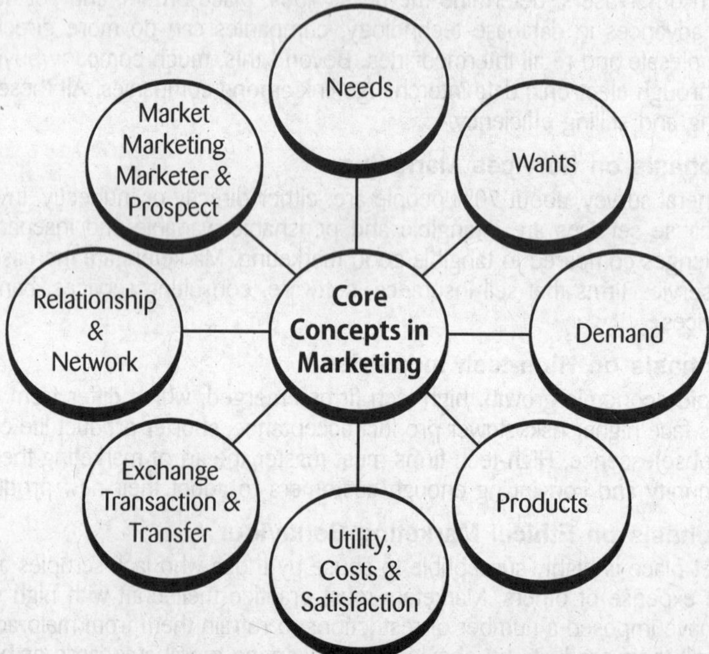

Figure 4: Core Concepts in Marketing

2. Wants

Wants are the options to satisfy a specific need. They are desire for specific satisfiers to meet specific need. For example, food is a need that can be satisfied by variety of ways, such as sweet, bread, rice, sapati, puff, etc. These options are known as wants. In fact, every need can be satisfied by using different options. Maximum satisfaction of consumer need depends upon availability of better options. Needs are limited, but wants are many; for every need, there are many wants. Marketer can influence wants, not needs. He concentrates on creating and satisfying wants.

3. Demand

Demand is the want for specific products that are backed by the ability and willingness (may be readiness) to buy them. It is always expressed in relation to time. All wants are not transmitted in demand. Such wants which are supported by ability and willingness to buy can turn as demand. Marketer tries to influence demand by making the product attractive, affordable, and easily available. Marketing management concerns with managing quantum and timing of demand. Marketing management is called as demand management.

4. Product

Product can also be referred as a bundle of satisfaction, physical and psychological both. Product includes core product (basic contents or utility), product-related features (colour, branding, packaging, labeling, varieties, etc.), and product-related services (after-sales services, guarantee and warrantee, free home delivery, free repairing, and so on). So, tangible product is a package of services or benefits. Marketer should consider product benefits and services, instead of product itself.

Marketer can satisfy needs and wants of the target consumers by product. It can be broadly defined as *anything that can be offered to someone to satisfy a need or want*. Product includes both good and service. Normally, product is taken as tangible object, for example, pen, television set, bread, book, etc. However, importance lies in service rendered by the product. People are not interested just owning or possessing products, but the services rendered by them. For examples, we do not buy a pen, but writing service. Similarly, we do not buy a car, but transportation service. Just owning product is not enough, the product must serve our needs and wants. Thus, physical product is just a vehicle or medium that offers services to us.

As per the definition, anything which can satisfy need and want can be a product. Thus, product may be in forms of physical object, person, idea, activity, or organisation that can provide any kind of services that satisfy some needs or wants.

5. Utility (value), Cost, and Satisfaction

Utility means overall capacity of product to satisfy need and want. It is a guiding concept to choose the product. Every product has varying degree of utility. As per level of utility, products can be ranked from the most need-satisfying to the least need-satisfying. *Utility is the consumer's estimate of the product's overall capacity to satisfy his/her needs*. Buyer purchases such a product, which has more utility. Utility is, thus, the strength of product to satisfy a particular need.

Cost means the price of product. It is an economic value of product. The charges a customer has to pay to avail certain services can be said as cost. The utility of product is compared with cost that he has to pay. He will select such a product that can offer more utility (value) for certain price. He tries to maximize value, that is, the utility of product per rupee.

Satisfaction means fulfillment of needs. Satisfaction is possible when buyer perceives that product has more value compared to the cost paid for. Satisfaction closely concerns with fulfillment of all the expectations of buyer. Satisfaction releases the tension that has aroused due to unmet need(s). In short, more utility/value with less cost results into more satisfaction.

6. Exchange, Transaction, and Transfer

Exchange is in the center of marketing. Marketing management tries to arrive at the desired exchange. People can satisfy their needs and wants in one of the four ways – self-production, coercion/snatching, begging, or exchanging. Marketing emerges only when people want to satisfy their needs and wants through exchange. *Exchange is an act of obtaining a desired product from someone by offering something in return.* Obtaining sweet by paying money is the example an exchange. Exchange is possible when following five conditions are satisfied:

i. There should be at least two parties
ii. Each party has something that might be of value to the other party
iii. Each party is capable of communication and delivery
iv. Each party is free to accept or reject the exchange offer
v. Each party believes it is desirable to deal with the other party

Transaction differs from exchange. Exchange is a process, not event. It implies that people are negotiating and moving toward the agreement. *When an agreement is reached, it is transaction. Transaction is the decision arrived or commitment made.* For example, Mr. X pays ₹ 25000 and obtains a computer. There are various types of transactions, such as barter transactions, monetary transactions, commercial transactions, employment transactions, civic transactions, religious or charity transactions. Transaction involves following conditions:

i. At least two things of value
ii. Agreed upon conditions
iii. A time of agreement
iv. A place of agreement
v. A law (legal system) of contract to avoid distrust

Transfer involves obtaining something without any offer or offering anything without any return. For example, Mr. X gives gift to Mr. Y. Transfer is a one-way process. But, pure transfer is hardly found in practice. One transfers something with some unexpressed expectations. Offer of money to beggar is to get the favour of God. Donor gives donations and receives honour, appreciation, and special invitation, or even special influence in administration. Gift is rewarded in terms of gratitude, a good behaviour, saying, "thank you" or with the expectation that the receiver of the gift will offer the same in the future. Almost all transfers are same as transactions. Transfer and transaction both are important for marketer.

7. Relationships and Network

Today's marketing practice gives more importance to relation building. Marketing practice based on relation building can be said as relationship marketing. Relationship marketing is the practice of building long-term profitable or satisfying relations with key parties like customers, suppliers, distributors, and others in order to retain their long-term preference in business. A smart marketer tries to build up long-term, trusting, and 'win-win' relations with valued customers, distributors, and suppliers. Relationship marketing needs trust, commitment, cooperation, and high degree of understanding. Relationship marketing results into economical, technical, social, and cultural tie among the parties. Marketing manager is responsible for establishing and maintaining long-term relations with the parties involved in business.

Network is the ultimate outcome of relationship marketing. A marketing network consists of the company and its supporting stakeholders – customers, employees, suppliers, distributors, advertising agencies, colleges and universities, and others – whose role is considered to be essential for success of business. It is a permanent setup of relations with stakeholders. A good network of relationships with key stakeholders results into excelling the marketing performance over time.

8. Market, Marketing, Marketer, and Prospect

In marketing management, frequently used words are markets, marketing, marketer, and prospects. A market consists of all potential customers sharing a particular need or want who might be willing and able to engage in exchange to satisfy this need or want. (For more detail refer to definitions in the same chapter)

Marketing is social and managerial process by which individuals and groups obtain what they need and want through creating and exchanging product and value with others. (For more detail, refer to definitions of marketing in the same chapter).

Marketer is one who seeks one or more prospects (buyers) to engage in an exchange. Here, seller can be marketer as he wants other to engage in an exchange. Normally, company or business unit can be said as marketer.

Prospect is someone to whom the marketer identifies as potentially willing and able to engage in the exchange. (In case of exchange between two companies, both can be said as prospects as well as marketers). Generally, consumer or customer who buys product from a company for satisfying his needs or wants can be said as the prospect.

MARKETING ORGANISATION

INTRODUCTION

To actualize marketing philosophy into practice, to coordinate marketing efforts with other departments of business organisation, and to exercise control over marketing operations, a company needs suitable formal structure for marketing department. The company needs innovative, responsive, and adaptive structure for smooth functioning of business operations. An appropriate marketing organisation is instrumental in realizing marketing objectives effectively in time. An enterprise comes to existence when formal framework or structure is prepared. Structure facilitates decision-making, implementation of decisions, coordination of marketing efforts, and control. It is like an effective instrument to adjust and readjust constantly with environment. Success of marketing activities depends on how they are organised. In fact, marketing organisation decision is taken along with other functions. However, it is one of the most crucial business decisions as marketing is in centre of business.

DEFINITIONS

Marketing organisation is a formal structure of marketing department. The structure is made of people, activities or functions, authority-responsibility relationship, interrelations between position holders, resources, and other aspects. It is prepared on the basis of products, geographical areas, marketing functions, customer groups, or other considerations.

DEFINITIONS OF ORGANISATION

Concept of organisation is important to define marketing organisation. Prior to marketing organisation, let us define term 'organisation.'

1. **John Pfiffner:** "Organisation is essentially a matter of relationships of man-to-man, job-to-job, and department-to-department."
2. **Chester Bernard:** "Organisation is a system of cooperative activity of two or more persons."
3. **Based on above definitions, we can say:** *Organisation is a structure or mechanism, set-up, arrangement or framework made of men, tasks, authority, and responsibility to facilitate coordination to achieve specific purposes.*
4. It involves mainly classifying, grouping, and assigning activities. It helps decision-making, implementation, and control. So, we can define as: *Organisation can be created through classification of the activities into groups and assigning each of the groups to individuals to facilitate decision-making, implementation of decisions, and control.*

DEFINITIONS OF MARKETING ORGANISATION

When concept of organisation is applied to marketing area, it is marketing organisation. In all above definitions, we add word 'marketing' before word 'organisation' and we can easily define marketing organisation.

1. We can define the term as: *Marketing organisation establishes authority relations among employees responsible for marketing decisions and their implementation.*
2. Marketing organisation is a base to implement marketing plan. In this regard, we can define the term as: *Marketing organisation is a deliberate and conscious creation of structure or mechanism to translate (implement) marketing philosophy into practice.*
3. More clearly, we may say: *Marketing organisation is a systematic and purposeful arrangement of marketing activities and functions. It involves assignment of marketing tasks to individuals, specification of authority and responsibility, establishing superior-subordinates relations, and clarifying roles and statuses of employees.*

Marketing organisation answers following questions:

1. Who performs which function?
2. Who can order to whom and who is answerable to whom?
3. How does communication take place?
4. What is role/or status of each of employees in marketing department?
5. Which is more suitable type of structure to company's marketing situation?

THE EVOLUTION OF MARKETING ORGANISATION

Over the years, marketing activities have grown from a very simple into much a complex group of activities. Now, it is not just a part of business management, but business management itself. Marketing has been recognized as the business activities. Marketing department is not a part of business organisation; rather it is centre of business organisation. Here, in this part, we examine how marketing department has evolved in business organisation and what is its status and position in modern business units.

Evolution Stages of Marketing Department

In views of Philip Kotler, marketing department has evolved through six stages. The stages show the changing role of marketing organisation and marketing manager over time. Evolution stages have been briefly discussed as follows:

1. Simple Sales Department

Normally, small companies follow this type of organisation. Here, marketing manager is called as sales manager and his primary work consists of managing sales and distribution activities. Company can hire help from external experts for other marketing functions like advertising, marketing research, etc.

2. Sales Department with Ancillary Marketing Function

It is applicable in expanding firms. When company expands its operations, it needs to add certain marketing functions. Sales and distribution remain main tasks, but other experts are also appointed for performing other functions.

3. Separate Marketing Department

Here, a separate and full-fledged marketing department is created. Marketing vice-president is the head and other managers perform several marketing functions under him. Normally, marketing department includes sales and distribution, marketing research, new product development, advertising and sales promotion, and sales force functions.

4. Modern Marketing Department

Marketing department is formed according to modern marketing theory and practice. A full-fledged marketing department considers all crucial issues and performs all marketing functions. Modern marketing department seeks cooperation from other departments to achieve maximum customer satisfaction. All marketing activities are systematically integrated to achieve marketing goals effectively.

Marketing vice president appoints marketing manager for carrying out various marketing activities. Marketing manager is responsible for identifying marketing opportunities and preparing suitable marketing mix. Sales, distribution, marketing research, advertising and sales promotion, sales force, public relations, etc., activities are performed under the direct supervision of marketing manager. The entire department struggles to achieve maximum possible customer satisfaction. Integration among various subdivisions of marketing department and between marketing department and other departments of organisation is key element of modern marketing department.

5. Effective Marketing Company

Effective marketing company follows modern marketing philosophy in practice. Effective marketing company is also known as integrated marketing department. A modern marketing department may fail if it fails to integrate efforts of other (finance, personnel, and production) departments. Effective marketing company considers marketing as a main function and other functions like finance, personnel, and production reduce to supplementary functions. Entire company is made market-driven. Here, business operations are replaced by marketing, that is, 'business' is considered as 'marketing.' Effective marketing company exists for realizing marketing goals. All employees of all the departments concentrate on realizing marketing goals (customer satisfaction). Thus, customer satisfaction is not the sole duty of marketing department but of whole organisation. Along with internal relations, external relations are given more priority in pursuit of maximum consumer satisfaction.

6. Process and Outcome Based Company

This is the advanced theme in designing marketing organisation. Many companies concentrate on key processes rather than department. Here, fundamental business processes are given more importance and attempts are made to remove departmental barriers. Main marketing processes include new product development process, customer creation and retention process, customer service, etc. For every process, process leaders are appointed to achieve specific process outcomes. Marketing personnel performs a key role right from planning to final outcomes.

MARKETING ORGANISATION PROCESS

To organise marketing department is not as simple as it was. Organisation structure for marketing is formulated along with other functions like finance, personnel, and production. However, marketing organisation seems difficult and complex as it affects other departments, and is affected by the rest of departments. Manager is required to consider a number of related and relevant aspects. Usually, following steps are followed to formulate marketing organisation:

1. Specification of Marketing Objectives

Marketing organisation process begins with specification of general and marketing objectives. A manager must know why the structure is needed. Types of objectives shape the structure. There may be many marketing objectives like customer satisfaction, market leadership, prestige and goodwill in market, maximizing sales volume and profits, etc. The structure must be capable of achieving the objectives.

2. Listing of Marketing Activities

Once objectives are specified, the next step calls for listing marketing activities. Irrespective of type of marketing division and decisions, a manager has to prepare a comprehensive list of all marketing activities. Note that important activities must not be missed and no activity should be repeated (duplicated).

3. Classifying and Grouping of Marketing Activities

Now, according to the nature and types of activities, they are to be classified or grouped into several groups or classes. They can be said as functions also. As a result, several groups of activities can be formed such as sales force activities, advertising activities, sales promotion activities, marketing research and information activities, etc. Each group must contain similar type of activities.

4. Assigning Responsibilities

On the basis of various groups of activities, divisions or departments are formed. Each division deals with only a specific type of activities. General manager assigns responsibility of each department to a person. The person is solely responsible for the outcomes the department assigned to him. Now, every division or department has responsible officer.

5. Delegation of Authority

Every responsible officer is equipped with sufficient authority. Authority is authorization to direct and order subordinates. Due to authority, one can take decisions independently. Delegation moves from top to bottom. The superior delegates the authority to his subordinates. Various levels and positions come into being. There must be balance between authority and responsibility.

6. Establishing Interrelations

After delegating authority to responsible marketing officers, now, interrelations are established. Interrelations indicate superior-subordinate relations. Horizontal and vertical relations are established. Statuses and positions are defined. Direction of communication is specified. Now, the structure is ready to work.

7. Preparing Organisation Chart

Organisation chart is a pictorial or diagrammatic presentation of interrelations among all employees working at different levels. Marketing organisation chart is considered as a supplementary or functional chart and it shows details about marketing department only. Way of presentation depends on general chart. The chart shows types of functions, levels in departments, way of communication, and title of every position holder. If organisation manual is prepared, it describes every position holder.

Here, it is decided what type of marketing structure is suitable. Based on size of operations, type of products, and geographical areas, an appropriate marketing structure is selected. Various options include product organisation, geographical organisation, functional organisation, matrix organisation, combined organisation, etc.

8. Creating and Maintaining Suitable Organisation Culture and Climate

The structure does not work automatically. Top management and key position holder(s) in marketing department must create conducive organisation culture and climate in which people can perform their duties effectively. There must be frank and friendly work climate to generate team spirit. Climate of confidence and trust boosts employees' morale. In the same way, regularity, discipline, and order are equally necessary. There must be clear-cut reward and punishment policies and practices. Clear rules, suitable policies, systematic procedures, etc., are necessary for creating and maintaining healthy organisation climate and culture.

TYPES/FORMS OF MARKETING ORGANISATION STRUCTURE

Modern marketing organisation can be prepared in variety of forms. It may be organised by function, geographical area, products or brand, and/or markets. Sometimes, more than one base is considered for designing the structure, for example, product and geographical area used to design the structure. This part describes main forms/types of marketing organisation.

1. Functional Marketing Organisation

Functional organisation is the most common and widely practiced form of marketing organisation. It consists of functional-marketing specialists (functional heads) reporting to marketing manager. Marketing manager (marketing vice-president) is the head of marketing department and is responsible to coordinate marketing activities.

Normally, marketing activities are arranged or grouped into five functions – sales manager, marketing administrative manager, advertising and sales promotional manager, new product manager, and marketing research manager. However, the number of experts (specialists) depends on size of organisation and management philosophy. Every function is under the charge of expert manager under whom necessary subordinates (supporting officers) are appointed. He is expert as well as administrator of his functional area. This form has its strong and weak points. Figure 5 shows structure of functional marketing organisation. In the figure, two officers are place under sales manager. Under every functional manager, needed officers can be appointed.

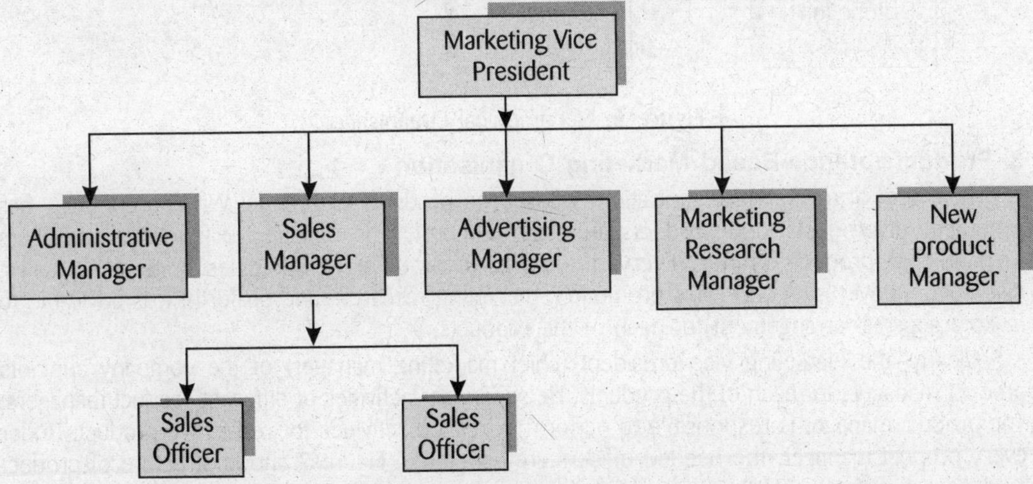

Figure 5: Functional Organisation

2. Geographical Marketing Organisation

When company sells its limited number of products in national market (sometimes, international market), it organises its marketing activities according to geographical areas. National marketing manager (also called marketing vice president) appoints area managers for different geographical areas of market (may be zones, states, or specified areas). He supervises activities of area managers. The area manager is responsible for his respective territory. Sales and distribution officer, advertising and sales promotion officer, marketing research officer, and administrative officers work under the area manager. Number of area managers and officers in each area depend on size of market, management philosophy, as well as types of operations. Area manager is fully responsible for the performance of his territory. Practically, this form is used only for sales and distribution activities, and other functional (like research, advertisement, new product development, etc.) are centrally performed by the parent organisation. Figure 6 shows structure of geographical marketing organisation. In the figure, two officers are place under West Zone Marketing Manager. Under every geographical (zonal) manager, needed officers can be appointed.

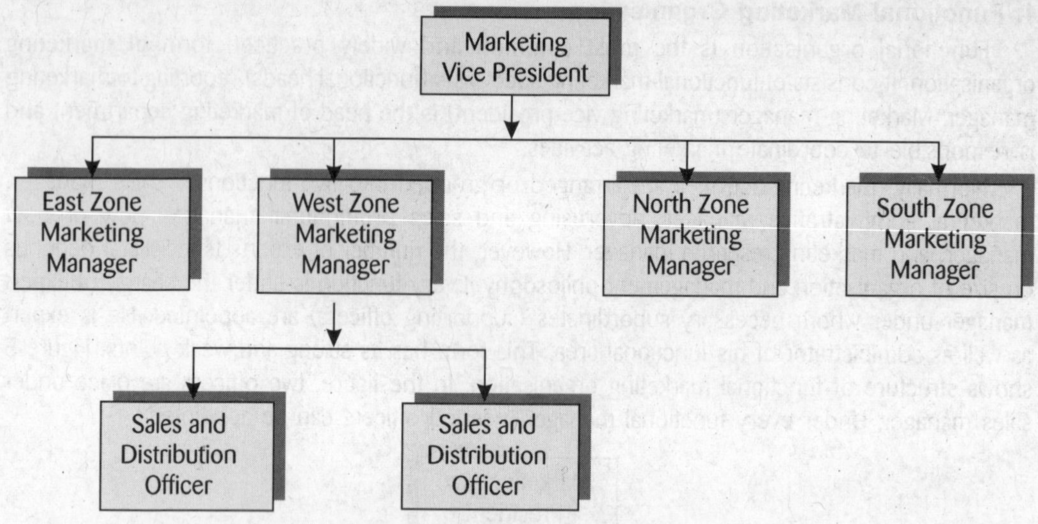

Figure 6: Geographical Organisation

3. Products/brands-Based Marketing Organisation

This form of marketing organisation is based on products or brands. When a company has a number of products, and products are quite different, it is difficult for functional managers to handle all products/brands. Every product calls for different strategies in terms of sales, distribution, advertising and sales promotion, marketing research, and so forth. It is advisable to make a separate arrangement for each of the products.

Clearly, the marketing vice president (chief marketing manager) of the company appoints product managers for each of the products. He supervises activities of different product managers. The product manager is responsible to perform all related activities for respective product. Under every product manager, the needed officers are appointed. Figure 7 shows structure of product marketing organisation. In the figure, four officers are placed under Product 'A' Marketing Manager. Other product managers can also appoint same officers as per need. And, every officer appoints necessary subordinates under him.

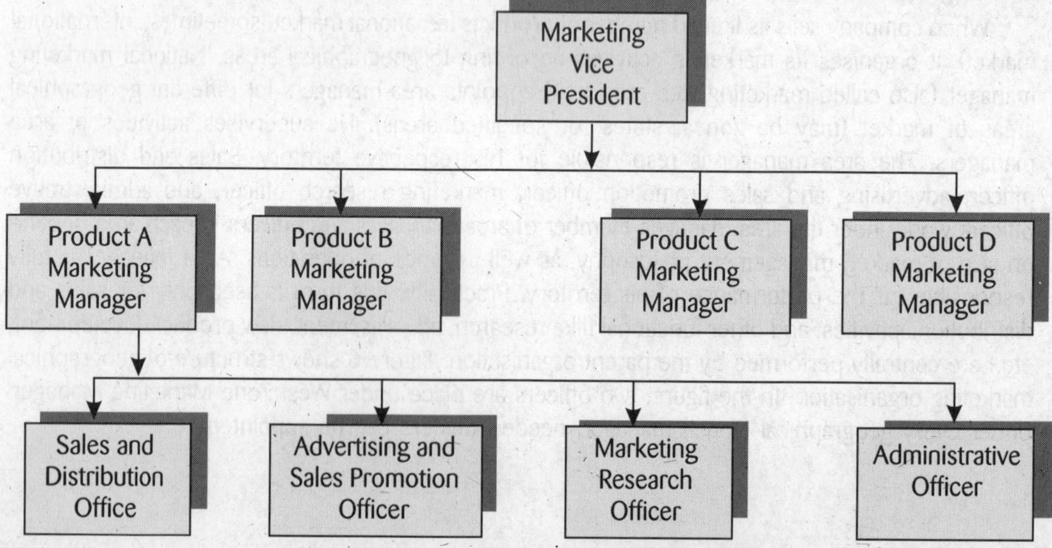

Figure 7: Product Organisation

4. Customer-Based Marketing Organisation

Some companies organise its marketing activities on the basis of customer groups. This form makes sense when the company has distinct groups of buyers (like government, industrial buyers, institutional buyers, retailed buyers, rural v/s urban buyers, domestic v/s foreign buyers, etc.) and each group requires different marketing (mix) strategies. Product, price, promotion, and distribution decisions are taken according to types of customer groups.

Marketing vice president appoints marketing managers for different groups of buyers. He supervises performance of all managers. Every manager for the respective group of buyers takes all relevant decisions like products, price, promotion, and distribution. The manager for specific segment of buyers appoints necessary subordinates to assist him. Number of managers and subordinates under each manager depends on number of groups, and size and area of operation. Figure 8 shows simple customer-based marketing organisation with four customers groups. Under manager for industrial buyers, there are four managers. For other groups of buyers, same type and number or different managers are appointed to take care of the segment.

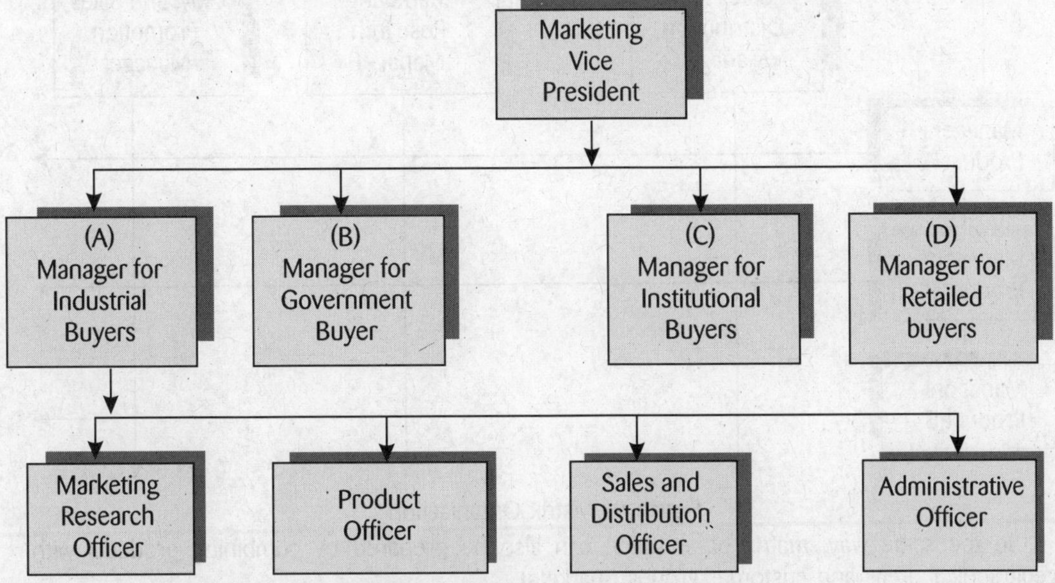

Figure 8: Customer Organisation

5. Matrix Marketing Organisation

It is a hybrid form of marketing organisation. Two bases are considered at a time to form a matrix. For example, products and functions, functions and geographical areas, function and customer groups or any other combination is used as a base to organise marketing activities. Here, the purpose is to share limited resources and to achieve economy in operation. Figure 9 shows that there are three functional managers (sales and distribution manager, marketing research manager, and advertising and sales promotion manager) working for all three products. There is no need to appoint independent functional manager for each of the products.

Companies producing many products in many markets for different groups of buyers follow this type of organisational structure. Thus, it is desirable in multi-product/multi-market/multi-customer companies. One manager has to take care of many products or many markets. Here, there are some practical problems to be tackled with care. There is possibility of conflict and confusion between two position holders as they have to work jointly. In the same way, it is, compared to other forms, a complex form. There is a problem of fixing authority and responsibility.

Marketing vice president is at top of the marketing organisation. Under him, functional heads or specialists (also known as staff managers), and other managers (known as line managers) are placed. Here, the staff means experts who extend expert advice to line managers. The line managers are responsible for specific products, geographical areas, or customers groups. In short, functional marketing organisation is extended with products, areas, or customer groups. Figure 9 shows matrix of functions and products. Under marketing vice president, there two types of manages – three functional managers and three product managers, who work jointly. All three product managers share resources with other functional managers.

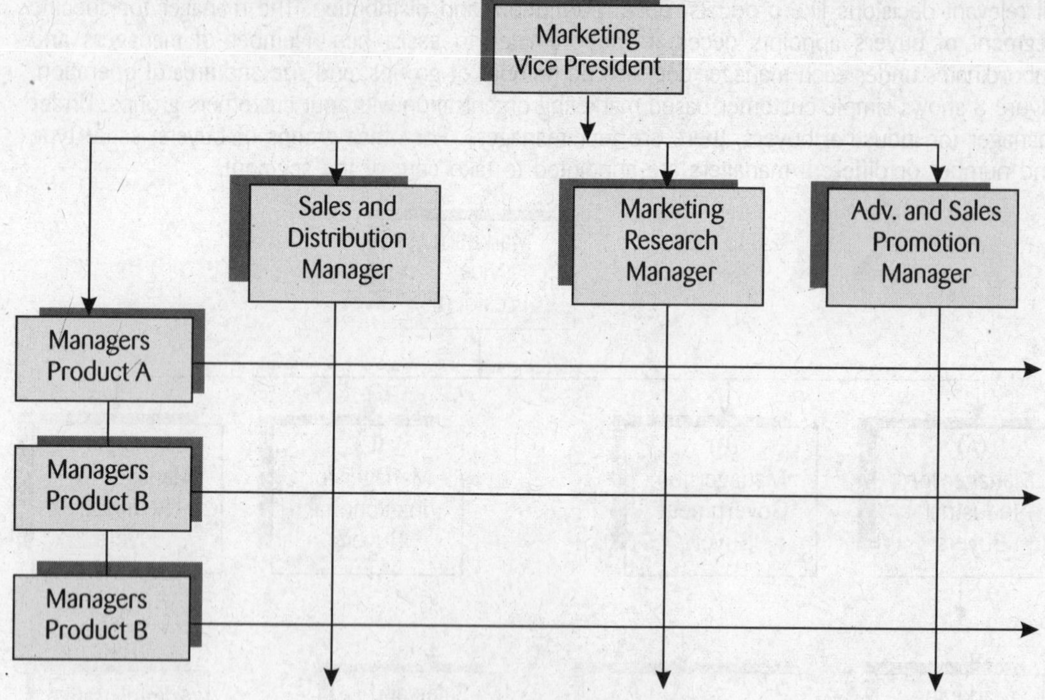

Figure 9: Matrix Organisation

In the same way, matrix organisation can also be prepared by combining products with geographical areas and customer groups (markets).

6. Combined Marketing Organisation

A combined marketing organisation consists of combination of various bases. More than two bases are used to form a structure. For example, marketing vice-president is at top. There are four regional managers (i.e., geographical organisation) under every regional manager, there are three assistant managers for the respective products (i.e., product organisation); and every assistant product manager appoints three functional officers (i.e., functional organisation) to assist him such as sales and distribution officer, marketing research officer, and advertising and sales promotion officer. In the same way, it may be combined with types of customer also. This type of organisation is normally used when a company has different products in different regions and requires different officers to perform varied functions for varied groups of buyers. Thus, it is applicable in large companies with a variety of products selling in several regions.

FACTORS AFFECTING SELECTION OF MARKETING ORGANISATION

Top level management has to consider many relevant factors while designing the best fit marketing organisation. Among most crucial factors include:

1. General and Marketing Objectives
2. Management Philosophy
3. Resource Capacity and Type of Employees
4. Recent Marketing Trend
5. Consumer Behaviour
6. Costs and Facilities
7. Type and Number of Products
8. Size of Operations
9. Type and Number of Customers
10. Geographical Areas of Operations
11. Availability of Infrastructural Facilities
12. Government Restrictions and External Business Environment

QUALITIES (FEATURES OR CONDITIONS) OF GOOD MARKETING ORGANISATION

Every business unit tries to set up a suitable organisation that helps achieve its goals.An ideal organisation is one, which fits or suits the current situations and requirements. It is natural that each organisation has different opportunities, challenges, and resource capability. So, concept of suitability is relative. Management theorist Henry Feyol, in his book *Administrative Management*, has given fourteen principles of organising. Many of them are equally applicable in marketing organisation, too. Qualities or principles affect structure as well as organising process. Both qualities and principles provide guideline or direction to create an effective organisation structure. Normally, qualities listed below can be suggested as principles, conditions, or features of a good marketing organisation:

1. Simplicity

The structure of marketing organisation must be simple to understand and apply. It must be free from unnecessary sophistication or complexities.

2. Flexibility

A good organisation is one that must be flexible, free from rigidity. Marketing organisation structure must be capable of coping with ever-changing business environment. Marketing manager must find it easy to make necessary changes to adjust with internal and external needs, or to meet challenging and absorb opportunities.

3. Stability or Principle of Continuity

Organisation must be stable. The structure must serve for a longer period. It may undergo minor changes, but the basic structure must be of permanent nature.

4. Suitability

For maximizing contribution, organisation must be suitable. Suitability is a relative term and can be discussed with reference to an individual business unit. Suitability principle suggests that the structure must be suitable to overall conditions of the business unit. More clearly, it can be said that organisation must be suitable with objectives, size, products, area of operations, nature of business, resources, activities, and other relevant criteria.

5. Provision for Top management

Top-level management is essential to guide, supervise, coordinate, and control efforts of marketing department. It is the apex body in business organisation. Therefore, there must be provision of top-level management for effective working of the entire marketing organisation.

6. Importance of Human Element

Organisation must accept important role of human element. People in organisation must be placed at center. It must be capable to meet human needs, motivate them, and to control their behaviour. In short, marketing organisation must be capable of getting the work done through people.

7. Specialization

The principle of specialization suggests that similar types of activities must be performed under one function or department. Similarly, each specific function or a set of activities must be carried out by qualified, experienced, and capable manager. Specialization results into a high degree of efficiency. Marketing research manager, for instance, performs all the relevant activities relating to marketing research.

8. Clear and Unbroken Line of Authority

The principle guides that line of authority from the top to bottom must be clear and must remain unbroken. This facilitates speedy action and better coordination.

9. Unity of Direction and Command

This is an important principle. Unity of direction implies that similar types of activities must be directed by one manager under one function/head. Whereas the unity of command guides that every subordinate must get orders, instructions, and guidelines only from one superior and is responsible to that superior only. It suggests one subordinate must have one boss.

10. Balance – Authority and Responsibility

Principle of balance guides a balanced approach between responsibility and authority. Authority should neither be more nor be less than responsibility. Authority must be just equal to the responsibility.

11. Application of Absoluteness of Ultimate Responsibility

The structure of organisation should be such that the ultimate responsibility can be fixed. For the final outcome, one must be held responsible. Authority can be delegated, not responsibility. Superior delegates to subordinates, but is responsible for final performance of his subordinates.

12. Proper Emphasis on Staff Function

Staff means a team/group of experts. For effective performance of various activities, there must be provision of proper staff function. The staff members guide the line managers in making decisions. Proper use of staff can contribute to overall efficiency.

13. Minimum Possible Levels

As far as possible, the number of levels within marketing department must be as minimum as possible. Minimum levels facilitate smooth communication and speedy actions. Complexity can also be minimized.

14. Proper Span of Control

Span of control, also referred as span of management, indicates how many subordinates can be effectively directed and control by one superior. Span of control depends on a number of factors. However, in most instances, 6 to 9 subordinates can be said as an ideal span of control. This principle must be considered while designing marketing organisation.

15. Other Principles/Qualities

The list seems much lengthy. Some minor principles or qualities of a good organisation have been just listed as under:

(a) Clarity and Precision
(b) Economy/Efficiency
(c) Objectivity – free from bias
(d) Coordination
(e) Provision of Feedback or Review
(f) Facility for Training and Development

The list is not complete. There must be more principles. Every manager, while dealing with day-to-day work, can also develop such principles. Managers should have knowledge of these principles. All these principles are not equally relevant to all organisations. One must apply only relevant principles for better performance.

MARKETING MANAGEMENT MODEL/SYSTEM

Figure 10 shows a model of interactive marketing system. It is also indicative of design of this book. The model exhibits all main chapters and sub-chapters covered in this volume.

In this book, all key components of the model have been logical arranged and adequately discussed in relevant chapters. Chapter 1 and chapter 2 deal with introductory conceptual aspects. They elaborate nature and scope of marketing. Chapter 3 describes issues related marketing environment. As depicted in the figure, marketing environment affects all other decision areas of marketing management, including objectives, inputs, target market, etc. Target market depends on consumer behaviour and market segmentation, described in chapter 4. Marketing mix – the core of marketing management system – occupies about 60% space in this volume. Marketing mix mainly include 4Ps, i.e., product, price, promotion and place decisions. Table 3 in this chapter gives outline of major areas and sub-areas of marketing mix. While chapter 5 and chapter 5.1 describe product mix, the chapter 6 deals with price. Chapters 7 to 7.4 discuss adequately all aspects related to market promotion (including advertising, personal selling, sales promotion, and publicity and public relations) while chapter 8 discusses place aspect of marketing mix and it involves physical distribution and channel of distribution.

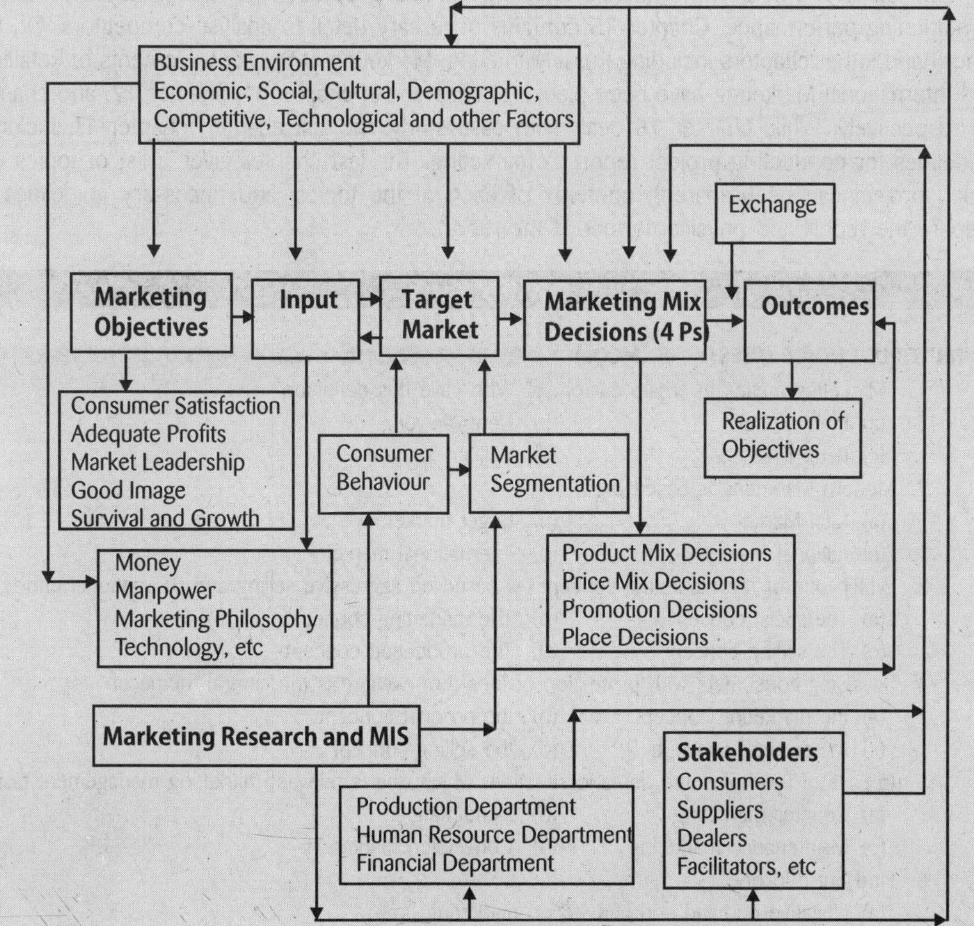

Figure 10: A Model of Interactive Marketing System®

Brief Comment: As shown in figure 10, marketing management process starts with objectives. A firm undertakes marketing activities for one or more marketing objectives. Objective selection depends on type of marketing environment. In order to achieve marketing, objectives the organisation needs to collect and organise productive resources (inputs). Types of resources are again reciprocally affected by the target market. Marketing environment affect the target market. Also, target market selection depends on consumer behaviour and market segmentation which are dependent on marketing research. Market segmentation bases depend on consumer behaviour. Marketing mix decisions (4Ps) are dependent on target market. Marketing mix is a tool that facilitates exchange. It is influenced by broad business environment, stakeholders, and other departments. Marketing information system and marketing research provide necessary information to formulate marketing mix. Effective marketing mix leads to realization of marketing objectives. To know whether firm's objectives have been achieved effectively, marketing research is necessary.

Key elements of marketing information system (MIS) and all basic issues of marketing research have been described in chapter 9. Marketing operations are regulated and controlled by a suitable control system. Some topics of this text have not been depicted in the model because they are not directly influencing marketing system. Chapter 14 descries key issues related to marketing control. Competition is one of powerful factors affecting marketing decisions, is also a key determinant of marketing performance. Chapter 15 contains necessary detail to analyse competitors. On the other hand, other chapters including Rural Marketing, Marketing of Services, Elements of Retailing, and International Marketing have been placed at chapter 10, chapter 11, chapter 12, and chapter 13 respectively. While chapter 16 deals with case study, the last chapter, chapter 17, includes guidelines for conducting project report in marketing. The last chapter gives a list of topics (on which project can be prepared), contents of each of the topics, and necessary guidelines to prepare the report and physical format of the report.

EXERCISES

MULTIPLE CHOICE QUESTIONS (MCQs)

1. "Marketing means to create customer." Who gave this definition?
   (a) Philip Kotler (b) Henry Feyol
   (c) Peter F. Ducker (d) William Stanton
2. Modern Marketing is based on
   (a) total Market (b) target market
   (c) national Market (d) international market
3. Which one of the marketing concepts is based on aggressive selling and promotional efforts?
   (a) The social concept (b) The marketing concept
   (c) The selling concept (d) The production concept
4. Satisfying consumers with protection of long-term welfare is the central theme of
   (a) the marketing concept (b) the product concept
   (c) the societal concept (d) the selling concept
5. In case of unwholesome demand situation, which one is relevant marketing management task?
   (a) Counter marketing (b) Demarking
   (c) Maintenance marketing (d) Conversion marketing
6. Find out odd one.
   (a) Negative demand and conversion marketing
   (b) Latent demand and development marketing

(c) Falling demand and synchromarketing
(d) Overfull demand and demarketing

7. In which of marketing mix elements does the personal selling fall?
(a) Promotion (b) Product
(c) Place (d) Price

8. Find out wrong statement.
(a) Need reflects the state of deprivation.
(b) Wants are options to satisfy a specific need.
(c) Exchange and transfer are exactly same.
(d) Utility implies product's capacity to satisfy need and want.

9. An organisation structure based on zones or places is known as
(a) Functional Organisation (b) Geographical Organisation
(c) Matrix Organisation (d) Customer Organisation

10. Which one is false?
(a) A product includes both a good and a service.
(b) Marketing starts and ends with consumers.
(c) Marketing starts before production and continues even after consumption.
(d) Maximum profit is the sole goal of modern marketing.

MATCHING TYPE QUESTIONS (MTQs)

11.

List I	List II
(a) Marketing Objectives	(1) A demand manager
(b) Target Market	(2) Maximum Consumer Satisfaction
(c) Market	(3) A circle of exchange
(d) Modern Marketing Manager	(4) A well-defined group of buyers

Codes: (A) (a)-(3), (b)-(1),(c)-(4),(d)-(2) (B) (a)-(1),(b)-(2), (c)-(4), (d)-(3)
(C) (a)-(2), (b)-(4), (c)-(3),(d)-(1) (D) (a)-(4),(b)-(1), (c)-(2), (d)-(3)

12.

List I	List II
(a) The Product Concept	(1) Long term social welfare
(b) The Selling Concept	(2) Aggressive selling and promotional efforts
(c) The Marketing Concept	(3) Product qualities and features
(d) The Social Concept	(4) Maximum consumer satisfaction

Codes: (A) (a)-(3), (b)-(2), (c)-(4), (d)-(1) (B) (a)-(2), (b)-(1), (c)-(3), (d)-(4)
(C) (a)-(1), (b)-(4), (c)-(2), (d)-(3) (D) (a)-(4), (b)-(3), (c)-(1), (d)-(2)

13.

List I	List II
(a) Negative Demand	(1) Development Marketing
(b) Unwholesome Demand	(2) Remarketing
(c) Falling Demand	(3) Counter Marketing
(d) Latent Demand	(4) Conversion Marketing

Codes: (A) (a)-(3), (b)-(4), (c)-(2), (d)-(3) (B) (a)-(2), (b)-(1), (c)-(4), (d)-(4)
(C) (a)-(1), (b)-(2), (c)-(1), (d)-(2) (D) (a)-(4), (b)-(3), (c)-(2), (d)-(1)

14.

List I	List II
(a) Consumer orientation	(1) well-defined group of buyers
(b) 4Ps	(2) Love your customer and not your product
(c) Target market	(3) Marketing raises living standard of society
(d) Role of marketing	(4) Elements of Marketing Mix

Codes: (A) (a)-(4), (b)-(3), (c)-(1), (d)-(2) (B) (a)-(4), (b)-(1), (c)-(3), (d)-(2)
(C) (a)-(3), (b)-(1), (c)-(2), (d)-(4) (D) (a)-(3), (b)-(4), (c)-(1), (d)-(2)

ANSWERS KEY: 1(c), 2(b), 3(c), 4(c), 5(a), 6(c), 7(a), 8(c), 9(b), 10(d), 11(C), 12(A), 13(D), 14(D)

QUESTIONS FOR DISCUSSION

(**Note:** These long questions can be asked for 10 to 20 marks)

15. Define term 'market' and 'marketing'. Discuss characteristics of modern marketing.
16. What is marketing? Explain importance of marketing for overall development of the country.
17. State five alternative Marketing Concepts. Differentiate between Societal Concept and Marketing Concept.
18. Write a detailed note on evaluation stages (Marketing Concepts) of development of marketing
19. What is Marketing Management? 'Marketing Management is essentially the management of demand'. Discuss the statement with reference to different demand situations and marketing management tasks.
20. What is do you mean by Marketing Management Tasks? Describe marketing management tasks relevant to different demand situations.
21. "Consumer Satisfaction is the only objective of modern marketing." Do you agree? Why? What should a manager do to ensure maximum consumer satisfaction?
22. What is marketing mix? Explain marketing mix elements. Also enlist factors affecting marketing mix decisions.
23. What is marketing organisation? Discuss types of marketing organisation. Which are the factors to be considered while deciding on marketing organisation?
24. Define marketing organisation. Explain qualities of a good marketing organisation.
25. What is Marketing Environment? Discuss factors affecting Marketing Environment.
26. Explain:
    (a) Exchange, transfer and transaction
    (b) Utility, value and satisfaction
    (c) Need, want and demand
27. Write Notes:
    (a) Marketing Concept
    (b) Societal Concept
    (c) Marketing and economic development
28. Discuss interactive marketing model.

✧✧✧

CHAPTER

2

EMERGING ISSUES IN MARKETING

- Consumer Orientation
- Integrated Marketing
- Business Ethics in Marketing
- Direct and Online Marketing (Cyber Marketing)
- Green Marketing
- Quantitative Techniques for Marketing Decisions
- Consumerism
- Consumer Relationship Building

INTRODUCTION

There are some contemporary issues and developments in marketing that have drawn attention of marketing students and teachers, writers, and practitioners. Most marketing writers and experts use these aspects to enrich marketing theories, and practicing managers use such issues to improve marketing practices. This part considers a few such issues to assist teaching and learning communities to get elementary idea about them.

CONSUMER ORIENTATION

Consumer (or customer) orientation is the focal issue (or central theme) in today's marketing practices. There are four pillars of the modern marketing concept – consumer orientation (may be said as consumer satisfaction), target market, integrated marketing, and profitability. Consumer orientation is a key to achieve business goals. A firm can achieve marketing goals by concentrating on customer satisfaction. Those companies who actualize consumer orientation can achieve better marketing performance.

We can define the term as: *The consumer orientation is modern marketing philosophy and approach that guide the marketing managers to formulate marketing programme (4Ps) in such a way that the firm can offer maximum possible satisfaction to target consumers.*

More clearly, the term can be explained as: *The consumer orientation is modern marketing philosophy that guides the practicing managers to carry out marketing efforts in a manner that result into maximum consumer satisfaction.*

The consumer orientation emphasizes on understanding consumers' real needs, and satisfying them better than any competitor. It requires the company to define the consumer needs from consumer's point of view. Company must do every thing possible to meet expectations of the target consumers.

Mahatma Gandhi's Famous Passage: More than a half century back, Mahatma Gandhi, the Father of Nation, has expressed his views on customer orientation. A famous passage of Mahatma Gandhi emphasizes on the critical place of customers in business.

> "A customer is the most important visitor in our premises.
> He is not dependent on us. We are dependent on him.
> He is not an interruption in our work. He is the purpose of it.
> He is not an outsider to our business. He is part of it.
> We are not doing him a favour by serving him.
> He is doing us a favour by giving us an opportunity to do so.
>
> A customer is not someone to argue with.
> Nobody ever won an argument with the customer.
> A customer is the person who brings us his wants.
> It is our job to handle profitably to him and to ourselves."
>
> – Mahatma Gandhi

Consumer orientation assumes the consumer satisfaction as a guiding philosophy. It is similar to devotion, dedication, and commitment toward consumer satisfaction. It makes the marketers think:

- "Customers are king in our business."
- "Satisfy customer needs to satisfy company's needs."
- "Customers are the best judges of our offers (goods and services)."
- "Customer is the most important person in our business."
- "He never complains... but suggests. He complains for company's benefits. He complains on behalf of product."
- "Customer is not dependent on us...we are dependent on him."
- "He is our business partner, he is our well-wisher. He is doing favour by giving us opportunity to serve him."

MANAGERIAL ACTIONS

Consumer orientation is not just a concept. It carries many important managerial implications. Maximum consumer satisfaction requires systematic marketing efforts. Consumer orientation involves designing entire marketing programme (4P's) in such a way that maximum consumer satisfaction can be achieved. Marketing efforts are directed to satisfy consumers. Every decision is aimed at satisfying needs and wants of the target consumers. Due to competition, the marketer tries to satisfy customers more effectively and efficiently than the competitors. Consumer orientation calls for following actions:

1. Define the target market carefully and collect relevant information.
2. Find out customers' needs and wants.
3. Produce products as per their expectations.
4. Ensure fair deal with customers and ensure commitment toward them.
5. Establish and maintain long-term relations with consumers.
6. Provide them correct information when demanded.
7. Safeguard their long-term interest/welfare.
8. Treat them as business partners.
9. Take care of consumers' suggestions and tackle their complaints.
10. Find out the best way to entertain them, and meet their expectations.

BENEFITS OF CONSUMER ORIENTATION

Note that consumer orientation is not a marketing philosophy only, but it is a dominant business philosophy and it deserves many practical implications for better managing. Company can achieve its goals effectively by practicing consumer orientation philosophy. Consumer orientation leads to consumer satisfaction. Consumer satisfaction offers several benefits to company. The basic question is: Why is company interested to satisfy consumers? Company can have following benefits if it satisfies its consumers:

1. Satisfied consumer buys more quantity of company's products.
2. Satisfied consumer buys the company's products more frequently.
3. Satisfied consumer talks favourably about the company and its products.
4. Satisfied consumer is not easily impressed or attracted by competitors.
5. Satisfied consumer tries and buys new products as and when the company introduces them.
6. Satisfied consumer extends necessary support during bad (adverse) time. He compromises with the company's offer and continues buying the product even at a little loss.
7. Satisfied consumer remains loyal to the company, gives valuable suggestions, and protects company's interest in all possible ways.
8. Satisfied consumer extends all possible support to the company to carry out its operations effectively.

INTEGRATED MARKETING

Customer is the target to serve. Company exists for customer satisfaction. Marketing manager alone cannot satisfy customers; he needs cooperation from others. All the activities of a firm must be integrated in a way that the ultimate consumers are satisfied more effectively than competitors. Integrated (joint) efforts (by all the employees of each and every department) made by the company for a maximum customer satisfaction is called integrated marketing.

Integrated marketing is defined as: *Integrated marketing is the marketing philosophy or approach that guides the manager to integrate (coordinate) marketing efforts with others in a way that result into a maximum customer satisfaction.*

Other activities including finance, production, marketing, research and development, and others must be performed as supporting/supplementary activities to marketing. Further, marketing manager must be regarded as the CEO of the company and the firm must operate as per his direction. Production manager produces what marketing management demands; personnel manager performs human resource activities as per needs of marketing department; and financial manager manages financial matter as per the needs of marketing management. In the same way, today's marketing managers are actively involved in integrating marketing efforts with external parties, such as suppliers, dealers, service providers, etc.

Integrated marketing takes place at three levels. First, the various marketing functions, like sales force, advertising, product management, marketing research, distribution, and so forth, must work together, in the integrated manner. Second, marketing department must be well coordinated with other departments, including finance, production, and personnel. Third, marketing department must coordinate its efforts with external stakeholders like customers, suppliers, bankers, governments, and other relevant groups. In short, integrated marketing implies integrating marketing efforts within marketing department, between marketing department and other departments of organisation, and between marketing department and outside parties.

One can also witness that marketing management is emerging as a single most dominant academic disciplines which covers not only finance, personnel, and production functions, but also mathematics, statistics, engineering, computer science, organisational behaviour (including psychology, sociology, social-psychology, political science, anthropology, and economics), and many other disciplines. Marketing is multidimensional and multidisciplinary science. Curricula or syllabi of other subjects are designed as per marketing needs. Marketing must be the focus of other academic disciplines.

IMPLICATIONS

Integrated marketing implies:

1. Customer is the target to serve. Marketing is the base to satisfy him. Other managements – production management, financial management and personnel management – are reduced to just a branches of marketing management.
2. Business environment is a source of marketing opportunities and threats. There are nothing like financial, personnel, and production opportunities. They are reduced to supporting activities of marketing department.
3. Marketing goals are treated as the superordinated goals that incorporate goals of all other activities or functions. Consumer satisfaction is goal of business enterprise, not of marketing department alone.
4. Marketing manager enjoys the highest position after the GM (may be said as the CEO), even he can be treated as the GM and other departmental heads are considered as assistant managers/senior officers/staff functions. Role, status, position, and separate entity of other managers have been undermined.
5. Marketing manager is responsible to coordinate efforts of all the functions of all departments for fulfillment of common goals. He is finally responsible for ultimate performance of the business enterprise.
6. Business goal to make profits has been replaced by consumer satisfaction. Consumer satisfaction is the only goal and is instrumental for other secondary goals. It is not the goal of marketing but of the entire business. Marketing manager integrates and coordinates efforts of all departments to achieve a maximum consumer satisfaction.
7. Marketing management is emerging a single most dominant academic discipline with not only internal integration but also integrating knowledge of mathematics, statistics, engineering, computer science, organizational behaviour (including psychology, sociology, social-psychology, political science, anthropology, and economics), and many other disciplines to enrich marketing theory and practice. Marketing is a multidimensional and multidisciplinary science. Marketing must be the focus of other academic disciplines.
8. Marketing manager is also required to integrate his efforts with external parties, including suppliers, dealers, service providers, government officials, etc., for excelling marketing performance.

DIRECT AND ONLINE MARKETING

Direct and online marketing is catching attention of businessmen and industrialists. Direct marketing and online marketing both are complementary terms and are taken together. (Online marketing is one of the options of direct marketing). However, both are different. Direct marketing is comparatively more effective and cheap. Similarly, most companies have developed their websites to facilitate their valued customers access goods and services. Not only hotels and resorts, airlines, railways travel, bank, etc., services, but consumable, jewelry, cosmetic, electronics and other products can also be sold through online marketing. Most companies prepare customer database (up-to-date computer-based information about customers) to treat customers more effectively.

DIRECT MARKETING

Direct marketing is, sometimes, known as direct-order marketing, too. It is at-home shopping system. Direct marketing is playing a broader role for building long-term relationships with the customers (direct relationship marketing). It is the way of dealing with customers directly, bypassing middlemen. It is a direct channel of ordering and distribution.

The Direct Marketing Association defines the term as: "Direct Marketing is an interactive marketing system that uses one or more advertising media to effect measurable response and/ or transaction at any location."

E (electronic)-commerce and Electronic market provide a support to describe needed products and services, allow buyers to search information and make queries, identify products they need and want, and place order using credit card. The product is then delivered physically to the customer at home or office (in case of software, it is send electronically to a customer's computer).

METHODS/CHANNELS OF DIRECT MARKETING

Different methods are used for direct marketing. These methods are used for getting information, sending orders, or lodging complaints. Most widely used methods for direct marketing involve:

1. Selling products by sales force or face-to-face selling.
2. Face-to-face selling at company's showrooms or retail outlets.
3. Direct mail to company for ordering or information (direct mail marketing).
4. Fax mail or E-mail to company for placing order or getting information
5. On-line marketing/cyber marketing. Connecting PCs with websites for dealings.
6. M-mail (mobile mail) or MMS/SMS through mobile phone.
7. Kiosk marketing (customer-order-placing machines). Electronic Kiosk provides needed information to customers and accepts orders from customers.
8. Automatic vending machine (for products like cold drinks, cigarette, travel tickets, candy, coffee, money etc.)
9. Telemarketing and voice mail, etc.

CYBER OR ONLINE MARKETING

Cyber marketing is one of the options for direct marketing. It is also known as online marketing, e (electronic)-marketing, e-commerce, Internet marketing, or, simply, Net marketing. Cyber marketing is the latest marketing development. It is a type of arrangement by which buyers and sellers can meet through electronic line via computers and modems. It is the method connecting marketers and customers through Internet. Both parties can exchange information necessary to arrive at exchange. Here, ordering and paying are made online. Normally, commercial online channels and Internet are used for online marketing.

Cyber marketing is used for both promotion tool as well as distribution tool. It can be used for marketing research purpose, too.

DEFINITION

Cyber marketing concerns with information technology. The main purpose is to exchange information. So, we can define it as: *Cyber marketing is an integrated form of Internet technology and direct marketing, used to find out profitable customers and develop rich contacts with them. Through contacts, one can know who, when, why, and with which conditions want to deal with business firm.*

In short, it can be defined as: *Cyber marketing is a system or arrangement of conducting marketing transactions through Internet Technology.*

Marketers (and customers) who want to practice cyber marketing require the latest computer with appropriate operating system and necessary software (programmes like web browser), modem, speakers, Internet connection, and primary knowledge of operating computer and Internet surfing.

Through online marketing, except software or programme, only information is exchanged, or order is placed. Actual delivery of physical products is made through different delivery systems (like post, courier, and person) with appropriate mode of transportation.

Online marketing is one that a person can reach the company via computer and modem. A modem connects the computer to a telephone (landline as well as mobile) line or data card so that the computer users (marketers and customers) can reach various online services. Online marketing only facilitates electronic transactions, but not delivery of physical products. Physical delivery can be made by any mode like person, transport agency, airline, rail, or private agencies. However, software can be sent directly to customer's computer.

ONLINE MARKETING ACTIVITIES

Online marketing involves following activities:

1. Collecting information (marketing research),
2. Sending information and promoting products,
3. Evaluation and selecting the right products,
4. Requesting quarries, seeking guidance and clarifications,
5. Lodging complaints,
6. Placing orders or making transactions – buying and selling,
7. Billing and paying,
8. Building, maintaining, and improving relationships with customers and other publics, etc.

APPLICABILITY

Nowadays, cyber marketing is widely used for all types of activities, like:

1. Buying and selling goods via Internet.
2. Downloading (sending/receiving) needed programmes or software
3. Medical profession (health care online)
4. Research (investigation) and development activities.
5. Online propaganda of political, social, or religious affairs.
6. Online advertising, publicity, and public relations.
7. Friendship and matrimonial related activities.
8. Banking, insurance, communication, transportation, etc., transactions.
9. Online emergency (fire brigade, police, and medical) services.
10. Investment (stock market –primary and secondary market, mutual fund, commodity market, savings, etc.)
11. Online education, training, and counseling.
12. Online examination (written tests or oral tests) and evaluation.
13. Online publications of books and articles (e-books and e-articles).
14. Travels and hotels (booking hotels and buying tickets of airways, railways, roadways, or seaways).
15. Entertainment (movies on demand, Internet games, online contests, and such other ways of entertainment).

BENEFITS OF DIRECT AND ONLINE MARKETING

Direct and online marketing have been increasingly used for consumable as well as durable products. Consumers report that direct marketing is fun, convenient, and hassle-free. It saves time and provides opportunities for a larger selection of merchandise. Most companies have designed their websites for the purpose. Easy and affordable excess to Internet made it more popular and, hence, widely used option to arrive at exchange. This option offers ease, economy, convenience, and speed in decision, actions, and transactions. It is beneficial to both marketer and customers. Let us list the benefits of direct and, particularly, cyber marketing:

1. Wide scope of selection for customers.
2. Presence of company's product in the global market.
3. Attractive presentation of complete information and all products.
4. Reliable and speedy access to information.
5. High convince.
6. Transaction with secrecy and safety.
7. Cyber marketing is multipurpose tool.
8. Relationship building.
9. No higher costs of approaching and information.
10. Reduced traffic problems and parking problems.
11. Easy access and speedy transactions at lower costs.
12. Less chances of cheating or fraud.
13. Damage-free products.
14. Availability of standard products.
15. Promotion of new products by direct and online marketing.
16. More suitable for demonstration and education. Online and direct marketing facilitate more convenient demonstration and education of the products.
17. It can be used for establishing good image or improving bad image.
18. Online marketing satisfies the esteem of customers. It is treated as the latest mode of accessing information about the products at fingertips.

CYBER MARKETING PROCESS OR IMPORTANT DECISIONS FOR CYBER MARKETING

A company planning to practice cyber marketing needs to decide on following five important aspects:

1. Designing Web Marketing Tool Box

This decision concerns with designing website for the company. In today's marketing practices, almost all firms, whether small or large, have their own websites. The firm must design the web carefully. Up-to-date marketing structure is designed with all key marketing aspects. The website must include necessary web pages that must be linked with home page. Normally, website consists of list of company details including name, address, registered office, phones, fax and e-mail address, products and detailed features of each of the product, price list and related incentives, special achievements, and other relevant information. Figures, numerical data, charts, brands, pictures, tables, etc., are used as per need to make the site attractive. Website must be supported with multiple link and multiple effects. It should contain moving or blinking pictures with necessary links to attract and arouse curiosity. The design of website must be such that one can easily access needed details. In short, the web marketing tool must be attractive, convenient, and perfect. Professional web designers can assist in designing a suitable web marketing tool.

2. Designing Web Address

When the website is ready, it must be given its name or address. It is known as URL-Universal Resource Locator. The address must be set carefully. It must not be too long or too short. In the same way, it must be meaningful to remember. It should indicate type of business (banking, insurance, company, educational institute, university, etc.), name of country (.in for India, .uk for United Kingdom, jp for Japan, etc.) Unnecessary symbols like slash (/), dash (-), star (*), hash (#) or any other symbols must be avoided. Only alphabets (a to z) and numbers (1 to 100) are used to design web addresses. In order to specify the group of business, specific words are used at the end of website like .edu for education, com. for communication/commerce, org. for organisation, etc. For example, HDFC Bank's web address is www.hdfcbank.com and www.hdfcsec.com. In short, address must be short, attractive, meaningful, and simple.

3. Presence in Search Engine and Directories

Once the Web is ready, it must be entered to the search engine so that web visitors can find it easy to access the company. In the same way, according to type of business, country, or any other criterion, it must be registered in directories so that people can easily reach the destination. There are many search engines like Google, AltaVista, Yahoo Search, Aj.com, MSN Search, etc. The address must be present in all the search engines. In same way, many directories are available like business, art, medical, publication, employment, film, sports, government, education, science and technology, and likewise. Website must be placed in suitable directories.

4. Advertising the Website

In order to make the website known to all, it must be properly advertised. Attempts must be made to popularize the website. For advertising purpose, it can be advertised by websites of other companies. In same way, web address must be communicated in advertising the products through different media. It can be advertised by placing on packaging and labeling of products. It can be placed in pen, card, calendar, reports, sticker, diary, label, and other articles.

5. Monitoring and Updating

Once the website is successful launched on the Internet, it must be observed and monitor regularly. Time to time, the web must undergo necessary modifications. The firm can employ expert staff to maintain the web. Sometimes, such work is assigned to outside professionals on contract basis. Regulating and updating website can meet changing needs of the company as well as the market.

Note that cyber marketing is not free from problems. Cyber crime (or fraud) is major issue. In the same way, quality of allied facilities determines effectiveness of cyber marketing. Some people argue that is a facility for availing necessary information, it is not a full-fledged marketing option to all marketing transactions. In addition, it cannot replace the place (or role) of a face-to-face dealing. It makes the deal between seller and buyer as mechanical ones; it lacks emotions and gestural expressions, like warm greeting, smile, welcoming, giving send off, etc. In case of problem with product or service, it multiplies customer's difficulties. Cyber marketing needs basic infrastructure, fair literacy rate, healthy mentality, and mutual trust. Only a few people can practice or adopt cyber marketing. However, it is fast developing mode of marketing, especially, for promotion and distribution. It is developing and advancing in our country. However, it can be a good option, and cannot replace entire marketing system.

GREEN MARKETING

Here, term 'green' is indicative of purity. Green means pure in quality and fair or just in dealing. For example, green advertising means advertising without adverse impact on society. Green message means matured and neutral facts, free from exaggeration or ambiguity. Green marketing is highly debated topic for lay people to highly professional groups.

Concept of green marketing concerns with protection of ecological environment. Modern marketing has created a lot of problems. Growth in marketing activities resulted into rapid economic growth, mass production with the use of advanced technology, comfortable and luxurious life, style, severe competition, use of unhealthy marketing tactics and techniques to attract customers, exaggeration in advertising, liberalization and globalization, creation of multinational companies, retailing and distribution by giant MNCs, etc., created many problems. Departmental stores, specialty stores, and shopping malls are flooded with useful as well as useless products. These all factors have threatened welfare of people and ecological balance as well. Particularly, giant factories have become the source of different pollutions. Production, consumption and disposal of many products affect environment adversely. Excessive pollution has provoked the Nature and the Nature starts behaving in unnatural ways (in form of global warming v/s global cooling, heavy rains v/s draught, and other natural calamities like frequent earthquakes and tsunami, cyclones, epidemics, and so forth). Economic growth via production and consumption threatens peaceful life of human being on the earth. Green marketing is an attempt to protect consumer welfare and environment (the nature) through production, consumption, and disposal of eco-friendly products.

Basically, green marketing concerns with three aspects:

1. Promotion of production and consummation of pure/quality products,
2. Fair and just dealing with customers and society, and
3. Protection of ecological environment.

Global ecological imbalance and global warming (also global cooling) have called upon environmentalists, scientists, social organisations, and alert common men to initiate the concrete efforts to stop further deterioration of ecological environment. The World Bank, the SAARC, the UNO, the WHO, and other globally influential organisations have started their efforts to promote and practice green marketing. The world environment summit at Copenhagen (2009) is the mega event that shows the seriousness of ecological imbalance. To increase awareness, 5th June is declared as the World Environment Day. Green marketing emphases on protection of long-term welfare of consumers and society by production and use of pure, useful, and high quality products without any adverse effect on the environment. Mass media have started their campaign for protecting the earth from further deterioration. Worldwide efforts are made to conserve natural water resources.

Thus, *green marketing is a marketing philosophy that promotes production and selling of pure (eco-friendly) products with protection of ecological balance.*

Green marketing involves multiple activities. Green Marketing encourages production of pure products by pure technology, conservation of energy, preservation of environment, minimum use of natural resources, and more use of natural foods instead of processed foods. Efforts of people, social organisations, firms, and governments in this regard can be said as green marketing efforts.

Green marketing raises the voice against production, consumption, and/or disposal of such products that anyway harm consumers, the society, and the environment. It is necessary that businessmen and users should refrain from harmful products.

EFFORTS AND ACTIVITIES

Green marketing concerns with following efforts:

1. Educating people to protect environment in all possible ways.
2. Use of natural substances, instead of synthesis, for production of useful products.
3. Use of environment friendly (pure) production technology or processes.
4. Minimizing use of plastic products and promoting use of paper, cloths, and leaves.
5. Recycling of wastes into useful products (best from waste) and applying pollution control systems.
6. Minimum and effective use of non-renewable natural resources like minerals, forests, water, etc.

7. Minimizing use of pesticides, chemical fertilizers and such farming techniques that damage natural constituents of land, and promoting organic farming and use of bullocks for agriculture.
8. People should be conveyed to use pure/harmless herbal products. Convincing people to use herbal shampoos, soaps, and washing powders, which have less adverse impact on environment. Neem, aloe-veera, etc., should be used for producing cleaning, washing, and bathing products.
9. Promoting companies to use special marks or symbols for indicating purity of the products. Different countries uses marks to indicate 'purity' of products, e. g., Eco Mark in Japan, Eco Loco in Canada, Blue Angle in Germany, etc. Green symbol or agmarks are used by marketers to indicate agricultural and pure products.
10. Educating and encouraging people to use solar cookers, solar heaters, battery-based vehicles, production and use of bio-gas and bio-diesel based on animal dung and/or agro-products.
11. More emphasis is given on promoting and using renewable energy sources like wind-power, hydroelectricity, solar energy, etc., instead of using mineral or non-renewable resources (coal, petroleum, natural gas, etc.).
12. Teaching and encouraging people to minimize use of chemical-based medicines and go for natural treatment and Yogas. Naturopathy and Ayurvedic treatment, and use of herbal medicines should be popularized.
13. Undertaking rigorous campaign to make people free from addictions of tobacco and tobacco-based products, morphine, cocaine, and other deadly substances.
14. Initiating world-wide campaign for preventing production and use of nuclear weapons (atom bombs), chemical weapons, and other mass destruction devices to protect living beings on the earth.
15. Government establishes, assists, protects, and encourages handcrafts, and tiny and cottage industries to produce pure products without any damage to ecological environment.
16. National and international organizations offer several certificates and awards to those business firms that take care of health of people and environment. ISI Mark/certificate by Indian Standard Institute, ISO 9000 series, ISO 14000 series (particularly for protection of environment), and ISO 21000 series issued by International Standard Organisation, Geneva, encourages production of pure products by pure technology. Additionally, governments, many reputed private agencies, and organisations also felicitate companies working for protection of environment.
17. Educating, counseling and convincing people to go for simple, healthy, and pure life. They are to be convinced to use balance diet – milk, fruits, vegetable, and green salads, etc. – and avoid junk or ready-made fast foods.

Green marketing consists of all efforts that make our life happy and healthy in all significant regards. It is not only restricted to production, distribution, and use of eco-friendly products; it basically includes promoting idea for the natural life, good habits, and healthy mentality. It restricts all practices that affect adversely the quality of life and ecological balance. It is a broad philosophy that ensures well-being of all living beings on the earth.

IMPACTS OR IMPORTANCE OF GREEN MARKETING

Green marketing affects positively the health of people and the ecological environment. People are aware of pure products and pure methods of producing, using, and disposing the products. It encourages integrated efforts for purity in production and consumption as well. We can witness following impacts of green marketing:

1. Now, people are insisting pure products – edible items, fruits, and vegetables based on organic farming. The number of people seeking vegetarian food is on rise.

2. Reducing use of plastics and plastic-based products.
3. Increased consumption of herbal products instead of processed products.
4. Recommending use of leaves instead of plastic pieces; jute and cloth bags instead of plastic carrying bags.
5. Increasing use of bio-fertilizers (made of agro-wastes and wormy-composed) instead of chemical fertilizers (i.e. organic farming), and minimum use of pesticides.
6. Worldwide efforts to recycle wastes of consumer and industrial products.
7. Increased use of herbal medicines, natural therapy, and Yoga.
8. Strict provisions to protect forests, flora and fauna, protection of the rivers, lakes and seas from pollutions.
9. Global restrictions on production and use of harmful weapons, atomic tests, etc. Various organisations of several countries have formulated provisions for protecting ecological balance.
10. More emphasis on social and environmental accountability of producers.
11. Imposing strict norms for pollution control. Consideration of pollution control efforts and eco-technology in awarding ISI, ISO 9000, or ISO 14000 certificates and other awards.
12. Declaration of 5th June as the World Environment Day.
13. Strict legal provisions for restricting duplication or adulteration.
14. Establishing several national and international agencies to monitor efforts and activities of business firms in relation pollution control and production of eco-friendly products.

BUSINESS ETHICS AND MARKETING

Business (or marketing) ethics are the moral principles generally found in forms of formulas, songs, anecdotes, statements, or words that indicate direct or indirect lessons or guidelines that businessmen have to observe while dealing with various interested parties. Business ethics and marketing seem clashing. But, it is not the case always. Nowadays, due to competition, consumer awareness, government compulsion, and self-restrictions imposed by the regulating body for the relevant associations, marketers have started observing business ethics in marketing practices. Marketing ethics are meant for ensuring fair dealings with marketing participants – customers, dealers, employees, government, and the society. Consumerism, a social movement, is directed toward compelling the marketing managers to practice such ethics. Ethics are either observed voluntarily or are forced by the Law. In order to protect consumer rights (for example, right to know, right to complain, right to be heard, right to safety, etc.) and ensure consumer welfare, government of India has formulated at least 30 Laws, of which, most of them have been amended several times to match the contemporary situations.

DEFINITIONS

In fact, it is not possible to define marketing ethics in the exact words as they exert many loose implications. There can be several definitions of marketing ethics.

In simple words, we can say: *Business ethics are standards or moral principles to judge right or wrong. They determine system of conduct or behaviour of businessmen in relation to customers and others parties involved in business activities.*

Ethics can be expressed in a variety of forms. It can be said: *Business ethics are the moral principles generally found in forms of formulas, songs, anecdotes, statements, or words that indicate direct or indirect lessons or guidelines that businessmen have to observe while dealing with various parties.*

Ethics put restrictions on dealings and decisions of manager. In this regard, we can define the term as: *Marketing or business ethics are moral restrictions prescribed by the relevant bodies, including associations, local authorities, or by the governments.*

In the same way: *Marketing/business ethics are the business conditions that a marketer is required to observe while dealing with customers and other participants. The ethics are self-observed or imposed by relevant bodies for the benefits of customers and society as a whole.*

At last, we can say: *Marketing ethics consist of those moral responsibilities of marketing managers related to protecting the rights and ensuring the welfare of consumers, and fair dealing with all other parties involved in marketing transactions.*

SOME BUSINESS ETHICS

There are a number of moral principles prescribed by different associations and governments. They include:

1. Do not cheat customers by defective or inferior products.
2. Avoid black marketing, hoarding, profiteering and speculation for the interest of buyers.
3. Refrain from unhealthy competition, or promote healthy competition.
4. Ensure honesty and precision while packaging, labeling, and advertising the products.
5. Do not defame the image and reputation of other rival firms by improper methods.
6. Create and maintain up-to-date records of economic transactions and produce them when asked by the relevant authority.
7. Pay taxes and duties honestly in time.
8. Discharge social responsibilities towards suppliers, governments, investors, employees, service providers, etc.
9. Do not make any contracts with others that affect adversely the long-term social interest and welfare of people. Do not work against national interest.
10. Extend all possible support and cooperation to the governments in implementing social and economic plans.
11. Contribute liberally for promoting socially significant activities.
12. Protect ecological environment in all possible ways.

Who form and promote business ethics? Various parties can contribute to formulation (development) and promotion of business ethics. Particularly, globally recognized organisations (like the WHO, the World Bank, the UNO, the UNESCO, the UNICEF, etc.), non-government organisations (NGOs), trade unions, governments, relevant associations of business units and industries, professionals, spiritual organisations and religious leaders, active and established political parties, academic and training institutes, business organisations (their founders/pioneers and managing bodies), customer organisations, any other registered or non-registered body of people, and a common man can have valuable direct or indirect contribution in development and promotion of business ethics. Business ethics are promoted through general or specific circulars, bulletins, reposts, speeches of well-known personalities, and all other mass media.

NEEDS AND OBJECTIVES OF BUSINESS ETHICS IN MARKETING

Business ethics are special type of regulatory guidelines. They are vital for making business operations more authentic. Today's marketing practices are full of deceptive packing, ambiguous offers, exaggerated advertising, and aggressive selling. Some marketers practice several unfair tactics to attract customers in pursuit of sales volumes and profits. Business ethics restrict these all things. Their presence and compulsion to follow them make a lot of difference in marketing activities. Business ethics are necessary for marketer as well as consumers. They have many direct or indirect purposes. Some common purposes may include the followings:

1. To prevent malpractices in business. Ethics make business activities more authentic.
2. To ensure uniformity in marketing practices among various business enterprises throughout the country.
3. To make marketers more aware, sensible, and liable to customers and society as a whole.
4. To ensure confirmation of marketing practices with the contemporary legal framework.
5. To enforce government, voluntary social organisations, and others to be alert regarding long-term interest and welfare of society.
6. To assist government to formulate necessary legal provisions and enforce the marketers to obey them.
7. To distinguish ideal firms from exploiting firms. They facilitate in taking needed actions against those firms indulging malpractices.
8. To decide on rewards, awards, certificates, prizes, and other encouragements for deserving business firms.

QUANTITATIVE TECHNIQUES FOR MARKETING DECISIONS

We know that decision-making is essential and dominating part of management. A person is called as manager because he is decision-maker. All functions such as planning, organising, staffing, directing, and controlling involve a series of decisions. Further, success of any business enterprise, to a large extent, depends on quality and timing of decision-making. Therefore, management can be said as decision-making. Quantitative techniques assist in making proper decisions in time.

Traditionally, decision-making was considered as an art or an experience-based talent to decide. During those days, business was very simple. But, today's situation is different. Business involves a lot of activities, is affected by several factors, and it is conducted in a rapidly changing environment. Modern business is much complex and dynamic. It needs a systematic and scientific approach to take the right decision in time. Another important issue is that modern business decisions involve a large number of variables and bulk amount of data. Modern business enterprises need to solve problems systematically that involves defining problem objectively, collecting data (facts, and figures), analyzing data thoroughly through the latest techniques, and deriving implications important for decision-making. Today's manager has to exercise available and suitable quantitative techniques for either data collection, data analysis, or both.

Any problem relating to any area of business operations can be solved by selecting and implementing the right alternative. Thus, decision-making involves selection of the appropriate option/alternative.

DEFINITIONS

We can define quantitative techniques as:

Quantitative techniques are basically mathematical and statistical methods, which can be used to identify, analyse, or to solve business problems.

Further, we can say: *Quantitative techniques are part of Operation Research (OR) that may be used to analyse and solve the quantifiable managerial problems.*

More clearly: *Quantitative techniques can be defined as the application of scientific methods, techniques, and tools for problem solving and decision-making.*

DECISION-MAKING AND QUANTITATIVE TECHNIQUES

Complexities in decision-making exist due to several factors such as economic, political, legal, technological, competitive and environmental; the limited resources of organisation; and the values, risks, attitudes, and knowledge of decision-makers. Due to these factors, the decision becomes multidimensional. Such situation requires use of quantitative approach to decision-making, which includes identifying and quantifying relevant factors. The general approach to solve business problems by using quantitative techniques is variedly designated as operations research, quantitative analysis, management science, decision science, mathematical approach, etc. Quantitative analysis is now extended to several areas of business operations and is probably considered as the most effective approach to handle some types of problems.

BENEFITS/ADVANTAGES OF QUANTITATIVE TECHNIQUES

If quantitative techniques are practiced for business decision-making, following possible benefits can be enjoyed:

1. Accuracy

Managerial activities and processes can be transformed into mathematical terms, data, or symbols. So, problem can be expressed in more precise manner. Managerial problems can be solved accurately, indiscriminately, and scientifically.

2. Consideration of Variables

Quantitative techniques consider all the possible variables and their interrelations involved in the problems. More comprehensive analysis is possible.

3. Economic

They are affordable by small and medium size firms. Models and software are cheaper and easily available. Quantitative techniques can be used for personal purpose, too.

4. Specialization

There are number of quantitative techniques. Depending on type of problem, the most appropriate method(s) can be used.

5. Speed

Proper use of models and computer-based software leads to accurate and speedy results. Problems can be analyzed and solved within limited time.

6. Reliability

Quantitative techniques are based on sufficient facts and figures. They give unbiased results, and, hence, are more reliable. Results are free from personal values, attitudes, needs, and other personality characteristics.

7. Simplification

Complex problems, involving bulk data, number of variables, and multiple relations, can be easily and accurately expressed and solved.

8. Clarity

Clarity and preciseness are possible. They offer more specific explanation of the problem under consideration.

LIMITATIONS

Users must be aware of their limitations. Main limitations of quantative techniques are:

1. Quantitative techniques can be used only when numerical (or quantifiable) data are available. There are many managerial problems, which cannot be expressed in quantifiable terms; hence, such techniques cannot be used.
2. There are some models, which have limited practical value. They are used to express problems in the sophisticated style.

3. Quantitative techniques are aid to decision-making. They do not take decisions. It is manager who takes decisions. So, impact of personal values, needs, and personality aspects cannot be eliminated.
4. Some techniques involve complex calculations and more time. Sometimes, it may lead to very strange results.
5. Certain models are costly. Even, use of such models need experts' services, which is costlier.
6. They show results, possible alternatives with outcomes, but final decisions cannot be taken automatically.

LIST OF QUANTITATIVE TECHNIQUES

The quantitative techniques listed under this topic are used for managerial decisions in varied areas of business operations. They employ mathematical and statistical tools to understand, analyse, and solve management problem in any area of business operations. Some are used in production area; some are used in marketing area; some are used in personnel area; some are used in financial; and some of them can be used in any area of business management. Since, marketing is treated as integrated function, which considers all the activities of business enterprise for marketing decisions, these techniques can be said as quantitative techniques for marketing decision-making. The techniques are used either for identification, analysis, or solution of managerial problems. These quantitative techniques can be used for various purposes such as (1) Quantitative techniques for forecasting and planning (2) Quantitative techniques for decision-making (3) Quantitative techniques for controlling.

1. Probability Distribution, including Binomial Distribution, Poisson Distribution, and Normal Distribution
2. Linear Programming – Graphical Method and Simplex Method
3. Transportation Problems (related to transportation)
4. Assignment Problems (related to assignment of work)
5. Sequencing Problems
6. Inventory Management and Economic Ordering Quantity
7. Queuing Theory or Waiting Line Theory
8. Replacement Theory (related to replacement of equipment)
9. Network Analysis/Project Management – PERT (Programme Evaluation and Review Technique) and CPM (Critical Path Method)
10. Decision Theory and Decision Tree
11. Theory of Game/Game Theory
12. Simulation
13. MARKOV Analysis
14. Investment analysis
15. Break-Even Analysis
16. Statistical Quality Control (SQC)
17. Others:
    i. Ratio Analysis
    ii. Times Series, and Regression Analysis
    iii. Input-output Analysis
    iv. Capital Budgeting Techniques
    v. Index Numbers
    vi. Expontial Smoothing, etc.

CONSUMERISM

Consumerism is not a recent phenomenon. It is assumed that the movement started in 1960s when President John Kennedy sent the Congress a special message on protecting consumer interest. The message included four consumer rights–the right to safety, the right to be informed, the right to choose, and the right to be heard. This message served as an important incident to launch the modern consumer movement. Initially, the movement started in Japan, Canada, Sweden, Britain, etc. Now, it is a global issue. In most of countries, this movement has been running in one or another form. It emerged because the consumer was not safe at market place. Societal concept has not been accepted as the marketing philosophy. Thus, it is an attempt to realize societal concept in practice. In the major part of the world, market is still dominated by producers and/or sellers. Obviously, when market is dominated by the marketers, consumers are more likely to be cheated or exploited. Due to over flooded products, severe competition to snatch market shares, intensive and exaggerated advertisement, lethargic and illiterate consumers, poor legal framework, inadequate role of social institutes, and many other such reasons, the consumers are observed helpless. They are more vulnerable to be cheated. Actually, consumerism is a social movement against malpractices indulged by marketers. It is the movement to protect consumer rights and interests. We must state that though this movement concerns with protecting the rights and interest of buyers against sellers, along with consumers, sellers, governments, and social organizations are actively involved in it. Indian government has so far formulated at least 30 Laws to protect interest of consumers against sellers.

DEFINITIONS

The term 'consumerism' has been defined as follows:

1. *Consumerism is the reaction of consumers against unfair trade practices carried out by the marketer. It shows consumer dissatisfaction toward the unjust business activities.*
2. *Consumerism is an evolving set of activities of government, business enterprises, independent organizations, and consumers that is designed to protect the rights of consumers.*
3. *Consumerism is a joint endeavor of government, businessmen, independent organizations, and consumers to enhance consumers' rights and to protect their interests.*
4. *Consumerism involves the united and organised efforts to fight against unfair marketing practices and to secure consumer protection.*
5. **Philip Kotler:** "Consumerism is a social movement seeking to increase the powers and rights of buyers in relation to sellers."

ROLE OR IMPORTANCE OF CONSUMERISM IN INDIA

(Causes Leading to Emergence of Consumerism)

We must mention that a pace of consumerism has been slow in India. Gradually, it has been recognizing as an important phenomenon to accept and practice. One can say that consumerism in India is in its childhood. Industrial revolution led to mass production, mass production led to intensive/aggressive marketing, which ultimately resulted into consumer exploitation. However, with reference to India, consumerism has a special role to play. Note that consumerism is not just to fight against traders to protect consumers' rights, but also it is important to educate consumers for their rights. It is aimed at increasing consumer awareness, enforcing government to exercise meaningful control over business activities, and to inspire independent social organisations to participate actively in this regard. Discussed on the next page are some of the reasons why consumerism has been recognized as an essential movement:

1. Indian market is still dominated by traders. Therefore, consumers are more likely to be cheated. Consumerism can influence traders' decisions for consumer interest or rights.
2. Indian consumers are backward. Most of them are not aware of products, their ingredients, price, and related services. If they are not protected, they can be easily cheated. Consumerism safeguards interests of innocent buyers.
3. Illiteracy is the basic reason that necessitates this social movement. Nearly 35% Indian consumers are illiterate. Description on product package is mostly in English. It is hard for them to read it. Consumerism prevents traders to refrain from any unfair practice.
4. Poverty and lack of information provide the traders an easy platform to mislead consumers. Consumerism safeguards poor and uninformed consumers.
5. Consumerism can impose compulsion on the government to be more active to protect consumer interest. Government is forced to prepare and implement more regulatory measures for the consumers' sake.
6. Basically, Indian consumers are lethargic. They are not very responsive. They hardly react strongly to unfair marketing practices. Consumerism can make them more responsive, alert, and active to fight against such practices.
7. Consumerism makes it possible for all the people to participate in the benefits resulting from economic development. Consumers and marketers both are mutually benefited.
8. It maintains balance between economic development and social welfare.
9. It can lead to safety, equality, and fairness in business activities, avoiding malpractices. Finally, consumerism becomes a very good tool to encourage cooperation between marketers and consumers. It improves entire market system, or quality of business practices. Harmony and peace prevail in market. Country can get recognition globally.
10. Now, Indian market has become a global market. LPG – Liberalization, Privatization, and Globalization–have necessitated the role consumerism to awake consumers for their rights and to fight against undesirable marketing practices indulged by Indian and foreign traders. Recent disinvestments/privatization policy of government, attacks of multinational companies on Indian market, and borderless trade throughout the globe have confused consumers. Consumerism has a long way to go to extend its help.
11. Invade of imported products, misleading advertising, attractive packaging, illusionary sales promotion techniques, intelligent hording and black marketing, and so forth can cheat poor, illiterate, and innocent Indian consumers. Both Indian and foreign traders take undue advantages of gullible consumers. Consumerism can have a wider role in such situations.
12. With tremendous march of science and technology, especially, revolutionary growth in information technology and professional marketing, and excessive market promotional efforts, consumers are found lost. They seem confused. Consumerism can serve as a guide to assist them to protect their interest by suitable buying decisions.
13. Public sectors services, public utilities, government companies, etc., have monopoly in many cases. When there is monopoly, exploitation is almost obvious. Individual consumers, even the local body of consumers, cannot raise voice against inferior quality, poor services, irregularity, overprices, etc. Consumerism can support consumers to protect their interest.

REASONS/PROBLEMS LEADING TO FAILURE OF CONSUMERISM

Though consumerism has a vital role in developing countries like India to awake consumers for their rights and prepare them to fight against any kind of unfair trade practices, its pace is far slow than expectation. Needless to state that consumerism has partially failed in India. This movement has not contributed to the extent it was needed. At present, Indian consumers are still cheated; erotic, senseless, and misleading advertisements are still exhibited openly through mass media; non-profit voluntary social organizations have been found diverted from the basic purpose for which they have been organised; partial failure of government machineries to implement the Laws formulated to protect consumers; prohibited products are distributed openly; and substandard and duplicate products are constantly over-flooded in the market. There are legal provisions, but are in government custody, not effectively and adequately implemented. Due to an inadequate role of consumerism, it can be said that consumerism is in the initial stage in India. It is expected to play more magnifying role. We haven't witnessed the real outcome of this movement. Failure of consumerism can be attributed to following reasons:

(These reasons are more closely related to the situations, which have, necessitated the active role consumerism as stated in the former part of this chapter.)

1. Lengthy, tedious, and less reliable legal procedures. Utter delay in the court verdict or judgment
2. Inactive, lethargic, and submissive nature of Indian consumers
3. Inadequate role of voluntary organizations
4. Poverty, illiteracy, lack of reliable information, and inadequate supply of certain products are among some cause-roots leading to failure of consumerism
5. Lack of patriotic attitudes of people – sellers and buyers
6. Shortage of goods and services, or monopoly
7. Senseless, excessive, and shortsighted liberalization and privatization policies and practices
8. Poor and inefficient role of public sectors
9. Failure of the government to implement the Laws and legal provisions successfully
10. Lack of marketers' willingness to fulfill social responsibility or social obligation. There are business ethics, but sellers are not willing to follow

SEVERAL ACTS FOR CONSUMER PROTECTION

Government of India has formulated and implemented at least 30 Acts so far to protect interest and rights of consumers. Most of these acts have undergone necessary amendments time to time to meet changing situations. Most important among them include:

1. The Consumer Protection Act, 1986
2. The Industries (Development and Regulation) Act, 1951
3. The Indian Contract Act, 1872
4. Monopolies and Restrictive Trade Practices Act, 1969
5. The Essential Commodity Act, 1955
6. The Prevention of Food Adulteration Act, 1954
7. The Standard of Weight and Measures Enforcement Act, 1985
8. Drugs Control Act, 1940
9. The Patents Act, 1970
10. Trade Names and Trade Marks Act, 1999

CONSUMER DISPUTE REDRESSAL AGENCIES

Chapter 3, Clause 9 to 27 of the Consumer Protection Act, 1986 deals with settlement of disputes. It provides for better protection of the rights and interest of consumers. The Act (the Clause 9) made provisions for establishment of proper machinery for the speedy settlement of consumer disputes and redressal of grievances. In the Act, three level redressal agencies work as judicial machineries for settlement of consumers' disputes.

1. Consumer Dispute Redressal Forum at the district level in each of the districts of every state (the District Forum).
2. Consumer Dispute Redressal Commission at the state level in each state of the country (the State Commission).
3. National Consumer Redressal Commission at the National level (the National Commission).

National Commission

The National Commission was established by the Central Government in August 1988. In the National Commission, a person who is or has been a judge of the Supreme Court appointed by Central Government is the president of the commission, and other two members with ability, experience, and knowledge to deal with problems relating to economics, law, commerce, accounting, industry, public affairs, etc., one of them should be woman.

State Commission

Clause 16 of the Act deals with formulation of the state commission. As per 2002 amendments, following provisions have been made:

Each state commission shall consist of:

1. A person who is or has been judge of high court appointed by State Government is a president of the Commission.
2. Other members, not less than two and more than limit specified, with qualifications, experience, and ability to deal with such matters like economics, law, commerce, etc. One of them should be woman.
3. Qualifications: Qualifications of other members are: (As per amendments 2002)
    - Their age must not be less than 35 years.
    - They must hold the graduation degree form the recognized university.
    - They must be honest, intelligent and respectable having required knowledge and at least 10 years experience to deal with matters related to economics, trade, commerce, law, accountancy, industry, and public administration.

District Forum

The Clause 10 to 15 of the Act makes provisions for formulation and functioning of the District Forum. Important provisions are:

1. The state government establishes district forum in each district. If government wishes, more than one district forum in each district can be established.
2. The District Forum shall consist of person who is or has been qualified to be district judge nominated by State Government. He is a president of such forum and two other members including a person who is eminent in education, trade, and commerce, one of them shall be a lady.
3. The District Forum shall work as semi-judiciary machinery. It cannot issue the Stay.
4. Qualifications of other members are: (As per amendments 2002)
    - Their age must not be less than 35 years.
    - They must hold the graduation degree from the recognized university.
    - They must have required knowledge and at least 10 years experience to deal with matters related to economics, trade, commerce, law, accountancy, industry, and public administration.
5. Other Provisions Related to Appointment of Members in the District Forum:
    - This act also specifies conditions under which one can be disqualified as a member.
    - Appointment must be made as per the recommendations of committee appointed for the purpose (Clause 1A).

- One can continue as a member of the forum for five year or up to age of 65 year whichever is earlier. One can be further appointed as member for the next five year or upto 65 year whichever is earlier.
- Provisions for resignation of member state that member can resign from the post by the hand-written application addressed to the state government and his resignation is accepted.
- Members of the District Forum are paid salary, honorarium and other benefits as per the state government rules.

SOME IMPORTANT ASPECTS

There are some important provisions relating to Consumer Dispute Redressal Agencies. The have been discussed as follow:

Provisions for Complaints

The Clause 12 specifies the manner in which complaint shall be made. As per Amendment 2002, one has to pay specified fees while registering the complaint with the District Forum. Within 21 days from the date of the receipt of complaint, the forum shall decide on whether to execute the complaint. Complainant is given chance to say before the complaint is rejected.

What is Complaint?

As per the Act, 'complaint' means any allegation in writing made by a complainant that:

1. An unfair trade practice or a restrictive trade practice has been adopted by any trader;
2. The goods bought by him or agreed to be bought by him suffer from one or more defects;
3. The service hired or availed of or agreed to be hired or availed of by him suffer from deficiency in any respect;
4. A trader has charged for the goods mentioned in the complaint a price in excess of the price fixed by or under any law for the time being in force or displayed on the goods or any package containing such goods with a view to obtaining any relief provided under this Act.

Who can complain?

Under clause 2(B) of the Act, a consumer, or one or more of consumers when they hold common interest, or any voluntary consumer association registered under the Companies Act, 1956 or under any other law for the time being in force, or the Central Government or any State Government can make complaint. In case of consumer's death, the representative or heir of the customer can also complain. (This clause has been added in the amendment 2002).

Jurisdiction of Agencies (as per the amendments 2002)

Jurisdiction of each of agencies is determined by the value of goods or compensation contained in the complaints.

A complaint with a value of goods or compensation is less than twenty lakhs to be dealt with the District Forum. In between twenty lakhs to one crore, it shall be dealt with the State Commission, and complaint involving more than a crore, it falls within jurisdiction of the National Commission.

Redressal of Dispute or Remedial Actions by Agencies

If any of the consumer dispute redressal agencies is satisfied that any of the allegations contained in the complaints is true, it shall issue an order to opposite party directing him to take one or more of following things such as:

1. To remove the defect pointed out by appropriate laboratory from the goods.

2. To replace goods with new goods of similar description, which shall be free from all defects.
3. To return price to the complainants.
4. To pay amount to the consumers for any loss or injury suffered by the consumer due to the negligence of opposite party.

Provision of Appeal

Appeal against order of any District Forum can be made to the State Commission. Appeal against order of State Commission can be made with the National Commission, and appeal against order of the National Commission can be made with the Supreme Court. The time limit for appeal is 30 days from the judgment by any of the redressal agencies. However, for certain valid reasons, such time can be extended.

Legal Actions

If a trader or person against whom a complaint is made fails or omits to comply with any order made by any of the redressal agencies, he shall be punishable with imprisonment for any term not exceeding three years or with a fine not exceeding ten thousand rupee or with both.

CUSTOMER RELATIONSHIP BUILDING

Relationship building is a broad term. It involves establishing and maintaining the long-term profitable relations with customers and those who can contribute to customer satisfaction. Customer relationship building is a part of broad relationship marketing. (For more detail, refer to chapter 7.4). Customer relationship building is also closely related to consumer orientation, discussed earlier in the chapter.

Company needs to establish and maintain long-term (or permanent) relations with following parties:

1. Customers
2. Employees
3. Suppliers
4. Distributors
5. Other companies
6. Government officials
7. Media and celebrities
8. Service providers, etc.

Marketers are concentrating their attention and efforts to build long-term-profitable relations with customers and all other participants in marketing. Particularly, with reference to customer relationship building, today's companies create, maintain and update a large customer database to design their offerings, and to know consumers' reactions. Direct mail (including e-mail), telemarketing, SMS, and active salesmanship are excessively emphasized to build, strengthen, and maintain long-term relations with valued customers. Customer relationship building is one of the basis objectives of marketing management.

CUSTOMER RELATIONSHIP BUILDING PROCESS

Relationship building is a lengthy and systematic process that involves step-by-step efforts. A firm desiring for relationship building must follow the steps, as stated by **Philip Kotler**:

1. **Suspects:** People who may buy the products of the firm. All buyers are considered as suspects.
2. **Suspect to Prospects:** People who have a strong potential interest in the products and the ability to pay. Target buyers can be the prospects for a company.

3. **Prospects to First Time Customers:** People who buy or try the product for the first time.
4. **First Time to Repeat Customers:** People who buy the product frequently along with products of competitors.
5. **Repeat Customers to Clients:** People who buy only from the company all the times.
6. **Client to Advocate:** People who behave as the advocate by praising and encouraging others to buy.
7. **Advocate to Partnering:** People who participate in company's prosperity and problems. They support the firm in all the possible ways and all the time. They behave as members of company with feeling of company's well-being.

EXERCISES

MULTIPLE CHOICE QUESTIONS (MCQs)

1. In relation to Mahatma Gandhi's famous passage on customer orientation, which statement is not fit?
   (a) A customer is the most important visitor in our premises.
   (b) He is not dependent on us. We are dependent on him.
   (c) He is an outsider to our business. He is a not part of it.
   (d) He is not someone to argue with.
2. In relation to integrated marketing, find out the true statement.
   (a) Marketing manager alone can satisfy customers.
   (b) Marketing is multidisciplinary science that integrates many disciplines.
   (c) Marketing, production, finance, and personnel functions have equal status in today business management.
   (d) Marketing goal is treated as subsidiary or secondary one.
3. Which one is not true?
   (a) Cyber marketing and online marketing are same.
   (b) Online marketing is one of the options of direct marketing.
   (c) Online marketing is applicable to services only.
   (d) Online marketing offers high convenience, reliability, and speed.
4. What does green marketing imply?
   (a) It implies marketing of only green coloured products.
   (b) It implies marketing of safe and eco-friendly products.
   (c) It implies complete ban on chemical products.
   (d) It implies punishing factory owners.
5. When do we celebrate the World Environment Day?
   (a) 6th June
   (b) 5th June
   (c) 15th June
   (d) 25th June
6. Which one is not a relevant consumer right?
   (a) The right to know
   (b) The right to complain
   (c) The right to safety
   (d) The right to beat the seller openly
7. Name the American president who, for the very first time, stressed on four consumer rights?
   (a) Abraham Lincoln
   (b) John Kennedy

(c) George Bush
(d) Bill Clinton

8. Who can be the president of the National Commission?
   (a) A judge of the Supreme Court
   (b) A judge of the High Court
   (c) A minister of civil supplies.
   (d) A member of the parliament
9. In relation to Philip Kotler's Customer Relation Building process, which one is not true?
   (a) Suspect to Prospect
   (b) Prospect to First Time Customer
   (c) First Time Customer to Repeat Customers
   (d) Repeat customer to Advocate
10. As per the provisions of the Consumer Protection Act, 1986, find out incorrect one.
   (a) Complaints with the value of goods or compensation more than a crore can be made to the National Commission.
   (b) Appeal against order of the District forum can be made to the State Commission.
   (c) There is no provision for appeal against the order of any of the redressal agencies.
   (d) There is provision of imprisonment and penalty if a person fails or omits to comply with any order by any of the redressal agencies.

MATCHING TYPE QUESTIONS (MTQs)

11.

List I	List II
(a) Consumer Orientation	(1) Moral Principles Observed Business
(b) Cyber Marketing	(2) Online Marketing
(c) Green Marketing	(3) A modern Marketing Approach
(d) Business Ethics	(4) Environmental Friendly Products

Codes: (A) (a)-(2), (b)-(1), (c)-(3), (d)-(4) (B) (a)-(3), (b)-(2), (c)-(4), (d)-(1)
(C) (a)-(1), (b)-(4), (c)-(3), (d)-(2) (D) (a)-(4), (b)-(2), (c)-(1), (d)-(3)

12.

List I	List II
(a) Linear Programming	(1) Integrated Marketing
(b) Consumerism	(2) It is OR Technique
(c) Joint Organisational Efforts	(3) Consumer Rights Protection Movement
(d) ISO 14000	(4) Related to Protection of Environment

Codes: (A) (a)-(2), (b)-(3), (c)-(1), (d)-(4)
(B) (a)-(3), (b)-(1), (c)-(4), (d)-(2)
(C) (a)-(1), (b)-(4), (c)-(2), (d)-(3)
(D) (a)-(4), (b)-(2), (c)-(3), (d)-(1)

ANSWERS KEY: 1(c), 2(b), 3(c), 4(b), 5(b), 6(d), 7(b), 8(a), 9(d), 10(c), 11(B), 12(A)

QUESTIONS FOR DISCUSSION

13. Define term 'Consumer Orientation and suggest marketing efforts needed to justify this concept.
14. What do you mean by Business Ethics? What is its significance? How do business ethics affect business decisions?
15. Explain Direct Marketing and Online Marketing. State merits and demerits of both.
16. What is Cyber Marketing? Write note on Cyber Marketing process.
17. What is Green Marketing? What is its importance? Which efforts are to be undertaken to actualize the Green Marketing?

18. "Today's marketing decisions are complex and difficult." Explain the statement. Also list the quantitative techniques used for making marketing decisions.
19. Define Quantitative Techniques and describe advantages and limitations of such techniques.
20. "Consumerism is reaction of unfair marketing practices." Comment. Discuss reasons for emergence of consumerism.
21. What is consumerism? Explain the role of consumerism in developing countries. Also state the facts responsible for partial failure of consumerism.
22. List some important Acts formulated by Indian Government and briefly discuss Consumer Protection Act, particularly Consumer Dispute Redressal Agencies.
23. What is Consumer Relationship Building? Explain its importance in the contemporary competitive marketing environment. Explain Consumer Relationship Building process.

CHAPTER

3 MARKETING ENVIRONMENT AND DEMAND FORECASTING

Marketing Environment

- Introduction
- Concept of Marketing Environment
- Variables, Forces, or Factors
- Impact Marketing Environment on Marketing Decision

Demand Forecasting

- Introduction
- Market Demand – Meaning and Definitions
- Elements of Market Demand
- Demand Forecasting – Meaning
- Method of Demand Forecasting

MARKETING ENVIRONMENT

Modern Marketing is treated as the open and adaptive system. Every system has its own environment. As an open system, marketer has to interact with outside forces (environment) for importing necessary inputs and exporting the outcomes. Marketing draws inputs from the environment and offers outcomes in form of products, services, and information. Environment affects tremendously the operations of the organisation. Environment consists of a number of variables, factors, or forces that are interdependent, interrelated, and interconnected. The degree of firm's success depends on how effectively it reacts/responses to its environment with given resources. A marketer needs to analyse the relevant environmental factors while deciding on any aspect related to marketing.

DEFINITIONS

1. In simple words, we can define the term as: *Marketing environment comprises of various factors or forces within which marketing manager has to decide. It offers both opportunities and threats.*
2. In other words, it can be defined as: *Marketing environment refers to the relevant forces that affect marketing decisions. It mainly includes external or uncontrollable forces, like political, legal, economical, socio-cultural, technological, competition, and so forth, on which a manager has no control.*

FORCES (FACTORS OR VARIABLES) OF ENVIRONMENT

The dynamic marketing environment involves three types of forces or factors, (1) External uncontrollable factors, (2) External partially controllable factors, and (3) Internal controllable factors. Figure 1 shows a three-tier (level) marketing environment.

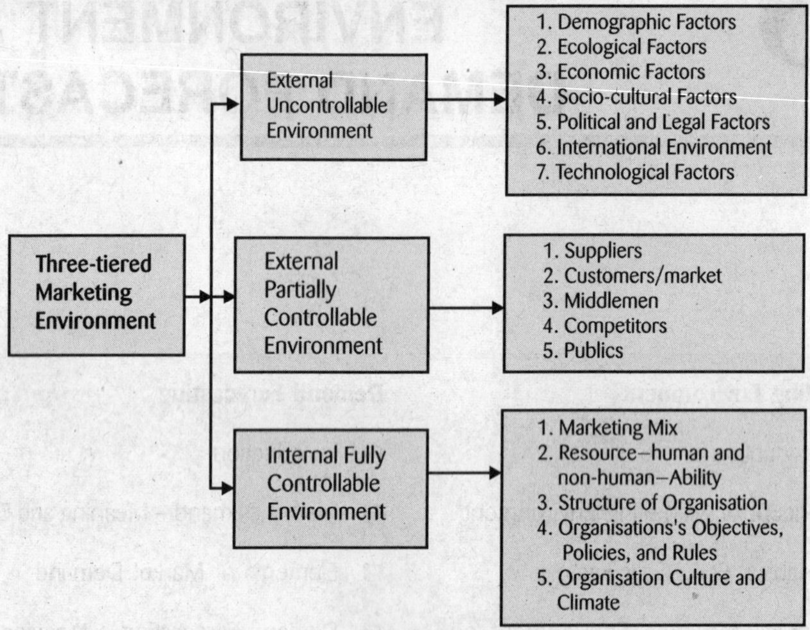

Figure 1: Three-tier Marketing Environment

EXTERNAL UNCONTROLLABLE FACTORS

A firm has no control over these factors. These factors constitute macro-marketing environment. For a firm, the only option is to accept and respect these factors, and adopt and adjust with them. Management must respond favourably to such environment in order to exploit the emerging opportunities. These factors include:

1. Demographic Factors

Demographic factors are related to population. Marketer must study these factors due to the fact that the market is made of people, and people constitute the population. Demographic study provides customer profile that is basic need for market segmentation as well as selecting target market. Therefore, demographic variables have direct and notable impact on firm's operations. A marketer must analyse demographic factors to get idea about number and type of people to be served as customers. Demographic variables include:

i. Total population and population growth rate
ii. Age groups and gender distribution
iii. Geographical (area-wise) concentration of population
iv. Proportion of rural v/s urban population
v. Literacy rate and level of education
vi. Population mobility (geographical shift) or migration rate
vii. Family system and household pattern
viii. Occupation-based classification of population.

2. Ecological Factors

These factors primarily concern with ecological (natural) environment. They are closely related to protection of ecological environment and pollutions – air, water, noise, and land pollutions. At present, the global-level efforts are made to protect environment. Such efforts can lay down certain restrictions in terms of use of natural resources, cost of raw material, quality of products, production process and technology, disposal of wastes, pollution control measures, and so on. Theses factors affect to the several aspects of production, distribution, and disposal of products. A firm must understand that people want better quality products at low price, but not at a cost of quality of life. Analysis of ecological environment involves:

i. Availability and use of natural resources
ii. Pollution and pollution control measures
iii. Contemporary legal provisions
iv. Ecological awareness and use of eco-friendly products
v. Contribution of corporate world for protection of environment
vi. Working of national and international agencies/organisations for protection of environment
vii. World-wide efforts for protection of environment.

3. Economic Factors

Economic environment consists of economic forces that affect company's costs, revenues, and profits on one hand, and customers' purchasing powers and willingness to spend on the other hand. Economic forces include a large number of variables, such as:

i. Economic growth rate
ii. Interest rates
iii. Inflation rate
iv. Functioning of stock markets and commodity markets
v. Industrial and agricultural policies
vi. Fiscal and monetary policies
vii. Export-import policies
viii. Liberalization, globalization and privatization processes
ix. Government's long-term planning and investment in infrastructural facilities
x. Quality and availability of basic facilities/services like transportation, banking, warehousing, insurance, communication, etc.

4. Socio-cultural Factors

Social and cultural factors affect consumers' tastes and preferences. People buy or favour those products which suit or complement their social and cultural norms, values, traditions, and habits. Knowing these factors of the target market, a manager can effectively design product-mix and promotional programme. Social-cultural environment is ever-changing and requires the manager to undergo adjustment and readjustment in his marketing mix to balance between what consumers want and what company offers. Ignoring or underestimating this environment can harm severely the company's interest. Socio-cultural variables are:

i. Cultural norms, values, beliefs, and rituals
ii. Castes, creeds, and racial aspects
iii. Social traditions, customs, habits, and superstitions
iv. Family and reference groups

v. Age and life-cycle stage
vi. Role of women
vii. Social classes
viii. Religious events and festivals.

5. Political and Legal Factors

A firm has to operate within the present political system and legal framework. Political factors affect economic policies. Every marketing decision is subject to be affected by political and legal factors. Governments have formulated a series of legislations to regulate business operations to restrict unfair trade practices and protect consumer and social interests. These laws may create new opportunities or challenges for businessmen. A manager must know business philosophy and approach of the current governments, and legal provisions that he has to observe while dealing with other parties. Some of political and legal factors are:

i. Political philosophy
ii. Political and legal reforms
iii. Government approach to different sectors
iv. Political stability
v. Acts or legal provisions relating to business operations and recent amendments
vi. Working of judiciary and administrative machineries.

6. International Environment

The world had become a global village. Most countries have permitted free trade (with little restrictions). A marketer has to deal with and satisfy cosmopolitan customers. Liberalization, globalization, and privatization promoted multinational companies that carry their operations in many countries. A businessman is required to follow global business theory – act locally, but think globally. Every firm, whether large or small, is, directly or indirectly, influenced by international economic and political forces. These variables include:

i. Working of international agencies and organisations (World Bank, UNO, etc.)
ii. Functioning of MNCs – Multinational Companies
iii. Export-import policies of different nations
iv. Availability of global aids and assistance
v. Global peace v/s conflict
vi. Liberalization, privatization, and globalization pace
vii. International agreements among countries
viii. Political stability in the dominant countries
ix. International business norms and values.

7. Technological Factors

Technological factors affect the firm's production process, product quality, cost effectiveness, and, hence, competitive ability. A wise manager must know the latest technology in the relevant field. Technology has released wonders in fields of business transactions, communication, entertainment, medical science, agriculture, and manufacturing systems. At the same time, it has released horrors in fields of hydrogen bombs, horrible chemical weapons, crime styles, deterioration of ecological environment, and so forth.

Every new technology is a force for creative destruction. New technology compels old one to exit. New technology brings superior products having more capacity to satisfy consumer needs. Following technological factors are important:

i. Suitability and availability of technology
ii. Pace of technological change
iii. Replacement costs
iv. Opportunities for innovation
v. Research and development (R & D) budget
vi. Government role in developing and/or importing new technology
vii. Regulations affecting technological change/reforms
viii. Technological transfer among nations.

EXTERNAL PARTIALLY-CONTROLLABLE FACTORS

These factors constitute a micro-marketing environment. They are not fully controllable. They can be made favourable by systematic actions. If they are treated effectively, more opportunities can be exploited. Partially controllable factors mainly include close stakeholders with whom a company must build, improve, and maintain healthy relations. Such factors include:

1. Suppliers

Suppliers are those stakeholders who supply necessary inputs to a company. The company must develop and maintain healthy relations with suppliers to seek needed cooperation. Suppliers' attitudes, relations, financial position, and other aspects have direct influence on company's operations.

2. Customers/market

Modern marketing is customer-centered. 'Satisfy customers and survive' – is modern business philosophy. Company exists to satisfy customers. Knowing company's target market (customers) adequately, more attractive offer can be presented. It should try to find out customers' needs and wants, and accordingly, products must be prepared. In short, a firm desiring to satisfy customers more effectively than competitors must follow the current and the future customer trends.

3. Middlemen

Middlemen, often known as the marketing channel, include wholesalers, retailers, agents, etc., who play active role in distribution system. Marketer must be aware of their expectations, attitudes, policies, resources, and overall behaviour.

4. Competitors

Most marketers have to operate within competitive situations. By formulating suitable offensive and defensive marketing strategies, more relative advantages can be gained. Company's performance depends on strengths and weaknesses relative to competitors. Every marketing decision must be taken with reference to the current and expected competition.

5. Publics

Publics include social organisations, local bodies, financial institutes, facility providers, workers, etc. These parties can create favourable situation for the firm if they are treated properly.

INTERNAL CONTROLLABLE FACTORS

Internal factors are under control of management. They are also a part of micro-marketing environment. Company has more freedom to treat these factors. These factors are manipulated by the company to respond external partially controllable and uncontrollable marketing environment. They are treated as resources, tools, or weapons to adjust, respond, or to fight with outside environment. These factors include:

1. Marketing Mix (product, price, promotion, and place)
2. Resource (human and non-human) Ability

3. Structure of Organisation
4. Organisation's Objectives, Policies, and Rules
5. Organisation Culture and Climate, etc.

Among three types of factors, the external factors are more critical to be considered. Company has to use internal-controllable variables and seek support of partially uncontrollable factors to adjust and readjust with powerful external-uncontrollable marketing environment.

MARKETING MANAGEMENT AND ITS ENVIRONMENT

Today's marketing is a dynamic and complex system working within social, economic, cultural, technological, legal and other forces. These forces constitute an environment. And, therefore, the organisation cannot live in a vacuum. Marketing management is responsible for scanning, analysing and responding its environment. To the extent the environment offers opportunities or threats depends heavily on how effectively the company responses or reacts its environment. The reaction or response of management is reflected in terms of marketing objectives, policies, programmes, strategies, and the quality of overall decisions. If it responds effectively, it can enjoy more opportunities and vice versa. Marketing manager has to monitor maketing efforts in light of changing marketing environment. He should try to adjust and readjust marketing efforts, including marketing strategies, as per dynamic need of its environment. Thus, the environment offers both opportunities, and threats and challenges depending upon the ability of business organisation to respond successfully. The business unit has to operate within limit of its environment. It can be said that the business unit has to accept/import what environment offers and has to offer what the environment accepts. Those firms fail to respond effectively cannot survive and grow. Adverse impact of the environment can be minimized by effective response in term of the right strategies. Every marketer must analyse the relevant marketing environment and acts accordingly.

OBJECTIVES OR IMPORTANCE OF ANALYSING ENVIRONMENT

Marketers analyse marketing environment to achieve one or more of following objectives:

1. To analyse overall marketing environment and identify relevant factors
2. To find out marketing opportunities to exploit and thetas to face
3. To segment the market and select the target market
4. To formulate long-term marketing plan
5. To initiate innovation and/or diversification
6. To determine marketing objectives and goals
7. To formulate marketing strategies for competitors
8. To identify key parties with whom to establish healthy relations
9. To assess company's strengths and weaknesses
10. To determine organisational response in term of marketing actions, within limit of given resources
11. To adjust and readjust continuously by making internal changes
12. To keep the marketing staff informed about the recent and expected developments in marketing environment

MARKET DEMAND FORECASTING

Market demand forecasting involves two aspects – market demand and market demand forecasting.

MARKET DEMAND

INTRODUCTION

Market demand is similar to industry demand. It is a broader concept and it involves total demand of a product in an industry. For example, demand of two wheelers in India implies demand of two wheelers produced and marketed by all the companies. It reveals the broader picture of demand. Marketer should keep in mind the wider scenario of industry/market demand to see his position, often called market share of company in an industry. Market demand plays a vital role in formulating the broad marketing programme.

DEFINITIONS

Term 'market demand' can be defined as:

1. **Philip Kotler:** "Market demand for the product is the total volume that would be bought by a defined customer group in a defined geographical area in a defined time period in a defined marketing environment under a defined marketing programme."
2. Thus, *market demand indicates total sales of the product to the specific groups of buyers in a specific period and in defined geographical areas in a given marketing environment.*

ELEMENTS OF MARKET DEMAND

Systematic analysis of above stated definitions necessarily reveals following elements:

1. Product

Market demand indicates the total demand of specific products in an industry. The place or scope of product must be specified. In which category or industry the product of company falls. It can be decided on the basis of who are the users and the purpose of using the product. Thus, we must mention the market demand in relation to the specific product.

2. Total Volume

It shows the total volume of sales in form of unit or value. It suggests the total sales of the product in the industry. For example, total volume means the amount (or units) of total demand of refrigerator in India.

3. Purchase or Buying

Only the quantity, that is ordered and purchased is included in market demand. Market demand includes units, which are ordered, delivered, or consumed.

4. Customer Groups

Market demand is expressed in term of different users. Total volume demanded by different groups of customers, such as industrial customers, institutional customers, and individual customers.

5. Geographic Area

Market demand can be specified in term of different geographical areas or localities. It may be in term of country, state, region, district, or any geographic unit.

6. Fixed Time Duration

Market demand is meaningful only if it is expressed in relation to time. For example, demand of two-wheeler during the year 2007. Time may be in term of week, months, quarter, or year.

7. Marketing Environment

Obviously, market demand is influenced by several factors. These factors constitute the marketing environment. So, it is necessary to mention assumptions about marketing environment comprising economic, cultural, social, political, etc., forces.

8. Definition of Marketing Programme

Market demand is affected by marketing programme/strategy. So, it is clarified with reference to a specific marketing programme including product, price, promotion, and distribution. Thus, market demand is stated in context with the definite marketing programme.

While estimating market demand, these all elements should be considered for meaningful picture of total demand. Here, we must distinguish market demand from company demand. Market demand is total demand of the product in an industry, and company demand means demand of the individual business unit's products. Market forecast relates with market demand and sales forecast relates with company demand. However, market demand forecast and sales forecast are taken loosely (i.e., more or less similar).

MARKET DEMAND FORECASTING

INTRODUCTION

Demand forecasting and sales forecasting are taken as synonyms. Demand forecasting is an important function of marketing management. Mostly, production is based on the future demand. Similarly, revenue, profits, investment, new technology, and, in general, development, alteration, or modification of the entire marketing programme depend on the future demand. Therefore, the estimate of the future demand or demand forecasting is a crucial function of today's marketing manager. It is not an easy task. To forecast demand accurately requires a manager to have a great deal of ability, knowledge, experience, imaginations, and expertise. He has to keep in mind a large number of internal and external factors. It is not an exaggeration to state that success of marketing strategy is, to a great extent, determined by ability of manager to estimate the future demand. In order to understand demand forecasting, we must clarify two terms - *market demand and demand forecasting.*

Demand forecasting and sales forecasting are taken as similar terms. Mostly, in marketing, estimating company's sales is more relevant and useful. Company demand (may be similar to sales potential) is the company's share of the market demand. **Our discussion is limited to company's sales forecast or company demand forecast.** We concern more with micro level demand forecasting. However, the broader picture of industry demand or market demand should never be ignored.

DEFINITIONS

1. Demand forecasting has been defined as: *Demand forecasting, in relation to company, simply means to estimate company's sales for a specific period of time.*
2. Company demand/sales forecast can be defined as: *Demand forecasting is the estimated demand of company's products in a given time. Company's marketing plan is largely based on sales/demand forecasting.*
3. More specifically, we can define as: *Demand forecasting is an estimate of a firm's sales turnover under defined marketing programme. The sales forecasting is the expected level of sales with given marketing strategy.*
4. Further, it can be stated: *A sales forecast is an estimate of sales, in monetary or physical units, for a specific future period under a given marketing plan and under an assumed set of marketing environmental forces outside the business organisation.*

Be clear that sales forecast may be for specific product item, product line, or for the product mix. It is an important part of market demand. Again, the time of sales forecast is not uniform. Company can estimate sales for any period. However, in most cases, company prefers to estimate sales for a year. Forecasting, being an estimate, is always subject to vary. Exact estimate of the future sales is almost impossible due to uncertainty of various internal and external forces. However, sales/demand forecasting is treated as instrumental for developing and modifying marketing strategies over time.

METHODS OR TECHNIQUES OF DEMAND FORECASTING

There are several methods to estimate the future demand. Selection of a method depends on analysis of many factors. Mostly, the choice of demand forecasting method depends on:

1. Availability of methods
2. Availability of data
3. Ability/expertise of manager
4. Experience of manager
5. Cost consideration
6. Accuracy level
7. Time and efforts
8. Management philosophy

Following part briefly describes popularly practiced methods for estimating the future sales. Each method has its merits, demerits, and applicability. Company can select the method as per its own situations.

1. EXECUTIVE OPINION/JUDGMENT METHOD

This is a traditionally used method. One or more top executives, including general manager, marketing manager, other departmental heads, sales officers, and some others, forecast the future demand based on their personal knowledge and experience. They may talk to customers, dealers and other relevant sources; refer to published reports and other sources; or may consult experts for estimating company sales volume in a given period. They may discuss jointly and pool their knowledge and experience to arrive at the round estimate of sales. Forecasting by executive opinion alone is risky. This method lacks scientific validity. The estimate may be subjective or biased.

Merits: Executive opinion method fetches following merits:

i. The estimates tend to be more balanced as various executives are involved.

ii. Sales forecasting is more accurate and reliable because the executives are well aware of company's strengths and weaknesses.

iii. It promotes cooperation and integration among the executives of various departments. They strive to meet the estimate they proposed.

Demerits: Below stated are the obvious limitations of the method:

i. Lack of time and knowledge to perform the task of forecasting is the prime problem.

ii. It may deteriorate relations due to possible conflicts or lack of consensus.

iii. Each department has its priorities, principles, and theories to work. So, result may be polarized.

iv. Prejudice, bias, and personal philosophy always affect the final estimate to a great extent.

2. SURVEY OF BUYERS' INTENTIONS METHOD

It is also known as consumers' expectations or opinions survey. It is commonly used method for sales forecasting. A sale is the result of consumer intention to buy the product. Many companies conduct periodical survey of consumers' buying interest to know when and how much they will buy. A sample of potential consumers is surveyed to know how much of the stated product they would buy at a given price during a specified future time period. Some firms maintains a permanent sample of buyers known as the panel to collect needed data on a regular basis.

Merits: This method offers following merits over the rest of methods:

i. More reliable and relevant information can be collected.

ii. This method is more suitable for industrial products.

iii. It is highly effective for short-run sales forecasting.

iv. This method is proved effective when consumers state their intention clearly and adhere to it.

Demerits: Following are the demerits of the method:

i. It is applicable only for short-run forecasting.

ii. It is expensive method and needs a lot of preparations. Also, it needs a large amount of time.

iii. Consumers may not express their intention clearly, or may not behave as per intention expressed.

iv. In case of highly scattered large number of consumers, it is not applicable.

v. Poor response rate is the major problem in our country. They do not respond to the questions asked and / or do not return questionnaire fully completed.

vi. Purchase intention is subject to change as per social and economic circumstances. One cannot expect consistent intention over time.

vii. Selection of the sample of potential buyers is difficult task as who, how many, and from which places respondents should be selected. Limitations of sampling become the limitation of the method.

It is especially more effective when (1) there are relatively few buyers, (2) buyers are willing to express buying intentions reliably, (3) company has enough time and money to spend, and (4) there is high probability that stated intention would result into actual purchase

3. COMPOSITE OF SALES FORCE OPINION METHOD

Sometimes, it is called sales force estimate method. Company can ask, either all or some of salesmen, to estimate demand for a given time. Each sales representative estimates how much each current and prospective customer will buy the company's product. They are offered certain incentives to encourage them better estimate. Here, for estimating the future demand, the company's sales force opinions are taken as a base. Since salesmen have direct and close contact with customers, competitors, dealers, and overall market environment, they can provide more reliable estimates of the future sales. However, company must be careful to avoid over optimistic or over-pessimistic opinions of salesmen. Their opinions should not be followed directly without investigating the market facts.

Merits: Company can enjoy following merits:

i. Salesmen have better insight into the recent market trend than any other groups. So, more accurate estimate is possible.

ii. It motivates and encourages salesmen as their opinions are considered by the company.

iii. It is suitable to all products and firms.

iv. No need to spend extra. Only limited incentives are sufficient to get desired results.

v. It is a speedy method to estimate sales.

vi. They can provide estimate in terms of products, territory, and customers.

vii. They struggle to fulfill the estimate they have given. High degree of commitment prevails.

Demerits: Demerits of the method include:

i. Salesman may not have time. Their regular work may suffer.

ii. Lack of experience and expertise to perform such task.

iii. Reliability is a question. There is posibility of manipulation of estimates.

iv. The future sales are affected by a large number of factors. Sales people may not be aware of them. Therefore, the sales estimates given by sales force may be less reliable.

v. For their protection, they may underestimate sales.

4. EXPERT OPINION METHOD

Company can also take assistance of experts to obtain forecasts. The experts include dealers, suppliers, distributors, consultants, and trade associations. These experts supply their estimate individually, or jointly in form of the pooled individual estimate. Along with the estimates, they also underline certain assumptions. Company contacts them periodically or occasionally for their opinions regarding level of company sales in the future. Some companies buy economic and industry forecasts from well-known economic firms. Even, they can employ or undergo contract with economists or experts on a professional basis for the purpose. The experts, taking into account strengths of company's strategies and market situations, exert their sales estimate for a give time period. The expert opinions on sales estimates and assumptions are accepted directly or they are reviewed further.

Merits: Expert opinion method offers following merits:

i. Less expensive and speedy estimates can be obtained.

ii. Balanced estimate is possible as more experts are involved.

iii. Pooled knowledge can be used. Experts of various fields contribute to sales forecasting.

iv. It is the only option when the past sales data are not available.

v. Estimates tend to be more neutral as experts are external to organisation.

Demerits: However, it suffers from following problems:

i. It is not a scientific method. Personal value, experience, and attitudes play vital role.

ii. It is based on opinions, and therefore, reliability is always doubtful.

iii. It is difficult to fix responsibility of the final estimates as many experts contribute to forecasting.

iv. It is not possible to get sales estimates in terms of products, customers, or territories.

v. Possibility of prejudice or bias cannot be ignored.

vi. All opinions, right or wrong, may be given equal importance.

5. MARKET TEST METHOD

It is popularly known as test marketing. It is an experimental method. Opinions are not considered but the real experiment is made. This is most reliable method. It is based on the actual study of market situation. In this method, neither buyers are asked to reveal their intention nor experts are contacted to give their opinion on the future sales, but a direct market test is conducted. Direct market test is desirable in case of a new product and existing products as well as existing products in new channel or territory.

The method is used to measure consumers' and dealers' reactions in handling, using, and repurchasing the product. Test marketing can be defined as, *an attempt to try the entire marketing programme in a limited number of well-selected markets, test cities, or different areas.* This help in testing viability of full marketing programme for regional and national market. A product is launched in a limited scale under normal market conditions to test consumers' reactions. Thus, test marketing essentially determines purchase interest in real situation. Test market provides valuable information such as (1) Reactions of consumers and dealers, (2) More reliable demand forecasting, (3) Measuring market share and size of market, and (4) Information regarding trial, first time purchase, repeat purchase, and frequency of buying.

Merits: Following are the merits of market test method:

i. Reactions of consumers and dealers can be obtained.

ii. Information regarding trial, first time purchase, repeat purchase, etc., can help in more accurate estimate of sales for a given time.

iii. Market testing or test marketing is advisable due to the fact that it is based on real situation.

iv. More reliable estimate of sales can be obtained as it is more practical method.

v. During market test, drawbacks related to product, packaging, price, promotion, and other aspects on can be identified which can be removed later on.

Demerits: Following are the problems associated with this method:

i. There are big "ifs". For example, if price is kept low, what happens? If more promotional efforts are undertaken, what will be the outcomes?

ii. It is expensive.

iii. It is time consuming.

iv. Danger of artificial response of consumers and competitors may mislead.

v. This method needs a great degree of expertise and experience.

vi. Market test result of one area cannot be equally applied in other areas directly.

vii. It is conducted in a limited scale. So, generalization is always doubtful.

viii. If it is conducted in controlled situation (laboratory experiment), the real position cannot be measured; and if it is conducted in natural setting (field experiment), impact of extraneous factors cannot be estimated.

6. TIME SERIES ANALYSIS

It is a popular statistical technique used for sales forecasting. It is called past-sales-trend analysis. It is entirely based on the past sales behaviour. It involves the projection of the past sales trends into the future. In order to predict future sales trend, we consider four historical variations/considerations, such as:

i. Long term variations due to population growth, technological changes, capital accumulation and so on

ii. Cyclical variation in demand occurring at regular interval.

iii. Seasonal variation in demand occurring due to seasonal effect

iv. Impact of some unpredictable variable on demand like war, riots, strikes, floods, earthquakes, etc.

It is statistically a sophisticated method for long-run and short-run projection of sales trend. Due to use of computer, now it is easy to use and, hence, consumes less time. Useful software is available at affordable rate to measure trend accurately and speedily. Data are expressed into two series, time and corresponding sales for a few years. On the basis of given sales for a few years, the future sales trend is estimated. Thus, the future sales are predicted on the basis of sales figures of the past five to seven years with the help of extrapolation.

Merits: Time series analysis enjoys following strong points:

i. This method is less costly.

ii. It takes relatively less time.

iii. Use of computer can multiply speed, reliability, and accuracy by manifolds.

iv. No need to collect opinions, it is simple method. If one has enough data, it is much easier method.

v. It gives more accurate results for short-term forecasting.

Demerits: Following are the limitations of time series method:

i. Statistical sophistication of long-run projection of trend may not yield an accurate estimate of the future trend.

ii. Statistical staff may be necessary, and, so it is costly.

iii. Very few marketing people can understand time series analysis. It is based on a lot of assumptions.

iv. It is erroneous to say that the past trends will be repeated. In rapidly changing marketing environment, the past becomes less relevant for measuring the future trends.

v. The tremendous effect of external factors is not taken into account for estimate purpose.

The methods discussed above are not the final list. And, no method is completely perfect or imperfect. Suitability of any of the methods depends upon situations. There are many other methods like regression analysis, factor analysis, statistical demand analysis, and so forth. Company should use one or more methods suit to its internal and external situations. It is advisable that company must estimate the future sales using more than one method to find out the degree of variation. One more important conclusion is that company should remember that estimates are always just estimates. The sales estimate must be interpreted and followed with care and caution.

EXERCISES

MULTIPLE CHOICE QUESTIONS (MCQs)

1. Which one is not included marketing environment?
   (a) External uncontrollable environment
   (b) External partially controllable environment
   (c) Internal controllable environment
   (d) Internal uncontrollable environment
2. Which one is a partially controllable factor?
   (a) Customers
   (b) Organizational resources and facilities
   (c) Organizational climate and culture
   (d) Ecological factors
3. Which is fully a controllable factor?
   (a) Product mix
   (b) Customers
   (c) Economic growth rate
   (d) Middleman
4. In which one group of marketing environmental factors does competition factor fall?
   (a) It falls in controllable factors.
   (b) It falls in partially controllable factors.
   (c) It falls in uncontrollable factors.
   (d) It does not fall in any of the groups.
5. Which is not true?
   (a) Demand forecasting and sales forecasting are same.
   (b) Market demand is similar as industry demand.
   (c) Market demand involves total demand of a product in an industry.
   (d) Company demand means total market demand.

6. What is implication of composite of sales force method?
   (a) Sales volume is forced to match the target.
   (b) Salesmen are forced estimate the sales volume.
   (c) Salesmen are asked to estimate demand for the product for a given time.
   (d) Salesmen's duty is to collect data from market.
7. Which method is called past sales trend analysis?
   (a) Time series method
   (b) Market trend method
   (c) Expert opinion method
   (d) One of them
8. Who are included in expert opinion method?
   (a) Only dealers, suppliers, and distributors
   (b) Only marketing manages and sales managers
   (c) Only marketing experts
   (d) Both internal and external experts

MATCHING TYPE QUESTIONS (MTQs)

9.

List I	List II
(a) Fully Uncountable Factors	(1) Marketing mix elements
(b) Partially Controllable Factors	(2) It contains several factors or forces
(c) Fully Controllable Factors	(3) Customers, suppliers and middlemen
(d) Marketing Environment	(4) Economic, political, and demographic

Codes: (A) (a)-(4), (b)-(3), (c)-(1), (d)-(2)
(B) (a)-(3), (b)-(2), (c)-(4), (d)-(1)
(C) (a)-(1), (b)-(4), (c)-(2), (d)-(3)
(D) (a)-(2), (b)-(1), (c)-(3), (d)-(4)

10.

List I	List II
(a) Political Factors	(1) A sources of opportunities and threats
(b) Product and pricing	(2) External uncontrollable factors
(c) Suppliers and customers	(3) Partially uncontrollable factors
(d) Marketing Environment	(4) Economic, political, and demographic

Codes: (A) (a)-(4), (b)-(3), (c)-(1), (d)-(2)
(B) (a)-(3), (b)-(2), (c)-(4), (d)-(1)
(C) (a)-(1), (b)-(4), (c)-(2), (d)-(3)
(D) (a)-(2), (b)-(1), (c)-(3), (d)-(4)

11.

List I	List II
(a) Total demand in an Industry	(1) All executives forecast the sales
(b) Expert Opinion Method	(2) Industry/market demand
(c) Market Test Methods	(3) A statistical method
(d) Time Series Method	(4) Based on real experiment in the market

Codes: (A) (a)-(2), (b)-(1), (c)-(4), (d)-(3)
(B) (a)-(3), (b)-(2), (c)-(1), (d)-(4)
(C) (a)-(4), (b)-(3), (c)-(2), (d)-(1)
(D) (a)-(1), (b)-(4), (c)-(3), (d)-(2)

ANSWERS KEY: 1(d), 2(a), 3(a), 4(b), 5(d), 6(c), 7(a), 8(d), 9(A), 10(D), 11(A)

QUESTIONS FOR DISCUSSION

12. What is marketing environment? Why is it necessary for marketing manager to analyse it. Explain micro and macro marketing environment.
13. Define marketing environment and discuss variables/forces affecting marketing environment.
14. What is market demand? Explain elements of market demand.
15. Explain the meaning of market demand and state elements involved in it.
16. State methods of demand forecasting and explain any three methods.
17. Explain demand forecasting in marketing. And write its methods.
18. Explain demand forecasting. Describe composite of sales force opinion method. Evaluate time series method and Expert opinion method for demand forecasting for demand forecasting.
19. Discuss various methods used for demand forecasting with merits and demerits.

CHAPTER

4 CONSUMER BEHAVIOUR AND MARKET SEGMENTATION

Consumer Behaviour

- Introduction
- Meaning & Definitions of Consumer Behaviour
- Importance of Consumer Behaviour
- Factors Affecting Consumer Behaviour
- Stages of Consumer Behaviour Process or Buying Process

Market Segmentation

- Introduction
- Definitions
- Importance
- Bases for Segmentation Consumer Market
- Bases for Segmenting Industrial Market
- Qualities of Good Segmentation
- Marketing Targeting – Meaning and Methods of Market Targeting
- Product Positioning – Meaning, Characteristics, Process and Importance

CONSUMER BEHAVIOUR

INTRODUCTION

Marketing starts and ends with consumers. In market-oriented marketing philosophy, consumers are placed in the center of business operations. Consumer satisfaction enjoys priority over goals of business. Consumers can be satisfied only when a marketer knows what consumers need and want. Consumer needs should be treated as the focus point. Also, demand creation is based on consumer satisfaction. As such, the study of consumer behaviour is the first step in designing marketing programme meaningfully and successfully. **Consumer behaviour studies how individuals, groups, and organisation select, buy, and dispose of goods, services, ideas, or experiences to satisfy their needs and desires.** Thus, the study of consumer behaviour (response or reaction) plays an important role in designing the marketing programme. Consumers favour those products, which suit their needs and wants. Here, consumer behaviour concerns with the study of the present or actual as well as the potential buyers.

Marketer can understand consumers through analysing the 7 O's framework propounded by Philip Kotler. The 7 O's are related with consumer behaviour. The 7 O's framework answers most of the questions about the market. Marketers can get enough insight by analyzing these O's.

1. Who constitutes the market? Occupants
2. What does the market buy? Objects/products
3. Why does the market buy? Objectives
4. Who participate in buying? Organisations
5. How does the market buy? Operations/buying process
6. When does the market buy? Occasions
7. Where does the market buy? Outlets/distribution centers.

Thus, consumer behaviour studies how the consumers react or respond to the products (or stimuli in general). Consumer behaviour is determined by consumers' characteristics. Individual consumer reacts or responds differently due to their distinguished set of characteristics. Consumer behaviour studies consumers' reaction patterns to company's offers.

DEFINITIONS

The term consumer behaviour can be defined as under:

1. **Frederic Webster:** "Buyer behaviour is the all psychological, social, and physical behaviour of potential customers as they become aware of, evaluate, purchase, consume, and tell other people about products and services."
2. **C. G. Walters and G. W. Paul:** "Consumer behaviour is the process whereby individuals decide whether, what, when, where, how, and from whom to purchase goods and services."
3. It can be said: *Consumer behaviour is a process through which the consumer interacts with his environment for the purpose of making market decisions on products and services.*
4. Moreover, we can say: *Consumer behaviour is a decision process and physical activity in which individual is engaged in evaluating, acquiring, using, and disposing the goods as well as services.*
5. Some experts consider consumer behaviour as the subject or study. Accordingly, it can be defined as: *Consumer behaviour is a separate academic discipline which studies what, how, why, where, when, and from whom the consumer buy the product. It is the study of total behaviour of consumers in relation to goods or services.*

COMMON CHARACTERISTICS OF CONSUMER BEHAVIOUR

Analysis of above stated definitions reveals following characteristics:

1. Consumer behaviour involves physical and mental activities which consumers undertake to acquire goods and services and obtain satisfaction from them.
2. It is considered as a powerful area of today's marketing management. The marketing programme is formulated on the basis of study of consumer behaviour.
3. It concerns with studying why, what, when, where, how, and from whom the consumer buys the product.
4. Consumer behaviour is a process through which the consumer interacts with his environment for the purpose of making decisions on products and services.
5. It is considered as an essential area in modern marketing study and practice.
6. It includes both observable (physical activities) like reacting positively or negatively, and mental activities such as forming attitude, perceiving advertising, learning, etc.
7. It is a complex and dynamic process, it is difficult to understand. It is also recognized as a multidisciplinary and relatively new discipline.

8. Consumer behaviour is affected by a large number of internal factors – needs, motives, perception, and attitudes, and external factors – economic, social, cultural, and business influences.
9. It is the study of reaction of consumers toward marketing stimuli. Marketing stimuli may be product, idea, appeal, activity, or any thing that can influence the consumers.
10. It is a separate discipline, a branch of study that concern with the study and analysis of consumer response to market offers.

IMPORTANCE OF (STUDY OF) CONSUMER BEHAVIOUR

As stated earlier, consumer behaviour plays an important role in modern marketing practices. Most of marketing decisions are based on the study of consumer behaviour. It provides valuable information to design marketing mix and modify it over time. Marketing managers can actualize marketing goals only by studying consumer behaviour and responding it by designing and redesigning marketing programme objectively. It is imperative to know how consumers react to marketing programme (4 P's) to serve them effectively. Role or importance of study of consumer behaviour can be explained with reference to the points stated as under:

1. Modern Philosophy

It concerns with modern marketing philosophy – identify consumers' needs and satisfy them more effectively than competitors. It makes marketing consumer-oriented. It is the key to succeed.

2. Achievement of Goals

The key to a company's survival, profitability, and growth in a highly competitive marketing environment is its ability to identify and satisfy unfulfilled consumer needs better and sooner than the competitors. Thus, consumer behaviour helps in achieving marketing goals.

3. Useful for Dealers and Salesmen

The study of consumer behaviour is not useful for the company alone. Knowledge of consumer behaviour is equally useful for middlemen and salesmen to perform their tasks effectively in meeting consumers needs and wants successfully. Consumer behaviour, thus, improves performance of the entire distribution system.

4. More Relevant Marketing Programme

Marketing programme, consisting of product, price, promotion, and distribution decisions, can be prepared more objectively. The programme can be more relevant if it is based on the study of consumer behaviour. Meaningful marketing programme is instrumental in realizing marketing goals.

5. Adjusting Marketing Programme Over Time

Consumer behaviour studies the consumer response pattern on a continuous basis. So, a marketer can easily come to know the changes taking place in the market. Based on the current market trend, the marketer can make necessary changes in marketing programme to adjust with the market.

6. Predicting Market Trend

Consumer behaviour can also aid in projecting the future market trends. Marketer finds enough time to prepare for exploiting the emerging opportunities, and/or facing challenges and threats.

7. Consumer Differentiation

Market exhibits considerable differentiations. Each segment needs and wants different products. For every segment, a separate marketing programme is needed. Knowledge of consumer differentiation is a key to fit marking offers with different groups of buyers. Consumer behaviour study supplies the details about consumer differentiations.

8. Creation and Retention of Consumers

Marketers who base their offerings on a recognization of consumer needs find a ready market for their products. Company finds it easy to sell its products. In the same way, the company, due to continuous study of consumer behaviour and attempts to meet changing expectations of the buyers, can retain its consumers for a long period.

9. Competition

Consumer behaviour study assists in facing competition, too. Based on consumers' expectations, more competitive advantages can be offered. It is useful in improving competitive strengths of the company.

10. Developing New Products

New product is developed in respect of needs and wants of the target market. In order to develop the best-fit product, a marketer must know adequately about the market. Thus, the study of consumer behaviour is the base for developing a new product successfully.

11. Dynamic Nature of Market

Consumer behaviour focuses on dynamic nature of the market. It helps the manager to be dynamic, alert, and active in satisfying consumers better and sooner than competitors. Consumer behaviour is indispensable to watch movements of the markets.

12. Effective Use of Productive Resources

The study of consumer behaviour assists the manager to make the organisational efforts consumer-oriented. It ensures an exact use of resources for achieving maximum efficiency. Each unit of resources can contribute maximum to objectives.

It is to be mentioned that the study of consumer behaviour is not only important for the current sales, but also helps in capturing the future market. Consumer behaviour assumes: Take care of consumer needs; the consumers, in return, will take care of your needs. Most of problems can be reasonably solved by the study of consumer behaviour. Modern marketing practice is almost impossible without the study of consumer behaviour.

FACTORS AFFECTING CONSUMER BEHAVIOUR

There are many factors affecting consumer behaviour. These all factors jointly shape consumer behaviour. Due to impact of various factors, consumers react or respond to marketing programme differently. For the same product, price, promotion, and distribution, their responses differ significantly. The factors do not affect equally to all the buyers; they have varying effect on their behaviour. However, some factors are more effective, while others have negligible effect on consumer behaviour.

Broadly, factors affecting consumer behaviour can be classified into three categories, like factors related to product, factors related to company, and factors related to consumers. This part discuses main factors influencing consumer behaviour. As shown in figure 1, factors affecting consumer behaviour can be classified into three broad categories – product characteristics, company characteristics, and consumer characteristics.

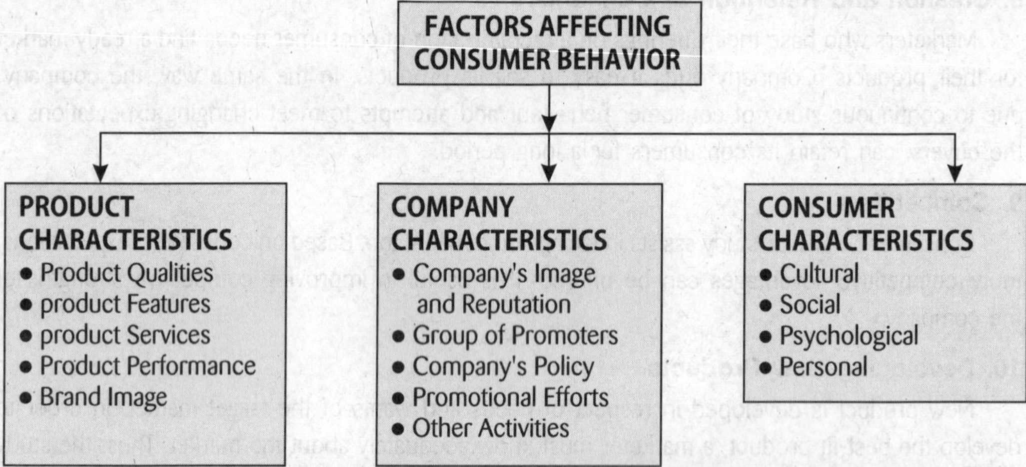

Figure 1: Factors Affecting Consumer Behaviour

The last set – consumer characteristics – is more relevant and significant; this class of factors has been given more space and weight in this chapter. Consumer characteristics are a popular set of factors affecting market behaviour. The reason is that the effect of company characteristics and product characteristics depends on consumer characteristics. So, it is more relevant to discuss only factors affecting to consumers/ consumer characteristics. Figure 2 shows an outline of factors affecting consumer behaviour.

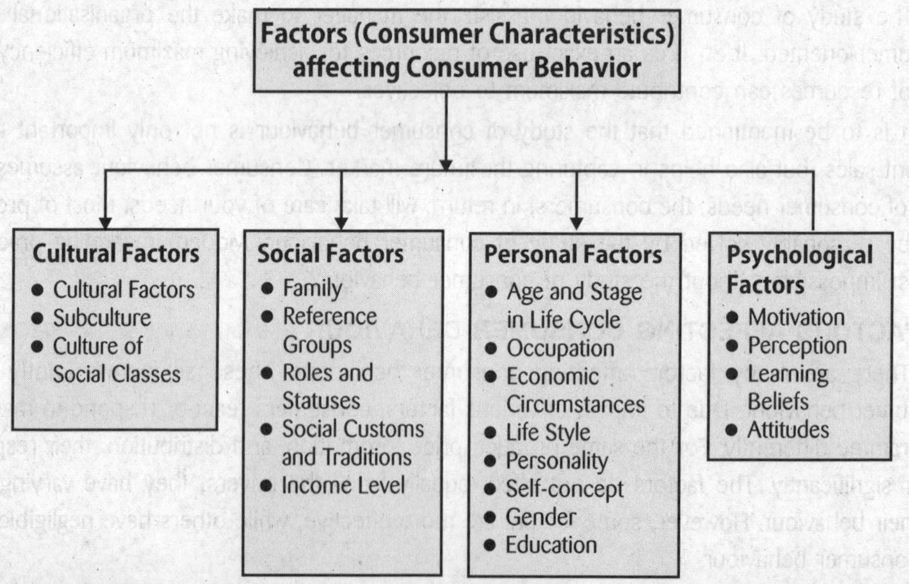

Figure 2: Factors (Consumer Characteristics) Affecting Consumer Behaviour

CULTURAL FACTORS

Cultural factors have the broadest and deepest impact on consumer behaviour. This set of factors mainly includes broad culture, sub-culture, and culture of social classes.

1. Broad Culture

Culture is a powerful and dominant determinant of personal needs and wants. Culture can be broadly defined as: *The way of living, way of doing, and way of worshiping. Culture determines the total patter of life.* Culture has a tremendous effect on needs and preference. People react according to the culture to which they belong. Every culture has its values, customs, traditions, and beliefs, which determine needs, preference, and overall behaviour. The child acquires a set of values, perception, attitudes, interest, preference, and behaviour from family and other key social institutions that control his/her behaviour. Every member is bound to follow cultural values to which he belongs. These cultural factors determine the way of reacting toward product and marketing strategies. Culture is reflected in terms of followings:

i. Family life/social system
ii. Role of women
iii. Woman education
iv. Approach to work and leisure
v. Approach to life
vi. Ethics in economic dealings
vii. Residence pattern
viii. Geographic factors
ix. Impact of other cultures, and so on.

These all factors affect what, when, where, how much, from whom, and how many times the product should be purchased and used. Marketer must be aware of the relevant cultural aspects, and marketing programme should be designed accordingly.

2. Subcultures

Each culture consists of smaller subcultures. Each subculture provides more specific identification of members belong to it. Product and marketing programme should be prepared in light of subcultures to tailor their needs. Subculture includes:

- **Nationality:** Every nation has its own unique culture that shapes and controls behaviour its citizens. For example, Indian culture, American culture, Japanese culture, Chinese culture, African culture, etc. Consumers of different nations hold different behaviour toward the company's products and strategies. The company can concentrate on one or more nations to serve.
- **Religion:** It is a powerful determinant of consumer needs and wants. Every religion has its culture in terms of rules, values, rituals, and procedures that have impact on its followers. Commonly, consumer behaviour is directly affected by religion in terms of products that are symbolically and ritualistically associated with the celebration of various religious events and festivals/holidays. Religious requirements or practices, sometimes, take on an expanded meaning beyond their original purpose. For example, Christians, Hindus, Muslims, Buddhists, etc., influence food preference, clothing choice, career aspiration, and overall pattern of life. Even, in each religion, there are several sub-religions. For example, Hindu Religion includes Vaishnav, Swaminarayan, Shivpanthi, Swadhiyai, and likewise; Christian Religion includes Protestants and Catholics; and similar is the case with Muslim and Jain.
- **Racial Groups:** In each culture, we find various racial groups; each of them tends to be different in terms of needs, roles, professions, habits, preference, and use of products. Each group responds differently to marketing offers due to different cultural backgrounds. For example, in our country, we find a number of racial groups like Kshatriya, Banya, Patel, Brahmin, Scheduled Caste, Scheduled Tribe, Shepherded, and so forth. These racial groups have their cultural values, norms, standards, habits, etc., that govern their overall response toward the company's products.

- **Geographical Regions:** Each geographic region represents specific culture and differs in terms of needs, preference, habits, usage rates, and uses of products. Clothing, residence, food, vehicle, etc., are determined by regional climate and culture.

3. Culture of Social Classes

Philip Kotler defines: "Social classes are relatively homogeneous and enduring divisions in a society, which are hierarchically ordered and whose members share similar values, interest, and behaviour." In many cases, social classes are based on caste system. Members of different castes have their cultures and, accordingly, they perform certain roles. Social classes reflect differences in income, occupation, education, their roles in society, and so on. Every social class has its culture that affects behaviour of its members. Social classes differ in their dress, speech patterns, recreational preferences, social status, value orientation, etc. They show distinct product and brand preferences in many areas like clothing, home furniture, education, leisure activities, and automobiles. Kotler identifies following social classes, each of them differs significantly in term of income, skills, needs, habits, preference, career orientation, approach toward life, etc.

i. Upper-upper
ii. Lower upper
iii. Upper middle
iv. Middle class
v. Working class
vi. Upper lower
vii. Lower-lower

Normally, with reference to India, on the basis of income level, or status in society, we can identity three social classes like upper class, middle class, and lower class.

In every society, percentage of each of these classes is subject to differ. Marketer should design his marketing programme to cater the needs of specific social classes.

SOCIAL FACTORS

Here, we examine the effect of social factors on consumer needs and preferences (behaviour). Social factors affect consumer behaviour. Consumer response to product, brand, and company is notably influenced by a number of social factors – family, reference groups, and roles and statuses. Marketer needs to analyse these social factors of his target market to cater its needs effectively. Let's briefly comment on some dominant social factors influencing consumer behaviour:

- **Family:** Family is one of the most powerful social factors affecting consumer behaviour. This is more significant where there is joint family system, in which children use to live with family for longer time. Values, traditions, and preferences are transmitted from parents to children inherently. Family members constitute the most influential primary reference group. From family, its member acquires an orientation toward religion, politics, ambition, self-worth, love, respect, and so on. Need, preference, buying habits, consumption rate, and many other aspects determined by family affect one's behaviour. In every family, elders, husband-wife, other members, and children have varying degree of influence on purchase decision, which is the matter of interest for the marker to appeal them. Some products are children dominant; some products are husband dominant; some products are wife dominant; while some products are equal dominant.
- **Reference Groups:** Philip Kotler states: "A person's reference group consists of all the groups that have a direct (face-to-face) or indirect influence on the person's attitudes or behaviour." Groups having a direct influence on the person are called membership groups. Normally, following reference groups affect behaviour of their members:

i. **Primary Reference Groups:** They are informal groups such as family members, friends, neighbors, relatives, and co-workers with whom the person interact fairly continuously. Habits, life-style, and opinions of these groups have direct impact on the person.

ii. **Secondary Reference Groups:** They tend to be more formal groups such as religious groups, professional groups, trade unions or associations, etc., that affect buying decisions of an individual buyer.

iii. **Aspiration (Aspired) Groups:** A person is not the member of such groups. But, he likes to belong to those groups. He imitates habits, preference and buying pattern of such groups. For example, college students imitate/like to belong to film stars, sportsmen, or professional groups.

iv. **Dissociative (Disliked) Groups:** Theses reference groups include such groups whose values or behaviour a person rejects or dislikes. He tends to behave differently than those groups.

A marketer should identify reference groups of his target market and should try to influence those groups. In case of television, automobile, clothing, home furniture, books and magazines, cigarettes, etc., the reference groups have more direct impact on buyers' purchase decision.

- **Roles and Statuses:** A person plays various roles in many groups throughout his life. He has to play different roles in family, club, office, or social organisation. A role consists of the activities that a person is expected to perform. For example, a person is father for his children, husband for his wife, son for his parents, friend for his friends, boss for his department, and a member of social organisation. Each role carries status. For example, sales manager has more status than sales officer. People choose those products that communicate or represent their roles and statuses in society. Therefore, marketer must be aware of the status symbol potential of products and brands. The marketer should also try to associate products and brands with specific roles and status.
- **Social Customs and Traditions:** Social customs, beliefs or traditions can be associated with religion, caste, or economic aspects. Such customs determine needs and preference of products in different occasions and, hence, affect consumer behaviour.
- **Income Level:** Income affects needs and wants of consumers. Preference of the rich consumers and the poor consumers differ notably. In case of quality, brand image, novelty, and costs, there is wide difference between the rich and the poor buyers. Marketer must be aware of expectations of different income groups of his target market.

PERSONAL FACTORS

Along with cultural and social factors, personal factors also affect one's buying decision. Personal factors are related to the buyer himself. These factors mainly include age and stage in life cycle, occupation, economic circumstances, life style, personality, and self-concept. Let us briefly examine the effect of personal factors on consumer behaviour.

- **Age and Stage in Life Cycle:** A man passes through various stages of his life cycle, such as infant, child, teenager, young, adult, and old. Need and preference vary as one passes through different stages of life cycle. For example, child and adult differ to a great extent in terms of needs and preference. Marketer may concentrate on one or more stages of his target consumers' life cycle. Use of different product depends on age and stage of buyers' life cycle.
- **Occupation:** Buying and using pattern of consumer, to a large extent, is affected by a person's occupation. For example, industrialist, teacher, artist, scientist, manager, doctor, supervisor, worker, trader, etc., differ significantly in term of need, preference, and overall

buying pattern. Company can specialize its products according to needs and wants of special professional groups.

- **Economic Circumstances:** Product preference, frequency of buying, quality, and quantity are largely affected by consumers' economic circumstances. Economic circumstances consist of spendable income, income stability, level of savings, assets, debts, borrowing power, and attitudes toward saving versus spending. People buy products keeping in mind these economic circumstances.
- **Life Style:** People with the same culture, social class, and occupation may differ in term of their life style. Knowledge of life style of the target market is essential for marketer to design more relevant marketing programme. Kotler defines: "Life style is the person's pattern of living in the world as expressed in the person's activities, interest, and opinions." Life style portrayed the "whole person" interacting with his/her environment. It is generally reflected in terms of activities, interest, clothing patterns, status consciousness, spending and savings, helping others, achievements, working style, etc. Every product has potential to suit different life styles.
- **Personality:** *Personality is a distinguished set of physical and psychotically characteristics that lead to relatively consistent and enduring response to one's environment.* Personality characteristics, such as individualism, difference, self-confidence, courage, firmness, sociability, mental balance, patience, etc., have a strong influence on needs and preferences. Every person buys that product which suits his personality. In case of clothing, automobiles, shoes, perfumes, etc., products are influenced by users' personality characteristics.
- **Self-concept:** It is also referred as self-image. It is what person believes of him. There can be actual self-concept, how he views himself; ideal self-concept, how he would like to view himself; and others-self-concept, how he thinks other see him. Person purchases such product that matches with his/her self-image. Marker must identify self-concept of his target buyers and must try to match the products with them.
- **Gender:** Gender or sex affects buying behaviour. Some products are male-dominated while some are female-dominated. Male customers react to those products which are closely suit their needs and styles. Cosmetics products are more closely related to female customers than male. Marketer must be aware of gender-effect on buying behaviour of the market.
- **Education:** Education makes the difference. Highly educated, moderately educated, less educated, and illiterates differ considerably in terms of their needs and preferences. In the same way, stage of education (like primary, secondary, college, etc.) affects buyers' behaviour. Education factor seems more relevant to academic institutes, book publishers, magazines, and newspapers. Education affects one's mindset. Buyers' colour choice, quality-orientation, services, and other aspects have more or less educational significance.

PSYCHOLOGICAL FACTORS

Buying behaviour is influenced by several psychological factors. The dominants among them include motivation, perception, learning, and beliefs and attitudes. It is difficult to measure the impact of psychological factors as they are internal, but are much powerful to control persons' buying choice. Manager must try to understand probable role the factors play in making buying decisions.

- **Motivation:** It has a significant impact on consumer behaviour. Motivation is closely related to human needs. One has many needs at a given time. Some needs are biogenic or physiological in nature arising from physiological states of tension, such as hunger, thirst, or discomfort. Other needs are psychogenic or psychological in nature arising from psychological state of tension, such as recognition, esteem, or belonging. Motivation comes from motive; motive is expression of needs; or intensified need become a motive. Thus, a motive is the need that is sufficiently pressing to drive the person to act. Satisfying the need reduces the felt tension. People hold one or more of following motives to buy:

i. To satisfy basic needs like hunger, thirst, or love
ii. To protect from economic, physical or mental hazards
iii. To get social status
iv. To be recognized or appreciated
v. To be respected
vi. To be self-actualized
vii. To avoid physical or mental stress

Motivation is, thus, a driving force that makes the individual to act to release the tension aroused from unmet needs. A motivated person is ready to act/react. Marketer should identify why people buy the products. What are the motives to purchase the products? If product is connected with their motives, they definitely respond positively. In fact, the product is a source of satisfying unmet needs. So, product is presented as a solution of tension resulted from unsatisfied needs. Several theories are available to understand motivation aspect. Most popular theories include Maslow Need Hierarchy, Herzberg's Two-Factor Theory, Stacy Adam's Equity Theory, Vroom's Expectancy Theory, Porter-Lawler Theory, McClelland's Achievement Theory, etc. Knowledge of these theories assists the manager to understand deeper motives the people hold for buying different products.

- **Perception:** Person's motivation to act depends on his perception of situation. It is one of the strongest factors affecting behaviour. The stimuli – product, advertising appeal, incentives, or anything – are perceived differently by different people due to difference in perception. Marketer should know how people perceive marketing offers.

  Bernard and Gary define: "Perception is a process by which an individual select, organize, and interpret information inputs to create a meaningful picture of the world." Perception depends on physical stimuli and stimuli's relation to surrounding field, too. People perceive the same stimulus differently due to selective attention, selective distortion, and selective retention. So, all consumers may not see the product or message in a way the marketer wants. Marketer should take these perceptual processes carefully while designing marketing programme. It is necessary that the product or marketing offer must be perceived in a way the market wants to be perceived. Marketer is also required to know the factors that affect people's perception. Tactful interview or questionnaire can help to measure perception of target groups.

- **Learning:** Most human behaviour is learned. Learning is basically concerned with experience of an individual. Learning can be defined as: *Relatively permanent changes arising from experience*. If an individual has satisfactory experience of buying and using the products, he is more likely to talk favourably or repeat the same. Most of purchase decisions depend on self-experience or experience of others, whose opinion carry value in buying decisions.

  Learning is produced through the interplay of drives, stimuli, cues, responses, and reinforcement. Learning theories help marketer to build up demand for the product by associating it with strong drives, using motivating cues, and providing positive reinforcement. New company can enter the market by using competitions' drives, cues and reinforcement. Sufficient knowledge of learning is an important input for the marketer to design the meaningful marketing programme.

- **Beliefs:** People hold beliefs about company, company's goods or services, and they act accordingly. Beliefs of the buyers affect product and brand image. We can define the term as: *Belief is a descriptive thought that a person holds about something.* Beliefs may be based on knowledge, opinion, or faith. Note that beliefs have nothing to do with facts or reality. People may have wrong beliefs for the superior product, or they hold positive beliefs for inferior product. Positive and negative beliefs have their impact on purchase decisions. Marketer can create positive belief by associating strong aspects related to product and brand, or can correct wrong beliefs by proper campaign. It is clear that people buy only if they believe it is worthwhile to buy. So, beliefs play decisive role in the buying decision. Marketer must try to know what type of beliefs people hold about company, products, and brands. Such knowledge must be incorporated in preparing an effective marketing programme.
- **Attitudes:** *An attitude is a person's enduring favourable or unfavourable evaluations, emotional feelings, and action tendencies toward some object or idea.* These emotional feelings are usually evaluative in nature. People hold attitudes toward almost everything, such as religion, politics, clothes, music, food, product, company, and so on. Attitudes decide liking or disliking of object. People can judge good or bad, beautiful or ugly, rich or poor, or desirable or undesirable about an object, a product, or a person. Attitudes play a vital role in accepting or rejecting, appreciating or criticizing the product or brand. People do not react to every object in a fresh way. Object is evaluated by attitudes. So, it is imperative that marketer must know what type of attitudes people hold about the company, products, and brands. Attitudes can be learned or developed. Learning plays an important role in developing attitudes. Even unfavourable attitudes can be changed into favourable ones by systematic campaign. Mostly, beliefs and attitudes are taken simultaneously.

We have discussed only main factors. There can be even more factors. Moreover, this is a loose classification. Cultural, personal, social and psychological factors are closely related and interdependent; sometimes, difficult to separate one from another. Some authors have included economic factors as a separate set of factors. In fact, economic factors are included in personal factors (economic circumstances). Marketer is required to know these all factors and their probable impact on consumer buying decisions. He must systematically identify and analyse relevant factors to formulate marketing strategies more effectively and meaningfully. He needs to study what is going in the mind of buyers. He has two options: (1) To change the consumer behaviour to suit the product or brand, and/or (2) To change the marketing programme to suit the consumer behaviour. Mostly, marketer tries to fit his offerings with consumers.

THE BUYING PROCESS OR STAGES OF CONSUMER BEHAVIOUR

Philip Kotler states: "To be successful, marketers have to go beyond the various influences on buyers and develop an understanding of how consumer actually makes their buying decisions." Marketers must identify three buyer-related aspects:

1. Who makes the buying decisions?
2. The types of buying decisions, and
3. The steps in the buying process

However, we will discuss the last issue, that is, the steps in buying process.

DEFINITION OF BUYING PROCESS

Simply, we can define the term as: *Consumer buying process consists of sequential steps the consumer follows to arrive at the final buying decisions.*

Mostly, consumers follow a typical buying process. Marketer must know how consumers reach the final decision to buy the product. According to Philip Kotler, the manager can learn about the stages in the buying process through four methods. Each method gives hint regarding the steps in the consumer buying process.

Methods to Learn about buying process are:

1. **Introspective Method:** Manager can think how he himself would react or buy the product.
2. **Retrospective Method:** He can interview the recent purchasers to recall the events leading to their purchase.
3. **Prospective Method:** He can locate consumers who plan to buy the product and ask them to think how they will follow buying process.
4. **Prescriptive Method:** He can ask the consumers to describe the ideal way to buy the products.

STAGES IN BUYING PROCESS

According to **Philip Kotler**, the typical buying process involves five stages the consumer passes through described as under:

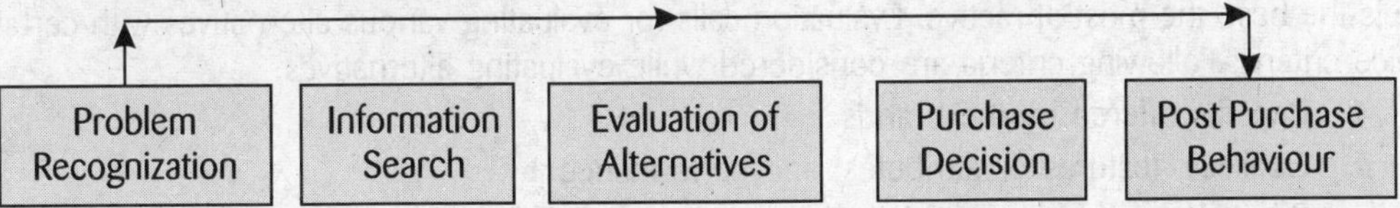

Figure 3: Consumer Buying Process

1. Problem Identification

This step is also known as recognizing of unmet need. The need is a source or force of buying behaviour. Buying problem arises only when there is unmet need or problem is recognized. Need or problem impels an individual to act or to buy the product. Buyer senses a difference between his actual state (physical and mental) and a desired state. The need can be triggered by internal or external stimuli. Internal stimuli include basic or normal needs – hunger, thirst, sex, or comfort; while external stimuli include external forces, for instance, when an individual watch a new brand car, he desires to buy it.

Marketer must identify the circumstances that trigger a particular need. He can collect information from a number of consumers regarding how stimuli spark an interest in products. Based on information, he can develop marketing strategies to trigger consumer interest.

2. Information Search

Interested consumer will try to seek information. Now, he will read newspapers and magazines, watch television, visit showroom or dealer, contact salesman, discuss with friends and relatives, and try all the possible sources of information. Mostly, the consumer can try one or more of following sources of information:

i. **Personal Sources:** They may include family members, friends, package, colleagues, and relatives.

ii. **Commercial Sources:** Advertising, salesmen, dealers, package, trade show, display, and exhibition are dominant commercial sources.

iii. **Public Sources:** Mass media (radio, TV, newspapers, magazines, cinema, etc.), consumer-rating agencies, etc., are main public sources.

iv. **Experimental Sources:** They include handling, examining, testing, or using the product.

Selection of sources depends upon personal characteristics, types of products, and capacity and reliability of sources. Each information source performs different functions in influencing buying decision. By gathering information from relevant sources, the consumer can learn about different products and brands available in the market.

Note that consumer will not collect detail information on all the brands available in the market. He scrutinizes all the brands in sequence, like total (brands) set to awareness set to affordable set, and to choice set. Consumer collects information only on limited brands, say, choice set.

Marketer must try to get his brand into the prospects' awareness set and choice set. Moreover, the company should identify sources and their relative importance. Company must ask the consumers regarding types of sources they exercise. They can elicit valuable information about sources they normally use and their relative value. On that basis, effective communication can be prepared for the target market.

3. Evaluation of Alternatives

In the former stage, the consumer has collected information about certain brands. Now, he undergoes evaluation of brands. He cannot buy all of them. Normally, he selects the best one, the brand that offers maximum satisfaction. Here, he evaluates competitive brands to judge which one is the best, the most attractive. Evaluation calls for evaluating various alternatives with certain choice criteria. Following criteria are considered while evaluating alternatives:

i. Benefits offered by the brands
ii. Qualities, features or attributes, and performance
iii. Price changed by various brands
iv. History of brands
v. Popularity, image or reputation of brands
vi. Product-related services offered by the brands, such as after-sales services, warrantee, and free installation
vii. Availability of brands and dealer rating.

Different criteria are used for different products. For example, if a person wants to purchase a motorbike out of Enfield Bullet 350; TVS Victor, TVS Centra, Suzuki Ferro; Hero Honda Spender, Ambition, and CBZ; Kawasaki Bajaj Boxer, Pulsar and Caliber; LML Freedom, etc., he will consider following criteria:

i. Price
ii. Pick-up and performance
iii. Facilities and comfort
iv. Gear-transmission system
v. Get-up/appearance
vi. Speed per hour
vii. Average per litre petrol
viii. Maintenance costs
ix. Image, status and novelty
x. Safety
xi. Resale value
xii. Services, guarantee, warrantee, etc.

The brand that meets most of the above conditions reasonably is more likely to be preferred. Marketer should highlights superior features of his brand. Some companies also advertise comparative table to help consumers evaluate various brands. For example, Yamaha, Maruti, and Hyundai provide comparative table in newspapers to show how the bike/car is superior to other brands.

4. Purchase Decision

This is the stage when the consumer prefers one, the most promising band, out of several brands. The former stage helps consumers evaluate various brands in the choice set. The brand that offers maximum benefits or satisfaction is preferred. Simply, the most attractive brand, that can offer more benefits in relation to price paid, is selected by comparing one brand with others. Comparison shows superiority/inferiority of the brands.

Now, consumer makes up his mind to purchase the most preferred brand. However, three factors further affect whether buying intension result into actual purchase. More clearly, the consumer' decision to avoid, modify, or postpone a purchase decision is influenced by these factors.

The first factor is attitudes of others. The impact of other persons' attitudes depends on degree of their negative attitudes toward the consumer's preferred brand, and consumer's degree of compliance with other persons' wishes. *The second factor is unanticipated situational factors*. Purchase intension may change due to certain unanticipated situational factors like price hike, loss of job, family income, major medical expenses, non-availability of the preferred brand, or such similar factors. *The third and the last factor is consumer's perceived risk*. Degree of risk depends on price, attribute uncertainty, entry of a new superior product, and his self-confidence.

Sub-decisions in Purchase Decision: Consumer's buying decision involves following five sub-decisions:

i. **Brand Decision:** For example, CBZ (model) motorbike of Hero Honda.
ii. **Vender Decision:** For example, XYZ Hero Honda Showroom.
iii. **Quantity Decision:** For example, One motorbike.
iv. **Timing Decision:** For example, on 1st December, 2007.
v. **Payment Decision:** For example, by cash.

5. Post-purchase Decisions

Consumer buys the product with certain expectations. Though he decides very systematically, there is no guarantee of a complete satisfaction. There is always possibility of variation between the expected level of satisfaction and the actual satisfaction. His subsequent behaviour is influenced by degree of satisfaction/dissatisfaction. Marketer must monitor the post-purchase experience of the buyers that includes:

a. Post-purchase Satisfaction
b. Post-purchase Action
c. Post-purchase Use and Disposal

Post-purchase Satisfaction: Actual satisfaction may not be equal to the expected one. He may find some problems or defects in the product while using. It is the matter of interest for marketer to know whether consumer is highly satisfied, somewhat satisfied, or dissatisfied. Consumer's satisfaction is the function of the relationship between expected/perceived performance (expectations) and actual performance. The larger the gap between expectations and performance, the greater the consumer's dissatisfaction will be. The consumer is satisfied when product meets or exceeds all the expectations and vice versa. If he is satisfied, he buys the product again, and talks favourably. In order to minimize the gap between expectations and performance, the seller must not exaggerate the product benefits; must make truthful claim of product's likely performance.

Post-purchase Action: Obviously, level of the consumer's satisfaction with the product affects his subsequent behaviour/action. If he is satisfied reasonably, he purchases the product again, and talks favourably to family members, friends, relatives, and coworkers. That is why marketer says: Our best advertisement is a satisfied consumer. Quite opposite to it, dissatisfied consumer responds differently. He may abandon product, complain to the company for compensation, resort to the court and warn other organisations, friends, relatives and coworkers to avoid product.

The task of marketer consists of taking certain steps to minimize amount of consumer's post-purchase dissatisfaction. Dissatisfaction can be reduced by:

1. Congratulating consumers for the right choice to justify their decision
2. Sending booklet to guide for effective use of the product
3. Inviting suggestions from consumers
4. Managing complaints by effective counseling and after-sales services
5. Informing about changes made in the product
6. Exchanging or returning amount, etc.

He must investigate where the product falls short. Close informal relations with consumers can yield valuable information. Remember that a dissatisfied consumer is more important than a satisfied one as his every problem regarding the product reveals a ready suggestion. Marketer must welcome complaints and tackle them carefully for the bright future.

Post-purchase Use and Disposal: Marketer should also monitor how the consumers use and dispose the product. Such information can be a very good guideline for the marketer. Marketer can learn possible problems and opportunities relating with the product. In normal situation, the consumer uses or disposes the product in followings ways:

1. He may not use the product immediately, store it for the future use.
2. Use the product fully immediately after purchase.
3. Resell or trade it.
4. Use the product differently than it is meant for. He may find new uses of the product.
5. Offer the product to others as a gift.
6. Throw the product away, considering as useless.

Marketer can change or modify marketing programme based on the study of how the product is used and disposed. In case, when consumers are much creative, it is important to investigate how the product is used or disposed.

Thus, buying process is a journey from problem recognization to reaction of buyers. The entire process is very meaningful to the seller. The process reflects most of factors affecting consumers. Marketer, therefore, must study the buying process from consumer's viewpoint. Company must take certain steps to support consumers in each stage to buy its product.

MARKET SEGMENTATION

INTRODUCTION

Modern marketers operate in a few target markets, not total market. The act of planning, implementing, directing, and controlling marketing efforts on target markets is call target marketing. Target marketing (focusing marketing efforts on the specific groups) involves three steps/decisions.

1. **Market Segmentation:** Market segmentation is an act of dividing the total market into distinct groups of buyers; each of them requires a separate marketing mix.
2. **Market Targeting:** Market Targeting is the act of developing measures for segments' attractiveness and selecting one or more market segments to enter or operate.
3. **Product Positioning:** Market positioning is an act of establishing a viable competitive plan to position the firm and its special offer in each target market.

These three decisions have been adequately discussed in the remaining part of the chapter. We begin with market segmentation, continue with market targeting, and end with product positioning.

Market segmentation is a part of target marketing. Modern marketing is consumer driven or consumer-oriented in nature. Consumers are placed in the center of marketing. The primary goal of marketing is to maximize consumer satisfaction. But, buyers in today's market are too numerous, widely scattered, and varied in their buying requirements. Company can do better if it serves only particular customer segments of the market. A marketer can satisfy his consumers only when he concentrates only on a limited number of well-defined groups of consumers. Therefore, he must define and select target market. The target market is the group or groups of buyers for whom the entire marketing programme is aimed at. Target market is targeted group of buyers whose needs and wants a company wants to satisfy. Selecting the target market calls for dividing total market into certain segments and selecting certain segments as target market. *The process used for defining and deciding target market is known as market segmentation.*

DEFINITIONS OF MARKET SEGMENTATION

Market consists of buyers, and buyers differ in many ways. Based on various characteristics of buyers, the total market is segmented into various groups or parts; some of these groups are selected as target markets. This act is known as market segmentation. Following are some of the standard definitions:

1. Market segmentation, in simple words, can be defined as: *A process of dividing a total market into different sub-markets, segments, or parts by using some definite criteria or bases is called market segmentation.*
2. Similarly, we can say: *Market segmentation is an act of classifying consumers on the basis of their significant characteristics, such as income, preference, location, profession, etc., to select target market. Separate marketing mix is developed for each segment or group of segments in the target market.*
3. *Market segmentation seeks the answer of the question: Which products are sold to whom ?*
4. **William Stanton:** "Market segmentation consists of taking the total heterogeneous market for a product and dividing it into several sub-markets or segments, each of which tends to be homogeneous in all significant aspects."
5. **Philip Kotler:** "The process of classifying customers into groups exhibiting different needs, characteristics, or behaviour is called market segmentation. Every market is made up of market segments."
6. **Frederic Webster:** "Market segmentation is a method for achieving maximum market response from limited market resources by recognizing difference in the response characteristics of various parts of the market. It is a strategy of 'divide and conquer' that adjusts marketing strategy to inherent differences in buyer behaviour."

CHARACTERISTICS OF MARKET SEGMENTATION

Definitions reveal following characteristics:

1. Market segmentation is a customer-oriented philosophy. The entire process of segmentation is based on customers.
2. Market segmentation is a process of dividing total market into similar segments, and selecting one or more segments as a target market.
3. Different bases are used to segment total market, such as income, geographical areas, psychological aspects, etc.
4. It is based on the theme, "divide and conquer." Success depends on matching the product with consumer needs.
5. It is an act of defining and selecting target market.
6. It is the study of different types of responses of buyers as they have different characteristics.

7. Marketing programme, including product, price, promotion, and distribution decisions, depends on market segmentation. It is a basic aspect of the modern marketing.
8. Market segmentation may be applied to industrial products as well as consumer products.

BENEFITS OF MARKET SEGMENTATION OR OBJECTIVES/IMPORTANCE OF MARKET SEGMENTATION

Companies are increasingly embracing (preferring) target market instead of mass marketing. It must be stated that market segmentation is an indispensable act to succeed in modern market place. No marketer, with whatever resource capacity, can satisfy all the needs of the mass market. If he wants to satisfy customers more effectively and efficiently than competitors, he needs to concentrate only on the limited number of well-defined buyers. He should limit his entire energy to certain groups of buyers to treat them more effectively. Target marketing helps marketers identify marketing opportunities better. They can develop the right offer for each of the target markets more efficiently. In the same way, pricing, promotion, and distribution strategies can be meaningfully designed. This is possible only by market segmentation. Benefits or importance of market segmentation can be better explained by below stated points:

1. More Precise Definition of the Market

Segmentation improves company's understanding of why consumers do or do not buy certain products. Marketer can have very clear understanding of his consumers. He knows adequately about the market. He can formulate and implement marketing plan more successfully.

2. Maximum Customer Satisfaction

Marketer can cater needs of customers more effectively. Market segmentation is relevant to the modern marketing practices. It ensures both maximum satisfaction to consumers and maximum sales to the company. Maximum consumer satisfaction is the master key to solve any problem. Marketer can cater needs of customers more effectively. Customers can have products as per their needs; they can get better products or services at lower costs.

3. Effective Marketing Strategy

Market segmentation provides an opportunity to understand needs and wants of different segments of the market. This can help in formulating marketing mix/programme more meaningfully. Company can gain a maximum market response.

4. Essence of Modern Marketing

Market segmentation strategy fits with modern marketing philosophy. If the marketer wants to satisfy his valued consumers, market segmentation is the only option. It is an essential condition for the successful modern marketing practice.

5. Improved Profitability

On the basis of the study on needs of specific group of buyers, the products are manufactured. Company can attract distinct groups of buyers and can increase sales. An increased sale has positive impact on its profitability.

6. Optimum Use of Productive Resources

Market segmentation leads to effective use of the valuable resources. Resources are allocated and used exactly as per market needs, avoiding mismatching between what marketer offers and what the market needs. So, valuable resources like man, money, material, space, technology, time, etc., can be utilized more effectively.

7. Benefit of Specialisation

It is easy to direct marketing efforts more clearly and specifically. Company designs its marketing programme for different products and for various groups of buyers. Specialisation in production and marketing can offer a lot of benefits to the company.

8. High Competitiveness

As a result of market segmentation, a company can treat its consumers more effectively than competitors. It improves competitive strength of the company. Company can respond strongly to the competitor; can prevent the entry of competitors; or can defeat competitors. Company can create and maintain the loyal consumers for long period of time.

9. Collection of Valuable Information

Market segmentation process elicits a lot of valuable information for the company. Such information is instrumental for marketing research, product development, and evaluation of marketing activities. It is also useful for measuring effectiveness of sales and distribution facilities.

10. Identifying Market opportunity

Market segmentation helps establish close relations with specific groups of buyers. Close relations facilitate a continuous interaction between consumers and company. Consumers inform the company regarding changes in their needs, wants, and habits on a continuous basis or whenever asked. Thus, it is easy for a marketer to project the future trends. He can identify opportunities to be available currently or in the near future, and can plan accordingly.

11. Benefits to Society and Nation

Market segmentation, if taken objectively, can contribute to social welfare and national development. Basically, it is a consumer-oriented philosophy, and it results into a win-win-win approach, that is, company, society, and nation, all three, are benefited. This can improve overall economic system by manufacturing the right products of the right quantity and quality for the right groups of consumers, made available continuously at the right price and place by the right distribution channel.

12. Benefits to Small Scale Industrial Units

We know that small-scale industrial units can function on a limited scale of operation. They can have only the limited manufacturing and marketing capacity. Industries working on a small-scale basis can take advantages of market segmentation. By concentrating on special demand of specific group of a limited number of consumers, they can afford products and get profitable market easily. They can compete with the large industrial units, too.

LIMITATIONS OF MARKET SEGMENTATION

No doubt, market segmentation is essential consideration in marketing programme, but is not free from limitations. Marketer must know possible practical problems (limitations) of market segmentation so as to minimize these limitations. Most common limitations of market segmentation include followings:

1. Limited Production

In each specific segment, customers are limited. So, it is not possible to produce products in mass scale for every segment. Therefore, company cannot take advantages of mass scale production; scale of economy is not possible. Product may be costly and affect adversely to the sales.

2. Expensive Production

Market segmentation is expensive in both production and marketing. In order to satisfy different groups/segments of buyers, producers have to produce products of various models, colors, sizes, etc., that result into more production costs. In the same way, the producers are required to maintain large inventory for different styles, colors, and sizes of products.

3. Expensive Marketing

Market segmentation also results into expensive marketing. Due to different groups of buyers, the marketer has to consider all the segments in terms of needs, interests, habits, preferences and attitudes. Marketer has to formulate and implement several marketing strategies for different segments.

4. Difficulty in Distribution

Company needs to make the separate arrangement for each of the products demanded by different classes of customers. Salesman's recruitments, selection, training, payments, and incentives are more difficult and costly. Company has to maintain separate channels and services for satisfying varied customer groups.

5. Heavy Investment

Market segmentation leads to heavy investment. In order to satisfy different needs and wants of various groups, a company has to produce variety of product lines and product items. For the purpose, the company requires to invest more on technology and other inputs that may demand heavy investment.

6. Promotion Problems

Market segmentation also creates promotional problems and multiplies promotional difficulties. It is obvious that different segments are made on the basis of distinguished characteristics of buyers. Each group differs in terms of advertising media, appeal or message. In order to influence various segments of buyers, the company is required to prepare a separate advertising programme or strategy. Similarly, personal selling and sales promotional activities become more complex. Company needs to spend more to take benefits of specialisation.

7. Stock and Storage Problems

To meet needs and wants of different consumer groups, the company must maintain adequate stock of various products on a continuous basis. This creates problem of stocks, storage, and working capital.

Most limitations reflect the impact of situation and inability of manager to segment the market purposively and meaningfully. But, limitations cannot restrict segmentation philosophy and practice. These limitations can be overcome by segmenting market carefully and objectively.

BASES OF SEGMENTING MARKET

Philip Kotler opines that market consists of buyers, and buyers differ in one or more respects. They may differ in their wants, resources, geographical locations, buying attitudes, and buying practices. Any one or more of these variables can be used to segment market. Note that bases for segmenting consumer market and industrial market may be different. Firstly, we discuss bases for segmenting consumer market. Bases for segmenting industrial market have been described in the later part.

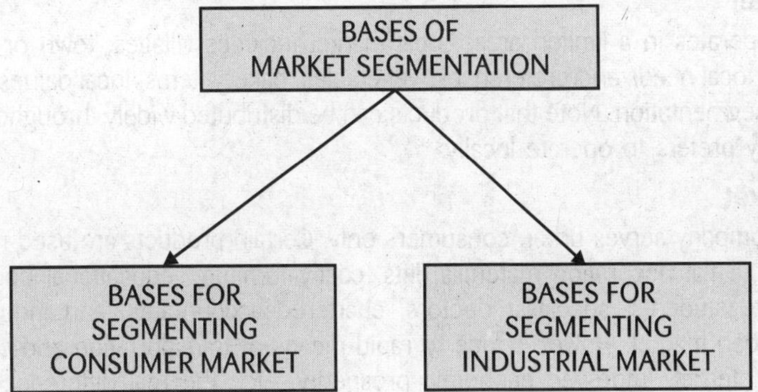

Figure 4: Bases of Market Segmentation

BASES FOR *CONSUMER MARKET* SEGMENTATION

Market segmentation, in simple words, is dividing consumers into various groups. There can be several such bases used for segmenting consumer market. Normally, as stated by Philip Kotler, bases can be classified into two categories as shown in figure 5.

1. People-oriented Bases for Segmentation, and
2. Product-oriented Bases for Segmentation.

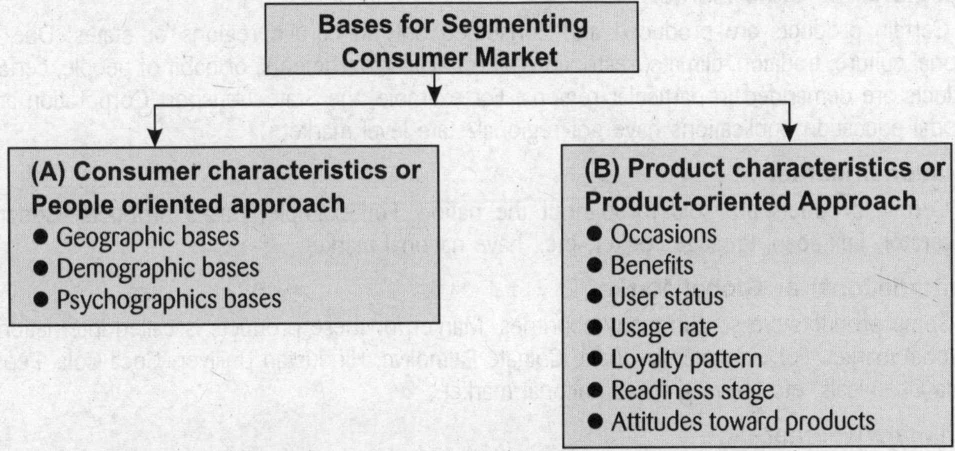

Figure 5: Bases for Segmenting Consumer Market

(A) PEOPLE-ORIENTED BASES

People-oriented bases for segmenting consumer markets are also known as consumer characteristics. Main bases in the category include:

1. Geographical bases,
2. Demographical bases, and
3. Psychographic bases.

GEOGRAPHICAL BASES

This segmentation is based on places or locations where consumers reside. Here, market segmentation calls for dividing the market into different geographical units, such as nations, states, regions, cities, climates, urban/village, etc. Needs and preferences differ significantly at different places. So, a company may operate in one or more geographical area as per its capacity. Typically, with regard to Indian situation, a company divides its market in following segments:

1. Local Market

Company operates in a limited area. Local market includes villages, town or city. Company concentrates on local needs and preferences. Vegetables, bakery items, local dairies, etc., products may prefer this segmentation. Note that products can be distributed widely throughout the country, but the company prefers to operate locally.

2. Urban Market

Here, the company serves urban consumers only. Certain products are used mostly in urban areas, for example flat decoration materials, lifts, costly furniture, educational books for college and postgraduate students, specialist doctors, chartered accountants, and industrial products mostly prefer urban market. However, due to rapid means of transportation and communication, easy access to Internet, improved economic prosperity, etc., the real difference between rural and urban markets is on decline. But, still rural and urban consumers differ significantly in several ways like habit, style, attitude, preference, and buying and bargaining ability.

3. Rural Market

Certain products are used in rural areas only, such as thick cotton cloths, cattle feeds, pesticides, fertilizers, etc. In most cases, the rural customers use cheaper, durable, and simple products. However, this conclusion is not strictly applicable. In the countries like India, where more than 65% population resides in villages, the rural market attracts not only national but also multinational companies.

4. Regional or State Market

Certain products are produced and consumed only in certain regions or states. Due to regional culture, tradition, climate, restrictions of regional governments, or habit of people, certain products are demanded in particular regions. For example, the State Transport Corporation and regional education publications have got regional/state level market.

5. National Market

Certain products are sold throughout the nation. For example, Bata's products, Goderej refrigerator, Lux soap, Prestige cooker, etc., have national market.

6. International or Global Market

Some products are sold in many countries. Market for these products is called international or global market. For example, Air India, Colgate Palmolive, Hindustan Uniliver, Coca-Cola, Pepsi, Nirma Chemicals, etc., have got international market.

7. Climate/Weather

Climate plays an important role in determining needs of people. Climate is based on cold, heat, rainfall, hills/mountains, jungle, sea, desert, and so on. Some products are used only in particular climate. Certain products like vehicles, cloths, foods, boats, camels, umbrella and rain suits, cold drinks, fans, air conditioners, etc., are used as per their suitability with the climate of specific region.

Thus, a company should formulate marketing strategy as per its market in different geographical areas. Product, price, promotion, and distribution decisions are considerably affected by geographic segmentation.

DEMOGRAPHIC BASES (SEGMENTATION)

Demographic means relating to population. In demographic segmentation, the market is divided on the basis of demographic variables, such as age, sex, family size, income, occupation, etc. It is the most popular and widely practiced set of bases. Needs, wants, preferences, and usage rate are highly associated with demographic variables. Also, it is comparatively easy to identify and measure market by demographic variables. Widely used demographic bases for market segmentation are discussed as under:

1. Age

Consumers of different age groups differ in terms of needs, preference, quantity, interest, habits, etc. An individual changes his needs, preferences, and habits as he grows from childhood to adulthood. Based on age criteria, we can classify the market in various segments as infants/children, teenagers, young, adults, and olds. For the products like chocolates, cloths, cycles and motorcycles, films, books and magazines, foods, medicines, clubs, etc., an age-based segmentation seems effective.

2. Sex/Gender

Sex or gender refers to male or female. This base is used for the products like cloths, cosmetics, magazines, cigarettes, two-wheelers, ornaments and jewelleries, garments, watches, and likewise. Male and female consumers differ significantly in terms of needs, attitudes, preference, and overall response to the product. However, this base cannot be strictly applied to all the products. Some products are used by both male and female.

3. Size of Family

Market can be segmented in terms of size of family also. Need, size/quantity, frequency packing, quality, etc., depend on the number of members in the family. In case of refrigerator, toothpaste, cars, flats, furniture, provisions, ice-cream package, etc., this type of segmentation makes sense.

4. Family-Life-Cycle

According to family life cycle, market can be segmented into several segments like single, newly married, family with one child, family with aged parents, and so on. At different stage of family-life-cycle, type, quantity, size, and preference of products are subject to vary.

5. Income

Income is a powerful determinant of needs and wants. It affects quantity, size, quality, novelty, and style. Companies dealing with automobiles, clothing, cosmetics, furniture, travels, footwear, electronics, clubs, hospitals, restaurants, hotels, etc., can use an income-based segmentation. It is quite obvious that poor, middle class, rich, and elite income groups differ significantly in term of quality, preference, services, and novelty.

6. Education

Education makes a difference. The market can be divided in terms of level of education also, such as illiterate, semi-educated, and educated. Illiterate cannot read and write; semi-educated can read and write with limited capacity; and the educated means more than matriculation. All three classes of customers respond differently to different products. Market for magazines, newspapers, books, movies, TV serials, schools, colleges and educational institutions, etc., can be segmented on education basis.

7. Castes and Social Classes

Sometimes, market segmentation takes place as per castes and social classes. Castes and social classes are based on social system and income both. As per social system, there may be higher class or lower class, while on the basis of income there may be lower class, middle class, higher class, etc. In Indian Society, we find a number of castes and classes. Caste or social class affects leisure activity, occupation, colour preference, habits, traditions, customs, rituals, etc.

8. Profession/Occupation

On the basis of profession or occupation, the market can be divided as businessmen, service class, farmers, laborers, professionals (such as lawyers, chartered accountants and doctors), actors, writers, etc. Consumers belong to various professions/occupations differ in terms of need, preference, life style, status, income, and so on. This segmentation is relevant to such products like two-wheeler, car, club membership, travels, furniture, magazines, and electronic appliances.

9. Religion

As per this base, the market is segmented on the basis of religions like Hindu, Muslim, Christian, Jew, fanatic, secularist, and many other religions. Even in each religion, there can be more sub-religions. Followers of each religion have different needs, habits, preferences, foods, clothing, rituals, reading materials, festivals, and what not. Producer keeps in mind of different religions and accordingly consumers of particular religion(s) must be selected.

10. Nationality

Use of products depends on nationality. Consumers of various countries differ in terms of habit, preference, food, clothing, festivals, religions, education, income, customs, beliefs and traditions, and life styles. They need different products of different style, price, quality, and taste. For example, Indians, Americans, Chinese, Japanese, African, etc., have completely varied needs and preferences.

PSYCHOGRAPHIC BASES

In psychographic segmentation, the market is divided into different groups on the basis of psychographic characteristics of buyers, like social class, life style, perception, learning, attitudes, and personality. Psychological characteristics refer to the inner or intrinsic qualities of the individual consumer. Consumers within same geographic and demographic group can exhibit quite different psychographic profile. Psychographic segmentation mainly involve following bases:

1. Social Class

Here, social class doesn't mean income-based social classes only. It implies a relative status in community. Consumers in different social classes vary in terms of values, product preferences, and buying habits. The concept of social classes implies a hierarchy in which individuals occupy different statues. Each class has specific values, traditions, and habits. In Indian context, community is divided into various classes like higher class, middle class, lower class, etc. However, many authors have considered this base in demographic segmentation. But, it has psychological implications.

2. Life-style

Life-style is a total pattern of life. It can be defined as one's own way of living. It is reflected in terms of interest, association, use of products, and way of influencing others. People purchase those products, which reflect their life styles. Car, motorbike, cell phone, magazine, cigarette, wine, cosmetic, clothing, etc., products are marketed on life-style base. Marketer tries to suit his products with life-style of consumers.

3. Personality

Personality and life-style go hand in hand. Consumers buy those products that suit their personality. Personality is a distinctive way to influence others. Personality is determined by certain physical and mental characteristics. However, mental or psychological characteristics are more relevant for market segmentation. Personality characteristics such as self-confidence, extrovert, firmness, individualism, balance, sociability, impressiveness, willpower, talent, and many other such characteristics affect product need and preference. This segmentation may be used for clothing, car, bikes, house, and glasses.

4. Buying Motives

Buying motives refer to the purpose of buying the product. What consumers expect from the product is the matter of interest for a marketer. People hold different motives for different product. They buy those products that can match with their expectations. Buying motives may be durability, reliability, taste, safety, ease, performance, services, prestige, status, and likewise. The market can be divided on the basis of these motives. This segmentation is applicable in automobile, furniture, electronic products, travels, gold and jewelry, hotels, charitable activities, etc.

Psychographic segmentation is more confusing as the views of various writers seem inconsistent. But, it is clear that personality, values, perception, attitudes, motivation, etc., have tremendous effect on consumers' buying decision. We have discussed only limited psychological/psychographic bases.

B. BEHAVIOURAL (PRODUCT-ORIENTED) BASES

Such segmentation is also called as consumer response segmentation, behavioural segmentation or product characteristics-based market segmentation. Clearly, the market is divided on the bases of product characteristics or consumer response to the products. (Consumer responds differently due varied product characteristics). In the former bases, we have considered consumer characteristics, here, we will consider product characteristics as the bases for segmenting the market. The popularly used behavioural bases have been discussed in following part:

1. Occasions

Many products are purchased and/or used occasionally. Therefore, a wise marketer associates the use of products with particular occasions. Occasions create demand. Clothing, furniture, firecrackers, eclectic appliances, gold, greeting cards, gift varieties, etc., products experience more demand during Diwali. Tours and travels companies organize special tours during vacations. So, the company finds an opportunity to segment the market on the basis of occasions. This is the reason why the most of companies introduces new models and varieties along with the special offers during various occasions. Occasions may be regular (birthday or marriage anniversary); may be special (achievement, special party, transfer/promotion, marriage, birth of child); or may be festivals like Kite-flying, Diwali, and Janmastami).

There can be various occasions such as festivals, elections, birthday, marriage anniversary, death, illness, outstanding achievements, examination results, change in employments, acquisition of home, and so many similar occasions. Company segments the market on one or more occasions and tries to meet needs and wants during such occasions.

2. Benefits

It is a widely used base of dividing the market. This segmentation is based on benefits the consumers seek the products. Benefits desired by the consumers may include quality, services, guarantee/warrantee, economy, ease, safety, performance, durability, and prestige/status. Company divides the market as per benefits expected by the buyers. For example, Colgate prevents cavity, Close-up offers freshness, etc. Most automobiles manufacturers use this segmentation. Firm can design its marketing programme in a way that different benefit-seekers can be satisfied.

3. User Status

Market may be segmented on the basis of user status, such as non-users, ex-users, potential users, first-time users, occasional users, and regular users.

i. **Non-users:** They are not using the company's products.

ii. **Ex-users:** They were using, but now are not using the products.

iii. **Potential Users:** They are not using, but there is potential that they may use the products.

iv. **First-time Users:** They have used the product only for the first time, if they are satisfied, they may use repeatedly.

v. **Occasional Users:** They use the product infrequently; they may buy when other brands are not available.

vi. **Regular Users:** They are regularly using the product.

The ultimate aim of the company is to convert all users into the regular users. All these different users need different marketing treatment. A company needs to formulate distinct product, price, promotional, and distribution strategies for each type of users.

4. Usage Rates

Market can be segmented on the basis of the usage rates like light, medium, and heavy product users.

i. **Light Users:** They are more in number, but purchase a small quantity.

ii. **Medium Users:** They are relatively more in number, and consume more quantity compared to the first one.

iii. **Heavy Users:** They are small percentage of the market, but account for high percentage of total consumption.

5. Loyalty Pattern/Status

Consumers' loyalty pattern can be used for dividing the market. Consumers hold varying degree of loyalty to the brand. Accordingly, buyers can be divided into four major groups:

i. **Hard-core Loyal:** Consumers who buy the same brand all the time. For example, they buying pattern may be A, A, A, A, A. They buy brand 'A' all the times.

ii. **Soft/split Loyal:** Consumers who are loyal to two or more brands. Their buying pattern may be A, A, B, B, A, B. Their loyalty splits between two brands.

iii. **Shifting Loyal:** Consumers who shift from one brand to another. Their buying pattern is A, A, A, B, B, B. Their loyalty is shifting from brand A to brand B.

iv. **Brand Switchers:** Consumers who show no loyalty to any brand. Their buying pattern is A, B, C, D, E, A, B. They are switching from one brand to next. They are variety seekers.

However, a company should conclude carefully these buying patterns as they do not always reflect the degree of loyalty. Company tries to create more hard-core loyal consumers.

6. Buyer Readiness Stage

Consumers show different stages of readiness to buy the product. They can be classified on the basis of readiness stages, too. Accordingly, the market is segmented as:

i. **Unaware:** They are not aware of the product.

ii. **Aware:** They are just aware, but don't have information about the product feature, quality, and price.

iii. **Informed:** This group has sufficient information to evaluate the offer.

iv. **Interested:** This group is interested to buy the product.

v. **Desirous:** This group is more likely to buy.

vi. **Intended to Buy:** They will buy, if they are convinced.

They all differ in terms of response to product, price, promotion, and distribution. Company has to prepare a separate marketing strategy for each group of buyers in varying readiness stages.

7. Attitudes toward Product

Different groups of buyers with different attitudes behave in different ways. The company, therefore, may segment the market on the basis of attitudes of consumers. Needless to mention, each type of attitude-holders should be tackled separately. Possible groups of consumers on the basis of the degree of favourableness of attitudes are:

i. **Enthusiastic:** They hold the most favourable attitudes toward the product brand and company. They favour the brand strongly.

ii. **Positive:** They talk positively, they favour the product and company reasonably.

iii. **Indifferent:** They hold neither positive nor negative attitudes toward the product and/ or brand. They are neutral.

iv. **Negative:** They do not favour the product. They may have prejudice for the product. They talk negatively, but do not react strongly as hostile.

v. **Hostile:** They react forcefully or have strong objections against product of the company. They try to harm the company in any way.

A company tries to convert other attitudes holders into enthusiastic and positive. However, hostile and, to some extent, negative groups are more detrimental.

In fact a company uses more bases to divide total market and select the target market. Practically, the target market of the company consists of multiple bases. That is to say that target market bears geographical, demographical, psychographic, and behavioural characteristics.

BASES FOR *INDUSTRIAL MARKET* SEGMENTING

Industrial products are used as the inputs by manufacturing units for further processes on the products, or manufacturing other products. Some products are both industrial as well as consumer products. Again, strict classification in term of industrial consumer and consumer products is also not possible, For example, electricity, petroleum products, sugar, cloth, wheat, etc., are used by industry as the inputs, while the same products are used by consumers for their daily consumption as well. Some companies, for example, electricity, cements, petrol and coal, etc., sell their products to industrial units as well as to consumers. This segmentation is more relevant to the business units that produce and sell industrial products to other firms, carrying manufacturing and processing operations.

In fact, all the bases used for consumer markets are equally applicable to industrial markets. Difference lies in definition of individual buyer. In case of industrial market, a business unit, agency, or company is considered as an individual buyer. More clearly, for example, Mr. X is an individual buyer for consumer market, while XYZ Ltd., can be an individual buyer for industrial market. Same bases can be used, but with different reference. However, some new variables can be used for segmenting industrial markets. Additionally, industrial buyers behave quite differently as factors affecting their behaviour are different. Practically, following bases (customer characteristics and/ or behavioural bases) are used for segmenting industrial markets:

1. Geographic Bases

Company needs to perform tasks differently to treat customers residing in different geographical regions. On the basis of geographical bases, industrial buyers can be segmented into following segments:

i. **Distance:** Local market, regional, domestic (national) market, and International market.

ii. **Location of Industrial Unit:** Rural and Urban Customers.

iii. **Area and Climate:** Area specific segmentation considers place-specific bases such as hilly, desert, valley, plains, etc., while climate-based classification includes segmenting market on the basis of level and intensity of humidity, heat, cold, rains, etc.

Different buyers located at different places need to be treated differently. Separate marketing programme must be prepared for each of these groups.

2. Types of Industry

Company's products are used in different industries. Relevant industries should be considered for segmenting market and, as per suitability, one or more industries can be selected as the target market to be served. Possible segments include:

i. Auto Industry
ii. IT Industry
iii. Chemical industry
iv. FMCG (Fast Moving Consumer Goods) Industry
v. Textile industry
vi. Iron and steel Industry
vii. Cement Industry
viii. Engineering Industry
ix. Agro-processing industry
x. Service Industry, etc.

As per company's products, it selects one or more relevant industry as target customers and formulates appropriate marketing mix for each of the segments.

3. Type of Business Operation

Industrial units perform different activities. Each of them differs in term of their nature of activities/operations and requirements. On that base, we can classify industrial customers into several segments, such as:

i. Manufacturing Units
ii. Assembling Units
iii. Processing Units
iv. Distributing units
v. Retailing Business
vi. Consultancies and Services Units, etc.

Some products are commonly used for different business operations. Companies dealing with these products can supply or sell to different customers. Different marketing strategies are necessary as these customers elicit different response patterns.

4. Consumption Rate/ Size

On the basis of order size and/or annual consumption, industrial buyers can be segmented in certain distinct groups. A company can select suitable one or more customer groups as target market. Sized-based segmentation includes:

i. Heavy Users
ii. Medium Users
iii. Light Users

Particularly, price and promotion strategies must be designed differently to meet expectations of varied groups.

5. Ownership Factor

Ownership exhibits different response. A firm needs to treat them differently. A company can select one or more customers to serve. Ownership-based segmentation leads to following segments:

i. Sole Proprietary Firms and Partnership Firms
ii. Private Companies

iii. Pubic companies and Public Sector Units (PSUs)
iv. Government as a Customer
v. Corporations
vi. Defense Department
vii. Cooperative Societies
viii. Community Organisations
ix. Religious and Missionary Organisations.

6. Buying Methods

Industrial buyers purchase products on different ways. Every method requires different treatment in terms of formality, timing of ordering and executing, profit margin, and overall procedures to be followed. Based on methods, industrial markets can be segmented on following bases:

i. Tender/sealed-bid Buying Units
ii. Service Contract Customers
iii. Leasing Customers
iv. Buying through Approved Agencies
v. Direct Purchasing Units.

7. Ordering Time or Frequency

Taking ordering time and buying frequency as the bases, industrial markets can be classified into several segments, such as:

i. **Annual Customers:** They put a large order (once in a year) and buy all quality at a time.
ii. **Regular Customers:** They buy regularly only from the particular firm. They are loyal customers.
iii. **Occasional Customers:** They buy company's products occasionally. They buy company's products just to try; they buy for change; or they buy when required products are not available from other sources.
iv. **Frequent and Infrequent Customers:** Frequent customers buy more frequently. They put repeated orders and are reasonably predictable. Infrequent customers are irregular in their buying pattern. They may or may not buy and are difficult to be predicted.

8. Payment Modes and Time

Industrial customers follow different modes of payment. They also take short or long time to pay their bills. Main segments are:

i. Cash Purchasing Buyers
ii. Credit Purchasing Buyers
iii. Partial Credit Purchasing Buyers
iv. Fully Trusted v/s Partially Trusted Buyers
v. Full (at a time) Paying Customers
vi. Gradual or Installment Paying Customers
vii. Short-term and Long-term Credit Buyers, etc.

Suitable marketing programme should be prepared to deal with these groups of buyers. Particularly, pricing policies are more relevant for this segmentation.

9. Legal Aspects

Legal or authenticity aspects can be relevant base to some companies for segmenting total market. The firm is directed to sell its products only to some agencies approved by the government. But, due to some reasons, it has to transact (willingly or unwillingly) with illegal customers, who have been restricted by the Law to buy, hold, or use some products. Company can earn more profits by dealing with unauthorized customers. In case of companies manufacturing some defense tools and devices (arms and ammunitions), or companies supplying products for national schemes for the BPL (Below Poverty Line) families or any other reserved categories, they may tempted to sell extra product to unauthorized customers. Sometimes, company is restricted to produce as per the fixed quota. Marketing strategies for legal and illegal customers seems quite different.

i. **Legal Customers:** These customers are free to use any quantity without any restriction.

ii. **Restricted (Partially Permitted) Customers:** There are permitted up to certain limit. They cannot buy more quantity beyond the specified limit.

iii. **Illegal Customers:** The Law puts ban on these customers. They cannot legally buy, hold, use, or resell some products.

10. Other Bases

Apart from these bases, some minor behavioural bases are also used for segmenting industrial markets. Some of them include:

i. Occasions

ii. User status

iii. Loyalty Pattern,

iv. Benefits Expected

v. Attitudes, etc.

These are main bases for segmenting industrial markets. There can be more minor bases for segmenting industrial markets. Besides, almost all bases used to segment consumer markets are equally applicable to segment industrial markets. It should be clarified that theses bases are too general and interrelated. This is a loose classification. One or more bases can be taken at a time to segment industrial products. All bases may not be relevant to every company, it should concentrate only on relevant bases.

QUALITIES OR CHARACTERISTICS OF A GOOD SEGMENTATION

With reference to India, task of segmenting the market is challenging due to large population and wide geographic, demographic, and socio-economic differences. A wise manager must, therefore, consider certain qualities or conditions for meaningful market segmentation. Philip kotler and other experts of the subject suggest following qualities for a good segmentation:

1. Substantiality

Substantiality implies that market must be lager enough to justify company's marketing efforts. It must offer attractive opportunities in terms of return on investment. Too small segments are not profitable as the firm has to make separate marketing programme (4Ps) for each of them.

2. Suitability

The segmentation must have overall suitability with firm's internal and external situation. It must suit with resources, objectives, and policies of the firm. There must be parity, compatibility, and balance between segments and firm's situations. Irrelevant criteria for segmenting market lead to mismatch.

3. Adequate Demand

It is the basic condition for successful segmentation. Different segments must exhibit adequate demand. Each of the selected segments must be able and willing to buy the company's offers.

4. Accessibility

The segmentation should be such that a firm can meet reasonably the expectations of selected segments. Firm must serve different segments efficiently. In short, the segments must be sufficiently homogeneous in terms of different bases to enable the company to reach them successfully.

5. Actionability

The segmentation must permit a company to take necessary actions effectively. The firm must be in position to respond different segments firmly. It must be able to tackle the problems and to absorb available opportunities.

6. Other Qualities

Over and above main qualities, there are some other qualities of an ideal segmentation. They include:

a. Potential for growth
b. Scale of economy
c. Differentiability, etc.

MARKET TARGETING

INTRODUCTION

A company cannot concentrate on all the segments of the market. The company can satisfy only limited segments. **The segments the company wants to serve are called the target market, and the process of selecting the target market is referred as market targeting.** Market segmentation results into dividing total market into various segments or parts. Such segments may be on the basis of consumer characteristics or product characteristics or both. Once the market is divided into various segments, the company has to evaluate various segments and decide how many and which ones to target. It is simply an act or process of selecting a target market

DEFINITIONS

Market is segmented using certain bases, like income, place, education, age, and life cycle, and so on. Out of them, a few segments are selected to serve them. Thus, evaluating and selecting some market segments can be said as market targeting. The quoted definitions are not available. However, we can define the term as:

1. We can define the term as: *Market targeting is a process of selecting the target market from the entire market. Target market consists of group/groups of buyers to whom the company wants to satisfy or for whom product is manufactured, price is set, promotion efforts are made, and distribution network is prepared.*
2. It involves basically two actions – evaluation of segments and selection of the appropriate market segments. In this relation, market targeting can be defined as: *Market targeting is an act of evaluating and selecting market segments.*
3. Finally, we define market targeting as: *Market targeting consists of dividing the total market into segments, evaluating these segments, and selecting the appropriate segments as the target market.*

PROCEDURE OF MARKET TARGETING

Market targeting procedure consists of two steps:

1. Evaluating Market Segments

Evaluation of market segments calls for measuring suitability of segments. The segments are evaluated with certain relevant criteria to determine their feasibility. To determine overall attractiveness/suitability of the segment, two factors are used:

i. **Attractiveness of Segment:** In order to determine attractiveness of the segment, the company must think on characteristics /conditions which reflect its attractiveness, such as size, profitability, measurability, accessibility, actionable, potential for growth, scale of economy, differentiability, etc. These characteristics help decide whether the segment is attractive.

ii. **Objectives and Resources of Company:** The firm must consider whether the segment suit the marketing objectives. Similarly, the firm must consider its resource capacity. The material, technological, and human resources are taken into account. The segment must be within resource capacity of the firm.

2. Selecting Market Segments

When the evaluation of segments is over, the company has to decide in which market segments to enter. That is, the company decides on which and how many segments to enter. This task is related with selecting the target market. Target market consists of various groups of buyers to whom company wants to sell the product; each tends to be similar in needs or characteristics. **Philip Kotler** describes five alternative patterns to select the target market. Selection of a suitable option depends on situations prevailing inside and outside the company. These alternative patterns have been discussed briefly in the remaining part.

ALTERNATIVE STRATEGIES (METHODS) FOR MARKET TARGETING

Basically five alternative patterns/strategies are available. Company may opt for any one of the following strategies for market targeting based on the situations:

1. Single Segment Concentration

It is the simplest case. The company selects only a single segment as target market and offers a single product. *Here, product is one; segment is one.* For example, a company may select only higher income segment to serve from various segments based on income, such as poor, middleclass, elite class, etc. All the product items produced by the company are meant for only a single segment.

Single segment offers some merits like, (1). Company can gain strong knowledge of segment's needs and can achieve a strong market position in the segment. (2). Company can specialize its production, distribution, and promotion. (3). Company, by capturing leadership in the segment, can earn higher return on its investment.

It suffers from following demerits like, (1). Competitor may invade the segment and can shake company's position. (2). Company has to pay high costs for change in fashion, habit, and attitude. Company may not survive as risk cannot be diversified.

Mostly, company prefers to operate in more segments. Serving more segments minimizes the degree of risk.

2. Selective Specialisation

In this option, the company selects a number of segments. *A company selects several segments and sells different products to each of the segments.* Here, company selects many segments to serve them with many products. All such segments are attractive and appropriate with firm's objectives and resources. There may be little or no synergy among the segments. Every segment is capable to promise the profits. This multi-segment coverage strategy has the advantage of diversifying the firm's risk. Firm can earn money from other segments if one or two segments seem unattractive. For example, a company may concentrate on all the income groups to serve.

3. Product Specialisation

In this alternative, a company makes a specific product, which can be sold to several segments. Here, *product is one, but segments are many.* Company offers different models and varieties to meet needs of different segments. The major benefit is that the company can build a strong reputation in the specific product area. But, the risk is that product may be replaced by an entirely new technology. Many ready-made garment companies prefer this strategy.

4. Market Specialisation

This strategy consists of serving many needs of a particular segment. *Here, products are many but the segment is one*. The firm can gain a strong reputation by specializing in serving the specific segment. Company provides all new products that the group can feasibly use. But, reduced size of market, reduced purchase capacity of the segment, or the entry of competitors with superior products range may affect the company's position.

5. Full Market Coverage

In this strategy, a company attempts to serve all the customer groups with all the products they need. Here, *all the needs of all the segments are served*. Only very large firm with overall capacity can undertake a full market coverage strategy.

Methods of Full Market Coverage

Philip Kotler identifies two broad ways for full market coverage strategy as under:

Undifferentiated Marketing: Company sells the same products to all the customer groups. It does not consider difference among buyers. Product and marketing programme remain common for all the segments. The firm relies on mass production, mass distribution, and mass advertising. So, it can considerably reduce production, distribution, and promotional costs. Similarly, reduced costs result into low price and the price-sensitive consumers can be attracted. This method is followed by pharmaceutical companies.

However, many experts and practicing managers have expressed strong doubts about the strategy. It is erroneous to believe that all the segments have similar needs. It is a rare case. Such strategy may invite competition to serve larger groups of buyers, and smaller groups are neglected. People, in different segments, differ significantly in terms of needs, preference, and advertising appeal.

Differentiated Marketing: Here, company operates in several segments and designs different marketing programmes for each of the segments. Various groups of customers are targeted by several types of products and marketing strategies. It is based on the notion that each group needs different products. This strategy is used by the most of automobile companies.

This strategy creates more total sales, but costs of doing business also on increase. Following costs are likely to be higher in **differentiated marketing** strategy:

i. Marketing research cost
ii. Administrative costs
iii. Manufacturing costs
iv. Inventory costs
v. Promotional costs
vi. Product modification costs

Here, costs and sales both increase. So, profitability is doubtful. However, it is less risky. Loss in one segment can be offset against profitable segments. Most of companies prefer this option.

Thus, market targeting is an essential aspect of marketing programme. A manager needs a lot of experience, knowledge, and expertise to take decision on target market. The alternative to be used depends upon a large number of internal and external variables. Careful and objective analysis of these variables can assist in selecting target market.

PRODUCT POSITIONING

INTRODUCTION

Every marketer has to select the target market to position the product in that market at profit. Product positioning is simply an act to create an image of product in the mind of consumer. Product positioning implies occupying permanent position of the products in the target consumers' mind. Product positioning consists of describing the customers how the company differs from the current and potential competitors. It is one of the vital tasks of marketing manager in competitive market situation.

DEFINITIONS

We can define the term as:

1. **Philip Kotler** "The positioning is the act of designing the company's offering and image so that they occupy a meaningful and distinct competitive position in the target consumers' mind."
2. In simple words: *Product positioning is an act of promoting the superior aspects or the key differentiations of products in the mind of the target market.*
3. Thus, it can be said: *Positioning is the act of designing the company's image and value of offer so that the segments' customers understand and appreciate what the company stands for in relation to its competitors.*
4. Also it can be defined as: *Product positioning is the process of differentiating company's total offerings from competitors so as to make the consumer admire and favour those offers with reference to competitors.*

CHARACTERISTICS OF PRODUCT POSITIONING

We can find out following characteristics from the definitions stated above:

1. Product positioning implies positioning/placing of the company's product in the mind of consumers.
2. It is a way to differentiate the company's product as superior than competitors. Differentiation may be in forms of quality, service, distribution, etc.
3. Product positioning includes three aspects – positioning of product (i.e., features, services and qualities), positioning of brand (i.e., brand image or popularity), and positioning of company (i.e., name, fame, activities, achievements, and reputation).
4. It makes the consumers appreciate and understand the company's product.
5. Company generally uses product design and promotional media to position the product in consumers' mind.
6. Product is always positioned with respect to competitors. In absence of competitors, the question of product positioning may not arise.
7. It is a physical process undertaken by the company to improve mental state of consumers.

PROCESS OF PRODUCT POSITIONING

According to **Philip Kotler**, product-positioning process consists of three steps/phases discussed as under:

1. Identifying Potential Competitive Advantages

This is the first stage in product positioning process. Product is positioned by highlighting product benefits/advantages. So, the primary task is to identify which are the potential competitive advantages that a company can offer. Company can differentiate its product by competitive advantages.

Types Competitive Advantages

Competitive advantages consist of advantages relating to product, service, personnel, channel, and image. The key advantages of each of the sources have been listed below:

i. **Competitive Advantages Related to Product:** Such advantages include product features or distinctive characteristics, product qualities (including durability, reliability, design/style and reparability), and product performance.

ii. **Competitive Advantages Related to Service:** They may cover (1). Easy ordering, (2). Speedy, accurate, and careful delivering (3). Facility for free and safe installation (4). Training to customers for effective and safe use of the product; guarantee, warrantee, credit, and maintenance, and (5). Customer consultation, which includes information and advice, either free or at price to buyers.

iii. **Competitive Advantages Related to Personnel:** They consist of employees' competence, courtesy, credibility, responsiveness, communication, etc.

iv. **Competitive Advantages Related to Channel:** Such advantages may include coverage, accessibility, regularity, types and quality of services, expertise, and performance of channel members.

v. **Competitive Advantages Related with Image:** This type of advantages related to a company image or brand image. They consist of prestige, status, and identity offered by the product manufactured and marketed by a well-known and reputed company.

2. Developing Positioning Strategy or Choosing Competitive Advantages

It is natural that all the benefits stated above are not meaningful or worthwhile. Therefore, a company must carefully select certain basic competitive advantages. While selecting the competitive advantages, company must consider some conditions:

Conditions for Selecting Competitive Advantages

The advantages a company wants to position must satisfy following conditions:

i. Advantages must be important to consumers.

ii. They must be distinctive or unique.

iii. They must be superior.

iv. They must be communicable and visible to buyers.

v. They must be preemptive (defensive or preventive), cannot be easily copied by competitors.

vi. They must be affordable to pay by the buyers.

vii. They must be profitable to company.

Choosing competitive advantages calls for dealing with two questions – one is, related with number of competitive advantages, and the second is, which competitive advantages should be selected for positioning purpose.

How Many Advantages to Promote?

This question relates to the number of competitive advantages. It is very crucial decision in product positioning. Since all the competitive advantages are not equally important, a company has to select a few distinct advantages. Advantages a company wants to promote should be just adequate (not too more or too less) and clear (free from confusions or doubts). Depending upon what the market expects from the product, number of competitive advantages should be selected. In short, the list should be reasonable to convince the customers the superiority of the product.

Which Advantages to Promote?

The second important question relates to selection of promising competitive advantages. Each advantage has its value. Only valued, impressive, distinctive, and novel advantages should be selected. Only those advantages making difference from competitors' offerings must be given place. In fact, the decision of selecting of competitive advantages depends on type of product, types of competitors' products, and type of customers. For example, for middle class buyers, quality, durability, and price are more important. In case of two wheelers, fuel efficiency, price, style, services, performance, safety, etc., are more important advantages. After suitable analysis of overall situation, the right type of competitive advantages should be selected.

3. Communicating the Company's (Competitive Advantages) Positioning

This is the third and the last important phase of product positioning process. This step is also known as signalizing the competitive advantages. Once the company has decided on what and how many competitive advantages are to be emphasized for product positioning, the next task is to communicate them effectively to position them in the mind of consumers. Note that competitive advantages may not be positioned automatically. Appropriate physical signs and cues should be used to make consumers judge different advantages. For example, if a company wants to position its superior services, it must hire expert staff to serve the market, and such service must be communicated through the appropriate means of communication.

For each of the advantages to position, different methods should be used. Consumers must be explained and convinced the competitive advantages the product can offer. All the promotional tools – advertising, personal selling, sales promotion, and publicity – are used for the purpose. Effective market communication is an essential condition to reach the mind of people and convey the message how differently and in superior way the product meet their expectations. Competitive advantages, if not successfully communicated, cannot be positioned, and are of no use.

Thus, product positioning plays an important role to attract and satisfy customers. Company can make a permanent place in the mind of customers. Successful positioning is not an easy task, company needs to study what market needs and wants, identify competitive advantages that a product can offer, and communicating them so as to make them aware and appreciate company's offers in relation to competitors.

IMPORTANCE OF PRODUCT POSITIONING

In today's competitive environment, it is imperative for a marketer to differentiate his product from competitors. Product positioning is an attempt to position competitive advantages of product in the mind of target consumers. Through product positioning, a company can create an image in the mind of the market. Successful product positioning can contribute significantly to achieve marketing goals.

Product positioning refers to differentiating firm's product and brand from competitors to attract, convince, and satisfy consumers. Before the product or brand is launched in the market, it must be positioned in the market. And, in case, if the product is introduced in the market without positioning, it may not stand against competition. So, a company always formulates and implements product-positioning strategy for successful launching of the product. Following benefits of product positioning imply its importance or utility in marketing:

1. To Make Entire Organisation Market-oriented

Product positioning is a part of the broader marketing philosophy. It concerns with identifying superior aspects of product and matching them with consumers more effectively than competitions. This philosophy makes the entire organisation market oriented.

2. To Cope with Market Changes

Once the product is positioned successfully doesn't mean the task of manager is over. He has to constantly watch the market. As per new developments in the market place, new competitive advantages should be identified, discovered or developed to suit the changing expectations of the market. It makes the manager active, alert and dynamic.

3. To Meet Expectation of Buyers

Generally, the advantages to be communicated are decided on the basis of expectations of the target buyers. So, product positioning can help realize consumers' expectations.

4. To Promote Consumer Goodwill and Loyalty

Systematic product positioning reinforces the company's name, its product and brand. It popularizes the brand. The company can create goodwill and can win customer loyalty.

5. To Design Promotional Strategy

More meaningful promotional programme can be designed. Based on what advantages are to be communicated, appropriate means are selected to promote the product.

6. To Win Attention and Interest of Consumers

Product positioning signifies those advantages that are significant to consumers. When such benefits are promoted through suitable means of advertising, it definitely catches the interest and attention of consumers.

7. To Attract Different Types of Consumers

Consumers differ in terms of their expectations from the product. Some want durability; some want unique features; some want novelty; some wants safety; some want low price; and so on. A company, by promoting different types of competitive advantages, can attract different types of buyers.

8. To Face Competition

This is the fundamental use of product positioning. Company can respond strongly to the competitors. It can improve its competitive strength.

9. To Introduce New Product Successfully

Product positioning can assist a company in introducing a new product in the market. It can position new and superior advantages of the product and can penetrate the market easily.

10. To Communicate New and Varied Feature Added Later on

When a company changes qualities and/or features of the existing products, such improvements can be positioned against products offered by the competitors.

Product positioning improves competitive strength of a company. Normally, consumers consider product advantages before they buy it. So, product positioning proves superiority of company's offers over competitors. It may also help consumers in choosing the right product.

EXERCISES

MULTIPLE CHOICE QUESTIONS (MCQs)

1. Select the true statement.
   a. Consumer behaviour is not important for formulating marketing mix.
   b. Consumer behaviour means consumers' activities at home.
   c. Consumer behaviour studies how consumers select, buy, and dispose products to satisfy their needs and wants.
   d. Consumer behaviour concerns only with the past behaviour.
2. Which one of followings is not included in three broad categories of factors affecting consumer behaviour?
   a. Product characteristics
   b. Company characteristics
   c. Consumer characteristics
   d. Salesmen characteristics
3. Which is not social factor affecting consumer behaviour?
   a. Subculture
   b. Family
   c. Reference group
   d. Roles and statuses

4. Which one is psychological factor affecting consumer behaviour?
   a. Perception b. Social classes
   c. Personality d. Gender
5. Which is not personal factor affecting consumer behaviour?
   a. Attitudes b. Occupation
   c. Life style d. Self-concept
6. In which class of factors affecting consumer behavior does motivation fall?
   a. It is a social factor b. It is a cultural factor
   c. It is a psychological factor d. It is personal factor
7. Which is not included in methods to learn about buying process?
   a. Introspective method b. Retrospective method
   c. Introduction method d. Prescriptive method.
8. Which is not included in the post-purchase behaviour?
   a. Buying the product by post b. Post-purchase satisfaction
   c. Post-purchase actions d. Post-purchase use and disposal
9. In bases for segmenting consumer market, which one is not included in user status?
   a. Non-users b. Ex-users
   c. First-time users d. Heavy users
10. Consumer loyalty pattern of using brand 'A' and brand 'B' like A, A, A, B, B, B, is called
    a. soft or split loyal b. hard-core loyal
    c. shifting loyal d. brand switcher
11. In buyer readiness stage, which one is the forth stage?
    a. Intended to buy b. Interested to buy
    c. Informed d. Desirous
12. Consumers who hold the most favourable attitudes toward the brand is called
    a. positive b. enthusiastic
    c. indifferent d. hostile
13. Company sells a specific product to several segment is known as
    a. Selective Specification b. Product specification
    c. Market specification d. Single segment concentration

MATCHING TYPE QUESTIONS (MTQs)

14.

List I	List II
(a) Consumer Behaviour	(1) cultural, social, and personal factors
(b) Market Segmentation	(2) Consumer, company, and product related
(c) Broad Factors Classification	(3) An act of dividing total market into parts
(d) Consumer-related Factors	(4) Systematic study of consumers' reactions

Codes: (A) (a)-(2), (b)-(1), (c)-(4), (d)-(3) (B) (a)-(3), (b)-(2), (c)-(1), (d)-(4)
(C) (a)-(4), (b)-(3), (c)-(2), (d)-(1) (D) (a)-(1), (b)-(4), (c)-(3), (d)-(2)

15.

List I	List II
(a) Cultural Factors	(1) Age, occupation, life style, gender, etc.
(b) Social Factors	(2) Family, roles, status, reference groups, etc.
(c) Personal Factors	(3) Basic values, customs, and traditions
(d) Psychological Factors	(4) Motivation, perception, learning, etc.

Codes: (A) (a)-(2), (b)-(1), (c)-(4), (d)-(3) (B) (a)-(3), (b)-(2), (c)-(1), (d)-(4)
(C) (a)-(4), (b)-(3), (c)-(2), (d)-(1) (D) (a)-(1), (b)-(4), (c)-(3), (d)-(2)

16.

List I	List II
(a) Geographic Bases	(1) Age, gender, education, and nationality
(b) Demographic Bases	(2) Local, regional, and national market
(c) Psychographic Bases	(3) Occupation, benefits, and usage rates
(d) Product-related Bases	(4) Motivation, life style, and personality

Codes: (A) (a)-(2), (b)-(1), (c)-(4), (d)-(3) (B) (a)-(3), (b)-(2), (c)-(1), (d)-(4)
(C) (a)-(4), (b)-(3), (c)-(2), (d)-(1) (D) (a)-(1), (b)-(4), (c)-(3), (d)-(2)

17.

List I	List II
(a) Automobile, FMCG, Textile, IT, etc.	(1) Type of business operations
(b) Heavy users, medium users, and light users	(2) Payment modes
(c) Cash, credit, partial credit, and installment	(3) Consumption rate
(d) Manufacturing, retailing, processing, etc.	(4) Types of industries

Codes: (A) (a)-(4), (b)-(3), (c)-(2), (d)-(1) (B) (a)-(3), (b)-(2), (c)-(1), (d)-(4)
(C) (a)-(2), (b)-(1), (c)-(4), (d)-(3) (D) (a)-(1), (b)-(2), (c)-(4), (d)-(3)

18.

List I	List II
(a) One product-one segment	(1) Market specialization
(b) Many products-many segments	(2) Product specialization
(c) Many products-one segment	(3) Selective specialization
(d) One product-many segments	(4) Single segment concentration

Codes: (A) (a)-(3), (b)-(4), (c)-(2), (d)-(1) (B) (a)-(1), (b)-(2), (c)-(3), (d)-(4)
(C) (a)-(4), (b)-(3), (c)-(1), (d)-(2) (D) (a)-(2), (b)-(1), (c)-(4), (d)-(3)

ANSWERS KEY: 1(c), 2(d), 3(a), 4(a), 5(a), 6(c), 7(c), 8(a), 9(d), 10(c), 11(b), 12(b), 13(b), 14(C), 15(B), 16(A), 17(B), 18(C)

QUESTIONS FOR DISCUSSION

19. What is consumer behaviour? Explain characteristics and importance of consumer behaviour?
20. Define consumerism and briefly explain factors affecting consumer behaviour.
21. Write notes:
    a. Cultural factors b. Personal factors
22. Discuss social and psychological factors affecting consumer behaviour.
23. With reference to consumer behaviour, discuss (1) Motivation (2) Social class (3) Life style and (4) Age.
24. What is consumer buying process? Describe stages of consumer buying process.
25. Explain market segmentation. Describe its importance.
26. "Market segmentation is a double edged weapon." Discuss. Explain qualities of a good segmentation.
27. Explain meaning of market segmentation. Explain demographic and psychological bases for market segmentation.
28. What is market segmentation? Explain behavioural bases to segment the market.
29. What is market segmentation? Discuss bases for segmenting consumer market.
30. Write a Note: Behavioural bases of market segmentation.
31. What is product positioning? Explain stages involved in product positioning process. Briefly state its importance.
32. What is market targeting? Explain its procedure and tools?
33. Which one out of the five alternatives will you will you prefer for market targeting? Why?

✧✧✧

CHAPTER

5

PRODUCT DECISIONS

- Introduction
- Concepts of Product
- Types of Product
- Concept of Product Mix, Product Line, and Product Mix Dimensions
- Factor affecting Product Mix
- Product Mix Strategies, and Objectives of Product Mix Change
- New Products – Concept and Reasons for Developing New Product
- Why do New Products Fail?
- Stages in New Product Development Process
- Product Life Cycle and Relevant Strategies
- Importance and limitations of Product Life Cycle.
- Consumer Adoption Process – Concept and Stages

INTRODUCTION

Product is one of the important elements of marketing mix. A marketer can satisfy consumer needs and wants through product. A product consists of both good and service. Decisions on all other elements of marketing mix depend on product. For example, price is set for the product; promotional efforts are directed to sell the product; and distribution network is prepared for the product. Product is in the center of marketing programme. Therefore, product has a major role in determining overall success of marketing efforts. A marketer tries to produce and sell such products that satisfy needs and wants of the target market. Other words used for product are good, commodity, service, article, or object. In marketing literature, product has comprehensive meaning.

DEFINITIONS OF PRODUCT

Term product has been variously defined by the experts in the field. Let us examine some standard definitions:

1. **Philip Kotler:** "Product is anything that can be offered to someone to satisfy a need or a want."
2. **William Stanton:** "Product is complex of tangible and intangible attributes, including packaging, colour, price, prestige, and services, that satisfy needs and wants of people."
3. **W. Alderson:** "Product is a bundle of utilities, consisting of various product features and accompanying services."

4. **We can also define the term as:** *Product is a vehicle or medium that delivers service to customers.*
5. **Further it can be said:** *Product is a bundle of benefits–physical and psychological– that marketer wants to offer, or a bundle of expectations that consumers want to fulfill.*

Marketer can satisfy needs and wants of target consumers by products. Product includes both good and service. Normally, product is taken as a tangible object, such as a pen, television set, bread, book, vehicle, table, etc. But, tangible product is a package of services or benefits. Marketer should consider product benefits and services, instead of product itself. Importance lies in the services rendered by the product, and not tangible object itself. People are not interested just possessing products, but the services rendered by the products. For examples, we do not buy a pen, but writing service. Similarly, we do not buy a car, but transportation service. Just owning product is not enough. It must serve our need and want. Thus, physical product is just a vehicle or medium that offer services, benefits, and satisfaction to us.

Product can also be referred as a bundle of satisfaction, physical and psychological both. Product includes:

1. **Core Product:** Core product includes basic contents, benefits, qualities, or utilities.
2. **Product-related Features:** They include colour, branding, packing, labeling, and varieties.
3. **Product-related Services:** They include after-sales services, installation, guarantee and warrantee, free home delivery, free repairing, and so forth.

As per the definition, anything which can satisfy need and want of consumers is a product. Thus, product may be in form of physical object, person, idea, activity, or organisation that can provide any kind of services that satisfy some customer needs or wants.

PRODUCT DIMENSIONS

Different people view product differently. Similarly, their expectations are different. *The different views or ways to see or perceive the product can be said as product dimensions.* There are three dimensions, as stated below:

Managerial Dimension: According to management, a product is viewed as the total product. It includes all those tangible and non-tangible aspects that management wants to offer. Managerial dimension of product covers mainly core products, product-related features, and product-related services.

Consumer Dimension: To consumers, a product is a bundle of expectations. They view product as a source of expectations or satisfaction. Thus, for consumer, total benefits received from product are important. This view is very important for a marketer.

Social Dimension: Society considers the product as a source of long-term welfare of people. Society expects high standard of living, safety, protection of environment, and peace in society.

CHARACTERISTICS OF PRODUCT

Careful analysis of concept of product essentially reveals following features:

1. Product is one of the elements of marketing mix or programme.
2. Different people perceive it differently. Management, society, and consumers have different expectations.
3. Product includes both good and service.
4. Marketer can actualize its goals by producing, selling, improving, and modifying the product.
5. Product is a base for entire marketing programme.
6. In marketing terminology, product means a complete product that can be sold to consumers. That means branding, labeling, colour, services, etc., constitute the product.

7. Product includes total offers, including main qualities, features, and services.
8. It includes tangible and non-tangible features or benefits.
9. It is a vehicle or medium to offer benefits and satisfaction to consumers.
10. Important lies in services rendered by the product, and not ownership of product. People buy services, and not the physical object.

TYPES OF PRODUCT

A company sells different products (goods and services) to its target market. They can be classified into two groups, such as:

1. Consumer Product, and
2. Industrial Products

Consumer Products

Consumer products are those items which are used by ultimate consumers or households and they can be used without further commercial and engineering processes. Consumer products can be divided into four types as under:

1. **Convenient Products:** Such products improve or enhance users' convenience. They are used in a day-to-day life. They are frequently required and can be easily purchased. For example, soaps, biscuits, toothpaste, razors and shaving creams, newspapers, etc. They are purchased spontaneously, without much consideration, from nearby shops or retail malls.
2. **Shopping Products:** These products require special time and shopping efforts. They are purchased purposefully from special shops or markets. Quality, price, brand, fashion, style, getup, colour, etc., are important criteria to be considered. They are to be chosen among various alternatives or varieties. Gold and jewelries, footwear, clothes, and other durables (including refrigerator, television, wrist washes, etc.).
3. **Durable Products:** Durable products can last for a longer period and can be repeatedly used by one or more persons. Television, computer, refrigerator, fans, electric irons, vehicles, etc., are examples of durable products. Brand, company image, price, qualities (including safety, ease, economy, convenience, durability, etc.), features (including size, colour, shape, weight, etc.), and after-sales services (including free installation, home delivery, repairing, guarantee and warrantee, etc.) are important aspects the customers consider while buying these products.
4. **Non-durable Products:** As against durable products, the non-durable products have short life. They must be consumed within short time after they are manufactured. Fruits, vegetables, flowers, cheese, milk, and other provisions are non-durable in nature. They are used for once. They are also known as consumables. Mostly, many of them are non-branded. They are frequently purchased products and can be easily bought from nearby outlets. Freshness, packing, purity, and price are important criteria to purchase these products.
5. **Services:** Services are different than tangible objects. Intangibility, variability, inseparability, perishablility, etc., are main features of services. Services make our life safe and comfortable. Trust, reliability, costs, regularity, and timing are important issues. The police, the post office, the hospital, the banks and insurance companies, the cinema, the utility services by local body, the transportation facilities, and other helpers (like barber, cobbler, doctor, mechanic, etc.,) can be included in services. All marketing fundamental are equally applicable to services. 'Marketing of services' is the emerging facet of modern marketing.

Industrial Products

Industrial products are used as the inputs by manufacturing firms for further processes on the products, or manufacturing other products. Some products are both industrial as well as consumer products. Machinery, components, certain chemicals, supplies and services, etc., are some industrial products. Again, strict classification in term of industrial consumer and consumer products is also not possible, For example, electricity, petroleum products, sugar, cloth, wheat, computer, vehicles, etc., are used by industry as the inputs while the same products are used by consumers for their daily use as well. Some companies, for example, electricity, cements, petrol and coals, etc., sell their products to industrial units as well as to consumers. As against consumer products, the marketing of industrial products differs in many ways. Industrial products include:

1. Machines and components
2. Raw-materials and supplies
3. Services and consultancies
4. Electricity and Fuels, etc.

CONCEPTS OF PRODUCT MIX, PRODUCT LINE AND PRODUCT ITEMS

PRODUCT MIX

Product mix of a company is made of all product lines and items. It includes the total number of varieties or models offered by the company. Let us define the term:

Philip Kotler: "A product mix is the set of all product lines and items that a particular seller offers for the sale to buyers."

William Stanton: "The product mix is the full list of all products offered for the sale by the company."

Thus, product mix means total number of products items offered by the company. For example, HMT Company produces watches, machines, tractors, plants, tools, and equipments, and many other products. In each product group, a number of varieties are offered. The set of all these products (main range) and product varieties in each range can be said as product mix.

Product Mix Dimensions

Product mix of a particular company includes major product lines. Product mix has various dimensions, such as:

- **Product Mix Length:** It refers to the total number of items (in all the product lines) in product mix. For example product mix of Bajaj Compny has more than 100 items in various product lines, such as fans, bulbs and tubes, heaters, motorbikes, shooters, richshow, processing machines, and many other ranges.
- **Product Mix Width or Breadth:** It indicates the total number of product lines a company carries. For example, two wheelers (including various models) constitutes one of the product lines of Bajaj Company.
- **Product Mix Depth:** It refers to a number of varieties in forms of sizes, colors, and models offered within each product line. It can be said as the average number of product items offered by the firm in each product line.
- **Product Mix Consistency:** It refers to degree to which different product lines are related in one or other ways. It indicates how closely various product lines are related. The consistency can be judged on the basis of production requirements, uses of products, distribution channels, or some other ways. For example, product lines of Philips India

Ltd., include radios, bulbs and tubes, different television sets, VCR, CD-DVD player, tape recorders, etc., can have higher consistency. While Hindustan Machines and Tools produce wrist watches as well as tractors, it is called inconsistent product mix.

PRODUCT LINE

Product line is a group of product items that can satisfy the same needs and wants, they have more or less similar features. For example, Bajaj Auto Ltd., in its two wheeler product line, makes Discover, Boxer, Boss, Pulsar, Cub scooter, Bajaj Sunny, etc.

Philip Kotler: "Product line is a group of products that are closely related because they function in a similar way, are sold to same customer groups, are marketed through the same type of outlets, or fall within given price range."

Thus, product line is the group of similar products. The similarity may be seen in one or more ways. Product line consists of product items belonging to same class. The definition suggests following five ways the items are closely related:

i. They function in similar manner.
ii. They offer similar benefits, or meet similar expectations.
iii. They are sold to similar customer groups.
iv. They are marketed by similar outlets.
v. They fall within same price range.

Characteristics of Product Line

Main characteristics of product line can be listed as:

1. Product line consists of closely related product items. Difference is only found in terms of colour, size, shape, model, performance, weight, and capacity.
2. It is a compose of various similar items.
3. Product items are complementary to one another. For example, tube, tyre, and related materials.
4. There is difference in price. For example, Hero Honda charges different price for different models.
5. The purpose of offering similar items in each of the product line may be to attract customers by offering more varieties, and to create a good image or reputation.
6. Different items of a product line can be manufactured using same technology and/or inputs.
7. Product items in each of the product lines are distributed in same distribution channel. That is, similar outlets market them.
8. Product items in each product line function in same manner. They need same technical skills to use them.
9. They are sold to similar customer groups. They satisfy needs of the same groups.
10. They have more or less same use or utility. They are used for the same purpose.

CONCEPT OF PRODUCT ITEM

Product items are various varieties offered within product line, which are similar in one or other ways. Such varieties are based on quality, size, colour, capacity, price, model, performance, and so on.

Table 1: Product Mix, Product Line, and Product Items

No.	Name of product Lines	Product Items	Total Items in Each Line
1.	A	A1, A2, A3, A4, A5, A6, A7.	7
2.	B	B1, B2, B3, B4.	4
3.	C	C1, C2, C3, C4, C5, C6, C7, C8.	8
4.	D	D1, D2, D3, D4, D5, D6.	6
5.	E	E1, E2, E3, D4, E5.	5
		TOTAL	30

Number of product lines : 5
Number of product items : 30
Product mix length : 30
Product mix width : 5
Product mix depth : 30/5=6
Product mix consistency : ?

FACTORS AFFECTING TO PRODUCT MIX

Product mix refers to the total number of product lines and product items that a company wants to offer to its target market. Company's product mix must undergo necessary changes to meet its objectives or market trend. In relation to product mix, a company is required to decide in terms of product lines and product items. Product mix is expanded, contracted, or modified depending on following factors:

1. Profitability

Every business unit tries to maximize its profits. It makes certain changes in its product mix in a way to realize positive impact on profitability. Company prefers to introduce more product lines or product items in existing product lines to improve its profitability. Product mix is constantly adjusted to realize more profits

2. Objectives and Policy of Company

Company frames its product mix to achieve its objective. Product mix is prepared, modified, or changed in light of objectives. Therefore, addition, subtraction, or replacement of product lines or product items is based on what a company wants to achieve. Product mix is prepared and modified according to a company's policy.

3. Production Capacity

Marketing mix decisions, to a greater extent, depend on plant or production capacity of company. Company will design its product mix in a way that optimum production capacity can be utilized.

4. Demand

Product mix decisions are taken with reference to demand. Marketer should study consumer behaviour to find the popularity of products. Changes in consumers' preference, fashion, interest, habits, etc., must be reflected in product mix of company. Company, naturally, priories those products which have more demand. In case of falling demand, company must drop poor products gradually. Thus, product mix is constantly adjusted to meet consumer needs and wants.

5. Production Costs

Product mix is widened or narrowed depending upon production costs. Company will prefer those products, which can be produced within budgeted limit. Sometimes, for any reason, the manufacturing costs for existing products rise, the company decides to drop such products to reduce their production costs. It tries to balance selling price, profit margin, and production costs.

6. Government Rules and Restriction

Every company produces such products, which are not restricted or banned by the governments. Even, sometimes, company has to stop certain products or varieties when it is declared as illegal. In same way, social and religious protests also play a vital role in this regard. Contemporary legal framework has direct impact on size and composition of product mix.

7. Demand Fluctuation

Apart from consumer behaviour, demand is also fluctuated due to many reasons. Especially, demand is affected due to seasonal effect, non-availability of substitutes, increase in population, war, draught, flood, or any other reason. In order to meet with the changed demand of certain products, the company has to adjust its product mix.

8. Competition

It is one of the powerful factors affecting product mix. A company formulates its product mix in such a way that competitors can be strongly responded. Product mix strategy adopted by the close competitors has direct impact on company's product mix.

9. Impact of Other Elements of Marketing Mix

Over and above these factors, other elements of marketing mix such as price, promotion, and distribution are also equally important in designing product mix. Company tries to maintain consistency among these all elements to carry out marketing activities effectively and efficiently.

10. Overall Business Condition or Condition of Economy

Domestic as well as global economic conditions are also important considerations. Because of liberalization and globalization, no business can dare underestimate macro picture of the world economy. A company should keep in mind health of domestic economy with reference to the world economy. This is more relevant when a company is involved in international trade.

PRODUCT MIX STRATEGIES

Company formulates and changes it product mix strategies to get the desired response from the market. In light of overall market environment and internal situations, the firm should manage it product mix strategies. The major alternative product mix strategies (given by William Stanton and others) have been discussed briefly as under:

1. Expansion of Product Mix

Expansion of product mix implies increasing the number of product lines. New lines may be related or unrelated to the present products. For example, Bajaj Company adds car (unrelated expansion) in its product mix or may add new varieties in two wheelers and three wheelers. When company finds it difficult to stand in market with existing product lines, it may decide to expand its product mix. For example, Hindustan Unilever Limited has various products in its product mix such as (1) toilet soaps, detergent cakes, washing powders, etc. (2) cosmetic products, (3) edible items, (4) shaving creams and blades, (5) pesticides, etc. If company adds soft drink as a new product line, it is the example of expansion of product mix.

2. Contraction of Product Mix

Sometimes, a company contracts its product mix. Contraction consists of dropping or eliminating one or more product lines or product items. Here, fat product lines are made thin. Some models or varieties, which are not profitable, are eliminated. This strategy results into more profits from fewer products. If Hindustan Unilever Limited decides to eliminate particular brand of toilet shop from the toilet shop product line, it is example of contraction.

3. Deepening Product Mix Depth

Here, a company will not add new product lines, but expands one or more excising product lines. Here, some product lines become fat from thin. For example, Hindustan Unilever Limited offering ten varieties in its editable items decides to add four more varieties.

4. Alteration or Changes in Existing Products

Instead of developing completely a new product, marketer may improve one or more established products. Improvement or alteration can be more profitable and less risky compared to completely a new product. For example, Maruti Udhyod Limited decides to improve fuel efficiency of existing models. Modification is in forms of improvement of qualities or features or both.

5. Developing New Uses of Existing Products

This product mix strategy concerns with finding and communicating new uses of products. No attempts are made to disturb product lines and product items. It is possible in terms of more occasions, more quantity at a time, or more varied uses of existing product. For example, Coca Cola may convince to use its soft drink along with lunch.

6. Trading Up

Trading up consists of adding the high-price-prestige products in its existing product line. The new product is intended to strengthen the prestige and goodwill of the company. New prestigious product increases popularity of company and improves image in the mind of customers. By trading up product mix strategy, demand of its cheap and ordinary products can be encouraged.

7. Trading Down

The trading down product mix strategy is quite opposite to trading up strategy. A company producing and selling costly, prestigious, and premium quality products decides to add lower-priced items in its costly and prestigious product lines. Those who cannot afford the original high-priced products can buy less expensive products of the same company. Trading down strategy leads to attract price-sensitive customers. Consumers can buy the high status products of famous company at a low price.

8. Product Differentiation

This is a unique product mix strategy. This strategy involves no change in price, qualities, features, or varieties. In short, products are not undergone any change. Product differentiation involves establishing superiority of products over the competitors. By using rigorous advertising, effective salesmanship, strong sales promotion techniques, and/or publicity, the company tries to convince consumers that its products can offer more benefits, services, and superior performance. Company can communicate the people the distinct benefits of its products.

REASONS (OBJECTIVES) LEADING TO PRODUCT MIX CHANGES

Product mix once prepared may not serve the company's purpose for a longer period of time without any change. Company can satisfy its customers by constantly altering its product mix. There are a number of causes leading to change in the current product mix. Marketer tries to match its product mix with dynamic market situations. Due to some causes, marketer has to alter product mix. Altering or changing product mix may be in forms of expansion, contraction, widening product line or any other ways as required. Followings are the some of the most common reasons or objectives requiring a company to make one or more changes in its product mix:

1. Market Demand

To absorb changes in demand of the products, marketer changes its product mix. Demand changes due to a large number of factors, such as technology, demographic variables, competitions, development of new products, change in fashion, custom, attributes, and many other such reasons. In order to satisfy changing needs and wants of existing customers, the company opts for various changes in its product mix. Company fails to reflect market demand in product mix may not survive in a long run.

2. Competition

It is a powerful cause leading to product mix modification. Company formulates product mix to respond competitors strongly. Minor or major changes in product mix are made to prevent, remove, or to fight with competitors. Company changes its product mix to offer more competitive advantages and prove the superiority of products over competitors through product differentiation.

3. Attraction of New Customers

When company wants to increase number of customers, it has to cater the needs and wants of new customers. Existing product mix may not be capable to meet the expectations of new segments. It has to add new product lines or new varieties in its existing product lines to attract new customers.

4. Utilizing Excess Production Capacity

Sometimes, company prefers to alter product mix to utilize excess production capacity. By adding new products or varieties, a company can utilize its plant resources capacities. Optimum utilization of production capacity improves profitability.

5. Expansion of Market in New Territory

When company plans to expand geographically, it has to modify its present product mix. In different geographical areas, consumer needs and wants are different. Therefore, company has to improve existing products or add more varieties to match products with new territories.

6. Reducing Financial Risk

Reducing level of financial risk is also one of the strong reasons leading to change in product mix. Looking at the future market trend, a company changes its product mix to exploit emerging opportunities or to face challenges, or both. To reduce financial risks, a company may opt for eliminating less profitable product lines or items within existing lines; may add low-price products to survive in recession; or may reduce product varieties to reduce capital investment and costs.

7. Improving Image and Goodwill

Company can establish image and reputation in the market through changing product mix over time. By introducing high-price prestigious products, adding new varieties, latest modes, etc., company can create a good image in the market. Similarly, it can serve lower income groups by offering low-price prestigious products.

8. Effective Marketing

In some cases, a company prefers to change product mix to utilize sales force, warehouses, transportation facilities, distribution network, etc. But, it changes as long as the changes have favourable effect on its marketing performance. Such changes may be in terms of expansion, contraction, or improvements of product mix.

NEW PRODUCT

INTRODUCTION

Concept of a new product is important for the managers. Both newly established as well as existing companies face the problem of developing of a new product. Buyers do want some elements of newness in a product. Newness may be in terms of production, marketing, place, service, use, or price. New product is one that offers new benefits or features. It differs significantly from the products currently available in the market in terms of uses, appearance, performance, taste, price, and construction. New product is one, which is perceived as a new by consumers. It may be original product, improved product, modified product, or new brand. Various issues are related to a new product, such as how to develop a new product, how to launch it, how to manage it, why it fails, what precautions should be taken to reduce its failure rate, and many other such aspects.

DEFINITIONS

Term 'new product' has been defined as under:

1. *A product that is offered for the first time to particular groups of buyers is a new product.*
2. *A new product is one, which differs significantly from the products available in the market in forms of qualities, features, or both.*
3. *A product that is perceived by the consumers as a new can be said as a new product. It must be new for consumers.*

TYPES OF NEW PRODUCTS

A new product is one, which is perceived as a new by consumers. If we consider this definition, we may find various types of new products. **Allen and Hamilton** have identified six categories of a new products.

1. New to the World

It is really innovative, is entered for the first time in the world. The product was not previously available in the World. For example, pills to cure the incurable diseases like aids, diabetes etc., or completely pollution free vehicle may be a new product.

2. New Product Line

In an established market, when a new product line is introduced, it is a new product. For example, introduction of car in the market by Bajaj Auto Limited can be a new product.

3. Addition to the Existing Product Line

When some models or styles are added in the existing product line, it can be a new product. As per example, CBZ and PASSION models introduced by Hero Honda in its two-wheeler product line were new products.

4. Improvement in Existing Product

In this case, new features, qualities, or services are added in the existing product. Example is, Pentium IV computer is the improvement over Pentium III.

5. Repositioning

Repositioning consists of introducing the existing product in a new segment or a territory.

6. Cost reduction

Selling a high-priced product at a lower price or at a concessional rate becomes a new product. For those who could not afford the product in the past, now they can use the same product as a new.

BASIC CONDITIONS/FEATURES OF A NEW PRODUCT

A product can be said as a new one if it satisfies following conditions:

1. It must be perceived as a new one by buyers.
2. It must differ significantly from the products offered by the competitors.
3. Consumer must accept it.
4. It must be distributable safely and normally.
5. It must have effective packing, branding, and labeling.
6. It must provide satisfactory performance.
7. It must be produced within permissible limit of costs.

REASONS FOR DEVELOPING A NEW PRODUCT

A new product, may be called innovation, seems to be necessary due to an enormous number of factors. The dynamic nature of business environment offers only two options – be innovative, or die. Marketer has to search for superior ways to meet increasing expectations. Those companies fail to respect or respond the need of time have to withdraw from the market. Innovation or new product development directly concerns with firm's survival, growth, and development. A marketer continuously tries to offer superior product to his consumers. He desires to offer more satisfaction than competitors. He also attempts to match goods and services with changing needs and wants of the target market. As per change in the fashion, preference, habits, and attitudes of consumers, a company must change its offer/product. New products are primarily developed to meet market expectations. However, there are some other dominants factors forcing a marketer to go for developing new products. Main factors or reasons for developing a new product have been described as follows:

1. **Changes in Market:** Today's market is much dynamic as compared to the past. Due to increased education, borderless marketing, severe competition, and availability of a number of substitutes have posed tremendous challenges for today's marketers. Market fashion, preference, and habits are constantly changing and marketer finds no option except to respect such market changes, by positive response in terms of innovation. Thus, consumer behaviour is one of the dominant reasons for innovation.
2. **Changes in Technology:** Due to continuous technological development, new production methods are invented. Old technology and production methods are replaced by newer ones. A company spends a large amount of money for technological research. To match the technological changes, new products are developed.
3. **Increasing Competition:** Increasing competition is one of significant reasons leading to go for innovation. Every company struggles to attract and maintain consumers by offering superior products. To offer more competitive advantages and to satisfy consumer more effectively and efficiently, the product innovation seems to be necessary.
4. **Diversification of Risk:** In many cases, a company develops new products just to diversify risk. Existing products may not be capable to match with market needs and wants. By offering more varieties, a company can minimize the degree of obsolescence. Thus, the need for continuous innovation arises because older products are thrown out of market.
5. **Reputation and Goodwill:** To create image and reputation as an innovative and dynamic firm, the innovation is adopted. Company wishes to convince the market that it tries seriously to meet consumer's expectations. Obviously, a company developing new products periodically has more reputation, and can attract consumers easily.

6. **Utilization of Excess Capacity:** Excess capacity may be in form of production capacity or human skills. To utilize maximum plant and material capacity, a company may go for developing a new product. Sometimes, excess managerial or human capacity may also tempt the company to opt for innovation.
7. **Seasonal Fluctuations:** Sometimes, new products are developed just to minimize seasonal fluctuations in demand. By producing new product, a company can meet seasonal requirements of market. Market is satisfied due to matching products in each of the seasons, and company can get attractive business.
8. **Growth and Development:** Innovation is an effective way to win more market share or sales. Marketer can exploit emerging opportunities by innovative products. When it is not possible to accelerate growth rate by the existing products, a company prefers to develop new products to expand its market, maximize sales, and earn more profits.

CONSTRAINTS IN DEVELOPING NEW PRODUCTS

WHY DOES A NEW PRODUCT FAIL?

To develop a new product successfully is not an easy game. One has to make a lot of exercise to minimize the rate of failure. There are a large number of factors leading to failure of innovation. As per the rough estimate, in developing countries, more than half of newly developed products fail. Same is the case in developed countries. The fundamental question is: Why does a new product fail? Which are the reasons leading to a higher rate of failure? We may find following causes for failure of new products:

1. *Shortage of new ideas* is the main constraint. Because of shortage of new ideas, it is difficult to offer a distinct product to market.
2. *High cost of developing new products* is another obvious reason. Development costs and production costs are so high to offer new product at a competitive rate/price.
3. *Long time period requires for developing a new product*. When the product is introduced after considerable time tag, it fails to match the needs and wants of market.
4. *Fragmented or small market* is another problem leading to failure of new products. Due to small market or limited market, heavy expenses cannot be recovered.
5. *Social and government constraints,* play a vital role in producing and marketing of new products.
6. Due to *dynamic nature of market*, a new product has a shorter life span. A product introduced may not serve the market effectively for a long period of time. Before it reasonable establishes, it is replaced by the newer products. Competition has dominant role in this regard.
7. *Heavy capital investment* is one of the major problems in developing new products. Development, production, and marketing of new products need a heavy investment. Many firms are afraid of new products due to inability to invest the huge fund.
8. *Successful development of innovation requires integrated efforts*. In case organisation fails to integrate efforts of different departments and people, the failure is certain.
9. *Failure of company to formulate effective marketing strategies*, including product, price, promotion, and place.
10. Sometimes, *natural and man-made calamities* also contribute to failure of the innovation.

ESSENTIALS OR REQUIREMENTS FOR SUCCESSFUL DEVELOPMENT OF NEW PRODUCTS

Based upon possible causes leading to new product failures, following factors (also called essentials, precautions or requirements) must be considered:

1. Adequate market demand
2. Market trends and economic conditions
3. Compatibility with the present production and marketing structure
4. Availability of funds
5. Competitiveness
6. Managerial experience and ability
7. Suitability with objective, image, and goodwill of company
8. Time period, or gestation period
9. Legal and social aspects
10. Internal integration and cooperation

NEW PRODUCT DEVELOPMENT PROCESS

In today's marketing practices, new product development is a challenging task. New product development process is dynamic in nature. Number of steps and types of steps to be involved depend on a number of factors such as objectives, investment required, degree of risk, type of people available, current market situations, type of product to be developed, past experience, market changes, and so forth. Careful analysis of the relevant factors helps decide the suitable process of developing a new product. Note that the question of new product development arises only when a company wants to develop a new product by its own. New product development is an integrated process. It involves not only the employees of marketing department, but also from other departments. Assuming that a new product is being developed after studying needs and wants of target market, in normal situations, following steps – as shown in figure 1 – are to be followed (as described by Philip Kotler):

1. Idea Generation

A new product is the result of new ideas. New ideas are the basic requirement for developing new product. Manager who wants to develop a new product must search for new ideas from various possible sources. Idea generation must be within specified limits. Ideas must be generated in accordance with following factors:

i. Objectives of organisation
ii. Product definition
iii. Definition of market, or users
iv. Efforts and money
v. Time available, etc.

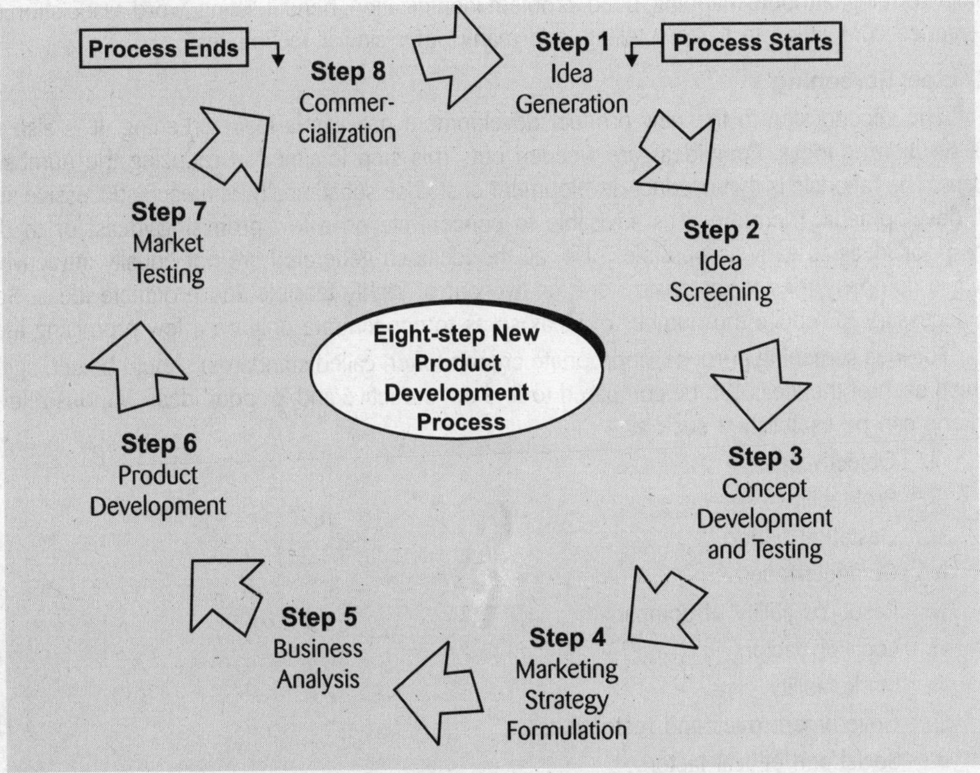

Figure 1: New Product Development Process

Sources of New Ideas: Within the stated limits, a manager should identify possible and affordable sources for new ideas. Most widely used internal and external sources have been listed below:

i. Top-level management
ii. Employees within marketing department
iii. Sales force or salesmen
iv. Scientists
v. Channel members or middlemen
vi. Competitors
vii. Investors
viii. Inventors
ix. Advertising agencies
x. Marketing research firms
xi. Government agencies and offices
xii. Commercial and general libraries
xiii. Private and government consultants
xiv. Industrial publications
xv. Mass media, including TV, Radio, Newspapers, Internet, magazines, etc.

Thus, in the first stage, attempts are made to generate or collect maximum number of possible ideas. Idea committee, idea manager, or the person in charge of product development should motivate employees to submit their ideas. Sometimes, certain techniques are used to collect new ideas from the people directly involved in marketing operations. Such techniques involve brainstorming, attribute mapping, need/problem identification, benefit-listing, word association test, sentence completion test, story telling, and many other similar techniques.

2. Idea Screening

The second step in the new product development process is idea screening. It is also said as scrutinizing ideas. Poor ideas are weeded out. This step is aimed at reducing the number of ideas. The rationale is that product development costs rise substantially with each successive stage of development. Therefore, it is advisable to concentrate on a few promising ideas, or to drop the poor ideas as early as possible. Also, all the ideas so generated are not equally attractive. In fact, a company tries to materialize one or two out of highly feasible and profitable ideas. So, it is necessary to reduce the number of ideas so as to concentrate only on a few promising ideas.

For idea screening purpose, appropriate criteria (often called standards) should be set, against which each of the ideas can be compared to find out attractive and/or poor ideas. Various relevant criteria can be established such as:

i. Objectives
ii. Profitability
iii. Gestation period
iv. Competitiveness
v. Resource ability of company
vi. Location factors
vii. Marketability
viii. Government rules and restrictions
ix. Social and ethical factors
x. Personal factors
xi. Availability of inputs.

Each of the listed ideas is compared with these preliminary criteria. Those ideas fail to suit the criteria are removed from the list, put aside. As a result, only attractive ideas can be retained. While screening the ideas, there is possibility of two types of errors, which must be avoided. First is, A DROP-error is one in which good/promising ideas, for any reason, are dropped. The second is, A GO-error that occurs when poor idea is permitted or selected for product development and commercialization.

3. Concept Development and Testing

Now, a company has a limited number of most promising ideas. For each of the ideas, concept is developed and tested to find out degree of success. All attractive ideas are refined into testable concept. At this stage, we must understand product idea, product concept, and product image. **Philip Kotler** states that product idea is a possible product that the company may offer to the market; product concept is an elaborated version of the idea expressed in meaningful consumer terms; and product image is the particular picture that consumer acquires of an actual or potential product. The step involves three sub-steps–concept development, concept positioning, and concept testing.

Concept Development: Each of the product idea is to be converted into several product concepts. The idea is expressed in consumer terms. Consumer terms mean from the viewpoint of consumers. Product concept may be expressed as:

i. Users of the product
ii. Possible uses of the product

iii. Primary benefits offered by the product
iv. Occasions of product use
v. Price range, etc.

Concept Positioning: Some companies go beyond mere concept development. They try to position the product concept against the competitors to find out how strongly the product stands in relation to existing competitive products. It is called product concept positioning. On the basis of product positioning, product positioning map or brand positioning map can be prepared to see the current position of the proposed product.

Concept Testing: As per **Philip Kotler**, concept testing calls for testing product concept with an appropriate group of target consumers, then getting those consumers' reactions. At this stage of development, we have only picture, symbol, sketch, or description of product. However, a computer-aided design or picture can make a strong sense. The use of virtual reality may help consumers to perceive the reality. In some cases, simple, less costly, and image reflective plastic or clay based models of the proposed product are prepared to get more reliable views and reactions of consumers. Target consumers are described the product or shown pictures to get their opinion. A company tries to test following aspects to measure consumers' views and reactions:

i. **Communicability:** Is the product concept conveying any meaning? It measures an ability of product concept to communicate the meaning to consumers.
ii. **Believability:** Do they believe that product is possible?
iii. **Need Level:** Can they see product as filling needs?
iv. **Gap Level:** Do they perceive the real gap between an existing product and a new product?
v. **Perceived Value:** Do they believe that price is reasonable in relation to the value (utility) of product?
vi. **Purchase Intention:** Are they going to buy a new product?
vii. **User Target:** Who will use the product?
viii. **Purchase Frequency:** When and how often will the product be bought?

Concept testing can be applied to any good or service. It provides valuable and meaningful information about possibility of success of the proposed product. Mark that consumers are the best judges who cannot be challenged. Only when product concept testing produces a favourable response or result, further process is carried on; otherwise the company drops the plan of developing a new product.

4. Marketing Strategy Formulation

When market testing produces favourable results, marketing manager moves to formulate marketing strategy for the proposed product. Remember that the company has, so far, not developed any product, but it is moving toward developing a new product. What strategy will be used if the product is to be launched? **Some companies do not follow this step at this level of development, but after development of product.**

The manager develops a preliminary marketing strategy statement for introducing a new product into the market. Marketing strategy is further refined in subsequent stage. Marketing strategy statement includes three sub-steps, such as:

a. Target Market Determination
b. Designing Marketing Mix
c. Preparing long-term Plan

Target Market Determination: This step describes the target market. Main points include:

i. Definition of target market

ii. Detail about target market's size, structure, and behaviour
iii. The plan for product positioning
iv. The sales, market share, and profit goals

Designing Marketing Mix: The second part of marketing strategy outlines various strategies on product, price, promotion, and distribution for the initial stage. Thus, marketing strategy for the first year is prepared.

Preparing Long-term Plan: The third step of marketing strategy statement describes a long-term plan for the product. It involves long-term sales and profit plans, and marketing mix strategies over time. It contains the company's plan for different stages of product life cycle.

Note that this is not the final and complete strategy for the product. The strategy formulated is taken as a base for the future. At the time of launching a product in the market, a lot of changes are necessarily made.

5. Business Analysis

In this stage of a new product development process, the manager tries to measure the business attractiveness of the proposal. Attempts are made to know what extent a proposed product is economically viable. The proposed product is checked with reference to overall business environment. It simply means measuring the ability of product to meet company's objectives (wants satisfying capacity and profitability aspects). This step calls for following aspects:

Estimating Sales: It is also known as sales forecasting. On the basis of sales history and current performance of similar types of products, or on the basis of expert opinion and preliminary consumer survey, the rough estimate of sales can be made. By this way, one can arrive at minimum and maximum sales to learn about range of risk. While estimating sales, care should be taken to deal with different products such as (1) one-time purchase product, (2) frequently purchase product, and (3) infrequently purchase product. In the same way, a manager should estimate (1) first-time sales, (2) replacement sales, and (3) repeat sales to estimate sales more accurately. Generally, the sales are estimated in form of quantity or number of units. For example, in the first year sales of the product will be 100000 units. And, during the life span of the product, sales will be 1000000 units.

Estimating Costs: Manager estimates total costs to find out cost per unit and profit margin. Practically, the person having adequate knowledge regarding the costing estimates costs. Following components of the cost are estimated:

i. **Development Costs:** Costs incurred for development of product including patent, buying copyrights, purchasing license, fees paid to experts, etc. They include pre-manufacturing costs.
ii. **Manufacturing Costs:** Such costs include fixed and variable costs incurred for processing or producing the product. Fixed costs remain fixed for any level of production. Fixed costs are depreciation on plant and buildings, interest on debt, office overheads, etc. Variable costs vary according to level of production, such as raw materials, labor costs, fuels, maintenance, storage costs, etc.
iii. **Marketing costs:** Marketing costs include the costs necessary to sell the products to consumers. Briefly, marketing costs covers all the selling and promotional costs, for example, packaging and labeling costs, transportation and distribution costs, and promotional costs including advertising, sales promotion, personal selling, and publicity.

Determining Selling Price and Profit Margin: On the basis of estimated sales and total costs, per unit cost can be calculated. Adding the desired per cent of profit on total costs, total sales revenue can be estimated for each of the proposals. Dividing sales revenue by number of sales units, per unit selling price can be arrived at.

Let's take an example:

Estimated Sales	:	100000 units
Development costs	:	₹ 5,00000.
Variable costs for 100000 units	:	₹ 10,00000.
Fixed costs	:	₹ 5,00000.
Total costs	:	₹ 20,00000.
Profit margin 25%	:	₹ (20,00000 × 25 %) = ₹ 5,00000.
Sales revenue	:	₹ (20,00000+5,00000) = ₹ 25,00000.
Selling price /unit	:	₹ (25,00000/1,00000)= ₹ 25.00
Amount of profits	:	₹ (25, 00000–20,00000)= ₹ 500000.

Evaluation of Product(s): On the basis of above statistics, now it is easy to find out feasibility of the proposed products. When we want to select one product from the two or more products, profitability of different proposals can be compared to find out the most attractive one. Along with profitability, other important variables should also be considered. If one has year-wise costs and sales data, the cash flow can be calculated; it can be used for evaluating the proposals. Various methods are used for evaluation purpose, such as Pay Back Period, Internal Rate of Return, Accounting Rate of Return, Present or Net Present Value, Profitability Index, Break-Even Analysis, and so forth. Nowadays, the use of computer and computer-based techniques is very common for the purpose. The product which is the most attractive in all the significant aspects is selected.

6. Product Development

Only when business analysis shows positive results, the company will move further in developing a new product for the selected proposal. This step calls for a heavy investment. Product development involves product design and testing. Company's research and development wing, marketing department, new product development officer, production department, outside experts, and others start their work for development of a new product. High degree of coordination and integration among these people plays a decisive role for successful development of a new product. This is the stage when new product idea may be translated into technically and commercial feasible product.

A company will not directly jump into mass production, but it concentrates on preparing a prototype (model) of the new product. Successful development of prototype takes long or short time depending upon the type of product. The prototype must satisfy following three conditions:

i. Attributes must be similar as described in product concept.
ii. It must perform safely and smoothly under normal conditions.
iii. It must be prepared within budgeted amount.

At the time of development of a prototype, functional as well as psychological characteristics should be considered. Colour, size, weight, status, image, physical clues, etc., must be given due attention. When the prototype is ready, it must undergo two types of tests:

i. **Functional Test:** It tests whether the prototype functions safely and effectively under normal uses and conditions.
ii. **Consumer Test:** Consumers are invited to laboratory to use or try the product. They are given samples to use at home. This test measures whether the consumers perceive the prototype as useful and beneficial.

7. Market Testing

If the prototype satisfies all expectations, a company proceeds further in new product development process. It is worth noted that many companies do not prefer market testing. They directly jump into the commercialization. But, it is advisable, even sometimes, indispensable to measure consumers' and dealers' reactions in handling, using, and repurchasing product. Product is dressed-up (wrapped with packing), and branding procedure is completed for testing it in more authentic consumer market. Market testing can be defined as: *An attempt to try the entire marketing programme for the first time in a limited number of well-selected markets, test cities or different areas.* This helps in testing viability of full marketing programme for regional and national market. A product is launched in a limited scale under normal market conditions to test consumers' reactions. Thus, market testing essentially determines effectiveness of all the key aspects of marketing programme.

Type of Information: Market testing produces valuable information. It reflects:

i. Reactions of consumers and dealers
ii. More reliable demand forecasting
iii. Measuring market share and size of market
iv. Effectiveness of (elements of) marketing mix
v. Whether brand, colour, packing, and labeling are appropriate
vi. Pre-testing of alternative plan(s)
vii. Information regarding trial, first time purchase, repeat purchase, and frequency of buying
viii. Competitive strength of the product.

Methods of Market Testing: Various methods are used for market testing purpose. Methods are different for consumer products and industrial products. Some popular methods for consumer products are sales-wave method, stimulated store techniques, controlled market testing, test market, etc., while trade show, distributor and dealer display room, product use test, etc., are used for industrial products. A company can select appropriate method depending upon the situation.

Important Decisions: Market testing involves a lot of vital decisions. Normally following decisions are more relevant:

i. **Purpose:** For what purpose, market testing is undertaken.
ii. **Costs:** Amount of money to be spent for market testing.
iii. **Place:** The region or state to be tested.
iv. **Type of cities:** Type of cities to be tested.
v. **Numbers of cities:** Number of cities to be tested.
vi. **Timing:** The time or season during which to test the product.
vii. **Duration:** The length of time for the test.
viii. **Actions:** Type of actions to be taken after market testing.

8. Commercialization

This is the stage of large-scale production and full-fledged marketing. This step is followed only if test marketing produces promising/desirable results. Now, the company makes necessary arrangement for mass scale production and full-fledged marketing. Commercialization calls for two sub-steps:

Production

Company prepares a plan for large-scale production. It makes necessary provisions for raw materials, working capital, labour, and other inputs. Minor and major problems related to production are mastered at the earliest possible. Packaging, branding, labeling, trademark, and similar activities are carried out. When full-fledged production starts, finished products are stored in warehouses for sell. In short, products are ready to be marketed or distributed to the consumers.

Marketing

Marketing of products is an essential part of commercialization. Products are now launched in the market. The company undergoes a lot of procedures for systematic marketing of the product. The contracts are made with middlemen, terms and conditions are decided, and a system for smooth distribution is developed. Similarly, promotion and pricing strategies are formulated for introducing a new product in desired segments of the market. Marketing of product involves following decisions:

- **When:** It concerns with a product entry time. This decision is related to timing of launching a new product in the market. Out of following alternatives, the suitable timing is selected:
  i. **First Entry:** Enter the market directly. As soon as the product is ready, it is marketed.
  ii. **Parallel Entry:** Company will wait for competitors. Company follows its competitors. Company assumes that competitors are right in deciding timing of marketing products.
  iii. **Late Entry:** Company deliberately delays it entry in the market. It allows competitors to enter the market, incurs the heavy expense for educating and convincing the consumers, and bears the risk. Company wants to learn the experience of competitors. This timing offers three advantages – competitors bear the costs of educating the market, company can avoid faults related to product and marketing, and company can learn the size of the market.
- **Where:** It indicates the place or geographic areas to launch a new product. A company has following options to decide on the place to enter the new product:
  i. Single locality
  ii. A region
  iii. Several regions
  iv. State
  v. National market
  vi. International market
- Depending upon level of risk, financial capacity and consumer behaviour, the company decides on a single or multiple areas to launch a product. It depends on speculation and ability of company.
- **To Whom:** It indicates the initial prospects or consumers. Company should decide who are the consumers to sell the new product for the very first time. On the basis of income, place, time they take to adopt the product, and many other such criteria, consumers can be classified into several groups. Company may concentrate on one or more of such categories. Company must concentrate its distribution and promotion on the best prospects, sometime referred as the prime prospects, having following characteristics:
  i. They are early adaptors.
  ii. They are opinion leaders.
  iii. They talk favourably about the product.
  iv. They are heavy uses.
- **How:** It indicates the product launching strategy. What strategy should be applied to enter the new product? It involves preparing an action plan to launch the product in the market. Basically, pricing and promotion elements are considered to design strategy for introduction stage.

When product is distributed to the market for the first time, it can be said that product has been borne in real sense. And, it starts its life cycle.

PRODUCT LIFE CYCLE (PLC)

In fact, no product is capable to satisfy needs and wants of consumers for an unlimited period of time. As such, its sales and profits are subject to differ over time. The life of product can be determined by its capacity to meet market expectations. It lasts or exists as long as it satisfies its users. The concept that studies the life span of product in relation to the demand is popularly known as product life cycle. We use 'PLC' as an abbreviation of Product Life Cycle. The concept PLC is important in marketing theory and practice. It is interesting to note that we can study the PLC only when product completes its entire life. No doubt, we can detect particular stage product life cycle on the basis of sales and profits. Product life cycle should be studied with reference to the broad picture of demand-technology life cycle. It provides insight into the competitive dynamics. It is a ready-made or expert prescription regarding what a marketing manager should do in different stages of the PLC. However, the concept may be misleading if it is not carefully understood and followed. Let's examine some definitions:

DEFINITIONS

The term 'product life cycle can be defined as under:

1. **Philip Kotler**: "The product life cycle is an attempt to recognize distinct stages in sales history of the product."
2. We can define PLC as: *PLC concerns with the study of the degree of product acceptance by the market over time. It includes major rises and falls of sales during its life.*
3. Product life cycle states relationship between sales volume and profits. So, we can define the term as: *Product life cycle concerns with the study of relationship between sales volume and profits in relation to time through entire span of the product's life.*
4. More clearly and comprehensively, we can define it as: *Product life cycle is the historical study of (sales of) the product. It includes when it was introduced; when it was getting rapid acceptance; when it was on the peak of its position; when it started falling from the peak; and when it disappeared.*

Product passes through certain stages during its life span. Typically, it passes through four stages as listed below:

1. **Introduction:** The product is introduced in the market.
2. **Growth:** The product is getting rapid acceptance and sales rise at the increasing rate.
3. **Maturity** (including Saturation): Sales rise, but at the decreasing rate. Saturation is marked with stable sales.
4. **Decline:** It is the stage when sales start falling.

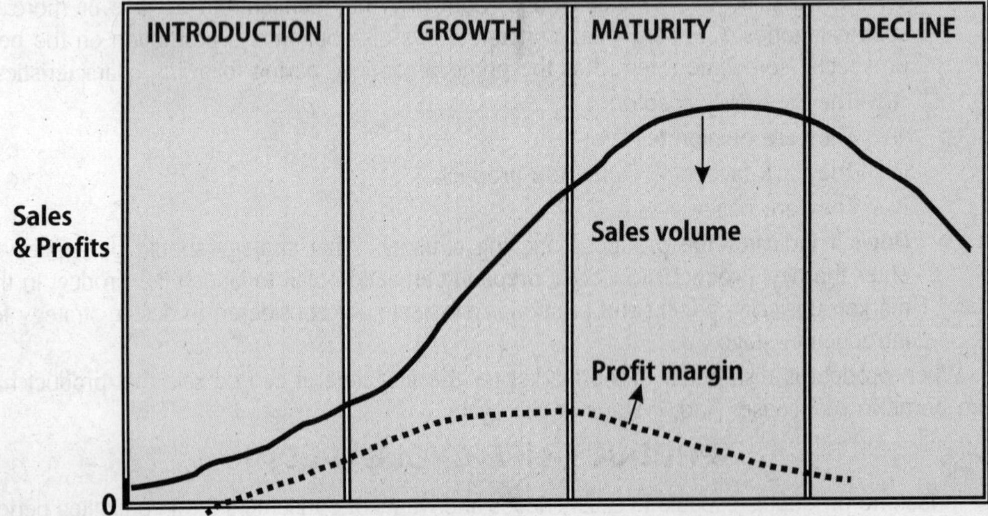

Stages of Product Life Cycle and Time

Figure 2: Product Life Cycle

Figure 2 shows that product life cycle has "S" shape curve. It indicates an ideal state.

ASSUMPTIONS

"S" shape cure is an ideal state, and is hardly possible. Such diagram – stages, sales curve, and profit curve– is possible only if following assumptions are fulfilled:

1. Product completes its entire life cycle. It passes through all four stages of its life.
2. Duration of each of the stages is equal or fixed.
3. There is no reintroduction of product.
4. Product passes through stages in chronological order, that is, one, two, three and likewise. There is no bypassing or overlapping of any of the stages.

STAGES OF PRODUCT LIFE CYCLE

Product life cycle comprises of four steps/stages. Each stage of product life cycle can be characterized in terms of at least four aspects – sales volume, amount of profits, level of promotional efforts and expenses, and degree of competition. Each stage demands the unique marketing strategy. Let us briefly describe each of the stages of the PLC.

Introduction Stage

Introduction stage starts when a new product is, for the very first time, made available for purchase. Consumers are not aware of product, or they may not have general opinion and experience regarding product. Moreover, a new product has to face the existing products. So, the sales remain limited. In the very initial stage, there is loss or negligible profit. During this period, the direct competition is almost absent. Company has not mastered production and selling problems. Price is normally high to recover/offset costs of development, production, and marketing with minimum sales. So, sales rise at gradually.

Characteristics of introduction stage include:

(i) Huge selling and promotional costs are required to increase awareness of customers.
(ii) Price is kept high to recover high development, production, and marketing costs.
(iii) Marketer has to tackle technical and production problems.
(iv) Sale is low and increasing at a lower rate.
(v) There is loss or negligible profit.
(vi) There is no competition

Growth Stage

This is the stage of a rapid market acceptance. Due to increased awareness, the product gets positive repose from market. This stage is marked by a rapid climb in sales. Sales rise at the increasing rate. Profits follow the sales. Seller shifts his promotional attempts from "try-my-brand" to "buy-my-brand." Company tries to develop effective distribution network. Here, the most of production and marketing problems are mastered. Due to rise in profits, competitors are attracted. At a right time, price may be reduced to attract the price-sensitive buyers. Company continues, even increases, its selling and promotional efforts to educate and convince the market and meet competition. At the end of growth stage, sales start increasing at decelerated rate, consequently, profits starts to decline.

Characteristics of growth stage include:

(i) Sales increase rapidly (or at increasing rate) as a result of consumer acceptance of the products.
(ii) Company can earn maximum profits.
(iii) Competitors enter the market due to attractive profits.
(iv) Price is reduced to attract more consumers.

(v) Distribution network is widened and improved.

(vi) Necessary primary changes are made in product to remove defects.

(vii) Company enters the new segments and new channels are selected.

Maturity Stage

This stage is marked with slow down of sales growth. Sales continue to rise but at decreasing rate. Competitors have entered the market and existing products face severe competition. Sales curve is pushed downward. It is just like an inverse "U." During this stage, for certain period of time, sales remain stable. This level is called the Saturation. Profits also decline. Normally, this stage lasts longer and marketers face formidable challenges. The stages may be divided into three phases:

i. **Growth Maturity:** Sales-growth rate starts to decline.

ii. **Stable Maturity:** Sales remain stable (i.e., saturation stage).

iii. **Decline Maturity:** Sales now start to decline.

Marginal producers are forced to drop out the products. Those who operate formulate various strategies to extend the stage. Market, products, and marketing programme are to be modified to sustain the stage.

Characteristics of maturity stage include:

i. Sales increase at decreasing rate.

ii. Profits start to decline.

iii. Marginal competitors leave the market.

iv. Customer retention is given more emphasis.

v. Product, market, and marketing mix modifications are undertaken.

Decline Stage

This is the last stage of product life cycle. Here, sales stat declining rapidly. Profits also start erasing. There is a minimum profit or even a little loss. Advertising and selling expenses are reduced to realize some profits. This stage is faced by only those who survived in maturity stage. Most products obsolete as new products enter the market. All products have to face the stage earlier or later. New products start their own life cycle and replace old ones. A number of competitors withdraw from the market. Those who remain in the market prefer to drop smaller segments, make minor changes in products, and continue selling the products in profitable segments and channels.

Here, logic has its own role. Management continues with the same product with expectation that sales improve when economy improves; marketing strategy is revised expecting that competitors will leave the market; or product is improved to attract new market segments. However, unless a strong reason exists, it is costly and risky to continue with the same products. Later on it is difficult of manage selling and promotional efforts. Marketer must check every possibility before dropping the product completely.

Characteristics of decline stage include:

i. Sales fall rapidly.

ii. Profits fall more rapidly than sales.

iii. Product modification is adopted.

iv. Gradually, the company prefers to shift resources to new products.

v. Most of sellers withdraw from the market.

vi. Promotional expenses are reduced to realize a little profit.

COMPARISON BETWEEN HUMAN LIFE CYCLE AND PLC:

Alike human being, product also has its own stages in its life. But, there is difference between them:

1. Human being has expected life, say 100 years; this is not the case with the product.
2. Compared to human being, the product has more uncertain life.
3. While human being's life cycle includes infant, child, and teenager, young, matured, and old, the product life cycle includes introduction, growth, maturity, and decline.
4. Each stage of human life cycle is marked with physical and mental growth. However, time duration is more important. On the other hand, the stage of product life cycle is marked with sales and profits volumes.
5. Human life cycle cannot be reversed, and/or overlapped; it is possible in case of product life cycle.
6. Rebirth of human being is (rationally) not possible, but reintroduction of product is possible.
7. In case of human being, the order of stages cannot be changed; it is possible in case of the product life cycle.
8. The time of each of the stages is almost fixed for human being; in case of product life cycle, the time is highly uncertain.
9. For human being, life span and the duration of any stage cannot be extended beyond limit; it is possible in case of product life cycle.
10. For sound health of human being, nutritious food, pure water, exercises, etc., are necessary; while improvements, modifications, market promotion and suitable marketing strategies are important for sound health of the product.

MARKETING STRATEGIES FOR DIFFERENT STAGES OF PRODUCT LIFE CYCLE

INTRODUCTION

Product passes through four stages of its life cycle. Every stage poses different opportunities and challenges to the marketer. Each of stages demands the unique or distinguished set of marketing strategies. A marketer should watch on its sales and market situations to identify the stage in which the product is passing through, and accordingly, he should design appropriate marketing strategies. Here, strategy basically involves four elements – product, price, promotion, and distribution. By appropriate combination of these four elements, the strategy can be formulated for each stage of the PLC. Every stage gives varying importance to these elements of marketing mix. Let us analyse basic strategies used in each of the stages of the PLC, as described by **Philip Kotler.**

MARKETING STRATEGIES FOR INTRODUCTION STAGE

Introduction stage is marked with slow growth in sales and a very little or no profit. Note that product has been newly introduced, and a sales volume is limited; product and distribution are not given more emphasis. Basic constituents of marketing strategies for the stage include price and promotion. Price, promotion or both may be kept high or low depending upon market situation and management approach. Observe Figure 3. Following are the possible strategies during the first stage:

		Promotion: High	Promotion: Low
Price	High	Rapid Skimming Strategy	Slow Skimming Strategy
	Low	Rapid Penetration Strategy	Slow Penetration Strategy

Figure 3: Marketing Strategies for Introduction Stage

1. Rapid Skimming Strategy

This strategy consists of introducing a new product at high price and high promotional expenses. The purpose of high price is to recover profit per unit as much as possible. The high promotional expenses are aimed at convincing the market the product merits even at a high price. High promotion accelerates the rate of market penetration. In all, the strategy is preferred to skim the cream (high profits) from market. This strategy makes a sense in following assumptions:

(a) Major part of market is not aware of the product.

(b) Customers are ready to pay the asking price.

(c) There possibility of competition and the firm wants to build up the brand preference.

(d) Market is limited in size.

2. Slow Skimming Strategy

This strategy involves launching a product at a high price and low promotion. The purpose of high price is to recover as much as gross profit as possible. And, low promotion keeps marketing expenses low. This combination enables to skim the maximum profit from the market. This strategy can be used under following assumptions:

(a) Market is limited in size.

(b) Most of consumers are aware of product.

(c) Consumers are ready to pay high price.

(d) There is less possibility of competition.

3. Rapid Penetration

The strategy consists of launching the product at a low price and high promotion. The purpose is the faster market penetration to get larger market share. Marketer tries to expand market by increasing the number of buyers. It is based on following assumptions:

(a) Market is large.

(b) Most buyers are price-sensitive. They prefer the low-priced products.

(c) There is strong potential for competition.

(d) Market is not much aware of the product. They need to be informed and convinced.

(e) Per unit cost can be reduced due to more production, and possibly more profits at low price.

4. Slow Penetration

The strategy consists of introducing a product with low price and low-level promotion. Low price will encourage product acceptance, and low promotion can help realization of more profits, even at a low price. Assumptions of this strategy:

(a) Market is large.

(b) Market is aware of product.

(c) Possibility of competition is low.

(d) Buyers are price-sensitive or price-elastic, and not promotion-elastic.

MARKETING STRATEGIES FOR GROWTH STAGE

This is the stage of rapid market acceptance. The strategies are aimed at sustaining market growth as long as possible. Here, the aim is not to increases awareness, but to get trial of the product. Company tries to enter the new segments. Competitors have entered the market. The company tries to strengthen competitive position in the market. It may forgo maximum current profits to earn still greater profits in the future. Several possible strategies for the stage are as under:

1. Product qualities and features improvement
2. Adding new models and improving styling
3. Entering new market segments
4. Designing, improving and widening distribution network
5. Shifting advertising and other promotional efforts from increasing product awareness to product conviction
6. Reducing price at the right time to attract price-sensitive consumers
7. Preventing competitors to enter the market by low price and high promotional efforts

MARKETING STRATEGIES FOR MATURITY STAGE

In this stage, competitors have entered the market. There is severe fight among them for more market share. The company adopts offensive/aggressive marketing strategies to defeat the competitors. Following possible strategies are followed:

1. To Do Nothing

To do nothing can be an effective marketing strategy in the maturity stage. New strategies are not formulated. Company believes it is advisable to do nothing. Earlier or later, the decline in the sales is certain. Marketer tries to conserve money, which can be later on invested in new profitable products. It continues only routine efforts, and starts planning for new products.

2. Market Modification

This strategy is aimed at increasing sales by raising the number of brand users and the usage rate per user. Sales volume is the product (or outcome) of number of users and usage rate per users. So, sales can be increased either by increasing the number of users or by increasing the usage rate per user or by both.

Number of users can be increased by variety of ways. There are three ways to expand the number of users:

i. Convert non-users into users by convincing them regarding uses of products
ii. Entering new market segments
iii. Winning competitors' consumers

Sales volume can also be increased by increasing the **usage rate** per user. This is possible by following ways:

i. More frequent use of product
ii. More usage per occasion
iii. New and more varied uses of product

3. Product Modification

Product modification involves improving product qualities and modifying product characteristics to attract new users and/or more usage rate per user. Product modification can take several forms:

i. **Strategy for Quality Improvement:** Quality improvement includes improving safety, efficiency, reliability, durability, speed, taste, and other qualities. Quality improvement can offer more satisfaction.
ii. **Strategy for Feature Improvement:** This includes improving features, such as size, colour, weight, accessories, form, get-up, materials, and so forth. Feature improvement leads to convenience, versatility, and attractiveness.

Many firms opt for product improvement to sustain maturity stage. Product improvement is beneficial in several ways like (1) it builds company's image as progressiveness, dynamic, and leadership, (2) product modification can be made at very little expense, (3) it can win loyalty of certain segments of the market, (4) it is also a source of free publicity, and (5) it encourages sales force and distributors.

4. Marketing Mix Modification

This is the last optional strategy for the maturity stage. Modification of marketing mix involves changing the elements of marketing mix. This may stimulate sales. Company should reasonably modify one or more elements of marketing mix (4P's) to attract buyers and to fight with competitors. Marketing mix modification should be made carefully as it is easily imitated.

MARKETING STRATEGIES FOR DECLINE STAGE

Company formulates various strategies to manage the decline stage. The first important task is to detect the poor products. After detecting the poor products, a company should decide whether poor products should be dropped. Some companies formulate a special committee for the task known as Product Review Committee. The committee collects data from internal and external sources and evaluates products. On the basis the report submitted by the committee, suitable decisions are taken. Company may follow any of the following strategies:

1. Continue with the Original Products

This strategy is followed with the expectations that competitors will leave the market. Selling and promotional costs are reduced. Many times, a company continues its products only in effective segments and from remaining segments they are dropped. Such products are continued as long as they are profitable.

2. Continue Products with Improvements

Qualities and features are improved to accelerate sales. Products undergo minor changes to attract buyers.

3. Drop the Product

When it is not possible to continue the products either in original form or with improvement, the company finally decides to drop the products. Product may be dropped in following ways:

i. Sell the production and sales to other companies
ii. Stop production gradually to divert resources to other products
iii. Drop product immediately

IMPORTANCE OF PLC

PLC is a valuable concept in marketing. It guides a manager to be dynamic. The concept emphasizes on competitive dynamics. It helps managers design the relevant marketing strategies for each stages of the PLC. The PLC concept advocates that marketer should be aware, alert, and conscious about market trends and accordingly he should attempt to get favourable market response. The concept, if followed carefully, is a ready-made guideline/formula for the practicing manager to exploit attractive opportunities and tackle fearful challenges. We can discuss the role of PLC concept as follows:

1. It is a Ready-made Guideline

It guides the manager to react effectively with market situations. He can interpret product and marketing dynamics in an objective manner. It is useful in making decisions as per market conditions.

2. It is a Forecasting Tool

It is very simple to predict the behaviour of market. Based on the study of the past PLC behaviour of the similar products and the current performance of the products, one can predict the future movements of sales, profits, challenges, competition, etc. The reliable forecasting is a base for the future actions.

3. It is a Planning Tool

It describes types of marketing challenges in each of the stages and also suggests major alternative marketing strategies a firm can select. Looking at sales volume, the manager can easily identify the stage in which product is passing through, and he can prepare strategies in advance to react effectively.

4. It is a Controlling Tool

The PLC concept is also useful for controlling purpose. A manager can compare performance of products against similar products of the past. It is easy even to compare overall marketing performance with competing firms. Based on level of performance, the appropriate strategies can be designed to excel company's performance.

LIMITATIONS OF PLC

As stated earlier, if PLC concept is not followed carefully, it is proved misleading and counterproductive. We must mention that the PLC is only a concept. It is not a foolproof tool to use for the better performance. The degree to which it is useful depends largely on how it is perceived and followed. The utility of concept is based on ability and experience of managers. It has been criticized on the several grounds:

1. One cannot study the entire product life cycle unless it completes; once the product completes its life cycle, it is of no use. The past behaviour has a little value in the contemporary market conditions. Over reliance on the past behaviour of product may be proved fatal.
2. The PLC pattern is highly variable. Practically, several patterns and shapes are possible. 'S' shape curve is the ideal state, which is hardly found in the real practice.
3. The stages don't have predictable duration, fixed sequence, and fixed length of each stage. Sometimes, the stages followed differently than the ideal pattern. One or more stages are repeated several times.
4. It is difficult to state the stage a product is passing through. It is not possible to say exactly which stage is running. And, any strategy formulated in this regard may be misleading.
5. Periodical, seasonal, or cyclical effect on the sales volume may lead to irrelevant decisions and actions.
6. It undermines the role of marketing managers and the marketing strategies. Marketers follow the stages of the PLC. In fact, effective strategies are such that can lead or manage PLC. PLC governs marketing managers, and not marketing managers can govern the PLC. It is the result, not the cause of marketing strategies. In fact, sales should follow marketing strategy; and marketing strategy should not follow the sales.
7. It is just a concept. It is better in book. It is conceptually rich, but practically it has a little value.

CONSUMER ADOPTION PROCESS

There are three important concepts related to new product development process – **product diffusion, consumer adoption,** and **product life cycle.** Consumer adoption is a significant concept for a marketer as he is required to support consumers to complete adoption process within the shortest possible time. Product passes through different stages of its life cycle due to consumer adoption of the product. It implies the mental process through which an individual consumer adopts the new product (innovation). It involves all the stages right from the first hearing about innovation to the final adoption.

Product life cycle, new product diffusion process, and consumer adoption process are interrelated terms. Product diffusion shows the typical pattern through which the innovation spreads into the entire society over time. It can be discussed in relation to entire society. Product life cycle describes the flow of sales and profits to the firm as a result of diffusion process. Consumer adoption process is a part of new product diffusion process that shows how individual consumer adopts the product. Diffusion indicates what happens to society as a result of introduction of a new product (i.e., response of society to a new product); product life cycle indicates what happens to the company' sales and profits as result of introduction of a new product (i.e., response of market to a new product); and consumer adoption indicates what happens to an individual as result of introduction of new product (i.e., response of an individual consumer to a new product).

CONCEPT OF PRODUCT DIFFUSION

E.M. Roger defines product diffusion as a process that describes relationship between number of consumers adopting innovation and the time they take to adopt innovation. Diffusion process can be expressed in form of normal distribution cure, a ball-shaped curve. On the basis of relative time the consumers consume, the consumers can be classified into five categories such as innovators, early adopters, early majority, late majority, and laggards. Such generalization can be applied to consumers of other countries equally but percentage of consumers differs. Period of diffusion-adoption depends on the degree of resistance of society in adopting the product. Innovators take the least time to adopt the product while laggards take the maximum time. Classification of (American) consumers and their percentage are depicted in figure 4.

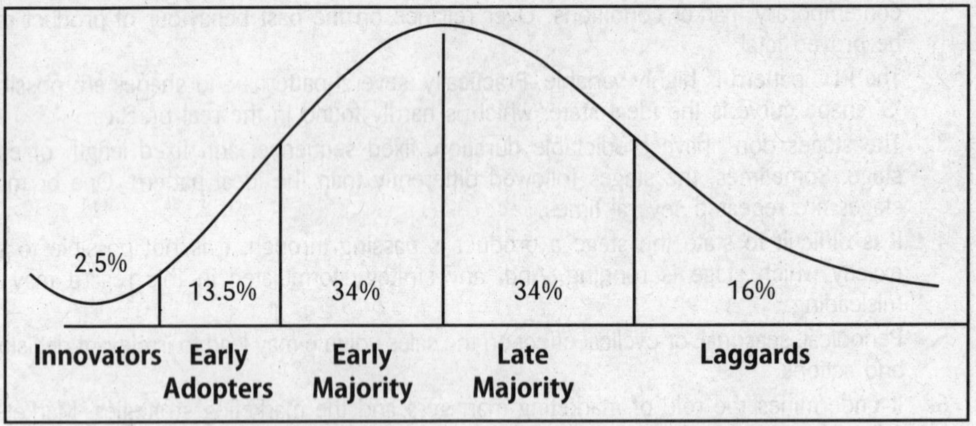

Figure 4: Consumer Diffusion Process – Types of Consumers

CONCEPT OF CONSUMER ADOPTION

Everett M. Roger defines: "Consumer adoption is a mental process through which an individual passes from first hearing about the innovation to final adoption. Thus, it is a decision of an individual to become a regular user of a product."

We can define the term as: *Consumer adoption process describes the steps that a consumer follows to adopt a new product.*

Philip Kotler considers five steps in consumer adoption process, such as awareness, interest, evaluation, trial, and adoption. On the other hand, **William Stanton** considers six steps, such as awareness stage, interest and information stage, evaluation stage, trial stage, adoption stage, and post-adoption stage. We will follow six steps.

(**Note:** Consumer adoption process is similar to consumer buying process The only difference is that consumer buying process concerns with one time buying while consumer adoption concerns with regular buying, he becomes a regular user of the innovation. However, there seems a negligible difference).

1. Awareness Stage

Individual consumer becomes aware of the innovation. He is exposed to innovation but knows very little regarding the innovation. He has only limited information about it. He is aware of either by discussion with friends, relatives, salesmen, or dealers. He gets idea about a new product from various means of advertising like newspapers, magazines, Internet, television, outdoor media, etc. At this stage, he doesn't give much attention to the new product.

2. Interest and Information Stage

In this stage, the consumer becomes interested in innovation and tries to collect more information. He collects information from advertising media, salesmen, dealers, current users, or directly from company. He tries to know about qualities, features, functions, risk, producers, brand, colour, shape, price, incentives, availability, services, and other relevant aspects. Simply, he collects as much information as he can.

3. Evaluation Stage

Now, accumulated information is used to evaluate the innovation. The consumer considers all the significant aspects to judge the worth of innovation. He compares different aspects of innovation like qualities, features, performance, price, after-sales services, etc., with the existing products to arrive at the decision whether the innovation should be tried out.

4. Trial Stage

Consumer is ready to try or test the new product. He practically examines it. He tries out the innovation in a small scale to get self-experience. He can buy the product, or can use free samples. This is an important stage as it determines whether to buy it.

5. Adoption Stage

If trial produces satisfactory results, finally the consumer decides to adopt/buy the innovation. He decides on quantity, type, model, dealer, payment, and other issues. He purchases the product and consumes individually or jointly with other members.

6. Post Adoption Behaviour Stage

This is the last stage of consumer adoption. If a consumer satisfies with a new product and related services, he continues buying it frequently, and vice-versa. He becomes a regular user of innovation and also talks favourable to others. This is a crucial step for a marketer.

In every stage of consumer adoption, a marketer is required to facilitate consumers. He must take all possible actions to make them try, buy, and repeat buy the innovation. Be clear that every type of consumer (innovators, early adopters, early majority, late majority, or laggards) follows all the stages of adoption process, but takes different amount of time to adopt the innovation.

FACTORS AFFECTING CONSUMER ADOPTION

There are a number of factors that affect consumer adoption. Number of consumers adopting the innovation and the time they take to adopt it depend mainly on four factors as stated below:

1. Individual Characteristics
2. Innovation Characteristics
3. Role of Others
4. Company Efforts

EXERCISES

MULTIPLE CHOICE QUESTIONS (MCQs)

1. "Product is anything that can be offered to someone to satisfy a need or want." Who has given this definition?
   a. S. A. Sherlekar b. Philip Kotler
   c. William Stanton d. None
2. Managerial dimension of product covers
   a. only core product
   b. both core product and product-related features
   c. core product, product-related features, and product-related services
   d. buddle of expectations
3. Which one is false?
   a. Core product includes basic contents, benefits, and qualities.
   b. Product related services include after-sales services such as free installation, free-home delivery, guarantee, etc.
   c. Product related features include colour, branding, packaging, labeling, etc.
   d. None of above statement.
4. Which one is only industrial product?
   a. Electricity b. Raw-materials and supplies
   c. Sugar d. Petroleum products
5. Average number of product items in each product line is called
   a. Product mix consistency b. Product mix length
   c. Product mix width d. Product mix depth
6. Which one of the followings is called product line?
   a. Closely related and similar product items. b. Total number of product items
   c. Average number of product items d. None
7. With reference to product mix strategies, which one is wrong?
   a. Product mix expansion implies adding more product lines and/or items in existing product mix.
   b. Product mix contraction implies dropping one or more product lines and/or items from the existing product mix.
   c. Trading up implies adding high-priced prestige product in the existing product mix.
   d. None
8. Which one is not a valid reason for developing a new product?
   a. Change in market b. Increasing competition
   c. Change in political party d. Diversification of risk
9. In view of Philip Kotler, which is the third step/stage in new product development process?
   a. Business analysis b. Product Development
   c. Concept Development and Testing d. Marketing Strategy Formulation
10. Find out false statement.
    a. Product life cycle consists of distinct stages in sales history of product.
    b. Product life cycle shows the degree of product's acceptance by the market.
    c. Product life cycle indicates the relationship between sales and profits in context with time.
    d. Product life cycle implies giving life to the people by products.
11. Saturation stage of product life cycle is a part of
    a. growth stage b. maturity stage
    c. introduction stage d. decline stage

12. The product life cycle stage in which sales volume is increasing at the increasing rate is called
    a. Growth stage
    b. Maturity stage
    c. Decline stage
    d. Introduction stage
13. Which stage of product life cycle is marked with slow down in sales growth?
    a. Introduction stage
    b. Growth stage
    c. Maturity stage
    d. Decline stage
14. Which one of following introduction strategies can make a sense when market is large, most consumers are price-sensitive, market is not much aware of product, and strong potential for competition exists?
    a. Rapid Penetration Strategy
    b. Rapid Skimming Strategy
    c. Slow Skimming Strategy
    d. Low Penetration Strategy
15. Of which product life cycle stage are Market Modification and Product Modification valid strategies?
    a. Introduction Stage
    b. Growth Stage
    c. Maturity Stage
    d. Decline Stage
16. Awareness – Interest – Evaluation – Trial – and Adoption are stages of
    a. New Product Development Process
    b. Product Life Cycle
    c. Consumer Adoption Process
    d. Consumer Diffusion Process

MATCHING TYPE QUESTIONS (MTQs)

17.

List I	List II
(a) Product	(1) Basic contents, qualities, and utilities
(b) Core product	(2) A bundle of utilities or benefits
(c) Product-related strategies	(3) Home delivery, guarantee, and repairing
(d) Product-related services	(4) branding, packaging, and labeling

Codes: (A) (a)-(2), (b)-(1), (c)-(4), (d)-(3)
(B) (a)-(3), (b)-(2), (c)-(1), (d)-(4)
(C) (a)-(4), (b)-(3), (c)-(2), (d)-(1)
(D) (a)-(1), (b)-(4), (c)-(3), (d)-(2)

18.

List I	List II
(a) Product mix	(1) It shows how products lines are related.
(b) Product mix width	(2) It implies in each product line.
(c) Product mix depth	(3) It contains major product lines
(d) Product mix consistency	(4) It is a full list of products.

Codes: (A) (a)-(2), (b)-(1), (c)-(4), (d)-(3)
(B) (a)-(3), (b)-(2), (c)-(1), (d)-(4)
(C) (a)-(4), (b)-(3), (c)-(2), (d)-(1)
(D) (a)-(1), (b)-(4), (c)-(3), (d)-(2)

19.

List I	List II
(a) Searching new ideas	(1) Idea Screening
(b) Reducing number of ideas	(2) Idea Generation
(c) Expressing ideas in consumer terms	(3) Business Analysis
(d) Analysing business attractiveness	(4) Concept Development

Codes: (A) (a)-(2), (b)-(1), (c)-(4), (d)-(3)
(B) (a)-(3), (b)-(2), (c)-(1), (d)-(4)
(C) (a)-(4), (b)-(3), (c)-(2), (d)-(1)
(D) (a)-(1), (b)-(4), (c)-(3), (d)-(2)

20. **List I** — **List II**

List I	List II
(a) Sales increase gradually	(1) Decline Stage
(b) Sales increase at a increasing rate	(2) Maturity Stage
(c) Sales increase at decreasing rate	(3) Growth Stage
(d) Sales stat declining	(4) Introduction Stage

Codes: (A) (a)-(2), (b)-(1), (c)-(4), (d)-(3)
(B) (a)-(3), (b)-(2), (c)-(1), (d)-(4)
(C) (a)-(4), (b)-(3), (c)-(2), (d)-(1)
(D) (a)-(1), (b)-(4), (c)-(3), (d)-(2)

ANSWERS KEY: 1(b), 2(c), 3(d), 4(b), 5(d), 6(a), 7(d), 8(c), 9(c), 10(d), 11(b), 12(a), 13(c), 14(a), 15(c), 16(c), 17(A), 18(C), 19(A), 20(C)

QUESTIONS FOR DISCUSSION

21. Explain concept of product and new product. Write a note on product dimensions.
22. "Strict classification between consumer products and industrial products is not possible." Comment the statement. Also write a note on classification of products.
23. Discuss following terms:
    i. Product items
    ii. Product line
    iii. Product mix
    iv. Product mix dimensions
24. What do you mean by new product? Explain systematic process for developing a new product.
25. Which are the reasons/objectives to develop a new product? Why a new product does fails? Explain.
26. Write short notes:
    i. Idea generation
    ii. Business Analysis
    iii. Market testing
    iv. Commercialization
27. Explain concept of product life cycle? In what different ways it is useful to manager? Also state-limitations of product life cycle.
28. Define term 'product life cycle.' Explain stages of product life cycle with the help of diagram.
29. Write a detailed note on marketing strategies for each of the stages of product life cycle.
30. What is Consumer Adoption? Explain steps consumer adoption process.

CHAPTER

5.1 PRODUCT-RELATED STRATEGIES

INTRODUCTION

Product is made of three elements – one is, core product that contains identifiable and comparable qualities, contents, and benefits of product; the second is, product-related strategies that contain branding, packaging and labeling decisions; and, the third is, product-related services that contain mainly post-sales services related to product, popularly known as the after-sales services. This chapter provides elementary detail on branding, packaging, labeling, and after-sales services.

BRANDING

INTRODUCTION

Branding is one of the important decisions in product mix in particular, and in marketing management in general. Manufacturers specially name the products prior to introduce in the market. The name is known as branding or brand name. The popular brands are Dalda Ghee, Xerox cyclostyle machine, Colgate toothpaste, Ambuja cement, Amul milk and butter, and Parle biscuits, Maruti car, Parker pen, and Thumps-up soft drink to name a few. World's top ten brands (in term of value in dollar) are Coca-cola, Microsoft, IBM, GE, Intel (all USA), Nokia, Disney (all Finland), McDonald (USA) Toyota (Japan), and Mariboro (USA).[1] Out of ten top brands, seven brands belong to USA. The brand is an identity by which product is known or recognized. Brand helps customers to identify the product and its sellers, can gain image and reputation, and is the aid to raise the sales. Due to brand name, sellers can distinguish their products from others. Note that branding is not compulsory. But, it is important as it offers a numbers of benefits. Marketer should select its brand carefully. It is the best means for advertising and positioning the product. A brand is a seller's promise to deliver a specific set of features, benefits, and services consistently to the buyers. Marketer can create brand loyalty, brand image, and brand equity for his product by an appropriate brand.

DEFINITIONS OF BRAND

Brand has been defined as:

1. **Philip Kotler defines:** "A brand is a name, term, symbol, logo, design, or combination of them which is intended to identify the goods or services of one seller or group of sellers, and to differentiate them from those of the competitors."
2. In simple words, we can say: *A brand is product's name, picture, symbol, sign, label, or number, by which the product differs from other products and consumers can identify it.*
3. More comprehensively, we can say: *The term 'brand' indicates all identifying marks such as trade names, trade marks, trade symbols, pictures, design of the package, distinctive colouring, or lettering with or without some attractive slogan.*
4. Similarly, we can say: *A brand is a special name or symbol by which consumer can identify the product from the rest of products, and marketer can distinguish his offer from competitors.*
5. Finally, it can be defined as: *The name, symbol, word, or picture given to the product to distinguish it from other producers and to help customers identify the product can be said as brand or branding.*

A brand is essentially a seller's promise to consistently deliver a specific set of features, benefits, and services to the buyers. The best brand conveys warrantee of quality. A brand conveys at least six meanings, as stated by Philip Kotler:

1. **Attributes:** Brand reflects the product's attributes – key features and qualities – such as expensiveness, durability, colour and shape, prestige, resale value, speed, safety, comfort, and so forth.
2. **Main Benefits:** Brand also indicates benefits offered by the product. People assign special benefits to specific brand.
3. **Value:** It says something about value or status of its producers. It shows the level of brand maker, and he/she is placed at high or low position.
4. **Culture:** A brand reflects the culture of producing company or country. It is like a symbol of one's culture.

5. **Personality:** Brand projects personality, actual or imaginary. It can have considerable impact on the personality of its users.
6. **Users Type:** Brand suggests type of its users.

BRAND AND BRANDING

A brand name must be distinguished from branding. Brand is a name, symbol, or sign by which a product can be distinguished. Branding is comprehensive term that involves a number of decisions and activities to brand the product. Branding can be defined as: *Branding is an act or process of deciding on brand. It consists of taking relevant decisions for brand name.*

BRAND AND TRADEMARK

Brand is a name or symbol of product while the trademark is any symbol, word, mark, or sign that indicates the origin or ownership. While brand concerns with product, the trademark concerns with company or producer. The trademark is a legal term. The brand registered under the Trade Names and Trade Marks Act, 1999 can be a trademark. It is given the legal protection. It is indicated by circle on 'R' like ®. Sometimes, circle on 'C' like © is used to indicate 'copy rights.' A registered brand (trademark) is the exclusive property of the seller and legal actions can be taken if it is copied or adopted by any producer or seller. Other Acts relevant to trade name and/or trade marks include the Copyright Act, 1957, the Patent Act, 1970, etc.

Note that brand has no expiry date. Patents and copyrights have expiry date or fixed time. Brand may be registered or non-registered. If it is to be registered, it must fulfill certain legal formalities.

CHARACTERISTICS OF BRAND/BRANDING

From various definitions given above, we can derive following characteristics of brand, or branding:

1. Brand consists of a wide range of pictures or symbols used for product identification.
2. Symbol or name is used as a brand. For example, Siddhi Cement, Ambuja cement, Rexona soaps, etc.
3. A brand is the practice of giving a specific name to a product or group of products by the seller. It creates individuality of the product.
4. Pictures are used to help illiterate customers identify the products, such as animal, gods, plant, bird, etc.
5. It may be in the form of multiple colour combination. Multiple coloured wrapper or label helps customer identify the product immediately.
6. Brand essentially identifies the seller or maker of that product.
7. A brand of the product is reflective of features, benefits, users, personality aspects, and the culture of the company producing the product.
8. A brand may be trademark if it is registered under the Trade Names and Trade Mark Act. Every trademark is a brand, but every brand is not a trademark.
9. The primary purpose of brand is to provide oral or pictorial identity to buyers and to distinguish the product from competitors.
10. It is relatively a permanent identity for the product. Brand has no expiry date.

Branding is an important decision in marketing. It helps sellers to distinguish the product from various brands available in the market. Likewise, consumers can easily identify the branded product. It is taken as one of the strategic decisions. However, it must be selected carefully,

BENEFITS/OBJECTIVES OF BRANDING

Branding is an act of symbolizing or naming the product for easy distinction and identification. In modern practice of marketing, branding has vital role to play. It is one of the most critical decisions in marketing. Branding offers a large number of benefits to both, sellers and buyers. Let us examine some of the important benefits:

BENEFITS TO PRODUCERS AND SELLERS

Branding offers following benefits to marketers or sellers:

1. Fixed Price

Branded product can be sold at a fixed price. For a popular brand, customers are ready to pay the fixed price. Branding avoids unnecessary bargaining.

2. Specific Customer Groups

It creates an exclusive market for the product. The popular and established brand creates and retains permanent groups of specific buyers. They are loyal to the brand and insist to buy that brand for a longer time.

3. Effective Advertisement

It makes advertising task easy and effective. Marketer can convince the buyer by limited information. Adverting becomes popular due to specific brand name.

4. Ban (Prevention) on Copying

One can prevent copy or imitation of brand by legally registering it. The Trade Names and Trade Mark Act protects the trademark (registered brand). The registered brand enjoys legal protection. The registered brand is exclusive property of the seller. Others cannot use or imitate it.

5. Expression of Product Benefits

The brand represents product benefits, services, and unique features. Customers automatically identify a particular brand as a set of guaranteed benefits.

6. Reduced Competition

Creation of brand image and brand loyalty lead to the reduced competition. Brand itself is a powerful weapon to protect the market from competitors.

7. Benefit of Price Differentiation

Company can charge different price for different brands for the same products. For example Hero Honda Motor charges different price for Honda CD, Spender, Passion, Street, CBZ, Ambition, etc. Price comparison is difficult and the firm has more freedom in fixing the price.

8. Improved Image and Reputation

Brand consciousness, brand awareness, and brand image popularize the name of product and company. Company with a reputed and established brand enjoys a strong position in the market. For example, Lux, Sony, Samsung, Philips, Colgate, Hero Honda, Maruti, Mercedes Benz, etc., are popular brands that represent their producers. People hold in highesteem the producers of popular brands.

9. Speedy Decision

Branded products are easily identified or distinguished. Similarly, price is also easily convinced to customers. It promotes easy buying decision and prompt action.

10. Marketing Strategy Formulation

Brand is also used for formulation of marketing strategies. It helps in deciding place of selling, customers for the products, and actions against competition.

11. Useful in Sales Promotion

Brand itself is a powerful source of information. It advertises products features, benefits, and status. Even, it is the most powerful tool for sales promotion.

12. Growth and Development

Introducing new product under the same brand enjoys all the benefits of the reputed and established brand.

13. Reduced Efforts of Middlemen

Middlemen, including wholesalers, retailers, agents, etc., can sell the branded product with minimum efforts. They do not need to provide more information to convince or to arrive at price fixing. Brand reduces level and amount of their efforts.

14. Easy Direct Selling

When brand becomes popular, a company can sell the product directly to customers. It leads to the reduced costs.

BENEFITS TO CONSUMERS OR BUYERS

Branding offers a lot of benefits to users and/or buyers. Some importance benefits have been listed as under:

1. Fixed Price

Mostly branded products are sold at a fixed price. It avoids bargaining and cheating.

2. Easy Identity

Customers can easily identify the branded product among the similar types of products.

3. Easy Buying

Customers can buy the branded product directly. Even, customers can buy the product through telephone, online transaction, letter, or by representative on the basis of (name, code, or symbol of) brand, without a detailed description of the product.

4. Quality Assurance

Manufacturers try to maintain quality of the branded products over a time as it enhances their image and reputation. Therefore, customers can buy the product with confidence and guarantee of quality and features.

5. Avoiding Cheating

When customers buy the product on basis of brand name or symbols, there is less possibility of offering similar type of products by the seller. Also, price for the branded product is fixed. So, customer cheating can be minimized.

6. Source of Status

It ensures exclusiveness. Reputed brand offers a sense of status and image. It gives more satisfaction to its buyers. The fame of company is the source of pride and status for buyers.

7. Wide Availability

Branded products are widely available in national as well as international market. So, customers can avail the products anywhere.

8. Better Packing

Mostly, branded products are offered in attractive and safe packing. It preserves product's qualities and contents. And, suitable packing also increases customers' convenience

Thus, branding offers a number of benefits to producers or sellers and consumers. The popular brands enable the company to achieve marketing objectives even at a high price. In today's competitive marketing environment, branding decision plays a crucial role.

LIMITATIONS/DISADVANTAGES OF BRANDING

Branding is an important decision in marketing. It is beneficial for both buyers and sellers. However, branding suffers from certain genuine limitations. We will assess limitations or problems relating to branding for consumers, and producers and sellers.

LIMITATION OF BRANDING – CONSUMERS' VIEWS

According to consumers, following are the main limitations or problems of branding:

1. Possibility of Cheating/Fraud by Company

Possibility of duplication is a common practice in today's market. Consumers cannot differentiate between original and duplicate brands as the duplicate brand seems original. We find duplicate brands for Colgate, Philips, Orient fan, Computer software, or programmes. Some producers sell their duplicate products with original brands. People do not distinguish the duplicate products from the original. They pay high price for substandard products.

2. Problem during Shortage

Consumers are habituated to use only popular brands. When, for any reason, shortage of particular brand arises, consumers find is difficult to find suitable substitutes. Many times, artificial shortage is created. For such a unfair game, consumers are the ultimate victims.

3. Difficulty in Selection

It is quite possible when a producer sells a number of products under only one brand. Consumers are confused and cannot take the right decision.

4. High Price

A company charges high price for its popular brands. Semi-monopoly situation is created. Thus, branding may lead to consumer exploitation.

5. Problems to Middlemen Initially

General trend is that consumers buy only those products, which have reputed and popular brands. At initial level, when the product is introduced, middlemen face a lot of difficulties to convince and sell the new product. Though the new product is all the way superior to the existing products and low in price, consumers do not buy it as it is not popular in the market.

6. Misleading in a Long Run

Once the brand is established, it is possible that the manufacturer may not care for qualities and standards. Consumers continue buying assuming that product is standard. Since they have the blind faith in particular brand, they hardly try any other brand. They may not come to know that superior products are available. They are emotionally exploited. Producers take advantages of their trust and faith in the brand.

7. Restricted Competition

Branding creates monopoly. It prevents the entry of a new product. Monopoly always results into consumer exploitation. Consumers have to compromise with price, quality, and service.

LIMITATION OF BRANDING – PRODUCERS' AND SELLERS' VIEWS

Producers and sellers perceive following limitations of branding:

1. Expensive

Branding is an expensive process. A company has to spend considerable amount to select and popularize the brand. To register the brand under The Trade Names and Trade Mark Act is lengthy and complicated process. Company has to pay high fees to the legal experts. It has to spend a lot of money for advisement and promotional efforts to get the brand popularized.

2. Restricting Business of Middlemen

Middlemen have to sell only popular brands. Even high quality products are available at a low price, they cannot convince the consumers. In many cases, producers lay the restrictions on middlemen to sell only their bands.

3. Brand Loyalty and Restricting of Preference

Buyers who are loyal to a particular brand do no prefer other brands of the same manufacturer. The manufacturer finds it difficult to introduce a new brand. Growth and development efforts of the company are restricted.

4. High Pressure for Quality

The manufacturer has to maintain high quality and standards for the popular brands. He has to constantly monitor quality and performance of the brand. If he fails to maintain standards, his reputation and image are affected adversely.

5. Rigidity

It cannot be changed. Any change may lead to heavy loss, or may adversely affect image and reputation.

6. Compromising with Middlemen

A company has to permit wholesalers to sell the products on their brands as long as the company's brand is not popular. In future, such agreement may be proved detrimental for the company.

7. Problem of Raw Materials

Manufacturer has to use only standard raw materials to maintain quality of the popular brands. In case of unavailability, or unfavourable terms and conditions of suppliers, the company finds it difficult to avail the required raw materials. Even, the company has to accept unfavourable conditions that affect its performance adversely.

It can be observed that branding offers a lot of benefits. But, it is not free from limitations. Marketer must be aware of these limitations. He should try to remove as many as possible limitations of branding.

QUALITIES OR FEATURES OF AN IDEAL BRAND

Brand name is a very sensitive and critical issue. A company needs to consider a number of aspects for selecting an effective brand name. It is a long-term and strategic decision. Company is known by its brand. Therefore, the brand must be selected consciously and carefully. Following are some of the important features, qualities, or conditions of an ideal/a good brand name:

1. Reflection of Product Qualities and Features

Brand name must be reflective of product qualities and features. The brand must suggest use, quality, purpose, performance or action. For example, Lijjat Papad reflects taste; Tiger locks reflect strength; and Tata Summo reflects sturdiness.

2. Simplicity

The brand name should be short to read or view; easy to pronounce and spell; and simple to identify and explain.

3. Meaningfulness

A brand must be meaningful. For example, Hathi cement is the indication of the strength.

4. Easy to Remember

Brand name should be such that one can remember easily. It should be interesting and attractive to catch the attention. The brand name should make a permanent place in the mind of people.

5. Novelty/Newness

Novel characteristic is one of the essential conditions for a successful brand name. It should be different, new, and unique, compared to existing/traditional brands in the market. Novelty characteristic attracts customers' attention.

6. Facility for Market Promotion

The brand should be such that supports in promoting a product. It should be simple and short to suit advertising in any of the popular media. Similarly, it must be fit with personal selling, sales promotion, and publicity.

7. Stability/long lasting

It should be stable or long lasting. It must remain unaffected in a long run. It should be free from fashion, style, or seasons as they have a shorter life. Change in brand leads the undesirable consequences.

8. Attractiveness

The word, slogan, picture, or colour used for brand name must be attractive. It should create a pleasant association. People must like to see or listen it.

9. Easy Registration

It must be capable of being registered and protected legally under the relevant legislations. It must be free from the controversial issues.

10. Variety

Company must use multiple brands for its various products. It should use different brands for different products. Because of variety of brands, failure of any brand will not affect other brands. Company can maintain its sales through other brands.

IMPORTANT BRANDING DECISIONS OR STRATEGIES

Branding is an important marketing decision. In today's marketing practices, branding plays a decisive role. In the age of cut-throat competition, branding has become a vital task to distinguish the product from the rest of products offered by the competitors. Branding is an integral part of marketing strategy. Note that branding is not only a means to sell the product; it has tremendous impact on image and reputation of company as well. Many products have made a stable and permanent place in the mind of buyers due to successful banding strategies. For example, Magi fast foods, Hero Honda motorbike, Titan watch, Ambuja cement, Nirma detergent powder and cake, Orient fan, Ramdev masala, Dalda ghee, Xerox photocopier, and Maruti car to name a few are very popular brands. Many companies fight by their brand names rather than qualities and features of the products. Therefore, a firm has to make a lot of exercise while deciding on brand name. Marketing manager has to take certain decisions relating to branding.

MAIN DECISIONS/STRATEGIES OF BRANDING

The main branding strategies or decisions include:

1. Decision on whether to Brand

The first primary decision is whether to brand. Sometimes, a firm sells the product as ordinary one without any brand. The base to sell product is quality, availability or use. Some products are sold without the brand name. For example, sugar, coal, fruits, vegetable, agricultural products directly sold by farmers, and many types of local accessories are sold without brand names. A firm is not required to spend on searching and preparing brand names, packing, stamping, and registering the brand. But, benefits of branding are not available. Generally, a company prefers to offer a suitable brand name to its products. If the product is branded, it offers many benefits as discussed in the earlier part.

2. Decision on Responsibility of Branding

The second important issue relating to branding is, who will take the responsibility to brand the product. Branding can be done by manufacturers, or distributors such as wholesalers and large retailers. Thus, brand label points out either the name of the manufacturer or the name of distributors but not both. There are two options:

(i) **Branding By Manufacturers:** It is a common practice to brand the products by manufacturers. Middlemen have to sell the products by brand names of manufacturers. For example, Philips radio, Philips tube, Philips bulbs, Philips T. V., Philips iron, etc., are branded by Philips India Ltd. In this case, manufacturers have more freedom to price, advertise, and distribute the products.

(ii) **Branding By Distributors:** In some cases, distributors perform branding task. In India, woolen, hosiery, sports goods, and other similar industries' distributors brand the product. Even in case of agricultural products, distributors give their own brand. Small manufacturers have to rely on the middlemen for marketing. Manufacturers merely produce the goods as per specifications and requirements of distributors and they need not to worry for marketing. Here, middlemen enjoy more freedom in pricing the product under their own brands.

3. Decision on Quality of Branded Products

The next strategic decision on branding involves the qualities of product. The firm has to decide on type and level of qualities of branded product. Which qualities are to be highlighted or associated with the brand name – is an important issue. Product qualities refer to an ability of product to meet the purposes for which it is produced. Qualities involve reliability, safety and durability, ease to operate, taste, contents, etc. In fact, qualities of the product are closely related to price at which it is to be sold. Level or degree of qualities may be premium, high, medium, low or substandard. Depending upon the groups of customers, the quality should be decided.

Even, when strategy on quality of branded product has been decided, the firm has to decide further on whether to alter the qualities over time. There are three options: (1). To maintain the same qualities over time, (2). To improve qualities gradually, and (3). To degrade the qualities. However, the third option is not desirable.

4. Decision on Family/Umbrella Brand Name

Here, the company has to decide whether the same brand name should be used for different product items and product lines. Following options are possible:

(i) **Family Brand:** Sometimes, a company uses family brand name that includes giving same brand name to various items of a specific product line. For example, 'Amul' for milk products, 'Acme' or 'Ponds' for cosmetic products, etc., use family brand. Family brand name can help in joint advertising and sales promotion. However, if one member (item) of family brand is rejected by the consumers, the prestige of all other products in family brand is adversely affected.

(ii) **Umbrella Brand:** A company may select same brand name for all the products (lines and items). For example, Tata Company uses same brand for all soaps, chemicals, engineering tools, textiles, salt, electronics products, etc. Similar is the case with Hindustan Machines and Tools Ltd. Such decision may minimize cost of promotion and marketing of products. Company can promote a new product under the same reputed brand easily and successfully. The umbrella brand is used when company has outstanding reputation and image in the market. However, the risk is that the bad experience with any of the products under umbrella brand will affect seriously the entire range of products.

(iii) **Individual Brand:** In this option, each product has a special, distinguished, and unique brand name. For example, Bajaj Company uses different brand names for its scooters and motorbikes such as Chetak, Super, Cub, Sunny, Caliber, Pulsar, Legend, etc. Company has to promote each brand separately. This option is very practical and safe compared to the previous options. But, it creates a lot of practical difficulties in selling and promotional efforts.

(iv) **Brand Name with Company Name:** In this case company uses the name of company with brand names. For example, Hero Honda CD, Hero Honda Passion, Hero Honda Spender, Hero Honda Street, Hero Honda Ambition, Hero Honda CBZ etc. Similarly, Tata Groups attach it name with each and every product it manufactures.

5. Decision on Brand Expansion or Extension

Brand extension refers to using the same brand name for the modified or new products introduced later on. By extending brand name for newly introduced product, the company can take advantages of its image, popularity and reputation. Sometimes, brand is extended for the products with new packages, different sizes, or new attributes. For example, Bajaj Auto and Hero Honda have extended its brands for the new models introduced later on. Parle Biscuit and Bornvita have extended their brand names for new packages, different sizes, etc.

6. Decision on Altering or Modifying the Brand

In some cases, a company has to change or alter brand name in the future. This option is preferred only when (1) company assumes that the brand name selected needs to be reviewed, (2) closely related brand name is used by competitors, and is difficult to distinguish the product from competitors, and (3) due to change in consumer interest and preference, it is necessary to change the brand name. The company must change its brand only as a last resort, that is, when all efforts fail to sustain the existing brand.

7. Decision on the Variety Brands

In this strategy, the company has to decide whether different brand names should be used for various types of its products. Company can fight with competitors by using different brand names. For example, Hindustan Uniliver Limited uses different brand names for its toilet soaps (product line) such as Lifebuoy, Lux, Rexona, Breeze, Lirin, etc. This strategy can offer following benefits:

(i) By periodical entry of new brands in the market, a company can retain its customers for a longer period.
(ii) Variety-seeker customers can be attracted by offering various brands.
(iii) Different types of customer groups can be satisfied by price and features differentiations.
(iv) Retailers can provide more variety to customers for better selection. Brand varieties attract more customers.
(v) Company can increase market share and sales.
(vi) It facilitates market promotion activities, etc.

Thus, branding decision or strategy is a critical issue for a manager. Appropriate branding strategy can help the manager achieve its marketing goals. Therefore, barding strategy should be prepared only after careful analysis of various related issues. Being a long-term and irreversible decision, it needs intensive and deliberate preparations.

PACKING AND PACKAGING

INTRODUCTION

Branding, packaging, labeling, product warrantee, and after-sales services are important product-related strategies. Especially, packaging and labeling represent product personality. Many marketers have called packaging a fifth 'P', along with Four P's – price, product, place, and promotion.

However, most marketers treat packaging and labeling as the elements of product strategy. In fact, packaging, labeling and branding are closely related. Branding is based on packing and/or packaging. In today's marketing activities, packing and packaging have vital role. Due to wide market, emphasis on customer satisfaction, competition, long or multi-level distribution network, extensive transportation, customer's desire for comfortable handling, protection of product and product contents, etc., packing and packaging have become integral part of product decisions. Virtually, the most of products cannot be sold without packing and packaging. Apart from these realities, now packing and packaging are treated as strategic decisions to differentiate products from competitors.

DEFINITIONS OF PACKING

The term packing can be defined in various ways. Some of the definitions of packing are as follows:

1. *The set of activities concerning with filling, putting, or covering the product in primary container for the purposes of protection of contents and qualities, and convenient handling from producers to buyers is called as packing.*
2. *Packing means the wrapping and crating of goods before they are transported or stored.*
3. *Packing is a task of putting product in a basic or primary container for protection and convenience.*

It is simply an act of placing the product in the container or covering it with wrapper. It is merely a physical action and provides a handling convenience, e.g., rice, cotton, wheat, or any other agricultural produce. It is necessary to prevent flowing out of such liquids like milk, drinks, sauces, etc. It is essential to maintain freshness and quality, e.g., butter, ghee, oil, cream, cheese, etc.

DEFINITIONS OF PACKAGING

Packaging has been defined as follows:

1. **Philip Kotler:** "Packaging includes the activities of designing and producing the container or wrapper for a product."
2. **Philip Kotler** in his old edition defines the term as: "Packaging is an activity, which is concerned with protection, economy, convenience, and promotional considerations."
3. **William J. Stanton:** "Packaging is a general group of activities, which concentrate in formulating the design of a package, and producing an appropriate and attractive container or wrapper for the product."

The colorful container or wrapper is called the package. The package includes three levels/layers of material – primary package including basic package or product's immediate container, for example, bottle, tube or internal wrapper (called as packing); secondary package which refers to additional layer of protection that is to be removed when product is ready for use, such as can, outer wrapper, or paper box; and shipping package that is a grand package, such as jute bag, cartoon or hard/wooden box or outer container, in which various primarily/secondary packed units are placed for handling, storing, or transportation. For example, in case of toothpaste, tube is primary package; paper box in which the tube is kept is secondary package; and the cartoon or large box in which 100 units each of 250 gram each are kept is shipping package. Packaging concerns with these all types of packages.

DIFFERENCE BETWEEN PACKING AND PACKAGING

Packing and packaging are closely related. Many people consider packing and packaging as similar, but they are different. Packing differs from packaging in many ways as show in the table 1.

Table 1: Showing difference between packing and packaging:

	Points	Packing	Packaging
1.	Meaning	To put products in the primary tins, boxes, plastic containers, peeps, or tubes is called as packing.	To design and prepare package and take relevant decisions can be said as packaging
2.	Need	It is must. Most of goods cannot be sold without packing.	It is optional. Goods can be sold without packaging.
3.	Branding and Labeling	Branding and Labeling are not included in the packing.	Branding and Labeling are used in packaging.
4.	Purpose	Packing is primary task. It protects product contents and qualities.	Packaging is marketing necessity. It is aimed at promotion device.It is more important in marketing strategy.
5.	Usefulness	It is useful for manufacturers or traders.	It is useful for manufacturers and customers.
6.	Scope	Packing is the initial task. It may be treated as a part of packaging activities.	It is a secondary task. First of all, product is packed and then packaging is applied. It is extension of packing function.
7.	Importance	Packing doesn't contribute in attracting customers.	It is informative and provides a lot of details. It attracts customers.
8.	Colorfulness	Mostly, it is simple but strong to protect quality and quantity of product.	It is colourful, attractive, and decorative with needed printed information.
9.	Picture of the product	Packing may not show what is inside the packing.	It shows colourful picture of product, demonstration, and useful guidelines.
10.	Example	Simple/plain plastic tube containing toothpaste can be said as packing.	Colourfully wrapped/labeled tube and outer paper box both with pictures and details can be said as packaging.

CHARACTERISTICS OF A GOOD PACKING/PACKAGING/PACKAGE

(**Note:** Now onward, throughout the chapter, packing (package) and packaging have been treated as similar. So, we may use both the terms interchangeably.)

Appropriate packing is necessary for producers to send the product in the hands of customers in a proper form, quality, and quantity. It offers protection and convenience benefits. Therefore, producer must care for packing the product. There are several guidelines to make packing task effective. They are also called as qualities or features of an ideal packing/packaging. Main features have been briefly explained as under:

1. Durability

Packing should be durable to protect contents for a longer period. The material used must be strong enough to protect the product inside it. Durability relates with type and nature of product.

2. Protectiveness

Packing must be protective. It must protect the product from linkage, evaporation, flowing out, damage of quality and contents, breaking or tearing, etc.

3. Attractiveness

Packing should be attractive. The attractive packing creates desire to purchase the product.

4. Suitable to Product

Packing should be selected according to type of products. For example, in case of a liquid product, jar, bottle, plastic container, etc., are recommended. But, one cannot use cotton or jute bag for liquid products. Similarly, for machine and tools, wooden box or hardboard is more suitable. Gaseous product must be packed in a special container to prevent linkage.

5. Suitable to Customer Needs

It should be suitable to customer needs. It must meet customer expectations. For liquid product and solid product, packing should be different. Similarly, depending upon need of protection, it should be packed.

6. Easy Handling/Carrying

It must be of suitable size to facilitate customers for easy handling or carrying. Customers can easily carry the product from retail outlet to their home. For example, rice bag should be 1 kg, 2 kg, 5 kg, 10 kg, or 20 kg. It is not fair to keep 100 kg or 250 kg bag.

7. Convenient to Customers

Packing should be convenient to buyers. It should facilitate the needs of customers. For example, edible oil should be packed in 1 kg, 2 kg, 5 kg, 10 kg, or 20 kg tin or container so that buyer can buy as per their need and capacity. It should be such that buyers can buy product as per their needs.

8. Light Weight

Weight of packing materials should be light to avoid unnecessary weight on the product. However, it should not be so light that affect its quality and strength.

9. Suitable to Use

Packing must be suitable for use of product. The size of mouth/cap of packing must be as per its use. For example, toothpaste tube should have small mouth, Bournvita or Boost must have large size mouth to use spoon.

10. Economy

It should be less costly. It should not be the heavy burden on price of the products. Costly packing affects its market adversely.

FUNCTIONS OR OBJECTIVES OF PACKING/PACKAGING

In recent times, packaging has become a potent or powerful marketing tool. A well-designed package of the product can create convenience value for the consumers and promotional value for the producer. Packaging is aimed at various purposes. **William Stanton** stated: "Packaging is aimed at protection, convenience, identification/promotion, and profit creation." However, there can be more functions or purposes as listed below:

1. Protection or Safety

To protect the product is the basic function of packaging. It protects product and its contents on the route from the producers to the consumers. Producers can distribute the products safely to ultimate consumers by the suitable package. Similarly, it is also aimed at storing the product for a long period of time. Packing makes national and international trade possible. It minimizes effect of water, cold, heat, light, passage of time, etc. Thus, it prevents product from spilling, spoilage, or evaporation.

2. Identification

It is a medium of identification for both producers/traders and consumers. One can clearly distinguish the product from one brand to another. Packaging helps identify a product. We know that the most packages bear the name of producer, picture of product, brand name, and its contents or ingredients. It may prevent substitution of competitive products. At the point of purchase, the package can serve as a silent sales person.

3. Preservation/maintenance of Quality

An appropriate package prevents contents and ingredients of product. It minimizes effect of time, light, water, and temperature on product contents. For example, medicines, chemicals, foods, cold drinks, etc., need airtight package to preserve contents or qualities. Even, certain products cannot be stored without a suitable packing.

4. Easy Handling

All the people involved in marketing the products such as producer, warehouse-keepers, middlemen, and consumers, need a suitable package. It facilitates opening, closing, reusing, storing, and easy handling of the product. A suitable size of package creates convenience in carrying and buying the product.

5. Product Differentiation

Package is an effective way to differentiate products. Various producers producing products having similar uses can differentiate their products from others. By highlighting certain dominant features on the package, a producer can easily distinguish his product from the rest of producers.

6. Attractiveness

Packaging enhances product appearance. The colourful design and label on the package, printed information, brand name or picture, colour combination, and overall getup of the package are the special means to attract the customers. Most packages are eye-catching, and demand the attention of buyers. Systematic colour combination can improve the appearance and appeal of the product. For cosmetic or garment product, an attractive package has major role for immediate impression on buyers.

7. Aid in Selling

Packaging can positively contribute to easily selling the product. It creates a good image of the product. The appropriate package performs a lot of tasks of sellers. It is a powerful aid to sell the product. It induces immediate buying decision.

8. Immediate Advertising

An attractive packaging is a powerful promotional tool. The size, shape, colour combination, picture, information on package, etc., draw the attention of customers. A systematic arrangement of the well-packaged product on retail counter can serve as a powerful sales person. The suitable product package itself is a means for sales promotion and advertising. Package speaks a lot on behalf of product and its producer. Packaging can be used effectively to introduce or promote a new product.

9. Cost Saving/Economy

It leads to more sales. Sometimes, customers buy the product just because of attractive package. Package costs range from 3% to 10%. Suitable package can reduce the costs, and finally the selling price. Sometimes, package can offer more than its costs by protecting contents and qualities. Scientific packaging reduces storage and maintenance costs. Similarly, the suitable package of the product also reduces wastage or spoilage.

10. Demonstration or User's Guide

Package of product bears necessary information regarding how to use product safely and effectively. It shows safety warning, limitations on use, and also demonstration about how to use. Wrapper or label on the product teaches a lot of things to the users.

11. Other Functions

Apart from above stated functions or purposes, there are certain minor functions, such as:

i. Reliability
ii. Price determination
iii. Storing facility
iv. Facility in using the product
v. Providing a base for labeling and branding, etc.

USES, BENEFITS, OR IMPORTANCE OF PACKING/PACKAGING

(**Note:** They are similar of objectives and functions discussed in the former part. But, here, they have been discussed separately for producers, customers and nation).

Packing is an indispensable function of marketing. Hardly products can be widely distributed without packaging. Nowadays, it is taken as a part of marketing strategy. Note that the suitable packaging is important not for producers and sellers, but is equally important for customers, society and nation as a whole. Due to its direct advantages for all the participants in marketing activities, the packaging has vital role to play. We will discuss the role, importance or benefits of packaging for three parties – producers, customers, and nation or society.

BENEFITS TO PRODUCERS AND SELLERS

The importance of packaging for producers and sellers can be explained with reference to following advantages:

1. Protection of Product

To protect the product is the main benefit of packaging for the producers. It protects product and its contents on the route from the producers to the consumers. It minimizes effect of water, cold, heat, light, passage to time, etc. Thus, it prevents product from spilling, spoilage, or evaporation.

2. Essence for Liquid Product

Liquid products, like milk, ghee, syrup, mineral water, acid, petroleum products and so forth, cannot be stored or distribute without package. So, packaging is almost indispensable for liquid products.

3. Easy Handling

All the people involved in marketing the products, such as producers, warehouse-keepers, and middlemen, can handle or transport products with ease. It creates a lot of convenience in handling the products. Suitable size creates convenience in carrying and selling the product.

4. Low Cost of Transportation

Naturally, packing reduces costs of transportation. A suitable package can avoid wastage/damage during transportation. Also, quality or ingredients can be protected. Suitable packaging facilitates a large number of units and/or more weight to transport. These all facilities offered by the packaging can result into low costs of transportation, and ultimately, low selling price.

5. Effective Storage

Most of the products cannot be stored without packaging. Producers and distributors can store the products to take benefits of the time utility by effective packaging system. Minerals, vitamins, smell, taste, colour, etc., can be preserved during storage.

6. Increased Product Attractiveness

Packaging enhances attractiveness of the product. The colourful design and label on the package, printed information, brand name or picture, colour combination, and overall getup (appearance) of the package are the special means to attract the customers. Most packages are eye-catching and demand the attention of buyers. For cosmetic and garment products, an attractive packing has major role in impressing buyers immediately.

7. Mean for Effective Advertising

An attractive packaging is a powerful promotional means. The size, shape, colour combination, picture, information on package, etc., draw the attention of customers. It provides a lot of important information printed on it. The suitable product package itself is a means for advertising. Package speaks a lot on behalf of product and its producer. Packaging can be used effectively to introduce or promote a new product.

8. Product Differentiation

Package is the significant way to differentiate products. Various producers producing products having similar uses can differentiate their products from others. By highlighting certain dominant features on the package, colourful picture, slogans, etc., the producer can easily distinguish his product from the rest of producers.

9. Standard Weight

Packing assures quality and standard weight of product. Weight printed on the packing reduces task of seller to weigh the product. He can sell the product easily.

10. Aid in Selling

Packaging can positively contribute in selling the product. It creates a good image of the product. An appropriate package performs a lot of tasks of sellers. It is a powerful aid to sell the product. It induces immediate buying decision.

11. Convenient for Sales Promotion

Packing is a powerful sales promotion technique. A seller can put gifts inside the packing. He can highlight special offers on the packing. Samples, coins, extra product, additional parts, and many other such incentives can be conveniently placed inside the packing.

12. Prevention of Adulteration

Packing and packaging prevent adulteration in the product. Middlemen or others cannot mix or add cheaper and inferior contents in original products. Many times, packing can be removed only once; repacking is not possible. So, people fear to be caught in case of any kind of malpractice.

BENEFITS TO CUSTOMERS

Packaging is beneficial for customers in several ways. Packaging offers following benefits to customers:

1. Reduced Adulteration

Consumers can get sealed and packed products. Generally, well-packaged products are safer from adulteration.

2. Quality Assurance

Systematic packaging is the guarantee of quality and standard. Packing protects the original contents or ingredients.

3. Easy Identification

Consumers can easily identify the product they wish to buy. Colour, picture, layout, slogan, etc., on the package can help buyers to separate the desired products from a large number of products.

4. Preservation of Product Ingredients

Scientific package maintains quality of product for a long time. Most of packages also state the expiry date. Packing preserves all ingredients, vitamins, taste, colour, smell, etc.

5. Easy to Carry

Consumers can purchase a large number of items due to packaging. It protects products from flowing out, braking, spoilage, leakage, or evaporation. Similarly, due to availability of products in convenient weight and size, consumers find it easy to carry the products with them.

6. Fixed Price

The packaged product shows printed price on it. Mostly, for well-packaged products, the price is fixed. So, it reduces the chance of cheating or charging overprice. Further, there is no need to bargain to arrive at the final price.

7. Reuse/multiple Uses of Package

When product is consumed, certain packages can be used for multiple purposes. Glass jars, bottles, paper boxes, wooden cartoons, etc., are used for variety of purposes. Sometimes, children use them as toys also!! For example, package offered by Bournvita and Boosts can be used for storing other grocery items.

8. Availability of Convenient Size

Since products are available in different sizes and weights, consumers find it easy to buy as per their needs. They find more options to suit their requirement.

9. Provision of Needed Direction

Mostly, a package provides useful information printed on it. It shows information about company, brand, features, benefits, warnings, direction to use, etc. Such information is vital for safe and proper use of product.

10. Easy Storage

Packaging can help in storing the product for the future use. Original quality and weight can be preserved during storage. It saves consumers' time, money, and efforts. For example, edible oil, ghee, soft drinks, biscuits, glossary items, etc., can be store for a year due to suitable packaging.

11. Effective Selection

A suitable package can speed up selection. Within limited time, consumers can complete the shopping. Outside getup of product facilitates immediate selection.

BENEFITS TO NATION

Packing and packaging offer a number of benefits to society or nation. Some important benefits have been discussed as under:

1. Reduced Wastage/Spoilage

Packaging minimizes overall wastage during distribution. It ensures optimum use of valuable resources. In developing and underdeveloped countries, there is shortage of resources. Packing can ensure effective use of productive resources.

2. Overall Economy

Packaging leads to overall economy. People can have standard products at a reasonable price. Time utility, low rate of waste, scale of economy, etc., result into overall economy.

3. National and International Market

Systematic and scientific packaging promotes national and international market. Increased national and international sales have positive impact on economic growth and welfare of people.

4. Raised Standard of Living

Packaging has direct and indirect contribution in raising standard of living of society. Easy availability, low price, rich contents, convenient buying, proper selection of products, and many other similar benefits offered by packaging have positive impact on the living standard of society.

Thus, packaging has major role in today's marketing practices. It offers the triple benefits – to producers, to customers, and to society/nation. This is the reason why producers assign more importance to packaging strategy.

LABELING

INTRODUCTION

Packaging and labeling give necessary information to users. Label justifies customer's right, i.e., "right to know." Generally, packaging, branding, and labeling decisions are taken together. However, label is a part of packaging and is applicable to non-branded products, too. The primary purpose of labeling is to provide useful information to users. It is directly stuck or attached on product, which is attractive and multi-coloured.

MEANING

Let us define term 'label' and 'labeling':

According to **Webster English Dictionary**: A label means a strip/piece of paper giving detail fixed on a thing. It is a paper or plastic piece that gives detail about name, use, instruction, etc., attached on a thing. Mostly, a label indicates name of company, name of product, weight, price, ingredients, uses, and recipe to use the product. It also describes precautions, or warnings to use the products. And, labeling is an act or a process of deciding on label for the product.

TYPES OF LABEL

There can be several types of label. Most common among them are:

1. **Brand Label:** It indicates brand name or symbol.
2. **Grade Label:** It indicates grade, class, group, quality group, or status of products.
3. **Descriptive Label:** It describes the products. It gives basic information about product.
4. **Informative Label:** It provides complete information related to product. It provides details, not only about product but also how, when, and why to use the product along with necessary precautions while using the product.
5. **Instruction and Warning Label:** Instruction label provides instructions necessary to use or operate the product. Warning label highlights precautions the user should observe while using the product.

CHARACTERISTICS OF LABELING

We can find out following common characteristics of label/labeling:

1. It is an advertising tool, too.
2. Label is made of plastic, cloth, or paper.
3. It is printed, attached, or stuck.

4. It describes product and its uses, shows MRP (Maximum Retail Price), and precautions.
5. Labeling decision is taken along with branding and packaging.
6. It justifies customer right, i.e., 'right to know.'
7. It is treated as the part of product.
8. It is in forms of multicoloured and attractive sticker.
9. It may be written in one or more languages.
10. It can increase product utility and is capable to increase customer satisfaction.
11. It is a part of marketing strategy to attract customers. It may be deceptive or misleading as only strong points are highlighted.
12. It is a multipurpose tool.

INFORMATION/DETAILS ON LABEL

Information on label depends on type of product. Normally, we find following details on label:

1. Name of producers or a group of producers, place of production, registered office with full address (phone numbers, fax, e-mail id, and websites)
2. Brand name and users
3. Category or class of product
4. Contents and ingredients of product with their proportion (percentage)
5. Uses or benefits of product, and manufacturing and expiry date
6. Recipe to prepare the product
7. Important instructions to follow while using product
8. Guarantee and warrantee details
9. Precautions to be observed and legal warnings
10. MRP, Weight, etc.

USES, IMPORTANCE, OR ROLE OF LABELING

We know that packaging, branding, and labeling are three integrated decisions that describe/decide product personality. In today's marketing practices, it is imperative to provide the users with necessary product-related information. It is especially true when product is technical and is distributed to the customers at distanced places. It can enhance product utility and attract customers. It is a multipurpose tool that offers a number of benefits to company as well as consumers. Following uses describe role of labeling:

1. It enhances product personality.
2. It helps to identify product or brand.
3. It shows grade of the products, like A, B, and C, etc.
4. It educates users. It makes it possible to use product without supervisor. If necessary, it shows warnings to use the product.
5. It describes product. The product can be marketed at distanced places directly.
6. It helps customers taking buying decision as it provides necessary detail to evaluate seller's offer.
7. It ensures the exact use of product. It tells how to use the product safely. It prevents manhandling and misuses of product.
8. It satisfies legal and ethical requirements.
9. It meets customers' right, that is, the 'right to know.'
10. It reduces task of sellers (middlemen and salesmen). Consumers can seek necessary information from the label.

11. It can promote product. It supports advertising, personal selling, and sales promotion.
12. It is a multipurpose tool.

AFTER-SALES SERVICES

INTRODUCTION

Company performs a number of activities to serve customers better than the competitors. Many companies try to improve competitive strengths by providing attractive after-sales services to customers. Even, customers buying decision is affected by type of after-sales services. Marketers can attract buyers by rendering post-sales services better than the rivals. Products like automobiles, machineries, electrical appliances, etc., after-sales services are considered as important aspects. After price and the quality, the third important consideration is after-sales services. For some customers, after-sales services are more important than price, style, getup, and many other factors.

DEFINITIONS

We can define after-sales services as: *A set of post-sales activities carried by a marketer that increase customer satisfaction and dealer effectiveness is called after-sales services.*

In the same way, it can be defined as: *After-sales services involve special efforts made by the marketer to meet consumer expectations, such as home delivery, free repairing, inspection, installation, instruction, demonstration, and so forth.*

TYPES OF AFTER-SALES SERVICES

Marketer can provide several types of after-sales services. Most common among them are as under:

1. Home delivery, installation, and demonstration
2. Free repairing and maintenance during warrantee period
3. Repairing at a fair rate after warrantee period
4. Providing training to use the product in proper way and repair them
5. Education and guidance to use the product safely and effectively
6. Periodical inspection and up-gradation (in case of durable products)
7. Assistance for replacement, or realization of any type of claim
8. Availing original spare parts and accessories at normal rate

SIGNIFICANCE OF AFTER-SALES SERVICES

After-sales services are treated as a part of marketing strategy to attract and retain customers on one end, and to fight with competitors on the other end. Most companies find it effective to opt for services competition. Marketer tries to offer more effective services than competitors can. Post-sales services are helpful to attract, satisfy, and retain customers. Following points explain how after-sales services can contribute to success of marketing efforts:

1. They are customer-oriented efforts that attract customers and meet their expectations.
2. They enhance product utility.
3. They ensure proper and safe use of products.
4. They assist in introducing a new product successfully. They promote product acceptability.
5. They strengthen competitive edge of product.
6. Marketer can distinguish his offer by service differentiation.
7. They promote company's image and goodwill.
8. They are used as a base to establish and maintain long-term profitable relations with customers.

9. Company can defend its high price, and/or inferior quality by proving attractive post-sales services.
10. They are a part of a total offer for technical products.

EXERCISES

MULTIPLE CHOICE QUESTIONS (MCQs)

1. Branding, packaging, and labeling, are called
   a. core product
   b. product-related strategies
   c. product-related services
   d. product decisions
2. Find our odd statement
   a. A brand can be registered under the Trade Names and Trade Mark Act, 1999.
   b. Trade Mark is a legal term.
   c. Actions cannot be taken if registered brand is adopted by others.
   d. Patents and copyrights have expiry date or fixed time.
3. Which one is not indicated by the brand?
   a. Symbol of the ruling party
   b. Company logo
   c. Product identification symbol
   d. Pictures to help the illiterate people
4. Which one of the followings the main purpose of branding the product?
   a. To help consumers identify the product among many products.
   b. To protect product from cold, heat, and rain.
   c. To provide complete detail about the product.
   d. None
5. Which one not correct?
   a. Branding is compulsory for every type of product and only branded product can be sold.
   b. Labeling justifies consumers' right, the right to know.
   c. Packaging is useful for protection of product, easy handling, and product differentiation.
   d. Branding is useful to both buyers and sellers.
6. Which one is an irrelevant branding decision?
   a. Decision on whether to brand the product
   b. Decision on responsibility of branding
   c. Decision on family or umbrella brand name
   d. Decision on long-term and sort-term branding
7. Which one in not a valid type of label?
   a. Brand label
   b. Grade label
   c. Descriptive label
   d. Entertaining label
8. The label that provide details not only about product but also how, when and why to use the product along with precautions is called
   a. the warning label
   b. the descriptive label
   c. the informative label
   d. the instruction label
9. "Cigarette smoking is injurious to health." In which class of labels does this information falls?
   a. Warning label
   b. Instruction label
   c. Informative label
   d. Descriptive label
10. Which one is incorrect?
    a. After-sales services enhance product utility.
    b. After-sales services ensure proper and safe use of products.
    c. After-sales services strengthen competitive edge of product.
    d. After-sales services reduce selling price.

MATCHING TYPE QUESTIONS (MTQs)

11.

List I	List II
(a) It helps identify the product	(1) Packaging
(b) It protects product contents and qualities	(2) Brand name
(c) It provides necessary information	(3) After-sales services
(d) Offering post-sales services	(4) Labeling

Codes: (A) (a)-(2), (b)-(1), (c)-(4), (d)-(3) (B) (a)-(3), (b)-(2), (c)-(1), (d)-(4)
(C) (a)-(4), (b)-(3), (c)-(2), (d)-(1) (D) (a)-(1), (b)-(4), (c)-(3), (d)-(2)

12.

List I	List II
(a) It indicates brand name of symbol	(1) Warning Label
(b) It indicates grade or class of product	(2) Descriptive Label
(c) It describes the product	(3) Grade Label
(d) It provides details about precautions	(4) Brand Label

Codes: (A) (a)-(2), (b)-(1), (c)-(4), (d)-(3) (B) (a)-(3), (b)-(2), (c)-(1), (d)-(4)
(C) (a)-(4), (b)-(3), (c)-(2), (d)-(1) (D) (a)-(1), (b)-(4), (c)-(3), (d)-(2)

ANSWERS KEY: 1(b), 2(c), 3(a), 4(a), 5(a), 6(d), 7(d), 8(c), 9(a), 10(d). 11(A), 12(C)

QUESTIONS FOR DISCUSSION

13. What is Branding? Explain its characteristics. Differentiate between branding and trademark.
14. What is Brand and Branding? Discuss important branding decisions.
15. Write a note: (1) Important decisions related to branding. (2) Alternative branding strategies.
16. Explain term 'banding' and discuss main decisions of branding.
17. Describe features of an ideal branding. And explain important aspects to be considered while selecting the brand.
18. What is branding? "Branding is not always beneficial." Discuss the statement with reference to limitations of branding.
19. Define branding and state its objectives. Explain benefits of banding.
20. What do you mean by branding? What are the benefits available to producers and consumers?
21. What do you mean by packing and packaging? Explain difference between packing and packaging.
22. Define packaging. Write a note on features of ideal packaging. Explain its functions
23. Differentiate between packing and packaging. What are the important aspects a marketer should considerer while deciding on packaging.
24. Explain term packing and write its functions.
25. Define packaging. Explain Objectives of packaging.
26. Explain importance of packing for the product
27. What is packaging? Discuss its advantages.
28. Define label. What type of information is provided through label? State importance of labeling.
29. What are after-sales services? State types of after-sales services. Also describe its significance in modern marketing practices.

✧✧✧

CHAPTER

6

PRICING DECISIONS

INTRODUCTION

Pricing decision is one of the most critical decisions of marketing mix. Price is an economic value or an exchange value of product expressed in forms of money. Many products fail not due to qualities, features, and performance, but due to faulty pricing policies. Price and pricing policies are of great importance for the manufacturers, middlemen, and consumers as well. It affects company's profits on one hand, and product purchase decision of consumers on the other hand. The price is one of the major determinants of purchase decision. Price is also a powerful tool for responding the competitors strongly. Price does not determine only quality and performance, but it also implies status and prestige aspects of product.

A company must determine appropriate price and must formulate effective pricing policies to get positive response of the market. By adjustment and readjustment in pricing related issues, a company can continue getting positive response during different demand situations. While deciding on price of the product, a company must take a balanced decision between two extremes – first is, the costs of production and marketing, and the second is, expectations and paying capacity of the target market.

DEFINITIONS OF PRICE

The exact and generally accepted definition of price is almost difficult. However, we can give following definitions of price:

1. *Price is the economic value of the product (good and service) normally expressed in terms of money.*
2. *Price is an agreement between sellers and buyers at which goods and services are exchanged for money.*
3. *Price is the specific value at which the product is exchanged. Thus, it is an exchange-value of product expressed in monetary form.*
4. *The price of product, according to marketer, indicates economic value of all the offers or benefits given by the seller to the buyers.*

5. *Price, according to consumer, is the perceived value of goods and services paid for the total (physical, economic, social, and psychological) satisfaction.*
6. *Price is the mechanism or device for translating perceived value of product into quantitative terms, i.e., in rupee and paisa.*

PRICING

Price is the economic value of the product while pricing describes the process to set that value. *Pricing is a process of setting the price for the product. It involves a series of steps to be followed to decide on price. Pricing is more relevant to marketing decisions than price.*

DIFFERENT VIEWS ON PRICE

Consumers and marketers (sellers) perceive the price for the product differently. Let's analyse their views:

Consumers' Views on Price

To consumers, price is a means for getting the product. They pay price for a number of expectations from the product. Price is perceived value of product that includes value of physical product plus other related benefits, like after-sales services, guarantee and warrantee, prestige of company, brand image, credit facility, installation, education, etc. According to them, the price is equal to all types of satisfactions or benefits derived from the product.

Marketers' Views on Price

According to marketers, price of the product is the value of total offerings. Price of the product includes cost of physical product, cost of promotion, cost of related services and brand image, and cost of distribution.

DIFFERENT NAMES OR WORDS USED FOR THE PRICE

The term 'price' indicates different things. Price is indicated differently for different type of products (goods and services). In short, for different types of exchange, different words/terms are used. Let us identify different names of price with reference to different products, such as:

1. Price of house/flat is rent.
2. Price of education is tuition.
3. Price of traveling by bus, train, plane or ship is fare.
4. Price of parking vehicle or passing through road/bridge is toll.
5. Price of insuring life or property is premium.
6. Price of services provided by doctors, chartered accountants, and other professionals is fees.
7. Price of workers is wage.
8. Price of employees is salary.
9. Price paid to guest/visiting lecturer is honorarium.
10. Price for privilege of making profit is tax or duties.
11. Price of services by public utilities is charges.
12. Price of salesman is commission.
13. Price of money is interest.
14. Price of illegal work is corruption or bribe.

PRICING OBJECTIVES

Pricing can be defined as the process of determining an appropriate price for the product, or it is an act of setting price for the product. Pricing involves a number of decisions related to setting price of product. Pricing policies are aimed at achieving various objectives. Company has several objectives to be achieved by the sound pricing policies and strategies. Pricing decisions are based on the objectives to be achieved. Objectives are related to sales volume, profitability, market shares, or competition. Objectives of pricing can be classified in five groups as shown in figure 1.

1. Profits-related Objectives

Profit has remained a dominant objective of business activities. Company's pricing policies and strategies are aimed at following profits-related objectives:

i. **Maximum Current Profit:** One of the objectives of pricing is to maximize current profits. This objective is aimed at making as much money as possible. Company tries to set its price in a way that more current profits can be earned. However, company cannot set its price beyond the limit. But, it concentrates on maximum profits.

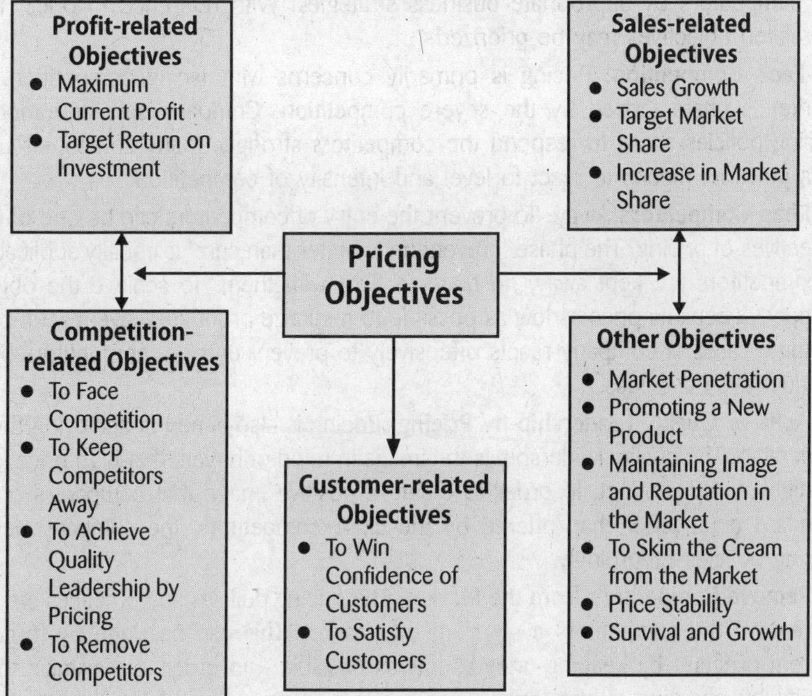

Figure 1: Pricing Objectives

ii. **Target Return on Investment:** Most companies want to earn reasonable rate of return on investment. Target return may be (1) fixed percentage of sales, (2) return on investment, or (3) a fixed rupee amount. Company sets its pricing policies and strategies in a way that sales revenue ultimately yields average return on total investment. For example, company decides to earn 20% return on total investment of 3 crore rupees. It must set price of product in a way that it can earn 60 lakh rupees.

2. Sales-related Objectives

The main sales-related objectives of pricing may include:

i. **Sales Growth:** Company's objective is to increase sales volume. It sets its price in such a way that more and more sales can be achieved. It is assumed that sales growth has direct positive impact on the profits. So, pricing decisions are taken in way that sales volume can be raised. Setting price, altering in price, and modifying pricing policies are targeted to improve sales.

ii. **Target Market Share:** A company aims its pricing policies at achieving or maintaining the target market share. Pricing decisions are taken in such a manner that enables the company to achieve targeted market share. Market share is a specific volume of sales determined in light of total sales in an industry. For example, company may try to achieve 25% market shares in the relevant industry.

iii. **Increase in Market Share:** Sometimes, price and pricing are taken as the tool to increase its market share. When company assumes that its market share is below than expected, it can raise it by appropriate pricing; pricing is aimed at improving market share.

3. Competition-related Objectives

Competition is a powerful factor affecting marketing performance. Every company tries to react to the competitors by appropriate business strategies. With reference to price, following competition-related objectives may be priorized:

i. **To Face Competition:** Pricing is primarily concerns with facing competition. Today's market is characterized by the severe competition. Company sets and modifies its pricing policies so as to respond the competitors strongly. Many companies use price as a powerful means to react to level and intensity of competition.

ii. **To Keep Competitors Away:** To prevent the entry of competitors can be one of the main objectives of pricing. The phase 'prevention is better than cure' is equally applicable here. If competitors are kept away, no need to fight with them. To achieve the objective, a company keeps its price as low as possible to minimize profit attractiveness of products. In some cases, a company reacts offensively to prevent entry of competitors by selling product even at a loss.

iii. **To Achieve Quality Leadership by Pricing:** Pricing is also aimed at achieving the quality leadership. The quality leadership is the image in mind of buyers that high price is related to high quality product. In order to create a positive image that company's product is standard or superior than offered by the close competitors, the company designs its pricing policies accordingly.

iv. **To Remove Competitors from the Market:** The pricing policies and practices are directed to remove the competitors away from the market. This can be done by forgoing the current profits – by keeping price as low as possible – in order to maximize the future profits by charging a high price after removing competitors from the market. Price competition can remove weak competitors.

4. Customer-related Objectives

Customers are in center of every marketing decision. Company wants to achieve following objectives by the suitable pricing policies and practices:

i. **To Win Confidence of Customers:** Customers are the target to serve. Company sets and practices its pricing policies to win the confidence of the target market. Company, by appropriate pricing policies, can establish, maintain or even strengthen the confidence of customers that price charged for the product is reasonable one. Customers are made feel that they are not being cheated.

ii. **To Satisfy Customers:** To satisfy customers is the prime objective of the entire range of marketing efforts. And, pricing is no exception. Company sets, adjusts, and readjusts its pricing to satisfy its target customers. In short, a company should design pricing in such a way that results into maximum consumer satisfaction.

5. Other Objectives

Over and above the objectives discussed so far, there are certain objectives that company wants to achieve by pricing. They are as under:

i. **Market Penetration:** This objective concerns with entering the deep into the market to attract maximum number of customers. This objective calls for charging the lowest possible price to win price-sensitive buyers.

ii. **Promoting a New Product:** To promote a new product successfully, the company sets low price for its products in the initial stage to encourage for trial and repeat buying. The sound pricing can help the company introduce a new product successfully.

iii. **Maintaining Image and Reputation in the Market:** Company's effective pricing policies have positive impact on its image and reputation in the market. Company, by charging reasonable price, stabilizing price, or keeping fixed price can create a good image and reputation in the mind of the target customers.

iv. **To Skim the Cream from the Market:** This objective concerns with skimming maximum profit in initial stage of product life cycle. Because a product is new, offering new and superior advantages, the company can charge relatively high price. Some segments will buy product even at a premium price.

v. **Price Stability:** Company with stable price is ranked high in the market. Company formulates pricing policies and strategies to eliminate seasonal and cyclical fluctuations. Stability in price has a good impression on the buyers. Frequent changes in pricing affect adversely the prestige of company.

vi. **Survival and Growth:** Finally, pricing is aimed at survival and growth of company's business activities and operations. It is a fundamental pricing objective. Pricing policies are set in a way that company's existence is not threatened.

FACTORS AFFECTING PRICING DECISIONS

An enormous number of factors affect pricing decisions. A marketing manager should identify and study the relevant factors affecting the pricing. Some factors are internal to organisation and, hence, controllable while other factors are external or environmental and are uncontrollable. Factors are also classified in terms of competition-related factors, market-related factors, product-related factors, and so forth. However, we will consider internal and external factors affecting pricing decisions. Due to these factors, price is set high or low, fixed or variable, and equal or discriminative. Figure 2 shows a list of internal and external factors. Let us analyse some of the main factors influencing pricing decisions.

INTERNAL FACTORS

Internal factors are internal to organisation and, hence, are controllable. These factors play vital role in pricing decisions. They are also known as organisational factors. Manager, who is responsible to set price and formulae pricing policies and strategies, is required to know adequately about these factors. Important internal factors have been discussed here:

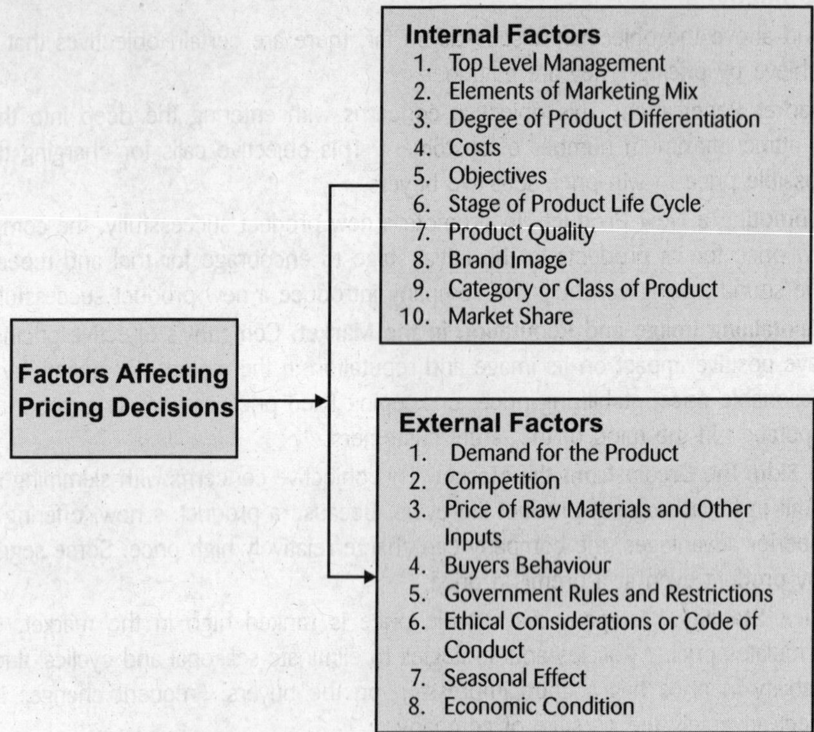

Figure 2: Factors affecting Pricing Decisions

1. Top Level Management

Top-level management has a full authority over the issues related to pricing. Marketing manager's role is administrative. The philosophy of top-level management is reflected in forms of pricing also. How does top management perceive the price? How far is pricing considered as a tool for earning profits, and what is importance of price for overall performance? In short, overall management philosophy and practice have a direct impact on pricing decision. Price of the product may be high or low; may be fixed or variable; or may be equal or discriminative depends on top-level management.

2. Elements of Marketing Mix

Price is one of the important elements of marketing mix. Therefore, it must be integrated to other elements (promotion, product, and distribution) of marketing mix. So, pricing decisions must be linked with these elements so as to consider the effect of price on promotion, product and distribution, and effect of these three elements on price. For example, high quality product should be sold at a high price. When a company spends heavily on advertising, sales promotion, personal selling and publicity, the selling costs will go up, and consequently, price of the product will be high. In the same way, high distribution costs are also reflected in forms of high selling price.

3. Degree of Product Differentiation

Product differentiation is an important guideline in pricing decisions. Product differentiation can be defined as the degree to which company's product is perceived different as against the products offered by the close competitors, or to what extent the product is superior to that of competitors' in terms of competitive advantages. The theory is, the higher the product differentiation, the more will be freedom to set the price, and the higher the price will be.

4. Costs

Costs and profits are two dominant factors having direct impact on selling price. Here, costs include product development costs, production costs, and marketing costs. It is very simple that costs and price have direct positive correlation. However, production and marketing costs are more important in determining price.

5. Objectives of Company

Company's objectives affect price of the product. Price is set in accordance with general and marketing objectives. Pricing policies must the company's objectives. There are many objectives, and price is set to achieve them. (For detail, see objectives).

6. Stages of Product Life Cycle

Each stage of product life cycle needs different marketing strategies, including pricing strategies. Pricing depends upon the stage in which company's product is passing through. Price is kept high or low, allowances or discounts are allowed or not, etc., depend on the stage of product life cycle.

7. Product Quality

Quality affects price level. Mostly, a high-quality-product is sold at a high price and vice versa. Customers are also ready to pay high price for a quality product.

8. Brand Image and Reputation in Market

Price doesn't include only costs and profits. Brand image and reputation of the company are also added in the value of product. Generally, the company with reputed and established brand charges high price for its products.

9. Category of Product

Over and above costs, profits, brand image, objectives and other variables, the product category must be considered. Product may be imitative, luxury, novel, perishable, fashionable, consumable, durable, etc. Similarly, product may be reflective of status, position, and prestige. Buyers pay price not only for the basic contents, but also for psychological and social implications.

10. Market Share

Market share is the desired proportion of sales a company wants to achieve from the total sales in an industry. Market share may be absolute or relative. Relative market share can be calculated with reference to close competitors. If company is not satisfied with the current market share, price may be reduced, discounts may be offered, or credit facility may be provided to attract more buyers.

EXTERNAL FACTORS

External factors are also known as environmental or uncontrollable factors. Compared to internal factors, they are more powerful. Pricing decisions should be taken after analysing following external factors:

1. Demand for the Product

Demand is the single most important factor affecting price of product and pricing policies. Demand creation or demand management is the prime task of marketing management. So, price is set at a level at which there is the desired impact on the product demand. Company must set price according to purchase capacity of its buyers. Here, there is reciprocal effect between demand and price, i.e., price affects demand and demand affects price level. However, demand is more powerful than price. So, marketer takes decision as per demand. Price is kept high when demand is high, and price is kept low when demand of the product is low. Price is constantly adjusted to create and/or maintain the expected level of demand.

2. Competition

A marketer has to work in a competitive situation. To face competitors, defeat them, or prevent their entry by effective marketing strategies is one of the basic objective organisation. Therefore, pricing decision is taken accordingly. A marketer formulates pricing policies and strategies to respond competitors, or, sometimes, to misguide competitors. When all the marketing decisions are taken with reference to competition, how can price be an exception? Sometimes, a company follows a strong competitor's pricing policies assuming that the leader is right. Price level, allowances, discount, credit facility, and other related decisions are largely imitated.

3. Price of Raw Materials and other Inputs

The price of raw materials and other inputs affect pricing decisions. Change in price of needed inputs has direct positive effect on the price of finished product. For example, if price of raw materials increases, company has to raise its selling price to offset increased costs.

4. Buyers Behaviour

It is essential to consider buyer behaviour while taking pricing decision. Marketer should analyse consumer behaviour to set effective pricing policies. Consumer behaviour includes the study of social, cultural, personal, and economic factors related to consumers. The key characteristics of consumers provide a clue to set an appropriate price for the product.

5. Government Rules and Restrictions

A company cannot set its pricing policies against rules and regulations prescribed by the governments. Governments have formulated at least 30 Acts to protect the interest of customers. Out of them, certain Acts are directly related to pricing aspects. Marketing manager must set pricing within limit of the legal framework to avoid unnecessary interference from the outside. Adequate knowledge of these legal provisions is considered to be very important for the manager.

6. Ethical Consideration or Codes of Conduct

Ethics play a vital role in price determination. Ethics may be said as moral values or ethical code that govern managerial actions. If a company wants to fulfill its social obligations and when it believes to work within limits of the ethics prescribed, it always charges reasonable price for its products. Moral values restrict managerial behaviour.

7. Seasonal Effect

Certain products have seasonal demand. In peak season, demand is high; while in slack season, demand reduces considerably. To balance the demand or to minimize the seasonal-demand fluctuations, the company changes its price level and pricing policies. For example, during a peak season, price may be kept high and vice versa. Discount, credit sales, and price allowances are important issues related to seasonal factor.

8. Economic Condition

This is an important factor affecting pricing decisions. Inflationary or deflationary condition, depression, recovery or prosperity condition influences the demand to a great extent. The overall health of economy has tremendous impact on price level and degree of variation in price of the product. For example, price is kept high during inflationary conditions. A manager should keep in mind the macro picture of economy while setting price for the product.

PRICING METHODS

Pricing method leads to a specific price. There are various methods used for setting price of the product. Some methods are cost-oriented while some are market-oriented. Each of the methods has its plus and minus points, and applicability. Marketing managers apply the appropriate method for setting the price. The appropriate method can be decided on the basis of the study and analysis of internal and external aspects as well as suitability of the method. Following part describes some widely used pricing methods. See Figure 3.

1. Mark-up Pricing Method

This is the most commonly used method. The method is also known as cost-plus pricing. In this method, a standard mark-up (or profit margin) is added to the product costs. This method is used in construction business, professions, and even for consumer goods. The method can be used only when company has necessary data about various costs and expected sales. Company may prefer fixed per cent of costs or fixed per cent of selling price. Let us illustrate the method:

XYZ Company Limited expects annual sales of 100000 units.

Variable cost per unit is ₹ 10.

Fixed cost is ₹ 500000.

Company wishes to earn 20 % mark-up on selling price, or 25% mark-up on costs.

∴ Cost per unit = variable costs + (Fixed costs/ Unit sales)
= ₹ 10 + ₹ 500000/100000
= ₹ 15

Now, company wants 20% mark-up on selling price,

Selling price = unit cost/ (1– desired mark-up)
= ₹ 15/ 0.8 = ₹ 18.75

Alternatively, suppose company wants 25% mark-up on unit cost,

∴ Selling price = unit costs + (15 × 25%)
= ₹ 15 + ₹ 3.75
= ₹ 18. 75.

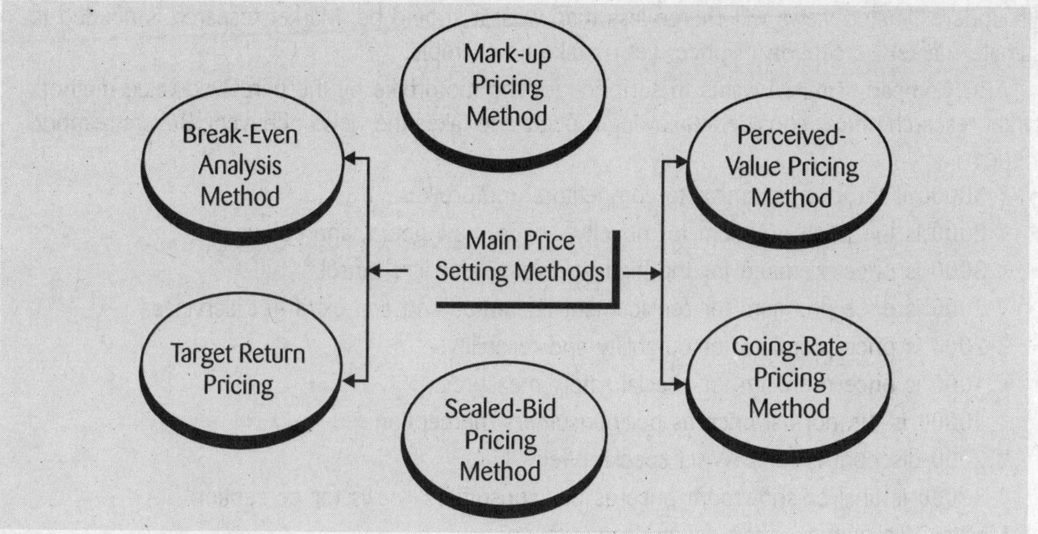

Figure 3: Price Setting Methods

Naturally, when cost is taken as a base, the rate should be high, as indicated in the example. Company may follow either of approaches, but must know the difference.

Merits: Keeping in mind a lot of forces affecting market, the mark-up rate may be kept high or low, fixed or variable. This method is widely used. It offers following merits:

i. It recovers costs as rapidly as possible.

ii. It is relatively a simple method to practice.
iii. If it is used by the entire industry, price tends to be similar. And, price competition can be minimized.
iv. Experts believe that cost-plus pricing method is fair for both – buyers and sellers.

Demerits: The method suffers from following limitations:

i. It ignores current demand.
ii. It ignores consumers' perception of price.
iii. It doesn't consider competition. (However, mark-up rate may be decided on the basis of competition).
iv. It is difficult to estimate exact sales.
v. The method is meaningful only if price of raw material and other inputs remain unchanged. Otherwise, the method may be misleading.

2. Perceived-value Pricing Method

Perceived-value pricing is a market-oriented method for setting the price. Here, price is based on the consumers' perceived value of the product. Consumers' views on price are given priority. Company takes consumers' perception of value as a key to set the price, and not its own cost and objectives. Company tries to measure the views of buyers regarding price of the product. Manager explains the cunsumers about total offers, including core product (key benefits and features), product-related aspects (like brand image, reputation, novelty, etc.), and product-related services (such as after-sales services like free installation, free home delivery, guarantee, etc.) and asks them to estimate price for that product or for total benefits offered by the product.

The key to the perceived-value pricing method is to measure accurately the market's perception of the offer's value. The seller with inflated views of his offers will overprice the product while with underestimated views will charge less than what it should be. Market research is needed to estimate market perception of price. Let us take an example,

ABC Company Limited wants to set price for the motorbike by the perceived-value method. Market research officer considers following aspects and takes the views of buyers. Buyers respond as under:

₹ 30000 if the bike is similar to competitors' motorbikes

₹ 2000 is the price premium for novelty, shape, new getup, and colour.

₹ 3000 is price premium for the highest milcage per litre petrol.

₹ 2000 is price premium for replacement guarantee and two extra free services.

₹ 2000 is price premium for durability and reliability.

₹ 1000 is price premium for special safety measures.

₹ 40000 is the normal price as per consumers' perception.

₹ 2000 discount is for DIWALI special offer.

₹ 38000 is final ex-showroom price as per consumers' views (or perception).

Merits: This method offers following merits:

i. Perceived-value method matches with consumer orientation.
ii. It considers indirectly competitors' offers.
iii. It is more realistic than any other method.
iv. Perceived-value can be taken as base, with little adjustment in costs and objectives, the most suitable price can be set.

Demerits: However, there are certain practical problems in setting price via this method. Main limitations include:

i. It is practically difficult to measure perception of the market. Unless relatively a large sample of consumers is contacted, views may be misleading.
ii. A lot depends on the person who estimates buyers' perception of price. Possibility of bias cannot be ignored.
iii. The method is based on the trust. If their response is not normal, it is a wasteful exercise.
iv. All the limitations of marketing research are equally applicable to this method.
v. It is, compared to the first method, difficult and complex to understand and apply.

3. Going-rate Pricing Method

This is also said as competitive parity method. Even, sometimes, it is called as competition-oriented pricing. The method is, normally, followed by small firms, said as 'the followers.' In going-rate pricing method, the company gives less attention to its own costs, objectives, or product demand. But, pricing decision is largely based on competitors' prices. The company may charge the same, more, or less than major competitors. The notion is "follow the leader," or "leader is right." One must note that company doesn't select a price, which is far below or much higher than the real. However, competitors' pricing is taken as a base. And, final price may be set slight high or low depending upon objectives, qualities of product, and services offered.

Merits: The method can be justified on the following grounds:

i. It is the only way to set the price when costs are difficult to measure and competitors' response is uncertain.
ii. It considers competitors pricing policies as a base. In contemporary marketing practices, it is more relevant method.
iii. Going rate pricing brings uniform pricing in the industry. It ensures fair return to sellers and harmony in industry.
iv. It may protect consumers' from cheating and misguiding. They can buy the similar product at a, more or less, same price.

Demerits: Going-rate pricing method has been criticized as under:

i. This is not an ideal method for pricing because it is one-sided, i.e., only competition factor is considered.
ii. Company's objectives, costs, qualities, services, and consumers' perception of value have been ignored.
iii. It is senseless to follow blindly the leaders or strong competitors as every firm has its special problems, opportunities, situations, and capabilities.
iv. Temporary pricing of competitors may lead to erroneous decision.

4. Sealed-bid Pricing Method

Sealed-bid pricing is followed in construction or contract business. It is also a competitive pricing method. Here, price is selected on the basis of sealed bids (quotation or estimated price) for the jobs. The firm sets its price on expectations of how competitors will price the product. The firm wants to win the contract requires submitting the lower price than competitors. However, costs and profits are not totally ignored. The firm cannot set price below the costs.

It is called as tender pricing also. In response to the proposal of jobs or works, interested parties (businessmen or marketers) have to fill the tender (send quotation or estimated costs) stating price and conditions of work and send in forms of sealed-bids. The bid is an offer of price for particular work or product. Generally sealed-bids (sealed envelops containing a bid) are invited for a competitive work. Offers or proposals come from charitable trusts, companies, organisations, or governments. In our country, we say this method as "tender," and proposal of jobs as a "tender notice." Mostly, the tender notice is published in newspapers or circulars. The offer or proposal for work contains type of work or job, time to complete the work, quality of work, and other similar conditions. In response to the tender or proposal, interested parties have to send sealed-bids stating their prices and conditions within the permitted time. In this method, the party inviting the sealed-bids is customer and those who bid by sealed quotations are the marketers (because they will serve the inviting party).

On a due date – either publicly or otherwise – the sealed-bids (or quotations) are opened, and the bid with lower price and more favourable conditions is selected. Rate of selected bid is the price for the job. The selected bid is given the business. The method has its plus and minus points.

5. Target Return Pricing

This is one of the cost-oriented methods for setting price of the product. Here, the firm determines that level of price at which it can yield the target return on investment. Here, return on investment is taken as a base for price determination. Attempts are made to recover the cost of investment. Mostly, government Companies, public utilities, cooperative societies, and the similar organisations fix pricing for their products on this basis to ensure minimum return on investment.

For example, Jai Hind Private Limited company expects to sell 10000 school bags of premium quality in the current year. Fixed costs allocated to this line is ₹ 5,00000. Variable costs estimated for each bag is ₹ 100. Total investment (covering development, production and marketing) on this line is ₹ 50,00000. Company wants 20% return on investment.

Return on Investment (ROI) = ₹ 5000000 x 20% = ₹ 1000000

Costs per unit = variable cost per unit + fixed cost per unit

= ₹ 100 + (₹ 500000 ÷ 10000 units)

= ₹ 100+ ₹ 50 = ₹ 150.

Target return (profit) per unit = ₹ 1000000 ÷ 10000 units = ₹ 100.

Selling price per unit = cost of product + Return on Investment.

= ₹ 150 + 100

= ₹ 250.

If company wants to earn 20% ROI (Return on Investment), the selling price should be ₹ 250. If RIO is more, definitely selling price will go up and vice versa.

This method can be used only when company is capable of estimating accurately the sales, variable costs, and fixed costs. The price so determined will be meaningful only if the company can achieve expected sales. Here, we assume that company might have estimated sales keeping in mind quality of product on one hand, and competition on the other hand.

6. Break-even Analysis Method

Some companies set the price for their products by Break-Even Analysis (BEP method). It is a managerial tool that establishes relationship among costs, volume of sales, and profits. It is also known as cost-volume-profit analysis. It involves developing tables and/or charts that help a company to determine at what level of sales, the revenue will be equal to the total costs. Under this method, attempts are made to find out volume of sales at which total costs are just equal to the sales revenue. This is such a level of sales at which there is no profit, no loss.

Sales Revenue = Total Costs.

This level is called BEP (break-even point), at which the firm has neither profits nor losses. The firm just covers its total costs. When sales revenue exceeds the total costs, the result is profit; and when sales revenue is less than total costs, the result is loss. Thus, BEP is the position of sales at which sales revenue is just equal to total costs. BEP can be calculated either by a formula or by a chart.

Formula Method: BEP can be calculated using formula as under:

For example,

Hindustan Products Pvt. Ltd. gives following details:

Selling price is = ₹ 200 per unit.

Variable cost is = ₹ 100 per unit.

Fixed cost is = ₹ 500000.

Contribution is = selling price – variable costs

= (₹ 200 – ₹ 100) = ₹ 100

Let's calculate BEP by using the Formula

BEP = Fixed Cost ÷ Contribution

= ₹ 500000 ÷ ₹ 100

= 5000 units.

Or

Sales Revenue is (5000 units x ₹ 200) ₹ 1000000.

If the company achieves sales of 5000 units, there is no profit, no loss position. Pricing is the decisive or critical factor in the break-even analysis. An increase in selling price enables the firm to reach break-even point much rapidly, that is, at less sales volume; and, lowering price needs to achieve more sales volume, assuming costs will be equal.

Based on ability of the firm to achieve sales, the price is set accordingly. By trial and error method, a table can be prepared with different level of price to see how much sales a company must achieve to offset costs against sales revenue. And, suitable price can be picked up.

Graphic Method: By trial and error method, a table can be prepared to find out the break-even point and can be presented graphically, the same result can be arrived at. We may take different level of sales at fixed price to find out break-even point.

BEP is essentially a tool for mark-up or cost-plus pricing. It can be said as an extension of mark-up pricing method. Here, it is assumed that sales will remain stable at different level of the selling price. (This is hardly possible). Similarly, fixed and variable costs remain unchanged. This method is used only when data on sales, costs, etc., are accurately available. While estimating sales, apart from the BEP at particular price, market forces should also be considered. But, all depends on the estimates. It is a useful tool. However, for setting price of the product, it should be used with care and caution. It may be used along with other price setting methods.

PRICING POLICIES

Pricing policies can be formulated on the basis of the price determined by any of the methods. Pricing policies are the general guideline for a manager to administer the pricing. The manager can take pricing decisions within the broad framework of pricing policies. He can adjust with pricing level as per contemporary situations, internal and external to organisation. Price determined is treated as a base to formulate appropriate pricing policies. Final price is adjusted or selected in relation to pricing policies. Following are alternative pricing policies:

1. Skimming pricing policy
2. Odd pricing policies
3. Every day low pricing policy

4. Penetration pricing policies
5. Psychological pricing policy
6. Brand image pricing policy
7. Market minus pricing policy
8. Price discrimination and pricing or fixed v/s variable pricing policy
9. RPM–Retailed Price Maintenance
10. Pricing policies, and discounts and allowances
11. Credit v/s cash pricing policy
12. Seasonal effects and pricing policy
13. Other elements of marketing mix and pricing policy
14. Pricing policies and geographical locations, etc.

EXERCISES

MULTIPLE CHOICE QUESTIONS (MCQs)

1. Which one is inconsistent?
   a. Price for professional services is called commission.
   b. Price for house is called rent.
   c. Price for money is called interest.
   d. Price for traveling through bus, rail or plane is called fare.
2. Which is a wrong statement?
   a. Price is exchange value of product expressed in form of money.
   b. Price is agreement between buyer and sellers at which a product is exchanged for money.
   c. Price is profit margin of the company.
   d. Price is perceived value of product paid for total satisfaction.
3. To increase market share is
   a. profit-related objective b. sales-related objective
   c. customer-related objective d. competition-related objective
4. Which is customer-related objective?
   a. To win confidence of customers. b. To increase sales.
   c. To earn target return on investment. d. To keep competitors away.
5. Which is an external factor affecting pricing decisions?
   a. Degree of product differentiation b. Product quality
   c. Buyer behaviour d. Brand image
6. Which is not an internal factor?
   a. Stage of product life cycle b. Top management philosophy
   c. Company objectives d. Competition
7. Name the price setting method in which there are more sellers than buyers.
   a. Sealed-bid pricing method b. Perceived value pricing method
   c. Mark-up pricing method d. Break-even analysis method
8. The price setting method that give more emphasis on consumes' views on price is known as
   a. Mark-up pricing method b. Going rate pricing method
   c. Perceived value pricing method d. Target return pricing method

MATCHING TYPE QUESTIONS (MTQs)

9.

List I	List II
(a) Price of Education	(1) Wage
(b) Price of workers	(2) Tuition Fee
(c) Prices of money	(3) Premium
(d) Price of ensuring life and property	(4) Interest

Codes: (A) (a)-(2), (b)-(1), (c)-(4), (d)-(3) (B) (a)-(3), (b)-(2), (c)-(1), (d)-(4)
(C) (a)-(4), (b)-(3), (c)-(2), (d)-(1) (D) (a)-(1), (b)-(4), (c)-(3), (d)-(2)

10.

List I	List II
(a) To keeps competitors away	(1) Sales-related pricing objectives
(b) To earn target return on investment	(2) Customer-related objective
(c) To win confidence of customers	(3) Profit-related pricing objective
(d) To achieve target market share	(4) Competition-related objective

Codes: (A) (a)-(2), (b)-(1), (c)-(4), (d)-(3) (B) (a)-(3), (b)-(2), (c)-(1), (d)-(4)
(C) (a)-(4), (b)-(3), (c)-(2), (d)-(1) (D) (a)-(1), (b)-(4), (c)-(3), (d)-(2)

11.

List I	List II
(a) The method based on cost and profit margin	(1) Mark-up pricing
(b) The method based on consumer opinion	(2) Target return pricing
(c) The method based on competition	(3) Going-rate pricing
(d) The method based on return on investment	(4) Perceived-value pricing

Codes: (A) (a)-(2), (b)-(1), (c)-(4), (d)-(3) (B) (a)-(3), (b)-(2), (c)-(1), (d)-(4)
(C) (a)-(4), (b)-(3), (c)-(2), (d)-(1) (D) (a)-(1), (b)-(4), (c)-(3), (d)-(2)

ANSWERS KEY: 1(a), 2(c), 3(b), 4(a), 5(c), 6(d), 7(a), 8(c), 9(A), 10(B), 11(D)

QUESTIONS FOR DISCUSSION

12. What is price? State different names of price in relation to different products. Why is pricing decision very significant?
13. Define price and pricing. Discuss pricing objectives.
14. "Pricing decision is very critical. Marketing manager has to take into account a large number of factors." Discuss the statement in relation to factors affecting pricing decisions.
15. Discuss internal and external factors affecting pricing decisions
16. Write explanatory note on various price setting methods.
17. Explain with example:
    a. Cost-plus pricing method
    b. Perceived-value pricing method
    c. Break-even pricing method

✧✧✧

CHAPTER

7

MARKET PROMOTION MIX

- Introduction
- Definition of Market Promotion
- Objective of Market Promotion
- Market Promotion mix – Definitions and Brief Idea of Elements
- Factors Affecting Market Promotion Mix.

INTRODUCTION

Promotion constitutes the third 'P' of marketing mix. It is also called as market communication. It involves providing necessary information to the target market. In today's competitive marketing environment, market promotion is not only useful but also indispensable. If adequate promotional efforts are not made, a company cannot grow and survive in a dynamic and competitive situation. Obviously, people buy the product if they think it is superior. Marketer has to communicate with the target market the competitive advantages of his product. The firm has to supply information about product qualities, features, benefits, availability, price, and so forth to enable customers buy the product. Again, due to centralised production and decentralised market, market promotion has become an inevitable activity. It happens that people do not buy the product simply because they do not know. So, marketers are increasingly engaged in market promotion activities. A large amount of money is spared for the purpose. It can be said that success and failure of the product, to a large extent, depends on how it is promoted.

DEFINITIONS OF MARKET PROMOTION

Term 'market promotion' – often refers as market communication – has been defined as under:

1. *Market promotion includes a set of efforts made by the manager to stimulate demand for the product without changing product mix, price, and distribution system. Market promotion is combination of advertising, sales promotion, personal selling (salesmanship), and publicity and public relations efforts.*
2. *Market promotion is basically a market communication process directed to stimulate demand for the products.*
3. **William Stanton:** "Promotion is the element of an organisation's marketing mix that is used to inform and persuade the market regarding the organisation's products and services."
4. **Alderson and Paul Green:** "Promotion is any marketing effort whose function is to inform or persuade actual or potential consumers about the merits of a product or service for the purpose of introducing a consumer either to continue or to start purchasing the firm's product or service at the same (given) price."

5. **Brink and Kelly:** "The coordination of all seller-initiated efforts to set up channel of information and persuasion to facilitate the sale of a product or service, or the acceptance of an idea."

OBJECTIVES OF MARKET PROMOTION

Market promotion is an integral part of marketing strategy. It is a powerful weapon used excessively by today's' marketers to achieve marketing goals in a competitive environment. Market promotion is essentially a way to communicate with the target market. Since the modern market is characterized by over-informed consumers, over-flooded products, cut-throat competition, and rapid changes, the market promotion has a crucial role to play. In nutshell, main objectives of market promotion can be described with reference to below stated points:

1. To Stimulate Demand

It is the primary objective of market promotion. Through the use of appropriate means of market promotion, such as advertising, sales promotion, personal selling, and so forth, the company can stimulate demand for the product. Market promotion efforts convert potential buyers into actual buyers. Company, by highlighting product benefits, tries to match the product with needs, wants, and expectations of buyers. As per need, various means of market promotion are used to establish the information link with the target customers.

2. To Inform Consumers

Promotion is aimed at informing consumers about features, qualities, performance, price, and availability of firm's products. Market promotion is also a valuable means to inform consumers the changes made in the existing products and introduction of new products. In the same way, market promotion, by various tools of market communication, is used for communicating the special offers, price concession, utility of products, and incentives offered by the company.

3. To Persuade Consumers

Market promotion is an effective way to persuade consumers the superiority of product over competitors. A firm can communicate competitive advantages the product offers to distinguish it from competitors' products. Obviously, market promotion can assist the firm to convince buyers that the firm's product is the best solution to their unmet needs and wants. Advertising is one of the most effective tools to distinguish the product from competitors' products.

4. To Promote a New Product

In a large and decentralised market, market promotion is an inevitable medium to promote a new product. By suitable promotional strategies, a company can successfully introduce a new product in the market as against existing products. Company can inform about availability, distinct features, and price of newly launched product. In every stage of consumer adoption of a new product, market promotion has critical role to play.

5. To Face Competition

Market promotion enables the firm to face competition effectively. In today's market situation, it is difficult to stand without the suitable promotional efforts. In short, it can be said that marketer can fight with competitors effectively, can prevent their entry, or can throw the competitor away from the market by formulating and implementing effective market promotion strategies.

6. To Create or Improve Image

Advertising, personal selling, and publicity and public relations – all promotional tools – are capable to create or improve image and reputation of the firm. Many companies have become popular in the market due to effective market promotion. Company can reach the customers at every corner of the world through market promotion. Brand image is purely an outcome of promotional efforts. For example, Hindustan Unilever, Colgate Palmolive, Sony, Philips, Hero Honda,

Ambuja Cement, and many national and multinational companies have made their permanent place in the market due to successfully launching of market promotion programmes.

Thus, market promotion can help company realize various objectives. Company can increase sales, improve its image, and maintain close and live contact with the market by suitable promotional efforts. A company's survival, growth, and development are based on how effectively it communicates with the market.

PROMOTION MIX

INTRODUCTION

Market promotion is one of the important decisions in marketing management. Market promotion is not only aimed at increasing the sales, but it is a multipurpose tool. Today's marketing managers undertake promotional efforts to increase sales with consumer satisfaction. Company's market promotion efforts include a large number of activities. Basically, market promotion involves four types of efforts like advertising, sales promotion, personal selling, and publicity (including public relations). A compose of these elements is popularly referred as promotion mix. Thus, promotion mix is a set of promotional efforts.

DEFINITIONS

Let's examine some definitions:

1. Promotion mix can be defined as: *Promotion mix is a combination of various elements of market promotion like advertising, sales promotion, personal selling, and publicity directed to promote the sales of the product.*
2. Likewise, we can say: *A set of promotional tools used by a manager to stimulate market demand for the product is known as promotional mix.*
3. More clearly, it can be defined as: *Promotional mix involves various promotional tools, such as advertising, sales promotion, personal selling, and publicity, to promote the sales of the company's products.*

ELEMENTS OF PROMOTION MIX

Elements of promotional mix are also called as tools, means, or components. Basically, there are five elements involved in promotional mix. Some authors have considered more elements, too. However, we will consider five elements as shown in Figure 1.

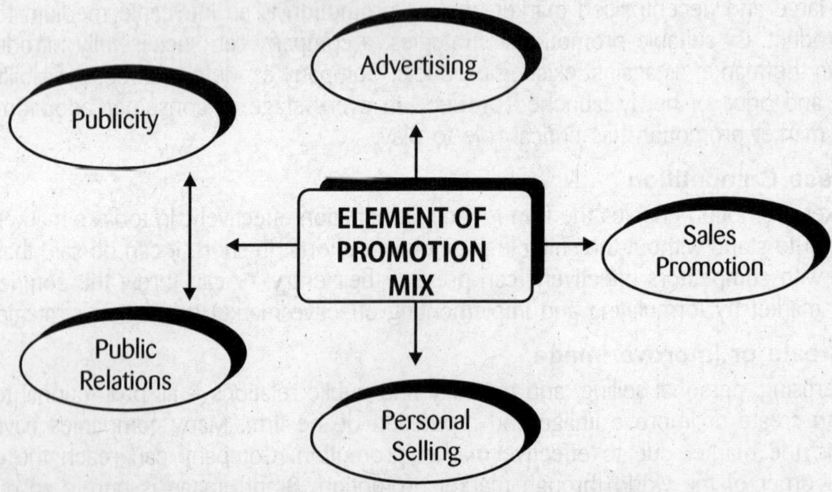

Figure 1: Elements of Market Promotion Mix

1. Advertising

Advertising is defined as any paid form of non-personal presentation and promotion of ideas, goods, and services by an identified sponsor. It is a way of mass communication. It is the most popular and widely practiced tool of market promotion. Major part of promotional budget is consumed for advertising alone. Various advertising media – television, radio, newspapers, magazines, outdoor means and so forth – are used for advertising the product. Characteristics of advertising are as follow:

i. Adverting is non-personal or mass communication. Personal contact is not possible.
ii. It is a paid form of communication.
iii. It is a one-way communication.
iv. Identifiable entity/sponsor–company or person gives advertising.
v. It is costly option to promote the sales.
vi. It can be reproduced frequently as per need.
vii. Per contact cost is the lowest.
viii. Various audio-visual, print, and outdoor media can be used for advertising purpose.
ix. It is a widely used and highly popular tool of market promotion.

2. Sales Promotion

Sales promotion covers those marketing activities other than advertising, publicity, and personal selling that stimulate consumer purchasing and dealer effectiveness. Sales promotion mainly involves short-term and non-routine incentives, offered to dealers as well consumers. The popular methods used for sales promotion are demonstration, trade show, exhibition, exchange offer, seasonal discount, free service, gifts, contests, etc. Characteristics of sales promotion are as follows:

i. The primary purpose of sales promotion is to induce customers for immediate buying or dealer effectiveness or both.
ii. Excessive use of sale promotion may affect sales and reputation of a company adversely.
iii. It is taken as supplementary to advertising and personal selling efforts.
iv. It involves all the promotional efforts other than advertising, personal selling, and publicity.
v. It consists of short-term incentives, schemes, or plans offered to buyers, salesmen, and/or dealers.
vi. It involves non-routine selling efforts.

3. Personal Selling

Personal selling includes face-to-face personal communication and presentation with prospects (potential and actual customers) for the purpose of selling the products. It involves personal conversation and presentation of products with customers. It is considered as a highly effective and costly tool of market promotion. Characteristics of personal have been listed below:

i. Personal selling is an oral, face-to-face, and personal presentation with consumers.
ii. Basic purpose is to promote products or increase sales.
iii. It involves two-way communication.
iv. Immediate feedback can be measured.
v. It is an ability of salesmen to persuade or influence buyers.
vi. It is more flexible way of market communication.
vii. Per contact cost is higher than advertising.
viii. It involves teaching, educating, and assisting people to buy.

4. Publicity

Publicity is also a way of mass communication. It is not a paid form of mass communication that involves getting favourable response of buyers by placing commercially significant news in mass media. **William J. Stanton defines**: "Publicity is any promotional communication regarding an organisation and/or its products where the message is not paid for by the organisation benefiting from it."

It is the traditional form of public relations. Publicity is not paid for by the organisation. Publicity comes from reporters, columnists, and journalists. It can be considered as a part of public relations. Publicity involves giving public speeches, giving interviews, conducting seminars, charitable donations, inauguration by film actor, cricketer, politician or popular personalities, stage show, etc., that attract mass media to publish the news about them. Main characteristic of publicity include:

i. Publicity involves obtaining favourable presentation about company or company's offers upon radio, television, or stage that is not paid for by the sponsor.
ii. It is a non-paid form of market promotion. However, several indirect costs are involved in publicity.
iii. It may include promotion of new product, pollution control efforts, special achievements of employees, publicizing new policies, etc., for increasing sales. It is primarily concerns with publishing or highlighting company's activities and products. It is targeted to build company's image.
iv. Mostly, publicity can be carried via newspapers, magazines, radio or television.
v. Company has no control over publicity in terms of message, time, frequency, information, and medium.
vi. It has a high degree of credibility. Publicity message is more likely to be read and reacted by audience.
vii. Publicity can be done at a much lower cost than advertising. Company needs to spend a little amount to get the event or activity publicized.
viii. Frequency or repetition of publicity in mass media depends upon its social significance or the values for news. Mostly, it appears only once.

5. Public Relations

The public relations is comprehensive term that includes maintaining constructive relations not only with customers, suppliers, and middlemen, but also with a large set of interested publics. Note that public relations include publicity, i.e., publicity is the part of public relations.

William Stanton defines: "Public relations activities typically are designed to build or maintain a favourable image for an organisation and a favourable relationship with the organisation's various publics. These publics may be customers, stockholders, employees, unions, environmentalists, the government, and people in local community, or some other groups in society." Thus, public relations includes organisation's broad and overall communication efforts intended to influence various groups' attitudes toward the organisation. Some experts have stated that the public relations are an extension of publicity. Main characteristic of publicity are as under:

i. Public relations is a paid form of market promotion. Company has to incur expenses.
ii. Public relations activities are designed to build and maintain a favourable image for an organisation and a favourable relationship with the organisation's various publics.
iii. It is an integral part of managerial function. Many companies operate a special department for the purpose, known as the public relations department.

iv. It involves a number of interactions, such as contacting, inviting, informing, clarifying, responding, interpreting, dealing, transacting, and so forth.

v. Public relations covers a number of publics – formal and informal groups. These publics may be customers, stockholders, employees, unions, environmentalists, the government, people of local community, or some other groups in society.

vi. Public relations activities are undertaken continuously. It is a part of routine activities.

vii. All the officials, from top level to supervisory level, perform public relations activities.

viii. In relation to modern management practices, the public relations is treated as the profession.

Thus, there are five major elements or promotion mix. Each tool/element has its advantages, limitations, and applicability. Depending upon company's internal and external situations, one or more tools are used. Mostly, company's promotional programme involves more elements, each element supplements others.

FACTORS AFFECTING PROMOTION MIX

Promotion mix is an important element of marketing mix. It involves various tools to inform, persuade, or attract consumers. The tools are primarily used to increase sales, face competition, and build brand image. As stated in the former part, there are five elements of promotion mix. Some writers have considered only four, such as advertising, sales promotion, personal selling and publicly. The important issues are: (1) how much to spend for promotion, (2) which tools are to be selected, (3) how to distribute the fund among various promotion tools, and (4) how long each of them are to carried on. These decisions depend on a large number of factors. Main factors influencing promotion mix has been briefly discussed as under:

1. Type of Product

Type of product play an important role in deciding on promotion mix. Product can be categorized in terms of branded products, non-branded products, necessity products, luxury products, new products, etc. All these types of products need different promotional tools. For example, advertising is suitable for the branded and popular products. Personal selling may be fit for non-branded products. Advertising, personal selling, sales promotion and publicity – all four tools – are used for a newly launched product to get a rapid consumer acceptance.

2. Use of Product

Product may be industrial product, consumable and necessity product, or may be luxurious product that affects selection of promotion tools and media. For example, advertising and sales promotion techniques are widely used for consumer goods while personal selling is used for industrial goods.

3. Complexity of Product

Product complexity affects selection of promotional tools. Personal selling is more effective for complex, technical, risky, and newly developed products as they need personal explanation and observation. On the other end, advertising is more suitable for simple and easy-handled products.

4. Purchase Quantity and Frequency

Company should also consider purchase frequency and purchase quantity while deciding on promotion mix. Generally, for frequently purchase product, advertising is used, and for infrequently purchase product, personal selling and sales promotion are preferred. Personal selling and advertising are used for heavy users and light users respectively.

5. Fund Available for Market Promotion

Financial capacity of company is a vital factor affecting promotion mix. Advertising through television, radio, newspapers and magazines is too costly to bear by financially poor companies while personal selling and sales promotion are comparatively cheaper tools. Even, the company may opt for publicity by highlighting certain commercially significant events.

6. Type of Market

Type of market or consumer characteristics determine the form of promotion mix. Education, location, income, personality characteristics, knowledge, bargaining capacity, profession, age, sex, etc., are the important factors that affect company's promotion strategy.

7. Size of Market

Naturally, in case of a limited market, personal selling is more effective. When market is wide with a large number of buyers, advertising is preferable. Place is also an important issue. Type of message, language of message, type of sales promotion tools, etc., depend on geographical areas.

8. Stage of Product Life Cycle

Product passes through four stages of its life cycle. Each stage poses different threats and opportunities. Each stage needs separate marketing strategies. Each of the promotional tools has got different degree of suitability with stages of product life cycle. It can be concluded that, in normal situations, (1) advertising, personal selling, and, even, sales promotion are used during the introduction stage. However, advertising is given more priority, (2) more intensive advertising and sales promotional techniques are used during the second stage, (3) more rigorous advertising along with personal selling are followed in the third stage, and (4) company prefers to curb the expenses in forth stage, and promotional efforts are reduced.

9. Level of Competition

Promotional efforts are designed according to type and intensity of competition. All promotional tools are aimed at protecting company's interest against competition. Level of promotional efforts and selection of promotional tools depend on level of competition.

10. Promotional Objectives

It is the prime factor affecting promotional mix. Different objectives can be achieved by using different tools of promotional mix. If company's objective is to inform a large number of buyers, advertising is advisable. If company wants to convince limited consumers, it may go for personal selling. Even, when company wants to influence buyers during specific season or occasion, the sales promotion can be used. Some companies use publicity to create or improve brand image and goodwill in the market.

11. Other Factors

Over and above these factors, there are certain minor factors that affect promotion mix. These factors may include:

i. Price of Product
ii. Type of Marketing Channel
iii. Degree of Product Differentiation
iv. Desire for Market Penetration, etc.

The list of factors stated above is not complete. There may be more factors. Promotional strategy should be formulated only after considering the relevant factors. Marketing manager must be aware of these variables. Note that these factors affect different firms in varying degree depending upon its internal and external marketing environment.

EXERCISES

MULTIPLE CHOICE QUESTIONS (MCQs)

1. Which marketing mix element is also called market communication?
   a. Product mix b. Promotion mix
   c. Price mix d. Place mix
2. Public relations is closely related with
   a. advertising b. publicity
   c. sales promotion d. personal selling
3. Which one of market promotion elements does involve offering short-term incentives to consumers, dealers, and salesmen?
   a. Sales promotion b. Personal selling
   c. Market promotion d. Publicity
4. Which one is not true?
   a. Advertising is the most expensive, prestigious, and effective promotional tool.
   b. As against personal selling, per contact cost in advertising is extremely low.
   c. Sales promotion doesn't have any positive impact on advertising and personal selling.
   d. Publicity is non-paid form of market promotion.
5. In relation to factors affecting promotion mix decisions, which one is not consistent?
   a. Political stability b. Type of product
   c. Size of market d. Stage of product life cycle
6. Which one is not the valid objective of market promotion for companies manufacturing consumer goods?
   a. To stimulate demand b. To inform consumers
   c. To face competition d. To entertain public
7. Which two elements of market promotion are closely related?
   a. Advertising and personal selling b. Personal selling and sales promotion
   c. Publicity and public relations d. Sales promotion and publicity
8. Find out the correct statement.
   a. Market promotion is part of sales promotion
   b. Market promotion and sales promotion are same.
   c. Publicity is more creditable and is not paid for by the firm.
   d. Public relations can be said as the part of publicity.

MATCHING TYPE QUESTIONS (MTQs)

9.

List I	List II
(a) Advertising	(1) Establishing long-term relations with publics
(b) Personal Selling	(2) Short-term and temporary incentives to buyers
(c) Sales Promotion	(3) Personal and face-to-face conversation with buyer
(d) Public Relations	(4) Non-personal mass communication

Codes: (A) (a)-(2), (b)-(1), (c)-(4), (d)-(3) (B) (a)-(3), (b)-(2), (c)-(1), (d)-(4)
(C) (a)-(4), (b)-(3), (c)-(2), (d)-(1) (D) (a)-(1), (b)-(4), (c)-(3), (d)-(2)

10.

	List I		List II
(a)	It is cost-free option	(1)	Personal selling
(b)	Highest per contact cost	(2)	Publicity
(c)	Lowest per contact cost	(3)	Public Relations
(d)	It is the task of PRO	(4)	Advertising

Codes: (A) (a)-(2), (b)-(1), (c)-(4), (d)-(3) (B) (a)-(3), (b)-(2), (c)-(1), (d)-(4)
(C) (a)-(4), (b)-(3), (c)-(2), (d)-(1) (D) (a)-(1), (b)-(4), (c)-(3), (d)-(2)

ANSWERS KEY: 1(b), 2(b), 3(a), 4(c), 5(a), 6(d), 7(c), 8(c), 9(C), 10(A)

QUESTIONS FOR DISCUSSION

11. What is market promotion? Explain its objectives.
12. Explain meaning of promotion mix and discuss its objectives.
13. What is market promotion? Describe its various elements briefly.
14. Write an explanatory note on elements of promotion mix.
15. Explain term 'promotion mix' and explain its main constituents/elements.
16. What is promotion mix? Discuss various factors affecting promotion mix decisions.

CHAPTER

7.1 ADVERTISING

INTRODUCTION

The world has become a global market. Modern market is more dynamic, competitive, and consumer-oriented. Entire marketing process is aimed at satisfying consumers more effectively than competitors. Consumer satisfaction can be achieved by receiving information from market and sending information to the market. In order to inform, attract, and convince the valued customers, a marketer undertakes a number of promotional means. Advertising is one of the powerful means to inform about company's total offers. Advertising is a dominant element of market promotion. Many times, the entire promotional efforts are replaced by advertising alone. Major portion of promotion budget is consumed by advertising alone. Advertising is so powerful and popular that it is taken as equal to marketing!! Mass media are used intensively to advertise various products. Marketing without advertising seems to be impossible. Advertising works like a magic stick to actualize marketing goals!!

DEFINITIONS OF ADVERTISING

1. We can define term 'advertising' as: *Advertising is a paid form of mass communication that consists of the special message sent by the specific person (advertiser or company), for the specific group of people (listeners, readers, or viewers), for the specific period of time, in the specific manner to achieve the specific goals.*
2. More clearly, advertising can be defined as: *Advertising includes oral, written, or audio-visual message addressed to the people for the purpose of informing and influencing them to buy the products or to act favourably toward idea or institution.*

3. **Philip Kotler:** "Advertising is any paid form of non-personal presentation and promotion of goods, services, or ideas by an identified sponsor."
4. **Frank Presbrey:** "Advertising is a printed, written, oral and illustrated art of selling. Its objective is to encourage sales of the advertiser's products and to cerate in the mind of people, individually or collectively, an impression in favour of the advertiser's interest."
5. **William Stanton:** "Advertising consists of all activities involved in presenting to a group a non-personal, oral or visual, openly sponsored identified message regarding a product, service, or idea. The message, called an advertisement, is disseminated through one or more media and is paid for by the identified sponsor."

CHARACTERISTICS OF ADVERTISING

Above stated definitions reveal following features:

1. Tool for Market Promotion

There are various tools used for market communication, such as advertising, sales promotion, personal selling, and publicity. Advertising is a powerful, expensive, and popular element of promotion mix

2. Non-personal

Advertising is a type of non-personal or mass communication with the target audience. A large number of people are addressed at time. It is called as non-personal salesmanship.

3. Paid Form

Advertising is not free of costs. Advertiser, called as sponsor, has to spend money for preparing message, buying media, and monitoring advertising efforts. It is the costliest option of market promotion. Company has to prepare its advertising budget to appropriate advertising costs.

4. Wide Applicability

Advertising is a popular and widely used means for communicating with the target market. It is not used only for business and profession, but is widely used by museums, charitable trusts, government agencies, educational institutions, and others to inform and attract various target publics.

5. Varied Objectives

Advertising is aimed at achieving various objectives. It is targeted to increase sales, create and improve brand image, face competition, build relations with publics, or to educate people.

6. Forms of Advertising

Advertising message can be expressed in written, oral, audible, or visual forms. Mostly, message is expressed in a joint form, such as oral-visual, audio-visual, etc.

7. Use of Media

Advertiser can use any of the several advertising media to convey the message. Widely used media are print media (newspapers, magazines, pamphlets, booklets, letters, etc.), outdoor media (hoardings, sign boards, wall-printing, vehicle, banners, etc.), audio-visual media (radio, television, film, Internet, etc.), or any other to address the target audience.

8. Advertising as an Art

Today's advertising task is much complicated. Message creation and presentation require a good deal of knowledge, creativity, skills, and experience. So, advertising can be said as an art. It is an artful activity.

9. Element of Truth

It is difficult to say that advertising message always reveals the truth. In many cases, exaggerated facts are advertised. However, due to certain legal provisions, the element of truth can be fairly assured. But, there is no guarantee that the claim made in advertisement is completely true. Most advertisements are erotic, materialistic, misleading, and producer-centered.

10. One-way Communication

Advertising involves the one-way communication. Message moves from company to customers, from sponsor to audience. Message from consumers to marketer is not possible. Marketer cannot know how far the advertisement has influenced the audience.

KEY DECISIONS IN ADVERTISING

Advertising is one of – but popular and powerful – tools of market promotion. It involves a several decisions. Some experts explain advertising decisions and activities in form of six 'M's as under:

1. The first 'M' stands for **Mission** – Advertising Objectives.
2. The second 'M stands for **Money** – Advertising Budget.
3. The third 'M' stands for **Message** – Creating Advertising Message and Copy.
4. The forth 'M' stand for **Monitoring** – Managing (organising) of Advertising Efforts.
5. The fifth 'M' stands for **Media** – Advertising Media Selection and Media Scheduling.
6. The sixth 'M' stands for **Measurement** – Measuring and Evaluating Advertising Effectiveness (MEAE).

However, most of experts agree that advertising consists of mainly eight decisions as shown in figure 1. Manager concerns with taking decisions on these areas of advertising. Remaining part of the chapter discusses some of important advertising decisions.

ADVERTISING OBJECTIVES

INTRODUCTION

Advertising is aimed at achieving various objectives. Objectives may be commercial or social in nature. Prof. Kelly gave the concept of DAGMAR – Defining Advertising Goals for Measuring Advertising Results – in relation to advertising objectives. Broadly, advertising objectives can be categorized into three classes, such as informative objectives, persuasive objectives, and reminder objectives. Prof. Sew and Prof. Smith have classified objectives as:

i. Sales objectives
ii. Aiding sales force
iii. Competition-related objectives
iv. Brand loyalty and reputation-related objectives

However, we will consider following objectives:

1. To Inform Buyers

This objective includes informing customers regarding product's availability, price, features, qualities, services, and performance. Besides, it also includes informing them about changes made in the existing product and introduction of new products. Company also highlights its location, achievements, policies, and performance through advertising.

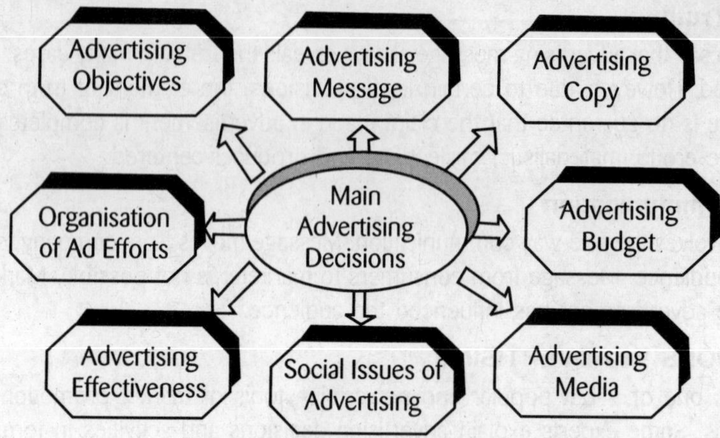

Figure 1: Main Advertising Decisions

2. To Persuade or Convince Buyers

Company uses advertisement to persuade or convince the buyers about superior advantages offered by its product. Company communicates competitive advantages the product offers to induce customers buy it. Comparative advertising is used to prove the additional benefits of product at a given price.

3. To Remind Buyers

Marketer uses advertising to remind the buyers regarding existence of company, products, maintenance of quality, superior services, and chasing customer-orientation. Mostly, the existing firms aim their advertising for this objective. Here, the purpose is to inform that the company is still in existence and serving customers in a better way. Due to huge information bombarded by a number of companies, customers are more likely to forget name of company and/or products and services it offers.

4. To Face Competition

Advertising is treated as the most powerful weapon to fight with competitors effectively. Advertising enables the firm to respond the competitors strongly. It helps the firm to distinguish its total offerings from competitors. In brief, the firm can face competition, can prevent the entry of competitors, or can remove competitors away from the market. In competitive marketing environment, the firm cannot survive without an effective advertisement.

5. To Achieve Sales Targets

Increase sales volume is one of the major advertising objectives. A company can advertise its products in various media to attract customers situated in different parts of the world. National and international marketing is the result of advertising. Even, non-users can be converted into users and usage rate can be increased. Thus, company can achieve its sales objectives by advertisement.

6. To Build and Improve Brand Image

Advertising is used for brand recognition and acceptance. A company can distinguish its brand by magnifying major benefits the product offers. Advertisement attracts customers toward the brand; they try it and accept it over time. In the same way, bad image related to brand can be changed by systematic presentation of facts and scientific evidences, and removing misunderstanding.

7. To Help or Educate People

Advertising is not always used only for company's benefits. It is meant for helping customers to make the right choice of product. It educates people about availability of new products, its features and qualities, price, services, and other related aspects. Such information is instrumental for purchasing suitable products. Thus, it guides customers to choose the most appropriate product.

8. To Build Company Image and Reputation

A company opts for advertisement to build prestige and reputation in the market. Most of the companies, though they are satisfied with the volume of sales, go for advertising to acquire fame in the market. Many companies advertise its policies, activities, and achievements to make a permanent place in the mind of people.

9. To Assist Sales Force and Middlemen

Advertising is an aid to middlemen and salesmen. Advertising also popularizes the name of dealers. Likewise, advertising provides necessary information to the buyers. Middlemen and salesmen are not required to do the same. It eases the task of sellers. In the same way, advertising encourages sales force.

10. Other Objectives

There are certain minor objectives of advertising, such as:

i. To promote new products.
ii. To build long-term relations.
iii. To remove misunderstanding.
iv. To expand of market.
v. To gain confidence of buyers.
vi. To request customers to compromise with unavoidable circumstances.
vii. To seek apology of the buyers for any undesirable events, etc.

Company has to select one or more objectives based on its situations. It should be clarified that the list is not exhaustive. New advertising objectives may emerge as per change in situations. However, the main objective of advertising is to increase sales and earn profits. Company must define it advertising objectives clearly and precisely.

ADVERTISING MEDIA

INTRODUCTION

Advertising message can be conveyed to the target audience through several advertising media. Advertiser must choose the right advertising media to carry the advertising message. A wide variety of media is used for publishing advertising message. Each medium has its relative advantages (merits), limitations (demerits), and applicability. Marketer can select those advertising media, which are suitable in all the important aspects. Let us define advertising media:

DEFINITIONS

1. Advertising media, also referred as ad media, can be defined as: *Advertising media are the means or vehicles through which advertiser communicates his message to prospective customers to influence their behaviour.*
2. **Brennam** defines: "The term 'media' consists of each and every method that the advertiser has at his command to carry his message to public."
3. Finally, more clearly, we can say: *Advertising media are the physical means whereby marketer tells the consumers about goods and services.*

TYPES (OR CLASSIFICATION) OF ADVERTISING MEDIA

Major advertising media, as shown in figure 2, include press media, direct advertising, outdoor media, audio-visual media, advertising specialties, and others. Several advertising media, its relative advantage and disadvantages, and relevant details have been discussed here:

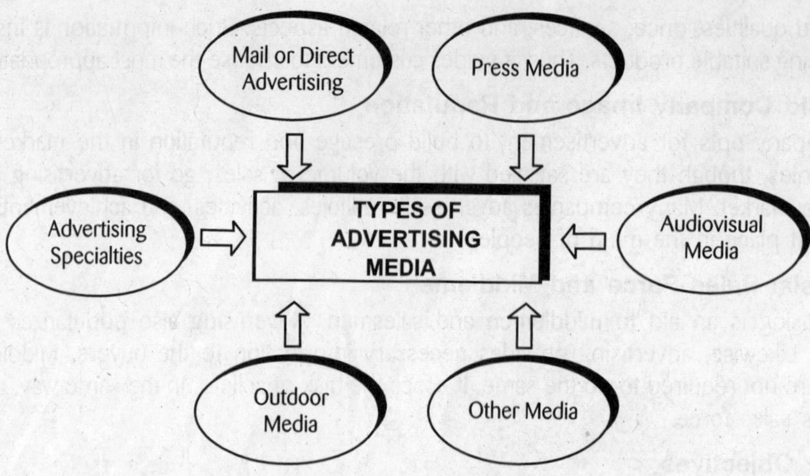

Figure 2: Types (or Classification) of Advertising Media

PRESS MEDIA

Press media are also called print media. Print media are popular and widely used for commercial advertising. A number of people can be addressed by print media. Attractive slogans, statements, words, figures, pictures, drawings, comparative statements, charts, etc., can be used for advertising the products in colourful and artful manner. Press media mainly involves newspapers, magazines, and other publications.

1. Newspapers

Newspapers are a popular medium to contact or inform a large number of customers. Newspapers may be morning or evening; may be in English, Hindi or in other regional languages; may be daily or weekly; may be local, regional or national; or may be routine or special edition. The company should consider circulation, language, geographical coverage, price, credibility, costs of buying space, and quality of printing while selecting a suitable newspaper. Pictures, slogans, figures, charts, etc., can be used. Company can used multi-coloured advertisement, too.

Merits

(a) Newspaper is fit for mass communication. Thousands and lakhs of people can be addressed at a time.

(b) Immediate or speedy message can be conveyed.

(c) Necessary changes can be made easily in regularly published advertisement and at low costs.

(d) Company can measure response immediately. Advertising effect can be assessed easily.

(e) Advertisers can take benefits of the credibility of newspapers.

(f) The medium is suitable for almost all types of products.

(g) It reduces tasks of salesmen and dealers.

(h) It is relatively a cheaper option. Per reader cost is very low.

(i) It is a more flexible advertising vehicle. As per need a company can prefer effective timings, languages, regions, and colour combinations.

(j) It is a simple and easy medium to access by advertiser and readers, etc.

Demerits

(a) Newspapers have a shorter life, normally, a day. Long-term effect cannot be generated.
(b) Message may not be read. Advertising message is more likely to be ignored or avoided.
(c) Quality of paper and printing may reduce the value of advertisements published in newspapers.
(d) It is treated as an ordinary advertising means. It is not as impressive (or prestigious) as magazines and periodicals.
(e) This advertising medium is not fit for the live demonstration and the fine quality pictures.
(f) It is costly when customers are limited in number.
(g) In case of written advertisement, the illiterate customers cannot read it. In countries like India, percentage of illiterate population is quite high.
(h) Normally, customers have to buy the newspapers. It is not cost-free medium like television or radio, etc.

2. Magazines

Magazine is another popular and wisely used advertising medium. It is similar to newspapers with regard to many aspects. To consumers, magazines are treated as source of information and entertainment. A large variety of magazines or periodicals are published weekly, fortnightly, monthly, quarterly, half-yearly or annually. Magazines are also published by religious and social organisations, schools, colleges, university or educational associations, professional and commercial associations, governments, companies, etc. Similarly, magazines are classified in forms of sex, age, profession, industry, entertainment, and so forth. Based on customer characteristics, a proper magazine should be selected for publishing advertising message.

Merits

(a) Magazines have a long life. They can be referred repeated by many users.
(b) They are more effectives as they are referred by educated and special class during leisure time. Advertising message in magazine is more likely to be read, considered, and reacted.
(c) They are printed in better quality papers and effective or fault-free language.
(d) Magazine can appeal to the special groups of customers. For example, children, women, or professionals.
(e) It is a prestigious and credible vehicle to send advertising message.
(f) It is a flexible, elastic, and multipurpose medium as readers may find page tag, receipt, guidebook, catalogue, picture, calendar, which can be detached and kept for the future reference.

Demerits

1 Many magazines have limited circulation and, hence, limited prospects are appealed.
2 Continuity or consistency is not possible as magazines are published weekly, monthly, or quarterly.
3 Most of the magazines are small in size; a large advertisement is not possible.
4 Compared to newspapers, magazine is expensive vehicle in terms of both space and per reader costs.
5 Advertising copy and money are to be sent in advance.

3. Other Print Media

Print media also include telephone directories, books, notebooks, reports, community and professional directories, bus or railway tickets and timetables, and special publications on the special events by schools, colleges, universities, local bodies, cooperative societies, companies, or governments. Local manufacturers, professionals, dealers, retailers, etc., mostly prefer these media to advertise their products. This set of media is relatively cheaper. Most of these print media are used by many people and have long life compared to magazines and newspapers. Further, more selective advertisement is possible. Such print media are more or less similar to newspapers and magazines.

DIRECT OR MAIL ADVERTISING

Direct advertising can be defined as: *Any form of advertising in which the message is directed to specific individuals directly by the advertiser. This medium consists of written, printed, or processed message delivered directly to the selected buyers.* This set of media is used to appeal the target market directly. In practice, it is not suitable for a large number of customers. This type of advertisement is mostly sent personally, or by post and courier services. In the age of information technology, fax, e-mail, and cell phone SMS are also famous modes to send direct mail in a limited scale. Most commonly used methods for direct advertising are:

1. **Sales letters:** The firm directly sends a written or printed letter to some or all customers. Such letters contain message, product description, special offers, etc. Sometimes, fully addressed and dully stamped reply envelope is also sent to get response. Sales letters can be sent to customers using different methods like courier services, paid persons, or postal services.
2. **Fax:** Catalogue, invitation, launching of new product or any message can be sent through fax machine. However, company must know fax number of the receivers. Now, fax is used widely for different purposes. Words, pictures, tables, charts, symbols, etc., can be sent through fax. It can be used for limited customers, and is normally applied for industrial products.
3. **E-mail:** E-mail is relatively new and popular tool for sending message. It is sent to special customers whose e-mail addresses are available or directly to all the account holders. For example, Hotmail or MSN Messenger services, G-Mail, Yahoo, e-patra, and many others provide free messenger services. However, advertiser has to pay for advertising his products.
4. **Cards:** Cards are used to carry brief messages, acknowledge orders, remind customers, answer enquiries, update mailing list or to make special offers. Cards may be plain or coloured; multifold or single fold; or may be in forms of greetings or business letters.
5. **Greetings:** Very popular means to establish relation with customers. The company maintaining a well-up-to-date customer database can send greeting cards on different events and occasions. Along with greetings, a brief message, picture of product or slogan with commercial value can be sent to customers and dealers.
6. **Circulars and Leaflets:** Mostly, they are typed or printed on one or both sides. They may be in coloured papers. Circulars and leaflets involve description or special features of products. Many companies send circulars or leaflets on regular basis.
7. **Catalogues, Folders, Booklets and Brochures:** They contain necessary information and are sent/offered to customers. Booklets are widely used by companies selling two-wheelers, refrigerators, television, or other technical products.
8. **Calendars and Diaries:** Companies offer calendars or diaries, specially prepared as per their requirements, free-of-costs to customers and dealers, containing their names, symbols, brand names, slogans or pictures of the products. Diaries are more informative and expensive compared to calendars.

9. **Others:** We may include other means used for direct advertisement. Such means or vehicle include:
   i. Data cards, samples, and gifts
   ii. SMS – Short Mobile Message through cell phone
   iii. House organs like story books, articles, cartoons, jokes, etc.
   iv. Pamphlets, etc.

They are in-house sources of information; they are made available to customers at their places (home or offices). In fact, a large number of media are used for direct advertising. Each of the media has its merits, demerits, and applicability. We will evaluate these media jointly.

Merits

(a) It involves a direct and personalized appeal to the customers, and, hence, it is more effective.
(b) Advertiser has more flexibility to adjust with different types of customers and their needs.
(c) Especially, catalogues, booklets, circulars, fliers, broachers, and house organs are effective and have educative value.
(d) Advertiser has complete control on these media. They can be sent as and when it is desirable to be sent.
(e) It can clearly explain the main features of products with statistical data.
(f) More varieties are available. Advertiser can use different means of direct mail to attract customers' attention and to arouse interest.

Demerits

(a) This method is costlier as advertising message is conveyed personally. It involves both preparation costs and distribution costs.
(b) It involves a lot of clerical work. Special wing/office should be maintained for the purpose for regular mailing.
(c) It is applicable when the customers are limited.
(d) Many times, this method results into waste of time, money, and efforts. People really do not have interest in such mails. They believe that direct mail is just to promote sales.
(e) It is meaningful only if customers are able to read and understand.
(f) Virtually, personalized appeal is difficult as the company doesn't have complete information of its buyers.
(g) Most people perceive e-mail, SMS, business letters, etc., as the nuisance. They hold negative attitudes toward those companies excessively practice this route for commercial ads. Some of these tools have more nuisance value than commercial value.

OUTDOOR OR MURAL MEDIA

Nowadays, outdoor advertising media are widely used for almost all types of goods and services. Outdoor media are excessively used by manufacturers and dealers, hotels, restaurants, academic institutions, airways, banks, insurance, etc. Cold drinks, cements, cigarettes, petroleum products, and cosmetics products widely use these media for advertisement. They are also known as mural media. Those companies, which are not in position to spend huge amount on television, radio, newspapers or magazines, may opt for these media. Most common outdoor advertising media have been briefly discussed below:

1. **Banners:** They are used at popular places like cricket matches, tournaments, stage shows, fairs, talent shows, and annual functions of school, colleges and universities, seminars and conferences, or public meetings.

2. **Special Signboards:** They are used at bus and railway satiations indicating route or platform number, or indicating name of roads and directions in the city. Most cell phone service providers including Vodafone, Idea Cellular, Airtel, etc., use this medium to popularize their name and brand.
3. **Kiosk:** Square or triangle shaped boxes with written words or picture on them are hanged on electricity or telephone polls.
4. **Billboards:** Special boards are prepared to advertise the product. Dealers or retailers put such boards nearby their shops, showrooms, shopping malls or on the upper sides of buildings.
5. **Handbills:** They are very common and too cheap. Advertisement is printed on a piece of paper of small size. These leaflets are distributed hand to hand by a paid man, along with newspapers, or otherwise.
6. **Station Posters:** Multi-coloured-printed posters with written message and pictures are stuck on walls, benches, insides the canteens, and inside and outsides bus stations, railway stations, and airports.
7. **Sky Writing:** It is a novel and expensive vehicle to advertise the product. It is not very popular in our country. It involves showing words, symbols, or picture through gas during the night using plane, ballon, helicopter, or bursting.
8. **Symbol of Product:** Giant size products, picture of products, or package of products are used for advertising purpose. Cadbury, Balaji Wafers, Coca-Cola, Maruti Car, Hero Honda, Nutraj Pencil, etc., use this medium.
9. **Neon Sign:** Neon tube lights are used for advertising. Words are written by neon tubes and are place on boards on buildings. Different coloured are used to make it attractive. This can be used only during the night. Cinema, business firms, banks, tuitions classes, and other professionals use neon signs to publish the advertising message.
10. **Other Outdoor Media**

Other common and popular outdoor advertising media include:

i. Posters and wall paintings
ii. Hoarding on the road
iii. Vehicle advertising
iv. Sandwich man
v. Trade fair
vi. Balloons, etc.

There may be more outdoor media than listed above. Each of these media has its merits, demerits, and suitability. But, we will discuss merits and demerits jointly for all the outdoor advertising media.

Merits

(a) Outdoor media do not require customers' special time and efforts to read or watch.
(b) Outdoor media are capable to attract mass. Number of people can be attracted at a time.
(c) They are cheaper than newspapers, radio, film, and television.
(d) They are prepared in attractive and colourful manners. They are large in size to draw attention. They are eye-catching.
(e) They are placed at a place where people are more likely to view the advertisement, such as public places, like gardens, hospitals, bus stations, railway stations, aerodromes, traffic points, railway crossing, highway turns, road crossing, corners, etc.

(f) Some of them have long life (for example, hoardings, billboard, wall painting, etc.) They continue to advertise the same product for relatively a long time. They remain before the eyes of people for a long time.

(g) They can be highly selective. Words, slogan, description, symbols, picture, etc., can be easily used. Even, advertiser can place it anywhere he likes.

(h) They indirectly protect historical walls and buildings. They beautify different areas or localities. On highway, they are source of information and entertainment.

Demerits

(a) People tend to overlook these media. People do not read or see such advertisements consciously and carefully.

(b) They may lead to accidents or mishaps. Interesting and exciting hoarding possibly leads mishaps.

(c) Hoardings, wall posters, station posters are not movable. They cannot be moved to other places.

(d) Direct effect cannot be measured.

(e) Use of these media in a large scale is expensive.

(f) Voice and live movements (i.e., audio-visual effect) like television and film advertisements cannot be presented.

AUDIO-VISUAL MEDIA

The media that can be seen and/or hear are known as audio-visual advertising media. In contemporary marketing environment, these media are the most popular means to send advertising message. Marketers are using aggressively the audio-visual vehicles to prove superiority of their products over the competitors. These media, though expensive, are considered as the modern and prestigious among all the advertising media. This set of media is excessively used for all types of goods and services. Audio-visual media mainly include television, radio, short films, Internet, moving slides, film slides, etc.

1. Radio

Perhaps it is the cheapest (in terms of per listener cost) and most pervasive among all media used for mass communication. It crosses the literacy barriers. Countrywide or on particular regions, the direct message is conveyed to the (desired group of) listeners. Radio is used not only for advertising national programmes by the Government for Family Planning, vaccination, woman education, ecological conservation, erosion of superstitions, or any other programmes of social and national interest, but is also used by many companies for commercial advertising. Insurance, banks, financial institutions, and manufacturers use radio to advertise their goods/services. Advertisements are broadcasted before, after, or during specific (regional or national) programmes. Some companies broadcast their own programmes or events of the social interest and get their products or activities advertised directly. Local radio (FM radio) is excessively used by local marketers like tuition classes, private colleges, hotels and restaurants, dealers and distributors of distributors consumer durables, and so forth.

Merits

(a) Radio is more effective than spoken words.

(b) Musical effects can be associated with message or slogan.

(c) Wide coverage, it reaches to every corner of the country or at particular region.

(d) Per contact cost is the lowest.

(e) The programme can be sponsored or purchased as per advertiser's needs and objectives.

(f) It is more credible. No advertisement is broadcasted against general interest of the public.
(g) It suits the low-cost products like foods, drugs, cosmetics, etc.
(h) It promotes goodwill and prestige of an advertiser.

Demerits

(a) Though per customer contact cost is the lowest, it is costly affair.
(b) Company has to compromise in terms of message, events, or time schedule.
(c) Only brief, sometimes not clear, message is conveyed.
(d) It is not suitable with all types of products.
(e) Mostly, advertisement appears during, before, or after the interesting programmes. People hear radio for programmes, and not for advertisement. So, message may not be properly attended. Advertising message is less significant than programme.
(f) It has a temporary effect. Hardly the customer inquires the products based on radio advertising message.
(g) It is not the sole medium to advertise the products. It is used as supplementary to other advertising media.

2. Television - TV

It is the newest, fastest growing, and most popular advertising medium. It is a powerful medium for entertainment and advertisement. Now, television set is available at affordable price. Most of TV channels and local cable operators carry commercial advertisements. It appeals the people through the eye and the ear, i.e., it creates audio-visual effect. Products can be demonstrated as well as explained. Written words, description, and slogans can also be depicted with pictures, package, and brand names and/or products. Now, film starts, cricketers, artists, and modeling personalities are excessively used to advertise different types of products. Shahrukh Khan for Santro car and Dishtv, Amitabh and Sachin for Pepsi, Sachin for TVS Motor bike, Mathuri Dixit and Amitabh Bachhan for Himani costmatics, M. Dhoni for Milkshakti Buscuit, and such others are popular TV advertisements. Camera and computer can create the highly impressive and effective combination of the events, words, slogan, and music. Advertisements appear in television during special events, like cricket match, film, thrilling news, or similar mega events, carry a heavy impression on customers. For example, TVS has earned the fame and sales in TVS Cup between India and West Indies in November, 2002.

Merits

(a) Millions of people can be exposed to the products.
(b) Company can appeal to the customers by two faculties (the eye and the ear) at a time. A long-term effect can be created.
(c) Live demonstration can be displayed. Customers are guided systematically.
(d) Television advertisement is also a great source of entertainment for children. Children are found uttering the slogans of various advertisements. It is an effective medium to popularize product within short period of time.
(e) Actual users can be demonstrated using the product. Users are shown using and enjoying the products.
(f) It is fit for the illiterate as well as the literate audience.
(g) Advertising during specific interesting events like films, cricket match, film fair, specific serials, or news carries a high degree of exposure.
(h) Television advertisement can be presented in the most effective and perfect way by using the latest animation technology or computer effect.

(i) Product can be attached to specific personality in the most effective way. For examples, Mathuri Dixit and Himani cosmetic products, Sachin Tendulkar and TVS Victor, Shahrukh and Santro car, Amitabh and Pepsi, etc. Personality of person becomes the identity of the product.

Demerits

(a) Advertisement of the firm appears before, after, or in middle of the programmes along with various advertisements. In the same way, various companies jointly sponsor a programme. Each company tries to impress its viewers. Advertisement may not be effective to catch the attention and to create the identity. All advertisements are not carefully attended.

(b) It is the costliest medium to advertise the product. Only financially sound company can afford the medium.

(c) In case of film or serial, people avoid seeing commercial break. They relax during commercial break, shift to other channels or even switch off TV for three to five minutes.

(d) Television is a source of entertainment. Many advertisements are viewed for joy. Its commercial value may be undermined.

(e) Frequent commercial breaks for a few minutes during interesting programme affect adversely the interest of audience. They are disturbed or irritated; cannot tolerate the disturbance in an interesting story. They may develop prejudice or negative attitude towards the company whose advertisement disturbs during climax.

(f) Many viewers opine that advertisements create a nuisance on television. They are more company-centered and have nothing to do with consumer interest and welfare. They waste the valuable time of people.

(g) Television advertisement seems more artificial, superfluous, erotic, misleading, and full of exaggerations due to use of animation, virtual reality or special effects created by computer. People perceive vast difference between actual performance of products as against the claimed performance. It creates a big question against credibility of the TV advertisement.

3. Internet

Internet is the latest medium to advertise products. Some companies put their advertisements on their websites; some companies buy web page of the popular websites. Even, sometimes, they place their advertising message directly on different websites. Viewers just clicking on the name, address, picture, product, logo, brand, or slogan and can get full detail of a product or a company. To develop their own websites on Internet is also very common due to rapid practice of e-commerce or online transactions. Most of the established companies, banks, insurance, and educational institutes have put their information of Internet. In India, use of Internet for advertising purpose is on increase. More than 100 million Indian access the Internet regularly.

Merits

(a) It has high credibility and prestige.

(b) Company can advertise its product globally.

(c) Advertisement can be prepared with multiple effects. Use of virtual reality makes advertisement interesting.

(d) It is highly suitable when the company wants to appeal to specific sophisticated groups of customers.

(e) Demonstration is possible.

Demerits

(a) It has a limited utility. A few people can access the Internet. In developing and underdeveloped countries, it has limited use.

(b) It is not automatic. One has to log on to access a particular website.

(c) Only limited firms can use this sophisticated advertising vehicle.

(d) Internet users are highly professional and distinguished class of people and they hardly care for advertisements.

(e) It is costly to both company as well as Internet users (customers).

(f) People access websites for detail information only after they are impressed or exposed by the message appears in other advertising media. Thus, the medium is complementary to the rest of media.

4. Moving Slide

This is mostly used in urban areas. Here, moving slides are used to advertise product. They are used for commercial or even for non-commercial purposes. Advertising message, picture of product, or logo of company moves either alternate or in one direction on the screen kept on private or public buildings. Such slides are based on electricity or battery. However, use of electric circuit is very common. Nowadays, computer-based slides are very effective. Normally, it is a visual device. Voice is not associated. These slides are located in densely populated locality, corners, or near public places where a maximum number of people passes through. Traffic points and railway crossing are among the most effective places. This medium is very effective during the night. Multicoloured slides attract pedestrians and people passing through vehicles.

Merits

(a) This medium is much cheaper as compared to print and audiovisual media.

(b) It is very flexible. The firm can change as per needs from one locality to another. Even, contents can be changed easily.

(c) It is a source of entertainment as well as information.

(d) For local advertising message, it is very effective.

(e) It is highly selective. Company can advertise its product only in special locality.

(f) It beautifies the corner or public places.

Demerits

(a) It is fit only for local advertisement.

(b) It has a limited exposure or reach.

(c) If company wants more slides at a different place, this medium becomes costly.

(d) Only visual message – but not voice – is transmitted.

(e) It is suitable for a short message.

(f) Live demonstration is not possible.

5. Film or Cinema

Film advertisement mainly involves cinema slides and short films. A large number of people can be exposed through this medium. Advertisements are shown at theatres or at different places by projectors.

Short Films: They are presented before films or during interval. Many companies use short films to advertise its products through cinema houses. It is a similar to television medium. Main difference between TV and short film is that film can expose only limited audience while TV is capable to contact millions of people at time. For example, popular advertisements are Vico cream, toothpaste and powder, Nirama detergent cake and washing powder etc. Short films are shown along with non-commercial films during various events or functions such as seminars and similar events.

Slides: The alternate way to advertise the product in the theatre consists of slides. This medium is also used for both commercial as well non-commercial ads. Alike TV, it is a slide-cum-sound medium. Only demonstration of products – but not live presentation – is possible. Here, slides consisting name of producers, products, logo, etc., are shown in theatres and at the place of special events. Advertisements are presented in theatre before and after film or during interval.

Merits

(a) It is less costly. Especially, slides are very cheaper.

(b) This medium is fit for literate as well illiterate people.

(c) Audiovisual effect is possible.

(d) It can be presented in different shows and in each show different people can be exposed to an advertising message. So, in case of the hit movies, a large number of people can be exposed.

(e) In short films, the live demonstration can be presented. Compared to TV, more information can be provided.

Demerits

(a) Inattention is the basic problem. Audience is more interested in the movie than advertisement.

(b) Advertising the products by short films is costly. Its preparation is more costly than presentation.

(c) Only those who spend money to see movie in the theatre or participate in seminar, functions, etc., are exposed to the advertising message. So, compared to radio, television, or print media, it has extremely limited coverage.

(d) Such medium cannot be used in the areas where theatres or projectors are not available.

(e) Slides are less effective. People avoid attending ad slides.

(f) If not prepared carefully, slides, short films, or documentary result into irritation, boring, and misleading.

ADVERTISING SPECIALTIES

There are near about 5000 such items used for advertising products. Here, some items, either related to products or not, are offered to customers at free-of-charge. On such items, brand names, logo, or company name have been stamped or inscribed. While using such products, consumers can know about name of company, brand, product, etc. Such items include pen, paperweight, lighter, purse, ring, belt, knife and other kitchenware, key-chain, bag, rain cap, or some extra accessories. These items can be offered to customers or dealers as the gift.

OTHER MEDIA

Apart from the media discussed in above part, there are various media frequently use for advertising the products. Most widely used common advertising media are:

1. Window Display
2. Product Package
3. Counter Display
4. Special Display and Shows
5. Showrooms
6. Trade Fair and Exhibition, etc.

Several media discussed in the former part are among popular ad media. There can be more ad media. Any tool capable of carrying the message can be treated as advertising medium. It must be stated that above classification of media is not very strict. Chance of duplication of one or more media cannot be completely ignored.

FACTORS AFFECTING MEDIA SELECTION

There are several factors a manager has to consider while selecting a suitable medium to carry the advertising message. Some factors are internal while some are external and uncontrollable. If the effect of these factors is dully assessed, the firm would be in better position to select the most suitable medium for its advertising programme. Important factors have been briefly stated as below:

1. Objectives of Firm

Company's general and advertising objectives are the prime considerations in media selection. Those media capable to meet company's expectations are likely to be selected. Advertising objectives may be to inform, remind, convince, create prestige, or to increase sales and profits. Different media have varying capacity to meet these objectives.

2. Costs Media and Company's Financial Position

Media selection decision is highly influenced by media costs and firm's ability to pay. Company has to pay for buying space or time and preparing advertising copy fit for the media to be selected. TV, radio, films are costly in terms of buying time and preparing advertising copy. Print media are relatively cheaper in both space and preparation of advertising message. Some outdoor media are quite low in cost. As per media costs and company's financial capacity, the appropriate media should be selected.

3. Reach or Number of People Exposed to the Message

It is an important criterion to choose among ad media. Reach means the number of different people exposed to a particular medium at least once during a specified time period. Mass media are capable to reach millions of people by just one exposure. Television has more exposure capacity compared to outdoor media in a particular time. Local media can expose the message to limited persons. In the same way, frequency (the number of times within a specified time period the average person exposed to the message), and impact (the impact created on audience by an exposure through given medium) are also key criteria to choose among advertising media. Reach, frequency, and impact are important variables that determine cost-effectiveness of various media.

4. Company's Advertising Policy and Approach

Company's advertising policy and approach determine which of the media should be selected. For example, if company's policy is not to spend more money for advertisement and to offer the product at a low price, it may go for cheaper media.

5. Type of Buyers

People to be influenced should be taken into account while selecting the media. Buyers can be classified into various classes as discussed in market segmentation. Each medium has its special viewers, readers, or audience. For the firm, it is important to know whether the target groups can be exposed by the particular medium. Television is the most common medium, but can be made more particular by selecting the special programme. Magazines are capable to appeal particular sex, age groups, or professionals. Daily newspapers are again very general in nature.

6. Condition under which Customers are Influenced

Readers'/viewers' mood and interest determine receptivity of message. Television is the best-fit medium to associate advertising message when people are watching or enjoying related programmes. For example, advertising TVS Victor motorbike on television during the live telecast of the TVS Cup One-day Series. However, it is difficult to determine mood or interest of readers for daily newspapers. It is relatively easy to determine mood of people during a specific programme in radio or television. In case of outdoors media, the place is very important to judge mood of people. For example, hoardings, posters, or banner near gardens or picnic places are more likely to be attracted.

7. Circulation/Coverage

The area covered by (or number of people exposed to) the medium is an important criterion. Some media are capable to cover the globe while some can cover only the limited locality. For example, the local newspapers cover limited areas, the national newspapers like The Time of India and The Economic Times cover the whole nation. Similarly, certain magazines have national and international circulation. And, the same is true with audio-visual and outdoor media. As per geographical concentration of customers, the suitable media should be selected.

8. Repetition or Frequency

Repetition or frequency implies the number of times within specific time period an average person is exposed to the message by specific medium. Most of the outdoor media hold the message for relatively long time. Magazines or periodicals publish monthly or quarterly; mostly they publish advertisements only in a particular edition. The more is the repetition of advertising message, the more is the effect of the medium on people. Naturally, advertisement appears frequently is more likely to read or attend than if it appears only once. However, repetition in case of newspapers, TV, radio, etc., depends on company's ability to pay.

9. Credibility and Image of Media

In case of newspapers and magazines, the factor is critical. Naturally, advertising message appears in the reputed newspapers or magazines carry heavy impression and effect than substandard media. People don't trust the appeal published in the lower standard media. Prestige of media becomes the prestige of advertiser. Firms opt for credible or prestigious media to carry the advertising message.

10. Past Experience

Company's own past experience may be instrumental to decide on advertising media. For example, if company has satisfactory experience of using a particular medium, there are more chances to use the same medium and vice versa.

11. Experience of other Companies

Experience of other companies is one of the important considerations in media selection. Company may try to know what other companies say about applicability and usefulness of various media. Views of other companies must be followed with care and caution.

12. Expert Opinion

Marketing experts or consultants who work on professional basis can be consulted to suggest an appropriate medium to carry the message. These experts, on the basis of analysis of market situations in relation to products to be advertised, can recommend the suitable media. Since they have experience and expertise in the field, they are in better position to judge the suitability of each of the media in relation to product and company's financial position. They charge fees for their consultancy services.

13. Type of Advertising Message

Each advertising message needs specific advertising vehicle. If a message is simple, print media are sufficient. If a message is complicated, and the company wants to demonstrate and explain, audiovisual media suit the needs.

14. Others

Apart from above mentioned factors, there are certain factors that affect media selection decision. They are listed as under:

a. Effectiveness of Media
b. Availability of Media
c. Government Rules and Regulations
d. Time and Place
e. Type of Products, etc.

Media selection is a crucial decision. It determines the cost-effectiveness of media. Failure of advertising programme, in many cases, is attributed to use of inappropriate media. Advertiser should consider all these factors carefully and should select the most favoured or suitable media.

MEDIA SCHEDULING

Media scheduling is one of the important decisions in advertising programme. Company should carefully decide on media timing for a maximum market response. Media scheduling is simply a time-table showing (1) the time decision – when to advertise, (2) the duration/space decision – how much to advertise each time, and (3) the frequency to advertise the message through different media – how many times in a year (or specified time period) the message should be advertised in each of the media. However, the first decision, i.e., time decision, is more relevant to media scheduling. Media scheduling calls for consideration of various factors to arrive at appropriate media timing. The decision is vital due to the fact that demand is subject to vary as per cyclical trend and/or seasons. To realize the maximum benefits of advertising costs, the most effective time is selected. Those executives or experts responsible to carry out advertising activities take a media scheduling decision.

TYPES OF SCHEDULING

The advertiser has to consider two types of media scheduling problems:

Macro-scheduling: The macro-scheduling involves allocating advertising expenditure and frequency (repetition/reproduction of message) in relation to season or broad picture of business cycle. The macro-scheduling problem concerns with how to schedule advertising in relation to seasonal and business cycle trends. The broad picture of seasonal and/or cyclical trend is considered. This is due to the fact that the demand is fluctuated as per seasons and/or business cycle. Therefore, it is desirable to vary advertising expenditures to follow seasonal patterns. Company, as per its calculation, can spend more or less during the season or particular phase of business cycle.

According to experts, advertising does not have immediate impact on consumer awareness, sales, or profits. So, one should study relationship between (1) timing of advertising and consumer awareness, (2) consumer awareness and impact on sales, and (3) sales and advertising expenditure. Advertising timing should be adjusted as per time gap exits between advertising time and its impact. Computer-based mathematical model can be formulated to study these time relations.

Advertiser has to decide on advertising time for different types of products, such as frequently purchased, seasonal products, and low-cost daily consumed products. Along with seasonal or cyclical aspect, an advertiser should also consider impact of the past advertising. Many consumers continue buying even without the present advertisement.

Micro-scheduling: The micro-scheduling problem concerns with allocating advertising expenditure and frequency within a short period to obtain the maximum response or impact. In other words, the problem deals with how to distribute advertising expenditure within the given time. For example, a company has decided to advertise specific message 60 times (that requires approximately Rs. 500000) through daily regional newspapers in a year. Now the question is to decide on which days/weeks/months/seasons the 60 times advertisement is to be allocated. Similarly, the same issue is related to radio or television spots.

ALTERNATIVE SCHEDULING STRATEGIES

A company has following alternative scheduling strategies to decide on micro-scheduling:

1. Continuous Advertising

This scheduling involves advertising the message evenly throughout a given period. For example, if company wants 48 television/radio spots, it will advertise 4 times in a month or once in a week, or on every Monday.

2. Concentrated Advertising

This scheduling involves giving all the advertisement in a single period. Thus, the concentrated advertising means to spend the entire advertising budget within one flight. It is applicable when product is sold in one season, event, festival or holiday. For example, the company advertises 48 spots within four days during Diwali festivals, 12 times a day.

3. Flighting Advertising

This scheduling involves giving advertisement at specific intervals. Company advertises for some period, followed by break of no advertisement, followed by the second flight of advertisement and likewise. Company with seasonal, cyclical, or infrequently purchase products follows such scheduling. Company with a limited fund prefers to advertise during a specific season or festival only.

4. Pulsing Advertising

This scheduling is the combination of both continuous and flighting advertisements. It includes continuous advertising at low-weight level, reinforced periodically by waves of heavier activity. In other words, the company spends certain portion of advertising fund for continuous advertising, and the remaining fund for flighting advertisement. For example, the company may advertise once in a day with a brief advertisement message. And, its detail advertisement appears for a week regularly after every three months. This timing is preferred by the financially sound companies.

FACTORS AFFECTING ADVERTISING SCHEDULING

The allocation of advertising expenditure/frequency over time depends on advertising objectives, nature of product, type of target customers, distribution channel, and other relevant marketing factors. But, mostly, following five factors are considered to decide on the timing pattern.

1. Buyer Turnover

It shows the rate at which new buyers enter the market. The rule is, the higher the rate of buyer turnover, the more continuous the advertisement should be.

2. Purchase Frequency

It shows the number of times during the specific period that the average buyer buys the product. The common rule is, the higher the purchase frequency, the more continuous the advertisement should be.

3. Forgetting Rate

It shows the rate at which the buyer forgets the brand. The rule is, the higher the forgetting rate, the more continuous the advertisement should be.

4. Financial Condition of Company

It shows an ability of a company to spend for advertisement. The rule is, the more is the ability to spend, the more continuous the advertisement will be.

5. Level of Competition

Company facing a severe market competition will opt for more continuous advertisement through multiple media. The rule is, the more is the intensity of competition, the higher the frequency of advertisement will be.

ADVERTISING MESSAGE

Message means a lesson or central idea of advertising. Message is also referred as the theme or appeal. The theme is the basic idea regarding products while the appeal is the systematical way to express the theme. However – more or less – advertising message, theme, and appeal are taken as same. The message is something that advertiser wants to convey the market. Message must be such that makes the viewers or readers to try and/or buy the products. Message or theme has different types of appeals like fear appeal, emotion appeal, beauty appeal, confidence or distinction appeal, economy appeal, health appeal, personality and image appeal, etc.

In short, an advertising message must touch needs, emotions, and attitudes of customers. Mostly, the message expresses major benefits the product offers. It shows superiority of company's product among the products of close competitors. Creativity plays an important role in advertising message. Advertisements differ in terms of the messages they carry with. It is the powerful factor determining effectiveness of overall advertising programme. Message must fulfill certain conditions:

(a) Message must be attractive.
(b) It must be suggestive.
(c) It must be appealing or motivating.
(d) It must fulfill legal and social conditions.
(e) It must be convincing.
(f) It must be memorable.
(g) It must indicate major benefits of products, etc.

PROCESS OF DEVELOPING ADVERTISING MESSAGE

Philip Kotler suggests four steps to develop an advertising message. Figure 3 shows the process of developing advertising message.

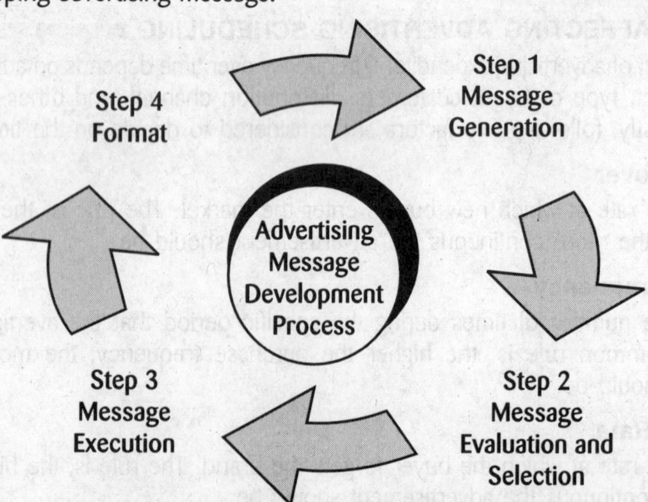

Figure 3: Advertising Message Development Process

1. Message Generation

In the first stage, the advertiser has to think about what he wants to appeal the market. He tries to generate as many as possible advertising themes/messages. Message creation involves discovering the key benefits a product offers. Sometimes, a marketer has to change benefits without changing the product when consumers seek new or different benefits. Marketer can talk to consumers, dealers, experts, or competitors directly or indirectly to prepare the themes. However, consumers are the major source of new ideas. Their views about strengths and shortcomings of existing products elicit clues to create the messages. Care should be taken to avoid irrationality and exaggeration.

2. Message Evaluation and Selection

The second step calls for evaluating the alternative messages. A good message must focus the basic aspects of product. While evaluating different messages, desirability, exclusiveness, believability, attractiveness, etc., criteria should be considered. In order to find out which appeal is the most effective, a marketer often conducts marketing research. Message should be evaluated from the viewpoint of customers. It must be selected in light of basic characteristics of the target market. In short, the most suitable or impressive message should be selected.

3. Message Execution

It is a challenging task. The message is the central idea/theme an advertiser wants to convey about the product. The impact of advertising message largely depends on how it is expressed. That is, "what is said" is not only important, but "how it is said." It may be positioned rationally or emotionally. Indian advertising messages are more emotional than rational. They express indirect benefits. Style, colour, getup, association, etc., are used to influence feeling of buyers. The message is executed in such way that consumers are made feel that the company offers products for their well-being or welfare. Use of word, slogan, style, tone, and so on makes advertising appeal attractive and effective. For effective execution, the choice of headlines, style, slogan, and so forth are important. Hero Honda, Hyundai, Raymond, Samsung, TVS, etc., have the impressive strategy to execute the message.

Message execution includes the use of following aspects:

- Styles
- Tone
- Words

Style: Style indicates method, approach, or manner. It has an important role in message execution. Some styles used for executing the message have been listed as:

(a) **Slice of life:** It shows one or more persons using the product in a normal setting, or a family seated at the dinner table might express satisfaction with the product. It is common in editable items like edible oil, ice-cream, rice, tea, or masala (spices).

(b) **Life style:** It shows how the product suits or fits with a life style. It is commonly used for whiskey, cold drinks, cigarettes, clothing, shoes, etc. Message carries the personality appeal.

(c) **Fantasy:** It consists of creating a fantasy around the product or its use. Perfumes, bathing soaps, beauty creams, goggles, hair oils, etc., use fantasy style.

(d) **Mood, Image, or Love:** The message is executed showing product's contribution to enhance mood, improve image or indicate love and affection. The message creates mood or image around the products. Healthcare, car, motorbike, toilet soap, cigarette, energy foods, and similar products use this style.

(e) **Music:** Music is the most common style to execute the message. Here, background music is used, or one or more persons or cartoon characters are shown singing a song with musical effect about/with products. It is commonly used in many products like chocolates, toys, cold drinks, motorbikes, and so forth.

(f) **Personality Symbols:** Attempts are made to associate the product with popular personality. Popular people like film stars, cricketers, musicians, political heroes, etc., are shown using of or appealing for the products.

(g) **Technical Expertise:** It shows technical excellence, expertise, and experience of the manufacturers. Along with products, the technical staff, plants, materials, and other related aspects are highlighted. Technical expertise helps build customers confidence on product or brand.

(h) **Scientific Evidence:** Scientific evidences or results of survey are linked with the products. Friendly Wash Chemicals, Colgate, and many other pharmaceutical and energy food companies use scientific evidences to reinforce their appeals.

(i) **Testimonials Evidence:** Testimonials evidences are commonly used in advertising message execution. To convince the customers, testimonials, awards, certificates, government recommendation, etc., are produced with the products. For example, along with products ISI or ISO certificates are highlighted.

Tone: Tone the means use of impressive sound with musical effect. Company sets tone for its advertisement for different appeals. Tone may be in forms of humor, fear, emotion, error, etc. In most of TV advertisements, we find tones. Tone indirectly forces or kicks the customers to try or buy the product.

Words: Impressive words or slogans are widely used in written, oral, and audiovisual advertisements. Words used are memorable and attention-catching. Words must be meaningful and attractive to draw the attention of the audience. They are placed on headlines. Words help recognizing products. For example, Virat Compressive Strength by Ambuja Cement; Dam Hai by Kinetic Boss; Des ki Dhadkan by Hero Honda, Hamara Bajaj by Bajaj Auto; Thanda Matab Coca-Cola by Coco-Cola Company, etc., are famous words or slogans used to execute the message.

4. Format

Company must care for the format of message. Format simply means arrangement of various items of the advertising message. Systematic format increases impression and reduces costs. Thus, a message format mainly includes arranging or designing all message-related items, such as ad size, colour, illustration, words, slogan, pictures, figure, and the order of these items.

Message Social Responsibility Review

Advertiser must care for social responsibility. While preparing and executing the message, care should be taken that legal and social norms must not be violated. Message must be truthful or claim must be honest. Words, slogans, and picture used must not be erotic, false, misleading, materialistic, exciting communal sentiments, etc. In short, a message must comply with the contemporary legal and social norms, that is, it must be free from legal constraints and social resistance. Many countries including India have formulated and implemented a number of statutory provisions to safeguard interest of consumers and society in general. Knowledge of relevant legal provisions and social norms, values, and traditions seems to be important to prepare and execute a non-controversial ad message.

ADVERTISING COPY

Advertising copy is known as ad copy. Ad copy is the core of advertisement. It is called as advertising documents. It involves the key information regarding advertisement. Before advertising message is sent to the media, it is presented in forms of a copy. It contains written, spoken, printed, recorded or pictured matters/materials related to advertising the product. Thus, it is the complete programme related to advertising. Advertisements for different media are prepared in accordance with the ad copy. Ad copy consists of main body, headlines, subheads, pictures, characters, cartoons, slogans, words, brand names, name of advertiser, logo of company, etc. Many companies prefer to take expert services of ad agencies to prepare ad copy.

Essential Conditions: An advertising copy should be drafted carefully. A scientifically drafted ad copy must satisfy following conditions:

1. Ad copy must be attractive to draw attention.
2. It must be believable.
3. It must stimulate interest.
4. It must have memory value.
5. It must convince or persuade the reader.
6. It must initiate action.

LAYOUT OF AD COPY

An ad copy consists of various parts, elements, or ingredients. Which parts and how many parts should be included depend on the media through which the advertising message is to be communicated. Layout of ad copy shows the coordination of various parts of ad copy like headlines, slogans, test, illustrations, pictures, sponsor, and logotype. It is a physical arrangement of presenting the message. It is like a map, design, or structure of advertising message. It is a technical job that requires a high degree of expertise, skills, and experience. All ingredients are presented in such a way that attracts the reader, listener, and/or viewer to attend the advertisement. Order must be decided carefully. Practically, an advertising copy includes one or more of the following parts:

1. Headlines

Headlines are crucial for print advertisements. They include attractive description written in colourful bold letters at the top or anywhere in the advertisement. Attractive fonts are used to make the headline eye-catching. Headlines may contain slogans. For example, More Smile per Mile by TVS Victor, Japanese quality, at Chinese price, available in India by Orpat Home Appliances, Elora Times Ltd. Mostly, headlines are written in bold letters. Headlines suggest major benefits, offers, or time limit. For example, special offers open only for two days.

2. Slogans

Slogans are made of words and sentences. They are expressed in a rhythmic manner. Slogans are used for every type of advertisement such as TV, radio, outdoor, and print media. Slogans are presented or written at the beginning, at the middle, or at the end of advertisement. In audiovisual media, a slogan is presented with musical effect by using persons or cartoon characters. For example, Hero Honda, Des Ki Dhadkan; TVS Victor, More Smile Per Mile; Raymond, The Complete Man; Sansui, Better than the best; Onida Television, Change the World; Coca-Cola, Life Ho To Asi, and Thanda Matalab Coca-Cola; Tata Namak, Desh Ka Namak, etc., slogans have popularized some brands and companies. Sometimes, songs are used. For example, Nirma Chemicals, MDS masala, etc., used songs in their advertisement. Slogans are indicative of key themes the advertiser insists to appeal the audience.

3. Text

The text is the central part of ad copy. It contains a description. It is prepared with reference to advertising objectives. For example, a company gives more description if company's objective is to provide more information. Text should neither be too lengthy nor be too short. Text includes theme or appeal to the customers. It describes major benefits of products. The claim must suggest an absolute or a comparative superiority of the products. Most text shows product benefits, special offers, time, availability, quality, etc. Text is prepared differently for different media. For example, space is important for print media; time is important for audiovisual media; size is important for outdoor media.

4. Illustration

Illustrations are used to make the advertising claim clear and attractive. Here picture, character, cartoons, charts, etc., are used to illustrate an use of the product. In the illustration, claims are made through celebrities. In many cases, they are shown using the products. TV advertisement uses film stars, artists, or cricketers to illustrate the use of the product. For example, Film stars Sharukh Khan and Priti Jinta are shown driving Santro Car. Children are used for illustrating different brands of toothpastes, chocolates, bicycles, and biscuits. Similarly, Coca-Cola illustrates its product through film stars and cricketers.

5. Pictures

Use of pictures is more or less similar to illustration. However, pictures are more relevant to print media. Pictures include products, brands, persons, etc., presented in systematic manner. Here, also, products and brands are associated with film stars, cricketers, and well-known cartoon characters.

6. Sponsor and logotype

Ad copy also includes name of company, sponsor, brand or logotype to assist customers recognize the name of producers and/or marketers. Name of producer or logotype is kept either at the beginning or at the end of advertisement. Some advertisements include full name and address of company, including registered office, regional offices, its website, e-mail, phone, fax, etc. Use of sponsor or logotype popularizes name of a company along with products and brands. In audiovisual advertisements, the name of company is shown and/or spoken.

ADVERTISING AGENCY

Advertising task has been increasingly difficulty. It requires a high level of creativity and imagination, and a great deal of expertise and experience. Today's advertisements are more sophisticated as well as complicated. They require a duly qualified and experienced special staff. Those companies desire to advertise their products on a continuous basis maintain a well-equipped advertising department to carry out advertising-related activities, such as preparation, execution, evaluation, and modification. However, to maintain a separate department is costly, and many companies can't afford. Companies that cannot maintain advertising department may opt for advertising agency. They use ad agency to do some or all the advertising jobs. However, the well-established and financially sound companies also prefer to assign the task to ad agencies (refer Table 1).

An advertising agency can be defined as: *An independent firm or organisation set up to render specialized services for advertising, in particular, and for marketing, in general. It is not an agent in legal sense, but is an independent firm.* The advertising agency, popularly known as ad agency, carries out all advertising-related activities on behalf of the client companies on professional basis. Since it specializes on advertising field, it can perform the advertising more effectively. It can hire specialized staff, and can maintain wide contacts to perform advertising activities more successfully.

FUNCTIONS OF AD AGENCIES

Advertising agencies perform a wide range of activities. Mostly, an advertising agency offers following services:

1. Ad agency determines the needs of advertisement for the client firms.
2. It prepares advertising message – theme and appeal.

3. It writes ad copy (copy writing).
4. It prepares art, picture, and photography.
5. It maintains close contacts with well-known personalities for advertisement and decides terms and conditions.
6. It prepares commercial spots for film, TV, or other media.
7. It deals with public relations.
8. It deals with media selection and buying pace/time.
9. It prepares advertising scheduling.
10. It assists in preparing advertising budget.
11. It provides marketing consultancy for clients.
12. It sends needed materials to company and media.
13. It carries out evaluation advertising effectiveness, etc.

BENEFITS OR REASONS FOR USING AD AGENCY

Ad agency offers following benefits:

1. Ad agency employs specialist staff to perform various activities related to advertisements, such as copywriter, artists, design-staff, and research experts. It provides expert services to client firms. All firms cannot maintain such services.
2. It analyses advertising in unbiased (bias-free) manner and objectively. It can assess neutrally the issues related to advertising. It is not possible if the firm performs advertising task by its own.
3. Ad agency works for many companies and products. It has a wide range of experience in handling different advertising issues. Client firms can get direct benefit of the agency's rich and varied experience.
4. Mostly, a company is busy with production and marketing. It cannot spare time for preparing, executing, and evaluating advertisement. The agency performs all the advertising tasks on behalf of the company.
5. It is a flexible option. If a company is not satisfied with any agency, the contract can be terminated easily.
6. Ad agency is cost-free. Company is not required to pay to ad agency for its services. Media owners pay to the agency. Company pays only to media owners. However, the recent practices are different.
7. Wide contacts, relations, and contracts of ad agencies with a number of well-known personalities like film stars, artists, cricketers, government offices, and various professionals offer a lot of direct and indirect benefits to the client companies.
8. Modern ad agencies perform a wide variety of functions over and above advertising activities, like marketing consultancy, research, new product development, etc. It deals with almost all the marketing areas.

Mudra Communication in Ahmedabad (Gujarat, India) is a popular and well-established ad agency. Mudra has launched a popular website 'magindia.com,' the first online Indian Advertising Gallery, provides any reference related to advertising. This is the only website that brings together the work of all ad agencies like press, TV, outdoor, direct mailer, PoP, logo, and symbols. The agency works for advertising industry, professionals, and students. Yahoo, Google, Lycos, and Excite have listed MAGINDIA.COM among the top online ad galleries worldwide.

At present, there are many ad agencies working for national and multinational companies. A few ad agencies working for reputed companies (clients) in India have been listed in table 1, along with registered offices and names of chief clients.

Table 1: A few ad agencies working for reputed business enterprises[2]

Name of Ad Agency	Registered Offices	Chief Clients
Adbur Pvt. Ltd.	Kaushambi, Sahibabad, Ghaziabad-201 010.	Sanat Products (Bioslim slimming agent); Dabur Pharmaceuticals (Lona Low-sodium salt). Dabon International Ltd (Lebon-Cheese)
Akshara Advertising	302-303-310 Meghdoot, 94 Nehru Place, New Delhi - 110 019	Rajasthan (University of Rajasthan); ONGC; MTNL., etc.
Chaitra Leo Burnett Pvt. Ltd.	9/11 NS Patkar Marg, AB Godrej Chowk, Mumbai - 400 036	ICICI; Bajaj Auto; Dabur India; BPL Ltd; Coca-Cola (Mazaa) Toyota (Qualis); Amtrex Hitachi(Air -conditioner)
Enterprise Nexus Communications Pvt. Ltd.	367, Sane Guruji Marg, Agripada, Mumbai - 400 011	Nimbus (Nirvanazone/youth portal); Daewoo (Matiz,Nexia/cars); Emami(Herbal skin & hair care range)
Euro RSCG Advertising Pvt Ltd.	Brady Glady's Plaza, Unit No 5, 1st floor, Senapati Bapat Marg, Lower Parel, Mumbai - 400 013	HDFC Securities (HDFCinvest.com/website); Pacific Online (portals); Rolta (roltanet.com/ISP); Weekender (weekender garments); Torrent Pharma (Dilzem Surge), etc.
Hindustan Thompson Associates	Lakshmi Bldg, Sir Pherozeshah Mehta Rd PO Box 541, Mumbai – 400 001, India	Apollo Hospital (Apollo Hospital & healthcare); DSP Merrill Lynch (Investment banking); Hero Honda (CBZ/automobiles); Indian Army; Indian Navy; News Television India Pvt Ltd (Star news/Media); Standard Chartered (Personal Banking & Cards); Ministry of Finance (VDIS); Ministry of Defence (Indian Army - recruitment); Pepsi Foods (7-UP, Mirinda, soft drinks); Star TV Network (Star Plus, Star Movies, Star News); Omega (watches); ESPN (Channel promo); Godrej GE (washing machines); Madura Garments (Van Heusen, garments); Hero Motors (Hero Winner, automobile); Parle (Monaco, biscuit); Hughes Ispat (telecommunication)
Mudra Communications	Mudra House, Sheth CG Rd, Ellisbridge,	Mahanagar Telephone Nigam Ltd (Corporate); Indian Express (News paper); Mid-Day (website); Global

[2]Internet Sources (2011)

Ltd.	Ahmedabad - 380 006	Trust bank (Banking);Indian Tourism Development Corporation (Hotels); Business Standard (Publications); Raj TV (TV Channel); Henkel Spic India (Detergents); Godrej Foods; Ahmedabad Electricity Co Ltd (corporate); LIC of India (Insurance - services); Honda Siel Power Products (gensets); Satyam Computer Services Ltd (Satyam - computer software); Satyam Infoway Ltd (Satyam - internet services); Compaq (Compaq - computers); Cadila Healthcare Ltd (EverYuth - healthcare); Blow Plast Ltd (VIP Skybags - luggage carrier); Dabur Ayurvedic Specialities Ltd (Nature Cure - Ayurvedic products); Henkel Spic India Ltd (Fa - soap); Hindustan Motors Ltd (Mitsubishi Lancer - automobile)
Rashtriya Advertising Agency.	Rashtriya tower, 38 Jhansi Road, Jhandewalan, New Delhi 110055.	Northern Railway; IRCON International Ltd(Govt); NHDC(Ministry of Textile); Power Finance Corporation; western railway; Reserve Bank of India; Airport Authority of India; Akai(electronics); Videocon (electronics); Food Corporation of India
MCS Communications Pvt. Ltd.	20/1 Bagirathi Ammal St, T Nagar, Chennai -600 017	Modi Xerox (photocopiers); Bajaj Auto Ltd (Bajaj/ motor bikes, scooter); HDFC Bank (Bank/Auto finance)
Moulis Euro RSCG (I)Pvt. Ltd.	4 & 5, 1st Floor, Rams, 27 West Cott Rd, Royapettah, Chennai - 600 014	Global Software Ltd(Software); Central railways (Railways); Banking service recruitment (recruitment); OBSI (Information Technology); board NIFT (Fashion Design Training); ONGC (Regional); LIC (LIC - insurance); Konkan Railway (Konkan Railway - rail transport); SmithKline Beecham (Smithkline Beecham - operational advertisements, southern region)

ADVERTISING BUDGET

Advertising budget (known as ad budget) is one of the most critical decisions of advertising in particular and of marketing in general. Ad budget is a part of promotional budget. Major part of promotion budget is spared for advertisement. Advertising budget deals with determining the right amount to be spent for a advertising activities for specific time period. Budget depends on many considerations. Every company wants to determine the optimum amount it should spend for advertising activities and efforts. Advertising budget can be defined as:

1. *Advertising budget consists of determining the total amount required for carrying out advertising activities for the defined time period.*
2. *Advertising budget is the estimate of fund to be spent for advertising activities for a specific time period.*

3. *Advertising budget is a detailed plan that determines the ideal amount the company should spend for advertising efforts for the specified time.*

ADVERTISING COSTS

Advertising budget covers following items/costs:

(a) Creation costs or advertising production costs
(b) Media costs
(c) Administrative overheads
(d) Research and development costs

FACTORS AFFECTING ADVERTISING BUDGET

A number of factors affect ad budget decisions. After proper analysis of these factors, the advertising budget should be set. Advertising manager has to take into account following factors while deciding on advertising budget:

1 Objectives of Company
2 Management Philosophy
3 Stage of Product Life cycle
4 Market Share and Consumer Base
5 Degree of Competition
6 Number of Advertising Frequency
7 Type of Media to be Used
8 Product Substitutability
9 Financial Condition of Company
10 Past Experience of Company, etc.

METHODS FOR ADVERTISING BUDGET

Several methods are used for setting advertising budget. Depending upon internal situations of the company, the suitable method is followed. Every method has its merits, demerits, and applicability. Commonly practiced methods have been briefly discussed in this part:

1. Percentage of Sales Method

It is a commonly used method to set advertising budget. In this method, the amount for advertising is decided on the basis of sales. Advertising budget is specific per cent of sales. The sales may be current, or anticipated. Sometimes, the past sales are also used as the base for deciding on ad budget. For example, the last year sales were Rs. 3 crore and the company spent Rs. 300000 for advertising. It is clear that the company has spent 1% of sales in the last year.

Company has the tendency to maintain certain per cent (or percentage) of sales as ad budget. Based upon the past, the current and the expected sales, amount for advertising budget is determined. This method is based on the notion that sales follow advertising efforts and expenditure. It is assumed that there is positive correlation between sales and advertising expenditure. This is not the scientific method to decide on advertising budget.

Merits: The method offers following merits:

(a) It is based on sales volume. Therefore, cost of advertising can be offset against profits earned from the sales. It satisfies financial management.
(b) This method encourages marketing manager to think in terms of relationship between promotional costs, selling price, and profits per unit.
(c) It maintains competitive parity. All firms in the industry spend approximately the same percentage of sales for advertising.

(d) It keeps the company in constant touch with the sales target to be achieved.

Demerits: The method has been criticized on following grounds:

(a) In absence of specific guidelines, it is not possible to decide the appropriate per cent of sales. It lacks a scientific base.

(b) Long-term planning is not possible because a long-term sales forecasting seems difficult.

(c) It neglects other objectives of advertising. Only sales are given priority. It doesn't consider the need of advertising.

(d) Stage of product life cycle is not considered.

(e) It is, to some extent, inflexible.

(f) It is assumed that only advertising affect sales. It is erroneous.

2. Objectives and Task Method

This is the most appropriate ad budget method for any company. It is a scientific method to set advertising budget. The method considers company's own environment and requirement. Objectives and task method guides the manager to develop his promotional budget by (1) defining specific objectives, (2) determining the task that must be performed to achieve them, and (3) estimating the costs of performing the task. The sum of these costs is the proposed amount for advertising budget.

The method is based on the relationship between the objectives and the task to achieve these objectives. The costs of various advertising activities to be performed to achieve marketing objectives constitute advertising budget. Under this method, following steps are to be followed to set advertising budget:

1. Determine main objectives of marketing department.
2. Set advertising objectives in terms of sales, profits, brand loyalty, competitive stability, etc.
3. Determine advertising task in terms of various advertising activities required to be performed to achieve the advertising objectives.
4. Estimate cost of each advertising activity for the defined period.
5. Make sum of costs of all the activities. It is the estimated amount for advertising.

Thus, advertising budget is set on the basis of the objectives a company wants to achieve and in what way it wants the objectives to be achieved. This method is logically consistent and practically applicable for all the companies. The method emphasizes on actual needs of the company. It is considered as a scientific method to set ad budget.

3. Competitive Parity Method

Competition is one of the powerful factors affecting marketing performance. This method considers the competitors' advertising activities and costs for setting advertising budget. The advertising budget is fixed on the basis of advertising strategy adopted by the competitors. Thus, competitive factor is given more importance in deciding advertising budget. For example, if the close competitors spend 3% of net sales, the company will spend, more or less, the same per cent for advertising. Here it is assumed that "competitors or leaders are always right." If not followed carefully, this method may result into misleading.

It is obvious that a company differs significantly from the competitors in terms of product characteristics, objectives, sales, financial conditions, management philosophy, other promotional means and expenses, image and reputation, price, etc. Therefore, it is not advisable to follow the competitors blindly. Marketing/advertising manager should take competitors' advertising strategy as the base, but should not follow as it is. The advertising budget must be adjusted to the company's internal and external situation.

Limitations: Manager must be aware of following limitations of the competition parity method:

(a) In case of a new product, the method fails to guide for deciding on advertising budget.

(b) It is difficult to know in which stage of life cycle the product of close competitor is passing through.

(c) Company differs in terms of sales, profits, challenges, financial conditions, and so on. To follow competitors directly may be erroneous.

(d) Advertising is not the sole factors that affect the sales; interplay of many factors determines sales.

(e) In case, when there are many competitors, it is difficult to decide as to whom the company should follow.

(f) The method is followed only when there are dominant competitors. In absence of competition, the method cannot be used.

(g) The method can make a sense only to followers and challengers. It is not applicable to a market leader.

4. Affordable or Fund Available Method

This is, in real sense, not a method to set advertising budget. The method is based on the company's capacity to spend. It is based on the notion that a company should spend on advertising as per its capacity. Company with a sound financial position spends more on advertising and vice versa. Under this method, budgetary allocation is made only after meeting all the expenses. Advertising budget is treated as the residual decision. If fund is available, the company spends; otherwise the company has to manage without advertising. Thus, a company's capacity to afford is the main criterion.

Limitations: Following are the limitations of the method:

(a) The method completely ignores the role or need of advertising in the competitive market environment.

(b) In long run, it leads to uncertain planning as there is no guarantee that the company will spend for advertising.

(c) Except company financial position, other factors like company's need for advertising, consumer base, competition, and so forth are ignored.

(d) This method only guides that a company should not spend beyond its capacity.

(e) This is not a method in real sense.

(f) There is possibility of bias in deciding advertising amount.

5. Expert Opinion Method

Many marketing firms follow this method. Both internal and external experts are asked to estimate the amount to be spent for advertisement for a given period. Experts, on the basis of the rich experience on the area, can determine objectively the amount for advertising. Experts supply their estimate individually or jointly. Along with the estimates, they also underline certain assumptions. Internal experts involve company's executives, such as general manager, marketing manager, advertising manager, sales manager, distribution manager, etc. Whereas external experts involve marketing consultants, dealers, suppliers, distributors, trade associations, advertising agencies, and other professionals related to the field. Marketing consultants and advertising agencies provide such services on professional basis. Advertising budget recommended by external experts is more neutral (bias-free) and, hence, is reliable. Experts considers overall situation and give their opinion on how much a company should spend. Mostly, the experts consider all the relevant factors related to advertising while deciding on advertising budget.

Merits: Expert opinion method offers following merits:

(a) The estimates tend to be more balanced as various executives and experts are involved.

(b) The budget is more accurate and realistic because the internal executives are well aware of company's strengths and weaknesses.

(c) It is the only option when a company is new, having no past experience.

(d) External experts tend to be more neutral as they are external to organisation

Demerits: However, the user must be aware of following possible demerits:

(a) It is not a scientific method. Personal value, experience, and attitudes play vital role.

(b) It is difficult to fix responsibility of the final estimates as many experts contribute to budget estimates.

(c) External experts are not fully aware of the company's marketing situations.

(d) When more internal experts are involved, it may deteriorate relation due to possible conflicts or lack of consensus.

(e) Possibility of prejudice or bias cannot be ignored.

(f) All opinions, right or wrong, are given equal importance

6. Other Methods

There are some other methods used for setting advertising budget. They have been listed below:

i. Arbitrary Allocation Method
ii. Profit Maximization Approach
iii. Incremental Method
iv. Sales Force Opinion Method, etc.

SOCIAL ISSUES OF ADVERTISING

Advertising has become an inevitable tool for both new as well as exiting companies. It is the single most powerful element of promotion mix and can enjoy major part of promotional budget. Obviously, it is a powerful weapon that can safeguard and augment company's interest. The fundamental issue is: How far such poliferation of advertising is socially desirable? To what extent does the advertising contribute to social welfare? There can be two types of arguments, in favour of advertising and against advertising.

ARGUMENTS IN FAVOUR OF ADVERTISING: The arguments imply social significance or usefulness of advertising.

1. **Stimulate Production:** Advertising has positive impact on demand. Demand for products can be increased. Naturally, an increased demand stimulates production. More production means more prosperity.
2. **Stimulate National Income:** Advertising can contribute to national income by generating more consumptions, demand, and production.
3. **Employment Opportunities:** It can ease unemployment problems by generating more employment opportunities.
4. **Commercialization of Inventions:** Advertising is useful to commercialize or materialize new useful inventions. New inventions benefit the society.
5. **Public Acceptance:** Advertising prepares people to accept and use new and standard products.
6. **Informative:** Advertisement is a good source of information. It can increase awareness about different products and special offers related to products. Availability of adequate information can help customers select the most suitable products/brands.

7. **Mass Production and Mass Distribution:** Advertising has significant role for mass production and mass distribution. It affects positively in all aspects of mass production and mass distribution.
8. **Educative Value:** It can educate the society about new products, new uses, improvements in products, and other aspects. People can learn a lot of useful things by advertising.
9. **Adaptive Value:** Advertising makes people start using new products. It has a high convincing value. Customers and company both have benefits.
10. **Improved Standard of Living:** Naturally, availability of useful information, mass production and mass distribution, and many other such positive outcomes of advertising improve living standard of people.
11. **National and International Market:** Advertisement is instrumental in generating national and international trade. People of the globe can access useful products easily.
12. **Entertaining Value:** Most advertisements are capable of entraining people. People like to see, hear, or read advertisements in different media. It provides the useful information in an interesting way. It helps release tension or stress.

ARGUMENTS AGAINST ADVERTISING: The arguments imply adverse impact of advertising on society.

1. **High Price to Consumers:** Advertising increases costs of product. Customers have to pay high price for the products heavily advertised. Companies do not forgo their profits. Thus, businessmen can earn more at a cost of customers.
2. **Wastage of National Resources:** Due to excessive use or proliferation of advertising, valuable national resources are wasted. In many cases, companies undertake rigourous advertising efforts without specific needs.
3. **Impulsive Buying:** It creates unnecessary needs. People are emotionally forced to buy the products. Sometimes, it instigates people to buy unnecessary products.
4. **Materialist Implications:** It promotes materialism. It makes people mad after things, whether useful or not.
5. **Fraud to Customers:** It has misleading/deceptive implications. Most claims are exaggerated. Advertising has a little truth and a lot false.
6. **Erotic, Unrealistic and Exaggerated:** It is difficult to justify the company's claims made in advertisement. Some claims or appeals are completely baseless. Advertising appeals related to biscuits, tonic foods, and herbal and pharmaceutical products are far from reality. Some advertisements are so vulgarly presented that have only erotic appeal than commercial.
7. **Company-oriented:** It is erroneous to believe that advertisement is always useful to customers. In most cases, it benefits only to advertisers, sometimes, even at a cost of buyers.
8. **Creation of Monopoly:** Effective advertising campaign creates permanent place for certain brands in the market. It blocks the entry of other competitors. Monopoly always has ill-effect on buyer's interest.
9. **Compulsion to Customers to View, Read or Hear:** It is a disturbance to people. Advertising carries nuisance value. People are not interested to watch, read or hear commercial ads, but they have to do it.
10. **Source of Confusion and Stress:** Due to over bombarding of advertising on different mass media, people are confused and feel stress in regard to selection of products.

EVALUATION OF ADVERTISING EFFECTIVENESS

Evaluation of advertising effectiveness is the last but most important decision of company's advertising programme. In today's context, almost all company's go for advertisement to achieve a variety of goals. They spend millions of rupees for advertising their goods, services, or names. Evaluation shows the rewards against money spent for advertising. Obviously, companies devote time, spend huge money, and put a plenty of efforts for advertising to get some sort of returns. Advertising effectiveness is measured against contribution of advertising to objectives. Every company is interested to know how each rupee spent for advertisement contributes to its objective(s). Measurement of advertising effectiveness shows net contribution of advertising in realizing marketing goals.

While measuring advertising effectiveness, one should be clear about various issues related to such task. In most cases, the advertiser considers following issues:

1. **Purpose:** Why to evaluate advertising effectiveness?
2. **Person:** Who is to perform this task?
3. **Time:** For what period the effectiveness is to be measured?
4. **Criteria:** Against which aspects the advertising effectiveness is to be measured?
5. **Methods:** How can the advertising effectiveness be measured?
6. **Action:** What actions will be taken after evaluating advertising effectiveness?

Evaluation of advertising effectiveness calls for assessing advertising benefits against money spent for it. Clearly, advertising is an expensive tool (element) of market promotion mix. Major part of promotional budget is consumed by advertising alone. It is imperative to check how far advertising has helped achieve marketing goals. Expenditure on advertising must result into profitable investment. Normally, the ultimate purpose of advertising is to sell product, increase sales, or to make profits with consumer satisfaction. Ability to generate sales is the acid test of advertising efforts. Success of advertising programme depends upon the effectiveness of communication in attracting, impressing, and convincing customers. If a company's advertisement creates the desired impact on sales volume, it indicates the effectiveness of advertisement. It is extremely critical to undergo periodical evaluation of advertising effectiveness.

DEFINITIONS

1. **In common words, we can define the term as:** *Advertising effectiveness is an attempt to assess the effect of advertising efforts and expenditure on company's sales, profits, and competitiveness.*
2. **In the same way, it can be said:** *Advertising effectiveness consists of measuring the contribution of advertising efforts on company's objectives. It involves establishing relationship between advertising efforts and advertising outcomes.*

TECHNIQUES TO MEASURE ADVERTISING EFFECTIVENESS

There are different tests and several techniques in each of the test to evaluate advertising effectiveness. Test depends on the aspects to be evaluated. Based on **Philip Kotler's** views, let us first discuss classification of tests (various ways or approaches) to evaluate advertising effectiveness.

1. **Pretest and Post Test:** Pretest implies testing advertising message before it is sent to specific media. Post test implies testing impact of advertising message after it is published in any of the media.
2. **Communication and Sales Effect Test:** Communication test measures communicability (ability to communicate) of the message. Whereas sales-effect test measures advertising impact on sales volume.

3. **Laboratory and Field Test:** Clearly, a laboratory test is conducted in a controlled environment in a limited scale. Respondents are invited in a laboratory to state their response. Quite opposite, a field test is conducted in original setting, artificial climate is not created. It is similar as conducting survey to measure what customers think about company's advertisement.
4. **Experimental and Survey Test:** Experimental test involves testing advertising effect by conducting test by manipulating independent variable (i.e., advertising efforts) and measuring the effect of the manipulation on other dependent variables like sales, profits, consumer satisfaction, etc. Experimental test may be laboratory or field test. Survey test involved knowing consumers' view's through a survey method.
5. **Message and Media Effect Test:** While message test involves measuring clarity, contents, believability, actionability, etc., of the message, the media test measures effectiveness/suitability of one or more media.

Mostly, a company is interested to measure advertisement's communication effect and sales effect. Therefore, it is worthwhile to discuss communication and sales effect test

COMMUNICATION AND SALES EFFECT TEST

Among several tests, the communication test and the sales effect test are more relevant because success of advertising campaign depends on how far advertising has influenced knowledge, attitudes and preference of the target customers. In the same way, a sales volume is the ultimate aim of all marketing efforts (including advertising). Advertising must increase sales. Therefore, evaluation of advertising effectiveness, in most cases, consists of evaluating communication test and sales effect test.

Methods for Communication Effect Test

Communication effect test seeks to determine whether advertisement is capable to communicate effectively. Following methods are used:

1. **Direct Rating Test:** In this method, consumers are asked to rate/rank alternative advertisements. They are exposed to different ads and are requested to rate them. Consumers can consider various criteria to rate the advertisement, like message contents, message clarity, coordination, and overall impression.
2. **Recall Test:** It measures the retention value of ad message. The consumers are asked to listen and/or view the particular advertisement. They are then asked to recall the same. The amount of contents and message they recall determines effectiveness of advertisement.
3. **Portfolio Test:** Here, the consumers are asked to view and/or listen to a portfolio of advertisements. They are given as much time as they need. They are then asked to recall all the ads and their contents. Their recall level indicates an advertisement's ability to affect consumers' knowledge and arouse interest.
4. **Laboratory Test:** The test is conducted in laboratory. Necessary equipments are used to measure consumers' physical reactions in terms of heartbeat, blood pressure, perspiration, etc., to an ad.

Methods Sales Effect Test

While the communication effect test measures communicating ability of the ad, the sales affect test measures ad's ability to influence sales. Ad must affect sales positively. In fact, advertising's sales effect is difficult to test because sales are influenced by many factors besides advertising, including product's features, price, availability, and competition. Following two methods are used:

1. **Historical Test:** The test involves correlating the past sales to the past advertising expenditures using advance statistical techniques. The results can reveal how far

advertisement was effective in generating or increasing sales. The test can be used for different products, territories and ad media, or in general.

2. **Experimental Test:** Experiment is conducted to assess impact of advertisement on sales. Instead of spending the same per cent of sales for advertisement in all territories or products, a company spends different percentage of sales for advertisement. Company can easily judge whether high-spending territories have resulted in increasing sales and vice-versa.

EXERCISES

MULTIPLE CHOICE QUESTIONS (MCQs)

1. Which one is a dominant mean of market promotion?
   a. Publicity b. Public relations
   c. Advertising d. Personal selling
2. "Advertising is any paid form of non-personal presentation and promotion of goods, services, or ideas by an identified sponsor." Who has defined it?
   a. William Stanton b. Frank Presbrey
   c. Philip Kotler d. None
3. Which is not a characteristic of advertising?
   a. Two-way communication b. Non-personal market promotion tool
   c. Expensive and prestigious tool d. Wide applicability
4. In which class of ad media do hoardings, wall paints, trade fairs, and station poster fall?
   a. Audio-visual advertising media b. Outdoor advertising media
   c. Print advertising media d. Direct advertising media
5. Sales letter, e-mail, fax, and cards, etc., are called
   a. press media b. outdoor media
   c. audio-visual media d. direct or mail media
6. Which is not correct?
   a. Direct media are also known as mail media.
   b. Press media are also known as print media.
   c. Outdoor media are also known as mural media.
   d. Internet is called as outdoor medium.
7. Advertising of all spots within three-four days during Diwali festival is called
   a. continuous advertising b. concentrated advertising
   c. flighting advertising d. pulsing advertising
8. In views of Philip Kotler, which is the third step of advertising message development process?
   a. Message Evaluation and Selection b. Message Generation
   c. Format d. Message Execution
9. Which area of advertising do headlines, slogans, text, illustration, pictures and logotype fall?
   a. Layout ad copy b. Advertising message
   c. Advertising budget d. Advertising agency
10. Name the advertising budget method in which amount of adverting depends on company's objectives and amount of costs to achieve them.
    a. Percentage of sales method b. Competitive parity method
    c. Objectives and task method d. Expert opinion method
11. Which is the most appropriate and scientific method of advertising budget?
    a. Fund available method b. Competitive parity method
    c. Expert opinion method d. Objectives and Task method

12. Which is not a valid argument in favour of advertising?
    a. Advertising has educative and entertaining value.
    b. Advertising always offer quality product at low price.
    c. Advertising improves living standard of society.
    d. Advertising creates employment opportunities.
13. Which one is baseless argument against advertising?
    a. Commercial advertising instigates communal riots and terrorism.
    b. Consumers have to pay high price for products.
    c. Commercial advertising tends to be erotic, unrealistic, and exaggerated.
    d. Commercial advertising is more beneficial to the sellers than the buyers.
14. Name the most relevant technique to measure adverting effectiveness.
    a. Pretest and post test b. Communication and sales effect test
    c. Laboratory and filed test d. Message and media test
15. The advertising effectiveness test that measures retention value of advertising message is called
    a. Direct Rating Test b. Portfolio Test
    c. Laboratory Test d. Recall Test

MATCHING TYPE QUESTIONS (MTQs)

16.

List I	List II
(a) To inform, persuade and recall buyers	(1) Advertising Budget
(b) To estimate advertising expenditure	(2) Advertising Objectives
(c) To decide on message transmission vehicles	(3) Advertising Copy
(d) To prepare an advertising document	(4) Advertising media

Codes: (A) (a)-(2), (b)-(1), (c)-(4), (d)-(3)
(B) (a)-(3), (b)-(2), (c)-(1), (d)-(4)
(C) (a)-(4), (b)-(3), (c)-(2), (d)-(1)
(D) (a)-(1), (b)-(4), (c)-(3), (d)-(2)

17.

List I	List II
(a) Press Media	(1) Sales letter, e-mail, cards, fax, etc.
(b) Audio-visual Media	(2) Station poster, hoarding, and station poster
(c) Outdoor media	(3) Radio, Television, and films
(d) Mail Advertising	(4) Newspapers and Magazines

Codes: (A) (a)-(2), (b)-(1), (c)-(4), (d)-(3) (B) (a)-(3), (b)-(2), (c)-(1), (d)-(4)
(C) (a)-(4), (b)-(3), (c)-(2), (d)-(1) (D) (a)-(1), (b)-(4), (c)-(3), (d)-(2)

18.

List I	List II
(a) Ad Agency	(1) It provides advertising consult services.
(b) Ad Copy	(2) It is a theme or appeal of advertisement
(c) Media Scheduling	(3) It is a media time-table
(d) Advertising Message	(4) It is advertising blueprint or document.

Codes: (A) (a)-(2), (b)-(1), (c)-(4), (d)-(3) (B) (a)-(3), (b)-(2), (c)-(1), (d)-(4)
(C) (a)-(4), (b)-(3), (c)-(2), (d)-(1) (D) (a)-(1), (b)-(4), (c)-(3), (d)-(2)

ANSWERS KEY: Chapter 7.1: 1(c), 2(c), 3(a), 4(b), 5(d), 6(d), 7(b), 8(d), 9(a), 10(c), 11(d), 12(b), 13(a), 14(b), 15(d), 16(A), 17(C), 18(D)

QUESTIONS FOR DISCUSSION

19. Explain term 'advertising.' Discuss it characteristics and objectives.
20. What do you mean by advertising media? Write an explanatory note on various advertising media.
21. Show classification of advertising media. Also discuss factor affecting media selection.
22. Write notes: (1) Advertising media (2) advertising objectives.
23. Write notes:
    i. Print Media
    ii. Audio-visual media
24. Define advertising budget. Explain factors affecting advertising budget.
25. Explain various methods for setting advertising budget with relative advantages and disadvantages.
26. "Advertising task is increasingly difficulty." Comment the statement and justify need of advertising agency.
27. What is ad agency? Describe its functions and benefits.
28. Discuss social views (advantages and disadvantages to society) of advertising.
29. Discuss:
    i. Advertising Message
    ii. Advertising Copy
30. "Advertising expenditure must result into increased sales, profits and customer satisfaction." Explain the statement with reference to need of assessing advertising effectiveness. Suggest methods for evaluating advertising effectiveness.

CHAPTER

7.2 PERSONAL SELLING AND SALES FORCE MANAGEMENT

Personal Selling
- Introduction
- Definitions
- Characteristics
- Importance
- Sales/Selling Process
- Difference between Personal Selling and Advertising

Sales Force Management
- Introduction
- Definitions
- Sale Force Management Decisions
  - Sales Force Objectives
  - Sales Force Size
  - Recruitment and Selection of Sales Force
  - Sales Force Training
  - Sales Forces Remunerations
  - Sales Force Control

PERSONAL SELLING

INTRODUCTION

Personal selling, popularly known as salesmanship, is considered as one of the options for distribution and also a tool for market promotion. Company can distribute its product either with the help of middlemen or by hiring salesmen. It is also one of the market promotion tools; market promotion involves four tools, such as advertising, personal selling, sales promotion, and publicity/public relations. Personal selling is increasingly used for consumer products as well as industrial products. Nowadays, advertising is treated as a source of awareness and information. It is not as powerful as personal selling to persuade customers. Many companies, manufacturing and marketing consumer products, use both the means – advertising and personal selling – to get the maximum possible customer response. It is a powerful means to sell the products. The branch of marketing management that deals with managing personal selling efforts is known as sales force management, which covers a wide range of activities related to salesmanship, such as sales force size, sales force recruitment, selection, training, remuneration and motivation, and control of personal selling efforts.

DEFINITIONS

We will, throughout the chapter, refer personal selling and salesmanship interchangeably. We can define the term 'personal selling' in several ways.

1. In common parlance, we can define the term as: *Salesmanship is the act of influencing customer via face-to-face communication. It is one of the methods to promote and/ or distribute the products.*
2. Some people define salesmanship in term of its role like: *Salesmanship is an art of teaching and helping buyers to buy the product.*
3. Marketing experts believe that salesmanship is the ability of a person to sell. Accordingly, it can be said: *Personal selling is the personal ability to influence buyers' attitudes, preferences, and behavior for inducing them to buy the product at mutual benefits.*
4. Salesmanship involves functions or activities of salesman. So, we can say: *Salesmanship is what a salesman does.*
5. Further it can be said: *Personal selling is personal power to persuade the people to purchase company's product pleasurably and permanently at a profit.*
6. **American Marketing Association**

"Salesmanship is the process of inducing and assisting perspective buyers to buy a commodity or service or to act favourably upon an idea that has commercially significance to the seller."

7. **National Salesman's Training Society of USA**

"Salesmanship is an ability to persuade people buy goods or services at a profit to seller and with a benefit to buyer."

DISTINGUISHED CHARACTERISTICS OF SALESMANSHIP

Careful analysis of above stated definitions necessarily reveals following features:

1. Salesmanship is one of the options to promote and/or distribute the product. It is an optional technique. Company may or may not practice it for promotion and/or distribution of products.
2. It is aimed at increasing sales.
3. It involves an oral and face-to-face presentation of a good or service.
4. It is the ability or power of a person to persuade buyers.
5. It facilitates the two-way communication – providing information to buyers and collecting the same from buyers.
6. It is dynamic and much flexible. Salesman can adjust his sales presentation as per need or situation.
7. It is an act of influencing attitudes, preference, and behavior to win buyers' confidence.
8. It is a profession. It is treated as professional activities as it satisfies the most of conditions of a profession.
9. It is a creative and educative process. It is slow but effective and impressive process.
10. It can be applied for commercial as well non-commercial purposes.
11. It is aimed at mutual benefits, profits to seller and benefits to buyers.
12. It is capable of measuring an immediate feedback of buyers.

IMPORTANCE OF PERSONAL SELLING

In today's marketing practices, personal selling has much important role to play. For many consumer products like home appliances, cosmetics, pharmaceuticals, publications, etc., salesmanship is considered as an indispensable technique to promote product as well as to increase sales. Due to increased expectations of consumers on one end and customer orientation approach of companies on the other end, the personal selling is given more priority. Many companies enjoy a strong position in market only due to effective personal selling. Salesman can personally attend each customer to convince as well to solve problems. Note that personal selling in not only important to sell the products, but also to create permanent customers. Salesman can renew customer relations each time. People have more faith on salesman than exaggerated advertisement. Following points explain importance of personal selling:

1. Two-Way Communication

It is the best tool for two-way communication. Salesman can provide necessary information to customer about company's offer, and also can collect information from customer. Customer can actively involve with salesman to solve his doubts and objections. It is not possible in any other methods of market promotion.

2. Personal Attention

Advertising and publicity are among mass communication tools. They do not cater individual needs. Personal selling focuses on personal problems of customers. It is comparatively more effective and result-oriented.

3. Detail Demonstration

Except television advertisements, demonstration is not possible. However, television demonstration is much limited. Salesman can provide a detail demonstration and can supervise when customer is making the actual use of products. For technical products, it has more relevance.

4. Complementary to other Promotional Tools

Personal selling can support advertising, sales promotion, and publicity. It removes the drawbacks of advertising and sales promotion. Advertising increases awareness while personal selling reinforces the advertising message. Similarly, it can make sales promotion tools more effective by personal guidance or conviction.

5. Immediate Feedback

This is the only market promotion technique that provides an immediate feedback. At the end of every call/visit, a salesman can easily judge whether the customer is interested or indented to buy.

6. Individual Services

Salesmanship offers individual services. It can meet personal expectations of buyers. It leads to customer satisfaction.

7. Flexibility

Sales talks and presentation can be adjusted according to situation to suit individual nature, motives, and problems.

8. Customer Confidence

By systematic sales talk and presentation, a capable salesman can remove all doubts, quarries, objections and misunderstandings, and can win customer's confidence. It increases customers' faith in company and its offers.

9. Triple Rewards

Salesmanship offers triple rewards. It benefits all parties, including customer, salesman, and company. Customer is satisfied with products and services; salesman can achieve his targets; and company can improve its market share and profits.

10. Improving Image

Note that salesmanship can remove bad image or misunderstanding by highlighting company's achievements and offers. The detailed explanation about company and its products removes all doubts and misunderstandings. It helps in restoring company image and reputation in market.

SALES PROCESS

Salesman has to follow a systematic process to sell the products to customers. This process is applicable to salesmen working in showroom or retail outlets as well as salesmen selling products by a door-to-door selling. However, it is more relevant to a door-to-door selling. Sales/selling process involves specific steps to sell the product to customers. Number of steps and types of steps depend on following factors:

1. Type of salesmen (qualifications, experience, training, and other personality aspects),
2. Types of products (technical or non-technical, consumable or durable, hazardous or safe, etc.)
3. Time available v/s work pressure
4. Product/brand popularity and customer awareness about product
5. Consumer behaviour (consumer characteristics)
6. Number of customers to be attended at a time
7. Current trend in selling and marketing
8. Company's policies, rules, and practices
9. Company's image and goodwill
10. New v/s existing product
11. Competition (number of competitors and intensity of competition)

STEPS IN SALES PROCESS

Experts have suggested a five-staged formula known as A-I-D-A-S for effective selling process. However, this formula is more closely related to sales presentation (only one step in selling process), and not the entire selling process. The formula has been briefly discussed here:

i. **'A' – Attention** calls for drawing attention or attracting of prospect. Salesman should try to adjust his talk with the needs of prospect or should talk according to the interest of potential buyers.
ii. **'I' – Interest** calls for making the customer interested in products. Salesman should do all possible efforts to arouse customer's interest in product.
iii. **'D' – Desire** calls for arousing and increasing desire for product. Customer can ask for more information. Salesman must handle problems, doubts, and objections with patience. Here, buyer can be prepared to buy the product.
iv. **'A' – Action** calls for getting positive action of customer in terms of placing order. Here, the prospect becomes the actual buyer.
v. **'S' – Satisfaction** calls for taking necessary post-sales steps to satisfy the buyer.

Taking clues form the formula, and ideas of other experts, we suggest a specific practically applicable and logically consistent selling process. Normally, a systematic selling process consists of eight steps as depicted in Figure 1.

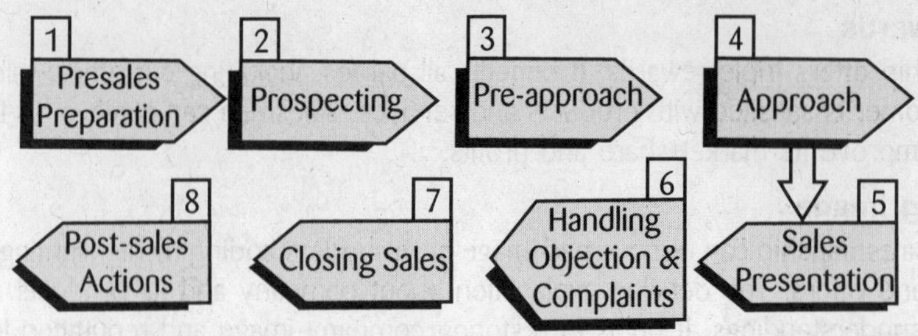

Figure 1: Typical Sales Process

1. Presales Preparations

Presale (before sales) is the step of getting ready to serve customers. A wise sales person must be well-prepared or well-equipped to treat the customers effectively. He must be aware of prospects to be served in terms of their buying motives and buying behaviour. He must know about the company's products, pricing policies, promotional efforts, and distribution network. Similarly, he must have complete detail about the company's history, goodwill and reputation, achievements, objectives, and general policies. In the same way, he must be familiar with competitors' offers and overall marketing environment. In short, he must prepare himself to deal with customers successfully. It is like the homework before the examination.

2. Prospecting

Prospecting means finding or locating the potential customers. A prospect is a probable buyer with unmet needs, ability to pay, and willingness to buy.

Sources: There are a number of sources to locate prospects, such as:

i. Present customers
ii. Other salesmen
iii. Company's present employees
iv. Use of telephone directories
v. Directories of professional and other associations
vi. Customer database prepared by companies or other professional agencies
vii. Other relevant sources.

Prospects must be qualified in terms of needs, purchasing power, and motivation to buy.

3. Pre-approach

Once the prospect is located, now, salesman has to collect necessary detail about him. Such detail helps him prepare his plan for sales presentation. Salesman collects adequate information about customer's nature, needs, problems, personal habits, preferences, and other aspects of behaviour. Salesman's sales talk and sales presentation must be consistent with the nature of prospect. In brief, a salesman must know everything about the potential buyer to whom he has to meet in the near future.

4. Approach

Now, a sales representative has to seek advance appointment/permission for personal meet. Sometimes, he can use phone or send business (visiting) card to take advance appointment. In many cases, salesman can directly meet prospect without advance permission. Approaching method depends on type of prospects. Anyway, this is the step where a salesman comes in a direct (and face-to face) contact with potential customer. At the time of the first meet, he has to greet him in an appropriate manner and has to briefly introduce himself. Immediately, he must initiate brief talk and adjust with the situation. The first contact is very critical. Salesman must be able to attract the prospect's attention and get him interested in the product. Note that he must not directly jump to sales talk.

5. Sales Presentation

This steps calls for a formal presentation of product. It includes sales talk and demonstration. Salesman should describe the offer in a suitable language, show the product, and, if needed, demonstrate it. In case of edible product, he may offer sample to taste. Sales presentation is closely related to buying process (for detail, refer to chapter 4 on consumer behaviour, buying process). In this step, a salesman must get attention of customer and make him interested in the product. Salesman can do it through a lively and interesting sales talk as well as a systematic demonstration of product or offering samples to use and taste. Visual device can be used for sales demonstration. He can produce authentic evidences to prove the product's superiority. All queries must be adequately solved.

Qualities of a Good Presentation

A wise salesman must observe following qualities to make sales presentation effective:

i. Sales presentation must be complete. It must cover all aspects related to company, product, competitive offers, etc.
ii. Sales presentation must be clear. He should explain every aspect clearly. In case of technical product, important aspect should be clearly explained. Talk must be free from confusion, misunderstanding, and vagueness.
iii. Sales presentation must be consistent. Salesman should present all things relevant/ consistent with buyer's needs and situation. Salesman must avoid the matter inconsistent to customers and/or company.
iv. Sales presentations must be precise. He must avoid overexplanation. Easy aspects must not be repeated. Depending upon type of buyer, he must present the sales talk.
v. Sales presentation must prove superiority of products. He highlights all strong aspects of product to prove that the product is superior to that of competitors. He should use comparison and test for the purpose.
vi. Sales presentation must be confidence winning. Prospect must believe that statements of salesman are authentic and true.
vii. Sales presentation must be supported with evidences. A salesman must produce testimonials, awards, and guarantees issued by government, celebrities, and other reliable sources.

6. Handling Objections and Complaints

Once a salesman completes his sales presentation, normally, customer raises objections and place complaints. Salesman may confront objections during his presentation, too. Objections and complaints show that customer is interested in the products, and is more likely to place an order. Salesman must always welcome objections, interpret them clearly, and remove tactfully. Unless the objections and complains are satisfactorily answered, the sales cannot take place. Genuine objections should be interpreted correctly and removed tactfully. Prospects must be convinced about benefits, superior performance, and strong aspects of the product. A great deal of expertise, experience, skills, and patience are important qualities to face buyer's objections and complaints successfully.

7. Closing Sales

Closing of sales refers to completing sales procedure. It concerns with purchase decision. The close can be defined as: *An act of actually getting the prospect's assent. It is the climax, or the desired outcome of the entire sales process.* Sales process ends with getting orders. A successful salesman must close the sales. An alert salesman must find out the right moment to get customer's consent, it is called the reaction moment. Salesman must not wait for customer to ask for product, initiative must come from salesman.

8. Post-sales Actions

It is known as follow-up actions. Virtually, sales process ends with getting the order from buyers. But, getting order is not the ultimate goal of salesmanship, the transaction must take place. The step involves two actions – one is, completing of selling formalities and, the second is, taking other post-sales actions.

Salesman writes order, arranges for dispatch and delivery of the product, and decides on the mode of payment. Sometimes, the product is handed over immediately or is delivered thereafter. Bill and guarantee card are issued. Sometimes, he provides extra guidance for proper and safe use of product. In short, all selling formalities are completed.

Once product is delivered and sales formalities are completed, it doesn't mean that sales process has ended forever. Delivery of product to customer is not the end, but an event. The event must be repeated. Salesman-customer relationship doesn't end with one transaction, but is the beginning of long-term relationship. Customers repeat orders only if they are satisfied with products and post-sales services. Customers' future response depends on salesman's post-sales behaviour and services. Therefore, salesman must undertake necessary actions to ensure maximum customer satisfaction and to avoid unexpected behaviour of buyers. Salesman must remain in live contact with customer to know whether he is satisfied. If customer is not fully satisfied, the salesman must find our reasons or problems and must try to provide satisfactory solution. Even, dissatisfied customers can be prepared to try/buy the product again with suitable follow-up actions.

DIFFERENCE BETWEEN SALESMANSHIP AND ADVERTISING

Both personal selling and advertising are used for promoting the products or increasing sales. Salesmanship differs from advertising in several ways. Table 1 shows how the advertising differs from personal selling:

SALES FORCE MANAGEMENT

Sales force means a team of salesmen. Salesmen are also called sales representatives, sales executives, market representatives, or sales persons. Personal selling is an expensive medium of promotion as well as distribution. The effectiveness of personal selling depends on how it is managed. Sales force management concerns with managing personal selling activities.

DEFINITIONS

1. In simple words, we can say: *Sales force management means management – planning, organising, staffing, directing, and controlling – of personal selling activities of the organisation.*
2. Sales force management performs all tasks of personnel management. In this connection, it can be said: *Sales force management is essentially the personnel management applied to personal selling activities of the company.*
3. All management fundamentals are applied to firm's personal selling activities. So, we can say: *Sales force management is the management of salesmen.*
4. **The American Marketing Association:** "The planning, direction, and control of the personal selling activities of business unit including recruitment, selection, training, equipping, assigning, rating, supervising, motivating, and paying as these tasks apply to sales force."
5. **Albert, Johnson and David:** "Sales force management refers to the planning, implementation, and control of selling efforts."

Table 1: Difference between Personal Selling and Advertising

No.	Key Points	Advertising	Personal selling
1.	Method/mode communication	It is the method of mass communication. It is the way of indirect communication.	It is the method of personal communication. It is the way of face-to-face communication.
2.	Direction of communication	One-way, from seller to buyer, communication.	Two-way, from seller to buyer and buyer to seller, communication.
3.	Degree of flexibility	It is less flexible. Once advertising programme prepared and implemented, there is less chance to alter or adjust it.	It is more flexible. Salesman finds it easy to adjust with situation. He can alter his presentation as per situation.
4.	Cost per contact	Per contact cost is extremely low.	Per contact cost is considerably high.
5.	Time taken to convey message	It is a fast method. Millions of people can be conveyed the advertising message by using mass media.	It is a slow process. At a time, one salesman can talk to one or limited people.
6.	Amount of information	Limited information can be communicated.	Comparatively more information can be communicated.
7.	Degree of explanation	Minimum. Clarification is not possible. It is less effective	Maximum. Clarification is possible. On the spot, matter is clarified. It is more effective.
8.	Suitability	Mostly, it is suitable for non-technical products.	It is suitable for almost all the consumer products.
9.	Tasks performed	It is a promotional device.	It is both promotional and distribution device.
10.	Feedback	Immediate feedback cannot be measured. Even, net impact cannot be known.	Immediate and direct feedback can be measured. Salesman can know the buying intention of buyers.
11.	Degree of control	Company has complete control over it. Advertisement takes place as per company's plan.	It is not controllable. Salesman can present his talk and product as per his skills, knowledge and experience.
12.	Degree of creativity and influence	It permits maximum creativity in preparing theme, message and spots. It is comparatively less influential.	Creativity depends on ability of individual salesman. Comparatively, it more influential.

FEATURES

Main features of sales force management have been listed below:

1. It is management of personal selling activities of the firm.
2. It is optional. It is necessary only when company opts for personal selling.
3. It is not same as sales management, but a part of sales management.
4. Main objectives are to make personal selling efforts effective.
5. Sales force objectives, size, recruitment, selection, training, compensation, assignment, control, etc., are the main decision of sales force management.

MAIN SALES FORCE DECISIONS

Sales force management consists of a lot of activities to make personal selling efforts effective. Main decisions of sales force management have been exhibited in Figure 1.

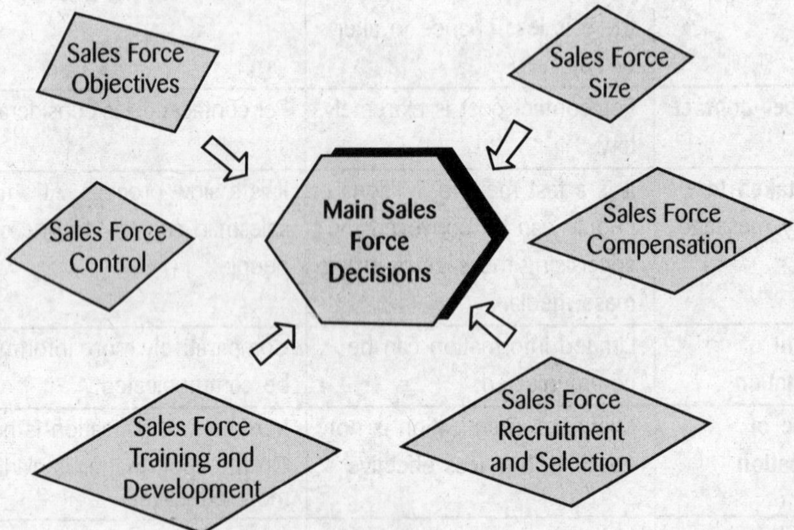

Figure 2: Main Sales Force Decisions

SALES FORCE OBJECTIVES

A firm must carefully set the specific objectives that sales force has to realize. Sale force is not expected to sell the products only; they are required to achieve many objectives. Normally, sales force is expected to perform following tasks:

1. **Prospecting:** It concerns with searching for prospects – potential buyers.
2. **Targeting:** It concerns with allotting time for prospects and customers.
3. **Communicating:** It concerns with providing necessary information about company, products, and services to customers and dealers.
4. **Promoting:** It concerns with performing necessary activities to promote new products.
5. **Selling:** It concerns with selling the product skillfully. It consists of approaching, presenting, handling objections, getting orders, and follow-up actions.
6. **Servicing:** It concerns with rendering technical and non-technical services to buyers. Salesmen provide a number of after-sales services to customers.
7. **Information Gathering:** It concerns with collecting useful information for the company from relevant respondents.

8. **Allocating:** It concerns with allocating the scarce products to customers.
9. **Image Creation:** It concerns with talking positively and favourably about company. Sales people try to create and improve company's image and reputation. They must remove customers' misunderstandings about company and products.
10. **Supplementing other Promotional Efforts:** It concerns with supporting all promotional efforts of the company.
11. **Educating:** Salesmen educate the customers to use the product properly. They also teach them a lot of product-related matters.
12. **Relations Building:** Salesmen are expected to build and maintain healthy and permanent relations with the valued customers.

SALES FORCE SIZE

Sales force size is like a manpower (or human resource) planning applied to sales force activities. It decides how many salesmen a company needs during specific time for effective selling and distribution activities. We know that personal selling is more effective as well as expensive medium to sell and distribute company's products. A company must have the adequate number of salesmen to carry out selling activities effectively.

Factors Affecting Sales Force Size: Sales force size (i.e., number of salesmen) depends on several factors, listed below:

1. Company's general and marketing objectives
2. Current and expected market shares
3. Degree of competition
4. Sales force practices of market leaders and market challenges
5. Types of products
6. Degree of product differentiation
7. Level of other promotional efforts
8. Functions performed by salesmen
9. Geographical concentration of customers
10. Types of customers and market trend
11. Personal selling costs and firm's financial capacity
12. Skills and abilities of salesmen
13. Availability of salesmen and their expectations
14. Methods of paying salesmen
15. Number and types of tasks a company wants the salesmen to perform.

METHODS OF DETERMINING SALES FORCE SIZE

There are some methods to decide on sales force size.

1. Equalized Workload Method

For this method, the workload means the calls the salesmen have to make. The method depends on total workload (i.e., calls). Here, salesmen's duties, functions, or activities are said as 'calls.' A call may include a number functions like pre-approach, approach, sales presentation, abjection handling, and closing sales. However, a call can be defined by the company as per its requirements or expectations. The method can be applied only if a company is in position to decide on (1) different groups of customers based on size of purchase, (2) number of calls required by the different groups of customers, and (3) average number of calls a salesman can make in a year.

Steps: Equalized workload method involves following steps:

i. **Classification of Customers:** Customers are classified into several groups on the basis of their average annual consumption.

ii. **Deciding Desirable Call Frequency:** Number of calls for each of the groups of customers is determined.

iii. **Calculating Total Workload:** To calculate total workload, different customer groups are multiplied by corresponding call frequency.

iv. **Determining Average Number of Calls:** Average number of calls a salesman can make in year is determined.

v. **Determining Sales Force Size:** Sales force size (number of salesmen) is determined by dividing total workload (calls) by average number of calls a salesman can make in a year.

Illustration: Let's take an example to understand the method.

ABC Ltd provides following information:

The company has three groups of buyers, such as:

i. **Class A – Heavy Users.** There are 500 heavy users and desired call frequency is 10 calls a year.

ii. **Class B – Medium Users.** There are 2000 medium users and desired call frequency is 6 calls a year.

iii. **Class C – Light Users.** There are 5500 light users and desired call frequency is 4 calls a year.

Based on experience and study, a company has concluded that in an industry an average salesmen can make 1000 calls in a year.

Let us calculate sales force size for ABC Ltd,

Table 2: Table Showing Calculation of Total Workload

Types of customers customers		Number of each class	Desired Call Frequency (Number of Calls)	Total Workload (calls)
Class A	Heavy Users	500	10	500 x 10 = 5000
Class B	Medium Users	2000	6	2000 x 6 = 12000
Class C	Light Users	5500	4	5500 x 4 = 22000
Total		8000		39000

Sales force size can be calculated as:

Sales force size = Total workload ÷ Average number of calls per salesman

= 39000 ÷ 1000

= 39

Company's sales force size is 39 salesmen. It needs 39 salesmen to meet its workload.

2. Incremental Productivity Method

In this method, additional (incremental) cost of salesman is compared to additional (incremental) sales revenue. Thus, additional contribution of additional salesman is calculated. First of all, a company can appoint any number of salesmen (normally minimum number). Then, it will continue adding more salesmen as long as the additional sales revenues are greater than additional selling costs. This method is not much useful as it requires a lot of calculations and it is based on the notion that increase in sales revenue is due to additional salesmen, which is always not true.

3. Experts' Opinion Methods

Here, experts are asked to suggest the right number of salesmen a firm requires. Experts may be internal such as general managers, marketing manager, sales managers, senior salesmen, marketing research officer, etc., or external like marketing consultants, advertising agencies, and marketing research firms. The experts are provided with needed details about company's objectives, market share, profitability, financial condition, competition, and other relevant aspects. On the basis of their experience and research, they suggest specific number of salesmen a company should appoint. This is not scientific methods as their opinions depend on their perception. There is possibility of bias. Company must follow experts' opinion carefully considering its own situations.

4. Affordable Methods

In real sense, this is not a method. The number of salesmen depends on a company's financial capacity to spend. Obviously, a company with sound financial position appoints more salesmen and vice versa. Its actual needs are not taken into account. The fact is, a company's financial position depends on sales and profits; sales and profits depend on selling efforts. Ironically, a company with poor financial position needs more salesmen, instead of less, to increase sales and profits!

5. Arbitrary Fixation Method

Here, sales force size is determined arbitrarily or randomly. A sales manager doesn't relate sales efforts to any other aspects, neither takes opinion of experts. He can determine any number of salesmen that seems appropriate according to his views. His experience, assumptions, and calculation play important role.

SALES FORCE RECRUITMENT AND SELECTION

Right salesmen can help company achieve marketing objectives. Recruitment and selection are two important decisions in sales force management that concern with ensuring the right type (right qualities, right qualifications, and right experience) of sales personnel. Problem of recruitment and selection arises when:

1. Starting a new company
2. Resigning and retiring of existing salesmen
3. Death of existing salesmen
4. Suspending of existing salesmen
5. Growth and development of company's operations
6. Entering into new territories
7. Developing and introducing new products

Note that salesman is not only employee of a company, but he is its responsible representative; he is not dealing only with selling products, but also with goodwill and reputation of company. A right salesman can create positive effect on sales volume, profitability, customer satisfaction, dealer effectiveness, company's goodwill, promotional efforts, and so forth. While recruiting and selecting salespersons, job analysis (consisting of job description and job specification) is to be made for better selection. Recruitment and selection are interdependent decisions. Let us discuss both terms separately.

RECRUITMENT

Recruitment means searching for prospective candidates and inspiring them to apply for the post. Recruitment ends on the last day/date of receiving applications. Salesmen can be recruited through a number of sources.

Sources of Recruiting Sales Force: Main sources, widely practiced in India, include:

1. Advertisement

2. Other firms
3. Middlemen
4. Personal recommendations
5. Recommendation of existing staff
6. Special recruitment agencies
7. Private training institutes
8. Colleges and academic institutes, etc.

Types of sources to be used for recruiting the salesmen depend on certain criteria, like type of products to be sold, types of customers to be served, paying capacity of company and type of remuneration plans, and other relevant factors.

SELECTION

Selection means selecting the fixed number of suitable candidates from those who applied for the posts. Selection process starts as soon as recruitment ends. Recruitment considers all applications received in a due date while selection considers only the required number of most suitable candidates.

There is no ideal selection process that most companies can follow. Normally, for selecting salesmen, the simple and short selection process is followed. However, some companies, when more salesmen are to be selected at time, also follow lengthy and systematic selection process. Selection process depends on types of salesmen, cost and financial position of company, time available, company's objectives, and so forth.

Steps in Selection Process: Systematic selection process consists of following steps:

1. Receiving applications
2. Screening applications
3. Preliminary interview
4. Written tests
5. Final interview
6. Medical examination
7. Final selection
8. Appointment and induction

Important Conditions: At the time of final selection or appointment of salesmen, following conditions must be made clear:

1. Time to resume the duty
2. Company' marketing objectives, policies, and strategies
3. Duties and restrictions
4. Place of work
5. Reporting system or procedure
6. Bill collecting system
7. Remuneration and incentives
8. Training and expenses
9. Other relevant conditions, if any.

SALES FORCE TRAINING AND DEVELOPMENT

Training is an act of imparting skills and knowledge necessary for performing the work better. Training is necessary to both new and experienced salesmen. A new salesman requires training due to the fact that he is not knowing how, when, and, what to sell. He needs skills and knowledge to deal with customers effectively. An experienced salesman requires training to keep him up to date.

Objectives and Importance of Training

Training the sales force is important to increase sales volume, improve morale, reduce selling costs, improve relations, enable them to adjust with changing work, improve image of company, and so forth. Below stated points indicate objectives and importance of training the salesmen:

1. To explain the sales people about basic principles of salesmanship.
2. To provide information about market territories and customers.
3. To tell them regarding the company's policies, objectives, reputation, strategies, problems and prospects, etc.
4. To inform them about products of the company.
5. To explain them about their duties, types of tasks, authority, and restrictions.
6. To provide salesmen the complete details about company's competitors.
7. To teach them how to report, how work with colleagues, and how to behave with superiors.
8. To teach them effective techniques to contact customers, make effective sales presentation, convince customers, get orders, and to handle their complaints and objections.
9. To make them aware of themselves.
10. To change or modify their attitudes, and remove prejudices and wrong beliefs.
11. To motivate them for maximum efforts and build high morale.
12. To refresh or update them periodically, etc.

Training Contents

Sales force training programme consists of training salesmen about what they have to do, when and why to do, where and how to do, and with whom to do. Salesmen are trained about following aspects:

1. Knowledge about company
2. Knowledge about market (customers characteristics)
3. Knowledge about products
4. Knowledge about marketing channels
5. Knowledge about themselves
6. Knowledge about competition
7. Knowledge about overall marketing environment
8. Knowledge about selling methods and techniques, etc.

Training Method

Several methods are used for training salespeople. Some methods are internal while some are external. Some companies prefer to maintain a well-equipped separate training department for the purpose. The department is headed by training manager. The companies that cannot afford separate department can send sales representatives to training institutes. Some companies do not go for systematic training and use simple training programme in which senior salesmen, sales manager or external experts train sales people as and when required. In all the cases, popular training methods include:

1. On-the-job training (i.e., working under experienced salesman)
2. Lectures and discussion
3. Professional training and educational institutes
4. Correspondence or distanced education
5. Providing the salesmen the sales literatures like manuals, books, reports, sales letters, complaint notes, etc.

6. Sales plays and dramas
7. Conferences, seminars and workshops
8. Sales conventions
9. Role playing
10. Case study
11. Product analytical tests
12. Brainstorming
13. Visit to exhibitions, big stores, shopping malls, trade fairs, etc.
14. Deputation or temporary appointment
15. Audio-visual devices (to show sales films, advertisement, speeches, etc.)

SALESMAN'S COMPENSATION PLANS

Decision regarding remuneration to sales force is crucial in sales force management. Overall performance of sales force/salesmen is largely determined by amount of pay. Level of efforts, degree of loyalty, honesty, stability, and so forth depend on the amount and timing of remuneration. In fact, amount of salary paid to salesmen is reflected in forms of sales volume. Undoubtedly, money has remained a major source of motivation. Therefore, it is imperative to formulate the best-fit remuneration policy to satisfy company's salesmen. In the same way, at the right interval, remuneration policy must undergo necessary changes.

Remuneration paid to sale force must be adequate to cover living expenses and must be paid regularly. Carefully designed remuneration plan is an important part of total motivation programme for sales personnel. One must remember that just to formulate a sound remuneration plan is not only important, but it must be successfully implemented and managed to gain its full benefits.

Components of Salesman's Compensation Plan

A compensation plan of a company consists of one or more of following components:

1. **Basis Pay (plus Dearness Allowance):** It consists of a time-based fixed payment made to all the salesmen on an equal basis. Mostly, dearness allowance (D.A.), as certain per cent of the basis pay, is also paid to meet the increasing living expenses.
2. **Commission:** Commission is the payment made for the actual work. It is a form of the piece-based payment. Commission is paid on the basis of sales volume. And, the rate of commission may be fixed or variable depending upon policy of a company.
3. **Expenses:** Over and above basic pay and commission, the expenses are paid extra. In most cases, companies pay the actual expenses or a lump-sum amount to meet expenses. Expenses include traveling, lodging and boarding, sales expenses like telephone, telegram, and expenses made for customers, entertainment allowances, etc.
4. **Bonus:** Some companies pay bonus. Note that bonus is not a part of regular payment and is not compulsory to pay. It is the extra payment made for extra work done by the salesmen and/or for their outstanding achievements. Bonus may be paid equally or in relation to sales.
5. **Fringe Benefits:** Companies pay some amount to salesmen as the fringe benefits for better living. Fringe benefits cover paid vacation, free holiday-home, insurance premiums, provident fund, car or scooter allowance, gratuity, medical allowance, club membership, educational expenses for children, and so forth.
6. **Profit Sharing:** Certain portion of net profit (profit remained after meeting all the statutory provisions) is distributed among salesmen.

Company, by combining one or more of these components, formulates a suitable remuneration plan. The remuneration plan must be adequate, attractive, and motivating.

Methods of Remunerating Salesmen or Alternative Remuneration Plans

Remuneration plan must be attractive to attract and motivate salesmen. Using different components, various methods are possible to suit different requirements of a company and/or the expectations of salesmen. Each remuneration method has its merits, demerits, and suitability. There are main five methods:

1. Straight Salary Method
2. Straight Commission Method
3. Salary plus Commission Method
4. Combination Plans:
   a. Salary and Bonus
   b. Commission and Bonus
   c. Salary plus Commission plus Bonus Method
   d. Profit sharing
5. Point or Merit-Based Method

(**Note:** Every method is inclusive of allowances and out-of-pocket expenses. Expenses are paid extra or included in salary. Fringe benefits depend upon willingness and ability of a company. Therefore, it is assumed that benefits and expenses – whatever ways they are paid – are included in every method. We may not mention the same in every method.)

Commonly practiced methods, along with merits, demerits and suitability, have been discussed as under:

Straight Salary Method

It is the most common method for remunerating sales force. Here, payment made to salesman is called salary. Mostly, salary includes basic pay plus dearness allowance. The salary is the payment made to a person for carrying out his job or performing his duties over a given period of time. It is based on total time or units of time (for example, days, weeks, or months) spent on the work. For example, salary is paid monthly, weekly, fortnightly, or may be any other duration of time. Salary is paid according to fixed scale of pay. It involves a stable and guaranteed payment regardless of amount of work. It is free from business fluctuations. However, there is provision for increments in the basic pay. Increment benefits are granted as increased length of service improves salesmen's ability and experience. Scale is decided on the basis of proper consideration of increment, for example, 3000-200-4000-400-6000. All other expenses are paid extra.

Merits: Straight salary method offers following merits to both company as well as salesmen:

1. It is very simple to understand and administer.
2. It gives a definite guaranteed income. It is a stable income. Business fluctuations do not affect salesmen's remuneration. Salesmen can work without tension of any reduction in payment.
3. It gives security. Salesmen can have a tension-free life. They can concentrate on their work.
4. This method enables a company to make necessary provisions in advance for amount of salary as it is easy to estimate.
5. High level of cooperation exists among sales force as they are earning equally.
6. Salesmen do not resist to transfer at any place or to carry out other assignments as their income will not be affected by change in place or work. Company has more freedom to adjust with the changing needs.
7. It ensures stability in staff.

8. It is not necessary for salesmen to resort to aggressive salesmanship. They give more attention to needs and expectations of customers than on their targets.
9. Salesmen do not tantalize to resort any dishonest way to raise sales volume.
10. Under this method, management is able to direct and control the salesmen better than any other method.

Demerits: Following are demerits of this method:

1. Basic drawback of this method is lack of incentives for better performance.
2. Generally, those salesmen who are capable, enthusiastic, and ambitious are discouraged.
3. Highly ambitious salesman may not stay with the company in a long run. Ultimately, staff stability is affected adversely.
4. Salary is paid irrespective of sales volume. Company has to incur fixed expenses regardless of sales or profits.
5. Salesmen may develop a tendency to avoid work because they are paid fixed amount. Sales force may be inactive or rigid.
6. In case when adequate increment is not granted regularly, it is difficult for salesmen to cope with rising living expenses.
7. This method does not lead to self-motivation and self-control. Company has to direct and control them on a continuous basis to make them active and interested to carry out assigned work in time.
8. In a slack season, a company cannot reduce selling costs. It is not advisable for a company. On the other hand, during prosperity, salesmen are not benefited with additional income.
9. Salesmen are not interested in prosperity of company. Their interest is only to earn fixed pay. They are found less interested to develop new techniques and tactics to attract customers. They are reluctant to undergo for training programmes or to attend seminars and conferences organized for developing required skills to boost sales. They pay only easy game and may not spare time and energy to do anything extra for the benefit of company.
10. This method is not suitable for hard-selling products or hard-selling territories.

Suitability

Straight salary method is suitable under following situations:

1. When salesmen are newly recruited and are under training.
2. When a company wants to enter a new territory.
3. When a company wants to launch/promote a new product.
4. When a company wants to utilize services of its salesmen to build image, goodwill, and reputation.
5. When a product is complex and technical that requires the salesmen to educate, train, and provide presales and post-sales services.
6. When a company wants salesmen to promote product, solve customers' complaints, and to educate them rather than to sell the products.
7. When salesmen are ready to work as per fixed salary and a company is capable to pay fixed salary regardless of sales volume.

Straight Commission Method

The alternate way to remunerate salesmen is straight commission method. It is quite opposite to the former method. Remuneration under this method is based on the piece-rate system. Payment is based on amount of work regardless of time taken to complete the work. Salesmen are paid according to their ability and performance. Mostly, income/payment of salesmen depends on total sale achieved. There are two options – one is straight commission plus expenses, expenses are paid extra, and the second is straight commission inclusive of expenses. In the second option, obviously, the rate of commission is kept high. In actual practice, commission is treated as a part of total payment, which is paid along with the fixed salary. Pure commission method is hardly practiced by any company.

Amount of commission is calculated as certain per cent of either total sales an individual salesman has achieved or on the basis of sales of particular territory. Commission is also associated with new account opened (number of new customer generated). Company may prefer fixed or variable commission rates for different products (new or existing, hard-selling or easy-selling products), for different territories (new or existing territories, difficult or easy territories) and for any level of sales. Sometimes, the rate of commission is associated with the volume of sales. Commission is paid as per the time period decided in advance. For example, a firm may pay commission to its sales force monthly along with minimum fixed salary or otherwise.

Merits: Followings are the merits of this method:

1. It motivates salesmen to do a better job. This method acts as a greater incentive for efficient and capable salesmen.
2. Alike straight salary method, it is also simple to understand and implement.
3. This scheme provides unlimited opportunities for capable and skillful salesmen. There is no ceiling of income. Payment under this method is usually higher than the previous one.
4. There is freedom of activities for the salesman. He is not bound for specific hours of work in a day. He can draw up his own plan and prepares schedule accordingly. He can acts as an independent businessman.
5. There exists close and direct relationship between efforts and rewards. This method leads to the increased productivity. Company and sale force both are benefited.
6. Salesman can easily be prepared to undergo for training, or to attend/participate seminars, discussions, and conferences organised for improving better skills to achieve more sales.
7. Under this method, due to freedom and incentives, the salesmen of better ability and caliber can be attracted. A company has enthusiastic, industrious, up-to-date, and confident sales people. Salesmen, along with sales and profits, also improve firm's image.
8. There is no complaint for overwork and underpayment. Every salesman can earn as per his ability to generate sales.
9. The most important plus point of this method is that selling costs can be controlled in direct relation to volume of sales. During recession, selling costs can be reduced. Selling costs remain parallel to sales.
10. By applying variable commission rates, a firm can promote new product or new market.
11. Attractive commission rate can attract salesmen of competing firms. It can multiply company's gain.
12. Company is not required to supervise and control them. Salesmen develop a sense of self-motivated, self-directed, and self-controlled.

Demerits: However, following are the weak points of straight commission method:

1. From management point of view, it is difficult to manage sales force as it has no direct control over salesmen. They are independent.
2. In order to increase sales, salesman may resort to some unfair practices. He may work against interest of company and/or customers by compromising with company's original policy. It spoils both company's image and relations with customers. For example, salesman may offer price concession against the company's pricing policy.

3. Salespeople concentrate only on the easy-sold products and territories. They, unless strong incentives are provided, are found less interested to promote a new product or territory.
4. Since they are constantly engaged in raising sales volume, they do not provide satisfactory services to customers or attend customer complaints.
5. They do not collect information for the company. They may not spare time for any other activities important for a company except selling the products.
6. Salesmen avoid promotional work and creative salesmanship. They remain persistent to achieve sales.
7. This method doesn't guarantee steady income. Income is highly fluctuating. In recession, salesmen find it difficult to cover living expenses.
8. Sometimes – in order to increase sales volume and earn more commission – salesmen may employ some tactics such as cheating, false promises or misleading information that affect company's reputation adversely.
9. Salesmen develop the money-oriented mentality. They frequently change the jobs.
10. Company cannot plan in advance regarding sales expenses.
11. This method is not suitable for new salesmen. Also, there may be conflict among salesmen working in the same territory with same products.
12. This method is time-consuming and expensive because a company has to maintain sales records of each salesman in terms of different products and territories to calculate amount of commission.

Salary Plus Commission Method

This is a popular and widely practiced method/plan to remunerate sales force. Under this method, over and above fixed and regular salary, a salesman is paid commission, too. Rate of commission may be fixed or variable, may be common or different to all products and territories. Proportion of fixed salary and commission depends upon types of products, territories, company objectives and policies, and other relevant factors. The strongest aspect of this method is that it combines elements of a regular fixed payment and an incentive to do better. It satisfies both a new salesman, and experienced and enthusiastic salesman. All other selling expenses and fringe benefits are paid extra, directly or indirectly. This plan combines merits of two methods discussed in the former part. Similarly, the method removes drawbacks of only straight salary and only straight commission. For example, a company pays fixed monthly salary Rs. 5000 to each salesman and 5% commission on total sales achieved. Expenses are paid extra as per actual spending.

Merits: This plan offers following merits:

1. It satisfies both types of salesmen – fixed regular income seekers, and industrious and ambitious salesmen.
2. Company has to bear minimum fixed costs of selling. Cost of commission is compensated with increased sales.
3. It is suitable for both salesmen – a new salesman and an experienced salesman.
4. It ensures stability in staff. After training and experience, they continue with the company as they find the scheme fit with their expectations.
5. They devote full time and energy for selling the products. They are not required to do any extra activities to earn extra.
6. All other merits of individual plans are equally applicable here.

Demerits: However, one must be careful of following drawbacks:

1. The major problem with this method is to determine the proportion of fixed salary and rate of commission. What should be the minimum salary – is difficult to decide. In absence of suitable formula (guideline), it is difficult to find out a satisfactory combination.
2. It is comparatively a complex plan. Company has to maintain record of individual salesman to decide on rate of commission and/or amount of commission.
3. Lack of uniformity among various companies neutralizes benefits of both plans. For example, some companies pay commission for any level of sales; some pay commission after certain level of sales; some pay at fixed rate, while some pay at variable rate.
4. Sometimes, when companies pay minimum amount as a fixed salary, it is difficult for salesman to achieve more sales during slack seasons. It leads to exploitation.
5. Company, to adjust with its own need, frequently changes the proportion of fixed salary and rate of commission. Ultimately, salesmen's interest is victimized.
6. In some cases, company pay commission not only for achieving sales, salesmen have to perform certain tasks extra. It gets its several activities done for the same amount of commission.

Combination Plans

In combination plan, various aspects are combined to make remuneration plan more attractive. Bonus and profit sharing are used with straight salary and/or commission. Combination plan involves combination of one or more of following elements:

1. Salary and bonus
2. Commission and bonus
3. Salary plus commission plus bonus method
4. Profit sharing with salary, commission and/or bonus.

What is BONUS?

Remuneration to salesmen consists of fixed salary/commission and bonus. Note that bonus is different than commission. Bonus is paid over and above the usual salary paid to salesmen. It is paid for achieving certain results beyond specific limit. Commission is paid on the basis of volume of sales while bonus is paid for fulfilling a certain sale quota. Note that bonus is not as powerful as commission. Generally, bonus is paid for following activities:

1. Bonus is paid for performing certain promotional activities like demonstration, extra services, extra visits or any other special work for company.
2. Achieving extraordinary sales volume.
3. Obtaining certain number of new customers.
4. Cutting down selling expenses.
5. Discovering new modes and methods of selling that lead to low selling costs, and less efforts and time.
6. For special achievements like defeating competitors, proving competitors' product as inferior, and winning competitors customers.
7. Helping the company in any other way.
8. Carrying out any other assigned work.

Important Aspects: While adopting bonus with salary, commission, or with both, a company should consider following aspects carefully:

1. Company should clearly lay down conditions, which entitle salesmen to a bonus. Terms and conditions must be thoroughly communicated and explained.
2. It should not lead to ambiguities in any situation. It should not be source of misunderstanding and dispute.

3. Proper procedure should be laid down to calculate bonus.
4. Salesmen should be informed time to time in the matter of bonus.
5. In case of any dispute, there should be proper machinery to deal with grievances and dispute. They should be handled with sympathy and fairness.

Salary Plus Bonus

Salary is a major part of remuneration and bonus is only an incentive to perform certain tasks. It is advantageous when a company wants to encourage salesmen to perform certain tasks for short period of time.

Commission Plus Bonus

Bonus is paid when a salesman earns certain amount of commission. It is, sometimes, adopted to eliminate drawback of only commission method. Bonus may be paid when a salesman reaches certain level of sales.

Salary Plus Commission Plus Bonus

Some companies may adopt this plan to make remuneration plan more attractive. It combines merits of all three individual plans:

1. Fixed salary ensures stability, security, and control over salesmen.
2. Commission provides incentives and promotion to do better job.
3. The bonus provides further stimulation to carry out the given assignments.

These three components make remuneration plan perfect and attractive. In many cases, bonus and commission jointly serve as powerful incentives.

Profit Sharing

This is not much popular mode of payment. It is not a part of regular payment to salesmen. Profit sharing is used occasionally or in exceptional cases. Profit sharing can be linked with salary and bonus, commission and bonus, or salary, commission and bonus, or with any other combination. This benefit is offered either on product-wise profits, territory-wise profits or total profits. It is not obligatory on part of a company. It depends on attitude and intension of management. If there is adequate profit, and if the company wants to share the profit with salesmen, profit sharing is possible. Normally, a company shares certain per cent profit equally among salesmen.

Merits: Combination plan offers following merits:

1. Bonus is paid for extra work. So, it is not expensive.
2. Amount of bonus can be determined easily on the basis of conditions laid down for the purpose.
3. Company enjoys full freedom in changing conditions related to bonus.
4. Commission, bonus, and profit sharing along with fixed salary improve salesmen's morale and, hence, performance.
5. This method combines merits of all three individual plans and also adds advantages of profits sharing.
6. Capable and all rounder salesmen are easily attracted.
7. Company can have good image and reputation in market.

Demerits: Demerits of combination plan are as under:

1. It is much complex plan as it involves a number of calculations. Sometimes, it may be source of confusion and conflict.
2. Selling costs are variable and they create difficulties in financial planning and control.
3. A lot of clerical work increases administrative costs; ultimately such costs are transferred to selling costs.

4. When salesmen are sufficiently paid by the way of fixed salary, commission rate is kept lower to keep selling cost down, commission may not be served as sufficient incentives; and when commission rate is raised, they are not interested to perform extra assigned work to earn bonus.
5. It is difficult to decide the proportion of fixed salary, rate commission, and amount of bonus.
6. Bonus and profit sharing may lead to dispute between the salesmen and the company management when salesmen treat these benefits as a part of regular income.
7. It is difficult of evaluate (costs and benefits) impact of each of the components of plan on sales volume, morale and dedication of salesmen, and customer satisfaction in general.

Point or Merit Based Method

In India, this is not a popular method. It is relatively a new method to remunerate salesmen. Here, amount of remuneration to be paid to salesmen depends on merits, marks, or point the salesmen have obtained. Company fixes rate per merit/mark/point in advance and communicate the same with salesmen. Opinion of salesmen may be considered to decide the acceptable rate or price of each unit. Amount of salary can be arrived at by multiplying points with rate per point. For example, company assigns points with tasks as:

- Creating a new customer: 5 points.
- Winning competitors' customer: 10 points.
- Handling customer objections tactfully: 15 points.
- Collecting useful information: 20 points.
- Selling products: 5 points per unit.

Rate per point: ₹ 10.00

If a salesman has achieved 500 points, his income is (500 × 10) 5000 rupee.

Company decides and communicates rate of per point. Rate may be fixed or variable. Company may set rate based on type of products or territories. A capable salesman can bag more points by his excellent overall performance and, hence, can magnify his earning. When each work has been defined carefully and precisely, the method can work effectively. It indirectly bears merits of all other individual plans. However, if it is not planned and implemented with care, it may be complicated, confusive, and possibly lead to conflict. Note that it is not a scientific method. However, it can be an effective alternative plan to remunerate sales force.

FACTORS INFLUENCING REMUNERATION PLAN

Salesmen's performance depends on remuneration plan. The remuneration plan must be suitable to the prevailing market condition, must be attractive to salesmen, and must be affordable for the company. A manager has to consider a number of factors while designing suitable remuneration plan for sales force. Below discussed are some of the important factors that affect company's remuneration plan:

1. Objectives and Policies of Company

Amount of pay to salesmen is directly affected by objectives a company wants to achieve and its remuneration policy. If the company's objective is to solve consumer problems via sale force and to raise sales volume, the company pays more fixed salary and attractive commission. Similarly, the company will pay attractive remuneration when it has liberal policy toward employees.

2. Type of Products

Salesmen who are engaged in selling different products must be remunerated differently as different products need different amount time and efforts. Certain products are 'easy-sold products' that require less efforts and time, while some products are 'hard-sold products' that requires comparatively more efforts and time. Likewise, a completely new product requires salesmen to struggle more to convince consumers. Even in case of technical products, more efforts and time are needed to teach them how to use products safely in normal a condition. Based on type and nature of products to be sold by salesmen, remuneration plan is prepared.

3. Qualification, Experience and Ability of Salesmen

Quite obviously, a salesman with higher qualifications, rich experience, and better ability to sell expects attractive pay package. Company must pay a fair and adequate remuneration to qualified and able salesmen as it is benefited by them.

4. Nature and Amount of Tasks

Compensation to salesmen is based on what a company wants its salesmen to do. Amount differs significantly if salesmen have to perform variety of tasks over and above selling the products. For example, salesmen may be required to generate new customers for existing products, to promote new products, to introduce products in new territories, to collect information of competitors' policies, to win competitors' customers, to conduct market survey, to handle special problems of consumers and dealers, etc. These extra efforts must be compensated by paying higher remuneration. Not only different tasks, but also the intensity of these tasks affects amount of remuneration.

5. Competition and Competitors' Remuneration Policy

A manager has to consider the degrees of competition and competitors' remuneration policy to decide on the company's remuneration policy. It is quite obvious that salesmen need to put more efforts when there is competition. Their efforts must be compensated with the attractive pay. Likewise, no company can completely ignore competitors' remuneration policy.

6. Availability of Sales Personnel

Availability of the required sales personnel is one of the important factors influencing the remuneration plan for salesmen. When company finds it difficult to recruit the needed salesmen at low payments, it has to offer high salary and other attractive benefits.

7. Legal Provisions and Restrictions

Naturally, each company has to formulate and practice the remuneration plan within limit of the contemporary legal framework. Legal provisions and restrictions of the relevant Acts like the Payment of Minimum Wage Act, the Bonus Act, etc., must be considered while deciding on remuneration to avoid any legal problem.

8. Current Remuneration Practices in Industry

No company dares ignore the current practices followed in the industry. Companies prefer to maintain parity with the industry. So, company's remuneration plan consists of such features similar to the industry.

9. Area and Types of Customers

In certain areas where product is either not familiar or is facing a severe competition, a salesman requires more efforts. Obviously, salary must be high in such a territory. When salesmen are paid mainly by commission on sales volume, the rate of commission must be kept high. Similar is the case with the types of customer. Different types of customers need different treatment to be convinced. So, the pay must be linked with the types of customers.

10. Financial Condition of Company

Along with above stated factors, a manager should also consider financial health of the firm. Firm's payment policy must be complementary to its financial position. Financially sound companies adopt an attractive package for salesmen.

11. Other Factors

Apart from the factors discussed so far, there are some additional factors, which have been list below:

(a) General business and economic conditions
(b) Nature of market for the product
(c) General market trend, etc.

REQUISITIONS OR QUALITIES OF A GOOD REMUNERATION PLAN

A good remuneration plan is one that must satisfy following conditions, qualities or requirements:

1. Provision for Adequate Income

It must be adequate to meet living expenses. Inadequate payment makes salesmen to work elsewhere to earn extra income.

2. Provision for Incentives

In order to encourage salesmen to perform job actively with interest, they must be offered attractive incentives, such as variable commission rates, fringe benefits, awards, bonus, etc.

3. Flexibility

Remuneration plan must be flexible to absorb useful changes. It must be changed periodically to suit with dynamic environment.

4. Simplicity

Pay plan for sales force should be simple to design, understand, and implement. It should not involve unnecessary complexities leading to confusion or misunderstanding.

5. Regularity

Remuneration must be paid regularly. Salesmen must be paid as per the schedule fixed in advance.

6. Suitability

The remuneration plan of a company must have overall suitability. In short, it must be suitable to company's objective, policies, current industry practices, and nature of job on one hand, and expectations, tasks, qualifications, experience, etc., of salesmen on the other hand.

7. Competitiveness

Salesmen's remuneration plan must enjoy competitiveness. It must be equal or more attractive than the competitors to sustain salesmen's interest to work with the company.

8. Consideration of Legal Provisions

Remuneration plan must be formulated in accordance with the legal provisions in force. It must fulfill the legal conditions or norms.

9. Fair and Economic

Pay plan must be fair to both, company and salesmen. It must not be beyond the ability of company to pay. It must involve reasonable costs to formulate and administer.

10. Provision for Security

Salesmen do not want only better pay but security, too. They want job security. Along with their job security, their feeling and self-respects must also be secured.

11. Motivating Salesman

Pay plan should be such that makes salesmen to work more. It must motivate salesmen to develop interest in job and put maximum possible efforts. It must lead to job satisfaction.

12. Attractiveness

It must be attractive. Able, qualified, and experienced salesmen can be attracted to work with the company. Similarly, attractive remuneration plan ensures the stability in sales force.

CONTROLLING SALES FORCE

Effectiveness of sales force management, to a large extent, depends on controlling mechanism practiced by the company. Control keeps sales people alert, active, creative, and regular in their efforts. Suitable controlling system is essential to both, company and salesmen. It is to be mentioned that very strict or very liberal controlling system is not advisable. After analysis of nature of sales people, type of work, degree of cooperation, and other relevant variables, an appropriate controlling system should be designed. Note that control is not for fault-finding or punishing others, but is meant for keeping them right. Its purpose is not to keep unnecessary watch on them, but to prevent them make mistakes, and, if necessary, to take suitable corrective actions. This topic has been adequately discussed in the chapter 14 Marketing Control.

Sales force control includes verifying sale force performance and taking corrective actions, if needed. It can be defined as: Sales force control involves measuring sales force performance, comparing it with standards, detecting deviations and causes, and, if necessary, taking corrective actions so that performance takes place as per plan.

For exercising control over sales force, mostly, sales volume, time, expenses, discipline, activities, etc., are used as bases for measuring and comparing performance.

CONTROLLING PROCESS

Sales force controlling process involves four steps:

1. Setting Sales Force Standards
2. Measuring Actual Sales Force Performance
3. Comparing Actual Performance with Standards
4. Correcting Deviations and Taking Follow-up Actions

SALES FORCE CONTROLLING METHODS

Several methods are used for controlling sales force efforts. Methods depend on areas, criteria, or aspects used for measuring and comparing. In every method, the same steps are followed. Widely practiced methods include:

1. Establishing sales territories
2. Allocating of sales quota
3. Maintaining continuous contact with salesmen
4. Determining authorities and rights of salesmen
5. Routing and scheduling sales personnel
6. Salesmen's reporting
7. Complaint and objection notes

8. Analysing sales expenses
9. Observation and visits or field trips
10. Providing materials and literature such as sales literature, sales manuals, visiting cards, order forms, showing small-shorts films to teach the way to work and behave.

EXERCISES

MULTIPLE CHOICE QUESTIONS (MCQs)

1. Which one of following market promotion tools is both a promotion tool as well a distribution tool?
   a. Advertising b. Personal selling
   c. Sales promotion d. Publicity
2. Which one is characterized by two-way communication, higher flexibility, immediate feedback, triple reward, and detail demonstration?
   a. advertising b. personal selling
   c. publicity d. public relations
3. In AIDAS formula related to sales process, alphabet 'D' stands for
   a. demand b. desire
   c. direction d. development
4. With reference to sales process, which is the last step?
   a. Closing sales b. Handling objections and complaints
   c. Post-sales actions d. None
5. Which one of the sales force decisions does concern with deciding the number of salesmen?
   a. Sales force objectives b. Sales force size
   c. Sales force control d. Sales force recruitment and selection
6. State the most suitable method for deciding on sales force size.
   a. Incremental Productivity Method b. Equalized Workload Method
   c. Expert Opinion Method d. Affordable Method
7. Which is an ideal method for compensating salemen?
   a. Straight Commission Method b. Straight Salary Method
   c. Salary, Commission and Bonus Method d. Salary and bonus Method
8. Name the sales force compensation method which is not very popular in India?
   a. Straight Salary Method b. Straight Commission Method
   c. Straight Salary and Commission Method d. Point or Merit Based Method
9. Which is not a method to exercise control over the sale force?
   a. Appointing a private detective to keep watch on salesmen's activities
   b. Allocating sales quota
   c. Routing and scheduling sales personnel
   d. Maintaining continuous contact with salesmen
10. Select the odd source of recruiting sales force?
   a. Promotion b. Recommendation from existing staff
   c. Special recruiting agencies d. Private training institutes

MATCHING TYPE QUESTIONS (MTQs)

11.

List I	List II
(a) Getting ready to serve customers	(1) Prospecting
(b) Finding or locating customers	(2) Presales Preparations
(c) Presenting products systematically	(3) Post-sales actions
(d) Undertaking post-sales actions	(4) Sales Presentation

Codes: (A) (a)-(2), (b)-(1), (c)-(4), (d)-(3) (B) (a)-(3), (b)-(2), (c)-(1), (d)-(4)
(C) (a)-(4), (b)-(3), (c)-(2), (d)-(1) (D) (a)-(1), (b)-(4), (c)-(3), (d)-(2)

12.

List I	List II
(a) Decision on number of salesmen	(1) Sales Force Control
(b) Decision on paying and rewarding	(2) Sales Force Training
(c) Decision on improving salesmen's skills	(3) Sale Force Compensation
(d) Decision on regulating salesmen's behaviour	(4) Sales Force Size

Codes: (A) (a)-(2), (b)-(1), (c)-(4), (d)-(3) (B) (a)-(3), (b)-(2), (c)-(1), (d)-(4)
(C) (a)-(4), (b)-(3), (c)-(2), (d)-(1) (D) (a)-(1), (b)-(4), (c)-(3), (d)-(2)

13.

List I	List II
(a) Paying fixed amount regularly	(1) Profit Sharing Method
(b) Paying salesmen on the basis of sales	(2) Straight Commission Method
(c) Distributing profits among salesmen	(3) Straight Salary Method
(d) Paying for carryout out special jobs	(4) Bonus Method

Codes: (A) (a)-(2), (b)-(1), (c)-(4), (d)-(3) (B) (a)-(3), (b)-(2), (c)-(1), (d)-(4)
(C) (a)-(4), (b)-(3), (c)-(2), (d)-(1) (D) (a)-(1), (b)-(4), (c)-(3), (d)-(2)

ANSWERS KEY: 1(b), 2(b), 3(b), 4(c), **5(b)**, 6(b), 7(c), 8(d), 9(a), 10(a), 11(A), 12(C), 13(B)

QUESTIONS FOR DISCUSSION

14. What is personal selling? Discuss its characteristics and importance.
15. Discuss steps involved in systematic selling process.
16. Define personal selling. Explain difference between personal selling and advertising.
17. What is meant by sales force management? Discuss sales force objectives and sales force size.
18. Why is sales force remuneration decision critical one? Explain factors affecting sales force remuneration decisions.
19. Explain alternative plans for remunerating sales force. Which is an ideal plan? Why?
20. Write notes:
    i. Recruitment of sales force
    ii. Selection of sales force
21. Discuss issues (meaning, needs, contents, methods, etc.) related to sales force training
22. "Sales force control ensures righteousness in sales force efforts." Elaborate the statement in relation to need of sales force control. State methods for exercising sales force control.

✧✧✧

CHAPTER

7.3

SALES PROMOTION

❒ Introduction	❒ Methods
❒ Definitions	❒ Merits/Benefits
❒ Characteristics	❒ Limitations
❒ Importance/Needs or Objectives	

INTRODUCTION

Market promotion consists of four major tools, such as advertising, personal selling, sales promotion, and publicity (and public relations). Sales promotion includes the short-term incentives offered to middlemen, salesmen, and/or consumers. Sales promotion implies a wide variety of promotional activities. In the current marketing practices, the role of sales promotion has increased tremendously. Companies spare and spend millions of rupees to arrest consumer attention toward products and to arouse purchase interest. Sales promotional efforts also improve firm's competitive position. Such efforts seem inevitable in today's marketing situation. It can also reduce the degree of consumer dissatisfaction. Nowadays, sales promotional efforts are undertaken for variety of purposes. It is among the most critical and expensive marketing decisions.

Sales promotion covers those marketing activities other than advertising, publicity, and personal selling that stimulate consumer purchasing and dealer effectiveness. Sales promotion mainly involves short-term and non-routine incentives offered to dealers as well as consumers. The popular methods used for sales promotion are demonstration, trade show, exhibition, exchange offer, seasonal discount, free service, gifts, credit facilities, contests, and so on.

DEFINITIONS

The term 'sales promotion' has been defined as under:

1. **Philip Kotler:** "Those marketing activities other than personal selling, advertising, and publicity that stimulate consumer purchasing and dealer effectiveness, such as display, shows, demonstrations, expositions, and various other non-current selling efforts, not in ordinary routine."
2. **Robert C. and Scott A.:** "Sales promotion consists of a diverse collection of incentive tools, mostly short-term, designed to stimulate quicker and/or greater purchase of particular products/services by consumers or traders."

3. Thus, it can be defined as: *Sales promotion involves non-routine promotional devices to stimulate and re-stimulate demand of the products.*
4. Finally, we can say: *Sales promotion includes non-routine selling efforts (incentives) for temporary period of time to maintain or increase sales during particular time interval.*

CHARACTERISTICS

Special characteristics of sales promotion are listed below:

1. It is a part of market promotion. It involves all the promotional efforts other than advertising, personal selling, and publicity.
2. The primary purpose is to induce customer for immediate buying or dealer effectiveness or both.
3. It is optional. Many companies do not practice it.
4. It is directed for multiple objectives, like to maintain sales during off-season, to increase sales, to face competition, to clear stocks, to improve image, to promote new products, etc.
5. It consists of offering, wide variety of tools/incentives.
6. Sales promotion efforts consist of special selling efforts for the specific time period in forms of short-term incentives and schemes undertaken at consumer level, dealer level or at salesmen level.
7. It involves the non-recurrent selling efforts. They are not a part of daily activities. They are not undertaken repeatedly.
8. Sales promotion incentives are imitative. Competitors can easily imitate them.
9. Sales promotion is expensive. It may affect adversity the profitability of company.
10. Excessive use of sale promotion may affect sales and reputation of company adversely.
11. It supports personal selling and advertising efforts. It is like a bridge between advertising and personal selling. It can increase effectiveness of other promotional efforts.
12. It includes impersonal incentives. They are offered openly to all

IMPORTANCE (NEED OR OBJECTIVES)

The basic objective of sales promotion is to maintain, increase, or regulate sales. There may be some other related objectives to carry out sales promotional efforts. In nutshell, it can be said that sales promotion is aimed at satisfying customers, encouraging salesmen and middlemen, and achieving sales targets. We can enlist objectives as under:

1. To introduce new products.
2. To keep consumers satisfied.
3. To attract new customers.
4. To clear stocks of products. To sell out old stocks rapidly.
5. To induce consumers to try and buy certain products
6. To induce present customers to buy more quantity and/or times.
7. To strengthen competitive position.
8. To offset price competition.
9. To speed up sales of slow moving products.
10. To induce consumers to switch from competitors' brands.
11. To maintain or increase sales during off-seasons.
12. To inspires middlemen to keep more inventories/stocks.
13. To encourage middlemen to put more efforts in attracting customers.

14. To support personal selling. To motivate salesmen to work more.
15. To increase effectiveness of advertising.
16. To reduce the degree of dissatisfaction of customers.
17. To increase familiarity and popularity of product, brand or company name.

SALES PROMOTION METHODS

As shown in Figure 1, sales promotional efforts are carried out at three levels – consumer level sales promotion, dealer level sales promotion, and salesmen level sales promotion.

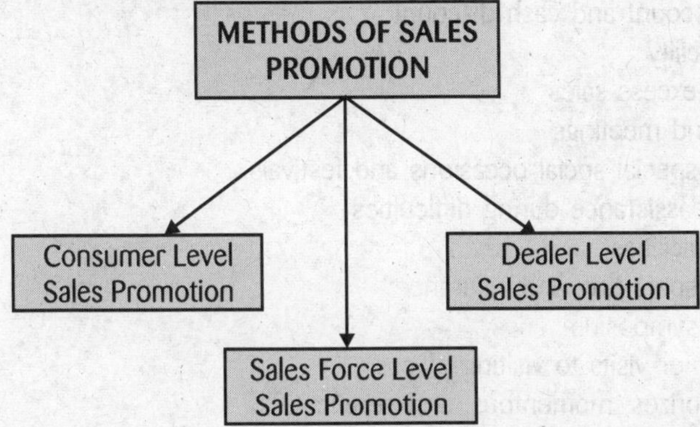

Figure 1: Sales Promotion Methods

Consumer Level Sales Promotion

To stay and grow in competitive market situation, producers offer several incentives to attract new consumers and maintain existing consumers. Selection of sales promotion tools for consumers depends on objectives of company, types of products, company's financial position, consumer behaviour, market trend, competition, and other relevant variables. Most popular tools of consumer level sales promotion include:

1. Free samples
2. Gift articles like balls, stickers, pens, cards, diaries, calendars, manuals, and other literature
3. Coupons
4. Credit facilities
5. Guarantee and warrantee
6. Exchange offer
7. Price discount and rebate or temporary price-cut
8. Seasonal discount
9. Loan facility
10. Installment payment scheme
11. Courtesy visit by sales representatives
12. Free accessories and parts
13. Extra quantity/excess product
14. Free demonstration
15. Display – arranging products in articulative and attractive manner
16. Free trial – permitting consumers to use product for short time
17. Premium – extra gift with product
18. Money refund offer
19. Cent-off promotion – reduction in regular price

20. Contests and prizes
21. Free home delivery and installation, instructions and other services.

Dealer/Channel Level Sales Promotion

Some companies offer short-term incentives to middlemen to make them active and interested. These incentives may be financial or non-financial. Such incentives encourage them to make more efforts to sell particular brands. Most common dealer level sales promotion tools are as below:

1. Bonus
2. Training to staff
3. Trade discount and cash discount
4. Credit facility
5. Gifts on excess sales
6. Parties and meetings
7. Gifts on special social occasions and festivals
8. Financial assistance during difficulties
9. Storage facilities
10. Free transportation and insurance
11. Dealers' symposium
12. Free tour or visits to visiting places
13. Awards, prizes, momentous, and certificates
14. Sales contests
15. Advertising materials
16. Gifts articles and samples for consumers
17. Premium on certain brand
18. Dealership rights (franchises)
19. Joint advertising, etc.

Salesman Level Sales Promotion

In this type of sales promotion, salesmen are offered certain incentives to encourage them to make more sincere efforts. Such incentives are not offered in regular course. The incentives are offered for a short-period of time. These incentives may be financial or non-financial. They include:

1. Extra commission – high rate or more amount
2. Free training
3. Sales materials and samples for customers
4. Gifts articles
5. Offering products at free-of-costs or at concessional rate
6. Bonus – extra payment for extra and/or excellent performance
7. Profit sharing (exceptionally, not regularly)
8. Special allowances and commissions
9. Free holiday-home
10. Customer entertainment allowances
11. Participation in formulating sales policies and strategies
12. Appreciation, recognition, and praise
13. Sales contests among salesmen
14. Awards, prizes and certificates
15. Sales force conventions (conferences, meetings, seminars, discussion, etc.)
16. Leave encashment etc.

MERITS

Sales promotion has proved as a powerful tool for increasing sales volume. In addition to this, it is used for variety of purposes. If sales promotional efforts are directed carefully and effectively, a company can have a lot of benefits. It offers following comparative advantages (merits):

1. Low unit cost
2. Effective sales supports
3. Rapid product acceptance
4. Reduced sales fluctuation
5. Immediate response
6. Better control
7. High flexibility
8. Consumers, dealers and salesmen can be encouraged at a time
9. It is complementary to advertising and personal selling.
10. High suitability

DEMERITS

Note that sales promotion is not always useful. It is like a double-edged sword. Company must practice it carefully and consciously. Manager should be aware of possible limitations (adverse impacts) of sales promotion. Improper and excessive sales promotional efforts have adverse impact on sales volume and image of company. Demerits of sales promotion include:

1. It is not as creditable as advertising and personal selling.
2. It cannot be carried out without advertising and personal selling.
3. Effectiveness depends on active interest of dealers, middlemen, and salesmen.
4. Consumers believe that sales promotion is associated with defective or inferior products.
5. Price discounts and allowances are not real but illusory. Such incentives are offered only after the price-hike.
6. Sales promotional techniques have short life.
7. From social consideration, it is a deceptive device to increase sales volume. It is more beneficial to traders than consumers.
8. It is expensive to a company. Also, it is expensive to consumers as benefits are illusory.
9. Articles and things offered to consumers are useless and of poor quality. It spoils company images and affects sales volume adversely.
10. Misuse of articles and things is very common. Dealers and salesmen sell them and earn money.
11. Immediate and accurate feedback is difficult to be measured.

EXERCISES

MULTIPLE CHOICE QUESTIONS (MCQs)

1. Choose incorrect statement
   a. Sales promotion and market promotion are same.
   b. Sales promotion involves short-term and temporary incentives.
   c. Sales promotion is expensive.
   d. Sales promotion is imitative.
2. Sales promotion techniques such as free samples, credit facility, exchange offer, free demonstration, etc., are included in
   a. sales force level sales promotion
   b. consumer level sales promotion
   c. dealer level sales promotion
   d. dealer and sale force level sales promotion

3. Free training to staff is
   a. a consumer level sales promotion technique
   b. a dealer level sales promotion technique
   c. a sales force level sales promotion technique
   d. both sales force and consumer level technique
4. Which one not true?
   a. Sales promotion techniques have short life.
   b. For sales promotion efforts, accurate feedback is difficult to be measured.
   c. Sales promotion cannot be carried out without personal selling and advertising.
   d. Sales promotion and market promotion are same.
5. Storage facilities, dealership rights, and training to staff are
   a. dealer level sales promotion techniques
   b. consumer level sales promotion techniques
   c. sales force level sales promotion techniques
   d. not sales promotion techniques
6. Which one is correct?
   a. Sales promotion efforts are not imitative.
   b. Sales promotion efforts are carried out regularly.
   c. Sales promotion is cost-free.
   d. Sales promotion is optional.
7. In relation to nature of sales promotion, find out odd one.
   a. Sales promotion is a part of market promotion.
   b. Sales promotion is expensive.
   c. Sales promotion doesn't support advertising and personal selling.
   d. Sales promotion increases familiarity of products.
8. Free training, free holiday home, sales contest, products at concessional rate, etc., are
   a. dealer level sales promotion techniques
   b. consumer level sales promotion techniques
   c. sales force/men level sales promotion techniques
   d. not sales promotion techniques

MATCHING TYPE QUESTIONS (MTQs)

9.

List I	List II
(a) Short-term and non-routing selling efforts	(1) Customer Sales promotion
(b) Gifts, exchange offer, and installment facility	(2) Sales Promotion
(c) Free training, free holiday home, and praise	(3) Dealer Sales Promotion
(d) Training to staff, trade discount, and gifts	(4) Salesmen Sales Promotion

Codes: (A) (a)-(2), (b)-(1), (c)-(4), (d)-(3)
(B) (a)-(3), (b)-(2), (c)-(1), (d)-(4)
(C) (a)-(4), (b)-(3), (c)-(2), (d)-(1)
(D) (a)-(1), (b)-(4), (c)-(3), (d)-(2)

ANSWERS KEY: 1(a), 2(b), 3(b), 4(d), 5(a), 6(d), 7(c), 8(c), 9(A)

QUESTIONS FOR DISCUSSION

10. What do you mean by sales promotion? State is salient features. What is its importance in today's marketing practices?
11. Explain term 'sales Promotion.' Discuss widely practiced sales promotional methods.
12. Write notes:
    i. Consumer level sales promotion
    ii. Merits and demerits of sales promotion
13. "Sales promotion efforts are supplementary to advertising and personal selling." Do you agree? How?

✧✧✧

CHAPTER

7.4 PUBLICITY AND PUBLIC RELATIONS

PUBLICITY

INTRODUCTION

Publicity is also a way of mass communication. It is not a paid form of mass communication that involves getting favourable response of buyers by placing commercially significant news in mass media. Publicity is not paid for by the organisation. Publicity comes from reporters, columnists, and journalists. It can be considered as a part of public relations. Publicity involves giving public speeches, giving interviews, conducting seminars, offering charitable donations, inaugurating mega events by film actors, cricketers, politicians, or popular personalities, arranging stage show, etc., that attract mass media to publish the news about them. Publicity is undertaken for a wide range of purposes like promoting new products, increasing sales of existing product, etc. It also aimed at highlighting employees' achievements, company's civic activities, pollution control steps, research and development successes, financial performance, its progress, any other missionary activities, or social contribution.

DEFINITIONS

Publicity has been defined as:

1. **William J. Stanton:** "Publicity is any promotional communication regarding an organisation and/or its products where the message is not paid for by the organisation benefiting from it."

2. **Philip Kotler:** "Non-personal stimulation of demand for the product or service, or business unit by placing commercially significant news about it in public medium or obtaining favourable presentation of it upon radio, television, or stage that is not paid for by the sponsor."

CHARACTERISTICS OF PUBLICITY

Key characteristics of publicity have been briefly described in following part:

1. Meaning

Publicity is not a paid form of mass communication that involves getting favourable response of buyers by placing commercially significant news in mass media. It involves obtaining favourable presentation upon radio, newspapers, television, or stage that is not paid for by the sponsor.

2. Non-paid Form

Publicity is not a paid form of communication. It is not directly paid by producer. However, it involves various indirect costs. For example, a firm needs some amount for arranging function, calling press conference, inviting outstanding personalities, decorating of stage, other related costs, etc.

3. Various Media

Mostly, publicity can be carried via newspapers, magazines, radio, or television. For example, in case a product is launched by popular personality in a grand function, the mass media like newspapers, television, radio, magazines, etc., will definitely publicize the event.

4. Objectives

Sales promotion is undertaken for a wide variety of purposes. They may include promotion of new product, pollution control, special achievements of employees, publicizing new policies, or increase in sales. It is primarily concerns with publishing or highlighting company's activities and products. It is targeted to build company's image. In a long run, it can contribute to increase sales.

5. Control of Producer

Company has no control over publicity in terms of message, time, frequency, information, and medium. It comes through mass media like radio, newspapers, television, etc. It is given independently by the third party. It is presented as a news rather than propaganda.

6. Credibility/Social Significance

Publicity has high degree of credibility or reliability as it comes from mass media independently. It is given as news for social interest. It has more social significance compared to other means of market promotion.

7. Part of Public Relations

Publicity is a part of broad public relations efforts and activities. Public relations includes improving, establishing, and maintaining direct relations with all publics. Publicity can help improve public relations.

8. Costs

Publicity can be done at much lower cost than advertising. Company needs to spend a little amount to get the event or function publicized.

9. Effect

Publicity message is more likely to be read, viewed, heard, and reacted by audience. It has a high degree of believability as it is given by the third party.

10. Repetition

Frequency or repetition of publicity in mass media depends upon its social significance or the values for news. Mostly, it appears only once.

DIFFERENCE BETWEEN ADVERTISING AND PUBLICITY

Publicity and advertising both are popular techniques used for market promotion. The key difference between the terms has been discussed in Table 1.

Table 1: The Table Showing Difference between Publicity and Advertising.

No.	Key Points	Publicity	Advertising
1.	**Payment**	It is not a paid form of communication.	It is paid by the sponsor who wants to advertise the product.
2.	**Media**	Mostly, publicity can be carried via newspapers, magazines, radio or television.	A large number of media are used. Based on various factors like cost, type of message, reliability, etc., media are selected.
3.	**Control**	Company has no control over publicity in terms of message, time, frequency, and medium.	Company has a complete control over advertising. Company can design its advertising as per its needs.
4.	**Objective**	It is undertaken for a wide variety of purposes. They may include promotion of new product, pollution control efforts, highlighting special achievement of employees, publicizing new policies, or increasing the sales.	Sales expansion and promotion of a new product are immediate and direct objectives of advertising.
6.	**Frequency- or Repetition**	It may not be repeated. It takes place only once.	Its frequency or repetition depends on company's need. It can be repeated if company wants.
7.	**Creditability**	It has a high degree of credibility or reliability as it comes from mass media independently.	Advertising has less credibility. It is considered as company's efforts to increase sales.
8.	**Form of Presentation**	It is in forms of news or reports presented differently than propaganda.	It is in forms of propaganda and it is presented more artificially and attractive manner as per producer's plan.
9.	**Costs**	Publicity can be done at a much lower cost than advertising.	Advertising is the most expensive promotional tool.
10.	**Sponsor**	It is not given by company or producer. It is given by the third party whose opinion carries more reliability.	It is always sponsored by company or its representatives.
11.	**Effect**	Publicity message is more likely to be read and reacted by audience.	Most of the advertising messages are not given more attention.
12.	**Usefulness**	It is useful for society. It has social significance.	It is exclusively useful for company and its dealers. To some extent, it may be useful to customers.

IMPORTANCE OF PUBLICITY

Like advertising and sales promotion, sales can be increased by publicity, too. Publicity carries more credibility compared to advertisement. Publicity is cost free; it doesn't involve direct cost. Publicity offers a lot of benefits to the producers and distributors. Importance of publicity can be made clear from the below stated points:

1. Publicity is an effective medium to disseminate message to the mass with more credibility. People have more trust on news given by publicity.
2. The creditability level of publicity is much higher than advertising and other means of market promotion. People express more trust on what the third party independently says. It appears directly through newspapers, magazines, television, or radio by the third party. It is free from bias.
3. It provides more information as the valuable information is free from space and time constraints. Similarly, publicity takes place immediately. No need to wait for time or space in mass media. It enjoys priority.
4. The firm is not required to pay for publicity. The indirect costs related to publicity are much lower than other means of promotion.
5. It is a part of public relations. It is free from exaggeration; it carries more factual information about company. It is more trustable. It helps establish public relations.
6. Generally, publicity covers the varied information. It normally involves name of company, its goods and services, history, outstanding achievements, and other similar issues. The knowledge is more complete compared to advertisement.
7. Publicity directly helps middlemen and sale persons. Their tasks become easy. Publicity speaks a lot about products on behalf of middlemen and salesmen. Sellers are not required to provide more information to convince the buyers.
8. It is suitable to those companies which cannot effort the expensive ways to promote the product.
9. Publicity increases credit or fame of the company. Publicity on company's assistance in relief operations during flood, earthquake, draught, and other natural calamities highlights its name and social contribution in mass media. People hold high esteem to this company.
10. Publicity can be used by non-commercial organisations/institutes like universities, hospitals, associations of blinds or handicaps, and other social and missionary organisations. They can publicize their noble works by the medium of publicity.

OBJECTIVES OF PUBLICITY

Publicity is aimed at a number of objectives. The most common objectives of publicity have been discussed in brief as under:

1. Building Corporate Image

Through publicity, a company can build or improve its corporate image. People trust more on what press reporters, columnists, or newsreaders say via mass media independently than what the company says. Publicity highlights the company's name and operations. It popularizes the name of the company.

2. Economy

It is a cost saving medium. Here, a company is not required to pay for message preparation, buying space and time, etc. The cost involved is much lower than other means of market promotion. Financially poor companies may opt for publicity.

3. Assisting Middlemen and Salesmen

Publicity can help middlemen and salesmen in performing the sales-related activities successfully. Information conveyed through publicity speaks a lot of things on behalf of sellers. Publicity makes selling tasks much easier.

4. Information with High Creditability

Sometimes, publicity is targeted to disseminate information more reliably. Customers do not express doubts on what publicity appeals. Customers assign more value to information supplied by mass media via publicity than by the advertisement.

5. Removing Misunderstanding or Bad Image

Company can defend the product that has encountered public problems. In many cases, publicity is aimed at removing misunderstanding or bad impression. Whatever a publicity conveys is more likely to be believed.

6. Building Interest on Product Categories

Publicity attracts attention of buyers. Due to more trusted news, people build interest in various products and activities.

7. Newsworthiness Information

Publicity publicizes the fact in an interesting ways. Publicity is eye-catching in nature. People do not skip the news presented by publicity that more likely happens in case of advertising. For example, when a new product is launched by the distinguished personalities like film star, eminent artist, or cricketer in a grand function, the product becomes popular within no time.

PUBLIC RELATIONS

INTRODUCTION

Company has to maintain close and constructive contacts with publics for carrying out various operations successfully. Company should behave in a manner that all the types of publics can be made happy. The public relations (a singular word) is a comprehensive term that includes maintaining constructive relations not only with customers, suppliers, and middlemen, but also with a large set of interested publics. Note that public relations includes publicity, that is, publicity is the part of public relations. Some experts have stated that public relations is an extension of publicity.

DEFINITIONS

Public relations (PR), also known as Marketing Public Relations (MPR), can be defined in several ways. Let us quote some dominant definitions.

1. **Philip Kotler:** "A public is any group that has an actual or potential interest in or impact on a company's ability to achieve its objectives. Public relations (generally written as PR) involves a variety of programmes designed to promote and/or protect a company's image or its individual product."
2. **William Stanton:** "Public relations activities typically are designed to build or maintain a favourable image for an organisation and a favourable relationship with the organisation's various 'publics.' These publics may be customers, stockholders, employees, unions, environmentalists, the government, and people in local community or some other groups in society."
3. It can also be defined as: *A public relations is an organisation's broad and overall communication efforts intended to influence various groups' attitudes toward the organisation.*

4. Finally, we can say: *Public relations concerns with a total process of building goodwill toward a business enterprise and securing a bright public image of the company. It is an extension of publicity. Publicity concerns with getting favourable response from mass media about company, its products, and its activities while public relations concerns with creating and maintaining constructive relations over a time.*

Many companies operate a special department for the purpose, known as public relations department to create and maintain constructive relations with different interested publics. A wise manager must take concrete steps to manage successful relations with the key publics. A public relations department monitors attitudes of the relevant publics and distribute information to build goodwill or image. The best PR department counsels the top management to adopt positive programmes and to eliminate questionable marketing practices so as to prevent negative public relations and to build healthy public relations.

According to **Philip Kotler,** normally, PR department performs the following activities; all of which may not support marketing objectives:

1. **Press Relations:** Presenting news and information about organisation in the most positive light.
2. **Product Publicity:** Sponsoring various efforts to publicize special products.
3. **Corporate Communications:** Promoting the understanding of the organisation with internal and external communication.
4. **Lobbying:** Dealing with legislators and government officials to promote or defeat legislations and regulations.
5. **Counseling:** Advising management about public issues and company positions and image.

CHARACTERISTICS OF PUBLIC RELATIONS

Following are the key characteristics of public relations:

1. Meaning

Public relations activities are typically designed to build and maintain a favourable image for an organisation and a favourable relationship with the organisation's various "publics." These publics may be customers, stockholders, employees, unions, environmentalist, the government, people in local community or some other groups in society

2. Important Managerial Function

It is an integral part of managerial functions. Many companies operate a special department for the purpose known as public relations department to create and maintain constructive relations with different interested publics. A manager must take concrete steps to manage successful relations with the key publics.

3. Publicity and Public Relations

It is an extension of publicity. Publicity concerns with getting favourable response from mass media about a company, its products, and its activities while public relations concerns with creating and maintaining constructive relations with various publics over a time.

4. Wide Range of Activity

Public relations includes a lot of activities to build and maintain long-term and positive relations with a large set of interested publics. It involves a number of interactions, such as contacting, inviting, informing, clarifying, responding, interpreting, dealing, transacting, and so forth.

5. Various Parties

Public relations covers a number of publics – formal and informal groups. These publics may be customers, stockholders, employees, unions, environmentalists, the government, people in local community, or some other groups in society. The purpose of public relations is to make these parties build positive attitudes about a company.

6. Continuous Process

Public relations is a continuous process. It starts with inception of business unit and lasts as long as it exists. The firm has to perform public relations activities on a continuous basis. Once the company has established a good image and reputation, such image and positive attitudes may extinguish if they are not monitored or maintained. Similarly, along with expansion of business, it has to build new relations with varied parties at different places.

7. Management Philosophy

It is fundamentally the management attitudes and managerial philosophy to build and maintain good relations with publics. A company formulates policy to establish public relations. This philosophy is based on building healthy relations with various groups for company's interest. Management must know the attitudes of publics toward the company's policy and practice. It considers general interest while taking decisions.

8. All Level Activity

All the officials from the top level to the supervisory level perform public relations activities. It obvious that officials working at various levels of management can contribute in developing positive relations with different publics like shareholders, customers, traders, service providers, government, and so on. It is the joint duty of all the employees from top to bottom.

9. Routine Activity

Note that public relations is a part of routine activities. It is not incidental or occasional. Further, it is not taken as distinct activity, but a part of day-to-day activities. It is treated as part of daily activities like purchase, administration, production, marketing, finance, and likewise.

10. Essence of Public Relations

It is an essential function of marketing department. A company can build, improve, and maintain its image through public relations. Due to the healthy public relations with several publics, the company can smoothly carry out its operations. It is treated as important as production and marketing.

11. Public Relations as a Profession

In relation to modern management practices, the public relations has become profession. It enjoys professional status. All the characteristics of profession such as specialized knowledge, need of formal education, ethical codes, service motive, continuous development, etc., are also prevalent in public relations. The professional is called PRO (Public Relations Officer). There are special courses intended to prepare and train successful professional public relations officers. There are professional public relations consultancies to guide businessmen how to build, improve and/or maintain public relations.

12. Public Relations as an Art

It is, no doubt, an art. To make publics think positively about the company, one must know how to deal with them. The officer – designated as public relations officer (PRO) – must have skills, special qualities, and knowledge to interact successfully with different groups of society to build the long-term constructive relations. He needs special qualities to be the successful PRO.

PARTIES (PUBLICS OR GROUPS) INVOLVED IN PUBLIC RELATIONS

Public relations activities involve generating positive attitudes of people toward the company. To make them think about and act with the company positively, public relations activities are performed keeping in view different groups. The medium or mode of interactions should be selected according to the basic characteristics of various publics. Education, activities, language, religion, traditions, and other relevant aspects related to different types of groups must be kept in mind while deciding on public relations with them. Public relations department needs the distinct public relations policies with each of the publics. Each type of group can be effectively influenced by the suitable tool, medium, and manner of interaction. A company should work out the broad guidelines for successful public relations. Following part describes what a public relations officer should do to maintain public relations with each of the groups.

Managers have to perform public relations activities with several groups. Main parties with whom the public relations are to be built and maintained have been shown in Figure 1.

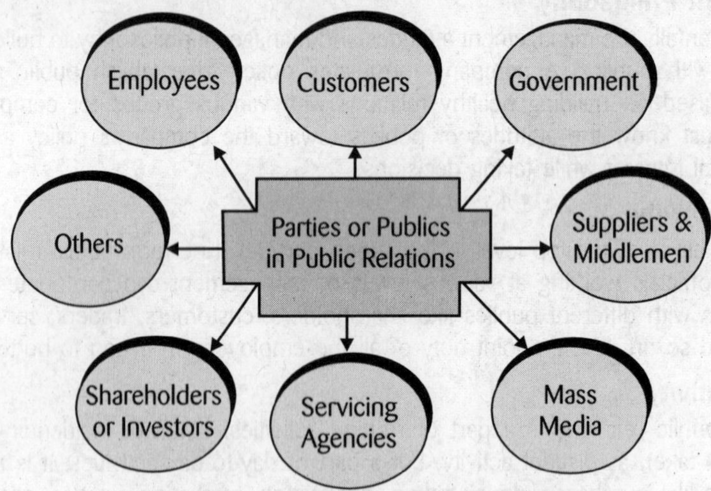

Figure 1: Various Publics in Public Relations

1. Public Relation with Employees

Success and failure of any business unit is largely determined by its employees. Most of business problems can be ended only by the enthusiastic, capable, and loyal employees. In order to maximize contribution of employees, the company needs to develop the sound public relations with them.

Company's efforts to develop public relations with the employees include:

1. To provide clear information to the employees about the rules and policies of the firm. Such information can improve their understanding and elicit respect toward the company.
2. To ensure two-way effective communication.
3. To provide basic facilities to improve their welfare.
4. To ensure better working conditions and security.
5. To allow their participation in company's management and economic progress.
6. To pay them adequately in time.
7. To maintain fair and just dealings, etc.

Benefits of public relations with the employees are:

1. They think and talk positively about the company.
2. They develop interest in work and enjoy working, and can get more job satisfaction.
3. There prevail the amicable industrial relations.
4. They extend unconditional cooperation during unfavourable situation/time.

5. Their morale can be boosted; they work within the limit of rules enthusiastically.
6. It leads to reduce turnover of employees, etc.

2. Public Relations with Customers

Customers are the base for any business. A firm exists for customers. Therefore, it should try to promote public relations with them. Here, customers include both the actual and potential buyers.

Company's efforts to develop public relations with the customers include:

1. To get information about their needs, localities, income, habits, traditions, festivals, language, religions, education, and so on to treat them effectively.
2. To provide the customers the truthful information on product, price, distribution, etc., to assist them take the right buying decision.
3. To invite them to visit to factory or showrooms.
4. To send them greetings, gifts, etc., on various occasions.
5. To attend their problems, quarries, and objections carefully.
6. To prevent marketing malpractices, such as creation of monopoly, adulteration, black-marketing, misleading, etc.

Benefits of public relations with the customers are:

1. Customer's complaints and suggestions help in removing product defects.
2. Company can know the attitudes of buyers toward product and policy.
3. Company can easily launch a new product in the market.
4. Satisfied customers can be helpful in a number of ways, like they talk favourable to others, remain loyal to company's product, and they do not tantalize to competitors offers.
5. Company's image and reputation can be improved or sustained.

3. Public Relations with Government(s)

The government plays a vital role in each of business activities. Its policies, rules, and administrative procedures affect the business in several ways. In order to avoid unnecessary restrictions or interference and to take maximum advantages of the government schemes/facilities, a businessman has to develop constructive public relations with the government. The government includes the central government, the state government, other government offices, and the local bodies including Panchayat, Municipality, Municipal Corporation.

Company's efforts to develop public relations with the government include:

1. To select proper media for developing public relations with government.
2. To invite the government officials to visit the company, or to participate in the special occasions.
3. To present practical difficulties of the government rules and policies, and make practical suggestions.
4. To offer gifts, convey letters of thanks, and attend various functions organized by the government offices.
5. To pay taxes and duties regularly, disclose necessary information, and to support in implementing the government policies.
6. To carry out business activities within limit of the government rules or guidelines.

Benefits of public relations with the government are:

1. Suitable presentation leads to removal of impractical difficulties related to rules and policies.
2. Availability of possible government facilities in time.

3. The unit can get sympathy of government in terms of various types relief schemes in case of unexpected events.
4. Unexpected interference can be minimized.
5. The government supports in solving internal problems of the firm.

4. Public Relations with Suppliers and Middlemen

Suppliers and middlemen have the dominant role in company's success. Suppliers provide inputs required for carrying out business operations effectively while the middlemen assist in distributing the products to ultimate consumers. A company should develop positive public relations with both suppliers and middlemen.

Company's efforts to develop public relations with suppliers and middlemen include:

1. To ensure fair dealings.
2. To assist during the odd time.
3. To offer credit facilities.
4. To provide needed information correctly in time.
5. To advertise or popularize their names, etc.

Benefits of public relations with suppliers and middlemen are:

1. They work with favourable terms and conditions with company.
2. They assist during bad time.
3. They extent their maximum possible cooperation and contribution for the success of business.
4. They can play a vital role in building and improving the company's image in the market, etc.

5. Public Relations with Mass Media

Mass media including radio, television, newspapers, etc., have prominent role to reach other parties. They are capable to carry company's message to several millions people successfully. They can change attitudes the people hold about the company.

Company's efforts to develop public relations with mass media include:

1. To provide necessary information regarding company's operations, product, general policies, and outstanding achievement.
2. To inform the media about public welfare activities a company undertakes.
3. To invite press reporters, editors, and columnists on important events/occasions.
4. To invite representatives of mass media on visit at factories, showroom, and offices.
5. To inform the media about company's contribution to cultural and educational activities, donations to missionary trusts, sponsorship to certain socially significant functions, conservation of environment, etc.
6. To maintain fair deal in business transactions with media. For example, using media as advertising vehicle.

Benefits of public relations with mass media are:

1. They disseminate information about company's business activities to the public.
2. The company is blessed with greetings of editors, reporters, columnist, or commentators.
3. The factual information of business unit can be made available to society at large.
4. They can create or improve image and goodwill of business unit.

6. Public Relations with Servicing Agencies

Such servicing agencies include banks and other financial institutions, warehousing, transportation, insurance, communication agencies like post, telephone, and courier services, and the local authority (Municipality or Municipal Corporation).

Company's efforts to develop public relations with servicing agencies include:

1. To disclose real position of the firm, avoiding manipulation of records.
2. To transact fairly with them.
3. To fulfill commitments or obligations adequately in time.
4. To cooperate and help them during the odd time.
5. To maintain live/close contacts with them to update useful details.

Benefits of public relations with servicing agencies are:

1. They like to deal with the company with favourable terms and conditions.
2. Assistance during awkward time.
3. Positive response and saving time while dealing with them.
4. Talk favourably with other parties, and can contribute to improve image of the firm.
5. Development of informal relations can be instrumental to opt shortcut way to get the work done.

7. Public Relations with Shareholders/Investors

Shareholders are the real owners of the firm. So, it is the duty of the business unit to maintain public relations with them. A company can build public relations with shareholders in a number of ways.

Company's efforts to develop public relations with shareholders/investors include:

1. To provide useful information to them about products, policies, progress, contracts, and other similar critical information.
2. To reply their letters properly in time.
3. To convey them invitation to attend meeting, to visit factories and showrooms.
4. To allow a special concession or discount on sales of products to shareholders.
5. To protect financial interest of shareholders by efficient use of their capital, regular payment of dividends, etc.
6. To prepare and present annul reports in simple language to enhance their understanding.
7. To organize welfare and entertainment programmes for shareholders.

Benefits of public relations with shareholders/investors are:

1. Company can know the attitudes of their investors.
2. Company can raise fund easily in the future.
3. Overall impression and image can be improved.
4. They cam be a powerful source of publicity, etc.

8. Public Relations with Others

Apart from above mentioned parties, there are some other parties with whom a firm should maintain public relations. Other parties may include local public, academic institutions, charitable trusts, environmentalists, artists, local political leaders, various unions, competitors, debtors, etc. A company has to undertake a wide variety of activities to build public relations with these parties.

MAIN MEDIA OR TOOLS OF PUBLIC RELATIONS

Public relations programme of a company consists of various decisions, such as establishing objectives of public relations, choosing message and vehicle, implementing the marketing public relations, and evaluating marketing public relations. Thus, choosing appropriate tools or vehicle is one of the important decisions of PR/MPR. Various media are used for market public relations. Selection of suitable means or tool depends on a large number of factors, such as objective, type of message to be conveyed, costs, time, parties with whom public relations are to be built, etc. After analyzing various relevant factors, suitable means/tools should be selected. Most popular and widely used tools for public relations, as stated by Philip Kotler, have been depicted in Figure 2.

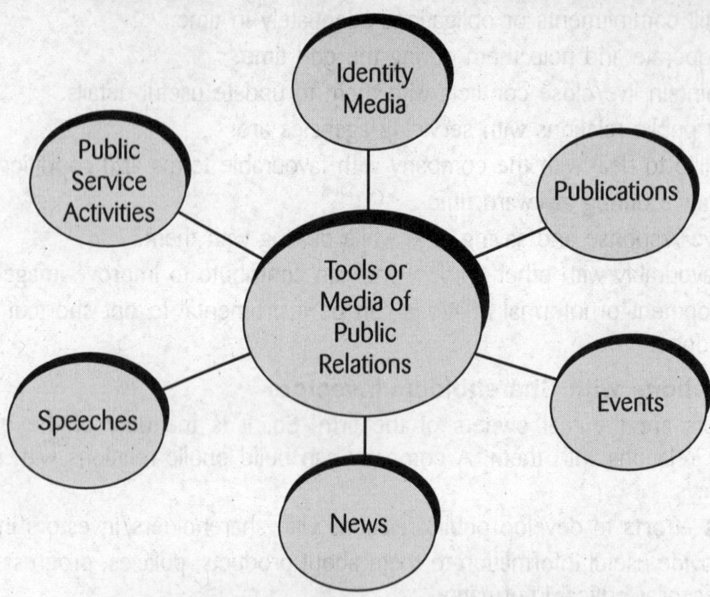

Figure 2: Main Media or Tools of Public Relations

1. Publications

Publications are widely practiced tools for developing public relations. Publications include publishing the annual reports, brochures, articles, company's newsletters, pamphlets and magazines, diaries, calendars, and audio-visual materials such as films, slides-and-sounds, video and audio CDs. Cost of audio-visual and multimedia materials is greater than printed materials, but audio-visual media have comparatively more impact on the audience. Using these all tools, the company tries to provide information on its products, services, facilities, schemes, achievements, etc. These all publications reach the shareholders, general public, employees, customers, traders, etc., and can create a good image.

2. Events

A company may highlight certain attractive events for developing public relations. It can draw public attention toward new products, other activities, and achievements by arranging special events. These events may include news (press) conferences, seminars, exhibitions, contests and competition, sport and cultural events sponsorships, anniversaries, etc. For example, Coca-Cola has sponsored the World Cup. Such events can gain high degree of popularity among the various publics.

3. News

Many times, public relations professionals prepare favourable and interesting news stories about the company – its activities, products, employees, achievements, and so on. Though news generation requires a great deal of skills, knowledge, and experience. The news stories must be interesting, attention getting, timely, and written well as per press media needs. Public relations officer needs to maintain good relations with reporters and editors for getting more favourable coverage to the company.

4. Speeches

Speeches are also widely used for public relations. Key position holders such as managing director, general manager, or outside experts deliver speeches on the company's products, policies, its outstanding achievements, etc., before a large audience to get popularity among various masses. Carefully prepared and effectively delivered speeches build the company's image. Speeches delivered during special functions can create a good impression on various groups of people.

5. Public-Service Activities

This tool includes various activities directed for the public welfare or interest. The firm can improve its goodwill by contributing money, time, and efforts to support community affairs where its offices and plant are located. Such activities involve running schools, colleges and charity-based hospitals, tree plantation programmes, organising medical/vaccination camps, events for offering charity or donation publicly, preparing and maintaining gardens for general public, taking villages as datak, provision of potable water at public places, etc. For example, Reliance Petrochemicals Limited has taken certain villages as datak for their overall development. These types of activities can contribute tremendously to popularize name of the company and its products.

6. Identity Media

In order to be easily identified in over-informed society, a company must create its distinctive visual identity. A company uses advertisements in forms of signboard, hoardings and wall-paints. It can use word, logo or symbol, slogan (in particular text format), picture, uniform of the employees, shapes, colour combination, and so on visual means to create a unique image or fame. They may be known as visual identities. The familiar logo of Ambuja Cement, Logo of LIC, our national flag, Desh Ki Dhadkan slogan by Hero Honda, and uniform of Indian Military are a few examples. Just by looking these visual identities, one can easily identify the company or its products. Such identities remain in the mind of people for relatively permanent period of time.

Each of the tools has its merits and demerits. A company should use the most suitable tools for successfully establishing public relations with various parties concern. Which tool is to be used depends on the overall suitability of the tool on one end, and policy decision of company management on the other end. Mostly, decision on public relations tools is taken after due consideration of relevant variables stated in the beginning of this topic. A company spends considerable amount for arranging events, hiring space and time of mass media, preparing and delivering speeches, and carrying out various activities in the interest of common public.

EXERCISES

MULTIPLE CHOICE QUESTIONS (MCQs)

1. Select the correct statement.
   a. Like advertising, publicity is also an expensive mean of market promotion.
   b. Like advertising, publicity is also a way of mass communication.
   c. Like advertising, publicity is also less creditable.
   d. Like advertising, publicity efforts are controllable.
2. Alike advertising, publicity appears in newspapers, magazines and journals, radio, television, and other mass media.
   a. The statement absolutely wrong.
   b. The statement is absolutely right.
   c. The statement is partially right.
   d. The statement is partially wrong.

3. Philip Kotler has suggested six tools of public relations. Which one is not included?
   a. Plays and dramas
   b. Identity media
   c. Publications
   d. Speeches
4. Publications, events, public service activities, identity media, news, etc., tools are used for
   a. Advertising
   b. Publicity and Public relations
   c. Sales promotions
   d. None
5. Which one is not true?
   a. Publicity is part of public relations.
   b. Public relations is an extension of publicity.
   c. Public relations is a singular term.
   d. Public relations and publicity are quite different terms.
6. Which one is the correct characteristic of publicity?
   a. Publicity is paid form of mass communication?
   b. Publicity is more creditable among all tools of market promotion.
   c. Publicity can be repeated as many times as the firm desires.
   d. Publicity is fully controllable.
7. In relation to role of publicity, find out odd one.
   a. Publicity doesn't help middlemen and salesmen.
   b. Publicity has high creditworthiness.
   c. Publicity provides more information as it is free from space/time constraints.
   d. Publicity is cost-free option of market promotion.
8. Pay taxes and duties, disclose necessary information, perform business as per legal norms, etc., are useful to develop public relations with
   a. Government(s)
   b. Employees
   c. Customers
   d. Suppliers and middlemen

MATCHING TYPE QUESTIONS (MTQs)

9.

List I	List II
(a) It is non-paid form of mass communication	(1) Public Relations
(b) Build and maintain long-term relations	(2) Publicity
(c) Customers, employees, suppliers, dealers. etc.	(3) Public relations tools
(d) Identity media, news, events, and publications	(4) Stakeholders

Codes: (A) (a)-(2), (b)-(1), (c)-(4), (d)-(3) (B) (a)-(3), (b)-(2), (c)-(1), (d)-(4)
(C) (a)-(4), (b)-(3), (c)-(2), (d)-(1) (D) (a)-(1), (b)-(4), (c)-(3), (d)-(2)

10.

List I	List II
(a) To pay them adequately in time	(1) Public Relations with shareholders
(b) To satisfy their needs and wants with care	(2) Public relations with governments
(c) To pay taxes and duties in time	(3) Public relations with customers
(d) To protect their financial interest	(4) Public relations with employees

Codes: (A) (a)-(2), (b)-(1), (c)-(4), (d)-(3) (B) (a)-(3), (b)-(2), (c)-(1), (d)-(4)
(C) (a)-(4), (b)-(3), (c)-(2), (d)-(1) (D) (a)-(1), (b)-(4), (c)-(3), (d)-(2)

ANSWERS KEY: 1(b), 2(b), 3(a), 4(b), 5(d), 6(b), 7(a), 8(a), 9(A), 10(C)

QUESTIONS FOR DISCUSSION

11. Define publicity. State its main characteristics and objectives of publicity.
12. Explain:
    a. Importance of publicity
    b. Differentiate between publicity and advertising
13. Define public relations. State its special characteristics. What is its significance?
14. "Relation building is a key to succeed in competitive market situation." Explain statement in relation to role of public relations. Suggest parties with whom company must build long-term relations.
15. Discuss company's efforts to develop public relations with various stakeholders.
16. What do you mean by public relations? Explain various tools/media of public relations.

CHAPTER

8 PHYSICAL DISTRIBUTION AND CHANNEL OF DISTRIBUTION

PHYSICAL DISTRIBUTION

INTRODUCTION

Today's businessmen are increasingly facing the problems of distribution, not problems of production. Due to consumer orientation as marketing philosophy, increased competition, decentralized and widely scatted market, urgent need to distribute the product in time, and fast-life approach have necessitated distribution of products to the ultimate users at the earliest possible and in the way they expect. Many products fail not because of quality, feature and price problems, but because of inefficient distribution system. Now, marketers have become conscious of the role of a proper distribution network in overall success of marketing programme.

Physical distribution, also known as product distribution, or distribution, involves a number of activities to make products available to the ultimate consumers. The right distribution can contribute to the total satisfaction of consumers. Physical distribution creates time and place utiltity, which utiltity, which maximizes value of products by delivering them to the right customers at the right time and at the right place. Companies can attract customers by offering better services at low price through improving physical-distribution system. Marketers, in an average, devote their 25% energy, costs, and time to distribute their products to the final users. Experts opine that substantial savings of costs can be affected in this area.

It is the last 4th 'P' of marketing programme. Business involves mainly two sets of activities – production and distribution. Distribution decision is considered as a vital in today's competitive age. Due to a suitable distribution network, the products can be made available to the customers at a low cost and in time.

DEFINITIONS

We can define term 'physical distribution' as under:

1. In simple words, physical distribution can be defined as: *Physical distribution relates with all those activities involved in making the product available at the right place, at the right time, for the right people (market), and in the right form or manner in pursuit of marketing goals.*
2. More clearly, we can say: *Physical distribution involves all those activities and services directed to make the products available from the primary producers to the ultimate users. These activities consist of physical transfer/movement of products plus other ancillary services, such as warehousing, transportation, communication, insurance, banking, and middlemen.*
3. **Philip Kotler:** "Physical distribution involves planning, implementing, and controlling the physical flows of materials and final goods from points of origin to points of use to meet customer needs at a profit."
4. **William Stanton:** "Physical distribution consists of all the activities concerned with moving the right amount of the right products to the right place at the right time."

CHARACTERISTICS OF PHYSICAL DISTRIBUTION

Physical distribution concerns with the total activities involved in distributing products to ultimate users. It joins two ends, producers and sellers. Careful analysis of elements, activities and effects of physical distribution necessarily reveals following features:

1. Meaning

It is a comprehensive term. Physical distribution, also known as distribution network, refers to a range of activities and services required for moving products from producers to ultimate users.

2. Parties

Physical distribution involves various parties, such as producers, middlemen (wholesalers, retailers, agents, etc.), owners of warehouses, bankers, insurance companies, transporters, communication service providers, and many other similar parties, who can facilitate a smooth flow to goods from producers to consumers.

3. Activities/Functions

Physical distribution involves a large number of activities like grading or classifying; processing, packing and storing; ordering, transporting, and transfering of title; receiving, inspecting, storing, maintaining, and selling; and insuring and paying. It is applicable to raw materials and finished products. In short, it involves:

(i) Order processing
(ii) Handling products
(iii) Sorting and packing

(iv) Warehousing
(v) Transportation
(vi) Insurance and banking
(vii) Inventory control
(viii) Customer service, etc.

4. Costs

Distribution involves, in an average, 20% to 25% costs. Main components of costs involve grading or processing, storing, moving, charging, insuring, damage or loss during movement, delivering to customers, and clearing bills. These all costs can be reduced to a great extent by a suitable distributing system.

5. Utility Creation

Physical distribution creates time and place utility. Products manufactured at a particular point can be made available to different destinations in time. Consumers have more ease and freedom to buy the required quantity of products as and when they need. The right distribution can add to the total consumer satisfaction. Wide availability at all the times can help buyers and sellers.

6. Role

Physical distribution plays a decisive role in determining overall success of any product. Just by establishing a suitable distribution system, a company can offer additional benefits to buyers. Availing products regularly and at reasonable price where and when consumers demand depends largely on physical distribution. It is treated as an important tool for survival and growth.

7. Flexibility

Physical distribution is flexible in nature. How a product can be distributed is dependent upon various factors. So, distribution decision is the individual decision of the firm and it depends on nature of product, management philosophy, financial and human abilities of the firm, availability of quality and quantity of auxiliary services, demand of products, government rules and restrictions, and likewise. Every company designs its distribution network as per its needs and forces of external environment.

OBJECTIVES/IMPORTANCE OF PHYSICAL DISTRIBUTION

Basically, physical distribution is aimed at availing the products to consumers smoothly at low cost. It stresses on achieving the righteousness in all the significant aspects of physical distribution, i.e., the right product, at the right time, at the right place, in the right manner, for the right people, and at the right price/cost. It balances between the price and the services. The main objectives can be stated as under:

1. To Ensure Consumer Convenience

It is the primary objective of physical distribution. The right kind of distribution can increase consumer convenience. They can buy the product as per their needs at any time from the convenient place, even at reasonable price. Similarly, middlemen involved in physical distribution, who sell products of various companies, can offer consumers a chance to select the most suitable products. Smooth and continuous flow of goods can add to total consumer satisfaction.

2. To Facilitate Continuous Production

Distribution is directly beneficial to producers. Continuous production contributes a lot to distributors, consumers, and society at large. An efficient distribution network facilitates continuous production because of sophisticated storing facility, rapid means of transportation and communication, access to global market, advance ordering, buying incentives to sell in off-seasons, rapid ordering and executing, etc.

3. To Achieve Economy

To economize distribution is one of the objectives of physical distribution. A suitable distribution system results into lowering overall costs in a number of ways. Speedy order processing, availability of the latest transportation and communication, benefits of scale of economy, rapid sales turnover, insuring the products, and many other similar benefits lead to low costs, and ultimately low selling price.

4. To Reduced Degree of Damage/Wastage

A company can reduce product damage that takes place during storage, transportation, and handling. Also, availability of insurance at a lower premium can reduce considerable risk during storage and transportation. Use of cold storage, rapid and safe means of transportation, and other facilities relating to distribution can reduce damage or wastage of product. Reduced damage and better quality significantly contribute to success of product.

5. To Increase Competitiveness

Today's market is characterized by cut-throat competition. All sellers are fighting for better offers to their consumers. A company can increase its competitive strengths by a systematic distribution network. Many companies can distinguish their offers by availing products differently than competitors. Effective distribution affects positively to services, availability, timing, price, and similar benefits. Undoubtedly, if all the components of distribution work effectively, physical distribution can be a powerful means to fight with competitors.

6. To Lower Idle Stocks

This objective relates with inventory control. Producers and distributors can minimize reordering size or safety margin by effective distribution system. Due to speed and precision in placing and executing orders, and advanced ordering by distributors, they are not required to maintain more stock of the finished products. This facility can reduce overall inventory costs and need of working capital.

7. To Ensure Continuous Availability

This objective concerns with offering direct benefit to consumers. Due to wide availability of products, consumers are not required store the essential commodities. They can buy the right quantity as and when they need. It leads to several benefits to consumers.

8. To Achieve Rapid Turnover of Stock

Physical distribution is also targeted to speed up turnover of stocks. From investment of cash in raw materials to realization of cash through the sales of finished can be speeded up. Stocks can be speedily converted into cash. So, the duration of working capital cycle can be reduced, and need of working can be minimized.

COMPONENTS OF PHYSICAL DISTRIBUTION

Marketing manager attempts to plan for a systematic physical distribution. Customers priorise those sellers who deliver product regularly and reliably. Similarly, the time is an important determinant of effectiveness of the distribution system. Timely delivery multiplies customers' satisfaction. For effective physical distribution of the products, the marketer needs to coordinate/integrate various components related to physical distribution. Marketer has to take various decisions on these components.

The physical distribution system refers to the portion of logistics system concerned with the movement of product from the sellers outward to the customers. Physical distribution system involves following main components:

1. Order Processing
2. Storage and Warehousing
3. Transportation
4. Organisational Responsibility for Physical Distribution
5. Inventory Control/management
6. Other Components:
   i. Material Management
   ii. Communication
   iii. Sorting and packing
   iv. Customer service
7. Logistical Coordination (Market Logistics)

All these components are closely related. They affect each other. Therefore, the decisions regarding these components should be taken carefully to strengthen the entire distribution system. Some components have been discussed here.

ORDER PROCESSING

A company receives orders from other companies, middlemen, or directly from customers through mail, e-mail, fax, phone, or salesmen. Order processing is an importation component of the distribution system. It is considered as a key to customer service and satisfaction. Order processing mainly includes:

1. Receiving order
2. Recording order
3. Filing order
4. Executing order or assembling of products for dispatch
5. Credit and collection.

Thus, it concerns with processing the orders quickly, accurately, and efficiently. The time period from the receipt of an order to the date of dispatch of products must be as short as possible. Ideally, the order recycle time should be completed within 8 days. But, the use of computer and computer networks, for speedy and accurate order processing, can save time, money and efforts for the company and increases customer satisfaction. It is often called as electronic data processing that minimizes possibility of error and omission. Every firm should establish the standard order procedure.

The physical distribution must be customer-oriented. It starts with customer order. Note that order processing affects customer service in two ways – reordering time (interval between two orders) and consistency of delivery time (delivering products within the fixed time). Rapid order processing enables a company to attain economy in other areas of physical distribution. The person in charge of order processing must be careful for following aspects:

1. Assembling product must be exactly as per demand of customers in terms of quantity, quality, features, and price.
2. Execution must be as quick as possible.
3. The dispatch must be in appropriate mode of transportation.
4. Credit discount and other allied benefits must be offered as per policy.
5. Assessing the effectiveness of order processing. That includes feedback and follow-up.

WAREHOUSING

In today's context, production is made in expectation of demand. Therefore, products are to be stored or preserved safely for the future demand. And also, all the production is not sold directly. Warehousing plays an important role for balancing demand and supply. For example, most of the agricultural products are produced seasonally, but have demand throughout the year. It facilitates both continuous production and continuous marketing of the production. Warehousing service can contribute to customer satisfaction. Be clear that storage and warehousing are not similar terms, though are closely related. Storage is marketing activity that involves holding and preserving products from the time of their production until their sale. Warehousing embraces storage plus a broad range of functions, such as assembling, breaking the bulk, dispatching as per need of middlemen, sorting/classification, providing market intelligence, preparing product for reshipping, etc. Warehousing involves more activities.

Classification of Warehouses

Warehouses may be classified on two bases, on the basis of commodity and on the basis of ownership. Let's have overview of different warehouses.

On the Basis of Commodity: On the basis of commodity stored, there can be:

1. Special Commodity Warehouses provide facility for storing special types of commodities, e.g., cotton warehouses, potato warehouses, grain warehouses, tanks for liquid products, explosive product warehouses, etc.
2. Cold Storage Warehouses provide facility for storing perishable products, e.g., fish, flowers, vegetable, fruits, etc.

On the Basis of Ownership: According to the ownership, there may be various types of warehouses, like:

1. Private Warehouses are owned by individual, or firms. They are owned by retailers and wholesalers, or by manufacturers. Retailers and wholesalers store finished products while manufacturers store raw materials, provision, tools-equipments, and finished products.
2. Cooperative Warehouses are owned on cooperative basis by two or more private parties to utilize storage facility jointly.
3. Public Warehouses owned by local authorities such as municipality, or by the state and central governments. Such warehouses are used by public/traders as well as by government. Traders can use these warehouses on the rents fixed by the government. Government uses these warehouses to buy and maintain stock of certain essential commodities.
4. Household Warehouses are temporary in nature owned by household/family to store and protect furniture, paintings, furs, tapestry, etc.
5. Bonded Warehouses are used to store product until payment is made or documents are cleared. They are situated near the Port for export and import business.

Many companies set up their distribution centers in each of regions around the market and integrate its distribution network with them for smooth, safe, and speedy delivery of products. The latest technology is used for maximum consumer benefits. Warehouses offer a number of direct advantages to manufacturers and sellers, and indirect advantages to customers.

Benefits Offered by Warehouses

Following are the important benefits offered by warehouses:

1. Protection of products from fire, sunlight, dust, theft, heat/cold, etc.
2. Modern warehouses enable to store or preserve perishable products, like milk, fruits, vegetable, flowers, and certain types of chemicals, for reasonably longer period.
3. Professional warehouses provide a lot of facilities, such as inspection, protection, records, displacement on demand, insurance, etc., at affordable charges. Such warehouses are well-equipped with human and mechanical devices.

4. Warehouses at different key centres can speed up order processing efficiently with less risk and costs.
5. Producers and sellers can avail loans on the product stored in warehouses.
6. Consumers have a number of indirect benefits like quick and continuous availability, low price, quality, etc. Producers, sellers, and users equally share all the benefits of warehousing.

Key Issues/Decisions in Warehousing

The manager should consider following aspects while utilizing warehouses:

1. Type of product
2. Time to store the product
3. Rent charged and facilities available
4. Location
5. Working capital requirement
6. Ownership
7. Risk, etc.

TRANSPORTATION

Transportation is one of the core components of distribution system. It consists of moving or transferring products from producers to final users. Transportation involves two parties, carriers and shippers. Carriers are those companies that provide transportation facilities to others, such as the Western Railway, Indian Airline, Indian Shipping Companies, and many other private carriers provide transportation services by road, rail, water, air and underground pipes. Shippers are those organisations and individuals such as manufacturers, middlemen, customers, and others to whom the carriers provide transportation services. For different modes of transportation, various regulatory bodies deal with various issues related to transportation of products. The Central and the State Governments have formulated a lot of Acts or legal provision to regulate transportation activities in the country. The main regulatory bodies may include:

i. The Civil Aviation Department, for air carriers.
ii. The Shipping Corporation of India, for water carriers.
iii. The Oil and Natural Gas Commission, for pipeline carriers.
iv. The Road Transport Corporation of the state, for land or road carriers
v. The Railway Authorities, for rail transportation, etc.

Transportation plays a crucial role in today's global marketing. It creates the place utility. In brief, transportation has positive impact in every facet of economic, social, and cultural development of the society. The key issues in transportation are type, costs, time, speed, risk, suitability, and availability. Marketer should take transportation decision carefully.

Key Issues in Transportation Decisions

A marketer needs to consider on following issues:

1. Mode of Transportation

This decision relates with selecting an appropriate mode of transportation. Main modes of transportation are road, railway, water, air, and pipeline. As per financial capacity, need, time available and overall suitability, the appropriate mode of transportation should be selected.

2. Costs and Availability

One should select such a mode of transportation that is the most suitable and low in costs. Similarly, the mode must be easily available.

3. Suitability and Credibility

It is an important consideration. The mode of transportation must fit to the products and company's overall internal situation, and must be reliable.

4. Relations

In the era of relationship marketing, the marketer must maintain long-term profitable relations with various transport agencies. A firm has to perform many activities to establish and maintain healthy and profitable relations with the transport agencies.

5. Legal Provisions and Restrictions

A firm must take transportation decisions within limit of contemporary legal provisions. Knowledge of legal provisions is essential.

6. Ownership

This issue concerns with whether a firm should own, contract, or hire transportation means. Depending upon a company's capacity and requirements, it may own its own means of transportation, may undergo the contracts, or may hire such facilities.

ORGANISATIONAL RESPONSIBILITY FOR PHYSICAL DISTRIBUTION

Physical distribution is an important decision in today's marketing management. It involves a wide range of activities. Therefore, an effective coordination of various activities, such as order processing, warehousing, transportation, inventory control, etc., is indispensable to contribute in overall success of marketing strategies. The entire range of physical distribution must be systematic and even scientific for effective distribution of products to the ultimate users. For the purpose, the systematic structure of organisation should be created to take care of physical distribution activities. Organisation of physical distribution must be well-equipped and properly organised to serve the purpose over time.

Type, nature, formation, and activities of organisational structure for physical distribution depend upon various factors like type of business, size of operation, resource availability, management philosophy, and so on. After proper analysis of various relevant variables, the suitable structure of organisation should be created and implemented. There may be practically two alternatives, physical distribution committee or physical distribution department.

Physical Distribution Committee

In order to manage distribution activities effectively and efficiently, many companies formulate a permanent committee. The committee consists of a group of people who work jointly for attaining marketing goals. The number of members in committee depends on types of key activities in distribution system. A physical distribution committee consists of experts on various areas of distribution like warehousing, transportation, communication, order processing, and so on. This committee is headed by distribution manager or marketing manager. Each of the experts in a committee has necessary skills and experience to handle specific group of activities. The committee, known as physical distribution committee, takes care of the entire range of activities related to distribution of products and is responsible for smooth distribution of products. The committee meets periodically and formulates policy to improve physical distribution system.

Physical Distribution Department

Some companies treat physical distribution as a separate area of marketing management and maintain a separate physical distribution department. This department is headed by physical distribution manager. He is solely responsible for managing physical distribution activities. He appoints needed experts in his department to assist him carrying different types of activities related to physical distribution. The physical distribution manager works under either production manager or marketing manager. Mostly, the companies engaged in production and distribution activities, appoint physical distribution manager under marketing manager. He may be line administrator, a manager with staff responsibility, or the combination of both staff and line function. This type of organisation is typically portrayed in Figure 1.

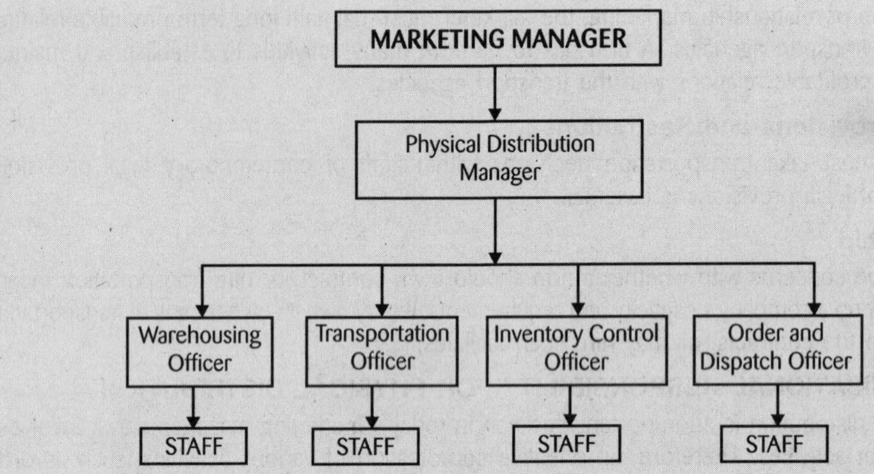

Figure 1: Physical Distribution Organisation

Marketing Manager: He, along with other marketing activities, also directs and controls physical distribution activities. Under him, the physical distribution manager is placed. Here, physical distribution is treated as a part of marketing. He takes care of marketing and distribution activities.

Physical Distribution Manager: He is a direct authority responsible for physical distribution. He works under marketing manager. His functions involve storage and warehousing, inventory management, transportation, order processing and dispatching, communication, etc. He coordinates various activities needed for effective physical distribution. Various officers are appointed under him for each type of activities. The officers who work under his direct supervision and control include:

1. Storage and warehousing officer
2. Inventory officer
3. Transportation officer
4. Order processing and dispatching officer
5. Communication officer, etc.

As per need, the required staff is appointed to assist each of these officers in performing their respective tasks. Sometimes, more officers are appointed for different types of works such as accountant, packing officers, and so on. The entire department headed by distribution manager works as a team to deal with total distribution system.

INVENTORY MANAGEMENT

Inventory refers to stock of goods meant for the future sales. It can also be said as reservoir of goods held in anticipation of sales. Demand is fluctuating and exact prediction is not possible. So, the primary purpose of holding inventory is to meet market demand continuously. The firm always maintains adequate stocks of products to meet customer orders immediately. It is considered as a link between ordering and production. Inventory management supports demand creation and consumer satisfaction.

Three types of costs are associated with inventory. The first is, holding costs (carrying costs), which include warehousing and storage costs, costs of capital tied up in inventory, costs of price decline, obsolescence, spoilage, pilferages, and taxes and insurance on inventory. The Second is, costs of stock out or shortage, which include loss of sales, adverse impact on goodwill, losing customers permanently due to shortage of stocks, and administrative costs. And, the third is, replenishing or reordering costs (order processing costs), such as preparing and placing order; transportation, insurances and wastage during movement; and costs of receiving, inspecting, and handling materials. However, carrying costs and ordering costs are more important, and if they are balanced, the total costs can be effectively reduced.

A company has to decide on total annual need of inventory, ordering size, and level of inventory (called as ordering level) at which new order should be placed. It must determine maximum and minimum quantity that may be needed at any time. The main issues are ordering size – how much to order, and (reordering) ordering level – when to order.

As stated earlier, ordering and carrying costs are important considerations in inventory management. Ordering and carrying costs are adversely related. If more inventory/stock is maintained, carrying costs are high and ordering costs are low. Quite opposite to it, when low level of inventory is maintained, carrying costs are low, and, due to more frequent order of smaller quantity, ordering costs go high. Therefore, the manager should decide on the optimum order size to reduce total cost of inventory. It is necessary to strike out balance between two types of costs to minimize total costs. The most popular technique to determine optimum size of order is Economic Ordering Quantity, which can be determined by using following formula

$$EOQ = \sqrt{\frac{2AO}{C}}$$

where,

A = Annual sales

O = Ordering costs

C = Carrying costs

Sometimes, ordering size or level is determined by trial and error or graphical method. The level of inventory at which costs are minimum, is taken as ordering size.

OTHER COMPONENTS

In fact, physical distribution consists of a lot of decisions. Some of minor decisions have been listed below:

i. Material Management
ii. Communication
iii. Sorting and packing
iv. Customer service, etc.

LOGISTICAL COORDINATION OR MARKET LOGISTICS

To distribute products from the point of production to the point of consumption (consumers) is traditionally called physical distribution. It starts from the factory and reaches the final destinations at the right time, in the right way and form, and at low costs. Distribution is treated as a separate function of marketing, and the special independent arrangement is made for smooth distribution. Problem of physical distribution is thought of only after products are produced. Thus, physical distribution concerns with systematically distributing products to final users. It involves all activities necessary (like warehousing, transportation, communicating, insurance, banking, ordering processing, inventory management, and services of channel members) to avail the products conveniently to ultimate users.

Market logistics (often called as supply chain management) is the modern form of physical distribution. Simple distribution is expanded into a broader concept of supply chain management. Supply chain management starts before physical distribution. Logistics means a detailed organisation of large and complex exercise. Here, distribution is not treated as an independent activity but as an integral part of the total business system.

Market logistics or supply chain management is a detailed programme attempting to procure the right inputs (raw materials, components, and capital equipments); covert them effectively into finished products; and distribute them to the final destinations. It can help a company identify superior suppliers and help improve its productivity. It leads to low costs and better quality products that ultimately results into better customer satisfaction and/or strengthening the competitive position. Market logistics system is prepared by considering target market's requirements. Thus, study of target market's requirements, preproduction (production planning), production process, and distribution are integrated to form market logistics system.

Market logistics involves (1) estimating target markets requirements, (2) procuring necessary inputs for producing the right products, (3) converting inputs into finished products (production process), and (4) systematically distributing the products to ultimate users.

Definitions

Market logistics can be defined as under:

1. **Philip Kotler:** "Market logistics involves planning, implementing, and controlling the physical flows of materials and final goods from points of origin to points of use to meet customer requirement at profit."
2. **The Council of Logistics Management:** "Logistics is that part of the supply chain process that plans, implements, and controls the efficient, effective, foreword and reverse flow and storage of goods, services, and related information between the point of origin and the point of consumption in order to meet customers' requirements."
3. In more systematic way, the term can be defined as: *Market logistics consists of estimating target markets requirements, procuring necessary inputs for producing the right products, converting inputs into finished products, and systematically distributing the products to ultimate users to achieve maximum customer satisfaction at profit.*
4. Market logistics is coordinated system that coordinates various parties involved in production and marketing. In this sense, we can defined the term as: *Market logistics is a broad system that involves coordinating activities of suppliers, purchasing agents, manufacturers, marketers, channel members, and customers to permit lower prices and yield higher profit margins.*

Objectives and Importance

Market logistics system is aimed at offering the right products to the right customers, at the right place, at the right time, in the right pattern, and at the least costs. It is an attempt to meet total customer expectations by systematically organising production and marketing activities. Let us list objectives of market logistics system:

1. To satisfy target customers by right products and right way of distribution.
2. To attract additional customers.
3. To reduce total costs and/or yield more profit margins.
4. To speed up trade cycle.
5. To integrate production and marketing with target market expectations.
6. To improve competitive strengths, etc.

Market Logistic Decisions

In fact, market logistics concerns with making the distribution system effective. It involves a lot of decisions to offer the right products to the right buyers, at the right time, at the right place, at the right price, and in a right manner. It includes all the decisions that can ensure the righteousness in all significant aspects. Market logistics is distribution related concept and mainly involves ordering processing, warehousing, and inventory and transportation decisions. But, distribution can not be meaningful without suitable products. So, virtually, it is not distribution system, but total business system including production, marketing, finance and personnel. Main decisions of effective market logistics system involve:

1. Determining target market requirements
2. Procuring appropriate inputs for producing the desired products
3. Producing the right products
4. Selecting suitable marketing channels
5. Order processing
6. Locating warehousing
7. Inventory management
8. Transportation
9. Handling, billing and payment
10. Maintaining relations among all parties involved

CHANNEL OF DISTRIBUTION

INTRODUCTION

One of the important features of a contemporary market is that centralized production and decentralized market. Customers are widely scattered throughout the world. In order to satisfy them, manufacturers must distribute products conveniently. Obviously, the prominent marketing goal, i.e., customer satisfaction, can be achieved only when the most desired products are distributed conveniently at reasonable price in time. Additionally, producers specialize on production, may not have time and expertise to distribute products to cater needs of final users. In such situations, role of middlemen or marketing channel is more crucial. Most producers take assistance of middlemen to distribute products to their valued customers. Even, the firm takes marketing channel as a strategic decision to distinguish their offers from the rest of competitors.

Most of producers do not sell their products directly to the final users. A host of intermediaries perform a variety of functions between primary producers and ultimate consumers. They can be named as wholesalers, retailers, agents, merchants, etc. They are often called as middlemen or marketing channel. Those who buy, take title, and resell the merchandise are called *merchants* (middlemen/channel members); other brokers or manufacturers' representatives who search for the customers, negotiate on their behalf, but do not take title of the product are called *agents*; and some others who do not take title of the product, and do not negotiate on producers' behalf, but facilitate physical movement of the product such as transportation companies, independent warehouses, banks, and insurance companies are called as *facilitators*.

DEFINITIONS OF MARKETING CHANNEL

Marketing channel, also known as channel of distribution or trade channel, can be defined in variety of ways. Some common definitions have been stated as under:

1. In simple words, marketing channel can be defined as: *Route or pathway through which products flow from producers to consumers is called marketing channel.*

2. Further, it can be said: *The link, medium, or bridge that joins two extremes – primary producers and ultimate consumers – is known as distribution channel.*
3. **Philip Kotler:** "Use of intermediaries like wholesalers, retailers, agents, etc., between manufacturers and consumers for the purpose of facilitating availability of goods and services is known as distribution channel."
4. **Stern and el-Ansary:** "Marketing channels are set of independent organisations involved in the process of making a product or service available for use or consumption."
5. **S. A. Sherlekar:** "Distribution channel refers to the set of marketing institutions participating in marketing activities involved in the flow of goods or services from the primary producers to the ultimate consumers."
6. **Cundiff and Still:** "A channel of distribution (sometimes called as a trade channel) for the product is the route taken by the title of the product as it moves from the producer to the ultimate consumer or industrial user."

TYPES OF CHANNELS

Several marketing channels are used to distribute products from the primary producers to the ultimate users. Table 1 shows typical intermediaries used for availing or distributing different products. Manufacturers can use one or more of three main alternative channels as shown in Figure 2.

Table 1: Products and Relevant Marketing Channels.

No.	Type of Products	Appropriate Channels
1.	Products (physical things or objects)	Wholesalers, agents, stockiest, retailers (including shopping malls), and online (or cyber) marketing
2.	Travel Services (Airlines, Railways, and Travel Companies)	Booking counters, hotels, travel agents, and online booking
3.	Life and General Insurance	Branch offices, online services, development officers, and agents
4.	Financial Services	Banks, agents, financial institutions, private financers, and online services.
5.	Employment	Employment agencies, training institutes, contractors, and online services
6.	Shares and Securities	Broking companies and individual stock brokers, and online trading
7.	Consultancy (Professional) Services	Experts staff and branch offices, online consultancies
8.	Matrimonial Services	Marriage Bureau, community centres, social workers, online services
9.	Education (knowledge and skills)	Universities, colleges, training institutes, academicians at centres, online education, distanced learning (by reading materials), private tuition classes and personal tutors
10.	Healthcare Services	Hospitals, health centres and clinics, private physicians, gymnasiums, Yoga centres, nursing rooms, mobile health services (e.g. 108 emergency ambulances), online health and medical constancy, etc.

1. Direct Channel

No middlemen are involved. Company sells its products directly to consumers. It is, as its name suggests, a direct mode of distribution. There are four types of direct channel:

i. Distribution from factory gate
ii. Distribution via showroom and retail outlets
iii. Distribution by salesmen
iv. Online marketing/cyber marketing

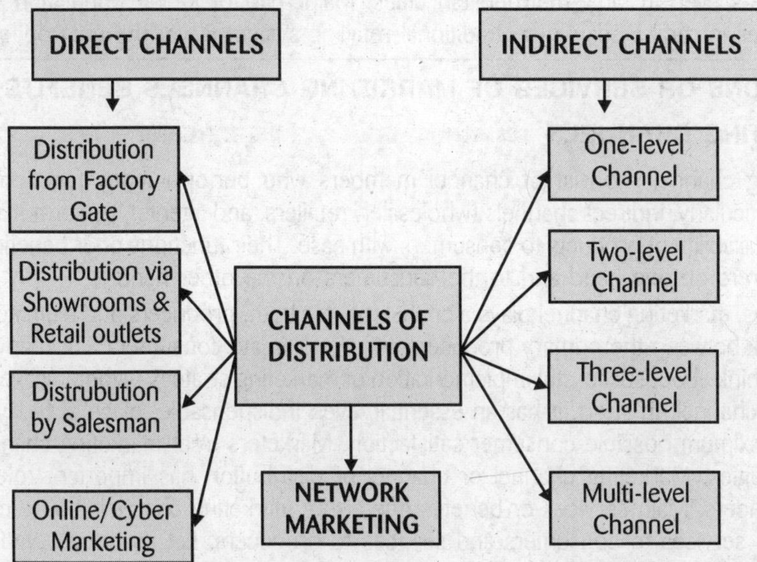

Figure 2: Channels of Distribution for Products

2. Indirect Channel

Here, middlemen, such as wholesalers, retailers, agents, etc., are involved in distribution of products. There are four types of indirect channel:

i. **One-Level Channel:** Company – retailers – consumers
ii. **Two-Level Channel:** Company – wholesalers and retailers – consumers
iii. **Three-Level Channel:** Company – agents, wholesalers, and retailers – consumers
iv. **Multilevel Channel:** Company – number of middlemen – consumers

3. Network Marketing

Here, products are distributed via members. Members are both sellers and users. They buy directly from the company. They can earn commission on their own consumption as well as consumption of other members working under them. A network is prepared to distribute products in the market. Every member tries to create more members under him. Members act as distributor as well as users. It has been claimed that members or users can access quality products at low price as middlemen are not included. For example, Modi Care, Amway, etc., are distributing products via network. It is an emerging option. However, it can be applicable only for the giant organisation like multinational companies.

> Note: Shopping Malls (Points or Centers) by corporate retailing houses are the special and advanced form of traditional retailing system. They offer more or less similar services that retailers have been offering since a long. They are multipurpose shopping centers, sell branded products of different companies, and are professionally managed to provide the

best possible services to customers. Mostly, malls sell multiple products. They facilitate the customers a one-stop-shopping facility. Shopping malls can be included in one-level channel as they intermediate manufacturers and ultimate consumers. Star Market, Big Bazaar, V-Mart, Reliance Mall, Reliance Fresh, Adani Shopping Malls are some of major corporate retail players in India. For consumable products, for example, grocery items, Indian consumers still prefer the known-nearby retailers to big shopping malls. Malls are situated only in big cities where the consumer population density is high. Shopping mall culture has, partially, failed to attract Indian buyers even in large-metropolitan cities. Major part of Indian population (more than 65%) resides in rural areas where traditional retailing system is yet the only option.

FUNCTIONS OR SERVICES OF MARKETING CHANNELS BENEFITS OF MARKETING CHANNELS

Marketing channels consist of channel members who perform many functions. Marketing channels, particularly, indirect channels (wholesaler, retailers, and agents), perform many functions to facilitate availability of products to consumers with ease. Their functions offer benefits or services to manufacturers on one hand and to the consumers on the other hand.

Nowadays, marketing channel plays a crucial role for both, producers and ultimate consumers. It is a vital link between the primary producers and the ultimate consumers. For many products, it is difficult to think about successful implementation of marketing strategy without active involvement of marketing channel. In short, it has an essential, even indispensable, place in today's marketing to achieve maximum possible consumer satisfaction. Marketers treat marketing channel as a part of their strategies. Marketing channel or channel of distribution has important role due to the services it renders. Main services or benefits offered by marketing channel can be classified into two groups – services to consumers and services to producers. Let us discuss various services offered by marketing channel individually:

Services to Producers

Followings are main services offered by channel members to producers:

1. Transporting

Middlemen are actively involved in transporting goods from producers to consumers. Channel members carry out transporting or physical movement of products. Channel members make all necessary arrangements to transport products from the producers to the distribution centers.

2. Place Constraints

Due to active role of middlemen, place constraints can be removed. Products can be made available at all the places where consumers reside. Thus, it increases place utility.

3. Concentration on Production

Since producers are not required to carry out distribution activities, they can concentrate their full attention on production side. Production efficiency can be improved. They are able to sell products of better quality at low price. Producers can improve their competitive strengths.

4. Information Link

Channel members are among the most reliable sources of information. Middlemen update company's knowledge about market. Producers can receive information about the latest developments at the market place. It facilitates the producers to adjust marketing strategy with market changes.

5. Promotion

Middlemen, including wholesalers, agents, and retailers, also carry out several market promotion activities on behalf of producers. They assist producers in implementing promotion strategies on one hand, and perform certain promotion activities by their own on the other hand. Sales promotion activities are not possible without middlemen.

6. Processing

To enhance product utility, middlemen perform necessary processes like grading, sorting, packing, cleaning, labeling, and other similar activities. Middlemen make necessary processes to suit products with consumer needs. Thus, they try to cater consumer needs more effectively.

7. Negotiating

They negotiate on a company's behalf. They communicate terms and conditions with buyers and try to arrive at transaction. Virtually, a company cannot directly negotiate with consumers.

8. Ordering and Financing

Apart from several important services, middlemen facilitate producers by placing advanced orders. Producers can find it easy to make successful production planning. In the same way, they also pay their bills in advance. This can meet their working capital needs. Many times, middlemen with sound financial position can lend money at a very liberal terms and conditions.

9. Risk Bearing

Once they place orders, all the risks associated with products are borne by middlemen. Producers are not required to worry.

10. Economy

Middlemen can provide better services to consumers than producers. Compared to commission changed or profit margin added by middlemen, more services are provided. Company can hardly do the same at the same rate.

Services to Consumers/users

List of services provided by middlemen to consumers may include:

1. Credit Facility

Middlemen sell products to consumer on credit. Consumers can postpone payment for a certain time. Consumers are not deprived of the necessary products due to temporary financial problems. They also help consumers borrow money from various sources.

2. Better Selection

Wholesalers and retailers sell products of many companies. So, consumers find it easy to select the most suitable products from any retail outlet nearby their residence.

3. Educating and Communicating

Consumers can get necessary information about products, price, and related benefits from middlemen. Also, middlemen educate and train consumers about how to use products safely.

4. Easy Accessibility

Wholesalers and retailers are spread everywhere. They are scattered according to the consumer density. So, it is more comfortable for consumers to buy products of the reputed companies anywhere.

5. After-sales Services

Middlemen provide a number of post-sales services to consumers, including home delivery, installation, repairing, exchanging and replacing, providing accessories, etc. Such services are valuable for consumers.

FACTORS AFFECTING CHANNEL SELECTION

Decision on channel of distribution is treated as strategic one as it plays a significant role to satisfy consumers and also to improve competitive strength. Choice of marketing channel, being very critical, must be made carefully. Marketing manager must take into account all the relevant factors to choose the best fit channel of distribution for the products. Dominant factors affecting channel selection are discussed below:

1. Factors Related to Products

Product is a prime factor in channel selection. Product-related factors are among most relevant and powerful factors affecting channel decision. Channel must be fit the type and nature of company's products. Such factors include:

a. **Perishability of Product:** Perishable products must be sold and consumed immediately after production. So, for perishable products, normally, direct or short channel is advisable. For durable products, indirect or multilevel channel is preferable. However, due to availability of rapid means of transportation and advanced cold storage facilities, the perishable product can also be sold by long-indirect channels.

b. **Technical Aspects:** Technical products cannot be used without sufficient information and direct supervision. Even, they need more frequent services. It is advisable to adopt indirect and multilevel channels to assist consumers to use the technical product properly and safely. For simple products, direct channels can be used.

c. **New v/s Existing Product:** Consumers need more information and attention for new products. More efforts and time are required to convince consumers. As a result, a company may opt for indirect channel to take help of middlemen in this task. For existing products, the company can use direct and/or indirect channels.

d. **Complexity and Risk Related to Use of Product:** Complex and risky products are sold via middlemen as consumers expect more direct supervision and assistance.

e. **Size of Product:** In case of heavy and bulky products, direct or short channel is more suitable. This is due to difficulties related to physical movement of the product.

f. **Divisibility of Product:** Mostly, indivisible products are distributed directly to customers. Divisible products can be conveniently distributed by middlemen.

g. **Unit Price of Product:** Precious products, like gold, jewelry, certain chemicals, software, etc., are distributed using direct or short channels of distribution. Use of direct and short channel can minimize risk of theft or robbery.

h. **Legal Aspect:** Quite obviously, permitted (legal) products can be distributed by any convenient channel of distribution. But, illegal products are distributed by direct channels for secrecy purpose.

2. Factors Related to Company

Company's internal situations have direct impact on choice of marketing channel. Manager has to analyse company-related factors to decide the best fit channel(s). Company-related factors include:

a. **Company's Financial Position:** Financially sound companies can maintain separate and well-equipped departments for distribution of products. Such companies can open and manage own retail outlets and can hire salesmen to manage distribution effectively. They do not require services of middlemen and, hence, can distribute the product directly. But, financially weak companies have to opt for indirect channels to share resources and expertise of channel members.

b. **Product Mix of Company:** A company's product mix consists of product lines and product items in each product line. Many product lines and several product items/ varieties in each of the product lines can enable the firm to offer multiple choices to a large number of consumers. Even, the firm can take benefit of the scale of economy.

In such case, direct channels are more advisable. Small companies with limited product lines and/or product items should distribute products via wholesalers and retailers, who sell products of many companies.

c. **Desire for Control:** If a company desires to have direct and close control over production and selling activities, direct channels are preferred and vice-versa.

d. **Experience and Expertise:** Successful distribution needs considerable experience and expertise. If a company possesses necessary experience, expertise, and staff, it can manage selling activities by its own. When a company lacks such experience and skills, it has to involve middlemen, and prefers indirect channels.

e. **Facilities and Staff:** Sufficient facilities and capable staff are essential for effective distribution of products. If a company manages for needed facilities and staff, direct channels are used, otherwise indirect channels are used.

f. **Company's Past Experience:** A company's past experience can also affect channel decision. When a company has favourable and satisfactory experience to work with middlemen, it may continue working with them. In case, if it is not satisfied with terms and services of middlemen, it would shorten its channel of distribution.

3. Factors Related to Middlemen

Companies consider several middlemen-related factors while deciding on channels. Most common factors include:

a. **Creditworthiness of Middlemen:** Middlemen's credibility is an important criterion to decide on the channel. If middlemen have good reputation and creditworthiness, a company can multiply its gain and, as a result, prefers to involve them in their distribution activities. Creditworthiness is a critical aspect while offering dealership or franchise for definite area.

b. **Attitudes of Middlemen:** Positive attitudes of middlemen make companies to involve them in distribution activities. Companies like to select indirect channel with one or more levels. Opposite situation leads companies to select direct channels.

c. **Services Rendered by Middlemen:** Channel decisions depend on number and quality of services offered by middlemen to customers. When the channel members are ready to provide several services to customers, like home delivery, free repairing, credit facility, installment payment schemes, and other post-sales services, the manufacturers like to involve them in distribution to avail such services to their customers. When middlemen do not provide the useful services to customers, companies prefer direct channels.

d. **Financial Capacity of Middlemen:** Strong financial capacity of middlemen attracts manufacturers. This is due to the fact that strong financial position benefits both manufacturers and customers. Strong financial position results into speedy recovery of bills receivable, less chances of bad debts, immediate payment, credit facility to customers, and also advanced payment.

e. **Terms and Conditions:** When terms and conditions laid down by middlemen are not favourable, the manufacturers don't like to involve them in distribution activities. They prefer direct distribution channels.

4. Factors Related to Market

Market (consumer behaviour) is a crucial factor in channel selection. Main factors related to market include:

a. **Size of Market:** In case of a large and concentrated market, it is economically affordable for a company to mange its own distribution setup. When market is small, it is advisable to assign distribution task to middlemen.

b. **Geographical Concentration:** When firm's customers are highly concentrated (living in nearby area) in particular region, it can directly deal with customers by using any of the direct channels. But, when customers are scattered in several regions, it is not convenient to use direct channels. Middlemen can do better job with less costs.

c. **Services Expected by Market:** Number and types of services expected by the target market, and company's capacity and readiness to meet them are important issues to be considered in this connection. For example, if the market expects a lot of services, and the company is unable and/or unwilling to satisfy them, indirect channels are preferred to avail the services from middlemen.

d. **Habits of Consumers:** Distribution channels must be fit with habits of consumers. Manager should find out why, how, when, where and from whom the consumers like to buy. For example, if consumers are habituated to buy a little quantity frequently from nearby retailer on credit, a company must involve retailers (along with wholesalers) to avail products at all the places where consumers reside.

e. **Current Market Trend:** Firm's distribution system must be compatible with the recent market trend. Trend includes a number of variables like policies and practices of giant national and multinational companies, functioning of departmental stores and corporate retailers, cyber marketing and network marketing, business partnering with banking, insurance, and other service providers, customers' awareness, and so on. Manager must observe these reforms and innovative practices minutely and accordingly a suitable channel should be selected.

5. Factors Related to Competition

Current and anticipated competition affects company's decision on marketing channel. Relevant competition-related aspects must be analyzed while selecting the channel. Competition-related factors include:

a. **Intensity of Competition:** When there exits a severe competition in the market, a company must consider competitors distribution strategies and practices while selecting marketing channels. In case of less competition, a company choice will be independent of competition.

b. **Response and Reactions of Competitors:** Reactions and response of the close competitors must be taken into account while deciding on distribution channel. A company must select such channels that can help availing competitive advantages.

c. **Company's Competitive Position in Market:** A leader company can design its own distribution network. It can select a specific channel of distribution as per its requirements. But, the follower companies have to follow market leader. Their choice depends on leader's practice.

6. Factors Related to Environment

Marketer has to consider overall business environment while deciding on marketing channel. Domestic and global environmental forces have direct or indirect impact on company's activities and operations. Main environmental forces that affect channel decision include:

a. **Economic Condition of Country:** Country's economic condition affects firm's operations. In economically poor countries, short or direct channels are used to sell product at low price. In developing and developed countries, normally, indirect channels are used to distribute products.

b. **Phases of Trade Cycle:** Phases of trade cycle, like recession, recovery, prosperity, etc., indicate the country's economic condition. Normally, in prosperity stage, long and indirect channels are used due to need for mass distribution and willingness of people to pay high price for the product. Direct and short channels are more suitable when the economy is passing through recession phase as direct and short channels keep the selling price low.

c. **Legal Provision:** Government policies and legal provisions have direct or indirect implication on firm's distribution activities. Manager must identify relevant provisions affecting distribution activities and, accordingly, an appropriate channel(s) should be selected. Taxes, charges, administrative procedures, restrictions, and other issues are worth noted in this regard.

d. **Availability of Facilities:** Availability, costs, and quality necessary facilities play decisive role in channel selection. Facilities like transportation, communication, warehousing, banking, insurance, supporting government agencies at national and international level, degree of harmony among states of the country, and relations among nations at large affect firm's channel decisions.

EXERCISES

MULTIPLE CHOICE QUESTIONS (MCQs)

1. In popular 4Ps marketing framework, with which of followings is a physical distribution related?
   a. Product Mix
   b. Place Mix
   c. Promotion Mix
   d. Price Mix
2. Find out the correct statement.
   a. Marketing channel is a part of broad physical distribution.
   b. Channel of distribution and physical distribution are unrelated.
   c. Physical distribution and channel of distributions are exactly identical.
   d. Physical distribution is part of a marketing channel.
3. Which one of marketing mix elements does involve a set of activities to make the product available to the ultimate consumers?
   a. Place
   b. Product
   c. Price
   d. Promotion
4. Which one is not a component of physical distribution system?
   a. Order processing
   b. Storage and warehousing
   c. Transportation
   d. Branding and packaging
5. A marketing channel containing a number of middlemen is called
   a. Direct channel
   b. One level channel
   c. Multilevel channel
   d. Two level channel
6. Find out odd one.
   a. Market logistics is also called as the supply chain management.
   b. Market logistics is a system that integrates production and marketing.
   c. Market logistics is aimed at offering the right product to the right customers in a right manner.
   d. Market logistics is logical explanation of marketing promotion.
7. In which class of distribution channels do corporate retailing houses (shopping malls) fall?
   a. Two level channel
   b. One level channel

c. Zero level channel
d. Multilevel channel

8. Online or cyber marketing is
   a. a from of direct marketing system
   b. a form of indirect marketing system
   c. a one level channel
   d. not a marketing channel
9. Name the channel of distribution in which the products are distributed via salesmen.
   a. Indirect channel
   b. One level channel
   c. Two level channel
   d. Direct channel
10. Which is not a relevant type of factors affecting channel decisions?
   a. Competition related factors
   b. Middlemen related factors
   c. Trade union related factors
   d. Product related factors
11. In which class of factors does geographical concentration of consumers fall?
   a. Factors related to product
   b. Factors related to middlemen
   c. Factors related to company
   d. Factors related to market
12. Economic condition, phases of trade cycle, availability of infrastructure are
   a. environmental factors
   b. product related factors
   c. market related factors
   d. middlemen related factors

MATCHING TYPE QUESTIONS (MTQs)

13.

List I	**List II**
(a) Place Decision is	(1) middlemen
(b) Chanel of distribution consists of	(2) 4th 'P' of Marketing Mix
(c) Physical distribution includes	(3) more than three middlemen
(d) Multilevel channel contains	(4) transportations, warehousing, banking, etc.

Codes: (A) (a)-(2), (b)-(1), (c)-(4), (d)-(3) (B) (a)-(3), (b)-(2), (c)-(1), (d)-(4)
(C) (a)-(4), (b)-(3), (c)-(2), (d)-(1) (D) (a)-(1), (b)-(4), (c)-(3), (d)-(2)

14.

List I	**List II**
(a) Channel containing only the retailers	(1) Network Marketing
(b) Chanel containing two middlemen	(2) 4th 'P' of Marketing Mix
(c) Shopping malls and corporate retailing	(3) Two-level channel
(d) Distribution through members	(4) One-level channel

Codes: (A) (a)-(2), (b)-(1), (c)-(4), (d)-(3) (B) (a)-(3), (b)-(2), (c)-(1), (d)-(4)
(C) (a)-(4), (b)-(3), (c)-(2), (d)-(1) (D) (a)-(1), (b)-(4), (c)-(3), (d)-(2)

15.

List I	List II
(a) Wholesalers, retailers, agents, and malls	(1) Products
(b) Broking companies, brokers, and online trading	(2) Healthcare services
(c) Marriage Bureau, community centers, etc.	(3) Matrimonial services
(d) Hospitals, health centres, Yoga centres, etc.	(4) Shares and securities

Codes: (A) (a)-(2), (b)-(1), (c)-(4), (d)-(3) (B) (a)-(3), (b)-(2), (c)-(1), (d)-(4)
(C) (a)-(4), (b)-(3), (c)-(2), (d)-(1) (D) (a)-(1), (b)-(4), (c)-(3), (d)-(2)

ANSWERS KEY: 1(b), 2(a), 3(a), 4(d), 5(c), 6(d), 7(b), 8(a), 9(d), 10(c), 11(d), 12(a), 13(A), 14(C), 15(D)

QUESTIONS FOR DISCUSSION

16. What is physical distribution? Explain its nature.
17. What is physical distribution? State its objectives.
18. Write a note: Objectives of physical distribution system.
19. Explain main components of physical distribution.
20. State various components of physical distribution. Explain order processing, and inventory management.
21. Write notes on: (1) Ordering, (2) Storing, (3) Transportation, and (4) Organisational responsibility.
22. Write a notes:
    a. Objectives of physical distribution
    b. Inventory aspect of Physical distribution.
23. What is channel of distribution? Explain types of marketing channels.
24. "Different products need different channels." Explain the statement with examples.
25. Define marketing channel. Write a detailed note factors affecting channel selection.
26. "Marketing channels are indispensable in modern marketing." Do you agree? State benefits of marketing channel.
27. Define market logistics. Briefly explain its objectives and main decisions.

CHAPTER

9 MARKETING INFORMATION SYSTEM AND MARKETING RESEARCH

Marketing Information Systems (MIS)

- Introduction
- Definitions
- Characteristics
- Elements

Marketing Research System

- Introduction
- Definitions
- Characteristics
- Importance
- Scope of Marketing Research
- Data – Types and Characteristics
- Data Collection Methods
- Data Collection Tools
- Questionnaire
- Sampling
- Marketing Research Process
- Research Report
- Limitations of Marketing Research

MARKETING INFORMATION SYSTEM (MIS)

INTRODUCTION

Information is like a life-blood of business. Quality of decisions depends on the right type of information. The right information implies the right quality, the right quantity, and the right timing of information. Circulation of needed information is as important as the circulation of blood in human being. Information keeps the organisation actively functioning, alive, and connected with internal and external marketing participants. It is a valuable asset for a firm as it is a base to manage other valuable assets. The firm fails to manage information (i.e., collecting, analysing, interpreting, storing, and disseminating of information) will definitely fail to attain goals. Today's marketing is dynamic, and manager has to undergo necessary changes to cope with the pace of changing marketing environment. Information is a basic input to know what is happening and what is going to happen. **Marion Harper** has rightly asserted: "To manage a business well is to manage its future, and to manage the future well is to manage the information."

A company needs information on a continuous basis to be aware of marketing developments taking place in the market. In order to learn about changing needs of customers, new competitors' initiatives, changing distribution practices, recent trends in promotion practices, etc., a manager requires the permanent arrangement to get the needed information on a regular basis. The system or arrangement that deals with providing the information regularly is known as marketing information system (MIS).

DEFINITIONS

Marketing Information System (MIS) has been defined as:

1. **Philip Kotler:** "A marketing information system is a continuing and interacting system of people, equipments, and procedures to gather, sort, analyse, evaluate, and distribute the pertinent, timely, and accurate information for use by marketing decision-makers to improve their marketing planning, implementation, and control."
   Philip Kotler gives alternative definition, such as: "A marketing information system (MIS) consists of people, equipments, and procedures to gather, sort, analyse, evaluate, and distribute the needed, timely, and accurate information to marketing decision makers."
2. **We can say:** *Marketing Information System (MIS) is a permanent arrangement (system or setup) for provision of regular availability of relevant, reliable, adequate, and timely information for making marketing decisions.*
3. **Finally, let us define the term more comprehensively:** *MIS concerns with setting and maintaining of a permanent system (network) to avail necessary information on regular basis. The system consists of people, equipments, facilities, and procedures directed to gather, analyse, evaluate, update, distribute, and preserve the information to assist marketing decision-making, i.e., analysing, planning, implementing, and controlling of marketing activities.*

COMPONENTS OF MIS

MIS is made of parts, subparts or subsystems which are called the components. Typically, according to Philip Kotler, a marketing information system consists of four interrelated components – Internal Reports (Records) System, Marketing Research System, Marketing Intelligence System, and Marketing Decision Support System, as shown in Figure 1. All components are interrelated and interdependent.

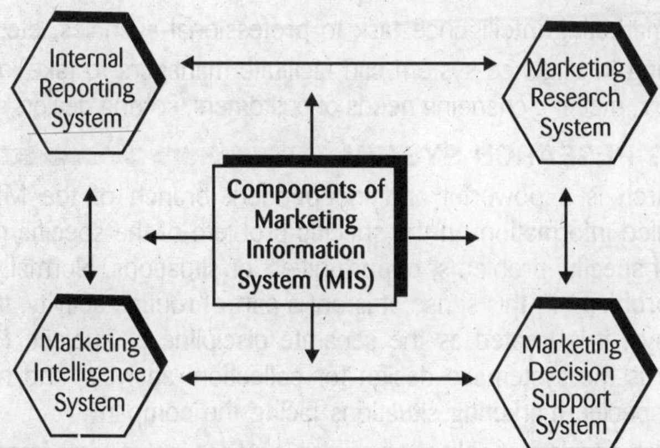

Figure 1: Components of Marketing Information System

1. INTERNAL RECORDS SYSTEM

Internal records system is a major and easily accessible source of information. It supplies the results data. It consists of all records of marketing operations available within organisation. This system concerns with collecting, analysing, interpreting, and distributing needed information from records of various departments of the company. Main sources include various records on sales and purchase, ordering system, sales force reporting system, inventory level, receivable-payables, marketing staff, costs, the past research works, and other literatures/reports available within organisation. Particularly, for sales orders and sales force reporting, the computer technology is excessively used for accurate, efficient, and speedy transmission of information.

To manage the internal record system, some companies appoint internal MIS committee to deal with all aspects of internal information. The committee (1) attends request for all type of information required by managers, (2) determines sources of the information and tools needed to collect, evaluate, and analyse information, (3) deals with presenting, distributing and updating the information, (4) handles complaints of employees , and (5) performs all types functions related to information.

Internal records system keeps regular circulation of the information throughout the organisation without much expense and efforts. Managers can get the up-to-date information about marketing operations. Once the system is set up properly, it can serve the purpose continually.

2. MARKETING INTELLIGENCE SYSTEM

While internal report system concerns with information available from internal records of organisation, the marketing intelligence system supplies the managers with happening data. It provides information about external happenings or external environment. Marketing intelligence system is: *The set of procedures and sources used by managers to obtain every-day information regularly about pertinent developments in the marketing environment.* A manager can try to expose external environment in various ways.

Marketing intelligence system consists of various methods. A manager can use one or more below mentioned methods:

i. Reading newspapers, books, and other publications.
ii. Watching TV, hearing radio, or Internet surfing.
iii. Talking to customers, dealers, suppliers, and other relevant parties.
iv. Talking to other managers and employees of his company as well as of other companies.
v. Maintaining live contacts with other officials and agencies.
vi. Purchasing useful information from professional sources.
vii. Assigning marketing intelligence task to professional agencies, etc.

Effective marketing intelligence system can facilitate managers to take immediate actions like reacting to competitors, meeting changing needs of customers, solving dealers' problems, and so on.

3. MARKETING RESEARCH SYSTEM

Marketing research is a powerful and independent branch of the MIS. In certain cases, managers need detailed information on the specific problem of the specific marketing area. Thus, it is a formal study of specific problems, opportunities, or situations. Normally, it is carried out for solving the specific problem. In this sense, it is not a part of routine activity. It collects need-based information. Nowadays, it is treated as the separate discipline or subject. **Philip Kotler** defines: "Marketing Research is the systematic design for collection, analysis, and reporting of data and findings relevant to specific marketing situations facing the company."

Marketing research consists of collecting primary and secondary data from various respondents using various tools through various methods for definite period of time, analysing data using appropriate statistics tools, and presenting findings in forms of a report. It is conducted by internal expert staff or external professionals. (For detail, refer to marketing research later on in the chapter)

4. MARKETING DECISION SUPPORT SYSTEM (MDSS)

Previously, the component was known as Analytical Marketing System. While former three components supply data, the marketing decision support system concerns more with processing or analysing available data. This component can improve efficiency and utility of the whole marketing information system. The system is used to help managers make better decisions. **John D. C. Little** defines: "A marketing decision support system (MDSS) is coordinated collection of data, systems, tools, and techniques with supporting software and hardware by which an organisation gathers and interprets relevant information from environment and turns it into a basis for making decisions." According to the definition, the MDSS includes tools, techniques or models used for (1) data collection, (2) data analysis, (3) interpreting results, and (4) supporting managerial decision-making. The MDSS can be applied to improve efficiency and usefulness of other three components discussed earlier in this chapter. In real sense, it is not a separate component, but extension of other components.

Statistical tools, new models, and software are used to help marketing managers analyse, plan, and control their operations. The MDSS consists of two sub-components – the statistical bank and the model bank.

The Statistical Bank

It consists of quantitative tools used in marketing decision-making. It is popularly known as Operations Research (OR). The statistical tools used for data analysis include:

i. Simple statistical techniques like averages, mode, mediun, etc.
ii. Regression-multiple regression analysis
iii. Discriminant analysis
iv. Correlation analysis
v. Factor analysis
vi. Cluster analysis
vii. Input-output analysis
viii. Conjoint analysis
ix. Multidimensional scaling, etc.

The Model Bank

This component includes decision support models. It is a collection of models and software that can help managers develop better marketing decisions. The model is a series of variables, their interrelationships, and programmes to represent some real systems. The models are developed by scientists who are known as operation researchers. For different purposes, different models are used. Widely used models include:

i. The Markov-Process Analysis
ii. Queuing Model
iii. New Product Pretest Models
iv. Sales Response Model
v. Discrete Choice Model
vi. Differential Calculus
vii. Mathematical Programming
viii. Statistical Decision Theory
ix. Game theory
x. Heuristics
xi. Decision Tree Model
xii. Feedback System Model
xiii. Linear v/s Non-linear Model, etc.

Using relevant variables, mathematical operators, and some techniques, the new models can be developed as per firm's needs. Sometimes, such models are also called packages. Some recently developed decision models include BRANDAID (marketing mix model), CALLPLAN (for sales force to determines number of calls), DETAILER (for sales force to determine type of customers to call), GEOLINE (for designing sales and service territories), MEDICAC (for advertising to select media), PROMOTER (for sales promotion programmes), ADCAD (for selecting type of advertising theme), COVERSTORY (for writing sales reports and memo writing), etc. Every model consists of variables and their relationships. Each of them can be applied in specific decision area and for specific purpose.

MARKETING RESEARCH

INTRODUCTION

Marketing research is one of the important functions of marketing management. It is also one of the components of MIS. We know that information is the basic input in making decisions. Every manager needs relevant, reliable, adequate, and timely information to take decision related to any area of marketing. Many companies maintain a well-equipped marketing research department to collect, analyse, and interpret data required for making marketing decisions at various levels. In today's marketing practices, marketing research plays a vital role as marketing starts and ends with the target market. A marketer needs to keep watch on marketing environment to find out opportunities and to face challenges. For this task, marketing research is inevitable. Note that marketing research provides need-based information. It is carried out to solve particular problems or to explore particular situation.

DEFINITIONS

Let us define the term:

1. **R. D. Crisp:** "Marketing research is the systematic, objective, and exhaustive search for and study of the facts relevant to any problem in the field of marketing."
2. **P. E. Green and D. S. Tull:** "Marketing research is the systematic and objective search for and analysis of information relevant to the identification and solution of any problem in marketing."
3. **W. B. Wentz:** "Marketing research is the process of gathering and analysing information to assist manager in making marketing decisions. These decisions involve manipulation of firm's pricing, product, promotion, and distribution variables."
4. **Philip Kotler:** "Marketing research consists of systematic design for collection, analysis, and reporting of data and findings relevant to specific marketing situation facing company."
5. **The Definition Committee of the American Marketing Association:** "Marketing research is the systematic gathering, recording, and analysing of data about problems relating to the marketing of goods and services."
6. **P. Cox and R. Good:** "Marketing research is a set of procedures and methods that are used to collect, analyse, and to record data about any problem in field of marketing."
7. Marketing research is aimed at solving business (marketing) problem. It helps to find out the best solution to problems. In this concern, we can define the term as: *Marketing research involves gathering, analysing, and interpreting data relevant to business operations to get the best possible answers to certain major questions like what to produce, when and how much to produce, where to place a product in market, where to direct sales efforts, and what price to charge.*
8. On the basis of various definitions, we can define the term as: *Objective and systematic collection, recording, and analysis of data relevant to marketing problems of business enterprise for the purpose of developing a base for marketing decision-making.*

Thus, marketing research consists of an application of scientific methods and procedures to study marketing problems, and to aid making decisions. Thus, it studies buyers and sellers (dealers) examining their attitudes, preference, habits and purchase potential. It is the task consisting of studying marketing problems, and collecting, analysing and interpreting data to solve these problems.

CHARACTERISTICS OR NATURE

Marketing research is an important area of marketing management. In today's marketing practices, it is considered as an indispensable activity. The main purpose of marketing research is to provide information about market on demand. It is one of the basic activities, or an integral part of modern marketing. Similarly, a large number of statistical techniques are used for tabulation, analysis, and interpretation of data. Nature of marketing research can be described in light of following points:

1. It is one of the important functions of marketing management. But, it enjoys a separate status in study and practice. It is considered as a separate subject or discipline.
2. It is a process of gathering, recording, and analysing data relevant to any marketing problem.
3. It follows scientific methods and procedures. It is a systematic and objective study of marketing problems that can provide bias-free results.
4. Objectivity is an essential element of modern marketing research. Results of marketing research should be free from personal value, needs, and emotion. It should emphasize on impersonal needs of organisation.
5. It is an art and a science. One is required to use the scientific methods for collection of data, and also qualities and expertise to conduct marketing research.
6. It is not a decision-making but an aid to decision-making. It provides the required information on which decisions can be taken.
7. It is a consumer-oriented activity. The entire process of marketing research is consumer-centered.
8. It is aimed at adequate, reliable, and timely availability of information. Its primary task is to provide necessary information on particular issue or problem.
9. It is a professional activity. It is conducted on a professional basis. There are many professional agencies conducting marketing research on behalf of marketing firms by fees. They hire qualified staff and conduct marketing research for the clients firms.
10. Use of computer and computer-based techniques is very common in modern marketing research activity.
11. Statistics is closely related to marketing research. For deciding sample, collection of data, tabulation, analysis and testing, interpretation, etc., statistics is widely used.
12. It is a powerful branch of marketing management, but it enjoys separate status and is treated as the independent discipline.

IMPORTANCE/OBJECTIVES OF MARKETING RESEARCH

Marketing research is a powerful branch of marketing management. It is clear that modern marketing is consumer-oriented. And, consumer orientation is almost impossible without marketing research. Similarly, consumer satisfaction is possible only if the marketer knows adequately about consumers, their needs, wants, preference, and habits. Marketing research provides such information. It is a valuable tool that links marketing efforts with needs and wants of the target market. Due to crucial role of marketing research, money spent on marketing research can be treated as valuable investment, and not expenditure. Based on marketing research, a marketer can maintain close contact with the market. Role of marketing research can be described on the basis of following points:

1. To Know Needs and Wants of Target Market

Knowledge of target market guides what a marketing manager should do to satisfy the market. Adequate knowledge regarding target market is basic requirement to satisfy consumers. Unless we know what they need and want, we cannot decide what to offer. Due to marketing research, marketing efforts can be effectively directed toward satisfying needs and wants of customers.

2. To Know Market Changes

Market situations are constantly changing. In order to match marketing efforts with changing needs and wants of consumers, a manager needs information that can be supplied by marketing research.

3. To Face Competition Effectively

Today market is chagarctersied by cut-throat competition. Facing competition strongly is one of the important tasks of modern marketing managers. Formulation of marketing strategies to defeat competitiors needs the accurate information about competitors' offers, price, promotion, and services that can be provided only by marketing research department.

4. To Realize the Marketing Concept in Practice

Marketing concept is based on consumer satisfaction. Consumers can be satisfied only when management has relevant and reliable information about consumers' needs, wants, attitudes, and expectations. Marketing research provides the required information to the manager regarding consumers. Therefore, marketing manager is in better position to design marketing programme to satisfy his valued consumers.

5. To Segment Market and Select Target Market

Modern marketing practice is based on the target market, and not on total market. Target market is the aimed market or well-defined groups of customers for whom product is manufactured, price is set, promotion efforts are made, and distribution network is prepared. For segmenting the total market and selecting the target market, the manager needs information on social, cultural, personal, and psychological aspects of customers. Marketing research can serve the purpose.

6. To Raise Standard of Living of Society

Marketing research can contribute in improving the standard of living of society. Due to marketing research, products are produced and distributed according to needs, preference, and priority of consumers. So, society at large can get what it needs and wants. Marketing research can also ensure the efficient use of resources and, consequently, quality product is available at reasonable price.

7. To Find out Opportunities, and to Prepare for Challenges and Threats

Marketing research helps in finding opportunities emerging from business environment. In the same way, a marketer can formulate appropriate strategies to face the challenges and threats in an effective manner.

8. To Formulate Marketing Programme (4Ps) and Improving it Overtime

Marketing research guides marketing manager find answers to several marketing problems – what to produce, how much to charge, how and in what way to promote the product, and where and how to distribute it. Decisions regarding product, price, promotion, and place largely depend upon marketing research. Also, improvement or alteration in any of these elements can be made on the basis of data gathered and analysed through marketing research.

9. To Reduce Risk Inherent in Decision-making

Every economic decision involves risk and uncertainty. Risk and uncertainty exist because of inability to avail necessary information in time. Note that risk cannot be eliminated. By marketing research, relevant and reliable information on the past, the present, and the future (projected) can be made available to decision-maker. Availability of needed information assists a manager to evaluate and select the most promising or attractive alternative. Naturally, decision based on facts and reality can reduce degree of risk.

10. To Assess Effectiveness of Marketing Strategies

Marketing research is not only useful to formulate and implement marketing strategies. But, it is also equally useful to assess the ongoing performance. A manager can find out the effectiveness of strategies he implemented. Further, it helps in detecting causes leading to poor performance.

11. To Reduce Wastage of Valuable Resources

Marketing research ensures the exact use of resources to satisfy customers. Every action is taken in light of need of the organisation. Exact and precise use of valuable resources ensures maximum contribution of each of the resources and at minimum possible wastage.

12. To Exercise Control

Marketing research is also important for exercising control over marketing operations. Controlling involves setting standards, measuring actual performance, comparing the actual performance with standards, finding deviation, if any, and detecting causes leading to the deviation. In the entire process of controlling, the role of marketing information seems to be inevitable.

SCOPE OF MARKETING RESEARCH

Scope of marketing research refers to the areas covered or the aspects studied under marketing research. In other words, it implies where or on which areas marketing research can be applied. In fact, marketing research concerns with almost each and every activity of marketing management. It has a wide and comprehensive scope. The scope of marketing research covers following areas:

1. Research on Products

Products involve goods and services. This branch of marketing research covers all the issues related to firm's products. It studies and solves the product-related problems, such as:

i. Study of products' qualities and performance
ii. Study of physical and psychological characteristics of product
iii. Determining uses of the existing products
iv. Comparative study of competitive products
v. Detecting consumers' problems related to the products
vi. Determining need for developing new products
vii. Assessing success of a new product in market, including market testing
viii. Product life cycle and consumer adoption study
ix. Study of branding, packaging, labeling, after-sales services, and remarking

2. Research on Market

This area of marketing research deals with market/consumers. It studies characteristics and compositions of the target markets. It covers both current as well as potential markets. This branch includes:

i. Defining and selecting target market
ii. Studying needs and wants of target market
iii. Study of size and location of current market
iv. Assessing the current market trends and projecting the future trend
v. Analysis of territorial sales opportunities and potential
vi. Setting sales territories and sales quotas
vii. Market share analysis

viii. Studies on relative profitability of different markets
ix. Estimating demand of a new product

3. Research on Sales Methods and Policies

This area of marketing research, particularly, concerns with study and analysis of the sales-related activities. Various aspects covered under this head may be listed as below:

i. Study and analysis of sales records
ii. Analysis of sales territories in terms of products, size of orders, times, terms and conditions and methods
iii. Study on activities and effectiveness of salesmen
iv. Evaluating existing selling methods
v. Sales force management including size, compensation, training, control, etc.
vi. Study on effect of various promotional tools such as advertising, personal selling, sales promotion, and publicity tools on sales
vii. Study on organisation structure of sales department

4. Research on Advertising

Advertising is one of the powerful methods of market promotion. Major part of promotional budget is devoted to advertising activities. Therefore, it is imperative to conduct research on various aspects related to advertising. Under this area, at least following aspects are covered:

i. Comparative study of various elements of promotion
ii. Study on advertising objectives, media and media selection, advertising message, theme, copy, and advertising agency
iii. Social aspects of advertising – negative and positive effects of advertising on society at large
iv. Advertising role in different stages of product life cycle
v. Government restrictions on advertising
vi. Study on costs and contribution of advertising or evaluating advertising effectiveness
vii. Study of competitors' advertising practices and strategy

5. Research on Pricing

Price is an important element of marketing mix. In developing and underdeveloped countries, price plays a vital role. Suitable pricing policies and methods can contribute positively in attainment of marketing goals. It is clear that price has remained a major determinant of buying decision. This branch covers:

i. Study on pricing objectives
ii. Study on effectiveness of pricing policies and strategies
iii. Study of various methods for setting price
iv. Quality v/s value analysis
v. New product and pricing policies
vi. Study on effect of discount, allowance, and seasonal variables
vii. Pricing strategies on different stages of product life cycle

6. Research on Distribution

In today's marketing, distribution has unique role to determine success of product. A marketer can contribute to total consumer satisfaction by designing appropriate distribution network. Physical distribution and distribution channel are two important components of such research. This area includes:

1. Assessing role of distribution decisions in achieving marketing goals
2. Comparative study of between direct and indirect distribution
3. Physical distribution and ancillary services
4. Study on various types of channels of distribution
5. Study on relevant factors affecting channel decision/selection
6. Comparing company's distribution strategies with competitors
7. Relevance of online marketing
8. Legal issues related to distributions

7. Research on Business Environment and Corporate Responsibility

This area is not concerned with solving any marketing problem directly. In order to collect and analyse data related to broad business environment, such research is conducted. The study on the area helps manager formulate strategies for the current and the future market as well. It also helps assess strengths and weaknesses of marketing department in relation to business environment. In today's dynamic business environment, the study on various economic, social, and cultural variables is extremely important. Similarly, it is necessary to analyse corporate responsibility. Main aspects covered under the head include:

i. Business analysis including demand, national income, per capita income, trade and industry, economic growth rate, fiscal monetary policies, and export-import policy
ii. Short-term and long-term business forecasting
iii. Technological aspects
iv. Availability and quality of productive resources
v. Impacts of legal provisions and Acts
vi. Study on consumerism and the consumer rights
vii. Social and cultural values affecting business policy
viii. Pollution and ecological imbalance, and social responsibility of business

DATA

Marketing research is a process of gathering, analysing, and reporting of data relating to any problem in the marketing field. Entire process involves the data-related activities. Data are the raw information. Webster's dictionary defines data as: "Facts, statistics, or information either historical or derived by calculation, or experimentation." For solving any marketing problem, adequate, reliable, relevant and timely data are necessary. Major part of research budget, efforts, and time is occupied in collecting data. Data, being raw information, cannot provide clear indication or implication. They are to analysed and interpreted to get meaningful implication. Only information developed from data can be used for taking decisions or formulating strategies.

Marketing research uses two types of data – primary data and secondary data. Both data have their uses and limitations. Also, different methods are used for collecting both types of data.

PRIMARY DATA

Primary data are those details, which are directly and completely related with the problem on hand. Primary data are original information and are treated as the basic input for analysing and solving any problem related to marketing activities. They are deliberately, rigorously, and consciously collected from the relevant respondents to generate original information that can be used directly to solve the marketing problem. They are collected as per company's plan. For example, if a company wants to solve the problem related to distribution activities, whatever data collected in light of this problem can be referred as primary data. Primary data are collected from relevant respondents. They are not readily available, their collection and analysis need rigorous efforts. Success of marketing research depends upon quality and quantity of primary data. In fact, no research project can be completed without primary data.

Characteristics of Primary Data

Primary data constitute the basis information to solve the marketing problems. With reference to primary data, it can be said that:

1. Primary data are original data.
2. Primary data are expensive.
3. Collection of primary data takes considerable time and efforts.
4. They are collected with reference to problem on hand.
5. They are collected deliberately from relevant respondents.
6. Specific methods (like survey methods, observation methods, experimental method, etc.) and tools (like printed forms, questionnaire, camera, etc.) are used for collecting primary data.
7. They constitute a basic input in the research project.
8. They are required be furnished, processed, or analysed before they are used.

Sources of Primary Data

Primary data are the basic input in solving problem. They are expensive, time consuming, and they need more efforts. Sources of primary data depend upon type of problem. They are collected by using specific methods and tools. Most commonly used sources of primary data may include:

1. Consumers
2. Retailers
3. Wholesalers
4. Dealers/agents
5. Suppliers
6. Employees of company
7. Salesmen
8. Trade associations
9. Professional experts
10. Top-level management
11. Competitors
12. Other business firms
13. Service providers like banks, transporters, insurance, etc.

SECONDARY DATA

Secondary data, on the other hand, are published data. They are readily available. They can be used directly without processing or analysis. They are collected rather than generated. Secondary data are those details which have been collected for the purpose other than specific research problem. They are also known as the recorded data. They are published data. They have been collected by other people for their contemporary problems. Sometimes, they are not useful. They are supplementary to primary data. They support primary data. Extent to which secondary data are used for marketing research depends upon suitability, accuracy, and time.

Secondary data consist of the information that already exists somewhere, having been collected for other purposes. Hardly problem can be solved only by secondary data. They are used for exploring, defining, and understanding problems, which can be solved by primary data. For collecting secondary data, there is no need for employing qualified, experience, and capable research officer. Similarly, special methods and tools are not used. Such data can be easily collected.

Characteristics of Secondary Data

Following are the key characteristics of secondary data:

1. Secondary data are published data, not original data, for the research on the hand.
2. They give the latest information
3. They can be easily collected from various internal and external sources.
4. They are relatively cheaper; they need less efforts, time, and money.
5. They have been collected by other people for their own problems and situation in the past.
6. They are used as a supplementary to primary data. Mostly, they are used for defining and understanding problems.
7. The use of secondary data is optional. Research can be conducted even without the use of this type of data.
8. They can be used without processing; no need to analyse them before they are used. They can be used directly.
9. Relevance, accuracy, and timing are the main problems related to secondary data.

Sources of Secondary Data

Secondary data can be collected from various sources. Mostly they are collected from published sources. There are two types of sources:

1. Internal Sources
2. External Sources

Internal Sources

i. Sales and purchase records
ii. Customers' complaint notes
iii. Sales orders
iv. Salesmen's reports
v. Past research work of company
vi. Other literature and publication work of company
vii. Information of the past special events, etc.

External Sources

i. Government publication and reports
ii. Advertising media – daily newspapers, magazines and periodicals, radio, television, etc.
iii. Advertising agencies and marketing consultants
iv. Universities and colleges
v. Commercial and general libraries
vi. Marketing research firms and consultants
vii. Trade associations and technical and professional groups
viii. Internet surfing
ix. Trade fairs and exhibitions
x. Consumer rating agencies, etc.

METHODS FOR COLLECTING DATA

Success of marketing research project depends upon quality and relevance of data. And, quality of data, to a major extent, depends upon methods and techniques used for collecting data. Selection and use of methods for conducting marketing research require a great deal of experience and expertise. Overall suitability of different methods plays a vital role in their selection.

Factors: Selection of methods for collecting data is based on following factors:

1. Overall objective of marketing department
2. Type of marketing problem and information needed
3. Time and cost factors
4. Research design to be followed
5. Ability and experience of employees involved
6. Sources or respondents of data, etc.

DATA COLLECTION METHODS

It is important to note that for collection of the secondary data, no need to use specific methods. They are easily collected from various published sources. The problem of method selection arises in case of primary data. So, discussion on data collection methods is relevant to primary data only. Practically, sample-based survey methods are used. Selection of an appropriate sample is important decision in almost all the methods for primary data collection. Commonly used methods have been depicted in Figure 2:

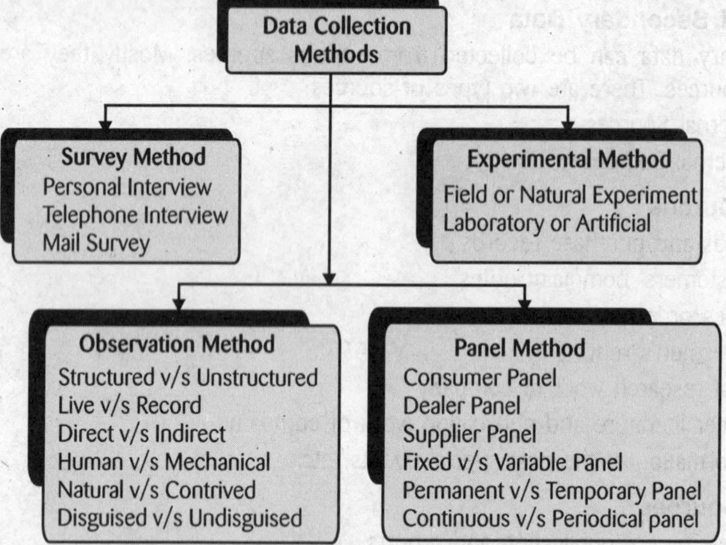

Figure 2: Primary Data Collection Methods

1. Survey Method or Questionnaire Method

Survey method is also said as communication method as the data are collected by communicating with the respondents, either by face-to-face oral communication or by other means like telephone, mails, etc. This is a widely used method for collecting primary data. It is fit for any kind of research problem. Major marketing research projects, more or less, follow survey method. Because of the intensive use of questionnaire in survey method, it is also called as the questionnaire method. The unique characteristic of a survey method is that the data are collected by asking questions to the relevant respondents. Commonly used options in the survey methods include interview, telephone interview, and mail survey.

i. **Interview:** Interview involves a face-to-face interaction with the respondents. Personal interview includes collection of data by personally contacting the respondents. Here face-to-face communication and free feedback are possible. It is a very effective and flexible method for conducting survey. Interview is conducted using questionnaire, containing different types of questions. Using probe questions like what, why, when, how much, where, with whom, etc., more information can be elicited from the respondents. Picture, chart, cartoons, products, and other similar devices are used to get more clear and precise information regarding their interest, attitudes, and opinions. Interviews may include personal interview, focus group interview, primary interview, and in-depth interview.

In personal interview, at a time, only one interviewee is interviewed while focus group interview includes interviewing more respondents at a time. Primary interview is conducted to collect the primary (elementary or brief) information. In contrast, the in-depth interview consists of the detailed discussion with the respondents. Success of interview depends on ability, training, experience, and competency of interviewer.

ii. **Telephonic Interview:** Nowadays, a telephone survey can be easily conducted due to wide spread telephone facilities provided by telephone department and private companies. Up-to-date telephone directories (in hard and soft copy format) can make the task easy. However, in urban areas, it can be conducted more effectively. Here, interview is conducted by asking questions through telephone (including cell phone), and response of the respondents is recorded systematically. This is an ideal method when one wants information on the current/live activities. For example, we can get information about the performance of the star cricketers when match is being displayed on television by asking question to viewers through telephone. Similarly, the effectiveness of advertisement can be measured by immediately contacting the respondents when advertisement is published during particular programme.

It is suitable when one wants short answers for a few questions. A large number of interviews can be conducted in a short time. This survey may be structured or unstructured. But, generally the structured telephone survey is used to get information on the specific aspects within limited time. Main problems associated with telephone survey are, (1) unwillingness, (2) no scope for further query, (3) limited information can be collected, (4) lack of attention or non-committed answer and misleading information, (5) only respondents with telephone (and or cell phone) facility can be contacted; not much fit for rural areas, and (6) limited utility due to certain practical problems in conducting such survey. In spite of these limitations, it can be a powerful option if it is conducted carefully.

iii. **Mail Survey:** In this method, data are collected by mail or letter. Well-designed printed copy of questionnaire is sent to known and unknown respondents with a request to return it back dully filled. The mail may work as a silent fieldworker. Certain gifts, rewards, or direct benefits are associated with the mail to inspire and prompt the respondents for quick and complete information. Sometimes, a coin, coupons, or draw tickets are sent with questionnaire. Follow-up with sweet reminders can create respondents' interest. Newspapers and magazines can also be used as medium for limited survey. Internet (putting quarries or questions on websites) and E-mail (electronic mail) are the latest computer-based devices to send and collect data on the relevant area. SMS by cell phone is also widely used for the purpose.

This method doesn't face geographical constraints. With same charge, by government postal service, national wide survey is possible. In fact, private mail service providers, like courier services, charge rates as per distance. It is, comparatively, less costly and convenient. For mail survey, questionnaire is prepared in regional language, and simple, short and direct questions are used.

Practical problems related to the mail survey are (1) time consuming, (2) careless completion of questionnaire, (3) minimum response rate, (4) incomplete response

(5) limited information can be collected, (6) SMS (cell phone), e-mail, etc., are costly and there are a lot of related practical problems, (7) expression or face reading is not possible, etc.

2. Observation Method

This is another type of widely used method for primary data collection. However, it is used as a complementary to survey method. It is used to furnish, revise or complement data collected through the survey. Observation can be defined as: *The act of carefully recognizing and noting facts or occurrence. The distinguished characteristic of this method is that no questions are asked to respondents for collecting data,* but their behaviour is observed minutely. Under this method, researcher can observe, measure, or note the original behaviour of respondents, mostly consumers and dealers.

There can be two types of observations – live observation and record observation. In case of live observation, on-going (live) facts or occurrence are recognized or noted. On the other hand, the record observation involves recognizing, or noting of the records. Observation carried out by the properly selected, trained, capable, and experienced observer can provide an objective information. A lot depends upon ability of observer. Various tools used for observing behaviour may include camera, movie camera, close-circuit camera, printed forms, etc.

Practical problems associated with observation methods are, (1) it is difficult of collect data objectively, (2) it doesn't measure the state of mind, which is more relevant for the study of intension, buying motive, or attitudes, (3) it depends heavily upon ability and experience of the observer; there is possibility of the biased outcomes, and (4) it is costly and time consuming.

Types of Observation: There can be various types of observation. Some popular forms have been stated briefly as under:

i. **Structured v/s Unstructured Observation:** Structured observation involves a detailed plan regarding what and when to observe; why and how to observe; and where and who is to observe. Printed forms are used to record the behaviour of respondents. Every aspects related to observation is predetermined in advance. It is known as planned or structured observation. Sometimes, the observer watches and notes the behaviour without any specific scheme or plan. Here, time, methods, place, and procedures of observing behaviour and recording data are not specified in advance. Such observation may turn as unstructured observation.

ii. **Lives v/s Record Observation:** In case of the live observation, on-going or live behaviour and activities are observed. The record observation consists of observing the recorded/past behaviour of the relevant respondents.

iii. **Direct v/s Indirect Observation:** Direct Observation involves observing behaviour of the respondents directly. There is no considerable physical distance between observer and respondents. Indirect observation is the distanced observation. Behaviour is observed at the distance place. Direct or indirect observation is applicable to both live as well as record observation.

iv. **Natural v/s Contrived Observation:** While natural observation is conducted in the original setting or situations, the contrived observation is based on artificially created environment. Artificial situation is created, people are informed, and their behaviour is observed. The natural observation provides more reliable and original information.

v. **Human v/s Mechanical Observation:** Obviously, human observation involves human being. Human organism is recognizing and noting the respondents' behaviour. On the contrary, the mechanical observation involves certain mechanical or electrical devices, such as movie camera, automatic recording close-circuit camera or robot is used to observe behaviour and activities of people.

vi. **Disguised v/s Undisguised Observation:** This is a very important classification of observation. Disguised observation is one in which the targeted people do not know that they are being observed. They will behave naturally and originally. Sometimes, the respondents are informed that their behaviour will be observed at a particular time. Thus, they know that they are being observed. It is a kind of an undisguised observation. Because they are aware, they may behave differently than regular. Depending upon situations, the suitable method of observation is used.

3. Experimental Method

Under this method of data collection, a cause and effect (i.e.,causal) relationship is established. The independent variables are manipulated to measure the effects of such manipulation on the dependent variables. For example, if marketing manager want to measure the effect of 10% price rise on sales, first, he raises price by 10% (manipulation of independent variable), and then he tries to measure the effects of the price rise on sales volume (impact on dependent variable). However, along with manipulation of independent variables, the impact of relevant extraneous factors should also be kept in mind to estimate the exact effect of manipulation. Many times, to minimize the effect of uncontrollable factors, the experiment is conducted in the controlled environment. Major problems associated with experimental methods for primary data collection are, (1) impact of extraneous factors that minimizes reliability of results, (2) experimental method is costly, (3) it is time consuming, (4) possibility of the strange (abnormal) results than normal because of effect of experiments; people may deliberately react abnormally, etc. Despite all these problems, the experimental method is very useful for certain marketing issues, for example, testing of new product in particular localities before it is lunched fully. It can be used to measure effectiveness of packaging and design, or measuring effect of particular promotional tool. Conducting a successful experiment for data collection needs a great deal of knowledge, experience, and ability.

Types of Experiment: Experimental method can be conducted in two ways:

i. **Field or Natural Experiment:** Such experiment is conducted in the real market situation. No attempts are made to create an artificial situation for manipulation and measurement of effects. In a natural way, the independent variables are manipulated in one or more market places to measure their impact of dependent variables. One of the prime problems is that here the researcher has no control on the situation and, consequently, outcomes of experiment may be misleading.

ii. **Laboratory or Artificial Experiment:** This experimental method differs significantly from the former one. Here, attempts are made to cerate artificial situations in which experiment is made. It is conducted in the controlled environment. The researcher has considerable control on the situations. The net or exact outcome may be obtained. But, it is conducted in a limited scale and it is difficult to derive general conclusions on the basis. For example, some customers and dealers are invited in a laboratory and are shown demonstration of proposed product to estimate product acceptability at particular price. There is full possibility that results may be quite imaging compared to real situation. Response during experiment and post experiment may produce contrasting results.

4. Panel Method

Panel method is a hybrid method. All aforesaid methods are used to collect data from the panel. Panel can be defined as: The fixed and relatively permanent sample/group of respondents to obtain information continuously or intermittently (periodical) basis. In case of panel method, data are collected only from panels of response groups or respondents. As and when information is needed, these panels are contacted. They are provided incentives; they are offered gifts or some rewards to encourage them provide relevant and accurate information willingly. The data are more reliable and up-to-date. Such panels provide necessary information about market trends, fashion, consumer attitudes and expectations, strengths of competitors, and also make valuable suggestions to improve the company's overall performance. Panel is relatively fixed and permanent sample of respondents. However, changes in terms of size, type, and location are made to suits the company's requirements.

Types of Panel: Commonly used panels are as under:

i. **Consumer Panel:** Such panel involves only consumers. They are consulted for the required data, or they provide data periodically on any issue related to market as per the contract.

ii. **Dealer Panel:** Dealer panel consists of middlemen, such as wholesalers, retailers, and agents. They can provide valuable information regarding consumers, competitors, and overall market environment.

iii. **Supplier Panel:** Suppliers are those parties who supply necessary inputs like raw materials, provisions, parts, and other inputs required for production and marketing of products. This panel also includes service providers like insurance companies, transporters, bankers, and so forth.

iv. **Continuous or Periodical Panel**: Continuous panel provides information on a continuous basis. They maintain live contact with a company and inform the company as and when they feel that the information is important. Periodical panel, on the other hand, provides detail at a fixed interval.

v. **Permanent or Temporary Panel:** Permanent panel is standing in nature. Such panel serves for relatively a long period to time. On the other hand, the temporary panel is ad-hoc in nature. It is terminated when the time is over.

vi. **Fixed or Variable Panel:** In case of a fixed panel, number and type of respondents are fixed. No changes are made in the panel. While in variable panel, number and types of respondents are subject to change.

TOOLS FOR DATA COLLECTION

For collection of data, various tools or instruments are used. However, the use of research tools for data collection purpose depends on various relevant factors like methods to be used; research problem to be solved; time, cost, and efforts needed; ability and experience of staff; and likewise. In actual practice of marketing research in India and abroad, one or more of following tools/instruments are used:

1. Questionnaire
2. Printed forms for recording response
3. Special forms used for recording live observation
4. Voice recorder
5. Telephone and fax machine
6. Computer with Internet connection
7. Close circuit camera
8. Cameras and movie cameras
9. Specially designed (or programmed) robots, etc.

Questionnaire is widely used tool for any type of research. In most marketing research projects, questionnaire is always used. Our discussion is limited to questionnaire only.

QUESTIONNAIRE

Questionnaire is the most popularly and widely used tool for collecting the primary data. It suits to any kind of research problem. In today's marketing research activities, the questionnaire has become indispensable tool. It is not used only in marketing field, but also all types of social research projects.

DEFINITIONS

Term 'questionnaire' can be defined as:

1. Dictionary meaning: *Questionnaire consists of the formulated series of questions.*
2. *Questionnaire is a set of questions systematically and deliberately prepared to investigate into the problem.*
3. *Questionnaire is a list of various types of questions related to specific area or problem, expressed in some logical patterns and order, which can be used for data collection purpose.*

KEY DECISIONS OR ISSUES IN QUESTIONNAIRE (PREPARATION)

We need to discuss several decisions – problems and issues – related to questionnaire preparation. Questionnaire preparation is a creative task. It needs a great deal of imagination, expertise, subject knowledge, and experience. It is prepared in light of response to be sought. The expert who has to design the questionnaire for the specific marketing problem should consider a large number of variables, such as research problem, cost, ability of field worker, time, characteristics of respondents, language, length of questions, number of questions, order of the questions, and so forth. The key issues related to questionnaire design may include:

1. Deciding on information to be collected by questionnaire.
2. Deciding on type of questionnaires to be used (e.g., questionnaire for mail, telephone, or personal interview).
3. Deciding on the content and necessity of each question, and determining whether respondents can answer it.
4. Deciding on methods of administering questionnaire and recording response.
5. Deciding on wording, sentences, and physical layout of questionnaire.
6. Deciding on size of questionnaire or number of questions.
7. Deciding on type of questions (e.g., open-ended, direct, multiple-choice, dichotomous, etc.).
8. Deciding on the order or sequence of questions.
9. Deciding on language to be used.
10. Deciding on pretest, review and final draft.

STEPS IN QUESTIONNAIRE DESIGN

The task of composing questionnaire may be considered more an art than a science. It needs a great deal of experience, expertise, and creativity. Systematic questionnaire preparation involves certain steps listed below:

1. Determine the Data to be Collected
2. Determine the Method to be Used for Data Collection
3. Evaluate the Contents of the Question
4. Decide on Type of Questions and Response Format
5. Decide on Wording of Questions
6. Determine on Questionnaire Structure or Physical Format
7. Pretest, Review and Final Draft

TYPES OF QUESTIONNAIRE

Questionnaire can be classified on the basis of several criteria as stated below:

1. **On the basis of structure and disguiseness,** there are four types of questionnaire:
   i. **Structured Undisguised:** This type of questionnaire involves structured and undisguised questions. Response is limited to certain options. A structured means that answers of the questions are predetermined. Respondents have to select answer from the given list of answers. Undisguised means questions are open-ended. They are asked directly. Respondents can know what the researcher wants to know. For example, there are four products a, b, c, and d. Customers are asked to select the most preferred product.
   ii. **Unstructured Undisguised:** Unstructured means free questions are asked. Their response is not limited to certain answers only. They have full freedom to answer the question. In short, answers of the question are not decided in advance. For example, customer is asked to name the most preferred products in particular category.
   iii. **Structured Disguised:** Structured means the answers of the questions to be asked are determined in advance. Disguised means indirect way of asking questions. Customers do not know the exact purpose/intension of question but can answer easily. For example, which of the following products is more harmful? Why?
   iv. **Unstructured Disguised:** Here, the response is not fixed. Respondents have full freedom to answer the question. Disguised means something hidden. For example, which motorbike is more risky? Why?
2. **On the basis of use/purpose of questionnaire,** there are three types of questionnaire:
   i. **Questionnaire for Personal Interview:** This questionnaire is prepared to administer for personal interview. It may involve more questions and indirect questions which requires explanation or clarification.
   ii. **Questionnaire for Telephone Survey:** This questionnaire is prepared to collect information via telephone. Obviously, such questionnaire involves a limited number of short and simple questions.
   iii. **Questionnaire for Mail Survey:** This questionnaire it meant for the mail survey. This questionnaire is sent to respondents with a request to return it dully filled. It also involves short and simple questions. However, it consists of more questions.
3. **On the basis of administration,** there can be two types of questionnaire:
   i. **Interviewer-administered Questionnaire:** When this questionnaire is to be administered, the presence of both interviewer and respondents is essential. Here, questions are asked to respondents one by one. Their response is recorded either in the same questionnaire or in the separate form. For example, picture or cartoon are shown to respondents and are asked to describe it. Personal interview and telephone survey are based on this type of questionnaire.
   ii. **Self-administered Questionnaire:** It is given to respondent by the interviewer to fill in her/his answers. This is possible even in absence of interviewer. For mail survey, this type of questionnaire is used.
4. **On the basis of type of questions,** there can be two types of questionnaire:
   i. **Simple Questionnaire:** This questionnaire involves certain number of questions of the same type. It may involve only dichotomous, multiple choice, or otherwise. It has limited utility.
   ii. **Multiple Questionnaires:** Obviously, it involves variety of questions. Such questionnaire consists of certain questions of different categories. It is a popular questionnaire.

TYPES OF QUESTIONS

Questionnaire consists of different types of questions. This part discusses some popular forms of questions, frequently used in marketing research. Each type of question has its merits, demerits, and suitability. A wise marketing research officer can select appropriate type and number of questions to design a meaningful questionnaire. Widely used questions have been discussed here.

1. Open-ended Questions

This question can be openly answered. No alternatives are provided. It is a versatile device to collect primary data. This type of question is structured but its answer is unstructured. It is not restricted to certain options stated at the end of each of the questions. Respondents have full freedom to imagine. For example: According you, who can be successful marketing manager? Respondents can answer as per their knowledge. This is the example of free-response.

Use of probing is also popular in the open-ended question. After one or a few questions on the particular subjects, the open end is reached. Then interviewer starts to probe to get more relevant or missing information. Probing at the right stage during replying can help to enrich the contents. Probe questions are used to elicit more information. They include how, how much, to/from whom, to what extent, when, why, where, who, anything else, etc.

2. Close-ended question

This question is closed, means its answer falls within the given limit. Respondents are not allowed to guess beyond limit. The limit is specified by providing certain options. For example: Which of the following qualities you think a successful marketing manager must possess? Respondents have to select one or more relevant qualities given at the end of question.

3. Direct and Indirect Questions

Direct question is one, which can be asked and answered directly. Question carries a very clear indication. Such question can be answered exactly and easily as it is free from ambiguity. No need to make any assumption. For example: Why do you like to buy Maruti Alto? While indirect question is asked indirectly to allow respondent guess and perceive the situations differently as per personality characteristics. Mostly, such question can be responded differently by different people. For example: If you want to buy a cheaper, fuel efficient, high resale valued, and the best sales-after-serviced car for a small family, which one is most suitable? Why?

4. Scale Type Questions

Scale types questions are very popular in conducting marketing research. Respondents are given a range of categories in which to express their opinion. This is a powerful method to convert qualitative response into a quantitative form. Note that respondents have to express their feeling by selecting only one option. They are used to measure intensity of respondents' feeling. Such questions are used to make comparative judgment about their motivation, attitudes, or behaviour. Mostly, the five-point scale and the seven-point scale are more popular. Scale is used to measure level or degree of attitudes or agreed upon opinion. For example, five-point scale may be 5, 4, 3, 2, and 1. For example, if we want to measure possibility of buying a particular product in a given situation, we may use words like highest (5), higher (4), high (3), low (2) and lowest (1). Sometimes positive and negative points are also used, such as 2, 1, 0, -1, -2. Use of words indicating intensity is also common in measuring response of respondents. For example, strongly agreed (2), agreed (1), indifferent (0), disagreed (-1), strongly disagreed (-2). Even, at the time of analysis of data, such scale along with weightage is considered to measure the intensity of opinion. In marketing research, Likert Scale and Thurston Scale are popular. Scale-based questions can be asked in different ways. Sometimes, scale along with points is used; sometimes, words indicting intensity are used.

5. Descriptive Questions

Descriptive questions can be attended by descriptive answers. Every question needs a detailed explanation. At the end of every descriptive question, adequate space has been given to write the answer. Mostly, question is open and responded are free to express their ideas. For example: Why is TVS Victor motorbike the most successful bike of the year? Respondents can answer the question by explaining the competitive or superior advantages of the bike.

6. Short questions

Short questions can be answered by just writing one or two words. Question may be lengthy but can be answered by one word only. For example: Name the cold drink you like the most?

7. Ranking Questions

In order to measure the priority among the listed items, ranking questions are used. The respondents are asked to rank comparatively the items listed. For example, if a marketer wants to measure priority of reasons to buy the product, he can ask: Please rank the following reasons from the most important (1) to the least important (7) to you, for buying motorbike. Seven reasons have been listed and against each reason a blank space has been given to facilitate ranking.

8. Checklist

Such questions involve more options and can be answered by selecting one or more options. For example: Motorbike is more preferable because of following benefits. Ten benefits have been listed. Respondents may tick mark one or more benefits they think appropriate.

9. Multi-chotomous Questions or Multiple-choice Questions

Such type of question involves more options, may be five or more. And respondents are asked to select any one by tick mark. They are not required to write any word. For example: Out of following five motorbikes, which is the most fit for college students? Consider the second example: For your personal use, which one of the following cell phone instruments do you use?

10. Dichotomous Questions

This involves three options such as 'yes,' 'no,' and 'indifferent.' Respondent are asked to select any one by tick mark or replying orally. For example: Are you using motorbike? You have only one option to select, say, 'yes,' 'no,' 'indifference.' However, in many cases 'indifference' is not used to force respondent to reply in term of 'YES' or 'NO.'

11. Projective techniques

Projective techniques are specific techniques to measure motives, desires, emotion, and urge of the respondents. Psychologists have recognized that direct questioning has a little value to collect information about desires, motives or attitudes. Such techniques are usually used when respondents are unable or unwilling to answer the direct question. Use of these techniques avoids stereotype answer. They are the non-structured and disguised techniques. Here, a relatively non-personal ambiguous stimulus object such as word, picture, or statement is given to respond the stimulus object by describing it. While describing the situation, automatically desire, motives, or attitudes are reflected. Responses are interpreted according to predetermined psychological framework. It is assumed that the respondents will project/guess their true motives, personality, and beliefs without knowing that they are revealing the facts about themselves. Some of popular projective techniques have been briefly discussed here.

a. **Word Association Test or Matching the Words:** This technique was developed by Wilhelm, a father of experimental psychology, in 1880's. For example: Please tell the popular band name for each of the following five products. Only name of product is given/asked, respondents can response with the first word comes to mind. Sometimes, products and brand are given in mismatched form to match them and prepare pairs. This can be used to study trade name, brand name, promotional slogan, or retention value of message. This can be administered either orally or in a written form.

b. **Sentence Completion Test:** It was developed by Payne in 1930's to overcome drawback of word association test. Instead of word, the first part of sentence is given to complete it. Here, the respondents are provided with an incomplete or a half-completed sentence and are asked to complete it in a manner they like. Respondents can reply according to their feeling, attitude, experience, or knowledge. For example: You don't like to travel by air because........................... Another example: You prefer motorbike to scooter because............... At the end of every incomplete sentence, enough space is given. This can be administered orally, too.

c. **Picture Completion Test:** Here, an incomplete picture or a sketch is given and the respondents are asked either to complete or to interpret it. For example: Incomplete picture used in advertisement is given to complete it or picture is shown to interpret it.

d. **Story Telling/Completion Test:** Respondents are told a part of story – enough to center attention on particular issue – to complete it or given hint or situation to tell a story about what is/was happening and why. From the story discussed, a researcher may be able to draw conclusion.

e. **Pictorial Test:** In pictorial test picture, paired-picture, symbol, cartoon, etc., are used to elicit what is going into the mind of respondents. In this technique, respondents are shown a picture, paired-picture, symbol, or cartoon to imagine what it implies about. Mismatching or awkward picture is shown to find out what is not suitable or what is improper. Film star or cricketer is shown with particular products. This is to know whether respondents have knowledge about products, brand, or company.

SAMPLING

INTRODUCTION

Today's marketing research projects are large, and, sometimes, indefinite number of items are involved. Practically, it is not possible to study all the people or items under study. For less time, less money, and ease, the sample seems more practical. Most marketing research projects depend on the sample survey rather than the totality survey. Whether to use a census or a sample depends on a number of factors, such as type of census, degree of homogeneity/heterogeneity, costs, time, feasibility to study, degree of accuracy needed, and some others. Normally, the census is preferred under following situations:

1. When population is small.
2. Variance in characteristics being measured is high.
3. The cost of error is high.
4. Fixed cost of sampling is high.

BASIC TERMS RELATED TO SAMPLING

Now, first, let's define related terms:

Sample: Sample is a part of universe/population/census, which represents the characteristics of the whole universe under study. Thus, sample is a small portion of the population/universe from which it has been drawn that may represent that population.

Population: A group from which the sample is drawn is called the population or universe. In different words, the universe is the entire group of items about which researcher wishes to study and about which he plans to generalize. Population may be made up of individuals, groups, associations, areas, or households. If population is not defined, it seems infinite.

Sampling: Sampling is a process of selecting a few items from a given population to be investigated. There are four basic questions related to sampling:

1. What constitutes the population?
2. Should we take sample or census?
3. What type of sample would be taken?
4. What should be the size of sample?

BENEFITS OR REASONS FOR SAMPLING

Sampling offers several benefits over the census. The main benefits have been listed below:

1. Only possible method in case of a very large population.
2. It is a time-saving option.
3. Speedy assessment/investigation is possible.
4. It may be more accurate as each item under study is given more attention due to a manageable number of items.
5. It is the economic way to conduct survey. Costs of investigating sample are far low than the population.

TYPES OF SAMPLING PROCEDURES/TYPES OF SAMPLES

There are several ways to draw a sample from the definite or indefinite population. Each type of sampling procedure has its merits, demerits, and applicability. Depending upon need, an appropriate sampling procedure may be followed. In real practice, not single type, but a combination of several types of sampling procedures is used. Sampling procedures can be categories into two broad classes:

1. Probabilistic Sampling Procedure
2. Non-probabilistic Sampling Procedure

Probabilistic Sampling Procedures

It has been developed after 1950's. It is a bias-free method of selecting sample unit as it depends on a chance rather than a judgment. Each sample unit of the population has known chance of being selected for the sample. Sampling procedure is based on the mathematical decision, which leaves no discretion to researcher. One can estimate in advance about chance/probability of the sample unit to be selected. Here, 'known chance' does not mean 'equal chance.' 'Equal chance' is possible in a special case, say, only in case of simple random sampling. This method permits measurement of sampling error.

1. **Simple Random Sampling:** It is the simplest type of probability sampling. The most fundamental feature of simple random sampling is that each sample element has known and equal chance (probability) of being selected. More specifically, we can say that every possible sample of given size drawn from a specified universe has known and equal chance of being selected. The sample is drawn by randomly (haphazardly) from the sample frame (a list of exclusive and exhaustive enumeration of all sample elements). It is used only when population under study is relatively small.
2. **Stratified Sampling:** In case of the stratified random sampling, the population under study is divided into certain groups known as 'strata' or parts. Then, from each stratum, an appropriate sample is drawn randomly. Number of strata depends on degree of heterogeneity in the population under study. The higher is the degree of heterogeneity, the larger the number of strata will be and vice versa. For example, if we want to know

attitudes of students toward private tuitions, we divide the total number of respondents (students) of Gujarat State in various parts or strata such as college students and school students; stratification may follow level of education such as first year students, second year, third year, post graduate level, diploma level; it may be on the basis of technical and non-technical disciplines; may be city-wise or university-wise classification. Stratification takes place in a several ways. Now, from each of the stratum, a sample of appropriate number of students is selected. Sample drawn from each of the stratum represents only that stratum. Final generalization is drawn by combining response of all the samples drawn from each of the strata.

3. **Systematic Sampling:** Here, a specified system or pattern is followed to draw a sample. For example: If population consists of 100 items, every item multiple of five can be selected, such as 5, 10, 15, 20.... Sometimes, odd or even numbers are selected. In short, a system is followed to select the sample. It is possible when the population under study is well-defined and items are properly arranged, and population is definite. Sometimes, specially prepared tables are also used.
4. **Cluster Sampling:** It is also known as block sampling. In the sample methods discussed so far, the units of sample are selected individually, for example, a customer. But in case of cluster sampling, each sample unit is not individual unit but cluster or a group of units. For example, a household containing 5 members constitutes a sample unit. So, population must be divided into mutually exclusive and collectively exhaustive groups. In short, it is similar to simple random sampling with the difference of a cluster as a sample unit. It may be one-stage or two-stage sampling depending upon the procedure followed.
5. **Area Sampling:** It is also a form of the specified stratified sampling. The word 'area' in area sampling originally refers to a piece of the land. An area sampling is actually sample of areas. It extensively used in actual practice. It suggests primary sampling of geographical area like a sample of countries, states, towns, villages, blocks, societies, apartments, or other areas of discretion. Here, people reside in particular piece of land are studied. Area sampling is also of two types, one-stage area sampling and two-stage area sampling. One-stage area sampling involves choosing a simple random sample of n areas from population of N areas of particular region. In case of two-stage area sampling, first areas are selected and then certain households from each of the selected areas are selected. It can be multi-staged areas sampling if more stages are followed.

Non-Probabilistic Sampling Procedures

Here, selection of sample is based on some sort of judgment of researcher. There is no chance of any particular element to be selected. In case of non-probabilistic sampling, one must rely on experience and expertise of the person drawing the sample. In case of this sampling procedure, we are unable to measure sampling error. Therefore, we are unable to say that sample estimates calculated from non-probabilistic sample are accurate. They include:

1. Convenience Sampling
2. Judgment Sampling
3. Quota Sampling
4. Snowball Sampling

RESEARCH DESIGN

INTRODUCTION

The word 'design' has various meanings. But, in relation to the subject concern, it is a pattern or an outline of research project's workings. It is the statement of essential elements of a study that provides basic guidelines of conducting the project. It is same as the blue print of architect's work. The research design is similar to broad plan or model that states how the entire research project would be conducted. It is desirable that it must be in written form and must be simple and clearly stated. The real project is carried out as per the research design laid down in advance.

DEFINITIONS

1. We can define the term as: *Research design is a broad framework that states the total pattern of conducting research project. It specifies objectives, data collection and analysis methods, time, costs, responsibility, probable outcomes, and actions.*
2. More clearly, research design can be defined as: *A research design is a broad plan that states objectives of research project and provides the guidelines what is to be done to realize those objectives. It is, in other words, a master plan for executing a research project.*

CONTENTS OF RESEARCH DESIGN

The most common aspects involved in research design include at least followings:

1. Statement of research objectives, i.e., why the research project is to be conducted
2. Type of data needed
3. Definition of population and sampling procedures to be followed
4. Time, costs, and responsibility specification
5. Methods, ways, and procedures used for collection of data
6. Data analysis – tools or methods used to analyse data
7. Probable output or research outcomes and possible actions to be taken based on those outcomes

TYPES OF RESEARCH DESIGNS

As stated earlier, the research design is a broad framework that describes how the entire research project is carried out. Basically, there can be three types of research designs – exploratory research design, descriptive research design, and experimental (or causal) research design. Use of particular research design depends upon type of problem under study. Let's have glimpse of each of them:

1. Exploratory Research Design

This design is followed to discover ideas and insights to generate possible explanations. It helps in exploring the problem or situation. It is, particularly, emphasized to break a broad vague problem statement into smaller pieces or sub-problem statements that help forming specific hypothesis. The hypothesis is a conjectural (imaginary, speculative, or abstract) statement about the relationship between two or more variables. Naturally, in initial state of the study, we lack sufficient understanding about problem to formulate a specific hypothesis. Similarly, we have several competitive explanations of marketing phenomenon. Exploratory research design is used to establish priorities among those competitive explanations.

The exploratory research design is used to increase familiarity of the analyst with problem under investigation. This is particularly true when researcher is new in area, or when problem is of different type. This design is followed to realize following purposes:

1. Clarifying concepts and defining problem
2. Formulating problem for more precise investigation
3. Increasing researcher's familiarity with problem
4. Developing hypotheses
5. Establishing priorities for further investigation

Exploratory research design is characterized by flexibility to gain insights and develop hypotheses. It does not follow a planned questionnaire or sampling. It is based on literature survey, experimental survey, and analysis of selected cases. Unstructured interviews are used to offer respondents a great deal of freedom. No research project is purely and solely based on this design. It is used as complementary to descriptive design and causal design.

2. Descriptive Research Design

Descriptive research design is typically concerned with describing problem and its solution. It is more specific and purposive study. Before rigorous attempts are made for descriptive study, the well-defined problem must be on hand. Descriptive study rests on one or more hypotheses. For example, "our brand is not much familiar," "sales volume is stable," etc. It is more precise and specific. Unlike exploratory research, it is not flexible. Descriptive research requires clear specification of who, why, what, when, where, and how of the research. Descriptive design is directed to answer these problems.

3. Causal or Experimental Research Design

Causal research design deals with determining cause and effect relationship. It is typically in form of experiment. In causal research design, attempt is made to measure impact of manipulation on independent variables (like price, products, advertising and selling efforts or marketing strategies in general) on dependent variables (like sales volume, profits, and brand image and brand loyalty). It has more practical value in resolving marketing problems. We can set and test hypotheses by conducting experiments.

Test marketing is the most suitable example of experimental marketing in which the independent variable like price, product, promotional efforts, etc., are manipulated (changed) to measure its impact on the dependent variables, such as sales, profits, brand loyalty, competitive strengths product differentiation and so on.

MARKETING RESEARCH PROCESS

INTRODUCTION

Marketing research is a systematic process of colleting, analysing, and recording data relevant to any problem in marketing. This process involves certain steps to be followed in sequence. Experts on the filed have suggested almost similar process. Type and number of steps in marketing research process depend on many factors, such as objectives, type of problem, costs, time, people, and so on. However, in real practice, medium and large size companies follow following steps to carry out marketing research, see Figure 3:

1. Objective Specification

Marketing research starts with objective specification. It is obvious that marketing research is carried out for certain ends/objectives. Here, general and marketing objectives must be clearly and precisely specified. Objectives determine scope and intensity of marketing research. Objectives may be short-term or long-term, may be specific or general, may be individual or group, and may be related to entire organisation or part thereof. Those people involved in the research project must be aware of these objectives. There are many marketing research objectives, such as to study the problem, solve the problem, satisfy customer, earn profit, formulate sound strategies, or to improve competitiveness. Marketing research is aimed at one or more such objectives. Thus, in the first step, marketing research objectives are specified.

2. Problem(s) Identification

Actual marketing research process starts with problem identification. Marketing research is meant for solving the marketing problem(s) on hand. If there is no problem, there is no need to carry out any research.

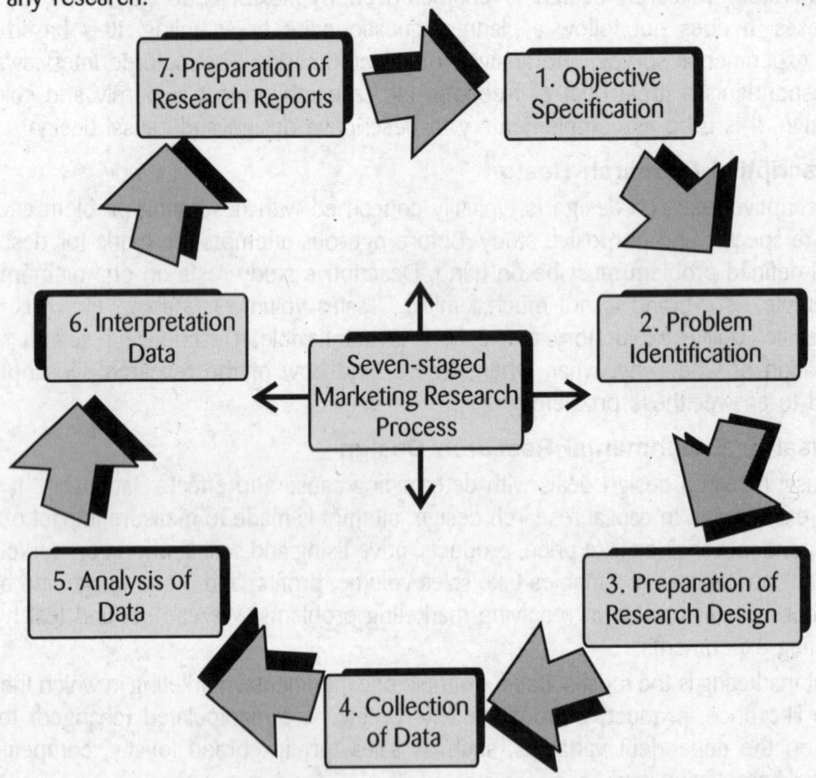

Figure 3: Seven-staged Marketing Research Process

Problem must be identified, properly defined, and be understood in a right perspective. It is said that the problem well defined is half solved.

In order to detect and understand problem, one should go for diagnosis of the situation and analysis of problem. Diagnosis is the medical term that is concerned with identifying problem on the basis of signs and symptoms, and analysis deals with a detailed study of problem so identified. This step calls for following issues:

i. What is the problem?
ii. Where is the problem?
iii. How old is the problem?
iv. How serious is the problem?
v. How many people are involved/affected by the problem?
vi. If not solved, what are the possible consequences of problem?
vii. How can the problem be solved?
viii. Time, efforts and costs consideration, etc.

3. Preparation of Research Design

Once problem is identified and properly understood, the next step is to prepare a detailed plan/design to solve it. It is a pattern or an outline of research project's workings. It is same as the blue print of architect's work. Generally, it is in written form. The research project is carried out as per the research design laid down in advance. It is, in other words, a master (or broad) plan or framework that states the total pattern of conducting research project. It specifies objectives, data collection and analysis methods, time, costs, responsibility, probable outcomes and actions. Research design involves at least following aspects:

i. Type and nature of problem
ii. Type of information needed
iii. Who is to collect data
iv. Sources of data
v. Data collection tools
vi. Pattern of analysis
vii. Sampling decisions
viii. Time and costs aspects
ix. Methods to be used for collection and analysis

4. Collection of Data or Fieldwork

Now, in order to solve the problem, needed data are collected as per the research design. This step involves collection and furnishing of data. Data are the raw information. Data can be defined as facts, statistics, or information either historical or derived by calculation, or experimentation. For solving any marketing problem, adequate, reliable, relevant, and timely data are necessary. Major part of budget, efforts, and time is devoted to collecting data. Four issues are worth mentioned in this stage:

i. Data collection methods
ii. Tools for data collection
iii. Sources of data
iv. Fieldwork/data collection work

Marketing research uses two types of data – primary data and secondary data. Both data have their uses and limitations. Also, different methods and sources are used for collecting both types of data. For collecting secondary data, specific methods are not used. They are published data and can be easily collected. But, the primary data, being the basic input, need an intensive field work. They must be collected deliberately and rigorously. Main methods used for primary data collection include communication method (including personal interview, telephone interview, and mail survey), observation method, experimental method, and panel method. Depending upon overall suitability, appropriate methods and tools (like questionnaire, printed forms, tape recorder, camera, movie camera, and other electronic devices) of data collection are used. These methods are used for collecting data from one or more sources. (A list of sources has been given earlier in the same chapter).

Field officer tries to collect adequate data. He has to tackle different situations, such as no response, inadequate response, absence of respondents and selection of substitutes, duplication, etc. In this step, time, costs, reliability, amount of data, etc., are critical issues.

5. Analysis of Data

Analysis of data gives some outcomes or results. It generates information that can be used for decision-making. When data collected are assumed to be adequate and reliable, the next step is to analyse the data. Analysis enables to establish interrelations among variables involved. It is clear that raw-data, if not analysed, convey nothing. In order to draw some meaningful conclusions, the data must be analysed by using appropriate statistical or mathematical techniques/tools. There are a number of data analysis techniques. Use of any of these techniques depends on type of data collected, time, and costs, reliability of techniques as well as ability and expertise of the data analyst. Sometimes, for analysis purpose, outside experts are assigned the task on professional basis. Nowadays, computer-based software (or package) is available at affordable price for speedy, unbiased, and accurate analysis of data.

Depending upon type of data, analysis may be uni-variate (in case of single variable), may be bivariate (in case of two variables), or may be multivariate (in case of more than two variables). Most commonly practiced statistical tools for data analysis have been listed below:

(A) Techniques for Uni-variate Analysis

(i) Z-test
(ii) Standard deviation
(iii) Mode
(iv) Mean
(v) Mediun
(vi) Chi-square test, etc.

(B) Techniques for Bivariate Analysis

(i) Time series
(ii) Correlation
(iii) Input-output analysis
(iv) ANOVA-Analysis of Variance
(v) Regression, etc.

(C) Techniques for Multivariate Analysis

(i) Multiple regression analysis
(ii) Multiple discriminant analysis
(iii) Multiple analysis of variance–Multi ANOVA
(iv) Canonical analysis
(v) Factor analysis, etc.

6. Interpretation

(**Note:** Sometimes, the interpretation is considered as a part of analysis. That is, analysis and interpretation are taken together. Here, for the ease of understanding, we consider interpretation as a separate step. Students and teachers may take the step as a part of step number five).

When task of analysis is over, based on final outcomes, certain meaningful inferences or conclusions are drawn, which are known as interpretation (of results). In order to specify the situation, certain assumptions are also made. Interpretation involves explaining results and drawing conclusions. Thus, it is a process of explaining relations among variables, clarifying situations, identifying causes, and making recommendations. Interpretation can be used directly for marketing decision-making or formulating strategies. Charts, tables, diagrams, etc., can be used for the purpose.

7. Preparation of Research Report

This is the last and the most critical step in marketing research process. Researchers are frequently required to make both oral and written presentation. However, written presentation is more important. Acceptance of research project does not depend on quality alone, but the way it is communicated with relevant audience, the way research work is presented. The research work presented in a written form is called as research report. Research report can be defined, as the systematic, articulate, and orderly presentation of research work in a written form. Marketing executives are not interested in methodology used to conduct research; they want the results presented systematically. Final outcomes and interpretations must be presented in way that the target people are convinced. While preparing research report, one must consider objectives, costs, users, time, and other relevant factors. For more detail, refer to research report in the next part.

RESEARCH REPORT

INTRODUCTION

Mostly, research work is presented in a written form. The practical utility of research study depends heavily on the way it is presented to those who are expected to act on the basis of research findings. Research report is a written document containing key aspects of research project. Research report is a medium to communicate research work with relevant people. It is also a good source of preservation of research work for the future reference. Many times, research findings are not followed because of improper presentation. Preparation of research report is not an easy task. It is an art. It requires a good deal of knowledge, imagination, experience, and expertise. It demands a considerable time and money.

DEFINITIONS

1. In simple words: *Research report is the systematic, articulate, and orderly presentation of research work in a written form.*
2. We can also define the term as: *Research report is a research document that contains basic aspects of the research project.*
3. In the same way, we can say: *Research report involves relevant information on the research work carried out. It may be in form of hand-written, typed, or computerized.*

REPORT FORMAT

There is no one best format for all reports. Format depends on several relevant variables. One must employ a suitable format to create desirable impression with clarity. Report must be attractive. It should be written systematically and bound carefully. A report must use the format (often called structure) that best fit the needs and wants of its readers. Normally, following format is suggested as a basic outline, which has sufficient flexibly to meet the most situations. Research report is divided into three parts as:

I. First Part (Formality Part)

(i). Cover page
(ii). Title page
(iii). Certificate or statement
(iv). Index (brief contents)
(v). Table of contents (detailed index)
(vi). Acknowledgement
(vii). List of tables and figures used
(viii). Preface/forwarding/introduction
(ix). Summary report

II. Main Report (Central Part of Report)

(i). Statement of objectives
(ii). Methodology and research design
(iii). Types of data and its sources

(iv). Sampling decisions
(v). Data collection methods
(vi). Data collection tools
(vii). Fieldwork
(viii). Analysis and interpretation (including tables, charts, figures, etc.)
(ix). Findings
(x). Limitations
(xi). Conclusions and recommendations
(xii). Any other relevant detail

III. Appendix (Additional Details)

(i). Copies of forms used
(ii). Tables not included in findings
(iii). A copy of questionnaire
(iv). Detail of sampling and rate of response
(v). Statement of expenses
(vi). Bibliography – list of books, magazines, journals, and other reports
(vii). Any other relevant information

KEY CONSIDERATIONS/FACTORS

While preparing research report, following issues must be considered:

(i). Objectives
(ii). Type of problem/subject
(iii). Nature and type of research
(iv). Audience or users of research work
(v). Size of report
(vi). Form of writing – handwritten, typed, or computerized.
(vii). Time and cost
(viii). Language
(ix). Contents of report
(x). Order of contents
(xi). Number of copies
(xii). Format – type and size of paper; lengths width, and depth of report; and pattern of writing including paragraph, indent, numbering, font size and type, colouring, etc.
(xiii). Binding (for soft, and, particularly, for hard copy) – type, quality of material, colour, etc., related issues.

PRINCIPLES OF A GOOD RESEARCH REPORT

Report writing differs from person to person depending on personality, imaginative and creative abilities, experience, and training. However, most researchers agree that following general principles must be kept in mind to produce a better research report. These principles are often called as qualities or requirements of a good report.

1. Selectiveness

It is important to exclude the matter, which is known to all. Only necessary contents should be included to save time, costs, and energy. However, care should be taken that the vital points should not be missed.

2. Comprehensiveness

Report must be complete. It must include all the necessary contents. In short, it must contain enough detail to covey meaning.

3. Cost Consideration

It must be prepared within the budgeted amount. It should not result into excessive costs.

4. Accuracy

As far as possible, research report must be prepared carefully. It must be free from spelling mistakes and grammatical errors.

5. Objectivity

Report must be free from personal bias, i.e., it must be free from one's personal liking and disliking. The report must be prepared for impersonal needs. The facts must be stated boldly. It must reveal the bitter truth. It must suit the objectives and must meet expectations of the relevant audience/readers.

6. Clarity

Report must reveal the facts clearly. Contents and conclusions drawn must be free from ambiguities. In short, outcomes must convey clear-cut implications.

7. Preciseness

Research report must not be unnecessarily lengthy. It must contain only necessary parts with adequate description.

8. Simplicity

Report must be simple to understand. Unnecessary technical words or terminologies (jargons) should be avoided.

9. Proper Language

Researcher must use a suitable language. Language should be selected as per its target users.

10. Reliability

Research report must be reliable. Manager can trust on it. He can be convinced to decide on the basis of research reposts.

11. Proper Format

An ideal repost is one, which must be prepared as per commonly used format. Parts or chapters must be orderly presented. One must comply with the contemporary practices; completely a new format should not be used.

12. Attractive

Report must be attractive in all the important regards like size, colour, paper quality, etc. Similarly, it should use liberally the charts, diagrams, figures, illustrations, pictures, and multiple colours.

LIMITATION OF MARKETING RESEARCH

Marketing research plays a crucial role in excelling marketing performance. In fact, it is inevitable to understand and treat customers more effectively than competitors. Marketer can satisfy customers by maintaining close contact with the target market by marketing research. It is one of the basic tasks of modern marketing. However, it is not free from limitations. Marketing manager must be aware of these limitations. Main limitations or practical problems have been discussed as under:

1. Effect of Extraneous Factors

Extraneous means external and uncontrollable factors. In most of the cases, the extraneous factors affect marketing research results adversely. Due to impact of such factors, the net impact cannot be estimated. For example, if marketer wants to study the impact of 10% price rise on demand and he raises price by 10%. As a result, demand falls by 20%. Here, decrease in demand cannot be fully attributed to price hike only. Demand might have been affected by other factors like introduction of new superior product, attractive offer of competitors, availability of powerful substitutes, etc., over and above price rise. Whatever degree of precaution is taken, one cannot eliminate effect of such factors completely, and as a result, marketing research cannot serve the purpose.

2. Time Gap Makes Research Irrelevant

Systematic marketing research project needs more time. It takes weeks, months, even years. When marketing research is carried on to investigate or solve the problem, final outcomes are available after considerable time. When outcomes are made available, situations might have been changed thoroughly or problem for which research was made might have been solved automatically. Decision-maker needs information in time. But, practically, it is not possible. Sometimes, time, money, and efforts contribute nothing.

3. Cost Consideration

To conduct marketing research systematically is a luxury. A firm needs money for research design, data collection, data analysis, interpretation, and report preparation. Statisticians and computer experts charge heavy fees. When research is conducted regularly, a company has to maintain a separate well-equipped marketing research department. Marketing research has become costlier. So, it is difficult for medium and small companies to afford.

4. Problem of Rapid Change

Today's market is characterized by tremendous changes. Whatever is applicable or relevant today is outdated tomorrow. Due to rapid changes, marketing research cannot serve the purpose. Research results or outcomes available after the specific time period seem irrelevant or meaningless.

5. Problem of Trust and Accuracy

Marketing research is based on trust and accuracy. Right from the identification of problem to the final outcomes, all depends on trust. Company has to trust on marketing research officer; research officer has to trust on field officer; and field officer has to rely on response of respondents. At any stage of marketing research, accuracy is vital issue. To the extent inaccuracy prevails, marketing research results suffer.

6. It is not Problem Solving Technique but an Aid to Solve the Problem

It is interesting and shocking to state that marketing research does not solve any problem directly. It is not a problem-solving technique but can assist to solve it. It is not a magic stick to solve marketing problems. It is a source of information. To the extent source is reliable and is used properly, it is useful. Even, an excellent research project is useless if outcomes are not considered.

7. Subjective or Biased Result

When human being is involved, a completely bias-free response or result is not possible. Effect of personal value, prejudice, attitudes, needs, and other socio-cultural factors affect the objectivity of research adversely. Subjectivity may lead to utter chaos.

8. It cannot Eliminate Risks Inherent in Decision-making

In every economic decisions, there exists risk and uncertainly. Marketing research cannot eliminate risk and uncertainty. It is an attempt to minimize degree of risk. So, heavy costs on marketing research don't guarantee safety and certainty.

9. Applicability or Use

Contribution of research project depends not only on quality and reliability alone, but also the proper use of information. Many times, marketing research reports remain just a formality for top management. Recommendations are neither considered seriously nor implemented fully.

10. Difference between Filed Officers, Data Analysts, and Decision- makers

Marketing research activity involves a number of people such as marketing manager, fieled officer, data analysts, and finally decision-maker. All these people have different objectives, backgrounds, and perspectives. Consistency or parity among them is a vital issue. Unless high degree of integration and intimacy among them exit, one cannot expect a success. In fact, it is difficult.

Marketing manager and those involved in marketing research activity must be aware of these limitations/practical problems. Note that these limiting factors cannot be completely eradicated. Attempts should be made to minimize adverse impact of these limiting factors. Careful plan, adequate budget, teamwork, accuracy, timeliness, proper use and implementation, *etc.*, have a strong prospect to contribute in successful marketing research.

EXERCISES

MULTIPLE CHOICE QUESTIONS (MCQs)

1. "To manage a business well is to manage its future, and to manage the future well is to manage the information." Who stated it?
   a. Philip Kotler b. Peter F. Drucker
   c. William Stanton d. Marion Harper
2. The statistical Bank and the Model Bank are components of
   a. Internal Records System b. Marketing Intelligence System
   c. Marketing Decision Support System d. Marketing Research System
3. Which component of MIS does supply the managers with happening data?
   a. Internal Records System b. Marketing Intelligence System
   c. Marketing Decision Support System d. Marketing Research System
4. What are BRANDAID, CALLPLAN, DETAILER, and MEDICAC?
   a. They are decision models (or packages). b. They are data collection methods.
   c. They are mathematical operators. d. They are marketing research tools.
5. Which one component of MIS does provide the detailed information on specific problem of specific marketing area?
   a. Internal Records System b. Marketing Intelligence System
   c. Marketing Decision Support System d. Marketing Research System
6. Which one is not an objective of Marketing Research?
   a. To know market changes b. To predict natural calamities
   c. To face competition d. To exercise control
7. Primary data are basic input for analysing and solving marketing problems, and are less expensive compared to the secondary data.
   a. The statement is absolutely false. b. The statement is absolutely true
   c. The statement is partially true. d. The statement is not related to marketing research.
8. Which one is not the true characteristic of secondary data?
   a. Secondary data are required to be furnished, processed or analyzed before they are used.
   b. Secondary data are supplementary to primary data.
   c. Relevance, accuracy, and timing are the main problems related to secondary data.
   d. Secondary data are published data.

9. Find the correct statement.
   a. Secondary data are basic input to solve the problem.
   b. Primary data are optional.
   c. Secondary data can be used without processing.
   d. Primary data are supplementary to primary data.
10. Which one is not included in survey method?
   a. Personal Interview   b. Telephone Interview
   c. Mail survey   d. Observation Survey
11. Survey method, observation method, experimental method, and panel method are
   a. data analysing methods   b. primary data collection methods
   c. secondary data collection methods   d. components of MIS
12. Which one of the followings is the most popular and widely used data collection tool?
   a. Tape Recorder   b. Questionnaire
   c. Close circuit camera   d. Phone and fax machine
13. Which types of questions are capable to measure intensity of respondents feeling?
   a. Close-ended questions   b. Short questions
   c. Ranking questions   d. Scale type questions
14. Which one is not included in projective techniques?
   a. Word association test   b. Sentence completion test
   c. Checklist   d. Pictorial test
15. The sampling procedure in which the population under study is divided into certain groups and then sample is randomly drawn form each of the groups is known as
   a. Systematic sampling   b. Stratified random sampling
   c. Cluster sampling   d. Area sampling
16. Which one of the following research design is used to increase familiarity of the analyst with problem?
   a. Exploratory research design   b. Causal research design
   c. Experimental research design   d. Descriptive research design

MATCHING TYPE QUESTIONS (MTQs)

17.

	List I	List II
(a)	It supplies results/records data	(1) Marketing Intelligence System
(b)	It supplies happening data	(2) Internal Records System
(c)	It supplies specific problem-related data	(3) Market decisions Support System
(d)	It contains analytical tools and models	(4) Marketing Research System

Codes: (A) (a)-(2), (b)-(1), (c)-(4), (d)-(3)   (B) (a)-(3), (b)-(2), (c)-(1), (d)-(4)
(C) (a)-(4), (b)-(3), (c)-(2), (d)-(1)   (D) (a)-(1), (b)-(4), (c)-(3), (d)-(2)

18.

	List I	List II
(a)	They are problem-related original data	(1) Sources of Primary Data
(b)	They are published data	(2) Secondary Data
(c)	Consumers, middleman, suppliers, salesmen, etc.	(3) Primary Data
(d)	Sales records, ad media, libraries, etc.	(4) Sources of Secondary data

Codes: (A) (a)-(2), (b)-(1), (c)-(4), (d)-(3)   (B) (a)-(3), (b)-(2), (c)-(1), (d)-(4)
(C) (a)-(4), (b)-(3), (c)-(2), (d)-(1)   (D) (a)-(1), (b)-(4), (c)-(3), (d)-(2)

19. **List I** / **List II**

List I	List II
(a) Questionnaire	(1) A list of questions
(b) Consumer panel and dealer panel	(2) Observation Method
(c) Cause-effect relationship	(3) Experimental Method
(d) Questions are not asked; behavior is noted	(4) Panel Method

Codes: (A) (a)-(2), (b)-(1), (c)-(4), (d)-(3) (B) (a)-(3), (b)-(2), (c)-(1), (d)-(4)
(C) (a)-(4), (b)-(3), (c)-(2), (d)-(1) (D) (a)-(1), (b)-(4), (c)-(3), (d)-(2)

20. **List I** / **List II**

List I	List II
(a) It is attempted just selecting one from the list	(1) Open Question
(b) It provides freedom to answer	(2) Checklist question
(c) It permits measuring response intensity	(3) Dichotomous Question
(d) Yes, No, Indifferent options	(4) Scale Type Question

Codes: (A) (a)-(2), (b)-(1), (c)-(4), (d)-(3) (B) (a)-(3), (b)-(2), (c)-(1), (d)-(4)
(C) (a)-(4), (b)-(3), (c)-(2), (d)-(1) (D) (a)-(1), (b)-(4), (c)-(3), (d)-(2)

ANSWERS KEY: Chapter 9: 1(d), 2(c), 3(b), 4(a), 5(d), 6(b), 7(c), 8(a), 9(c), 10(d), 11(b), 12(b), 13(d), 14(c), 15(b), 16(a), 17(A), 18(B), 19(D), 20(A)

QUESTIONS FOR DISCUSSION

21. Define Mis-Marketing Information System. Discuss components of MIS.
22. What is marketing research? Explain its nature and scope.
23. Define marketing research system. Discuss its importance and practical problems (limitations).
24. Define primary data and secondary data. Write a note on sources of both types of data.
25. Explain various data collection methods.
26. What is questionnaire? Which are the important issues related to questionnaire formulation? State the qualities of an ideal questionnaire.
27. Discuss different types of questions with examples.
28. Describe steps involved in marketing research process.
29. What is research report? Explain its format/structure. Also suggest qualities of a good research report.
30. Write notes:
    a. Sampling – meaning and types of sampling procedures
    b. Research design – meaning and types

CHAPTER

10

RURAL MARKETING

INTRODUCTION

The emergence of rural markets as highly untapped potential emphasizes the need to explore them. Marketers over the past few decades, with innovative approaches, have attempted to understand and tap rural markets. Some of their efforts paid off and many markets still an enigma.

Rural marketing is an evolving concept, and as a part of any economy, has untapped potential; marketers have realized the opportunity recently. Improvement in infrastructure and reach, promise a bright future for those intending to go rural. Rural consumers are keen on branded goods nowadays, so the market size for products and services seems to have burgeoned. The rural population has shown a trend of moving to a state of gradual urbanization in terms of exposure, habits, lifestyles, and lastly, consumption patterns of goods and services. So, there are dangers on concentrating more on the rural customers. Reducing the product features in order to lower prices is a dangerous game to play. Rural buyers like to follow the urban pattern of living.

Astonishingly, as per the census report 2003-04, there are total 638365 villages in India in which nearly 70% of total population resides; out of them 35 % villages have more than 1000 population. Rural per capita consumption expenditure grew by 11.5 per cent while the urban expenditure grew by 9.6 per cent. There is a tremendous potential for consumer durables like two-wheelers, small cars, television sets, refrigerators, air-conditioners and household appliances in rural India. Let's have a glimpse on Rural Index 2005 figures:

Table 1: Rural Urban Penetration–Rural Index 2005*
(Some Consumer Durables)

Criteria/Products	Rural House Holds (000) Number (%)	Urban House Holds (000) Number (%)	Total House Holds (000) Number (%)
Car/Jeep or van	1603 (1%)	7241 (12%)	8844 (4%)
Two-wheelers	16195 (11%)	25813 (42%)	42008 (20%)
Colour TV sets	18152 (12%)	38572 (63%)	56724 (27%)

Criteria/Products	Rural House Holds (000) Number (%)	Urban House Holds (000) Number (%)	Total House Holds (000) Number (%)
Refrigerators	11014 (8%)	29515 (48%)	40529 (20%)
Washing Machines	1870 (1%)	14447 (24%)	16317 (8%)
Room air-conditioners	76 (0.025%)	2936 (5%)	3012 (1%)
Bicycles	80533 (55%)	36835 (60%)	36835 (60%)
Gas stoves	27390 (19%)	40964 (67%)	68354 (33%)
Pressure cookers	37883 (26%)	45192 (74%)	83075 (40%0
Ectricity Connection	59928 (41%)	46981 (77%)	106909 (52%)
Drinking water In the household	39549 (27%)	35073 (57%)	74622 (36%)
Fuel LPG/electricity/ biogas	8544 (6%)	26090 (43%)	34634 (17%)

*Sources: FK Urban (Internet)

CONCEPT OF RURAL MARKETING

The concept of Rural Marketing in India Economy has always played an influential role in the lives of people. In India, leaving out a few metropolitan cities, all the districts and industrial townships are connected with rural markets. The rural market in India generates bigger revenues in the country as the rural regions comprise of the maximum consumers in this country. The rural market in Indian economy generates almost more than half of the country's income. Rural marketing in Indian economy can be classified under two broad categories. These are:

- The market for consumer goods that comprise of both durable and non-durable goods
- The market for agricultural inputs that include fertilizers, pesticides, seeds, and so on

The concept of rural marketing in India is often been found to forms ambiguity in the mind of people who think rural marketing is all about agricultural marketing. However, rural marketing determines the carrying out of business activities bringing in the flow of goods from urban sectors to the rural regions of the country as well as the marketing of various products manufactured by the non-agricultural workers from rural to urban areas. To be precise, rural marketing in India Economy covers two broad sections, namely:

- Selling of agricultural products in the urban areas
- Selling of manufactured products in the rural regions

The rural market in India is not a separate entity in itself and it is highly influenced by the sociological and behavioural factors operating in the country. The rural population in India accounts for around 627 million, which is exactly 74.3 percent of the total population.

Conceptually, rural marketing is not significantly different to urban marketing. Marketing manager has to perform the same tasks, but differently in rural marketing. It can be said that marketing is not different, but markets (buyers and users). In rural marketing, a firm has to undergo marketing efforts to satisfy rural segments, which notably differ from urban segments in some aspects. At the same time, we must note that increasing literacy rate, improved sources of income, awareness due to improved and increased means of communication and transportation, high rate of mobility within and between countries due to liberalization and globalization, and many other such reasons, some customers are likely to be identical. Even, a few rural customers seem cosmopolitan! So, one can find customers of different behaviour patterns within a village or a town. In the same way, most of products are commonly used in both urban and rural areas.

In some aspects, both rural and urban customers behave in homogeneous pattern. Some Indian customers have become global and cosmopolitan!

DEFINITIONS

'Rural marketing' is similar to simply 'marketing.' Rural marketing differs only in terms of buyers. Here, target market consists of customers living in rural areas. Thus, rural marketing is an application of marketing fundamentals (concepts, principles, processes, theories, etc.) to rural markets.

1. Let us define the term in simple way as: *Rural marketing concerns with planning and implementing marketing programmes (often referred as marketing strategies or simply 4P's) for rural markets to achieve marketing goals.*
2. In more specific words: *Rural marketing is a process of developing, pricing, promoting, and distributing rural specific goods and services leading to desired exchange with rural customers to satisfy their needs and wants, and also to achieve organizational objectives.*
3. Marketing efforts remain same, only important aspect is type of buyers. So, the term can be defined as: *When marketing activities are undertaken for rural segments, it is turned as rural marketing and the management is called rural marketing management.*
4. Since marketing manager has to carry out similar tasks. So, definition of marketing stated by American Marketing Association can be equally applicable in relation to rural segments. We will add only specific word 'rural' to define the term: *Rural marketing is a process of planning, and executing the conception, pricing, promotion, and distribution of ideas, goods, and services to create exchange (for rural segments) that satisfy individual and organizational objectives.*

   (Only the word 'rural' has been added to the definition adopted by the AMA. The word implies that marketing activities are undertaken in rural areas to satisfy rural segments.)
5. More specifically, it can be said: *Rural Marketing means to produce products (goods and services) for the rural customers and to make necessary arrangement to supply them.*
6. At last, we can say: *Rural marketing is the marketing for the customers residing in rural areas. It involves designing marketing programme (4P's) to arrive at desired exchange with the rural customers that satisfies their needs and wants.*

CHARACTERISTICS OF RURAL MARKET/MARKETING

Mostly, major part of rural market holds a very divergent pattern of reacting to marketing. So, marketer needs to design a specific marketing mix for the rural segments. For rural market, a marketing manager has three options – one is, to design marketing programme common for all types of customers; the second is, to design marketing programme purely for rural customers; and the third is, to design marketing programme for customers residing in rural but reacting as if they were global.

Excepts some villagers of some progressive states like Maharastra, Gujarat, Hariyana, etc., most rural customers are poor, backward, illiterate, and orthodox. They vary significantly in terms of preference and habits. They are to be treated in different patterns. Our discussion emphasizes on major rural markets with rural characteristics.

1. More Prospective

With the initiation of various rural development programmes, there has been an upsurge of employment opportunities for the rural poor. One of the biggest cause behind the steady growth of rural market is that it is not exploited and also yet to be explored.

2. Size

The rural market in India is vast and scattered, and offers a plethora of opportunities in comparison to the urban sector. It covers the maximum population and regions, and thereby, the maximum number of consumers. Rural market is account for about 74% of total Indian population.

3. Nature

The social status of the rural regions is precarious (uncertain) as the income level and literacy is extremely low along with the range of traditional values and superstitious beliefs that have always been a major impediment (obstacle) in the progression of this sector.

4. Response to Products

Product-related features of rural segment are:

i. Rural markets (buyers) believe in product utility rather than status and prestige. However, they like novel products with distinctive features.
ii. Most village customers consider tastes rather than usefulness in long run.
iii. They like simple and long-life products. They are interested in immediate results. Products must offer immediate benefits.
iv. They respond to those products that suit their religious faith, and social norms and customs.
v. They ask for such products which can assists in their traditional occupations and life style.
vi. They have minimum urge for individuality. They prefer family-used products than personal-used products.
vii. They strongly prefer such products that can change and improve their life-style.
viii. They are less concerned with product services associated with products like after-sales services, guarantee and warrantee, home delivery, and other similar services. Branding, packaging, and labeling have less influence compared to urban segments.

5. Response to Price

Price-related features of rural segments include:

i. Rural customers are price-sensitive and highly influenced by level of pricing. Price is the strongest factor that affects their buying decision.
ii. They buy those products which are low in price and medium in quality.
iii. They are easily attracted by price discounts and rebates.
iv. They prefer credit facility. They normally have strong desire to postpone payment for certain period.
v. Some middle class rural customers are attracted by installment and loan facility.

6. Response to Promotion

Promotion-related features of rural segment include:

i. Rural customers are highly attracted by local and regional promotional efforts.
ii. Their reference groups consist of educated and non-educated family members and relatives living in urban areas and foreign countries as well.
iii. Personal selling seems more influential to convince rural mass.
iv. They are attracted by such sales promotional tools or articles which are useful in their routine life such as knife, gas lighter, rings, key-chains, caps, photos of local actors, calendars and cards with religious impression, etc.
v. They have a strong faith on local religious and spiritual leaders. Such leaders are among the most influential reference groups.

vi. Publicity efforts related to local vocational and agricultural activities can impress them.

vii. They can be appealed by visual or pictorial advertisements published in local and regional languages.

7. Response to Distribution

Distribution-related features of rural segment include:

i. Normally, they buy from familiar retailers and salesmen. They are hesitant to buy from big shopping malls or departmental stores. However, situation is changing gradually.

ii. Rural customers strongly favour relations. They continue buying from known and established retailers who maintain close family relations with them.

iii. Mostly they buy from retail outlets situated in rural or sub-urban areas. However, some rural customers like to buy products from nearby cities also.

iv. Normally they place frequent orders of small in size. They lack storage facilities.

v. They are not interested in home-delivery. They want immediate possession. They lack patience. They are found eager to possess and use the products immediately.

vi. Caste, religion, political party, relations, etc., play important role in selecting the retailers.

vii. Online and direct marketing are not much popular in rural areas. Sometimes, a few of them are interested in network marketing.

8. Predictability

Unlike urban markets, the rural markets are difficult to predict, and possess special characteristics. The featured population is predominantly illiterate, have low and irregular income, lack of monthly income, and flow of income fluctuating with the monsoon winds. They don't have a stable pattern of reacting due to income factors.

9. Role of Government

Demand of products depends on availability of basic facilities like electricity, transportation, schools, hospitals, etc. The steps taken by the Government of India to initiate proper irrigation, infrastructural developments, prevention of flood, grants for fertilizers, and various schemes to cut down the poverty line have improved the condition of the rural masses. Rural market depends on government's contribution to the rural sector.

10. Rigidity

Most rural customers are illiterate, backward, and orthodox. It is very difficult to convince them to buy the products. They believe in the present and lack ambitions.

11. High Level of Heterogeneity

We find different types of buyers in rural areas. Some are simple, while some are sophisticated; some are extreme rich, while some are extreme poor; some are highly educated, while some are complete illiterate; some are dynamic and modern, while some are very rigid and orthodox; some believe in quality and status, while some believe in availability and price.

Rural customers are gradually transforming into urban, metropolitan, and even cosmopolitan customers. Improved education, rapid means of transportation, access to advance communication, raised living standards, craze to follow modern (even ultramodern) life pattern, and many similar factors have drastically changed rural consumer behaviour. The gap between urban and rural segments tends to be notably narrow. Sometimes, rural and urban customers exhibit no difference at all.

IMPORTANCE OF RURAL MARKETING

Rural marketing implies applying marketing theory and directing marketing efforts to create and satisfy needs and wants of rural market (customers). Importance of marketing indicates the contribution of rural as well urban marketing. As we know that rural market is growing faster than urban, rural marketing results into overall balanced economical and social development. Rural marketing turns beneficial to business units, people residing in rural areas, people residing in urban areas, and to the entire nation. Let's see how growth and development of rural marketing contribute to overall prosperity and welfare.

1. Reduced Burden on Urban Population

Rural marketing can contribute to rural infrastructure and prosperity. People can also live confortably in villages due to availability of all goods and services in villages, even comparatively at low price. People, due to growth of marketing activities, can earn their livelihood in rural places. Population pressure on urban can be reduced.

2. Rapid Economic Growth

Naturally, marketing acts as catalyst agent for economic growth. There exists more attractive business opportunities in rural than urban. Rural market is more potential for consumer durables and services. Rural population largely depends on agriculture and it can contribute nearly 50% to total national income. Agriculture enjoys significant portion in export business, too. Rural marketing improves agricultural sector and improved agricultural sector can boost whole economy of the country.

3. Employment Generation

At present, nearly 70% of total Indian population feeds on agricultural activities in rural areas. Rural marketing can generate more attractive employment opportunities to rural and urban people. Growth of rural marketing leads to increased business operations, professional activities, and services that can generate a lot of employment opportunities.

4. Improved Living Standard

Due to rural marketing system, rural buyers can easily access needed standard goods and services at fair prices. In the same way, rural marketing improves rural infrastructure. Additionally, rural marketing can also improve their income. These all aspects can directly improve living standard.

5. Development of Agro-based Industries

Rural marketing leads to set up agro-based processing industries. Fruits, vegetables, cereals, pulses, etc., are used as raw-materials. Such industries can improve farmers' profit margin and employment opportunities.

6. Optimum Utilization of Rural Untapped Resources

There are unlimited businesses opportunities exist in rural areas. Untapped and underutilized resources can be utilized at optimum level and that can further accelerate overall economic growth.

7. Easy Marketability of Agricultural Produces

Growth of rural marketing improves whole marketing system. Multiple options are available to farmers and local producers to market their products. Big domestic corporate houses and multinational companies prefer to buy agricultural products directly from villages by their own or through agents and small firms. Rural producers can sell their produces easily at satisfactory prices. Their improved income level can improve their purchasing power that can further fuel to industrial demand.

8. Improved Rural Infrastructures

Rural marketing and basic infrastructures go hand to hand. Growth of rural marketing leads to improved transportation, insurance, banking, communication, entertainment, and other facilities. Due to availability of basic infrastructural facilities, business units can easily reach the target rural buyers.

9. Price Stability

Marketing results into better transportation, warehouses, and communication facilities. Agricultural products can be systematically marketed throughout the year. Huge gap between demand and supply can be avoided and, as a result, prices of most of commodities remain more or less stable.

10. Quality of Life and Reduced Crime

Marketing can refine entire living style and system. Better quality products at reasonable price, improved income level, availability of facilities, etc., have direct positive impacts on quality of life. Quality of life improves and level crime reduces.

11. Balanced Industrial Growth

The gap between rural and urban development can be reduced gradually. Rural development improves rural life and reduces pressure on urban life.

12. Others

Apart from these points, there are a number of ways that rural marketing can significantly contribute to economic and social development. Some points have been listed below:

i. Creating self-reliant villages
ii. Increased literacy rate and overall development
iii. Attracting giant business groups in rural places
iv. Rigorous research and development in agricultural sector
v. Growth of academic and training institutes in rural areas
vi. Increased representation of rural population, and increased political influence, etc.

RURAL MARKETING MIX

Marketing mix (programme) comprises of various controllable forces (often referred as elements) like product, price, promotion and place. Success of any business enterprise depends on marketing mix. These four elements are like powerful weapons in the hand of manager to defend his market and/or attack on rivals. A manager needs to understand his rural market carefully, considering all important characteristics of rural customers. We have analyzed some features of rural markets (buyers) in the former part of the chapter. Since behaviour of rural consumers is different and less predictable, the marketing manager has a challenging task to design marketing mix strategies for the rural segments. Due to considerable level of heterogeneity, a manager needs to design tailor-made programme to cater needs and wants of specific groups.

Dynamics of rural markets differ from urban market types, and similarly rural marketing strategies are also significantly different from the marketing strategies aimed at urban or industrial buyers. This, along with several other related issues, has been subject matter of intense discussion and debate in countries like India and China, and even the focus of international symposia organized in these countries. Following part deals with marketing mix elements for rural segments.

1. PRODUCT MIX

Product is a powerful determinant of firm's success. The products must be suitable to rural customers in all significant aspects. The company must produce product according to the present and the expected state of rural buyers. Product features (size, shape, colour, weight, etc.), qualities, brand name, packaging, labeling, services, and other relevant aspect must be fit with needs, wants and capacity of buyers. Product must undergo necessary changes and improvements to sustain its suitability over time. Note that effectiveness of other decisions like pricing, promotion and place also depends on the product.

2. PRICE MIX

Price is the unique element of marketing mix, particularly, for rural markets. As stated in the former part of this chapter, rural customers are most price sensitive and, hence, price plays more decisive role in buying decisions. Pricing policies and strategies must be formulated with care and caution. Price level, discounts and rebates, credit and installment faculties, and so on are important considerations while setting and altering prices. Normally, the low-priced products attract rural buyers. However, some rural customers are quality and status conscious.

3. PROMOTION MIX

Rural markets are delicately powerful. Certain adaptations are required to cater to the rural masses. The promotion strategies and distribution strategies are of paramount importance. Ad makers have learned to leverage the benefits of improved infrastructure and media reach. The television airs advertisements to lure rural masses, and they are sure it reaches the target audience, because majority of rural India possesses and is glued to TV sets!

Marketing manager has to decide on promotional tools such as advertisement (objectives, message, media, budget, scheduling, etc.), sales promotion (sales promotion tools, levels, costs, timing, etc.), personal selling (including objectives, sales force size, recruitment and selection, training and development, remuneration, training, controlling, etc.), and publicity and public relations.

The method of promotion needs to be tailored to suit the expectations of the market. Van/vehicle campaigns, edutainment films, generating word of mouth publicity through opinion leaders, colourful wall paintings, etc., techniques have been proved effective. The wide reach of television has exposed the conservative audience to westernization. Similarly, puppet-shows, dance, dramas and mythological songs, specially developed for product-promotion purpose, are now being used in rural markets. These traditional art forms readily render for communication with the rural society. Village fairs and festivals are ideal venues for projecting these programmes. In certain cases, public meetings, too, are used for rural promotion. Music cassettes (CDs) are another effective medium for rural communication. It is an appealing medium and a comparatively less expensive medium. Different language groups can be reached with a low budget. They can be played in cinema houses or in other places where rural people assemble. It is also essential that in all rural communication, the rural genius must be kept in view. The theme, the message, the copy, the language, and the delivery must match the rural context.

Evidently, rural communication needs creativity and innovation. In rural marketing, usually a greater time lag is involved between the introduction of a product and its economic size sale. This is because the rural buyer's adoption process is relatively more time consuming.

Opinion leaders play a key role in popularizing products and influence in rural market. Nowadays educated youth of rural also influences the rural consumers. Rural consumers are influenced by the life style they watch on the television set. Their less exposure to outside world makes them innocent and fascinated to novelties. The reach of mass media, especially, television has influenced the buying behaviour greatly

4. PLACE MIX

Rural markets face the critical issues of distribution. The marketer has to strengthen the distribution strategies. Distributing small and medium sized packets through poor roads, over long distances, into deep pockets of rural India and getting the stockiest to trust the mobility is a herculean task.

Both physical distribution and channel of distribution should be decided carefully to ensure easy accessibility of products for rural buyers. Choosing suitable mode of transportation, locating warehouses at strategic points, sufficient insurance, maintaining adequate inventory, maintaining a sufficient number of retail outlets at different regions, and deploying specially trained sales force are some of the critical decisions in rural distribution.

Normally, indirect channels (particularly one or two level) are more suitable to serve scattered rural customers. In two level channels wholesalers are located at urban and semi urban to serve urban and rural retailers. However, not only in backward states, but also in progressive states, local producers (farmers and others) distribute directly to customers.

For service marketing, employees of rural branches and agents can do better jobs. Banking, insurance, investment, satellite and cable connection, cell phone, auto sales and services, etc., the market is booming in villages of some states. Service industries are trying to penetrate the rural segments by deploying the specially trained employees and local agents. Surprisingly, online or cyber marketing is making its place gradually in rural areas of the progressive states. Marketer must design and modify time to time its distribution strategies according to nature of rural segments, may be quite differently than that of urban markets.

REASONS RESPONSIBLE FOR THE RURAL MARKET BOOM

Television has done wonders to rural India. Today, especially in the south, the penetration of satellite television is very high, which is around 50 per cent unlike 25-30 per cent in the rest of the country.

Television is the most sought consumer item in rural India followed by two wheelers. Gradually, they are moving to small cars.

Prime Minister Manmohan Singh recently talked about his vision for rural India. He asserted: "My vision of rural India is of a modern agrarian, industrial and services economy co-existing side by side, where people can live in well-equipped villages and commute easily to work, be it on the farm or in the non-farm economy. There is much that modern science and technology can do to realise this vision. Rural incomes have to be increased. Rural infrastructure has to be improved. Rural health and education needs have to be met. Employment opportunities have to be created in rural areas."

'Go rural' is the slogan of marketing gurus after analyzing the socio-economic changes in villages. The rural population is nearly three times the urban. So, rural consumers have become the prime target market for consumer durable and non-durable products, foods, construction, electrical, electronics, automobiles, banks, insurance companies and other sectors besides hundred per cent of agri-input products, such as seeds, fertilizers, pesticides and farm machinery. The Indian rural market today accounts for only about ₹ 8 billion of the total ad pie of ₹ 120 billion, thus claiming 6.6 per cent of the total share. So, clearly, there seems to be a long way ahead. Although a lot is spoken about the immense potential of the unexplored rural market, advertisers and companies find it easier to vie for a share of the already divided urban pie.

The success of a brand in the Indian rural market is a unpredictable as rain. It has always been difficult to gauge the rural market. Many brands, which should have been successful, have failed miserably. More often than not, people attribute rural market success to luck. Therefore, marketers need to understand the social dynamics and attitude variations within each village. It can be said that the future is very promising for those who can understand the dynamics of rural markets and exploit them to their best advantage. A radical change in attitudes of marketers towards the vibrant and burgeoning rural markets is called for, so they can successfully impress on the 72 crores rural consumers spread over approximately six lakh villages in rural India. Let us discuss important causes led to rapid growth of rural markets:

1. **Population Growth:** Increased in population and, hence, increase in demand. At present rural population is account for nearly 72 crores of total Indian population, three times more than urban population. More population means more demand.
2. **Agriculture Prosperity:** Market increases due to agrarian prosperity. Profitable farming and better marketing options in some states have made a large number of villagers the

potential consumers for FMCG (Fast Moving Consumer Goods) companies. The greater the agriculture development in an area, the greater the rural market.

3. **Rural Development Programme:** Large inflow of investment in rural development programme from government and other sources contributed to improved life style of rural segments.
4. **Intensive Interaction with Urban Population:** Increased contacts of rural people with urban counterpart due to rapid development of transportation and telecommunication.
5. **Increased Population Mobility:** Mobility of rural population to urban areas, metro cities and foreign countries intensified incomes and, hence, purchasing power of rural people.
6. **Increased Rural Attraction:** Increasing attraction of rich people to stay temporary or permanently in rural areas for better and peaceful life. Agricultural land is being converted into luxurious farm-houses. Such move is leading to tremendous development of rural market.
7. **Improved Literacy Rate:** Increased literacy rate and education level among rural folks, and growth of academic and training institutes in rural places have accelerated growth of rural market. Literacy level 25% before independence – is now more than 67%.
8. **Improved Rural Infrastructure:** Improved infrastructure has positive impacts on rural market in several ways. Availability of electricity, education, health, transportation, communication and entertainment, and so on contributed to rural development and, hence, rural market.
9. **Growth of Agro-processing Industry:** Establishment and growth of agro-processing industries, and active involvement of the giant business units (For example, Reliance Fresh) in distribution of agro-products like fruits, vegetables, serials, etc., have changed income and life style of rural people.
10. **Political Influence of Rural Population:** Improved and increased political influence of rural people can significantly contribute to rural development.
11. **Foreign Income:** Inflow of foreign remittance (transfer funds) and foreign-made products into rural areas significant fueled to rural market boom.
12. **Reforms in Land Tenure System:** Significant changes in land tenure system causing a structural change in ownership pattern affected positively the life of farmers.
13. **Rural Development Priority:** Liberal assistance from national and international financial institutions and agencies for rural development has changed rural lifestyle. World Bank has granted billions of rupee for rural infrastructure.
14. **Role of Giant Business Tycoons:** Increased corporate business interest in rural areas resulted into rapid rural development and, consequently, has fueled to growth of rural market. Corporate tycoons are liberally donating for improving rural infrastructures.
15. **Rapid Socio-economic Changes:** Socio-economic changes (e.g., lifestyle, habits and tastes, economic status, etc.) resulted into drastic changes in living pattern of rural people resulted into greater potential for cosmetics and durable products along with automobiles. After the basic needs of food, cloth and shelter, they are looking at how to live better.

PRESENT RURAL MARKET PICTURE

Rural India accounts for more than 50% of the GDP and out of total 62.97 million households, having income more than 5 lakhs per annum; nearly 28.68 million households (46%) live in Rural India. The rural market is projected to be bigger in India than the urban market for the fast moving consumer goods, with an annual size of ₹ 48000 crore ($12 billion) in 2004 and growing. Rural consumption expenditure is accounted for around 60 per cent, or ₹ 9, 13,500 crore ($228 billion), of the country's total consumption expenditure. The figures show the significance of rural marketing.

Out of the 593 rural districts in India, 67 were classified as urban cousins (similar as urban), 118 close to rural economic centers; around 160 with basic minimum infrastructure and 248 are deprived.

Many giant companies are planning to link India's agricultural products to the world markets. These companies, particularly, include those venturing into the domestic retail sector like Reliance, Godrej, Field Fresh (Sunil Mittal's 50:50 joint venture with Rothschild), Snowman Frozen Food (a joint venture with the Mitsubishi group), Amalgam foods and HUL, Radhakrishna Group, DCM Sriram, Gufic Labs, Jain Irrigation, Tata Group, Dabur, Blue Star, Voltas and many others.

Tax incentives being given by the government for food processing, including income tax and excise holidays for industries involved in the processing of fruits and vegetables have led to interest in the sector. These companies are establishing direct contact with farmers to source their requirements, by eliminating middlemen, and cutting down costs to offer higher yields to farmers.

A look at the marketing scenario indicates that most of the products are sold in local rural haats. Besides these haats, the government at various levels has also helped in promoting the sale of these products outside the confines of the local environs. For example, State Government established societies (at state and district level) like the District Supply and Marketing Societies (DSMS) have made significant contribution to the sale of these products. Furthermore, the State & District government departments extend preferential treatment to these products at the time of procurement, thereby increasing the sale of these products. The respective state governments extend further assistance to the rural poor by organizing melas/trade fairs and exhibitions in major urban centers where these products are publicized and promoted.

These people may not be literate in the true sense, but they know what is happening around the world because of television. They know how the rest of the country lives. It has been reported that by 2009-10, the number of urban households is projected to grow by 4 per cent, while rural households are expected to grow by 11 per cent. The total expenditure of urban India is almost equal to what has been spent by rural India. But what is being spent by urban India is only a small percentage of the population.

The Indian rural market has a huge demand base and offers great opportunities to marketers. Two-third of Indian consumers live in rural areas and almost half of the national income is generated here. The reasons for heading into the rural areas are fairly clear. The urban consumer durable market for products like colour TVs, washing machines, refrigerators and air conditioners is growing annually at between 7 per cent and 10 per cent.

The rural market is zooming ahead at around 25 per cent annually. "The rural market is growing faster than urban India now," says Venugopal Dhoot, the chairman of the ₹ 989 crore Videocon Appliances." "The urban market is a replacement and upgradation market today," adds Samsung's director, marketing, Ravinder Zutshi.

About 25 per cent of the urban India is spending as much as 75 per cent of what rural India is spending. This shows the potential exists in rural India. There is a huge market waiting to be tapped in rural India. Yes, corporate world cannot afford to ignore rural India. Unfortunately, they are only talking about it; they are not investing enough to get the maximum mileage out of it. For them, rural India is an unknown entity even today, and it calls for a lot of investment. Initially, the ratio between investment and returns will not be the same as you see in urban India. For urban India, one television spot is enough but it's not so in rural India. You have to slog it out there. You will not be able to survive without rural India in future. One company that conquered the rural market 50 years ago and has consistently ruled is Hindustan Unilever.

About 50-55 per cent of HUL's sales come from the rural market. Even today, it is constantly innovating and improvising. And Hindustan Unilever is marketing directly in the rural markets.

Rural India has changed tremendously. The data published by the National Council for Applied Economic Research shows that, in the last ten years, the income of rural India has grown several-fold. There is a definite shift from middle to upper middle class and from lower to middle class segments.

AGRICULTURAL GROWTH AND RURAL MARKET

For the last 10 consecutive years, we have had good monsoons. So, agriculture is prospering. Of course, there have been setbacks in the last couple of years.

Another interesting aspect is, today rural India is not 100 per cent dependent on an agrarian economy. Unlike in the past where the ratio between those who involved in agriculture and in other business was 75-25, today the estimated ratio is 50:50. So today, 50-60 per cent of the rural population is involved in other occupations. A lot of people belonging to the second generation are getting white-collar jobs in nearby towns. So, there is a growing middle class with a monthly income in rural India and it is a drastic change from the past where their income was totally dependent on the monsoon, cropping season, etc.

This has resulted in a definite growth in the prosperity level in rural India. Of course, there are still a lot of poor people, especially the agricultural laborers. But, there is a growing middle class with regular income and the rural rich are becoming richer.

In India, we have the developed rural India, and undeveloped rural India. Gujarat, Punjab, Haryana, Tamil Nadu, Andhra Pradesh, Kerala, and parts of Maharashtra come under the developed rural India but the rest of the states are undeveloped where power and other infrastructures are big problems.

The prosperity of Kerala has come from the NRI income and not from agriculture. Today, there is hardly any village in Kerala without foreign source of income. Tamil Nadu is prosperous as power and good roads are available. All the villages with proper infrastructure have developed fast. In such villages, people also have better access to towns and cities.

PROBLEMS AND CHALLENGES OF RURAL MARKETING

At present, three out of four of country's consumers are in rural market and one-half of national income is generated there. A number of corporate units have been trying to get grip on the rural market in a variety of ways. There is no doubt that rural market reveals opportunities and great attraction to marketers. But, it not as easy as it seems on surface. It is not so simple to enter and succeed in this market in a smooth way. This market poses a variety of challenges, and, therefore, the marketer has to work hard to tackle these challenges tactfully. A company planning to enter and/or expand rural market must consider these problems seriously. Some of genuine problems associated with rural market include:

1. Wide and Scattered Market

Wide and scattered market is difficult to reach in both the aspects – promotion and distribution. Rural India is spread in the entire county in around 6 lakhs villages of different sizes while urban population is concentrated in around 3200 cities. Most of villages are extremely small with population less than 500 people. Only one percent (6300) villages have a population of more than 5000. It is challenging tasks to choose target markets and to serve them effectively.

2. Problem of Designing Products

Products sold successfully in urban markets, may not necessarily be successful in the rural markets due to difference in utility value of the products. Mindset of rural segments seems quite astonishing and different. Existence of considerable heterogeneity among rural folks poses challenges for marketers to incorporate their uneven expectations in the products.

3. Transportation Bottleneck

Transportation is the nerve centre for any type of business. Most of villages are not properly connected with main roads. Every year during monsoon thousands of villages are disconnected for a longer time. Lack of proper transportation hinders marketing activities. Agro-based products cannot be sent to marketing centers, and industrial products cannot be supplied to rural population safely in time. In certain areas, even construction of road or railway is difficult to construct and maintain.

4. Seasonal and Irregular Demand

Rural demand is characterized as seasonal and irregular. So, companies cannot concentrate on rural segments as it is difficult to plan. In the same way, demand depends on income of rural customers, and income is quite uncertain because they depend on agriculture, and agriculture depends on monsoon.

5. Uncertain and Unpredictable Market

Market response is difficult to scale. They don't have stable and predicted behaviour. In such a situation, the effective marketing strategies do not make a sense. Rapid changes are difficult to incorporate and, hence, there are more chances to suffer. Overwhelming response of rural population to some products experiences sudden fall. Market planning remains ever challenging in rural segments.

6. Low Living Standards

Rural customers have low income, low purchasing power, low literacy rate, and, therefore, low standard of living. But, picture is now changing and marketers can have better opportunities than ever. Low standard of living restricts their buying ability and pace of adopting products.

7. Lethargic Life Style

Lack of desire for a new life style is most critical issue for a marketer. They cannot be easily convinced to try, use and adopt certain products with better qualities and innovative features Product modification does not create desirable and positive effects on rural folks. Customs, established beliefs, superstitions, etc., restrict their behaviour. Unfortunately, their opinion leaders lack scientific approach. Innovative and superior products are difficult to be introduced successfully in rural areas.

8. Language Problem

Language is a main constrains in communication strategies. Multiplicity of languages spoken in rural areas makes marketing activities difficult. Languages differ from state to state, and area to area in the same state. While designing advertising, personal selling, and publicity strategies, marketers cannot fulfill linguistic expectation of all rural people. Promotion programme always lacks versatility.

9. Urban Marketers v/s Rural Customers

The executives in companies cannot understand the consumer psychology of rural markets. Lack of awareness and understanding about consumer behaviour in rural markets create problems in formulating marketing strategies. Rural and urban customers significantly differ in terms of habits, tastes, uses, preferences, and other such aspects. So, any attempt to satisfy rural customers with urban mind (marketing executives born and brought-up in urban climate) results into vain endeavor.

10. Backwardness

Rural customers are economically backward. More than 30 per cent of the rural masses live below the poverty line. Poverty confines them to spend even for basic necessities. Backwardness also affects their mentality to change. Their poor purchasing power and rigidity are main constraints for marketers to serve them.

11. High Inventory Costs

Since rural demand is limited and uncertain, an effective inventory management is difficult. Besides, the retailers serving in rural areas don't have adequate knowledge and aptitude to decide optimum inventory. Unnecessary stocks cut their profit margin, and they loose customers in case of inadequate stocks.

12. Inadequate Marketing Support

Normally, producers and wholesalers do not extend full support to rural retailers in terms of liberal credit, financial assistance, and other facilities that they offer to traders of urban areas. In same way, rural customers and retailers are not given adequate space in designing overall marketing programme.

13. Other Problems

Over and above these problems, there are many minor and major difficulties that rural marketers have to face. It is not possible to discuss them in detail. Let us list them:

a. Lack of vision in retailers
b. Ancient and obsolete business techniques
c. Raw and immature consumers
d. Difficulty in segmenting markets
e. Inadequate bank and credit facilities
f. Problems in organising marketing channels
g. Limited accessibility of media
h. Branding, packaging, and labeling problems
i. Pricing problems
j. Low turnover, etc.

EXERCISES

MULTIPLE CHOICE QUESTIONS (MCQs)

1. In relation to rural marketing, which one is not true?
   a. Rural population constitutes around 70% of total population.
   b. Rural per capita expenditure growth rate is less than that of urban.
   c. Rural market in Indian economy generates more than half of national income.
   d. There are more than 600000 villages in India.
2. With reference to response of rural market to product, find out a true statement.
   a. Rural buyers believe in product status and prestige rather than product utility.
   b. Rural buyers ask for the product which can assist them in their traditional occupations and life style.
   c. Most rural buyers give more important to product's taste than usefulness.
   d. Rural buyers strongly expect in after-sales services.
3. Which is not a valid feature of rural market?
   a. Rural consumers buy from known and nearby retailers.
   b. Rural consumers place limited number of orders of bulk size.
   c. Rural consumers consider caste, religion, political affiliation, etc., while selecting the retailer.
   d. Rural consumers are not interested in home delivery.
4. Which is the strongest reason for less predictability of rural market?
   a. Rural consumers have different pattern of living in different seasons.
   b. Rural consumers are dominated by customs and superstitions.

c. Rural consumers are mentally disturbed.

d. Rural consumers have uncertain and irregular source of income.

5. Which one is not a distinctive feature of rural market?

   a. Rural market is highly price-sensitive.

   b. Rural market prefers to buy on cash and is not interested in credit facility, installment scheme, and loan.

   c. Rural market holds strong faith in local religious and spiritual leader.

   d. Rural market is less predictable than urban market.

6. With reference to the impacts of growth of rural market, find out the odd statement.

   a. Growth of rural market generates employment opportunities.

   b. Growth of rural market increases population pressure on urban.

   c. Growth of rural market improves rural infrastructure.

   d. Growth of rural market improves living standard of villagers.

7. Which is not a valid cause/reason of rural market boom?

   a. Population growth

   b. Natural and man-made calamities

   c. Agriculture prosperity and improved literacy rate

   d. Rural development programme

8. Out of following companies, which one is not involved in linking Indian agricultural products to the world markets?

   a. Reliance Group

   b. Tata Group

   c. Godrej, Hinustan Unilever and Dabur Groups

   d. Maruti Udhyong Limited (MUL)

9. In India, Gujarat, Haryana, Punjab, Tamil Nadu, Andhra Pradesh, Kerala, etc., are considered as

   a. the developed rural India

   b. the developing rural India

   c. underdeveloped rural India

   d. none

10. Which is not justifiable challenge or practical problem of rural marketing?

    a. Unwillingness of rural segments to pay bill in time

    b. Backwardness and low living standard

    c. Seasonal and irregular demand

    d. Wide scattered market

MATCHING TYPE QUESTIONS (MTQs)

11.

List I	List II
(a) Size of Rural market	(1) Around 6 lakh
(b) Number of villages in India	(2) Around 627 million (74% of population)
(a) Projected growth of rural market	(3) 50% of GDP
(b) Rural India Account for more than	(4) Around 11%

Codes: (A) (a)-(2), (b)-(1), (c)-(4), (d)-(3)

(B) (a)-(3), (b)-(2), (c)-(1), (d)-(4)

(C) (a)-(4), (b)-(3), (c)-(2), (d)-(1)

(D) (a)-(1), (b)-(4), (c)-(3), (d)-(2)

ANSWERS KEY: 1(b), 2(b), 3(c), 4(d), 5(b), 6(b), 7(b), 8(d), 9(a), 10(a), 11(A)

QUESTIONS FOR DISCUSSION

12. Define rural marketing. Explain its characteristics in detail.
13. Explain term 'rural marketing' and discuss its importance
14. Write notes;
    a. Reasons leading to growth of rural marketing
    b. Present picture/scenario of rural marketing
15. "Rural marketing decisions are similar to urban marketing." Do you agree? Explain rural marketing mix.
16. "Rural marketing is not easy to game to play." Comment the statement in relation to problems and challenges associated with rural marketing.

CHAPTER

11

MARKETING OF SERVICES

INTRODUCTION

Today's is service era. Service sectors account for more than 70% employment opportunities. Even in the time of economic meltdown, unlike manufacturing sector, the service sector has registered employment rate up. Our economy is emerging as the service economy because service sector contributes more than 50 per cent to the GDP of the nation. This sector has major contribution in the national income. Note that services are no longer treated as an industrial by-product. The sector is booming. We cannot imagine our life in absence of services. Services create convenience to our economic activities and day-to-day life. Banking, health care, insurance, transportation, communication, entertainment, beauty-care, education, repairing, electricity, and a host of product-related services have become an integral part of our routine life. Some services are as old as human civilization; however, marketing focus to services is the recent phenomenon.

Booming Service Sectors in India: India is experiencing a service boom. Notable growth rate has been recorded in many service sectors, including insurance, transportation, telecommunication, IT sector, electricity, postal services, tourism, banking, health care, entertainment, education, consultancy, etc.

Causes Leading to Service Boom in India: Many reasons led to service sector boom in India. Main factors have been just listed below:

1. Economic Prosperity
2. Development of Agriculture Sector
3. Changing Role of Women
4. Cultural Transformation
5. Revolution in Information Technology
6. Emphasis on Conservation of Natural Resources
7. Improvement of Marketing System
8. Emphasis on Consumer Satisfaction
9. Competition and Market Promotion Services

10. Growth of MNCs
11. Increase Health Care Consciousness
12. Economic Liberalization
13. Growth of International Trade
14. Internal and External Migration, etc.

Good-Service Dilemma: Product consists of both tangible components and intangible services. Every product has more or less proportion of good or service. A goods-service relationship can be explained in term of five product categories, listed below:

1. **Pure Tangible Goods,** for example, sugar, detergent cake, etc.
2. **Tangible Goods with Accompanying Service,** for example, electrical appliances.
3. **Hybrid Goods,** for example, hotel and restaurant services.
4. **Services with Accompanying Goods,** for example banking, transportation, etc.
5. **Pure Services,** for example, consultancy, education, idea selling, etc.

It is almost impossible to distinguish clearly the pure physical object and pure service because every physical object offers services to the users and every service is offer via physical-tangible things. For example, salt is pure physical-tangible object, but it offers taste that cannot be said as physical object. Toothpaste is physical object, but is used for its services like cleaning and strengthening teeth, and freshening breath. Transportation is a pure service, but it is rendered through vehicles, pick-up stations, and staff. The banking services can be said as intangible but they include tangible objects like forms, statements, ATM card, draft, money transfer, cheque book, pass book, etc. Virtually, every product – physical object or intangible service – consists of major component of intangible service.

In our discussion, pure services are focused. This chapter contains several issues relating to intangible services and their marketing aspects and problems.

DEFINITIONS

We can define term 'service' as under:

1. **Philip Kotler:** "A service is any activity or benefit that one can offer to another that is essentially intangible and does not result in the ownership of anything. Its production may or may not be tied to a physical product."
2. **The American Marketing Association (AMA):** Services are activities, benefits, or satisfactions which are offered for sale or provided in connection with the sale of goods."
3. **William Stanton:** "Services are separately identifiable, intangible activities which provide want satisfaction when marketed to consumers and/or industrial users and which are not necessarily tied to the sale of a product or another service."
4. **The term can also be defined as:** *Any facility or assistance, whether pure (banking, insurance, transpiration, etc.), or product-related (installation, repairing, inspection, demonstration, etc.), offered to someone that satisfies any type of need or expectation can be a service.*
5. **More clearly, it can be said:** *A set of activities, benefits, facilities, and conveniences offered by any one to satisfy any type of need of any person can be said as service.*

CHARACTERISTICS OF SERVICES

We can list main characteristics of services as under:

1. Intangibility

Intangibility is a unique characteristic a service. Services cannot be seen, tasted, felt, heard or smelt before they are purchased. Buying decision depends on provider's staff, equipments, place, symbols, price, and the past experience.

2. Inseparability

Service cannot be separated from its producer. Services are rendered by their producers only, e.g., doctor's services to patients. Thus, service provider is a part of service. Both provider and client affect outcome of service.

3. Presence of Client

Some services require the presence of client. For example, heart surgery cannot be made without client's (i.e., patient's) presence. It cannot be sent via middlemen. However, many professional services can be rendered by staff, mail, or electronic devices.

4. Variability

Service variation is an important aspect. Especially, people-based services vary from person to person, such as washing, cleaning, nursing, teaching, cooking, etc. That is the reason that service buyers always insist a specific service provider. On the other hand, the equipment-based services may offer almost similar services, like automatic washing machine, ATM, airlines, medical, etc. Charges may be linked with person or institute. Besides, type of instruments, range of services, place, and type of staff also affect quality of equipment-based services.

5. Perishability

Obviously, services cannot be stored. If it is not rendered, it is wasted. For example, marketing consultant's time and energy are wasted if he remains free. That is why service firms face difficulty when demand fluctuates. Several strategies can help minimize degree of perishability.

6. Objectives

Every service provider differs in his or her objectives. Objectives may be monetary or non-monetary.

7. Charges/Fees

Services are provided for fees or charges. Service provider may be paid in different forms, such as commission, fees, rent, premiums, salary, and so forth. Charges depend on service provider, staff, equipment, place, time, turn (priority), image, etc.

8. Types

Services may be pure services like banking, insurance, medical, consultancy, and likewise. Whereas some services like installation, repairing, maintenance, inspecting, training, demonstration, etc., are product-related services.

9. Users

The users of the services may be called as clients (for management consultant), patients (for doctors), owner/master (for domestic servant), customers (for salesmen), or simply users. Users may be an individual, an institute, or a group.

10. Others Characteristics

In addition to above discussed features, there are some minor features of service listed as under:

i. Services include all activities, benefits, facilities, and/or conveniences that are offered to consumers.

ii. Services are identifiable.

iii. Services are marketed directly to consumers and to the industrial users.
iv. Ownership is not transferable.
v. Customer participation is important in services.
vi. Services may or may not be tied with the sales of goods.
vii. Services may or may not be tied with the sale of another service, etc.

CLASSIFICATION OF SERVICES

Different service providers offer different services. We can classify them in several types as:

1. Personal Services

Individual offers such services to owner like nursing, washing, tailoring, and hair cutting, cooking, and other personal care services. Mostly, the service provider is compensated with money or other benefits.

2. Office Assistance

Business firm needs certain services of clerk, peon, typist, secretary, accountant, security, and such others for office administration. Such staff is paid by salary.

3. Trade-aided Services

These services are offered by service industries, such as banking, warehousing, insurance, transportation, communication, etc. They charges fees or commissions.

4. Professional Services

Qualified and trained professionals, like chartered accountants, advocates, management consultants, doctors, and such others, provide expert services and charges fees from their clients.

5. Product-aided Services

Repairing, inspection, demonstration, installation, upgradaing, etc., offered by company, middlemen, and salesmen are product-aided services. Such services are called as after-sales services. The services may be offered with or without charges.

6. Educational Services

Educational institutes, like schools, colleges, training institutes, and universities, meet educational needs of people. The services include teaching, training, evaluating, and generation and dissemination of knowledge for development. They charges fees for their services.

7. Entertaining Services

Hotel, resort, circus, films, club, and other similar organisations provide facilities to entertain their customers. Charges depend on staff, quality, status, contents, location, and time.

MARKETING OF SERVICES

Marketing is not only applicable for physical tangible goods. It is equally useful to intangible offers like services. Marketing fundamentals, like concepts, functions, strategies, processes, etc., can be applied in service sectors to achieve goals. All service providers – individuals, institute, or industry – need to market their services. From marketing viewpoint, they can apply all marketing tactics and techniques for better consumer satisfaction. Banking, insurance, transportation (roadways, railway, pipe ways, and airways) hotels, resorts, postal, phone, consultancy, etc., rigorously apply marketing theory and philosophy to offer maximum satisfaction to their customers. In the same way, schools, colleges, training institutes, and hospitals having missionary goals also practice marketing fundamentals for better services to the society. Army, political parties, religious institutes, etc., also follow marketing principles. However, services are different than tangible objects. Due to perishability, heterogeneity, difference in production of services, simultaneous production, distribution and consumption, non-storability, non-transferable ownership, and such other distinguished features of services demand separate marketing strategies.

Here, different services, schemes, conveniences, facilities, etc., offered to customers by the relevant sectors can be said as products. In reality, even for tangibles-physical products, customers expect services or utilities. For example, we do not want just ownership of a motorbike or a car, but its services to go from one place to another. Virtually, all products – tangible or intangible – offer some services or utilities to the buyers. Any offer of marketer includes some part of service. Thus, the service components can be a minor or major part of total offer. So, marketing problems may be same for goods as well as services. It is obvious that managers who know marketing fundamentals can do better for their customers or clients. However, professionally managed service organisations practice marketing philosophy more intensively.

MARKETING MIX FOR SERVICES

All fundamentals of modern marketing, like concepts, processes, functions, principle, and so forth, are equally applicable to service sector. Most service providers face competition, and are required to improve qualities, contents, availability, and timing of their offers to attain goals with consumer satisfaction. Service providers need knowledge of marketing to attract, satisfy, add, and maintain customers. Service marketer, whosoever, is required to design the product (services and facilities), set price for the product (fees, commission, charges), apply market promotion, and to decide on place for rendering services. Thus, marketing mix is applicable to any service provider.

ELEMENTS OF SERVICE MARKETING MIX

Marketing mix for good or service, more or less, has same elements; only contents and reference of each of the elements differ. Let's examine marketing-mix elements for a service:

Product Mix: Service is an intangible product. Here, service or facility is considered as a product. Various services, schemes, plans (for example, cell phone and insurance industry), facilities, constancy, and so forth are products of service providers. Branding, guarantee, and after-sales services are also applicable. Unlike tangible product, a label cannot be directly attached with product. The label, in form of description or explanation, describes service conditions and qualities. Packing and packaging are not applied in direct form. Regularity, reliability, consistency, continuity, positive response/behaviour, relation building, responsiveness (attentiveness), assurance, empathy, convenience, presence of physical supporting facilities, and so forth are important qualities of service product.

Price Mix: Charge, fee, commission, or rate that service provider charges can be referred as price for the service. Discount, concession, special offer, etc., are also applicable in service marketing. Pricing objectives, price setting methods, factors, pricing policies, etc., are key aspects while setting price for the service.

Promotion Mix: Service promotion decisions are almost identical to physical product. Market communication is more crucial in service industry. A firm must design its communication network systematically to help customers access the services. Most service providers have their websites to serve customers better. Banking, software, insurance, cell phone, brokerage, travels, hotels, and other service sectors provide online services. Compared to tangible products, the Internet is excessively used in service industry to promote and distribute services. Advertising, personal selling, sales promotion, and publicity and public relations can be applied to service industry with or without little variation. Service promotion strategies are almost identical to physical product. Difference lies only in types of offers.

Place Mix: Physical distribution and channel of distribution decisions are somewhat different in service industry because of absence of physical entity of product. Branches, agents, sales executives, service centers, etc., can be said as middlemen for service marketing. Company must open the adequate number of branches or offices at several places so that customers can easily excess services. Logical and systematic physical arrangement of various counters or tables in the office, and deployment of trained staff play crucial role in offering of services conveniently. Services are rendered by employees/people. So, more emphasis is given on recruitment, training, behaviour, and motivation of employees. Market logistics system can be applied to services, too.

OTHER AREAS OF SERVICE MARKETING

In marketing, product consists of good and/or service. Consumer behaviour in service marketing, service demand management, consumer purchase decision in services, market segmentation for service sector, service positioning, service life cycle and strategies, marketing research in service marketing, sales force for service sector, international marketing of services, retailing of services, customer relationship management, etc., are more or less similar to that of product marketing. Modern marketing directly or indirectly involves services. All fundamentals of marketing science are equally applicable to goods and services. For detail, refer to relevant chapters of the book.

EXERCISES

MULTIPLE CHOICE QUESTIONS (MCQs)

1. In relation to service marketing in India, which is not true?
   a. Today's is service era.
   b. Service sector is account for more than 70 % employment opportunities.
   c. Service sector contributes more than 50% of our GDP.
   d. Service sector is still treated as an industrial by-product.
2. Which one is not a convicting cause of service marketing boom in India?
   a. Frequent natural calamities like tsunami, earthquake, heavy rain, etc.
   b. Economic prosperity
   c. Emphasis on consumer satisfaction
   d. Revolution in information technology
3. In which class of services do banking and transportation fall?
   a. Tangible goods with accompanying services
   b. Pure Services
   c. Services with accompanying goods
   d. Hybrid goods
4. Trade-aided services include
   a. Hotels, clubs, and films
   b. Schools, colleges and universities
   c. Nursing, washing, and cooking.
   d. Banking, insurance, and transportation
5. Nursing, hair-cutting, tailoring, and cooking are
   a. personal services
   b. product-aided services
   c. professional services
   d. entertaining services
6. Find out what is not true.
   a. Marketing is equally applicable to tangible goods and intangible services.
   b. Due to perishability, simultaneous production, distribution and consumption, non-storability, etc., services marketing require different marketing strategies.
   c. Price element of marketing mix is not applicable to services.
   d. Practically, it is difficult to distinguish between pure services and pure products.

7. Find out correct statement.
   a. Today's is commodity era.
   b. Service sector contributes more than 50 per cent to the GDP of the nation.
   c. Now, service sector is shrinking.
   d. None.
8. In context with nature of services, which one is inconsistent?
   a. Services are intangible.
   b. Services can be stored for the future use.
   c. Those who use services are called clients.
   d. Both service provider and client affect outcomes of the service.

MATCHING TYPE QUESTIONS (MTQs)

9.

List I	List II
(a) Service cannot be seen, tasted before they are bought.	(1) Inseparability
(b) Service cannot be separated from its provides,	(2) Intangibility
(c) Service cannot be stored.	(3) Variability
(d) Service quality varies from person to person	(4) Perishability

Codes: (A) (a)-(2), (b)-(1), (c)-(4), (d)-(3)
(B) (a)-(3), (b)-(2), (c)-(1), (d)-(4)
(C) (a)-(4), (b)-(3), (c)-(2), (d)-(1)
(D) (a)-(1), (b)-(4), (c)-(3), (d)-(2)

10.

List I	List II
(a) Nursing, washing, tailoring, hair-cutting, etc.	(1) Trade-aided Services
(b) Banking, insurance, communication, etc.	(2) Personal Services
(c) Chartered accountant, advocate, doctors, etc.	(3) Entertaining Services
(d) Hotels, films, club, circus, resort, etc.	(4) Professional Services

Codes: (A) (a)-(2), (b)-(1), (c)-(4), (d)-(3)
(B) (a)-(3), (b)-(2), (c)-(1), (d)-(4)
(C) (a)-(4), (b)-(3), (c)-(2), (d)-(1)
(D) (a)-(1), (b)-(4), (c)-(3), (d)-(2)

ANSWERS KEY: 1(d), 2(a), 3(c), 4(d), 5(a), 6(c), 7(b), 8(b), 9(A), 10(A)

QUESTIONS FOR DISCUSSION

11. "Service sector is booming." Explain the statement and discuss factors leading to service boom in India.
12. Define word 'service' and explain its characteristics.
13. Explain different types of services. Also write a note on marketing mix for service industry.
14. "Marketing of services is similar to marketing." Comment the statement with reference to product marketing and service marketing.

✧✧✧

CHAPTER

12

ELEMENTS OF RETAILING

INTRODUCTION

Retailing is not a recent phenomenon, it is as old as human civilization. However, modern retail business is different. Particularly, in service sector, retailing has transformed thoroughly. Now, retail business is among fast developing activities. India is ranked first among top thirty emerging markets in the world.[1] Across the world, retailing business is on rise. Retailing is no longer treated as the part of distribution system, a one decision of marketing management; now, it is recognized as an industry with a huge turnover. Tight work schedule, 24/7 type working pattern, excessive use of e-money, advancing information technology, improved incomes and standard of living, availability of quality products at reasonable price, attractive opportunities in retailing business, crazy shopping hobby of youngsters, adaptation of people with mall culture, and active and drastic change in overall living and buying pattern of consumers have fueled to retail industry in India and abroad.

RETAIL SCENARIO OF INDIA

In last one and half decades, many corporate giants have entered into retailing and have successfully professionalized this business. Many international retailers have entered Indian market and many are about to enter to explore retailing opportunities. Interestingly, apart from a unique industry, retailing has been emerging as a discipline, a branch of study. In almost all B-Schools, many students specialize on retiling field every year. Even, primary and secondary schools have introduced retailing related topics in their curricula in one or other form. Now, retailing activities have transformed into promising business worldwide. Retail business occupies an important place in the world economy. Retailing industry, accordingly to Global Industry Classification Standard (GICS), is growing at the rate of 5%. In year 2009, total turnover of retail industry in the world is

[1] A.T. Kearney, "Emerging Market Priorities for Global Retailer," The 2005 Global Retail Employment Index.

estimated to be $12,104 billions. It is one of the major sources of employment, too. It enjoys 6% to 7% share in total employment in India and China. In some developed countries, its contribution in total employment much higher than India. For example, share of retail in total employment in Brazil, U.S.A., Korea, and U.K. is 15%, 12%, 18%, and 11% respectively.[2] Wal-Mart Stores is ranked first in terms of revenues ($ 287989 millions, 2004), and number of employees (1700000 employees in 2005) among leading multinational retailers across the globe.

Indian retailing system exhibits considerable variety. We find giant shopping malls and a small retail shops operating simultaneously in nearby area. Interestingly, some small sole proprietary retailers are competing successfully with retail corporate giants in neighboring areas. Medium and large departmental stores also operate in retailing field amidst many small retailers and a few corporate retailers. In the same way, service sector retailing business is also booming. Most service sectors, including banking, stock markets and securities, insurance, healthcare, communication, tour and travels, hotel and restaurants, and so forth, have started concentrating their attention on effective retailing to survive and grow.

Retail Sector is the most booming sector in the Indian economy. Some of the biggest players of the world are going to enter the industry soon. It is on the threshold of bringing the next big revolution after the IT sector. Retail market is expected to grow manifolds by the year 2010. The sector contributes 10% of the GDP, and is estimated to show 20% annual growth rate by the end of the decade as against the current growth rate of 8.5%. A CRISIL report says that the Indian retail market is the most fragmented in the world and that only 2% of the entire retailing business is in the organized sector. This suggests that the potential for growth is immense. There are about 300 new malls, 1500 supermarkets and 325 departmental stores currently being built in the cities across India.

GROWTH OF RETAIL COMPANIES IN INDIA: OVERVIEW

Growth of Retail Companies in India is still not yet in a matured stage with great potentials within this sector still to be explored. Apart from the retail company like Nilgiri's of Bangalore, most of the retail companies are the sections of other industries that have stepped in the retail sector for a better business. The growth of retail companies in India is most pronounced in the metro cities of India; however, the smaller towns are also not lagging behind in this regard. The retail companies are not only targeting a few metros in India, but also are considering the second graded upcoming cities like Ahmedabad, Baroda, Chandigarh, Coimbatore, Cochin, Ludhiana, Pune, Trivandrum, Simla, Gurgaon, and others. The South Indian zone have adopted the process of shopping in the supermarkets for their daily requirements and this has also been influencing other cities as well where many hypermarkets are coming up.

Reasons for the Fast Growth of Retail Companies in India

The retail companies are found to be rising in India at a remarkable speed with the years and this has brought a revolutionary change in the shopping attitude of the Indian customers. The growth of retail companies in India is facilitated by certain factors, like:

- Existing Indian middle classes with an increased purchasing power
- Rise of upcoming business sectors like the IT and engineering firms
- Change in the taste and attitude of the Indians
- Effect of globalization
- Heavy influx of FDI in the retail sectors in India

[2] ICIER Publication, 2002, p.31.

Estimates and Predictions for Retail Sector in India

Some studies conducted by reputed groups have made following prediction:

- At present, the industry is estimated to be at more than US$ 400 billion by a study of McKinsey.
- The Economist Intelligence Unit (EIU) estimates the retail market in India will increase to US$608.9 billion in 2009 from US$394 billion in 2005.
- KPMG Report says that the organized retail would grow at a higher rate than the GDP in the next five years.
- The retail sector would generate employment for more than 2.5 million people by the year 2010, as predicted by Ma Foi Management Consultants Ltd.

Major Players in Retail Industry: Major leading Indian companies in retail business include Archies, Bata India Ltd, Big Bazaar, Crossword, Ebony Retail Holdings Ltd., Fabmall, Food Bazaar, Globus Stores Pvt. Ltd., Health and Glow, Liberty Shoes Ltd., MTR Foods Ltd., Music World Entertainment Ltd., Pantaloon Retail India Ltd., Shoppers Stop, Style SPA Furniture Ltd., Subhiksha, Tital Industries, Lifestyle, etc. New entrants entering the market soon will be Reliance Retail Ltd, Wal-Mart Stores, Carrefour, Tesco, Boots Group, etc.

DEFINITIONS OF RETAILING

Word 'retail' implies to sell or to vend to ultimate users. Term 'retail' is derived from the French word 'retaillier,' which means to cut off a piece or to break the bulk. Retail implies selling of goods to many ultimate users repeatedly in small quantity. Let's examine some definitions:

1. **Philip Kotler**: "Retailing includes all the activities involved in selling goods or services to the final consumers for personal or non-business use. A retailer or retail store is any business enterprise whose sales volume comes primarily from retailing."
2. **The North American Industry Classification System (NAICS)**: "The retail trade sector comprises of establishments primarily engaged in retailing merchandise, generally without transformation, and rendering services incidental to the sales of merchandise."
3. **We can defined the term as**: *Retail is a final step in distribution system that involves selling merchandise (goods and services) in original form in small quantity directly to the consumers for their personal, family or household use. It is the only stage where consumers come in direct contact with sellers (or retailers).*

Retail is the last stage of business activities. Successful retailing contributes to business success on one hand and consumer satisfaction on the other hand. It is the only stage where the target market is availed the products. The person who is involved in retailing is called retailer and his business is called retailed business. Retail shops, departmental stores, showrooms, visiting salesmen, shopping malls, cooperative societies, and government approved fair-priced stores, the Canteen Stores, the Post Office, mobile vendors, multiplexes, and many others are called retailers. Retailing is the last stage in any mode of distribution system. Banking, transportation, telecommunication, cyber marketing, Internet, consumer guidance agencies, etc., facilitate retailing.

Key Elements of Retailing

Definitions imply following elements (features) of retailing.

1. Retail must be the ultimate stage of distribution. Product must not be sold after retailing.
2. Retailing must involve individual dealing or personal dealing between the consumers and retailers.
3. Products must be sold directly to consumers for their personal or family use.
4. Products must be sold in original form, without making any type of change.
5. Product must be sold to ultimate users in small quantity.

6. Retailing must involve repeat transactions. Retailer sells the same merchandise repeatedly to same group of consumers.
7. Customers must pay directly to the retailer.
8. All fundamentals of marketing can be applied to retailing, i.e., all marketing decisions can be applied to this sector.
9. Retail trade is carried out by manufacturers, their agents, or by independent organisations.
10. Retailing must involve the transfer of ownership or title.
11. Successful retailing needs various facilities such as banking, transportation, telecommunication, cyber marketing, Internet, and consumer guidance agencies.

EVOLUTION STAGES OF RETAIL FORMAT

In fact, it is difficult to explain stages of retail trade. Exact inception of retailing is difficult state. Retailing is assumed to be as old as human civilization. However, it has experienced the drastic changes during its evolution to reach today's position. New forms could improve retailing practices but could not replace old modes of retailing. For example, emergence of shopping malls cannot replace small retailers. Swapna Pathan[3] considers specific stages of retail trade evolution. With little variation, we can describe journey of retail trade – from very primitive stage to advanced stage – in following steps:

1. Barter System Stage

In fact, it is difficult to state when and where retailing emerged. It is as old as human civilization. It has been in existence since many centuries in one or other forms. Barter was the oldest form of trade. Most merchandise were sold in market places or by peddler (hawkers). Vendors or producers themselves used to come to market to sell their goods. During the time, local markets were dependent on sources of supplies of perishable items because of difficult and slow journey. Markets were seasonal due to lack of storage facilities. However, some customers prefer to travel considerable distances for specialty items. Handcraft items, grocery, fruits and vegetables, and other edible items were main merchandise during the period. At the end of 17th century, in major cities retailing started being more systematic. Retailers were treated as the entrepreneurs of those days.

2. Social Development Stage

Development of retail can be attributed to social development over the time. Development of railways and telegraph contributed positively to growth of retail trade. Retail traders started using telegraph to book orders from distance places and railways to receive or send goods to distance destinations. Due to improved transportation and telecommunication, and advent of traveling salesman, wholesale business came into existence. In the middle of 18th century, in America and Europe, systematic retailing began. Gradually, along with retail traders, departmental stores came into being. At the end of 18th century, retail business becomes more systematized. Improved communication and transportation supported growth of retail trade.

3. The Industrial Revolution Stage

Beginning of 19th century led to systematic growth of retail trade across the world. Industrial revolution resulted into mass production, and necessitated mass distribution. It brought dramatic changes in distribution and retailing. Due to urbanization, consumers clustered in smaller geographical areas that phenomenon led to emergence of a number of shops in market places. Middlemen (retailer and wholesalers) were responsible to sell products manufactured by big companies.

---

[3] Swapna Pathan, Retailing and Management, Tata McGraw-Hill Company Ltd., New Delhi-2006, pp.50-57.

4. The Emergence of Self-service Stores

20th century experienced the boom in retailing both in term of retailing modes and volumes of business. Self-service stores started in first couple of decades of 20th century in developed and some developing countries. At present, most departmental stores and retail shopping malls do practice self-service retailing. The primary purpose of self-service stores was/is to permit customers to see and choose the brand they like. Moreover, this type of stores can reduce costs as fewer sales people are required to serve the customers.

The Development of Supermarkets and Convenience Stores: Supermarkets started in the 1930s. This retailing system attempted to serve different types of customers. In supermarkets, well-packed products were displayed in attractive way. Necessary details such as price, weight, manufacturers, manufacturing and expiry dates, contents, and other relevant details are printed on the package.

On the other hand, convenience stores functioned on customer request. The stores were established at the place where customers could access merchandise conveniently. These stores worked for early morning to the late night and sold ice, cold drinks, groceries, drugs, bread, milk, etc. Invention of cold storage facilities and automobiles further helped growing retail activities. Most supermarkets and stores were working in leading cities of Europe and America.

5. Specialty Stores, Malls, and other Formats

After 1970, in many big cities of world, new modes of retailing started. Increased population and hence demand, rapid means of transportation and telecommunication, development of latest cold storage facilities, introduction of barcodes on package, improved banking and insurance, etc., further contributed to retail boom. Several retail malls were established in last two decades of 20th century and continued growing till today. Spacious retail malls sell all products of different brands in a single area. Many companies started retail chain in big cities to grab the retail opportunity. Full-fledged shopping mall with museum, swimming pools, arcades, well-trained and humble staff, refreshing facilities, parking, and so forth make the shopping an exciting experience. Malls become visiting destinations. Now, people are habituated to buy from shopping malls. After metrocities, retail giants are extending their operations to small cities. India and other developing countries actively joined in the booming stage of retailing.

6. The Rise of the Webs

Internet brought further revolution in retailing. With growth of World Wide Web, customers as well as retailers can excess suppliers and products from anywhere in the world. Most companies have their websites. Systematic linkage of one web with others and with search engines helps retailers to sell products globally. Cyber Marketing facilitates selection of products, placing orders of specific description, and paying bills. Not only durables, consumables like ice-cream, cold drinks, fast food items can be purchased through online. Internet marketing contributed significantly to service sector retail trade. Online availability of all services changed shopping pattern. Online shopping and online trading become the part of today's life.

We must note that along with modern shopping malls and online retailing, small traditional retailers have successful maintain their place, significance, and existence. Though they are small in size, they are capable to compete with retail giants. In the same way, wholesalers do work without threat from retail shopping malls.

KEY DECISION AREAS IN RETAILING

This part describes some of key decisions of retail trade. The decisions include:

1. Retail Modes
2. Understanding Retail Consumers

3. Retail Strategy Formulation
4. Retail Brand
5. Retail Store Locations
6. Merchandise Management (Retail Merchandising)
7. Retail Price
8. Organising of Retailing Operations
9. Retail Market Promotion/Communication
10. Servicing Retail Consumers
11. Retail Store Design and Visual Merchandising
12. Supply Chain Management

RETAIL MODES

Retail business has undergone a drastic shift in recent years. Dynamic business environment, changed consumer behaviour, entry of giant corporate players in retail business, development of information technology and wide practice of online marketing, improved infrastructures, and intensified competition – all affect the shape and mode of retail business.

Retail trade is practiced in several forms, formats, or modes. In the contemporary marketing environment, several retail modes are followed worldwide. Different retail modes differ in terms of their size of operations, location, ownership, type of merchandise offered, price charged, services offered, transactions (ordering and delivering merchandise) pattern, and in many other ways. The classification ranges from small independent local owner-operated stores to multinational giant category killers. Swapna Pathan[4] classifies retail modes on the basis of store-based retailers, non-stores based retailers, and service retailers. Figure 1 shows classification of popular retail modes.

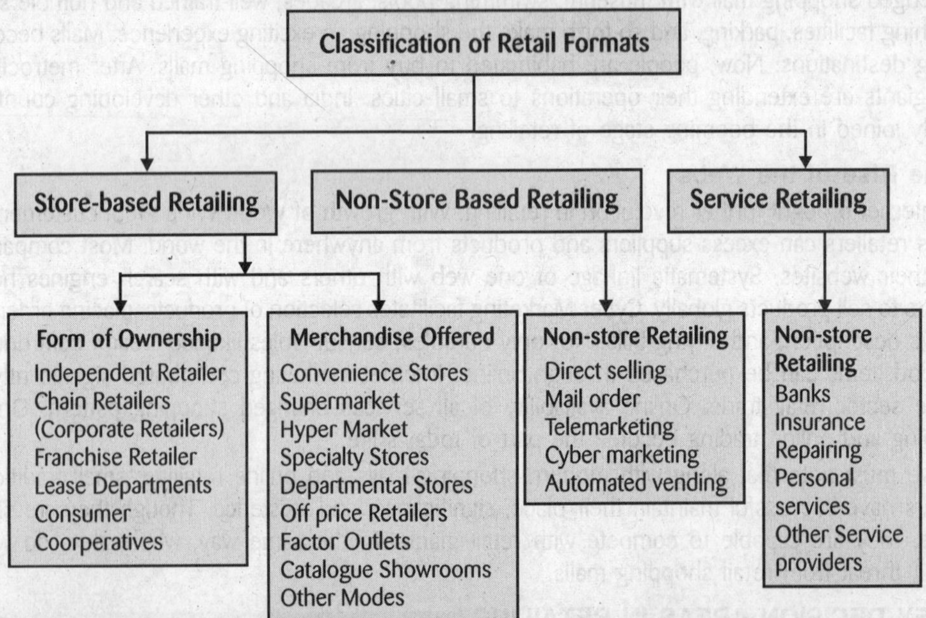

Figure 1: Classification of Retail Modes

[4] Ibid., p. 60

Classification is based on three major criteria, such as store-based retailing, non-store-based retailing, and service retailing.

STORE-BASED RETAILING: Store-based retailing indicates that retailers have their own specific shops, malls, or showrooms. They are retailing from their stores. Store-based retailing can be again classified into two categories as:

1. Form of Ownership
2. Merchandise offered

FORM OF OWNERSHIP

On the basis of ownership, there are five types of retail formats:

i. Independent Retailer
ii. Chain Retailers (Corporate Retailers)
iii. Franchise Retailer
iv. Lease Departments
v. Consumer Cooperatives

Independent Retailer: Independent retailer is a small trader who operates only on one retail outlet at particular locality. The outlet is owned by owner or proprietor, family members, and assistants. India's major retailing depends on independent retailers. Local Kirana store, panwala, clothe merchant, and some modern small-sized stores and showrooms are examples of independent retailers.

Chain Retailer: It is a type of ownership in which two or more retail outlets are under common ownership. It is also known as corporate retail chains. The stores exhibits similarity in term of merchandise they sell, advertising, services, etc. For example, Arrow of Arvind Mills, Wills Sport of ITC, Shopper's Stop, Food World, etc.

Franchise: A franchise is a contract or agreement between franchiser (company or producer) and the franchisee (retailer) to conduct business under the established name as per specific business format. There can be two type of franchising – trade mark franchise and business format franchise. Archie's stores, Pizza Huts, Subway, McDonald, etc., are example of franchise retailing.

Leased Departments: When a retail department is leased or rented to an outside party, it is turned as leased department. Many malls, departments, multiplexes, etc., are operating on lease.

Consumer Cooperatives: Consumer cooperatives or consumer cooperative societies are owned by their member consumers. They run on cooperative basis. Sahakari Bhandar and Apana Bazaar in Mumbai, Super Bazaar in Delhi, Kendriya Bhandar by the government, etc., are example of consumer cooperatives.

MERCHANDISE OFFERED

On the basis of merchandise (commodities) offered, there can be several modes of retailing, such as:

i. Convenience Stores
ii. Supermarket
iii. Hyper Market
iv. Specialty Stores
v. Departmental Stores
vi. Off price Retailers
vii. Factory Outlets
viii. Catalogue Showrooms
ix. Other Modes

Some of these modes have been briefly described here.

Convenience Stores: Small retail stores offering essential goods which remained open for long hours and all the days of week and located near residential areas are referred to convenience stores. They sell bread, milk, grocery products and other essential items.

Supermarkets: They are large in size, self-service operations, and based on high volume and low margin. They sell food, healthcare and beauty care products, groceries, and other non-food items. Nilgiri's, Food world, Food Bazaar, and others are major supermarkets in India.

Hypermarket: It is a combination of supermarket and departmental stores. They offer variety of food and non-food items like clothes, jewelry, hardware, sport equipments, cycles, motor accessories, books, electronics and electrical appliances, etc. It is similar to one-stop shopping. They offer products at cheapest possible prices. Carrefour, Wal-Mart, Meijer, Target, Tesco, etc., are famous supermarkets. Big Bazaar, Star India Bazaar, Giant, etc., are example of India's supermarkets.

Specialty Store: This retail store specializes in a particular merchandise or single product of consumer durable like furniture, jewelry, household goods, consumer electronics, sport goods, fabrics, etc. Proline Fitness Station and Gautier Furniture are big players in India. Even, many local small retail players can develop specialty stores.

Departmental Store: It sells different types of goods all under one roof. Along with products, they also offer new customer services like reading rooms, restrooms, home delivery, wrapping services, etc. Some of major departmental stores in India include Shopper's Stop, Globus, Websites and Lifestyle, etc.

Off Price Retailers: They sell merchandise at less than retail prices. They buy from manufacturers the seconds, overruns, and off seasons at a deep discount. Such stores are owned by manufactures or departmental stores. Pantaloon Factory Outlets and Levi's Factory Outlets are example of off price retailers.

Catalogue Showrooms: Normally, they specialize in hard goods like house ware, jewelry, and electronics. Customers walk into the showroom and refer catalogue of products they want to buy. Sometimes, they have to write the product code number on a chit and handover to salesmen.

Others: Apart from above store-based retailing modes, we find many other forms of retailing like discount store, super warehouse store, limited assortment store, super center, wholesale club, etc.

NON-STORE RETAILING

It is form of direct retailing without any kind of store or retail outlet. There are several forms of non-store retailing:

i. Direct Selling
ii. Mail Order
iii. Telemarketing
iv. Cyber Marketing
v. Automated Vending
vi. Other Forms

Direct Selling: It consists of making direct contact with the end consumers at home, at work, at office, or at any convenience place. Cosmetics, jewelry, garments, foods, home appliances are sold directly to customers. For example, salesmen can sell these products to consumers. It also includes network marketing in which every the consumer is both a consumer as well as a seller.

Mail Order Retailing: Here, customers demand for products of specific description through mail and are delivered the products at their places.

Telemarketing: Order for the product is placed by phone and/or cell phone. Television shopping is also a type of telemarketing. Products are displayed and demonstrated on television. Full description of products is shown on TV and phone numbers are provided for each city to place order.

Cyber Marketing or Electronic Shopping: It is also known as online or Internet marketing. Transactions are made by Internet. Full detail is placed on the web.

Automated Vending: Customer can access the products round the clock. It is suitable for soft drinks, ice-cream, coffee, candy, cigarette, newspapers, etc. It is not very famous in India. Tea and coffee is offered by this mode at the airport in India. ATM (the automated teller machine) by banks is popular example of this type of retailing.

SERVICE RETAIL

It involves retailing of services to the end users. They mainly include:

i. Banks
ii. Insurance
iii. Repairing Services
iv. Rental Services
v. Personal Services
vi. Other Service Providers

The classification may not be perfect and/or exhaustive. It seems difficult to classify all retailing modes as there may be more criteria. There may be other modes of retailing.

UNDERSTANDING RETAIL CONSUMERS

Consumer satisfaction is the key to succeed. A firm exists for its consumer satisfaction. Retailer has to understand consumers for developing successful retailing strategy. He can satisfy consumers only when he understands them in terms of consumers' needs, wants, habits, paying ability mode of payment, attitudes, services they expect, and so forth. Knowledge about consumers seems critical due to intense competition. In short, a retailer needs to know about following aspects:

1. Who constitute the retail market?
2. What the retail market needs and wants?
3. Where do consumers reside?
4. How do they place order and pay bills?
5. What services do they want?
6. When, where and how much do they buy?
7. Which are the factors that affect their buying decisions?

Above behaviour is affected by consumers cultural, social, economic, psychological and personal factors, which are more or less similar to factors discussed in chapter 4.

Factors Influencing the Retailer: The extent to which the retailer is capable to meet consumer expectations depends on following retailer-related factors:

i. Type of Merchandise
ii. Range/variety of Merchandise
iii. Ability and Experience
iv. Location
v. Facilities or Resources
vi. Financial Conditions
vii. Relations with Others
viii. Attitude and Behaviour, etc.

Buying Process: Retail shopper needs to study how the consumers make buying decision. In fact, consumer buying process remains identical. Stages of consumer buying process discussed in chapter 4 are equally applicable for retailing, too.

Marketing Research: Marketing research assists in formulating retail strategy. Most retailing decisions are information based. Relevant, adequate, reliable, and timely information can improve retail business performance. Retailer must know every thing – buyers, competitors, environment, recent trend, and so forth. Retail store location, type of merchandise, variety, services, etc., depends on information collected through marketing research. All marketing research issues have been discussed in chapter 9.

RETAIL STRATEGY FORMULATION

A retail strategy can defined as: *The broad, clear, and definite plan that a retailer formulates to tap the retail market effectively and build long-term relationship with the consumers. The strategy guides what a retailer should do to satisfy consumers.*

Carefully prepared retailed strategy helps the firms formulate policies and determine tactics to serve the consumers better than competitors. Basically, the retail strategy involves:

1. Store Location, where to set up retail outlet?
2. Merchandising, what merchandise to sell?
3. Pricing, how much to charge?
4. Marketing, how to promote and sell the merchandise.

Steps in Retail Strategy Formulation: Strategy formulation is similar to any corporate business enterprise. Normally, the process consists of following steps:

1. Define Goal
2. Analyse Business Environment
3. Identify Strategic Options
4. Set Objectives
5. Obtain and Allocates Needed Resources
6. Develop Strategic Plan
7. Implement Strategic Plan
8. Evaluate and Follow up Actions

RETAIL BRAND

Brand is one of the crucial decisions in retailing. It is a promise of seller to deliver specific features, qualities, performance, and services consistently to buyers. Brand decision in retail marketing is much complex due to several ways to brand the product. Some retailers sell merchandise under manufacturer's name, company's own retail outlet finds it convenient to sell under its own brand, sometimes, retailer gives its brand name to product, and some products like groceries are sold without any brand name. Brand creates a distinct image. Retailer can sell popular bands without difficult. Brand creates a distinct image which attracts consumers. Customer can buy established brand anywhere at the same price. For example, if one wants to buy a pair of Levi's jeans, he can buy them from company's retail outlet, from any departmental stores like Shopper's Stop, Lifestyle, Piramyd, or from any retailer at the same price. Retailers selling popular brands can gain good business without much effort.

In case of retailing, a company can enhance brand image or popularity with company's heritage, location of retail outlet, the store environment, the services provided, and the advertising and promotion efforts.

Brand related issues have been described in chapter 5.1.

RETAIL STORE LOCATIONS

Alike modern marketing mix, in retailing, too, the store location is an important 'P' in marketing mix. Store location is a decisive factor that affects consumer buying decisions. Due to crowded market places, frequent traffic jams, parking problems, tight work schedule, concept of fast life, cost of traveling, and many other issues, the retail location has its own unique place in retail business. Actually, retail location is a strategic decision that affects company's effort of offer product more conveniently than competitors. It is irreversible decision; once a store comes into existence, it is fairly difficult to change the location. Location adds value to retailer's offer. Retail store location decision must be taken with due consideration of several significant variables. Retail store location is among most critical decisions.

Important decisions are:

1. In which state to locate the store? It implies selection of region.
2. In which business district to locate the store? It implies selection of district in particular region.
3. In which part of district centre to locate the store? It implies selection particular area of business district.
4. In which area or locality of selected district, city, or town to locate the store? It implies exact location (site) of store in selected areas, for example, central part of city, or in newly developed commercial centre of a particular city.
5. At how many places in the city to locate the store? It implies one or more stores in a selected city or locality.

Factors affecting Store Location: As stated earlier in the chapter, store location is strategic decision and must be taken with care and caution. Decision-maker must carefully analyse relevant factors to arrive at the right choice of location. Among most important factors include:

1. Economic Prosperity of Region
2. Demographic Features of Population
3. Characteristics of Household in the Area
4. Competition and Compatibility
5. Costs of Establishing Retail Store
6. Possibility of Development of Site
7. Laws and Regulations
8. Transportation Facilities
9. Price-sensibility of Consumers
10. Traffic and Costs of Traveling
11. Amenities Available
12. To Buy or to Lease
13. Accessibility to Market or Centre
14. Product Mix to be Offered
15. Total Number of Stores in the Area, etc.

Methods or Theories: There are some methods or theories to evaluate a trading area/store location. Retailers can use any one or more of below listed several methods to evaluate potential store locations.

1. The Harfindahl-Herschman Index
2. The Index of Retail Saturation
3. Reilly's Law of Retail Gravitation

4. Central Place Theory
5. Huff's Model of Trading Area Analysis.

MERCHANDISE MANAGEMENT (RETAIL MERCHANDISING)

Along with the right location, the products to be sold are also very important in retail trade. Merchandise management involves the planning, buying, and selling merchandise. Merchandise is the core of retail. **The American Marketing Association** define merchandising as: "Merchandising is the planning involved in marketing the right merchandise at the right place, at the right time, in the right quantity at the right price."[5] A retailer must decide on the "five rights" such as the right products in the right quantity available at the right place, at the right time, and at the right price. These five rights are instrumental to attract and satisfy his valued consumers. More clearly, merchandise management, as defined by **Swapna Pathan**, is: "The analysis, planning, acquisition, handling, and control of the merchandise investments of a retail operation."[6] Thus, success of retail store depends on ability of retailer to sell the right merchandise to consumers, at the right location, and at the right price.

Key Decision of Retail Merchandise: Retail merchandising or merchandising management covers:

1. Identifying the Right Products for Retailing, (what to sell?)
2. Procuring the Right Products, (from whom and how to buy)?
3. Reaching the End Consumers, (how to sell to consumers?)

RETAIL PRICE

After deciding where to locate the store and what to sell, the next critical decision is at what price to sell the merchandise. Unquestionably, price is an integral part of retail marketing mix. Price is key factor that affects retailer's profits on one hand and consumers' buying decision and satisfaction on the other hand. The right price improves competitive strengths of retailers and it attracts consumers. Concept of retail price is similar to concept of price in marketing. Price is economic value of retail merchandise normally expressed in monetary form. Retail price is inclusive of costs of products, company's image, and facilities offered and convenience to consumers. For detail refer to chapter 6.

ORGANISING OF RETAILING OPERATIONS

Organisation of retailing efforts is the key factor which affects performance of retailer's business. A well-thought organisation facilitates smooth retailing operations. Organisation of retailing consists of assigning duties to people, delegating authority, defining roles and statuses, and establishing relationship among position holders. Retail organisation consists of following levels or posts:

1. Top management
2. Buying and Merchandising authority
3. Store operations (dealing with consumes)
4. Administration and human resource
5. Supporting functions

Main Functions: While designing organisation structure for retail store, a retailer must consider following key functions:

---

[5] Visit: www.ama.org.

[6] Swapna Pathan, p. 68.

1. Buying and merchandise
2. Store operations (consumer services, store administration, management of premises, management of inventory and display, managing relations, managing promotions, handling events, maintaining alliances and relations)
3. Administration and legal functions
4. Human resource activities
5. Finance and accounting,
6. Supporting functions, like advertising and promotion, public relations, etc.

The store manager has a sole role in retail business. He organises and controls efforts of other employees. Note that type of organisation and its structure depends on a large number of factors, like size of retail store, ownership, type of merchandise, top management philosophy, geographical areas of operation, etc.

Human Resource Management in Retail: All fundamentals of HRM are equally applicable to retail stores. Key activities include identifying various roles, deciding on number and types of posts, recruitment and selection, training, compensation and motivation, welfare and human relations, etc. The retail store must be equipped with the right type (right number and right qualification and skills) of human resources.

RETAIL MARKET PROMOTION/COMMUNICATION

Communication is one of basic issues in retail marketing. Communication is a tool to inform, to convince, and to remind consumers. It can also contribute to relation building. Primarily, market communication is used to inform the consumers about retailers, their locations, merchandise they sell, and special benefits and services they offer. Openly availability of customer care phone numbers, excessive use of telemarketing, and positive response of customer care cells have magnified the role of communication in retailing. Most companies offer toll-free numbers to facilitate contact, query, or to registering complaints. Companies are found active and eager to know what their valued customers believe about their offers. Retailer can use various channels or tools for market promotion, such as:

1. Advertising
2. Personal Selling
3. Sales Promotion
4. Publicity and Public Relations
5. Direct Marketing

Retail market promotion task is similar to marketing management. All market promotion issues of marketing management are equally applicable to retailing. For detail refer to chapter 8 to 8.4. Assessing internal and external situation, the right promotion mix should be formulated. As per need, time to time, necessary changes are made to suit the changing situation.

SERVICING RETAIL CONSUMERS

Servicing retail consumers implies providing a suitable treatment to customers. A retailer must do everything to satisfy consumers or serve them better than competitors. Customer service (or servicing customer) may include all functions and activities performed by retailer to satisfy his customers. Normally, a retailer has to offer three types of services, (1) before customers visit the store, (2) during customers' visit to store, and (3) after-sales services (after customers leave the store). Level of services a retailer can offer depends on type of products sold and retail outlet itself. For electrical and electronics products, services are more important. For FMCG and grocery products, a retailer is required to do a little for in-store services. A retailer must deploy properly trained and humble staff to assist customers at every level of dealing.

Rom Zemke and Dick Schaff have suggested five principles of distinctive customer services:

1. Identify key customers and listen and respond them.
2. Define superior service and establish a service strategy.
3. Set standard and measure performance.
4. Select, train, and empower employees to work for the customers.
5. Recognize and reward complements (to employees)

A retailers' customer service must match with customers' expectations. Their expectations depend on their past experience, personal needs, competitive offers, and word-of-mouth communication. There should be a little gap between what customers expect and what a retailer offers. A retailer needs to reduce four types of gaps such as (1) the knowledge gap, (2) the standard gap (in term of time, quality, after-sales services, behaviour, etc), (3) the delivery gap (when they want delivery of goods and when the retailer supplies the same), (4) and communication gap (what it promises and what it does).

In-store Selling Process: Service staff of retail store must be aware of a systematic retail selling process. Normally, the retail selling process (or in-store selling process) consists of following steps:

1. **Acquiring Complete Knowledge of Merchandise,** i.e., a service staff or salesmen must know everything about store's or mall's products.
2. **Identifying and Understanding the Customer Needs,** i.e., understanding customers' needs in term of type of product, quality, size, price, colour, etc.
3. **Approaching Customers,** i.e., to meet the customer as soon as he/she enter the store.
4. **Presenting Merchandise,** i.e., showing, describing, and demonstrating the product.
5. **Overcoming Resistance,** i.e., dealing with customer's queries, objections, and problems.
6. **Suggestive Selling,** i.e., displaying and demonstrating the customer the new and related products.
7. **Closing Sales,** i.e., getting customers consent and finalizing the order.

RETAIL STORE DESIGN AND VISUAL MERCHANDISING

A retailer's task consists of satisfying customers. A retail shopping mall exists to cater customer needs and expectations. Internal design of retail store plays a crucial role for satisfying retail customers. The design should be different, distinct, and attractive to catch the customers' attention. Interestingly, today's shopping is a hobby, a fun, an excitement, and, in all, a sensory experience. A retailer can appeal to the senses of sight, touch (feel), sound, smell, and, even, taste. Clearly, the store design tells a lot to customers what the store is all about. It is a powerful tool to communicate about stores and create the image. Store design is like a store personality that influence viewers and visitors. Retailer must consider both aspects – exterior store design and interior store design.

Exterior Store Design: Exterior design concerns with outside layout or look of the retail store. Important aspects constituting to of external store design may include location of store site, decent and clean store frontage and marquee, inviting entrance, convenient and safe parking facility, health and safety (security) standards, eye-catching window display, glaring lighting, impressive, decorated and multi-coloured building, etc.

Internal Store Design: It involves space planning, i.e., arrangement of merchandise, facilities, and staff at the right places. It shows the inside arrangement of the retail mall. In short, internal store design is function of the aesthetics (including actual size of stores, the colour, textures, etc.), the merchandise sold within and space used for the same, and overall layout of the store.

Interior store design shows layout of various departments, space for preserving customers' belongings, location of products, fixtures (tables, racks, stands, shelves, gondolas, bins, etc. used to display products), atmospherics aspects (lighting, colour, music, and scent, etc., used to influence customers emotional response), flooring and ceiling, lighting, graphics and signals (to guide customers), deployment of staff, location of trolleys, billing and cash counters, drinking waters and urinals, and other facilities. These all aspects must be arranged systematically to give customers a pleasant shopping experience.

RETAIL MIS

MIS – management information system – is a permanent system designed to collect, analyse, interpret, disseminate, and store necessary information. Retail is the final destination of business operations. All those who involve in producing, handling, moving, storing, and selling merchandise need the relevant, reliable, adequate, and timely information to actualize their objectives. Information seems vital for efficient stocking of merchandise, knowing customers needs and wants, market intelligence, and keeping entire operations functioning smoothly. For more detail, refer to chapter 9.

SUPPLY CHAIN MANAGEMENT

Retail is not an end, it is an event. Retailing should not be treated as independent of other business activities. A retailer has to develop direct link with customers on one hand and with suppliers on the other hand to transact effectively. Supply chain indicates a systematic managing of supply side of various commodities. In retailing, it seems a challenging task as a retail shop, a departmental store, or a shopping mall sells fairly a number of products. For example, a departmental store has a number of departments like apparel, gift articles, stationary, cosmetics, kitchenware, appliances, electronics, groceries, and so forth. In every category there are sub categories. For example, in apparel, there may be different section for male, female, and children. Further, there are sub-sections such as casual wear, formal clothes, and accessories. In addition, each sub-section, there are different groups based on price, colour, size, price range, brand, company, etc. This all about only apparel department; assume, how many items will be there if there are ten to fifteen departments. Perhaps, to manage supply of all these items is more difficult than to sell them. Therefore, retailer has to set a system that links company's requirement with different suppliers. JIT – Just in Time, TQM – Total Quality Management, ZI – Zero Inventory, ECR – Efficient Consumer Reponse, VMI – Vendor Managed Inventary, and some other concepts and techniques have become the integral part of today's retailing business. Applying supply chain management can improve overall business system, including retailing.

DEFINITIONS

A supply chain is a network or systematic arrangement of various facilities and distribution options that performs (1) the functions of procurement of raw-materials, (2) transformation of these materials into intermediate and finished products (i.e., production), (3) the distribution of these products to the ultimate consumers, and all those facilities and activities that support these operations. Retailing deals with only one aspect of supply chain system, i.e., distribution. Let's define it.

1. **Ellram and Cooper:** "Supply chain management is an integrated philosophy to manage the total flow of a distribution channel from suppliers to ultimate consumers.
2. **Quinn:** Supply chain involves all those activities associated with moving goods from the raw-materials stage through the end users. This includes sourcing and procurement: production scheduling, order processing, inventory management, transportation, warehousing, and customer service. Importantly, it embodies the information systems so necessary to monitor all those activities."

3. **The APICS Dictionary:** "Supply chain is the process from the initial raw-materials to the ultimate consumptions of the finished product linking across suppler-user companies; and the functions within and outside a company that enable the value chain to make products and provide services to the customers."

Logistics management is a part of supply chain management. Thus supply chain management involve systematic linking or integrating three core business processes such as procuring inputs for production, manufacturing of finished products, and, finally, making arrangement for effectively distributing finished product to ultimate users. Essentially, all these activities need information system.

Supply chain management ensures that the right product reaches the right place at the right time and in the right form. It satisfies both consumes and retailers. Retailer can minimize chances of short-fall and excess of merchandise in his retail store. It helps in continuity, consistency, and low costs. Now, planning, sourcing, scheduling, buying, transporting, storing, selling, etc., are not treated as independent functions, but the integral parts of a supply chain system.

TOP TEN PLAYERS (COMPANIES) IN RETAIL SECTOR[7]

India top ten retail players include:

1. Shoppers' Stop
2. Westside (Trent)
3. Pantaloon (Big Bazaar)
4. Lifestyle
5. RPG Retail (Foodworld, Musicworld)
6. Crossword
7. Wills Lifestyle
8. Globus
9. Piramals (Pyramid & Crosswords)
10. Ebony Retail Holdings Ltd.

PROFILE OF TOP RETAIL PLAYERS IN INDIA

This part gives brief outline of top ten retail companies in India.

1. Shoppers' Stop

K. Raheja group of companies founded Shoppers' Stop on October 27, 1991. The organisation had already made its presence felt in the hospitality and real estate sector, and now it has created a landmark in the Retail sector with Shoppers' Stop. Shoppers' Stop is famous for the expertise and acumen relating to the current practices of the industry. It provides quality services, products and the right kind of shopping environment. It has developed itself as a household name and has set high standards for itself with the mission statement: "Nothing but the best." In 2005, the company had 25 stores with a turnover of Rs. 1000 crore and 7 lakh sq. feet retail space in the year 2005. The average age of the employees in the organisation is 25 years.

Products: Main products offered by the organisation include:

- **Apparel (Clothes):** Men, Women, and Kids
- **Accessories:** Men, Women
- **Home Decor:** Appliances & Adornments, Bed, Bath & Kitchenware, etc.
- **Gift Ideas:** Gift vouchers; Birthday, corporate and wedding, etc.
- **Other services:** Colour studio, CRY bags, Nail studio, Music, Books, etc. etc.

[7] Sources: Internet

Stores: The organisation operates in all part of country. It has its stores in Delhi, Jaipur, Lucknow, Bangalore, Banglore, Chennai, Hyderabad, Mumbai, Pane, Kolkata etc.

Company's corporate office is situated in Mumbai (W). For more detail visit company's official website: www.shoppersstop.com

2. Westside/Trent

Tata Group founded Trent Ltd. (Westside) in 1998. The acquisition of a London-based retail chain Littlewoods by the Tatas was followed by the establishment of Trent Ltd, which was later renamed as Westside. It is one of the largest and fastest growing chains serving the customers in various categories, including men's wear, women's wear, kid's wear, footwear, cosmetics, perfumes and handbags, household accessories, lingerie and gifts. The company offers products with a balance between style and price. There are 25 Westside departmental stores operating in various cities like Mumbai, Hyderabad, Pune, Delhi, Banglore, Noida, Gurgaon, Nagpur, Kolkata and many others.

Trent had established a hypermarket business with Star India Bazaar which provides them products at lower price and better shopping experience. Star India Bazaar offers customers a variety of products in categories, such as staple foods, fruits, vegetables, consumer electronics, health and beauty products and many more at affordable prices.

In the year 2005, Trent acquired 76% stake in Landmark, which is one of the largest books and music retail chains in the country.

Honours: Some of the honours given to the company include:

- Lycra Images Fashion Awards 2005 awarded it with the Most Admired Large Format Retail Chain of the Year.
- 'Brand Leadership Retail' given by India Brand Summit.
- NDTV Profit Business Leadership Awards 2006 in Retail category.
- Aiding the community
- IFA Visionary of the Year Award, 2002, honoured Mrs. Simone N. Tata.
- Balanced Scorecard Hall of Fame.

Westside Stores: Company operates in many leading cities, including Ahmedabad, Banglore, Banglore, Banglore, Chennai, Delhi, Ghaziabad, Gurgaon, Hyderabad, Jaipur Kolkata, Lucknow, Mumbai, Nagpur, Noida, Pune, Surat and Vadodra.

Company's corporate office is situated in Mumbai. For more detail log on: www.mywestside.com

3. Pantaloon Retail (India) Limited

Pantaloon Retail is the flagship enterprise of the Future Group. Pantaloon Retail (India) Limited has spread across various businesses and cities in India. Pantaloon owns multiple retail formats and is able to cater to a large section of the society. The company has over 140 stores across 32 cities in India and 14000 employees. The headquarters of the company are situated at Mumbai. The organisation made an incursion into the modern retail (fashion) in 1997. Big Bazaar, a hypermarket chain, was introduced in the year 2001, with an Indian touch of convenience and hygiene. Food Bazaar, food and grocery chain, and Central Mall located at various Metros are other important parts of the group.

Others include Collection (home improvement products), E-zone (consumer electronics), Depot (books, music, stationery and gifts), Blue Sky (fashion accessories) and Shoe Factory (footwear). The company has also launched a retailing venture known as futurebazaar.com. The vision of Future group is to "Deliver Everything, Everywhere, Every time to Every Indian Consumer in the most profitable manner."

Honours: Some of the awards given to Pantaloon Retail (India) Limited includes:

- National Retail Federation gave Pantaloon the 'International
- Retailer of the Year' Award
- Images Retail Awards 2005
- PRIL – Most admired retailer of the year
- Central – Retail launch of the year
- Mr. Kishore Biyani – Retail Face of the year
- Big Bazaar – Best Value Retail Store
- Readers Digest and Awaaz Consumer Award
- Big Bazaar – Best Retail Destination
- Readers Digest Platinum Trusted Brand Award
- Big Bazaar – Earning a trusted Place in the everyday lives of consumers
- Food Bazaar – Retailer of the year (food and grocery)
- Big Bazaar – Most preferred, large, Food and Grocery store
- Business Today selected PRIL among India's 100 biggest wealth creators; India's top 75 most investor-friendly companies; Top 20 companies in India to watch in 2005

4. Lifestyle International

Lifestyle is an international fashion store of the Landmark Group, a Dubai-based company. Lifestyle created a revolution in the Indian Retail Industry by bringing a truly international shopping experience. It was launched in Chennai, and now it is one of the largest professional retailers spread across 3,25,000 sq. ft. in various cities such as Chennai, Gurgaon, Mumbai, Hyderabad and Bangalore. It is a heaven for shoppers with a vibrant and spicy lifestyle. It provides a wide choice of products at affordable prices with a convenient world-class environment and a friendly layout. Being one of the best shopping destinations, it has won the ''Most Respected Company in the Indian Retail Sector' and the 'Most Admired Large Format Retail Company' awards in India. Lifestyle operates in many leading Indian cities, including Bangalore, Chennai, Gurgaon, Hyderabad, Mumbai, etc.

5. RPG Retail

The history of RPG Enterprises goes back to the 19th century. In 1979 Mr. RP Goenka took the initiative to set up RPG Enterprises. Presently it has a turnover of US$ 1.65 billion (Rs. 7472 crore) and assets worth US$ 1.8 billion. Among the fastest growing groups in India, it is operating successfully through more than 20 companies in 7 business sectors, namely Retail, IT & Communications, Power, Transmission, Entertainment, Life sciences, and Tyre.

The organisation believes in responding to a business opportunity, making optimum utilization of resources, and inspiring people to foster teamwork. Quality is another important parameter for the enterprise to improve continuously and satisfy customers in the best possible manner.

Performance, excellence and entrepreneurship are ingrained in the organisation as core values. It is a place where the employees are aware of the Corporate Social Responsibility, involving in various social activities, sports and arts. The organisation operates through various retail formats such as supermarkets, hypermarkets, music stores and health and beauty products outlet.

Its largest chain of Spencer offers a complete array of products and durables. It is operating through 80 stores spread in 20 cities, and is still growing rapidly. Every month nearly 2.6 million people walk in its stores. The stores are located in Bangalore, Mumbai, Delhi, Chennai, Trivandrum, Hyderabad, Faridabad, Vizag, Aurangabad, Pune, Ghaziabad, Cochin, and many more.

The music store of RPG Enterprises - MusicWorld delivers its products through 170 outlets spread in 21 cities. The enterprise has also set up a training institute for Front Line Staff and Staff

Managers known as RPG Institute of Retail Management (RIRM).Its corporate office is in Mumbai. Visit company's website for more detail: www.rpggroup.com

6. Crossword

Crossword, the largest bookseller in India, came into existence on 15th October 1992. Crossword Bookstores Ltd., is a subsidiary of Shopper's Stop Ltd. It is widely known in various countries for its achievements. It featured in Advertising Age International, USA, as one of the Marketing Superstars for 1994. It has established itself as a lifestyle bookstore, with bright interiors and enough space for movement, suitable for all kinds of people. The simple and intelligent modifications in the store such as electronic POS, proper classification, a dedicated helpdesk, inventory control systems and smart displays have won the hearts of the people visiting the store.

The enterprise strives to give value to the customers and make the visit a pleasant experience by providing a customer centric environment including a proper café, reading tables, and toilets within the store.

The name 'Crossword' came up from the actual crossword puzzles, which provide both fun and a learning experience. The name symbolizes that the seeker would get knowledge, information and pleasure of reading. The gamut of products offered by the store mainly includes books, music, stationary, magazines, toys and CD- ROMs. The products and services like Dial-a-book and Email-a-book have helped customers buy directly from their homes. Other facilities like gift vouchers, friendly 'Return, Exchange & Refunds' policy make shopping a pleasant experience for the customers.

Crossword has 93,000 loyal customers retained through programs with points, discounts, promotional offers and monthly e-newsletters which provide them more 'eWords' to update them about news, new books, events, and best seller lists.

It is a centre for social and cultural gatherings, debates, discussions, and readings on various subjects to enlighten and entertain people. Subjects ranging from war and peace, travel, business and management are generally the topics of discussion.

Accolades (Honours) Received

- Business World has ranked it 6th among the most admired retailers for the year 2006.
- Awarded Reid & Taylor Best Retailer of the year – Leisure & Specialty at the India Retail Summit 2005.
- Crossword was honoured by the Federation of Indian Publishers for excellence in Publishing for the year 2004.

Crossword spreads through forty-three stores across cities like Mumbai, Kolkata, Chennai, Pune, Ghaziabad, Bangalore, Ahmedabad, Vadodara, Gurgaon, and Hyderabad. For detail log on company website: www.crosswordbookstores.com

7. Wills Lifestyle

ITC has made a presence in the Retail sector through its exclusive specialty store - 'Wills Lifestyle'. It has developed itself as a fashion destination offering a range of apparels and accessories. Top designers of the industry design these clothes. The store offers Wills Classic work wear, Wills Sport relaxed wear, fashion accessories and bath & body care products. Wills Lifestyle has also developed John Players as a brand that offers a fine collection of clothes for dynamic and vibrant people. ITC believes in the philosophy of enjoying the changing environment. This season Wills Lifestyle has brought a complete array of products for very aspect and mood of life be it work, relaxation or party. The store offers a truly 'International Shopping Experience' through world-class environment and a robust portfolio of offerings.

Superbrands Council of India awarded the title of Superbrand 2006 to Wills Lifestyle. It is the title partner of the premier fashion event – Wills Lifestyle India Fashion Week. Leading designers such as Rahul Khanna, Manish Malhotra and Monisha Jaising have been promoting the brand. Wills Sport was designated as the 'The Most Admired Brand Launch of the Year' at the Images Fashion Awards 2001. ITC entered the youth fashion market with the brand known as John Players in December 2002. John Players is available across the country in over 125 exclusive stores and over 1500 multi-brand outlets; also declared as 'The Most Admired Shirt Brand of the Year' at the Images Fashion Awards, 2005. ITC Limited Company's corporate office is situated in Gurgaon.

Honours Received

Quality, marketing and product excellence are the areas on which the company emphasises. Lifestyle Retail Business Division has won several Images Fashion Awards; some of them are:

- NID Awards for Design Excellence 2006 for Best Packaging Design in the FMCG Category for John Players.
- 2005: Most Admired Shirt Brand of the Year - John Players
- 2004: Rising Star Brand of the Year – John Players
- 2003: Most Admired Exclusive Brand Retail Chain of the Year – Wills Lifestyle
- 2002: Most Admired Women's Wear Brand of the Year – Wills Sport
- 2001: The Most Admired Brand Launch of the Year – Wills Sport
- The Most Admired Exclusive Brand Retail Chain of the Year – Wills Lifestyle

8. Globus

Globus was launched in 1998 as a part of the Rajan Raheja Group. The company opened its first outlet in Indore followed by two more in Chennai. The flagship store was opened on 1st November 2001 in Mumbai, followed by a vibrant store in New Delhi. Subsequently, its stores were launched in Bangalore, Ghaziabad, Kanpur, Ahmedabad, Noida, Lucknow, Varanasi and Hyderabad.

The organisation has an innovative and adaptive environment. Globus has achieved customer delight by presenting value products and services through continuous improvement. It has a team of dedicated and passionate employees maintained by constant training. Globus has developed long lasting relationships with its business partners. It employs the best practices of the industry through cost analysis. It has brought about a veritable revolution in the retail industry through its constant efforts and innovation in apparels. It has been a benchmark for many upcoming retailers. It has brought about an important change in the industry and has distinguished itself from others. Globus has acquired the best processes and procedures in various fields, such as Marketing & Brand Development, Research & Design, Human Resources, Services, Administering Policies & Procedures and Production & Merchandising.

The group wishes to add 100 fashion stores by the end of 2008. It has blended its resources of technology and people in such a way as to get a competitive advantage over others. Its registered office is located at Santacruz (West), Mumbai. For more detail, visit its website: www.globus.in

9. Piramals

Piramals Enterprises made its foray into the retail industry in 1999. It entered the market with a lifestyle department store called Piramyd Megastore, a shopping mall called Crossroads and a family entertainment center called Jammin. The current annual turnover of the organisation stands at $20 million. The company has over 50 retail outlets across the country, first of them launched in North India. The CEO of the company is Mr. Ajay Piramal. The flagship company of Piramals is Nicholas Piramal. The organisation owns a shopping mall in Mumbai known as Crossroads. The mall is spread over 1,50,000 square feet in four buildings across the city. The stores will also be located in Ludhiana, Delhi, Pune and Ahmedabad.

It is on a land acquisition spree and has bought a number of properties throughout the country. The company has decided to scale up its operations and plunge itself in the retail sector. The company has been signing up contracts with many other organisations to expand its operations.

Piramals is planning to restructure its management into two independent business units. The lifestyle retailing, food, home and personal care would be split into Piramyd Megastore and Tru-Mart with their own business heads. As the company is planning to expand its operations over the next few months, it needs to split business units to exercise better management. The company is expected to own 13 Megastores and 61 TruMarts by 2008. Its corporate office is situated at Mahim (W), Mumbai.

10. Ebony

Ebony launched its store in 1994 at South Extension, New Delhi. Its main goal is to give world-class shopping experience to the Indian consumer. It has successfully opened seven stores across seven cities in India.

Ebony Retail Holdings Ltd has initiated several industry trends, making a distinguished place for itself in the industry. The most prominent and successful Ebony in-house brand are ETC and a special books and music venture called Wordsworth. Ebony has opened its stores in Chandigarh, Noida, Ludhiana, Jalandhar, Amritsar and Faridabad apart from New Delhi.

Almost 8000 people visit its stores everyday and the figures double during the weekends. It is known for its value added benefits, promotions, and discounts throughout the year. It keeps its employees motivated and encouraged through regular promotions and incentives.

The range of products and services offered by the company include well known apparel brands, household items, cosmetics and personal care products, jewellery, fashion accessories, household items, cosmetics, furnishing, crystal wear, books and music, sourced from across the world. Ebony also has a marketing tie-up with Planet M.

The company has formed 'Ebony Elite Club,' which comprises of 55000 Ebony loyalists. The club introduces various promotional schemes, privileges, and discounts through Ebony Gold card issued for the club members.

DS Group is the promoter of Ebony Retail Holdings Ltd., which is a multinational company founded in the 1940s. It is known for its operations in various verticals but in India the group is making its imprints in retailing and infrastructure. It is Delhi-based Company. For detail, visit its website: www. ebonyclick.com

EXERCISES

MULTIPLE CHOICE QUESTIONS (MCQs)

1. Among many factors which fueled to growth of retail industry in India and abroad, which one is not relevant?
   a. Advanced information technology
   b. 24/7 type working pattern
   c. Crazy shopping by youngsters
   d. Poor traditional retailing services
2. In relation to retailing, which is not true?
   a. Sole proprietary retailers and departmental stores cannot survive due to corporate retailing.
   b. Retailing sector enjoys 6% to 7% share in the total employment in India and China.
   c. Only 2% of total retailing business in India is managed by organised sector.
   d. Retail sector contribute around 10% of GDP.
3. Which is not a consistent element of retailing?
   a. Retailing must involve repeated transaction.
   b. Products must be sold to other traders in a huge quantity to for sale.

c. Retailing must involve personal dealing between consumer and retailer.

d. Retailing must be the final stage of distribution.

4. According to Swapna Pathan, (the author in retail marketing), the Emergence of Self-service Stores is
   a. the last stage of retail trade evolution
   b. the second stage of retail trade evolution
   c. the forth stage of retailed trade evolution
   d. the third stage of retail trade evolution
5. In modern retailing activities, which one is not included?
   a. Retail brand
   b. Retail store locations
   c. Maintaining contacts and relations with other retailers and wholesalers.
   d. Retail strategy formulation
6. Which type of retailing mode is known as one-stop shopping?
   a. Specialty stores
   b. Supermarkets
   c. Convenience stores
   d. Hypermarkets
7. Name the retail mode in which Big Bazaar, Star India Bazaar, Giant, Wal-Mart, Target, etc., fall?
   a. Hypermarket
   b. Departmental Stores
   c. Convenience Stores
   d. Specialty Stores
8. Name the retailing mode in which direct selling, mail order, telemarketing, cyber marketing, and automated vending fall.
   a. Non-store Retailing
   b. Service Retailing
   c. Store-based Retailing
   d. None
9. The integrated system/philosophy to mange the total flow of a distribution channel from suppliers to intimate consumers is called
   a. Supply Chain Management
   b. Merchandise Management
   c. Retailed Store Locations
   d. Retailed Store Design and Visual Merchandising
10. Wills Life Style is owned by
    a. The Tata Group
    b. ITC Group
    c. The Future Group
    d. K. Raheja Group
11. Name the corporate retailer who sells only books, magazines, music, stationary, CDs/DVDs, etc.
    a. Crossword
    b. Wills Lifestyle
    c. Westside or Trent
    d. Pantaloon Retail
12. Which business group in India found Westside/Trent in 1998?
    a. ITC Group
    b. Tata Group

c. Future Group
d. Landmark Group

MATCHING TYPE QUESTIONS (MTQs)

13.

	List I		List II
(a)	Contribution of retail sector in employment	(1)	Around 10%
(b)	Contribution of retail sector in GDP	(2)	Around 6 to7%
(c)	Contribution of organized retailing in India	(3)	Around 20%
(d)	Estimated growth of retailing in the next decade	(4)	Around 2%

Codes: (A) (a)-(2), (b)-(1), (c)-(4), (d)-(3)
(B) (a)-(3), (b)-(2), (c)-(1), (d)-(4)
(C) (a)-(4), (b)-(3), (c)-(2), (d)-(1)
(D) (a)-(1), (b)-(4), (c)-(3), (d)-(2)

14.

	List I		List II
(a)	Store-based and non-store-based retailing	(1)	Retail MIS
(b)	Deciding on location or cite retail outlets	(2)	Merchandise decision
(c)	Deciding on product to be sold in retailing	(3)	Retail location decision
(d)	Deciding retail information needs	(4)	Retail mode decision

Codes: (A) (a)-(2), (b)-(1), (c)-(4), (d)-(3)
(B) (a)-(3), (b)-(2), (c)-(1), (d)-(4)
(C) (a)-(4), (b)-(3), (c)-(2), (d)-(1)
(D) (a)-(1), (b)-(4), (c)-(3), (d)-(2)

ANSWERS KEY: 1(d), 2(a), 3(b), 4(c), 5(c), 6(d), 7(a), 8(a), 9(a), 10(b), 11(a), 12(b), 13(A), 14(C)

QUESTIONS FOR DISCUSSION

15. "Retailing is booming in India." Explain the statement with suitable examples and evidences.
16. Define retail trade and enlist its features. Write a note on Indian retail scenario.
17. Enlist major decisions of retail trade. Explain any three decisions.
18. Give a list of ten retail players in India. Write note on any two major retail players.

CHAPTER

13

INTERNATIONAL MARKETING

INTRODUCTION

Availability of the advanced communication and transportation facilities has reduced the physical distance among the nations of the world, and has made the world as a global village. Countries of the world are nearing to participate in the global market opportunities. Customers' needs and wants are not limited to the products produced and marketed within the boundary of country. Today's buyers can access goods or services produced and marketed by the foreign companies. For example, Sony TV, Gucci purses, Coca-Cola, Rayban Glasses, Toyota and Ford vehicles, Arrow shirts, Levy's Jeans, Oxford's books, McDonald's Fast Food, and many other products of foreign companies are easily available anywhere. Similarly, producers' products are not meant for domestic market only. Development of computer network (Internet), e-commerce, e-business, network marketing, rapid means of transportation and other similar advancements have made it possible to access or avail products of any company throughout the world. All components of business have acquired the global status, i.e., global market, global demand, and global supply. Cultural diversities tend to reduce considerably. Customers have become cosmopolitan. Nowadays, to export or import is not as difficult as it was. Instead of restricting, most of nations encourage international trade/marketing. (International, multinational, transnational and global marketing are used interchangeably).

EXPORT MANAGEMENT AND INTERNATIONAL MARKETING

Export management and international marketing are closely related but are different. Export management only involves managing international trade from the host (exporting) country to the guest (importing) country. It is limited to managing of flow of goods or services. While international marketing is comprehensive and integrated term that also covers exporting products. In brief, it can be said that export management is a part of international marketing management. Export management more closely related to selling products in the international market. It is similar to international trade. International marketing deals with identifying needs and wants of international (customers) market, producing products to satisfy those needs and wants, and adopting the most appropriate way to price, promote and distribute for the product to satisfy those needs and wants. Modern marketing doesn't involve only selling or distributing, but also include production, finance, and personnel activities. Further, post-sales activities are also equally crucial. However, management practitioners and experts use both terms loosely and treat, more or less, as the similar. The conceptual controversy has a little relevance to the real practice.

DEFINITIONS

(Most of the writers have defined international marketing similar as export management. Virtually, both are different). Let's examine some definitions.

1. **The American Marketing Association** defines the term: "International marketing is multinational process of planning and executing the conception, pricing, promotion, and distribution of ideas, goods, and services to create exchange that satisfy individual and organisational objectives."

   (Only the word 'international' has been added to the definition adopted by the AMA. The word implies that marketing activities are undertaken in several countries and such activities should somehow be coordinated across nations)
2. We can define the term as: *International marketing means to produce products (goods and services) for the foreign customers and to make necessary arrangement to supply them.*
3. International marketing concerns with marketing products in foreign counties. In this reference, we can define it as: *Marketing activities across the border can be said as international marketing. Marketing activities among the countries of the world can be turned as international marketing.*
4. Finally, it can be said: *International marketing is the marketing for the customers of other countries. It involves designing marketing programme (4P's) to arrive at desired exchange with foreign customers that satisfies their needs and wants.*

FEATURES

We can identify following simple features of international marketing:

1. Marketing activities are undertaken across the borders.
2. It is directed to facilitate exchange between the firm and the customers of foreign countries.
3. It is aimed at satisfying needs of international/global customers.
4. International marketing decisions are taken with reference to the global business environment.
5. It involves two or more nations.
6. Tailor-made marketing mix is necessary for each of the nations.
7. It is more complex and, hence, difficult.
8. Role of international trade agencies seem very critical in marketing products in other countries.
9. It offers attractive opportunities along with challenges and threats.
10. All other characteristics of modern marketing are also applicable to international marketing, etc.

NEED AND IMPORTANCE

In relation to the need or importance of international marketing, views of **Philip Kotler** are worth noted. According to him, two forces essentiated the international marketing are pull forces and push forces. **Push forces** lead to force the nation to sell its goods and services in other nations. The push forces include lower national income, low per capita income, low domestic demand, unfavourable approach of government, high rates of tax and duties, government force to export to earn foreign exchange, tough local market, etc. These forces force the marketer to opt for international market. Another set of forces is pull forces. **The pull forces** pull (attract) businessmen to sell their products in the foreign market to exploits attractive opportunities in the foreign countries. To take benefits of more profitable opportunities, they are pulled to business in other nations. The variable lead to international market may fall either in pull forces or push forces or both. Let's have brief explanation of several benefits available due to international marketing:

1. It ensures survival for a company and a country.
2. Nations can get benefits of division of work and specialization.
3. It also helps in balancing unequal distribution of natural resources.
4. Extending product life cycle by selling products in other nations.
5. It is important for controlling inflation and achieving price moderation.
6. Balancing demand and supply.
7. Promotion of invention and innovation globally.
8. Companies can take benefits of taxes and duties.
9. Technological Transmission among countries of the world is easily possible.
10. International marketing can improve standard of living of people.
11. Growth of international marketing results into social and cultural development.
12. Worldwide peace is possible due to interdependency among countries of the world
13. Global employment opportunities can help ease unemployment problems.
14. Growth of overseas market leads to global prosperity.

FORCES/VARIABLE LEADING TO THE NEED OF INTERNATIONAL MARKETING

The world has become the global market. The opportunities emerging in any nation are not enjoyed by the nation only. Other nations of the world can take benefits of them. Due to global thinking, liberal dealings with others, positive attitudes toward privatization, available of necessary guidelines, facilities, and encouragement have ultimately resulted in growth of international marketing. Main forces led to need of international marketing are:

1. Unequal distribution of natural resources
2. Specialization and need for marketing surplus
3. Craze for global political empowerment
4. Rapid means of communication and transportation
5. Liberalization
6. Globalization or global thinking
7. Trend for privatization
8. Improved understanding and cooperation among nations for mutual benefits
9. Satisfactory functioning of several international organisations or agencies such as International Monetary Fund (IMF), World Bank, United Nations Organisation (UNO), UN Security Council, etc.
10. Growth and Development of Multinational Companies (MNCs)
11. Emergence of global marketing opportunities
12. Technological advancement and transfer of technology

INTERNATIONAL MARKETING ENVIRONMENT

Environment consists of forces. Environment is made of such controllable and uncontrollable forces. It is the environment that determines favourable or unfavourable conditions, and hence, provides either opportunities or threats and challenges. Degree of one's success, to a large extent, depends on effect of marketing environment and ability of the firm to respond effectively. International marketing environment covers all the relevant global forces influencing international marketing decisions. These forces may be internal (such as resource ability and management attitudes), may be domestic (such as government policy toward international business and facilities), and global (such as overall international business environment of relevant part of the world). However, discussion of global forces is more relevant as they are major considerations in international marketing.

DEFINITIONS

We can define the word 'international marketing environment as under:

1. *International marketing environment is a set of controllable (internal) and uncontrollable (external) forces or factors that affect international marketing. International marketing mix is prepared in light of this environment.*
2. *International marketing environment consists of global forces, such as economic, social, cultural, legal, and geographical and ecological forces, that affect international marketing decisions.*
3. *International marketing environment for any marketer consists of internal, domestic, and global marketing forces affecting international marketing mix.*

Figure 1: Three-level International Marketing Environment

FACTORS OF INTERNATIONAL MARKETING ENVIRONMENT

Factors or forces involved in the international marketing environment can be classified into three categories as stated in the figure 1. Manager dealing with international marketing has to design his marketing mix and marketing (mix) strategies in accordance with these forces. He has to keep in mind the present the and expected impacts of such forces while taking international marketing decisions. The environment determines the degree of favourableness for any marketer for international marketing; determines level of opportunities and threats.

1. Global Factors

Such factors are related to the world economy. Broader picture of global phenomenon affects every decisions of international marketing. Main global factors include:

i. Customer-related factors
ii. Political and legal factors
iii. Social factors
iv. Cultural factors
v. Competition
vi. Global relations among nations and degree of the worldwide peace.
vii. Geographic/ecological/climate-related factors
viii. Functioning of international organisations like UNO, World Bank, WTO, etc.
ix. Availability of marketing facilities and functioning of international agencies, etc.

2. Domestic Factors

Domestic factors are related to the economy of the nation. Overall economic, social and cultural, demographic, political and legal, and other domestic aspects constitute domestic environment for international marketing. This environment affects international marketing mix in several ways. Important domestic factors include:

i. Political climate/stability/philosophy
ii. Government approach and attitudes toward international trade
iii. Legal system and business ethics
iv. Availability and quality of infrastructural facilities
v. Availability and quality of raw-materials
vi. Functioning of institutions and availability of facilities
vii. Technological factors
viii. Ecological factors, etc.

3. Internal or Organisational Factors

These are internal and controllable factors. They are related to internal situation of the company dealing with international trade. International marketer needs to use, adjust, and organise these factors to satisfy needs and wants of the (international) target markets. These factors include:

i. Objectives of company
ii. Managerial philosophy of company
iii. Personal factors related to management
iv. Managerial attitudes toward other nations, customers, social welfare, etc.
v. Company's policies and rules
vi. Resource ability of company and marketing mix
vii. Form of organisation and organisational structure.
viii. Nature and types of employees
ix. Internal relations with other departments
x. Company's relations with other stakeholders and service providers.

INTERNATIONAL (GLOBAL) MARKETING DECISIONS

International marketing decisions are same as domestic marketing; only difference is that all marketing decisions are taken with reference to foreign or international markets (or customers).

More clearly, product, price, promotion, and distribution decisions are made for international buyers. Those firms planning to enter the global markets have to decide on following key decisions:

1. **International Markets Decision:** Whether to go for international market?
2. **Market Selection Decision:** To whom of which country to sell?
3. **Market Entry Decision:** How to enter the international market?
4. **Marketing Mix Decision:** Which type of marketing mix should a firm prepare?
5. **Organisation Decision:** What type of organisation should a firm adopt to manage international business?

Let's describe in brief these key decisions.

International Markets Decision

The first few important questions a firm has to answer are: Should a company go for international market? Why should a company prefer to enter global market? Does company capable to transact in international markets? Obviously, answers come from company's current domestic market position and types of opportunities available in the foreign markets. When international markets seem to more attractive and the company is capable to exploit these markets, the company decides to enter the international markets. In short, a company prefers to enter the international market in following situations:

1. When company's has excess production capacity and there exists attractive opportunities outside, and/or
2. When, compared to domestic markets, foreign markets seem more attractive or profitable, and/or
3. When company has enough capabilities to deal with international markets, and/or
4. When domestic governments insist, force, and/or encourage businessmen for international markets.

Market Selection Decision

Once a firm has decided to enter the international market, the next important marketing decision is market selection. As per company's present product mix, production capacity, and proposed expansion strategy, it selects one or more countries to operate in. In the same way, it has to decide on type of foreign buyers to be served. Market segmentation and target market selection are two basic issues in the decision. Initially, a firm targets the most attractive and comparatively easy international markets. Global marketing research can help a company to study international consumer behaviour, segment international market, and select a few most profitable markets. To assess international markets, following criteria may be used:

1. Present market opportunities
2. Future market opportunities
3. Market share
4. Uncertainties and challenges
5. Cost-profit estimates
6. Return on investment

Market Entry Decision

A firm has selected international markets to operate in. Now, the next imperative marketing decision is market entry, i.e., how to enter the market; which of the options to be used for foreign market entry. There are several options to choose an appropriate entry strategy.

1. **Exporting:** Exporting involves selling domestic products in foreign markets. It is easier and common entry option. Exporting consists of producing the products in home country and selling or exporting the same in the international market. There are two options in exporting, the first, company itself exports products in foreign markets, and, the second,

company exports through intermediate agency or agent. Some entry options in exporting, as suggested by Philip Kotler, include:

i. **Export Department:** A company maintains a full-fledged export department to sell its products in foreign markets. The department is responsible for searching export opportunities, promotion and selling products, and performing all activities related to export business.

ii. **Opening Branch in Foreign Market:** Some companies open their branches or shops in foreign markets to serve consumers. The head of the branch is responsible for all activities related to promotion and distribution of the company's products.

iii. **Appointing Traveling Salesmen:** Some companies appoint salesmen to search customers in foreign market and serve them. They collect orders and manage necessary procedures. They can help develop relations with foreign agencies, retailer, and customers.

iv. **Appointing Distributors:** In this entry option, a firm appoints agents, representatives, or middlemen in foreign markets. They are responsible to carry out all activities to promote and sell the company's products.

2. **Direct Foreign Investment:** A company sets up its own factory in other countries. Its carries out all production and marketing activities in foreign land. But, the option depends on a lot of factors such as market stability, costs of production and marketing, competition, government policies, and other factors determining favourableness of situation. Company should select this strategy carefully as there are considerable risk and uncertainties in some countries.

3. **Joint Venture:** The joint venture is jointly owned and managed by host and foreign companies, by two companies of two nations. A foreign company holds necessary equity to get voice in management but not enough to completely dominate the venture. Structure of joint venture depends on government policies and approach of host country. In underdeveloped and developing countries, many multinational corporations are operating as joint ventures. For example, HMT represent joint venture with Swiss Machines and Tools, Proctor and Gamble has joint venture with Godrej, Suzuki of Japan has with Maruti Udyog, etc. At present Indian governments and companies operate with more than 50 countries as joint ventures. When a giant company invests directly in many countries, it is called multinational companies (MNCc). There are several forms of joint venture, such as mixed companies, joint ownership companies, licensed companies, contract manufacturing, management contract, etc.

Marketing Mix Decision

Marketing mix decision involves preparing marketing mix (strategies) for international market. Marketing mix consists of 4P's – product decisions, pricing decisions, promotion decisions, and place or distribution decisions. Marketing mix decisions remain same as domestic market except the target market. Here, all marketing mix decisions are taken with reference to foreign customers and global marketing environment. (For detail on key issues of marketing mix, refer to marketing mix, chapter 1.)

Organisation Decision

Organisation for global marketing is an important decision. In order to implement, direct, and control international marketing efforts, a company must adopt an appropriate organization structure. The organisation is responsible to regulate foreign trade. It is same as domestic marketing organisation; the only difference is that it is prepared to administer international marketing operations and activities. Structure depends on a lot of factors such as type of products, number of countries, type of buyers, etc. Sometimes, it is treated as the department or part of main organisation, for example, foreign trade department. There are different types of organisation structures suit with international marketing such as:

i. Product-wise Organisation
ii. Country-wise Organisation,
iii. Customer-wise Organisation
iv. Place-wise organisation
v. Matrix or Mix Organisation, etc.

All issues related to international marketing organisation are similar to marketing organisation discussed in the last part of chapter 1.

SPECIAL DIFFICULTIES (BARRIERS) OR PRACTICAL PROBLEMS

International marketing is not as easy as domestic marketing. International marketing environment poses a number of uncertainties and problems. As against, national markets, international markets are more dynamics, uncertain, and challenging. Especially, cultural diversities and political realities in several nations create a plenty of barriers that need special attention. In the same way, geographical constraints cannot be totally undermined. Widespread terrorism has created a new threat to international trade. Though the world is advancing in terms of information technology, innovative and superior methods of organising marketing efforts (like horizontal organisation, network organisation, virtual organisation), global efforts for smooth international trades, and so forth, yet international marketing is not that much easy to pursue, it has become a challenge to accept.

1. Tariff Barriers

Tariff barriers indicate taxes and duties imposed on imports. Marketers of guest countries find it difficult to earn adequate profits while selling products in the host countries. Sometimes, to prevent foreign products and/or promote domestic products, strategically tariff policies are formulated that restricts international marketing activities. Frequent change in tariff rates and variable tariff rates for various categories of products create uncertainty for traders to trade internationally. Antidumping duties levied on imports and defensive strategies create difficulty for exporters.

2. Administrative Policies

Bureaucratic rules or administrative procedures – both in guest countries and host countries – make international (export and/or import) marketing harder. Some countries have too lengthy formalities that exporters and importers have to clear. Unjust dealings to get the formalities/matters cleared create many problems to some international players. International marketers have to accustom with legal formalities of several courtiers where they wants to operate.

3. Considerable Diversities

Different countries have their own unique civilization and culture. They pose special problems for international marketers. Global customers exhibit considerable cultural and social diversities in term of needs, preferences, habits, languages, expectations, buying capacities, buying and consumption patterns, and so forth. Social and personal characteristics of customers of different nationalities are real challenges to understand and incorporate. Compared to local and domestic markets, it is more difficult to understand behaviour of customers of other countries. In the same way, as against domestic markets, to design and modify marketing mix over time for international markets seem more difficult. Market segmentation, product design, pricing, and distribution need more information and efforts. Promoting products in international markets is a formidable task.

Message preparation and execution in suitable media in international markets is not easy game to play.

Language and religious diversities are the real challenge for international business players. There are 6000 languages in the world. China (20%) is the largest in term of native speakers, followed by English (6%), and followed by Hindi (5%). Yet English is recognized as global business language. English speaking countries can contribute the largest share (40%) in global business. Religious diversities seem difficult to cope with as they determine needs and wants of people. At present Christianity is the largest in the world (1.7 billion), followed by Islam (1.0 billion), followed by Hinduism (750 millions), and followed by Buddhism (350 millions).

4. Political Instability or Environment

Different political systems (democracy or dictatorship), different economics systems (market economy, command economy, and mixed economy), and political instability are some of real challenges that international markers have to face. Political atmosphere in different courtiers offer opportunities or pose challenges to international marketers. Governments in different nations have their priorities, philosophies, and approaches to the international trades. They may adopt restrictive (protectionist) or liberal approach to international business operations. Especially, political approaches of dominant nations have more influence in international marketing activities. Long-term trend of global political environment is unpredictable and uncertain. Economic policies of different nations (industrial policies, fiscal policies, agricultural policies, export-import policies, etc.,) do have direct impact on international trade. Drastic change in these policies creates endless difficulties to international traders. While dealing with international markets, international political and legal environment needs a special attention.

5. Place Constraints (Diverse Geography)

Trade in foreign countries of far distance itself practically difficult. In case of perishable products, it is a real challenge. Exporting and importing products via sea route and making arrangements for effective selling involves more time as well risks. Segmenting and selecting international markets require the marketers to be more careful.

6. Variations in Exchange Rates

Every nation has its currency that is to be exchanged with currencies of other nations. Currencies are traded every day and rates are subject to change. Indian Rupee, European Dollar, US Dollar, Japanese Yen, etc., are appreciated or discounted at national and international markets against other currencies. In case of extraordinary and unexpected moves (ups and downs) in currency/exchange rates between two courtiers create serious settlement problems.

7. Norms and Ethics Challenges

Ethics refers to moral principles, standards, and norms of conduct governing individual and firm's behaviour. They are deeply reflected in formal laws and regulations. In different parts of the world, different codes of conduct are specified that every international business player has to observe. However, globalization process has emphasized some common ethics worldwide. Corruption is another issue relating to business ethics.

8. Terrorism and Racism

Terrorism is a global issue, a worldwide problem. People of the world are living under constant fear of terrorists attracts anywhere in the world. To trade internationally is not economically risky, but there is the threat to life. Racism also restricts international trade activities.

9. Other Difficulties

Besides these problems, there are many obstacles in international markets, such as:

a. Changing ecological environment and global warming
b. Difference in weathers and natural climates
c. Inappropriate or inadequate role of international agencies supporting and regulating international trades
d. Natural and man-made calamities
e. Difference in currencies, weights, standards, measures, and marketing methods
f. Protectionist approach of some countries
g. Economic crisis across the globe

ROLE/FUNCTIONING OF INTERNATIONAL AGENCIES IN THE INTERNATIONAL MARKETING

There are many agencies situated in India and abroad that have a vital role in facilitating international trade/marketing. Such agencies are expected to remove obstacles or hindrances related to international marketing. Some of important international agencies and organisation have been listed below:

1. The FIEO – The Federation of Indian Export Organisation
2. The WTO – The World Trade Organisation
3. The ADB – The Asian Development Bank
4. The IDA – The International Development Association
5. The IFC – The International Finance Corporation
6. The EXIM Bank – The Export Import Bank
7. The IMF – The International Monetary Fund
8. The World Bank
9. The EU – The European Union
10. The Reserve Bank of India
11. The Export Houses
12. The Asian Dollar Market.

FUNCTIONS OF INTERNATIONAL AGENCIES

Such agencies and organisations perform one or more of following functions:

1. Regulatory functions –regulating and controlling international trade activities
2. Providing technical, administrative, and (loans) financial assistance
3. Consultative function
4. Counseling and Promotional activities
5. Financial functions
6. Processing and transporting
7. Security or protection to traders
8. Regulating exchange rates of foreign currencies and maintaining of exchange stability

EXERCISES

MULTIPLE CHOICE QUESTIONS (MCQs)

1. In relation to international marketing, find out the correct statement.
   a. Due to growth of international marketing, the world has become a global village.
   b. Nowadays, export and import are more difficult compared to the past.
   c. International marketing and export marketing are completely different.
   d. Customers' needs and wants are limited to domestic products only.
2. In context with international marketing, find the odd one.
   a. International marketing activities are undertaken across the boarders.
   b. International marker can serve many counties with the same marketing mix.
   c. International marketing offers attractive opportunities along with challenges and threats.
   d. International marketing involves two or more nations.
3. Lower national income, low per capita income, low domestic demand, high tax rates, tough competition, and unfavourable government approach are called
   a. pull forces b. push forces
   c. pull and push forces d. neither pull nor push forces
4. Which two of followings are pull forces?
   a. Low national and per capita income
   b. High tax and tough competition
   c. High overseas demand and low tax rates
   d. Low local demand and governments' pressure to increase export
5. In which level/class of international environmental factors do company policies, nature and type of employees, managerial attitudes, and resources ability fall?
   a. They are global factors.
   b. They are domestic factors.
   c. They are organisational factors.
   d. They are not the factors of international marketing environment.
6. Which one is not an international marketing decision for a firm planning to enter the international markets?
   a. Market Selection Decision b. Market Entry Decision
   c. Marketing Mix Decision d. Market Exit decision
7. In context with barriers in international marketing, find out inconsistent statement.
   a. Considerable market diversities of international market make the marketing manager's task easy.
   b. Terrorism and racism are global issues that affect international trade.
   c. Diverse geography is a challenge for international marketer to sell product in foreign market.
   d. Business ethics differ from country to country.
8. Name the country having the largest (nearly 20%) native speakers in the world?
   a. India b. China
   c. America d. Russia
9. At global level, which religion has the largest number (nearly 1.7 billion) of followers?
   a. Hinduism b. Islamism
   c. Buddhism d. Christianity
10. Which one of the following set of functions is not performed by international agencies like the WTO, the World Bank, the Export Houses, the EXIM Bank, etc?
    a. Consultative functions b. Entertaining and spiritual functions
    c. Security to traders d. Financial functions

MATCHING TYPE QUESTIONS (MTQs)

11. **List I** / **List II**

List I	List II
(a) The forces lead to sell products in other nations	(1) Pull forces
(b) The forces that attract foreign marketers	(2) Push forces
(c) Trade between two or more countries	(3) Multinational companies
(d) Coca-cola, Samsung, Sony, Oxford, etc.,	(4) International Trade

Codes: (A) (a)-(2), (b)-(1), (c)-(4), (d)-(3)
(B) (a)-(3), (b)-(2), (c)-(1), (d)-(4)
(C) (a)-(4), (b)-(3), (c)-(2), (d)-(1)
(D) (a)-(1), (b)-(4), (c)-(3), (d)-(2)

12. **List I** / **List II**

List I	List II
(a) Company's resource ability and marketing mix	(1) Global Factors
(b) Country's legal system and political philosophy	(2) Domestic Factors
(c) Functioning of international agencies	(3) Internal Factors
(d) Internal, domestic and international factors	(4) Environmental Factors

Codes: (A) (a)-(2), (b)-(1), (c)-(4), (d)-(3)
(B) (a)-(3), (b)-(2), (c)-(1), (d)-(4)
(C) (a)-(4), (b)-(3), (c)-(2), (d)-(1)
(D) (a)-(1), (b)-(4), (c)-(3), (d)-(2)

ANSWERS KEY: 1(a), 2(b), 3(b), 4(c), 5(c), 6(d), 7(a), 8(b), 9(d), 10(b), 11(A), 12(B)

QUESTIONS FOR DISCUSSION

13. Define international marketing. Explain its characteristics and importance.
14. What is international marketing environment? Discuss variables constituting international marketing environment.
15. Write Notes:
    a. Importance of international marketing.
    b. Role of various institutions in international marketing.
16. "International marketing is not as easy as domestic marketing." Discuss the statement with reference to special difficulties related with international marketing practices.

CHAPTER

14

MARKETING CONTROL

- Introduction
- Definitions
- Need or Importance of Marketing Control
- Tools or Types of Marketing Control:
  - Annual Plan Control
  - Profitability Control
  - Efficiency Control
  - Strategic Control

INTRODUCTION

Marketing control is an important task of marketing department. It is indispensable for effective working of marketing department, achieving marketing objectives in time, and continuous development. Controlling mechanism (or system) can prevent mistakes to occur and also help in rectifying mistakes, if any. It ensures that everything is going on as per plan and the organisation is achieving its objectives. Due to marketing control, entire department remains active and alive.

Marketing controls seeks answers of following questions:

- What should happen? It shows expected (ideal) situation.
- What is happening? It shows on-going actual current performance.
- What has happened? It shows the result achieved.
- Why has it happened? It shows the reasons responsible for the results.
- What is required to do? It shows the corrective actions to be initiated.

Marketing control implies application of controlling system (controlling mechanism) to marketing activities. Controlling of any type activities or operations involves the same steps like:

1. Setting standards (setting expected results or objectives)
2. Measuring actual performance/results.
3. Comparing actual results with standards (and detecting causes responsible for the results).
4. Taking corrective actions.

DEFINITIONS

Definitions involve more or less same activities like setting standards, measuring performance, comparing actual performance with standards to detect degree of deviation, and taking corrective actions as per degree of deviation.

1. Marketing control can be defined as: *Marketing control is a process of comparing actual performance of marketing department with standards to find our degree of deviation, and, if necessary, corrective actions are taken.*
2. We can also define the term as: *Marketing control involves verifying and rectifying marketing performance.*
3. Sales volume is the main criterion to evaluate marketing control. In relation to sales, it can be said: *Setting sales standards, measuring sales, finding degree of deviation by comparing estimated sales with actual sales and detecting causing responsible for the deviation, and taking corrective action is called marketing control.*
4. Finally, in systematic way, we can define: *Marketing control calls for verifying or checking of marketing programmes and, if needed, taking suitable measures to endure that the activities are going on as per marketing plans.*

NEED OR IMPORTANCE OF MARKETING CONTROL

Marketing control acts as a preventive as well as corrective device; it prevents errors to occur and, in case, if errors occurred, it can rectify them. Need and importance of marketing control can be explained in relations to the points listed below:

1. To achieve objectives.
2. To make the plan successful.
3. To prevent mistakes to occur.
4. To formulate and modify marketing strategies.
5. To rectify mistakes.
6. To adjust with external environment.
7. To take maximum advantages of company's strengths.
8. To verify policies, rules, objectives, and strategies.
9. To measure and evaluate effectiveness of marketing efforts.
10. To keep employees alert and active, or to apply psychological pressure.
11. To achieve better coordination.
12. To keep the organisation active and engaged.
13. To make managers responsible, regular, and disciplined.
14. To apply new ideas and methods for better performance.
15. To prevent unexpected events to occur, etc.

TOOLS/TYPES/METHODS OF MARKETING CONTROL

On the basis of types of criteria – sales, profits, efficiency, and strategic considerations – used for measuring and comparing results, there are four types or tools of marketing control. In every type of control, the same procedure is applied, i.e., setting standards, measuring actual performance, comparing actual performance with standards, and taking corrective active actions, if required.

Philip Kotler considers four types of marketing control:

1. Annual Plan control
2. Profitability control
3. Efficiency Control
4. Strategic Control

Each type of control, its methods, and related aspects have been adequately discussed in the remaining part of the chapter.

ANNUAL PLAN CONTROL

In this method, annul plans are prepared for various activities. Each plan includes setting objectives (expected results or standards), allocating resources, defining time limit, and formulating rules, policies and procedures. Annual plan control relates to sales. Periodically (mostly annually) the actual results are measured and compared with standards to judge whether annual plans are being (or have been) achieved. Depending on the degree of difference between the planned and the actual results, causes are detected and suitable corrective actions are undertaken. Thus, it contains checking ongoing performance against annual plan and taking corrective action. Figure 1 shows five measures of annual plan control.

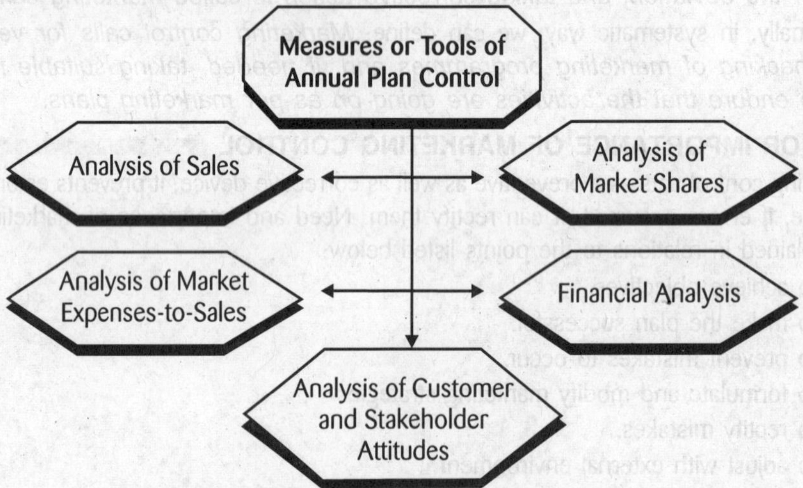

Figure 1: Five Measures of Annual Plan Control

Measures (Evaluation Tools) of Annual Plan Control

Following five measures are used in annual plan control:

1. Analysis of Different Sales

Analysis of different sales contains measuring and evaluating different sales (total sales, territory-wise sales, distribution channel-wise, product-wise sales, customer-wise sales, etc.) with annual sales goals. Targets are set for different types of sales and actual sales of different categories are compared to find out how far company can achieve its sales goals.

2. Analysis of Market Share

Here, market share is used as base for measuring, comparing, and correcting results. *Market share is a proportion of company's sales in the total sales of the industry*. It helps to know how well the company is performing relative to its close competitors. Thus, the performance is assessed against expected market share and competitors' market share. It involves considering three types of market shares:

i. Overall market share
ii. Served market share
iii. Relative market share

3. Analysis of Market Expenses-to-Sales

This type of control checks marketing expenses. It ensues that the firm is not overspending to achieve its annual sales goals. Different marketing expenses are watched in relations to sales.

Normally, company considers five components to calculate expenses-to-sales ratios and compares them with standard ratios to find our how far expenses are under control, such as:

i. Sales force-to-sales ratio
ii. Advertising-to- sales ratio
iii. Sales promotion-to-sales ratio
iv. Marketing research-to-sales ratio
v. Sales administration-to-sales ratio

Marketing managers needs to monitor these expenses in relation to sales. If the expenses fall beyond permissible limits, it should be taken as a serious concern and needed steps are taken to keep them under control.

4. Financial Analysis

Financial control consists of evaluating sales and sales-to-expense ratios in relation to overall financial framework. It means net profits, net sales, assets, and expenses are studied to find out rate return on total assets, and rate of return on net worth.

Financial analysis determines firm's capacity of earnings, profits, or income. Attempts are made to find out factors influencing firm's rate of return on net worth. Here, various ratios are calculated such as profit margin ratio (net profits ÷ net sales), asset turnover ratio (net sales ÷ total assets), and return on assets ratio (net profits ÷ total assets), financial leverage (total assets ÷ net worth) and return on net worth (net profits ÷ net worth). Profit margin can be improved either by cutting expenses and/or increasing sales.

5. Analysis of Customer and Stakeholder Attitudes

The measures of annual plan control discussed in former part are financial and quantitative in nature. Qualitative measures are more critical because they give early warning about what is going to happen on sales as well as profits. Manager can initiate precautionary actions to minimize adverse impacts of forces on the future outcomes. Under this tool, customers' attitudes are tracked to project the way they will react to the company's offers. Alert company prefers to set up a system to monitor attitudes of customers, dealers, and other participants. Base on their attitudes, preference and satisfaction, management can take early actions. This tool is preventive in nature as adverse impact on the future results can be prevented by advanced steps. Market-based preference scorecard analysis is used to measure (score) attitudes of customers and other participants. Such analysis reflects actual company's performance and provides early warnings.

Measuring Customers' Attitudes: Here, a firm tries to measure attitudes of customers by using various methods like, complaints and suggestions, customer panels, customer survey, etc. It provides details about new customers created, existing customers lost, dissatisfied customers, relative product quality, relative service quality, target market awareness, target market preference, and other valuable information.

Measuring Stakeholders' Attitudes: It consists of measuring or recording stakeholders' attitudes. It shows the pattern of stakeholders' preference, attitudes, and overall response toward company and its offers. Stakeholders include suppliers, dealers, employees, stockholders, service providers, etc. They have critical interest and impact on company's performance. Without their cooperation and contribution, a company cannot realize its goals. When one or more of these stakeholders register dissatisfaction, management must take suitable actions. Methods used to track attitudes of customers can also be used for measuring attitudes of stakeholders.

PROFITABILITY CONTROL

In this method, the base of exercising control over marketing activities is the profitability. Certain profitability (and expenses) related standards are set and compared with actual profitability results to find out how far company is achieving profits. Profitability control calls for measuring profitability of various products, channels, territories, customer groups, order size, etc. It provides necessary information to management to determine whether products, channels, or territories should be expanded, reduced, or eliminated.

Process of Marketing-Profitability Analysis

Systematic and logical process is used for analysis of profitability. It involves:

1. Identifying Functional Expenses

It consists of determining expenses to be incurred for the marketing activities like salaries, rents, advertising, selling and distribution, packing and delivery, billing and collection, etc.

2. Assigning Function Expenses to Marketing Entities

Simply, expenses of particular head (for example, salary or advertising) are associated with different entities like products, channels, territories or customers groups.

3. Preparing Profits and Loss statement

A profit and loss statement is prepared for each type of products, channels, territories, etc., to evaluate their relative performance. Based on relative performance in form of profitability, management can decide on products, channels or territories to be expanded, reduced or eliminated. For example, a firm has five products, like A, B, C, D, and E. If profit and loss statement shows that (1) product C is more profitable, and therefore, it must be expanded; (2) product B is poor, and, therefore, it must be reduced; (3) product D is making loss, and therefore, it must be eliminated, and (4) product A and product E are satisfactory, and therefore they must be maintained. In the same way, it can be applied to different territories and segments. Table 1 shows how to prepare profit and loss statement for different products.

4. Taking Action

On the basis of the profit and loss statement, necessary actions can be directed. Actions include one or more of followings:

i. Expanding product(s)
ii. Reducing product(s)
iii. Eliminating product(s)
iv. Reducing any of the expenses
v. Increasing sales, etc.

Table 1: Profit and Loss Statement for Products (in ₹ 00,000):

Particulars	Products					
Total	**A**	**B**	**C**	**D**	**E**	
Sales	—	—	—	—	—	—
Cost of good sold	—	—	—	—	—	—
Gross Profit	—	—		—	—	—
<u>Expenses:</u>		—	—	—	—	—
Selling	—	—	—	—	—	—
Distribution	—	—	—	—	—	—

Advertising	—	—	—	—	—	—
Packing and delivery	—	—	—	—	—	—
Billing and collection	—	—	—	—	—	—
Total costs:	—	—	—	—	—	—
Net profit margin (%)	—	—	—	—	—	—

(**Note:** The same table can be prepared for different channels, segments, and territories also.)

EFFICIENCY CONTROL

This control, particularly, concerns with measuring spending efficiency. While profitability control reveals the relative (in relation to different entities like products, territories, channels, etc.) profits a company is earning, the efficiency control shows the ways to improve efficiency of various marketing entities like sales force, advertising, distribution, sales promotion, and so forth. Sometimes, a post of marketing controller is created to work out a detailed programme to measure and improve efficiency of expense-centered marketing activities. Here also, in order to evaluate efficiency level of different marketing activities, the efficiency standards (of ideal performance) are set and are compared with actual performance. Efficiency control can improve efficiency of marketing department in two ways – one is, improving ability of various marketing activities to contribute more in reaching the goals, and the second is, reducing expenses or wastage.

Types of Efficiency Control

Figure 2 shows major types of efficiency control. Main types of efficiency control involve controlling sales force efficiency, advertising efficiency, sales promotion efficiency, distribution efficiency, and marketing research efficiency.

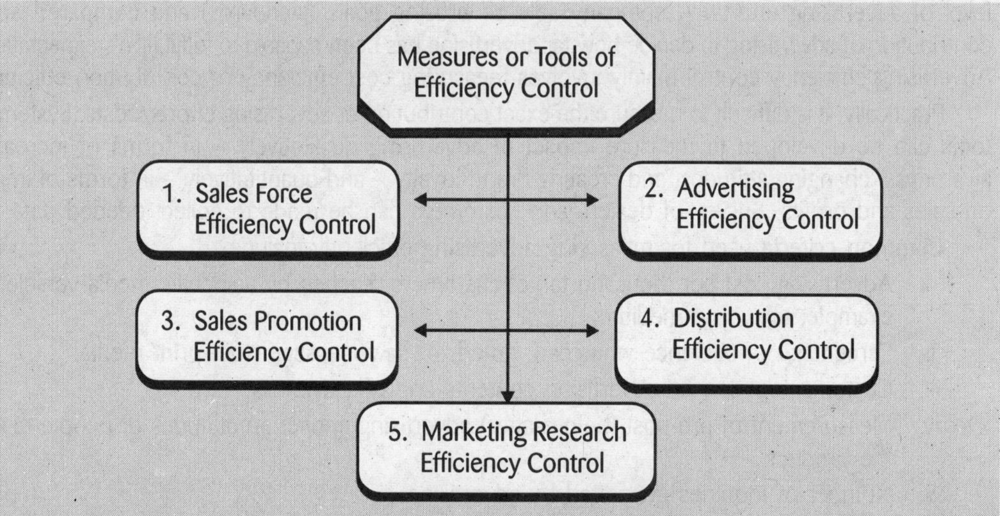

Figure 2: Major Types of Efficiency Control

1. Sales Force Efficiency Control

To measure efficiency of sale force (salesmen), certain key indicators/criteria are developed. A manager has to make a lot of calculations and paperwork.

Common criteria used to measure and evaluate the sales force efficiency include:

i. Average number of sales calls per salesman in a day
ii. Average sales calls time spared per contact
iii. Average revenue generated per call
iv. Average costs incurred per call
v. Entertainment cost per calls
vi. Percentage of orders per specific number of calls, i.e., how many orders have been received from 100 calls made
vii. Number of new customers created during specific period
viii. Number of customers lost in a given period
ix. Contribution of salesmen in total sales, revenue, and profits
x. Sales force costs as percentage of total sales.

Questionnaire, discussion, inspection, observation, salesman's report, etc., methods are used for the purpose. However, most companies use salesman's report. A unique computer-based programme or software can also be developed for speedy and accurate measurement of sales forces efficiency on a regular basis. Simply, actual performance of sales force is compared with these criteria to find out deviation, and, accordingly, necessary actions are taken.

This measurement of sales force efficiency can provide satisfactory answers of following questions:

i. What is role/contribution of sales force in selling efforts?
ii. Who are the most efficient, less efficient, and inefficient sales people?
iii. Which are reasons responsible for poor efficiency of sales force?
iv. What can/should be done to improve efficiency?

2. Advertising Efficiency Control

Advertising is the most expensive among all the promotional tools. Major part of promotion budget is consumed by advertising alone. So, it is extremely necessary to find out efficiency level of advertising efforts. A company sets advertising goals (standards) and compared actual contribution of advertising to decide how far advertising has been capable to fulfill firm's expectations. Advertising efficiency control mainly involves measuring cost efficiency or contribution efficiency.

Practically, it is difficult to measure the exact contribution of advertising efforts/costs. Systematic tools can be developed to measure impact of advertising qualitatively – in forms of increasing awareness, changing attitudes, and creating brand loyalty – and quantitatively – in forms of impact on sales and profits. Survey of dealers and customers can be made to collect needed data.

Common criteria used for measuring advertising efficiently include:

i. Advertising cost per thousand target customers reached by a specific media vehicle, for example, television medium.
ii. Percentage of audience who read, noted, or saw message from print media.
iii. Customer opinion on advertising contents and effectiveness.
iv. Measurement of pre-post (before-after) advertising impact on attitudes of people toward the product.
v. Number of inquiries generated by advertising.
vi. Cost per inquiry.

vii. Media suitability.

viii. Impact of advertising on personal selling, sales promotion, public relations, publicity, and distribution.

ix. Need and performance of advertising agency, etc.

Manager can compared efficiency of advertising programme with internal as well as external standards to judge comparative efficiency. He must find out causes leading to inefficiency. One or more of following actions are initiated:

i. To changes advertising objectives and policies.

ii. To change advertising message.

iii. To change advertising media.

iv. To change media scheduling and frequencies.

v. To change and/or train the staff.

vi. To change advertising agency.

vii. To change advertising budget, etc.

3. Sales Promotion Efficiency Control

This control is exercised by sale manager. Sometimes, sales promotion manager is also appointed to deal with the issue. Sales promotion efficiency measures the impact of sales promotion efforts on sales, profits, competitiveness, and consumer satisfaction. Such efforts include offering a wide range of short-term incentives to stimulate buyer interest and consumer trial. Sales promotion is, no doubt, costly, but it seems essential. Here, manager tries to measure costs and impact of each of sales promotion tools. Normally, sales promotion tools are applied at three levels – customer level, dealer level, and sale force level.

Common criteria used for measuring sales promotion efficiency include:

i. Percentage of total sales promotion expenses to sales.

ii. Costs of display, sample, coupons, and other tools per unit selling price.

iii. Number of inquires generated due to display, demonstration, other such incentives.

iv. Joint and individual impact of various tools on dealer interest, consumer purchase, and competitiveness.

Analysis of costs and contribution of sales promotion tools helps in selecting the most cost-effective sales promotion tools to use. A firm can reduce unnecessary costs and/or can improve contribution of each of the tools of sales promotion. It helps design suitable sales promotion strategies in term of costs, level of sales promotion, timing, and types of techniques at each of the levels.

4. Distribution Efficiency Control

In an average, distribution costs account for 20 to 30 per cent of selling price. By a suitable distribution network, company can improve its profitability on one end and consumer satisfaction on the other end. Therefore, it is necessary to review or assess the entire distribution system periodically. Distribution efficiency control measures how far company's distribution system is efficient to achieve marketing goals.

Common criteria used for the purpose include:

i. Percentage of total distribution costs per unit price.

ii. Percentage of physical distribution (warehousing, inventory, ordering, transportation, communication, insurance, etc.) costs per unit price.

iii. Percentage of channel members' (wholesalers, retailers, agents, etc.) costs per unit price.

iv. Costs and contribution of direct v/s indirect channels.

v. Potentials of using online marketing, network marketing, and by retailing chains.
vi. Assessing costs of marketing channels in relation to services they offer to the company as well consumers.

Distribution efficiency gives valuable information to select the most cost-effective distribution option and sub-options. Company can minimize distribution costs and/or improve profits and competitiveness. In the same way, it can increase consumer satisfaction, too.

5. Marketing Research Efficiency Control

Marketing research is process of gathering, analysing, and interpreting data relating to any marketing problem. Due to dynamic nature of marketing environment, a company needs data on various relevant variables time to time. Marketing research is an expensive option. It is imperative for a firm to know how far marketing research efforts and costs are instrumental in achieving marketing goals. It provides necessary details to improve research policies and practices.

Common criteria used to measure marketing research efficiency include:

i. Annual budget of marketing research department.
ii. Costs of research projects conducted in a year.
iii. Effectiveness of tools and methods used for collecting and analysing data.
iv. Usefulness of findings of marketing research in decision-making.
v. Relative advantages of company's research department v/s professional research firms, etc.

STRATEGIC CONTROL

Strategic control implies a critical review of overall marketing effectiveness in relation to broad and long-term objectives and firm's response to marketing environment. It deals with assessing firm's ability to define and achieve marketing goals, and response pattern to environment. Normally, strategic control verifies company's long-term performance with reference to the close competitors. Here, entire marketing system is reviewed to judge firm's overall strengths and weaknesses. It answers the question: How far is the firm capable to exploit emerging marketing opportunities and face challenges and threats?

Methods or Tools

As shown in Figure 3, four tools are used for strategic control – the marketing effectiveness review, the marketing audit, the marketing excellence review, and the ethical and social responsibility review. Let's discuss each of them.

Figure 3: Tools of Strategic Control

1. The Marketing Effectiveness Review

It involves a review of overall marketing performance. It helps finding effectiveness of several business plans in term of sales growth, market share, and profitability. Attempts are made to detect causes for good-performing marketing department and poor-performing department.

Common criteria: Some criteria are used to review marketing effectiveness. They include:

i. **Company's Customer Philosophy:** It shows company's approach toward customers.
ii. **Integrated Marketing Efforts:** It shows the way company integrates efforts of all divisions and departments for achieving marketing goals.
iii. **Marketing Information:** It studies company's policies and practices to collect, use, and disseminate critical information on a regular basis.
iv. **Company's Strategic Orientation:** It shows company's broad and long-term plans for survival and growth. It also indicates firm's long-term plans for profits, sales, and expansion.
v. **Operational Efficiency:** It shows how efficiently a company managing its current operations.
vi. **Public Relations Practices:** It shows company's policies and practices to establish, maintain, and improve relations with various publics, which have direct interest in the company's operations, and whose cooperation seems critical in achieving marketing goals.

Here, we have considered only six criteria. As per need, more criteria can be developed and used for the purpose.

A special instrument can be developed by using these criteria to measure marketing effectiveness. The instrument (a type of questionnaire or form with questions and certain number of options or intensity in each of the questions) is filled by managers of marketing and various other departments. On the basis of this instrument, controller can calculate score of each managers of each of the departments. Level of scores received by manager or department clearly indicates the effectiveness of particular manager and/or department. Accordingly, each department is awarded class like excellent, very good, good, fair, or poor. Necessary actions can be taken on the basis of performance.

2. The Marketing Audit

Another alternative tool for critical review of overall marketing performance is the marketing audit. *Audit means to examine systematically. It is systematic examination/investigation of all critical aspects of marketing department*. **Philip Kotler** defines: "A marketing audit is a comprehensive, systematic, independent, and periodical examination of a company's marketing environment, objectives, strategies, and activities with a view to determine problem areas and opportunities, and recommending a plan of action to improve the company's marketing performance."

Key characteristics of marketing audit have been discussed below:

i. **Comprehensive:** The marketing audit covers all the major marketing activities of a business unit.
ii. **Systematic:** It is a systematic examination of all marketing operations. It is a well-planned and orderly task. All aspects are audited minutely. It indicates corrective actions to improve firm's marketing performance.
iii. **Independent:** Marketing audit is conducted objectively (bias-free) or neutrally. It includes self-audit, internal, or external audit. However, the external audit is considered as the best one.
iv. **Periodical:** The marketing audit should be conducted regularly to detect problems and avoid crisis.
v. **Purposive:** Its purpose is to find out marketing problem areas and opportunities. It recommends actions to improve company's marketing performance.

Key Issues or Decisions of Marketing Audit

A detailed plan is prepared to conduct marketing audit. The main decisions/issues of marketing audit include:

i. Deciding on marketing audit objectives (why).
ii. Deciding on marketing audit responsibility (who).
iii. Deciding on data to be collected (what).
iv. Deciding on respondents (whom).
v. Deciding on time (when and how long).
vi. Deciding on areas of marketing audit (Where).
vii. Deciding on intensity of examination (How much).
viii. Deciding on methods and tools (how)
ix. Deciding on audit report format
x. Deciding on actions to be taken on the basis of report.

Components of Marketing Audit

The marketing audit examines six major components of company's marketing operations, such as:

a. **Marketing Environment Audit:** It examines impacts of micro and macro factors of marketing environment. Macro marketing environment consists of demographic, economic, environmental (ecological), technological, political and cultural factors. Micro marketing environment includes market segments, customers, competitors, dealers, suppliers, facilitators, and general publics.
b. **Marketing Strategy Audit:** It examines company's business mission, marketing goals and objectives, resources capacity, and marketing strategies.
c. **Marketing Organisation Audit:** It examines suitability of marketing organisation (structures) to implement marketing operations effectively. It includes level, relations, authority-responsibility, communication, facilities, organisation manual, etc.
d. **Marketing System Audit:** It examines major systems like marketing information and research system, marketing planning system, marketing control system, new product development system, etc.
e. **Marketing Productivity Audit:** It examines company's profitability for different products, territories, and channels. It also examines cost-effectiveness for various operations.
f. **Marketing Function Audit:** It examines marketing mix elements such as product, price, promotion (advertising, sales promotion, personal selling-sales force, publicity, and public relations), and distribution.

For each of the components, appropriate auditing questions are designed to examine how effectively the company is performing. All relevant respondents like customers, suppliers, managers, dealers, etc., are interviewed using these questions. Finally, the auditor prepares marketing audit report. The audit report contains individual and joint evaluation of main audit components (marketing areas). It detects strengths and weakness, and recommends actions for improving marketing performance.

3. The Marketing Excellence Review

This is more or less similar to market effectiveness review. But, here, some excellently performing business units are taken as the base for evaluating firm's performance. Here, performance is reviewed relatively. The marketing excellence review is used to judge how excellently the company is performing with reference to high performing business units. A special instrument with adequate number of criteria and appropriate scaling can be developed to judge poor, good or excellent performance.

Criteria used for the purpose include:

a. Market/customer orientation
b. Market segmentation
c. Product quality
d. Quality of services
e. Approach toward competition
f. Integration and alliance
g. Approach toward dealers
h. Dealing with other stakeholders
i. Social responsibility and national services, etc.

Depending on result of the marketing excellent review, necessary actions are taken. Company's actions mainly include undertaking all possible steps to reach the level of excellently performing business units.

4. The Ethical and Social Responsibility Review

This review/verification decides whether firm's marketing policies and practices are ethically and socially true. *Ethics are moral principles, norms, or standards of right or wrong.* Every business unit has social responsibilities toward a number of stakeholders. In same way, marketing practices should be ethical with reference to moral norms, standards, and values. Company's products, policies, and practices should not have adverse impact on customers, other stakeholders, and larger interest of society. Thus, here company tries to assess its ethical and social responsibility. As per need, necessary actions are taken.

Criteria used to review social and ethical responsibility include:

a. Clear definitions of illegal, immoral, and antisocial activities.
b. Company's active efforts to practice, promote, and disseminate moral principles and to hold its employees fully responsible to observe them in practice.
c. Company's direct contribution for social welfare of people.
d. Fulfillment of social responsibility toward various parties.
e. The adherence to all laws and regulations in force.
f. Use of business ethics in areas of product, price, promotion and distribution.

On the basis of ethical and social review, company can evaluate its performance in this regard and, if necessary, appropriate actions are taken.

EXERCISES

MULTIPLE CHOICE QUESTIONS (MCQs)

1. With reference to marketing control, find out odd one.
   a. Marketing control is indispensable for effective working of marketing department.
   b. Marketing control ensures that everything is going as per plan.
   c. Marking control is only corrective mechanism.
   d. Marketing control is preventive as well as corrective mechanism.
2. Which is the last step of Marketing control process?
   a. Measuring actual performance b. Setting standards
   c. Comparing actual results with standards d. Taking corrective actions.

3. Which is not included in Kotler's four types of marketing control?
   a. Annual Plan Control   b. Profitability Control
   c. Environmental Control   d. Strategic Control
4. Sales Analysis, Analysis of Market Share, Analysis of Market Expense-to-sales are tools of
   a. Profitability Control   b. Annual Plan Control
   c. Efficiency Control   d. Strategic Control
5. In relation to Analysis of Customer and Stakeholder Attitude, which is odd one?
   a. It is qualitative measure.
   b. It gives early warning about what is going to happen.
   c. It is purely a quantitative measure.
   d. It is one of the tools of annual plan control.
6. Which is not included in five tools of efficiency control?
   a. Product and Price Efficiency Control   b. Marketing Research Efficiency Control
   c. Advertising Efficiency Control   d. Distribution Efficiency Control
7. The Marketing Excellence Review, the Marketing Effectiveness Review, the Marketing Audit are the tools of
   a. Annual Plan Control   b. Strategic Control
   c. Efficiency Control   d. Profitability Control
8. Which one is used to judge how excellently the company is performing with reference to high performing business units?
   a. The marketing Excellence Review   b. The Marketing Audit
   c. The Marketing Effectiveness Review   d. The Ethical and Social Responsibility Review
9. Which one tool of Efficiency Control does measure efficiency of company's salesmen?
   a. Sales Promotion Efficiency Control   b. Distribution Efficiency Control
   c. Sale Force Efficiency Control   d. None of them
10. Which type control does deal with assessing firm's ability to define and achieve marketing goals and response pattern to environment?
    a. It is Annual Plan Control   b. It is Efficiency Control
    c. It is Strategic Control   d. It is Profitability Control
11. In which major type of marketing control is Marketing Audit included?
    a. Marketing Audit is included in Annual Plan Control
    b. Marketing Audit is included in Strategic Control
    c. Marketing Audit is included in Efficiency Control
    d. Marketing Audit is included in Profitability Control
12. The Ethical and Social Responsibility review is a tool of
    a. Profitability Control   b. Annual Plan Control
    c. Efficiency Control   d. Strategic Control

MATCHING TYPE QUESTIONS (MTQs)

13.

List I	**List II**
(a) What should happen?	(1) Actual ongoing situation
(b) What is happening?	(2) Expected situation
(c) What has happened?	(3) Reasons responsible for results
(d) Why has happened?	(4) The result achieved.

Codes: (A) (a)-(2), (b)-(1), (c)-(4), (d)-(3)   (B) (a)-(3), (b)-(2), (c)-(1), (d)-(4)
(C) (a)-(4), (b)-(3), (c)-(2), (d)-(1)   (D) (a)-(1), (b)-(4), (c)-(3), (d)-(2)

14.

List I	List II
(a) The Marketing Effectiveness Review	(1) Based on internal standards
(b) The Marketing Excellent Review	(2) Based on moral norms/principles
(c) The marketing Audit	(3) Based on systematic examination
(d) The Social Responsibility Review	(4) Based on excellent firms

Codes: (A) (a)-(2), (b)-(1), (c)-(4), (d)-(3) (B) (a)-(3), (b)-(2), (c)-(1), (d)-(4)
(C) (a)-(4), (b)-(3), (c)-(2), (d)-(1) (D) (a)-(1), (b)-(4), (c)-(3), (d)-(2)

ANSWERS KEY: 1(c), 2(d), 3(c), 4(b), 5(c), 6(a), 7(b), 8(a), 9(c), 10(c), 11(b), 12(d), 13(A), 14(D)

QUESTIONS FOR DISCUSSION

15. What is marketing control? How is it useful to marketing managers in achieving marketing goals?
16. Explain various (types) approaches to marketing control.
17. Write notes:
    a. Annual plan control
    b. Efficiency control
18. Discuss:
    a. Profitability control
    b. Ethical and social responsibility review.
19. What is strategic control? Write a brief note on types of strategic control.
20. Write a descriptive note on marketing audit.
21. Explain following:
    a. Sales force efficiently
    b. Advertising efficiency
    c. Marketing research efficiency
    d. Marketing excellence review

CHAPTER

15 ANALYSING COMPETITION

INTRODUCTION

Modern marketing theory and practice are characterized by cut-throat competition. Marketers are virtually attacking each other for market shares. Market place seems an arena or a battle-field. Albert W. Emery, in relation to competition, has stated: "Marketing is merely a civilized form of warfare in which most battles are won with words, ideas, and disciplined thinking." Marketing manager has four powerful weapons at his command to win in the battle, such as product, price, promotion, and place. Marketing strategies are formulated by combining and/or adjusting these four elements of marketing mix. Further, these weapons can be sharpened by continuous research and innovation.

A marketer needs to analyse his competitors to determine his position and role. Based on his position as leader, challenger, follower or nicher, he has to formulate relevant marketing strategy. Marketing strategy, as defined by **John Scully**, is: "Marketing strategy is a series of integrated actions leading to a sustainable competitive advantage."

ANALYSING COMPETITORS

Marketing planning depends on knowing adequately one's competitors. A manager must constantly compare his company's products, prices, promotional activities, and distribution system with those of its competitors to identify areas of competitive advantages and disadvantages. A company with adequate knowledge about its competitors can launch more precise attacks on the competitors as well as prepares a stronger defense against competitors' attacks.

Analysing competitors answer following questions:

1. Who are our competitors? (Identifying competitors).
2. What are their objectives? (Knowing competitors' objectives).
3. What are their strategies? (Analysing competitors' strategies).
4. What are their strengths and weaknesses? (Assessing competitors' strengths and weaknesses).
5. What are their reaction patterns? (Projecting competitors' reaction patterns).

PROCESS OF ANALYSING COMPETITORS

Analysing competitors calls for considering a lot of aspects. A company needs to know everything about its competitors. Note that analysing competitors is not incidental task, a manager must know about his competitors on a continuous basis. So, it must develop a system to facilitate the task on regular basis. A detailed and systematic process of analysing competitors, as described by **Philip Kotler**, consists of eight steps, see Figure 1.

1. Identifying Competitors

Process of analysing competitors begins with knowing who our competitors are. A company can easily identify its competitors. For example, Coca-Cola knows that Pepsi-Cola is its main competitor; Hero Honda knows that Bajaj Auto is its major competitor; Sony knows that Philips and LG are its competitors. Based on product substitutability, there are four levels of competition, (1) Brand competition, in which companies offer similar products and services to same customers at similar prices, (2) Industry competition, in which all companies makes similar products or class of products, (3) Form competition in which, companies. produce such products that offer the same services, and (4) Generic competition, in which companies are competing for the same consumer rupee.

Major Competitors: But, more meaningfully, we can identify two major types of competitors, industry concept of competitors and market concept of competitors.

Industry Concept Competitors: Competitors deal with industrial products. On the basis of production process, number of sellers and degree of differentiation, entry and mobility barriers, exit and shrinkage barriers, cost structure, degree of vertical integration, and degree of globalization, there are different industries in which a number of companies operate.

Market Concept of Competitors: They deal with consumer products. It indicates competitors trying to satisfy the same customers' needs. It includes the companies offering the products that can satisfy particular need of the same segments.

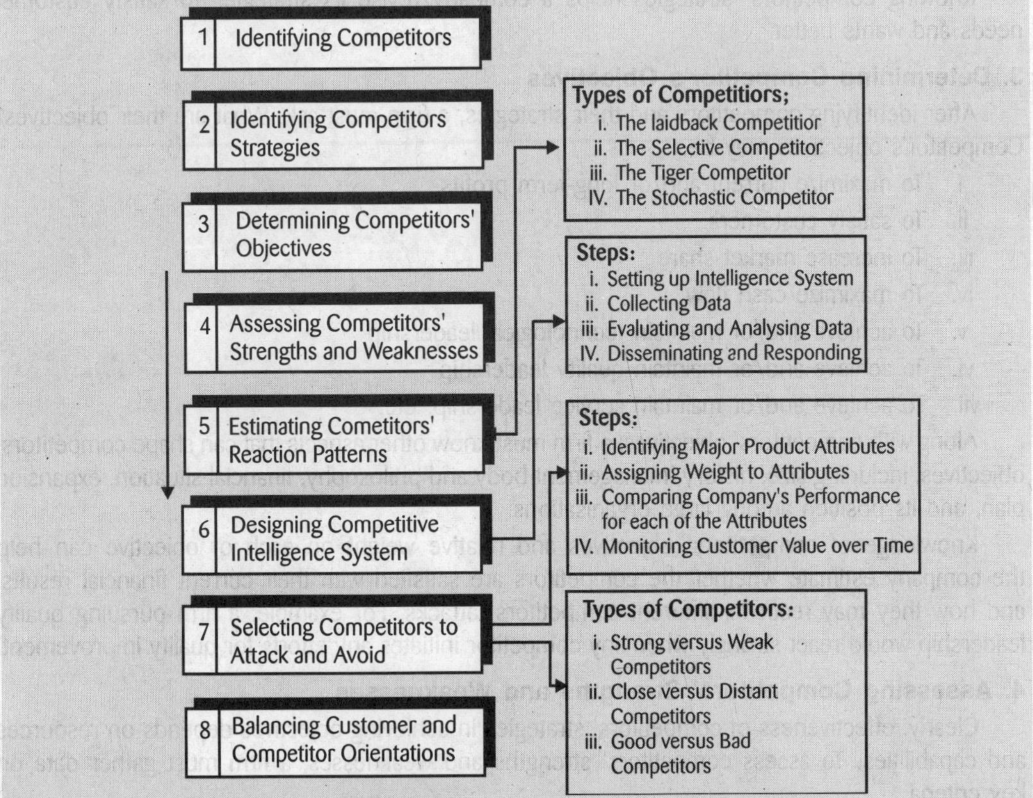

Figure 1: Eight-stepped Process of Analysing Competitors

In fact, meaningfully identification of competitors consists of liking industry analysis with market analysis. It involves (1) studying their areas of operations, (2) identifying the customer needs they are trying to satisfy, (3) finding the territories in which they are selling the products, (4) estimating their market share, and (5) assessing their capabilities, objectives, and strategies.

2. Identifying Competitors' Strategies

After exactly recognizing who are our competitors, the next step is to get insight into competitors' strategies. A firm needs to identify the strategic group – a group of firms that follows the same strategy in a given target market. A company requires a full profile of each of the competitors in terms of following aspects:

i. Competitors' main business
ii. Marketing activities of competitors
iii. Technology and manufacturing methods used by them
iv. Resources capabilities – financial, technological, and human resources
v. Product mix – types, qualities, and features
vi. Customer services
vii. Pricing policies
viii. Distribution network
ix. Sales force strategy
x. Publicity and public relations efforts
xi. Advertising and sales promotion strategies, etc.

Knowing competitors' strategies helps a company revise its strategies to satisfy customer needs and wants better.

3. Determining Competitor's Objectives

After identifying competitors and their strategies, a firm must ask: What are their objectives? Competitor's objectives may be:

i. To maximize current and/or long-term profits
ii. To satisfy customers
iii. To increase market share
iv. To maximize cash flow
v. To achieve and/or maintain technological leadership
vi. To achieve and/or maintain quality leadership
vii. To achieve and/or maintain service leadership, etc.

Along with competitors' objectives, a firm must know other aspects that can shape competitors' objectives, including size, history, management body and philosophy, financial situation, expansion plan, and its position among large organisations.

Knowledge of competitors' objectives and relative weight on each of objective can help the company estimate whether the competitors are satisfied with their current financial results, and how they may react to different competitors' attacks. For example, a firm pursuing quality leadership would react strongly when any competitor initiates any efforts for quality improvement.

4. Assessing Competitors' Strengths and Weaknesses

Clearly, effectiveness of competitors' strategies in achieving objectives depends on resources and capabilities. To assess competitors' strengths and weaknesses, a firm must gather data on key criteria.

Key criteria used to assess competitors' strengths and weaknesses include:

i. Competitors' sales
ii. Customer awareness
iii. Customer loyalty
iv. Market share
v. Product quality
vi. Distribution system
vii. Profit margin and return on investment and cash flow
viii. Sale force efficiency
ix. New investment capacity
x. Future plan
xi. Capacity utilization, etc.

Normally, a firm can learn about competitors' strengths and weaknesses through secondary data, personal experience, and hearsay. It may conduct marketing research with customers, suppliers, dealers, and other relevant respondents to collect primary data related to competitors. Alert and active marketing intelligence system can fulfill company's need for information on competitors.

Knowing adequately the competitors' strengths and weaknesses is necessary to detect the aspects on which they are poor, average, or strong. Mostly, a firm attacks on poor aspects (weaknesses), and avoids strong aspects (strengths).

5. Estimating Competitors' Reaction Patterns

Knowledge of competitors' strategies, objectives, and strengths and weaknesses can help manager anticipate (project) their likely reactions to the company's strategies. Additionally, each competitor has certain philosophy of doing business, specific culture, and guiding beliefs that determine its reaction pattern.

On the basis of reaction patterns, competitors can be classified into four categories:

i. **The Laid-back Competitor:** This competitor doesn't react quickly or strongly to any of the opponents' moves/attacks. There may be a number of reasons why the laid-back competitors don't react immediately, like they may feel that customers are loyal; they may be doing well in business; they are slow in noticing the move; they may lack funds to react; they are over engaged in their own development plan; and they have confidence that rivals any way cannot harm their interest.

ii. **The Selective Competitor:** A competitor that reacts only to certain types of attacks and not to all. For example, it may react to price-cut, but not to increased or improved promotional efforts.

iii. **The Tiger Competitor:** A competitor that react (like a tiger) swiftly and strongly to any attack on its terrain or arena. The tiger competitor wants to signalize the rival firms that it is a tiger and it would be better not to attack because defender (the tiger) will/can fight to finish them.

iv. **The Stochastic (Unpredictable) Competitor:** A competitor that doesn't exhibit a predictable reaction pattern. There may be many reasons why the stochastic competitor doesn't react. For example, it may not like to react on a specific occasion; it may not have favourable economic situations; it may want to prepare for a strong future attack, it may believe that it is better to concentrate on improving its position than to react; and/or it may have confidence that rival's attacks cannot have adverse impact on its performance.

It very critical for a firm to estimate competitors' reaction patterns and should select the future course of action accordingly.

6. Designing Competitive Intelligence System

Information regarding competitors is very critical for designing marketing strategies and improving them over time. Market intelligence is the system or arrangement that provides regular information on competitive dynamics. A firm must carefully design its market (competitive) intelligence system to avail necessary information regarding competitors on regular basis. In fact, customers, dealers, suppliers, and other stakeholders must be given incentives to spot competitive information and pass it on the relevant officials of the firm. Designing competitive intelligence system involves four steps:

i. **Setting up Intelligence System:** A full fledged setup – consisting of needed staff, resources, and facilities – is designed to deal with information need. A qualified, capable, and experienced manager is assigned the duty to manage this department.

ii. **Collecting Data:** Necessary data are collected from relevant respondents, like customers, sale force, suppliers, dealers, market research firms and trade associations. Likewise, data are collecting from rivals' employees and from those who interact with rivals. Online sources can also be used. A company must develop effective and smart ways of collecting data without violating the contemporary legal provisions.

iii. **Evaluating and Analysing Data:** When collected data seem adequate, they are checked for validity and reliability. Then, they are suitably analysed using suitable methods, and properly interpreted and organised underling reasonable assumptions. The information is properly presented in forms of soft copy (in forms of CD) and/or hard copy (in forms of report). If needed, the professional experts are contacted for proper analysis and interpretation.

iv. **Disseminating and Responding:** Important information is circulated to decision-makers. In the same way, managers are responded actively as and when they inquire about competitors. Useful information is stored for the future reference.

7. Selecting Competitors to Attack and Avoid

Now, managers find is easy to design competitive strategies. They can judge to whom they can effectively compete within the market. Sometimes, managers conduct customer value analysis to assess the company's strengths and weaknesses relative to competitors. The basic purpose of such analysis is to determine the benefits the customers in target market want, and how they perceive relative value of competitors' offers. The customer value analysis consists of five steps:

i. **Identifying Major Product Attributes:** This step includes identifying the major attributes (qualities, features, and performance) that the customers value (or want) It is necessary to find out what they expect from product and seller.

ii. **Assigning Weight to Attributes:** It includes assessing quantitative importance of the different attributes. It is necessary to find out relative significance of each of the attributes in terms of ranks or rates.

iii. **Evaluating Company's Performance:** It includes assessing company's performance on the different customer values against their rated importance. It is necessary to find out company's performance on each of the attributes.

iv. **Comparing Company's Performance for each of the Attributes:** It includes examining in what way customers in a specific segment rate the company's performance against a specific major competitor on an attribute-by-attribute basis to find out how far company's performance is better against competitors in terms of each of the attributes in a specific segment.

v. **Monitoring Customer Value over Time:** The last step consists of directing efforts to observe customer values periodically and competitors' state.

Types of Competitors: On the basis of customer value analysis, a company can classify competitors into different categories. It can focus its attack on any one or more of the following different competitors:

(a) **Strong versus Weak Competitors:** Normally, most companies prefer weak competitors to attack and avoid strong competitors as they require fewer resources and time. However, a company preferring to attack weak competitors can achieve a little. So, sometimes, a company selects some weaknesses of the strong competitors.

(b) **Close versus Distant Competitors:** Mostly, companies prefer close competitors to compete. To compete with close competitors is comparatively easy.

(c) **Good versus Bad Competitors:** Obviously, a firm should try to support its good competitors and attack its bad competitors. In order to distinguish good and bad competitors, a number of criteria are used, such as good competitors follow industry rules, make realistic assumptions about growth potential, set reasonable prices in relation to costs, support others to lower costs and improve differentiations, accept general level of their share and profits, take reasonable risks, invest according to their capacity, favour healthy industry competition, create and maintain healthy climate in the industry, etc.

8. Balancing Customer and Competitor Orientations

The last but much conclusive step of competition analysis process is to balance customer-orientation and competitor-orientation. A company must watch every movement of its competitors to grow and/or safeguard its interest. But, it should not be so competitor-centered that it loses its customer focus. It must maintain a balance between customer and competitor orientation.

A competitor-centered company's every move depends on competitions' actions and reactions. Basically, it focuses more on competitors. Its move is based on its competitors' move and not toward its own goals. Such company exists to fight. Outcomes are more uncertain. In contrast, a customer-centered company focuses on customers' needs and wants. Its move depends on customers' (behaviour) actions and reactions. Naturally, the customer-centered company can find better opportunities and can pursue long-term goals. Company should strive to serve its customers in better ways with given resources. While serving customers, it should be alert of competitors' actions and reactions. Finally, in today's marketing environment, a wise firm must monitor both customers and competitors. *A firm should compete to satisfy its customers better or should satisfy customers better by competing.*

MARKETING STRATEGIES FOR COMPETITORS

INTRODUCTION

Philip kotler, the eminent writer, has discussed the military-type marketing strategies for competitors. He adopted many terms from military science to suggest suitable strategic actions against the enemy. His work is based on many research projects and studies carried out in the United States of America. Though the strategies are based on American economic and marketing systems, they are equally applicable to other countries including India. He is the only expert and writer on this topic who provides sufficient insights into the competitive dynamics. The entire portion of the chapter is based on Kotler's views.

COMPETITIVE POSITIONS

Normally, a firm occupies one of six positions in the target market:

1. **Dominant:** The firm has control over other competitors. Naturally, it can enjoy more freedom to select suitable strategic options.

2. **Strong:** The firm doesn't control behaviour of other competitors, but can take independent actions without endangering its long-term position. Other competitors' actions do not have a notable impact on its positon.
3. **Favourable:** The firm is in position to exploit opportunities to improve its position. It has to constantly adjust its strategies to continue enjoying the better-than-average opportunities. It has to remain alert and struggle constantly.
4. **Tenable (Average):** The firm has satisfactory performance, but has to suffer due to dominant and strong competitors. It has less-than-average opportunities to improve its position.
5. **Weak:** The firm has unsatisfactory performance. However, there exists opportunities to improve its position. It must change or adjust constantly to exist.
6. **Nonviable (non-survivable):** The firm has unsatisfactory performance and has no opportunity to improve its performance and position.

Major Types of Competitors: On the basis of market position, market shares, brand image, resources_capacities, and domination power (degree of control over others), there are broadly four types of competitors, such as:

1. Market Leaders
2. Market Challengers
3. Market Followers
4. Market Nichers.

Every company must formulate different strategies to react with different competitors. Let us analyse relevant marketing strategies for different position holders. **Figure 2 shows broad** strategies for different competitors.

MARKETING STRATEGIES FOR MARKET LEADERS

Market leader has the largest market share in the relevant product in the industry. It has a a dominant position in the market. Obviously, it leads other firms in new product development, price change, distribution coverage, promotional activities, and novel experiments. The leader may or may not be respected by other firms, but other firm has to acknowledge its dominance. Other firms can challenge, follow or avoid the market leader. In India, well-known market leaders are Maruti Suzuki in cars, Hero Honda in two-wheelers, Hindustan Unilever in consumer packages goods, Coca-Cola in soft-drink, McDonald's in fast food, Life Insurance Corporation in life-insurance, and so forth.

A few market leaders have monopoly in the market. They have to remain alert all the time leadership to maintain their leader-position. Other firms are constantly challenging leadership position. A little mistake can plunge the leader into second or third position. It has to adopt innovative practices in all the marketing areas. Sometimes, it has to incur excessive costs to maintain the number-one position. Strategic options for market leader have been depicted in Figure 3.

Figure 2: Broad Marketing Strategies for Competitors

STRATEGIES

It is hard task to remain the number one in market. The firm desiring to maintain market-leader position has to adopt one or more of following three major strategies:

1. Expanding Total Market
2. Defending Current Market Share
3. Expanding Market Share

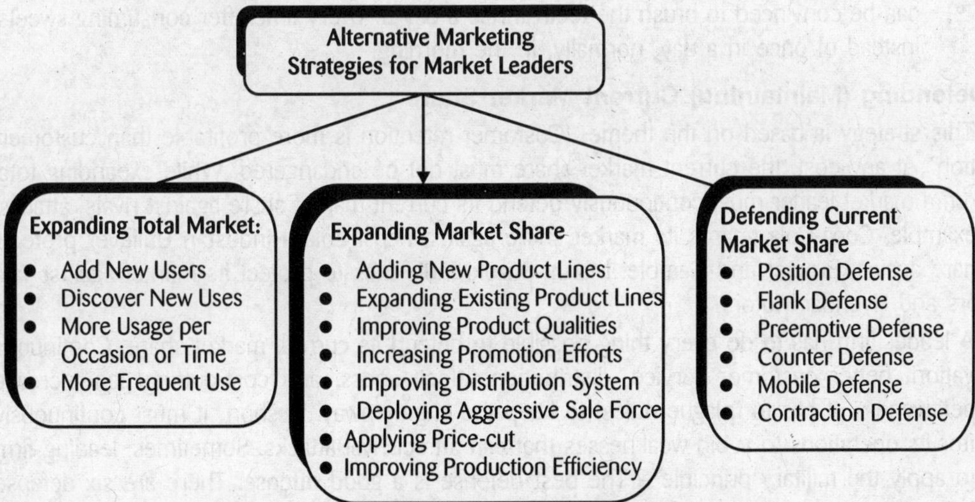

Figure 3: Alternative Strategies for Market Leaders

1. Expanding Total Market

The leader normally gains more when the total market expands. Naturally, when total market or the industry expands, major player will gain more. Total market can be expanded in four different ways:

i. **Add New Users:** The leader firm must try to add new users. Every product class has potential to attract new buyers who are either not aware of the product or are resistant due to high price and lack of desired features. New users can be added in several ways:
   - Convincing non-users to use the product (market penetration strategy).
   - Adding more users in user-class (new market strategy)
   - Winning competitors customers (aggressive strategy).
   - Selling product in other markets (geographical-expansion strategy).

ii. **Discover New Uses:** Another option to expand the total market consists of discovering and promoting new uses of the existing products. The strategy can be applied to industrial products as well as consumer products. A wise firm can get idea regarding new uses of product from customers tactfully. Users are encouraged to suggest the new/innovative uses of the product. In the same way, the company's research and development wing can also contribute in discovering the innovative uses of the product. After discovering new uses, a heavy advertising and publicity must be undertaken to popularize new uses of the product.

iii. **More Usage per Occasion/Time:** The third strategy to expand the market consists of convincing the present users to use more of the product per use occasion. It is more applicable to edible-class products. Similarly, it can be extended to durable products, too. More usage may be in forms of more quantity, numbers, time, amount, intensity, and so on. A firm has a lot of promotional offers at its command to encourage more usage per occasion.

iv. **More Frequent Uses:** Sometimes, a company tries to convince users to use the product more frequently to increase consumption. If a particular product is used once in a day, it can be used twice or thrice in a day. For example, in case gift articles, it is very common to discover different events when gifts can be offered. Likewise, customers can be convinced to brush the teeth thrice a day or every time after consuming sweets, instead of once in a day, normally, in the morning.

2. Defending (Maintaining) Current Market Share

This strategy is based on the theme: 'Customer-retention is more profitable than customer-creation.' At any cost, the current market share must not be endangered. While expanding total market, a market leader must continuously defend its current market share against rivals' attacks. For example, Coca-Cola guards its market share against Pepsi-Cola. Hindustan Unilever protects its share against Procter and Gamble. Maruti Suzuki India tries to protect its market against Tata Motors and Hyundai Motors.

A leader firm has to do every thing possible to defend its current market share. Continuous innovation, better customer service, distribution effectiveness, and cost-cutting can increase competitiveness. It has to 'plague holes' to keep the enemy away. In short, it must continuously monitor its operations to avoid weaknesses that can attract rival attacks. Sometimes, leading firm has to apply the military principle – The best defense is a good offense. There are six defense strategies:

i. **Position Defense:** The most basic defense strategy is to build an impregnable (indestructible, unconquerable, or unbeatable) fortification (protecting fort) around one's territory to keep the opponents away. It involves continuous innovation, diversification, price-cuts, improving distribution, and strengthening promotional efforts.

ii. **Flank Defense:** Here, the purpose is to protect weak sides or fronts. Flank defense consists of erecting/setting outposts to protect weak fronts that are vulnerable to be attacked. Such protection attempts serve as invasion base for counterattack, if needed. Quality improvement, introduction of low-price products, aggressive sales force, etc., can make sense.

iii. **Preemptive or Preventive Defense:** The basic idea of preemptive defense is to launch the attack before the enemy starts attacking. It is like: To attack the enemy earlier to avoid enemy's attack. Playing the psychological games is very common to discourage competitors' maneuver (movement). The company leaks the news by any of the media that it is considering to cut price and/or planning to build another plant. Such news intimidate (threaten) the competitors who decide to cut price or enter the market with the existing or new product.

iv. **Counteroffensive Defense:** Counteroffensive indicates responding enemy's attack with a counterattack. The leader cannot remain passive when competitor's attacks in forms of price-cut, product modification, promotion blitz (bombardment), or any time of invasion on its sales territories. Leader firm has to undertake frontal, i.e., head-on attack in case of rapid erosion of market share.

   When market leader's territory is attacked, an effective counter attack is to invade the enemy's territories so that it has to pull back some of its troops (resources) to defend the territories. Sometimes, leader exercises economical or political clout (influence, blow, or power) to discourage the attackers. Economical clout includes applying further price-cut or may announce product up-gradation to delay customers buying the competitors' products while political clout includes lobbing legislators to take political actions to hamper or slow down the enemy.

v. **Mobile Defense:** Mobile defense – also called shifting defense – is much more than simply protecting the territories. The leader stretches or expands its domain (area) over new territories that can serve as the future centers for offense as well as defense. A leader will deploy its resources in such a way to avoid the future invasion and create an impression in mind of competitors that leader is capable to safeguard its territories. There are two approaches to mobile defense:

   - **Market Broadening:** It involves shifting firm's focus from the current product to forthcoming new technology and concentrating more on research and development activities. However, too much focus on the future at the expense of the present is not advisable. Company must maintain its strengths today to fight in the future. It must go for reasonable broadening
   - **Market Diversification:** Market diversification calls upon moving quickly into unrelated industries to strengthen its position.

vi. **Contraction Defense:** Sometimes, even large companies can no longer defend all territories. The best strategy in this situation is a planned contraction, i.e., strategic withdrawal. Planned contraction doesn't mean market abandonment (fleeing from the market), but rather giving up weaker territories and concentrating on stronger territories.

3. Expanding Market Share

Instead of expanding total market and defending current market shares, sometimes, the market leader prefers to improve profitability by increasing market share. The extent to which the increased market share results into improved profitability depends on a lot of variables. Here, company must do something to snatch the market share from the pockets of competitors. There are several ways to expand market share:

i. **Adding New Product Lines:** In order to expand market share, the market leader can add new and diversified product lines to make the product mix comprehensive and attractive. However, there must be adequate demand for new product lines.
ii. **Expanding Existing Product Lines:** It is a product line extension strategy. It calls upon expanding current product lines by adding new models, varieties or items with attractive features (colours, sizes, shapes, weights, get-ups, etc.) and superior qualities (durability, taste, usefulness, safety, convenience, status, etc.) This strategy can attract more customers. Research and development department must be active to grab emerging market opportunities.
iii. **Improving Product Qualities:** Market share can be increased by improving qualities of current products so that customers expecting better qualities can be attracted.
iv. **Increasing Promotion Efforts:** Heavy advertising, aggressive sales force, effective sales promotion, and attractive publicity efforts can help expanding market share faster relative to competitors.
v. **Improving Distribution System:** Market share can be expanded via better distribution system. Both direct and indirect channels and overall physical distribution system must be modified so that customers can avail the products with the least difficulties. Similarly, effective distribution system can bring down overall selling costs which can further improve profitability.
vi. **Deploying Aggressive Sale Force:** Effective personal selling efforts also have positive impact on sales volume, market share, and profitability as well.
vii. **Applying Price-cut:** To attract price-sensitive customers, leader can practice price-cut strategy. This strategy is profitable only when the per cent of sales-rise is more than per cent of price-cut.
viii. **Improving Production Efficiency:** A leader must improve production efficiency to reduce overall costs. Due to improved production efficiency, a firm can sell better-quality products even at low price.

MARKETING STRATEGIES FOR MARKET CHALLENGERS

Market challengers are known as runner-up firms. They occupy second, third and lower ranks in an industry. Bajaj Auto in two-wheelers, Tata Motors and Hyundai in cars, Reliance Petro and Essar Oils in refineries, Pepsi-Cola in soft-drink, Procter and Gamble in consumer packaged goods, Vodafone in cellular service providers, Sony and Samsung in cell-phone instruments, etc., are some of the market challengers in India.

Market challengers are capable to attack the leader and other competitors. Sometimes, capable challengers can overtake the leader, too. Let us examine three-staged marketing strategies available to market challengers. Figure 4 shows the market challengers' three-stage marketing strategies.

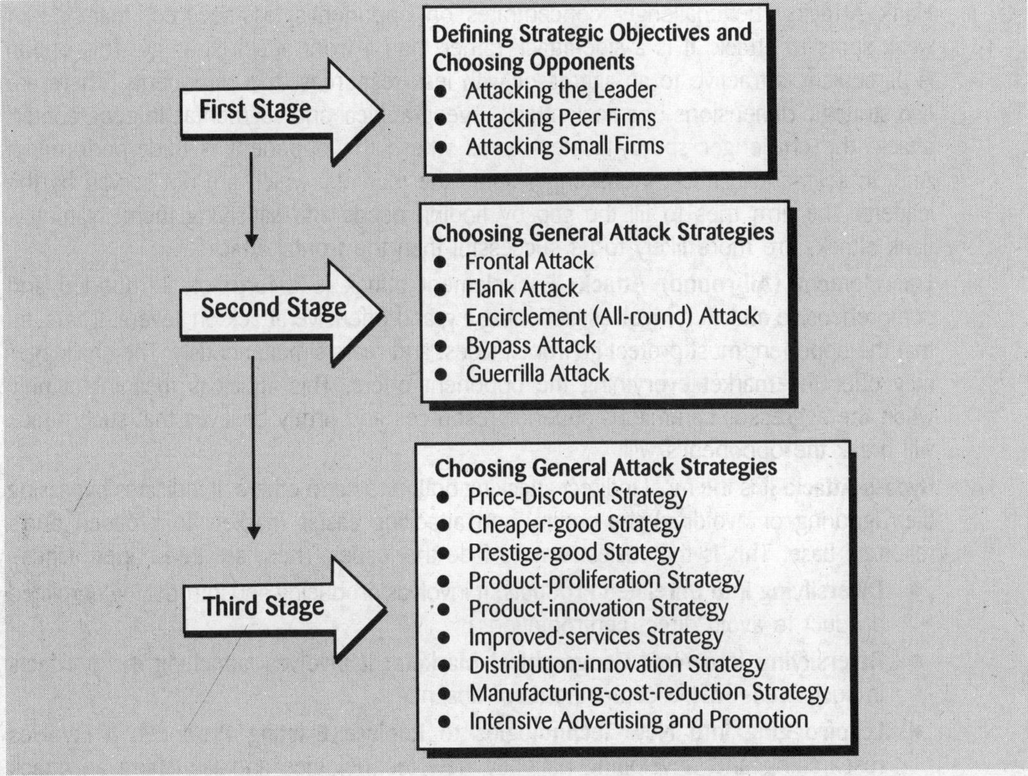

Figure 4: Three-stage Marketing Strategies for Market Challengers

STRATEGIES

The challenger can exercise following strategies:

1. Defining Strategic Objectives and Opponents

First of all, a market challenger firm must define its strategic objectives. Normally, most of market challengers' strategic objective is to increase market share. Then, the challenger has to decide on the opponents to attack. Like market leaders, the challengers can not fight against all opponents. Therefore, a challenger firm has to select the specific opponent to attack. A market challenger can attack any of the following opponents:

i. Attacking the market leader.
ii. Attacking the firms of its own size that are not doing the job well and are underfinanced.
iii. Attacking the small local and regional firms that are not doing the job well and are underfinanced.

2. Choosing General Attack Strategies

Once strategic objectives are defined and opponents are selected, the challenger can apply following attacking options:

i. **Frontal Attack:** A frontal or "head-on" attack is an aggressive attack strategy. A challenger attacks the opponent's strengths rather than its weaknesses. The outcomes depend on who has more strengths and endurance. This option is preferred by the firm with greater resources, otherwise it is proved as a suicide mission. Frontal attack involves attacking opponent's products, advertising and pricing, and lowering production costs with heavy investment, etc. IBM's attack on Microsoft is the best example of frontal attack. This attacking option is widely practices in Banking, insurance, cell-phones, airways, etc.

ii. **Flank Attack:** The challenger concentrates on opponent's less-secured, rear-side or weak spots to attack. It is a side-attack rather than a front attack strategy. This option is particularly attractive to an aggressor with less resources than opponents. There are two strategic dimensions of a flank attack – geographical and segmental. In geographical attack, the challenger spots (locates) areas where the opponent is underperforming. And, in segmental attack, a challenger spots the markets, which are not served by the leaders. The firm tries to fill the gap by finding needs and satisfying them. Naturally, flank attacks are more likely to be successful than the frontal attacks.

iii. **Encirclement (All-round) Attack:** Encirclement attack is a form of all-rounded and comprehensive attack. It involves launching a grand offensive attack on several fronts, so that the opponent must protect its fronts, sides, and rears simultaneously. The challenger may offer the market everything the opponent offers. This attack is meaningful only when the aggressor commands superior resources and firmly believes that such attack will break the opponent's will.

iv. **Bypass Attack:** It is the most indirect attacking option to harm others. It indicates bypassing (i.e., ignoring or avoiding) the enemy and attacking easier markets to broaden one's resource base. This is the easiest way to face the leader. There are three approaches:
- **Diversifying into Unrelated Products:** It involves producing and introducing unrelated product to avoid direct confrontation.
- **Diversifying into New Geographical Markets:** It involves launching the products in such areas where competitors are absent.
- **Leapfrogging into New Technologies to Replace Existing Products:** It involves researching and developing patiently new technologies and launching an attack with superior products.

v. **Guerrilla Attack:** This type of warfare contains making small and intermittent (sudden and irregular) attacks on enemy's different territories. A firm may undertake a few major attacks or continuous minor attacks for longer time. It is more preparation for war than war itself. Ultimately, the guerrilla attack must be backed by a stronger attack to beat the opponent. It is also expensive and requires a good deal of resources. However, it is less expensive compared to other attacks. The purpose of such attack is to confuse, harass and demoralize opponents, and finally make permanent place in the market. Guerrilla attacks include selective price cuts, intense promotional efforts, more attractive service offers, occasional legal actions, etc. Normally, such attacks are practiced by smaller firms against lager firms.

3. Choosing Specific Attack Strategies or Attacking Tools:

The five main attack strategies – frontal attack, flank attack, encirclement attack, bypass attack, and guerrilla attack – are very broad. These strategies consist of many specific attack strategies, some of them have been described as under:

i. **Price-Discount Strategy:** It consists of offering a comparable product at a lower price. Success of price-discount strategy works successfully if (1) the challenger can convince that products and services are comparable to that of leaders, (2) buyers must be price-sensitive and feel comfortable to buy, and (3) market leader must not cut its price in spite of challenger's attack

ii. **Cheaper-good Strategy:** It consists of offering average or low quality products at much lower price. The strategy works successfully only when there are sufficient number buyers who are interested in the low-priced and low-quality products.

iii. **Prestige-good Strategy:** It consists of launching the high quality products and selling them at premium price. This strategy succeeds if specific group of buyers are ready to pay high price for superior quality-prestigious products.

iv. **Product-proliferation Strategy:** It consists of attacking leader by launching a large number of product varieties to give buyers more choice.

v. **Product-innovation Strategy:** It consists of adopting product innovation to attack leaders' position.

vi. **Improved-services Strategy:** It consists of offering the customers new and better services with same products. Such strategy is widely practiced in consumer durables.

vii. **Distribution-innovation Strategy:** It consists of attacking leaders by discovering new ways or channels of distribution. A challenger can apply door-to-door selling, online selling, direct selling, opening stores at convenient places, etc., instead of tradition way of distribution.

viii. **Manufacturing-cost-reduction Strategy:** It consists of reducing manufacturing costs by more efficient purchasing, lower labour costs, modern production equipment, and improved technology. The market challenger can apply lower cost to aggressive pricing.

ix. **Intensive Advertising and Promotion:** It consists attacking the leader by increasing advertising and promotional expenditures. The success of the strategy depends on how far challenger can exhibit superiority over the leader.

MARKETING STRATEGIES FOR MARKET FOLLOWERS

The firms prefer to follow leader rather than to challenge are called the followers. They do not face the leader directly. Some followers are capable to challenge but they prefer to follow. However, market followers always react strongly in case of any loss. In some capital goods industries like steel, cement, chemical, fertilizer, etc., product differentiation is low, service qualities are similar, and price sensitivity is high. They decide to provide similar offers by copying the market leader. But, one must be aware that followership is not always rewarding path to pursue.

Market followers prefer to follow the leader doesn't mean that they don't require specific market strategies. They cannot be simply passive or a carbon copy of leaders. They must know how to hold current customers and win a fair share of new customers. Followers must keep manufacturing cost low and offer better quality products with satisfactory services. At the same time, they must enter new markets as and when there are opportunities. They have following strategic options:

1. **Counterfeiter or Fraudster:** It is a simple way to follow the leader. The follower who wants to be counterfeiter duplicates the leader's product as well as package and sells it in the market through disreputed distributors. Products are marketed secretly to avoid legal complications. The product seems exactly similar to original product except basic quality and features. This is common strategy in auto-parts and electronics products. People, knowingly or unknowingly, buy such duplicate products as they are made available at low price.
2. **Cloner or Emulator:** The cloner clones (emulates) the leader's products, distribution, advertising and other aspects. Here, product and packaging may be identical that of leader, but brand name is slightly different, such as "Colgete" or "Colege" instead of "Colgate" and "Coka-Cola" instead of "Coca-cola." This strategy is widely practiced in computer business also. The cloned products are openly sold in the market due to different brand names.
3. **Imitator:** Some followers prefer to imitate/copy some aspects from the leader, but maintain differentiation in terms of packaging, advertising, sales promotion, distribution, pricing, services, and so forth. Customers can easily distinguish imitated product from original

one. The leader doesn't care for imitator until imitator attack the leader aggressively. Quite obviously, such products are sold at low price.

4. **Adaptor:** Some followers prefer to adapt the leader's products and improve them. They make necessary changes/improvements in the original products and develop little different products. The adapter may choose to sell the products in different markets (country or area) to avoid direct confrontation with the leader. Many Japanese companies have practiced this strategy and developed superior products.

Followers can earn more as they do not bear innovation expenses. In the same way, they can conserve advertising and other promotional expenses. However, to be follower of a leader is not always better option to pursue.

MARKETING STRATEGIES FOR MARKET NICHERS (TINY FIRMS)

A niche is a more narrowly defined small market (limited number of buyers) whose needs are not being well-served by existing sellers. It is a small segment that has distinctive needs and is, mostly, ready to pay high price. Marketers can identify niches by dividing a segment into subsegments or by dividing a group with a distinctive set of traits. They may seek a special combination of benefits. Niches (small groups of buyers) are fairly small and normally attract a few competing firms (nichers). A nicher is the small firm serving only small specific groups of customers called as the niches. *The firm's marketing efforts to serve the niches successfully is called nichemanship.*

Nichers understand their niches' needs so well and minutely that their customers are willing to pay a premium price. They design special products with distinctive features, qualities, uses, and value for special group of limited customers. They have the special skills to serve the niches in a superior fashion and can gain certain economies through specialization. For example, a footwear company can create niches by designing shoes for different sports (like crickets, hokey, athletes, golf, etc.), and exercises (like cycling, running, jogging, waking, etc). In the same way, niches can be created in hotels, cosmetics, cloths, airways, hospitals, and others. Nichers can gain comparatively high returns. They can achieve high margin while large companies can achieve high volume.

Smaller firms normally avoid competing with larger firms by targeting small markets in which large firms have a little or no interest. Companies with low market shares can be highly profitable through effective niching. **Nichers have to perform three main tasks – creating niches, expanding niches, and protecting niches.** They have to remain alert for all the time as they can be invaded any time by the large competitors.

STRATEGIES

Specialization is the basic idea to serve niches. Nichers can apply specialization on various aspects. They can practice one or more of following marketing strategies:

1. **End-user Specialist:** It is very popular and widely used option to serve niches. The firm prefers to operate one-type of end-use customers, for example, a legal advisory firm can handle only criminal cases, or a fashion designer can work only for a few film stars.
2. **Vertical Level Specialist:** The firm can specialize at vertical level of production or distribution, for example, producing only raw-materials for specific companies, only warehousing services, or it may concentrate only on retailing. It can serve only a part of the total process.
3. **Customer Size Specialist:** The firm can sell products only to small, medium, or large size customers. For example, a firm can supply one or two components only to large companies.
4. **Specific Customer Specialist:** A firm supplies its products only to distinct group of buyers. For example, designing special two-wheeler for handicapped people or serving special foods to people who are suffering from certain diseases like diabetes.

5. **Geographic Specialist:** The firm serves customers of only specific region or area of the world, for example, specific need of the people living in the hilly area.
6. **Product or Product Line Specialist:** The firm produces or sells only one product or product line, for example, it sells only socks, ties, or tie pins. A small finance company deals with only car loans or personal loans.
7. **Event Specialist:** The firm concentrates its efforts only on particular events or occasions like marriage, grand inauguration, birthday, anniversary, or some festivals. It offers goods or services for celebrating the events of target buyers.

EXERCISES

MULTIPLE CHOICE QUESTIONS (MCQs)

1. According to Philip Kotler, how many steps does the process of analysing competitors involve?
   a. Six b. Seven
   c. Eight d. Nine
2. The competitor who doesn't react quickly or strongly to any of the opponents' move/attack is called
   a. The laid-back competitor b. The selective competitor
   c. The tiger competitor d. The stochastic competitor
3. How does the tiger competitor react?
   a. This type of competitor doesn't react quickly and strongly to any of the opponents' attack.
   b. This type of competitor only to certain type of attacks.
   c. This type of competitor doesn't exhibit a predictable reaction pattern.
   d. This type of competitor reacts swiftly and strongly to any attack.
4. Name the competitor who doesn't exhibit a predictable reaction pattern.
   a. The laid-back competitor b. The selective competitor
   c. The tiger competitor d. The stochastic competitor
5. Name the competitive position in which the firm has full control over other competitors.
   a. Dominant position b. Strong position
   c. Favorable position d. None
6. On the basis of market position, market share, brand image, resource capacity, and dominance, how many types are the competitors classified?
   a. Four b. Five
   c. Three d. Six
7. "To attack the enemy earlier to avoid enemy's attack." By which name is this defense strategy known?
   a. Flank strategy b. Preemptive strategy
   c. Counteroffensive defense d. Position Defense
8. Market broadening and market diversification are approaches of
   a. Mobile Defense b. Position Defense
   c. Contraction Defense d. Counteroffensive Defense
9. Which one is not a market leader's strategy?
   a. Expanding Total Market b. Defending Current Market Share
   c. Expanding Market Share d. Guerrilla Attack
10. By which name is the strategy that consists of protecting weak sides known as?
    a. Counteroffensive Defense b. Position Defense
    c. Flank Defense d. Contraction Defense
11. The attack strategy that consists of small, sudden, and irregular attack is known as
    a. Encircle Attack b. Guerrilla Attack
    c. Bypass Attack d. Flak Attack

12. Counterfeiter, cloner, imitator, etc., are relevant strategies of
    a. Market Leaders b. Market Followers
    c. Market Challengers d. Market Nichers
13. The small market players who follow specialists strategies like end-use specialists, customer size specialists, geographical specialists, etc., are called
    a. Market Followers b. Market Challengers
    c. Market Nichers d. None
14. Which one is not a strategic option of market followers?
    a. Market Fleeing b. Counterfeiter
    c. Cloner d. Imitator

MATCHING TYPE QUESTIONS (MTQs)

15.

List I	List II
(a) A firm who doesn't react to attack quickly and strongly	(1) Selective competitor
(b) A firm who react to only specific attacks	(2) Laid-back competitor
(c) A firm who react shiftily to any attack	(3) Stochastic competitor
(d) A firm who doesn't have predictable reaction	(4) Tiger competitor.

Codes: (A) (a)-(2), (b)-(1), (c)-(4), (d)-(3) (B) (a)-(3), (b)-(2), (c)-(1), (d)-(4)
(C) (a)-(4), (b)-(3), (c)-(2), (d)-(1) (D) (a)-(1), (b)-(4), (c)-(3), (d)-(2)

16.

List I	List II
(a) A firm has control over other competitors	(1) Dominant position
(b) A firm has better-than-average opportunities	(2) Non-viable position
(c) A firm has less-than-average opportunities	(3) Tenable position
(d) A firm has no opportunity	(4) Favourable position

Codes: (A) (a)-(2), (b)-(1), (c)-(4), (d)-(3) (B) (a)-(3), (b)-(2), (c)-(1), (d)-(4)
(C) (a)-(4), (b)-(3), (c)-(2), (d)-(1) (D) (a)-(1), (b)-(4), (c)-(3), (d)-(2)

17.

List I	List II
(a) A firm has the largest market share	(1) Market Challenger
(b) A firm occupies the second, third position in industry	(2) Market Leader
(c) A firm prefers to follow leader in industry	(3) Market Nisher
(d) A firm concentrate on small attractive segments	(4) Market Follower

Codes: (A) (a)-(2), (b)-(1), (c)-(4), (d)-(3) (B) (a)-(3), (b)-(2), (c)-(1), (d)-(4)
(C) (a)-(4), (b)-(3), (c)-(2), (d)-(1) (D) (a)-(1), (b)-(4), (c)-(3), (d)-(2)

ANSWERS KEY: 1(c), 2(a), 3(d), 4(d), 5(a), 6(a), 7(b), 8(a), 9(d), 10(c), 11(b), 12(b), 13(c), 14(a), 15(A), 16(D), 17(A)

QUESTIONS FOR DISCUSSION

18. What is meant by competition analysis? Explain its process.
19. Explain terms:
    a. Market leaders b. Market challengers
    c. Market followers d. Market nichers
20. Explain strategic options available for market leaders.
21. Discuss marketing strategies for market challengers.
22. What do you mean by market follower? Explain relevant strategies.
23. "Market nichers have also their strategies." Comment. Explain market nichers' strategies.

✧✧✧

CHAPTER

16 CASE STUDY — MARKETING CASES AND ANALYSIS

INTRODUCTION

Case study has been increasingly used in management education and training to prepare efficient junior managers. It has been proved as a powerful technique to enable students and trainees to perceive situations in the right perspective and help them develop decision-making ability. Analysis of cases, as part of training or education, can promote imagination power, initiativeness, analytical ability, and, in all, the balanced decision-making skills. While dealing with cases, students are confronted with real situations, which make them feel that they are facing the real practical problems. Due to its practical value, the case study has become the inevitable/integral part of the management curricula. This chapter deals with fundamental aspects relating to the case study and a few cases for practice.

DEFINITIONS OF THE CASE

In a common parlance, a case is the event or incident related to any field of human activities. Essentially, it describes some events or incidents that any organisation has been facing or has faced/resolved. Events or incidents may be in form of problems, opportunities, mistakes, or management actions. Thus, it is the study of events related to business management that calls managers to act upon.

More clearly we can define the case as: *A case is description of real life situation that mainly contains problems (facts, circumstances, objections, or constraints), people (managers, executives, or those responsible for decision-making), and situation (a set of variables or factors relevant to the problem in hand). It makes its readers and learners feel that they are facing some problems that need to be analyzed and solved through decision-making and actions.*

In other words: *A case is written description of the imaginary or real events/incidents (which had been occurred or have been occurring) concerned with business operations.*

Pfeiffer and Ballew, 1983, defined case in a comprehensive manner. According to them: "A case is a description of an administrative decision or problem that people are trying to solve, or record of an issue that actually has been faced by people involved, e. g., managers, executives, doctors, engineer, accountants, etc., to gather the surrounding circumstances, facts, opinions, or prejudice on which executive decisions depends. It is usually written (prepared) from the point of view of the decision-maker."

DEFINITION OF CASE STUDY

Now, we can define case study as: *A case study is simply the study of a given case (events and incidents). The study involves thinking, analysing, debating/discussing, drawing conclusions, decision-making or putting suggestions.*

We can also define the term as: *Case study is a study of a given case. The study consists of comprehension, discussion, debate, detecting problems, finding solutions, or analyzing the situation.*

More precisely, it can be defined as: *Case study contains application of knowledge, experience, and imagination to analyse the case in relation to the objective. It includes perceiving and understating the events or incidents involved in the case with reference to the prevailing environment, drawing conclusions, and making decisions.*

CHARACTERISTICS OF THE CASE/CASE STUDY

Definitions of case/case study reveals following common points that can be referred as the characteristics:

1. A case is in form of written description/recorded details/audiovisual matter that contains the details about some incidents.
2. A case study is based on certain assumptions, stated explicitly or implicitly.
3. A case may be actual or fractious. It shows historical incidents or, sometimes, current situations.
4. It is a way to learn and not to teach. However, it is used as learning as well as teaching technique.
5. It is used to develop a better decision-making ability.
6. A case study can be discussed in a group. However, an individual can also get insight or understanding by analyzing it.
7. It is one of the powerful techniques to impart managerial knowledge or training.
8. A case can have multiple solutions. Solutions or conclusions depend on who, when, how, and under which situations the case has been discussed.
9. A case study can be conducted in form of discussion in a group or analysis can be presented on individual basis.

ROLE OR SIGNIFICANCE OF CASE STUDY

Case study, in management education and training, has been treated as an important tool/ method to prepare managers of the time. In context with role of training, views of the International **Labour Organisation** are worth noted. It opines: "The case technique is based on the belief that the trainee can attain managerial understanding and competence through the study, contemplation, and discussion of actual situations. The rigorous analysis required, especially in the longer cases, is said to develop habit of logical thinking, and searching for as complete information as possible before reaching conclusions." The case study offers following benefits:

1. Case can be selected, or prepared as per the need. Based on managerial aspects to be taught and discussed, the case can be selected or prepared.

2. It is the teaching method that establishes balance between theoretical and practical knowledge. Students are made to use theoretical base to solve practical problems. It improves practical utility and relevance of theoretical aspects. In short, it makes theoretical knowledge more practice oriented.
3. Students/trainees can be exposed to a live situation. They are made feel that they are dealing with the real situations. It motivates them to behave as the actual decision-maker.
4. Case study is a powerful technique to develop decision-making ability. The case study forces the trainees to widen their thinking. It makes them think divergently to find out the best solutions out of available list of alternatives.
5. Case study generates important managerial qualities, such as initiative skills, creativity, communication ability, and leadership qualities. It can also promote team spirit.
6. It provides enough freedom to make assumptions about the situation. It makes students think in a broad sense. Students of different educational base, backgrounds, and personality characteristics can perceive the case situation differently. So, more interesting and divergent conclusions can be drawn. A case method can integrate multiple disciplines. It broadens students' perspective.
7. As per requirement, it can be used as teaching method or learning technique.
8. It is more flexible aid to impart practical knowledge or to train the trainees in a particular area of study. As pre need, it can be handled with individual as well as with group. Similarly, it can be selected according to ability, caliber, and level of students.
9. Case study is an effective method to improve interpersonal relations. Participants can develop listening skills, can understand and accept feelings of others. It is an aid to impart human qualities.
10. The real life situation can be created in the classroom that makes the learners feel that they are dealing with the real problems. It has a great potential to improve decision-making ability.
11. The case study provides an immediate feedback/response that increases students' interest and encourages active involvement.
12. The most attractive feature of the case study method is that it does not require much equipment or facilities. It can be conducted at any place like open place, classroom, conference hall, or any other place. Thus, it is the most effective with low costs.
13. It is a powerful source of research or findings for teachers. The teacher can accumulate a lot of valuable information related to particular topic.
14. It promotes informal relations between teacher/trainer and students. It makes students and teacher to come closer. It promotes maturity, self-discipline, and self-control among trainees.

LIMITATIONS OF THE CASE STUDY METHOD

Case study method is a powerful option to teach and train students. Particularly, it has become the integral part of management education and training programme. However, it is not a foolproof method. One must be aware of some obvious limitations to use it more purposefully. Important limitations have been listed below:

1. Case preparation and case presentation (handling) require a lot of time and money. It may be more costly compared to other teaching methods.
2. To prepare a case needs a great deal of experience, ability, and expertise. Similarly, handling case with students is also a challenging task. Only highly creative expert trainer can do it successfully. It is difficult to find such trainers.

3. A case study is very dynamic. It must be improved and updated time to time. It needs constant engagement on part of teachers and trainers. They have to remain alert, active and engaged with changing overall scenario.
4. It is not the only tool to impart knowledge. It should be treated as one of the several tools to teach and/or train. Overemphasis on the case study method may have adverse impact on education and training. It must be used as supplementary to other methods (particularly to lecture method).
5. Normally, case study needs certain basic facilities. In absence of facilities, students may take it granted; they may not takes it seriously, it loses its objectivity; it may be turned as time consuming faros or game.
6. Case study needs an active and able involvement of participants. It can be conducted only with a specific group of students having wiliness and ability to participate, self-discipline, self-control and high level of maturity. Such audience is normally difficult.
7. To accept and incorporate the case study as a part of curriculum requires a complete mental change among students, teachers, academicians, and authorities concern. It is hard to change education pattern thoroughly.
8. In absence of proper cases, trained and qualified teachers, and proper climate, there are more chances that the case study may remain just a formality, though it is part of syllabus.
9. Success of case study method, to a large extent, depends on teacher or trainer. His skills, experience, attitudes, knowledge, and personality affect motivation and morale of students. Only availability of better cases, facilities, etc., is not enough.
10. Mostly, case study can be used as teaching device. It is used to apply theoretical knowledge to practical problems. Case study should be used only when students have sound theoretical background. It is more suitable at postgraduate level than at graduate level.

CHARACTERISTICS OF AN IDEAL CASE

Usefulness of the case study method, to a large extent, depends on case itself. A case must be relevant to the objectives or skills to be developed; must be suitable to level/capacity of the students/trainees; must be meaningful to convey some implications; must be appropriate in size; must contain such a matter that needs attention, interest and analysis; and must be interesting to draw attention and arouse interest. Case must be prepared or selected carefully to enjoy the maximum benefits. Following are the some of the basic conditions or qualities of a good case:

1. Objectivity

The case must reflect impersonal needs of organisation. It must be free from personal bias. It should be fit with the objectives of case study.

2. Size

Case must be appropriate in size. The case must not be too lengthy or too short. The lengthy case duplicates matters and leads to confusion. Similarly, the short case cannot provide necessary contents to think and opine. However, the length of the case depends on type of event, and level and caliber of the trainees. At undergraduate level, case must be short.

3. Adequacy

It must be adequate to convey some implications or problems. It should be neither fully complete nor fully incomplete. The complete incident doesn't force the trainees to apply their logic or knowledge. In the same, fully incomplete case fails to provide hints, ideas, or situations that demands application or decision-making and hence fails to attract trainees. It must provide necessary materials to storm the brain.

4. Relevance

The case must be relevant to subject or topic under study. It must be related to subject or skills to be developed.

5. Suitability

The case must be suitable in all the significant aspects like type of trainees, capacity of trainer, facilities under which the case is to be conducted, and time within which it can be successfully completed.

6. Attractive

Attractiveness is an essential condition. It should not be boring. It must reflect needs and objectives of the students. It must contain such a matter, event, or story that tantalizes the trainees to think or suggest.

7. Optional Solutions

The case should be such that provides the students with an ample scope to assume, imagine and view the matter differently. It must contain such a problem or situation that can be dealt with differently.

8. Directive

The case must tell the learner what is expected of them. At the end of case, there must be clear direction what students are required to do. Mostly, three of four direct or indirect short questions are given that students have to attempt by analysing the case. Sometimes, there are asked to discuss and comment on problem or the situation. The case must assign some tasks to students.

9. Structure

Avoid jargons and technical terms. Language should not be classic or flowered. Language should be lucid. Sentences should be correctly structured and should be free from spelling/grammatical mistakes.

GUIDELINE FOR CONDUCTING CASE STUDY

Case study is excessively used in management training and education. But, there is no specific method of conducting the case study. Teachers, trainers, and experts exerted a lot of suggestions to make the case study more effective and purposeful. In absence of any specific model to conduct the case study, teachers and trainers have developed their own styles and methods to use this tool. Here are some important issues related to case study:

1. Seating Arrangement

Normally, 'C' shaped seating arrangement is recommended so that all participants can see each other comfortably. However, it is not compulsory; a case can be discussed in any type of seating arrangement.

2. Facilities Needed

There is no specific list of facilities. A full-fledged conference hall, containing microphone, inbuilt speakers, close circuit cameras, multimedia projector with computer, special multipurpose chairs arranged in desired manner, air conditioners and/or fans, suitable stage, and other needed facilities is desirable. This type of conference/seminar hall helps create a suitable climate for conducting the case study effectively. In case of lack of all standing facilities, an ad hoc arrangement can be done to serve the purpose. Note that facilities are necessary, but not indispensable. Case study method can be used successfully with or without these facilities. Instructor (teacher) and participants must be enthusiastic to practice case study.

3. Number of Participants

Alike other issues, there is no specific number of participants that can be referred as ideal one. Too many and too limited participants restricts discussion. But, case study method can be applied more comfortably with 20 to 30 participants.

4. Time for Discussion

Again, time limit for conducting case is more confused. Time requires for conducting case depends on various factors like size of the case, number of participants, level and background of participants, purpose for conducting case, qualities and qualifications of instructor, participants' interest and awareness, and other relevant issues. Normally, time requires should not be less than an hour.

5. Reading and Preparation Time

Time allowed to prepare note on the case depends, particularly, on size of case, subject matter, level of participants and other aspects. Following options are used:

(a) One full day to study case in detail and prepared the comments, or
(b) 30 minutes to an hour for reading and preparation, or
(c) Five to ten minutes time for preparation, or
(d) Any other time duration that an instructor thinks fit.

How to read the case?

Reading the case requires skills. A specific pattern is suggested to read the case. Normally, participants are advised to read the case thrice as under:

a. **First Time Reading:** Just overview the case within a few minutes to get only primary idea regarding a given case in term of area to which it relates, main problem, authority involved, etc. It is just to explore the case in brief.
b. **Second Time Reading:** Systematic reading with underlining/highlighting important aspects. It takes more time. Time depends on length of case as well as central idea of the given case.
c. **Third Time Reading:** Participants have to read the case in relation to the questions given in the exercise at the end of case, or in relation to task assigned by the instructor.

6. Way of Presentation

Method of presentation varies from person to person. (1) Students/participants can express their views from their own place or from the dais, one by one as per roll number or otherwise. (2) They can use transparencies and overhead projector to present their comment. Sometimes, when they are given enough time for preparation, they can prepare Power Point Slides and present through multimedia projector. (3) Students can discuss any question of his preference or he/she is asked by the instructor to comment on the specific question. (4) Many times, students have to prepare answers of all the questions given at the end of the case in written form and have to present according to their turn.

7. Who can initiates discussion?

Teacher or trainer has many options to initiate discussion, such as:

a. According to (registration/roll) number, or
b. According to present seating arrangement from first to last, or
c. Any student can be asked to begin, or
d. Any student who is willing to initiate, or
e. Group discussion (particularly when questions are not given and case is to be used as a tool to evaluate personality traits. Any participant can initiate discussion.)

8. How to prepare or write answers?

While commenting on the given case or answering the questions given at the end of the case, the student or trainee must follow some simple guidelines, such as:

a. Attempt questions in order – first, second, third...and likewise.
b. Use simple and short sentences which must be free from grammatical errors.
c. While answering, as and when necessary, put reasonable assumption(s) to support your conditional reply.
d. Use your theoretical base to comprehend the situation and apply your knowledge beyond the case contents.
e. Apply your creative idea and be original.
f. As and when possible, use numbers or bullets to separate points and ideas.
g. As and when required, highlight important line or words to be focused.
h. Never pick up any sentence directly from the case description. (However, quotations, figures, statements, etc., can be directly used to support answer.)

STEPS INVOLVED IN CASE STUDY METHOD

Mostly, in practical sense, a systematic procedure of conducting case study involves following steps:

1. Introduction by Instructor or Professor
2. Distribution of Printed Case Materials
3. Allowing Time Limit for Preparation
4. Presentation and Discussion
5. Brief Comment by Instructor
6. Winding up

MODEL CASES

In this part, some cases have been given to teach and train the management students or trainees. The cases have been prepared on the basis of main decision areas like product, price, promotion and places. Most of the cases are prepared for undergraduate students. However, they can be used at postgraduate level, too.

Case 1: (Salesmen's Compensation)

Mr. Manoj, a young and dynamic fresh M.B.A. with Marketing as a specialization, joined the Power Chemical Limited – a leading company manufacturing and selling washing powder and detergent cake of different qualities – as a junior sales officer. A company had a powerful team of 50 junior sales officers, one in each of the districts in several states of the country. The company had a policy to pay Rs. 10000 fixed monthly pay plus 2% commission on the net sales. Company had a tradition to appreciate and reward outstanding performance of salesmen.

Mr. Manoj struggled to reach the sales target of seven lakh rupees in three months. He sacrificed his pleasure time and continued traveling to meet dealers and stockiest. He visited them doubled than his colleagues. Even, he sacrificed his paid vacation for 15 days, available in the six month duration. At the end of three months, he could achieve sales of ten lakh rupees against the target of seven lakh. He was one among the ten most successful junior sales officers. However, his performance was far better than his colleagues. Company appreciated all the ten junior sales officers equally by raising fixed pay by Rs. 2500 monthly along with the prize of Rs. 5000 each and the certificate.

At the end of the next six months, sales manager was highly surprised and shocked to know that Mr. Manoj could hardly achieve the target while many of his colleagues had crossed the previous sales targets. He could not understand why Mr. Manoj's performance was much poor. While discussing with his friends and closely associated colleagues, he came to know that Mr. Manoj had been in search of a new job. He was found less interested in work. Further, he was on leave for 20 days over and above 15 days paid vacation.

Exercise

1. Which area of marketing the case is related with?
2. How will you evaluate the motivation policy of the company?
3. According to you, what is the main cause of his poor performance?
4. What a company was needed to do to sustain his excellent performance?
5. How would you evaluate Mr. Manoj's reaction pattern to company's policies? According to you, which are other ways to express his feeling?

Case 2: (Role of Salesmanship)

Marvelous Electronics Private Limited, manufacturing home appliances, was using excessive personal selling to offer the best after-sales services. Company had a trained and satisfied team of forty salesmen. Company was offering attractive pay, commission, and fringe benefits to satisfy salesmen. Commission and bonus were linked with number of calls, complaints attended, suggestions collected, and new customers generated. Personal selling costs accounted for 20% of sales. Company has been earning reasonable profits and fairly enjoying its position in the market. Mr. M. Sadhu, the marketing manager, was responsible for managing sales and distribution activities. Company management had full trust and confidence in Mr. M. Sadhu's marketing policy. Due to health problem, Mr. M. Sadhu, the most experienced marketing manager, who had been with the company since last two decades, decided to retire.

Mr. J. B. Sant was appointed as a marketing manager in the place of Mr. Sadhu. Within a week, Mr. Sant decided to cut sale force to reduce costs. According to him, poor profits were result of excessive selling costs. Suddenly, in spite of a strong oppose by the sale officers, he decided to reduce 50% personal selling staff. He believed that middlemen could do the better at low costs. In certain cities, he gave dealership and withdrew sales force.

Within a month, sales started to decline. Particularly, from the territories where sale force was withdrawn showed extremely poor sales. Dealers defended their poor performance by describing the actions they had taken to sell the products. According to dealers, sales declined due to competition. Mr. Sant didn't satisfy with the dealers' arguments. He ordered for a brief survey to investigate the main reasons.

Within a month, he got survey report. He came to know that most of dealers failed to meet customer expectations. He realized his mistake. He called officials of marketing department to review sales and distribution policy.

Exercise

1. What was the secret of success of Marvelous Company?
2. What made Mr. J. B. Sant to reduce sales force?
3. How do you evaluate Mr. Sant's new distribution/sales strategy?
4. Enlist possible reasons for declining the sales.
5. What is your expert advice to Mr. Sant to improve marketing performance?

Case 3: (Sales Promotion)

Mr. Shyamsundar was a successful marketing manager. Ever since he took charge as the marketing manager in Hindustan Food Limited, situated in GIDC Zone II, Rajkot, he continued following cost-plus pricing method to set price for chocolates, biscuits, breads, and other bakery items. He allowed liberally trade discounts, cash discounts, and other special concessions on the selling price. He practiced discriminative pricing policy to satisfy different groups of buyers. Additionally, he offered various other sales promotional incentives during Diwali, Janamastami, and other Hindu Festivals. He tried all the possible tactics to attract/satisfy customers. Continuously for ten years, the company had achieved nearly 25% growth in net profits. Mr. Satyajit, the GM of the company, was quite satisfied with the stable and gradual progress in the severe competitive environment. Looking to the stable and satisfactory performance of Mr. Shyamsundar, the GM had granted him all the powers to decide independently on price and pricing related issues. Everything went on as per the expectation.

On 25th December 2002, Mr. Satyajit met a car accident and died. Mr. Gopalchand, the MD, had to appoint a new general manager. Next month, Mr. Mangaldas 45, an ambitious and dynamic man, having 15 years experience as a senior marketing manager in a leading export company carrying diamond business, who was MBA from Harvard University, appointed as the GM in the company.

His style was quite different than his predecessor. Immediately after his appointment, he studied marketing audit report of last five years, analyzed marketing strategies, particularly pricing strategies, and realized the scope to reduce costs and/or to make more profits. He called on Mr. Shyamsunder and advised to make following two major changes in pricing strategies from the immediate effect:

1. Apply indiscriminative (uniform) pricing policy.
2. Reduce price allowances, discounts, seasonal offers and other incentives to realize more profits.

Mr. Shyamsunder strongly opposed these changes. He warned the GM regarding adverse impacts of such changes on customers satisfaction, dealers interest and, hence, on sales. But, the GM was firm to alter pricing strategies. All the changes were implemented immediately.

After three months, sales started declining. Those who were placing bulk orders started making small orders, sales department failed to clear bills of credit sales in time. Sales during Diwali were far below than previous years. Company experienced 10% cut in overall sales instead of gradual growth. Mr. Mangaldas disappointed with the performance of marketing department. Though product was standard, price was reasonable, and company spent a large amount for advertising, sales fell down. He called meeting to investigate the facts.

Exercise

1. What were the important elements of pricing strategy that achieved 25% stable growth in profits?
2. Why Shyamsunder was granted a complete freedom to frame pricing strategy?
3. Why did the new GM decide to change the pricing strategy?
4. How would you evaluate the new pricing strategy?
5. GM requests you to make suggestion to sustain the previous growth. Can you help him?

Case: 4 (Need for Market Survey)

Top-level management of Paradise Cosmetics Company limited – a well-established, a medium scale unit, located at Vapi, Gujarat, producing beauty-care products for women – decided to launch a new product. The company had five successful products in the market. Mr. Rajabhaya, the senior most marketing executive was given the charge to handle the matter related to new product development. He had a little faith in the latest marketing approaches, concepts, and philosophies. Mr. Rajabhaya called meeting all marketing officials to discuss the issue. In the meeting, officials were asked to suggest what type of new product a company should launch.

Immediately, Mr. Samir Sukla, young area marketing manager, objected saying that to decide a new product was the right of consumers and not of marketing officers. He recommended conducting market survey before taking any decision. He strongly believed that a new proposed product must be fit with expectations of consumers. In favour of his stand, he stressed on modern marketing theory and practice. But, Mr. Rajabhaya and some other senior officers were not ready to waste time in conducting market survey. According to them, since last 20 years, many products had been launched successfully and they had never asked the users to tell what they wanted. For them, it was meaningless to take market opinion before launching a new product, if the product to be launched was superior in quality and low in price. Mr. Samir reiterated his stand saying that the present condition was different than the past due to severe competition and increased consumer awareness. In spite of strong objection of Mr. Samir Sukla and some junior officers, Mr. Rajabhaya – assuming it was just philosophical talk having no value for real practice of marketing – decided to launch a new product without market survey.

Exercise

1. Why was Mr. Rajabhaya not interested to go for the market survey before taking any decision on a new product?
2. How can you justify Mr. Samir's stand to conduct market survey?
3. What is your suggestion? Why?
4. What type of market survey should the company conduct?
5. Do you think that market survey can always contribute positively? Why?

Case 5: (Product Life Cycle)

Mr. Rajpal, M. Sc. Chemistry and MBA with Production, an experienced general manager of a leading pharmaceutical company decided unanimously in the meeting held with the MD and other executives to launch a new product to improve profitability, market image and competitive strengths, though existing products had fairly dominant place in the market. He had been with the organisation since inception and played crucial role to excel the firm. With integrated efforts of all the departments concern, within next six month, a new product was developed. Mr. Yashpal, young marketing manager, who was MBA from IIM, Madras was assigned the task to position the product in the market. He prepared marketing strategy for introduction stage and discussed the same with the GM to seek approval. And, under his direct supervision, a new product was launched on 20th March, 2003.

Due to effective marketing strategy, the product was gaining market acceptance gradually as per expectation. Top-level management satisfied with Mr. Yashpal's strategies. Few months later, Mr. Yashpal met the GM to discuss about new marketing strategy for the second stage of the product life cycle. He recommended marketing strategy with following changes:

1. To reduce selling price by 10% to attract price-sensitive segment of the market.
2. To give more emphasis on comparative advertising to prove products' superiority over the competitors.
3. To offer liberally price discount, allowances, and adopt discriminative pricing policy.
4. To enter the new segments to widen market and increase sales.

The GM surprised at Mr. Yashpal's proposal. He couldn't understand why strategies were to be changed when product was getting acceptance, and sales were increasing. He declared openly that as long as sales had positive growth rate, no changes should be made in marketing strategy. Mr. Yaspal tried to convince the GM stating that different marketing strategies were required at different stages of product life cycles. But, the GM was firm to continue with the same. Though Mr. Yashpal was very enthusiastic, persistent, and ambitious to achieve sound result, he could not work as per his theory. He was highly disappointed. He started withdrawing from monitoring marketing activities.

Within three months, sales started suffering. Surprisingly, sales experienced negative growth rate. The MD invited Mr. Rajpal, Mr. Yashpal, and other marketing executives to review the situation. There was heated discussion. All area managers opined that sales suffered only because of irrelevant marketing strategies. Now, it was too late. In the same meeting, Mr. Yashpal declared to resign from immediate effect.

Exercise

1. What types of changes did Mr. Yaspal want to be introduced? Why?
2. How can you justify demand of Mr. Yashpal to alter strategy?
3. Why was the GM intended to continue introductory marketing strategies?
4. The MD is confused. He needs expert counseling. Can you help him?
5. "Mr. Yashpal should not resign at this time." Put your relevant arguments.

Case 6: (Marketing Theory and Practice)

Mr. Vedanta, 50, B. Com. from Bombay University, working as a Chief Marketing Executive in "We ARE FOR YOU," a famous departmental store situated in central Bombay, decided to upgrade his marketing knowledge. In fact, the departmental store was among the most popular and reputed stores in the city. Mr. Vedanta was known for his discipline, commitment, and better communication skills. Despite he had very tight schedule, he decided to advance his knowledge for better performance. He joined local college offering Marketing Management courses in the evening. On the very first day, Mr. Bhadu, an eminent marketing consultant and visiting faculty in several management institutes, delivered a lecture on needs of modern marketing thoughts for better marketing. He discussed following topics continuously for three hours.

- "Consumer satisfaction as a master key to succeed in marketing area."
- "Public relations as a platform to strengthen market position."
- "Essence of market survey to keep marketing efforts up to date."
- "Application of Operations Research Techniques/Models for better managing."

Mr. Vedanta was confused on the very first day due to the lecture. He had always thought that whatever he had been doing was the best marketing approach to succeed. He had never thought of these issues. His department had been continuously growing in terms of number of customers, sales, and profits. He could not convince himself that the lecture was just a philosophical talk as the lecture was delivered by the most successful marketing consultant. Vedanta had never thought of these issues and though he was successful. He was in dilemma whether he should continue attending lectures. Another problem was whether to practice so called contemporary advanced marketing philosophy being discussed in classroom. And, finally he stopped attending college within a week.

Exercise

1. Do you believe that an experienced and successful manager should join such management programmes?
2. How would you evaluate the topics Mr. Bhadu discussed on the very first day?
3. "Though Mr. Vedanta was unaware of modern marketing knowledge, he was successful in his job." Comment
4. Would you advice Mr. Vedanta to continue evening management course?
5. Do you think that Mr. Vedanta should use modern theory of marketing in the practice?

Case 7: (Personal Values v/s Marketing Practices)

Mr. Gaurishankar Joshi, a young MBA form B. K. School of Management, Ahmedabad, joined Best Care Pharma Pvt. Company, situated at Ankleshwar, as an assistant sales and advertising manager. Mr. Gaurishankar's family background was quite different. He had been grown in a joint family consisting of 20 members. His Grandfather and uncle were popular Kathakar (Spiritual Speaker) in India and abroad. His father was trustee in famous Shiva Temple in the city. His family culture was highly religiously dominated. Truth, honesty, justice, fairness, care for others, and such other virtues (moral values) were forcefully imparted in every member of his family. Every family member was expected to work as per these spiritual values or human qualities. He was the first to take management education in the family. He had strongly decided to prefer different profession. He made up his mind to settle in private field to show his caliber.

Since last two years, he has changed at least five companies due to more or less malpractices indulged by companies. He could not find any company running as per social/business ethics and spiritual norms. Spiritual values and family norms disqualified him to work in the companies.

During orientation for one month, he was exposed to quality and contents of products including tablets, injections, and syrups mostly used by the child specialists for treatment of patients under the age of 10 years. He studied advertising message, contents printed on the package and label, sales promotion techniques offered to doctors and stockiests, and training contents to medical representatives. Immediately after two weeks, he came to know the real quality and contents of products. He was shocked to know the following realities:

1. Quality of the products was far below than claimed in advertising.
2. Proportion of various components in each of the products was severely different that stated in actual description on the package.
3. Medical representatives were trained to exaggerate the facts. Most of the claims regarding the effect of products were baseless.
4. Doctors were offered a lot of incentives to use and/or prescribe a maximum quantity of products.
5. Advertising appeal was seriously misleading and exaggerating.

Mr. Gaurishankar found his values and family norms strongly clashing with marketing practices. He had worse experience than previous jobs. He was under the pressure of two forces; one is, his spiritual values and family norms, and the second is, job requirements. He didn't like to turn back to his family occupation, and he couldn't settle anywhere due to unjust job requirements. He was under extreme tension. Immediately after training, he went on medical leave for one week to decide whether to join the job.

Exercise

1. Would you appreciate his decision to prefer quite different occupation?
2. What is your advice to Mr. Gaurishankar? Should he resume the job?
3. How would you perceive overall marketing environment?
4. Is it possible to observe social norms in real practice? Why?

Case 8: (Need of Participative Management)

Mr. Avinash had been working as a distribution officer in Mangaldeep Electronics Company Pvt. Ltd., a Mumbai-based middle scale unit, since last 5 years. A company had been selling its products throughout the country. In the meeting of the Board of Directors, managing director decided to promote all senior officers as assistant managers for the respective posts. It was further decided to offer promotion benefits with transfer. Immediately, eight senior officers were relieved from the current posts and were issued promotion with transfer orders to join new posts at various territories throughout the country within a week. Mr. Avinash went on sick leave for a month. A company warned him to resume the post. On the next day, the MD received resignation letter from Mr. Avinash. The MD could not understand why Mr. Avinash resigned.

Exercise

1. Why did Mr. Avinash delay to resume the job?
2. What made him to resign?
3. What the MD could have been done to avoid such incident?
4. The MD requests you to counsel him.

Case 9: (Need of Market Survey)

Deshmukh Datta, 60, a successful marketing manager in Jayhind Food Ltd., located in Ahmedabad GIDC Area, ignored recommendations of Mr. Ramesh, a young and dynamic research officer to change features and qualities of products. Mr. Deshmuk denied his recommendations stating that it was meaningless to change when company was leading in the market and sales volume was increasing. Company had a strong position in market. Current performance was quite satisfactory. He stated that without internal need of organisation and external pressure of the present market, to make any change in products was foolish act. Mr. Ramesh argued that he recommended on the basis of the market trend measured in the last month by market survey of 100 customers and 25 dealers. The proposed changes were required as precautionary measures. Mr. Deshmuk was not ready to disturb marketing activities without any current needs. Mr. Ramesh disappointed. He worried for the future challenges, but was helpless to protect the interest of his company.

After six months, dealers started placing less number of orders of less quantity than previous. When asked, they stated that customers were demanding different features. More substitutes of varied features and superior qualities were available. They were not interested in the existing products. Mr. Deshmukh Datta highly shocked to know it. The company was losing customers. Now, it was too late to meet customers' expectations.

Exercise

1. How would you evaluate the decision of marketing manager not to change product quality and features?
2. What made Mr. Deshmukh to continue products without any change?
3. Why was Mr. Ramesh insisting to modify existing products?
4. Now, what is the way out to retain sales?
5. Do you think that a firm should always implement recommendation of market survey fully? Why?

Case 10: (Need of Integrated Marketing)

VISION MEDIA Limited, a well-known Mumbai-based company producing TV serials for national channels. Mr. Balyogi, the GM who was MBA with marketing, struggled since 15 years to create the most conducive organisational climate and culture in which integrated efforts could be made to achieve the highest possible performance. Company had mainly three departments Finance, Production, and Marketing. Though there were different departments, all departmental heads were acting as members of the team led by Mr. Balyogi. He had tried to make the company customer-oriented. Though he was the GM, he used to follow the instructions of Mr. Sunderdev, the Marketing Manager. Mr. Sunderdev is informally considered as the leader. The GM made entire organisation to obey Mr. Sunderdev's decisions. Practically, it seemed that Mr. Sunderdev was leader and Mr. Blayogi was coordinator. He made the company market-driven. The GM believed integrated efforts were the only master key to compete effectively. He invested his most of time for integrating the entire efforts and promoting team spirit. The company had completed 10 serials and had marketed half of them successfully within last one and half years. The company was enjoying a good reputation, image and goodwill along with sufficient profits.

On 25th July 2003, Mr. Y. A. Tyagi, who was MBA for California University, and was holding several diplomas related to production of films and serials, appointed as the GM as a successor of Mr. Balyogi. Formerly Tyagi was working as an assistant producer in international channel. Mr. Tyagi had different pattern of working. He believed that more freedom to managers lead to chaos. He was in favour of centralized decision-making. He did not allow any departmental head to decide independently. Marketing manager Mr. Sundardev was felt ignored. His task was to study several aspects of different serials shown in popular TV channels. He was responsible for research and marketing. The entire organisation was working as per his theory and guideline. His difficulties started multiplying. The GM was insisting the organisation to produce serial on sophisticated idea, far away from market need, interest, and habits of people and local culture. Marketing manager could neither get staff nor finance, nor support from other departments without approval of the GM. Within short period of time, due to rigid nature and strict behaviour, at least five senior employees resigned and the rest of them were waiting for better opportunities. Employees started assuming that the company would neither flourish nor survive under Mr. Tyagi's dictatorship.

Exercise

1. Comment on Mr. Balyogi's approach to work.
2. What according to you was the secret of success for Vision Limited?
3. What should marketing manager do under the leadership of the new GM?
4. Can you project the future of Vision Limited?
5. In case of the new GM, which reasons were responsible for a new pattern of management?

Case 11: (Distribution Channel)

Mr. Prabhakar, the GM of Beauty Care Ltd., a cosmetic company, situated in Indore (MP), held an urgent meeting of all the sales area officers of the state to discuss the proposed strategy for newly developed hair oil product. Since last five year, company had the strategy to sell the products via dealers. In the meeting, the GM asked the officers whether to go for dealership or salesmanship. The officers expressed their views one by one:

Mr. Shyamlal, the most experienced sales officer said, "Sir, company must go for dealership and should concentrate on quality and production."

Mr. Malik, a junior young sales officer sated, "Salesmanship is the most effective option to promote the product and accelerate sales. Door-to-door selling by lady salesmen is an effective option."

Mr. Deepak, the recently appointed sales officer said with confident, "Sir, first we must prepare a powerful team of salesmen to promote the product aggressively. Once the product become familiar and is accepted by the market, we should go for dealership. I strongly believe that dealer can sell, but can't promote the product."

Miss Malini, the only lady sales officer in the company, expressed her views, "Sir, I believe that retailers in different cities and towns can do a better job. They have live contacts with customers and can easily promote the products by convincing the regular customers to try the product. It is better to prepare retailers than salesmen. This is cheaper and the perfect way."

Exercise

1. What do you think about the current strategy of the company to sell new product via dealership?
2. How would you evaluate the GM's approach to discuss the issue with sales officer?
3. Of whose suggestion(s) the GM should follow? Why?

Case 12: (Diversifying Business)

Poonam Tea Enterprise had been in tea business since 1990. Poonam Tea was a well-established tea brand in Gujarat state. The brand was making a good business and had a large number of loyal customers. Mr. Ruchir, the General Manager of the company, was not satisfied with only single business. He was of the opinion that the firm must have multiple businesses to hedge risk. Instead of developing the current business, he wished to diversify the business into other related areas such as beverages and plantation. He had the plan to use the same brand Poonam for the new venture. He firmly believed that Poonam was well-known brand and new products would become famous within no time in the state.

During officials meet, he announced his plan. Immediately Mr. P. Patel, the senior marketing manager of the company, strongly objected the proposed move. He argued that instead of diversifying into other products, it would be easy to expand the market of Poonam Cha in other states. To his views, this could be easily done with little efforts and money while the new business seemed risky.

Despite of Mr. P. Patel's strong objection, Mr. Ruchir was firm to implement his plan. In next few days, he officially announced to diversify into the new business. Immediately, Mr. P. Patel found no option and resigned. The firm gradually started developing a new business of beverages and plantation. It was assumed that company would establish its position within short period of time. But, due to the promising future prospect and global opportunities, many giant companies entered the same business with the advanced technology and the huge investment. Poonam Tea Enterprise could not face the global competition and failed in the new business. The company found not option but to withdraw the product from the market. Also, Poonam Cha gradually started losing its sales and brand image due to utter failure in developing a new business.

Exercise

1. Evaluate the decision of Mr. Ruchir to expand into other area of business.
2. Do you think that company's tea business would not have suffered if the Poonam brand were not used for beverages and plantation business?
3. Would you advise Mr. Ruchir to request Mr. P. Patel to join the firm again?
4. Suppose, you are in place of Mr. P. Patel, would you joint the company again?
5. Which are your suggestions to the company to put the tea business back on the track?
6. Which, according to you, were the reasons for failure of a new venture?

Case 13: (Price for the New Product)

Prestige Chemical Pvt. Ltd., a medium size company situated at Baroda (Gujarat), has recently developed new premium quality soap with brand name GLORY. Now product is ready to be launched in the some part of Gujarat. Company has decided to advertise the product in leading newspapers to inform customers about the product. Market seems limited. It is assumed that company has to convince price-sensitive customers of this region in a competitive situation. Mr. Khanna, the marketing manager wants to set price for the introductory stage. He requests you to help him in this regard. He needs your expert comment on following issues. Can you help him?

Exercise

1. Which factors should he take into account while setting price for GLORY brand soap?
2. Which are the possible pricing methods for setting price of the product? Which is the best fit method for this type of product? Why?
3. Would you advise him to offer cash discount and trade discount? Why?
4. Suggest the appropriate pricing strategies for the introductory stage.

Case 14: (Improper Marketing Strategies)

Shri Shanabhai Patel, an NRI, owing two chemical units near Baroda and three ice factories, also owns one Mushroom Unit named MASIKA AGRI-TECH PVT LTD, situated near Itola Railway station on Bombay-Ahmedabad highway. He grows mushrooms and prepares mushroom powder and capsules which are supplementary food, and not a medicine for any diseases.

Mushrooms powder is useful as nutrient agent and works as anti-oxidant agent and also restricts ageing process in human body. He also manufacturers tasty biscuits with rich nutrition and high fiber contents, from five grains such as soyabeen, wheat, bajari, nachanee and juwar. Both mushrooms powder and biscuits are useful for nourishment of human body and recommended for curing constipation and other related diseases. Mushrooms capsules, powder, and biscuits are new products for most of people. Mr. Shanabhai Patel wants to introduce such products in central Gujarat and Saurashtra regions. He doesn't formulated systematic marketing strategies to introduce these products in the regions.

Mushrooms powder is sold at Rs. 180 per 250 grams bottle while biscuits are sold at Rs. 20 per 100 grams packet. The company offers 20% and with 25% discount per bottle of powder and a packet of biscuits respectively. 20 capsules pack is sold at Rs. 40 and no discount is offered. A company sells all products directly to customers and also through dealers.

To promote his products in Saurashtra area, Mr. Shanabhai Patel applied a novel strategy. He visited several colleges to appoint students and members of non-teaching staff as salespersons and distributors at district level. He visited a number of colleges thrice for the purpose, but was highly disappointed with response. He is confused. He needs expert counseling from you.

Exercise

1. What are the strong points of company's marketing strategies?
2. Find out loopholes of company's marketing strategies.
3. In order to promote the products rapidly in the area, what, according to you, should he do?
4. How would you evaluate Shanabhai Patel's plan to distribute novel products via college students and staff?
5. If you are appointed as a marketing manager for the Saurashtra region, what actions would you initiated?

Case 15: (Sales Force v/s Dealership)

Excellence Electronics Ltd., a large scale unit, manufacturing home appliances, has been using excessive personal selling to offer the best after-sales services. Company had well-trained and motivated sale force of sixty salesmen. The company offers attractive salary, commission, and fringe benefits to keep them satisfied. Commission and bonus are linked with number of calls, complaints attended and solved, innovative suggestions collected, and new customers generated. Personal selling costs accounted for 15% of sales. Company had been earning good profits and has maintained satisfactory position in the market. Mr. V. V. Patel had been managing sales and distribution activities successfully since last ten years. Company top management had full trust on marketing policy of Mr. Patel. Mr. Patel, due to health and aging problems, decided to retire.

Mr. Sunil Shah, the less experienced but highly ambitious young MBA from Bangalore, was appointed as a successor of Mr. Patel. Top management extended the same policy and allowed him to work independently. Within a week of his appointment, without any discussion and study, he decided to cut selling expenses by reducing 30% personal selling staff. According to his views, there is scope for cost reduction due to excessive selling costs. Senior sales officers strongly objected his decision. But Mr. Shah remained firm on his decision. He believed that middlemen could do better at low costs. He liberally offered dealership in many cities.

Within a few months, sales started declining, particularly, from those regions where sales force was reduced considerably. Dealers defended their poor performance by describing actions and efforts they had taken. To dealers, sales declined due to completion. But, Mr. Shah didn't satisfy with dealers' defense. He decided to conduct brief survey to investigate the facts.

He got survey report and was shocked to know that dealers had hardly taken effective steps to attract and satisfy customers. Most of dealers failed to provide satisfactory services after-sales. Customers posed strong problems of poor services of dealers. He realized his mistake. He called immediate meeting of sales officials to discuss the matter.

Exercise

1. What was the secret of success of Excellence Electronics Company?
2. Why did Mr. Shah decide to reduce sales force? Was it necessary to do so?
3. How would you evaluate Mr. Shah's new sales strategy?
4. Which could be other reasons for reduced sales volume, over and above, reduced personal selling staff.
5. Suggest appropriate actions to improve marketing performance.

Case 16: (Advertising Department v/s Advertising Agency)

Top management of Excel Auto Private Limited, a medium scale unit manufacturing and marketing auto parts for two wheelers, established in 1985 in Mumbai (East), is thinking to widen its domestic market. At present, the company sells its products in three states of country – Maharashtra, Gujarat, and Madhya Pradesh. Company advertises its products in local and regional newspapers and relevant journals. Mr. Manek Chaudhari, the most senior regional marketing manager for Maharashtra state manages all advertising related matters along with his routine selling and distribution activities. There is no separate advertising department. Company has enough excess capacity to increase production if there is market. Company management calls a meeting of top officials from respective states to discuss on company's market expansion plan. In the meeting, held on 23rd January, 2010, all official stressed on increasing advertising activities and expenditure. Meeting ended without any conclusion and decided to meet after a month.

Next meeting, under the chairmanship of Mr. R. K. Ramdoot, the MD, was held as per schedule. There was heated discussion particularly on the issue: Whether to manage separate advertising department or to opt for advertising agency. Dialogues of officials have been given below:

Mr. R. K. Ramdoot initiated discussion and said, "It is certain that we must expand our market share. We must penetrate our products in other states. I agree to intensify advertising efforts, but the question is how to do it."

Manek Chaudhari replied, "Sir, it is simple, we must increase ad budget and increase our advertising efforts. I can do it without any problem.

Mr. Kapil Tyagi, a young sales manager from Gujarat, objected. He argued, "It is not so simple. Advertising is not as easy as it was. Our advertising efforts are lacking systematic planning. We must have well-considered and systematic plan for national level advertising in leading media. We must have well-equipped department or we must go for advertising agency to take care of advertising-related activities. Advertising requires professional touch, unfortunately, we are lacking it.

Ms Richa Saxena, the only lady sales manager from Madhya Pradesh, supported Mr. Tyagi's arguments and complemented, "Mr. Tyagi is right. We are spending money but we are not gaining enough. Today's advertising needs the different approach and activities. We must professionalise our advertising efforts or take help of professionally sound advertising agencies. With the same budget, advertising can serve better."

Manek Chaudhari, reacting positively, said, "Its O.K. I don't have any objection if company management sets up separate advertising department or opt for ad agency. However, to my view, advertising agencies can offer better services at affordable rates."

Mr. R. K. Ramdoot smiled and stated: "Problem is ended. We must go for advertising agency to intensify our selling efforts. I assign the task to Mr. Mr. Kapil Tyagi to choose the right agency."

All cheered at Mr. R. K. Ramdoot's decision. Mr. Ramdoot expressed vote of thanks. Meeting ended with smile of every body's face.

Exercise

1. Comment on company's present advertising efforts.
2. "Today's advertising task is more challengeable." Discuss the statement on the basis of the case.
3. Why is ad agency more advisable than advertising department?
4. What types of functions does advertising agency perform for the client firm?
5. Do you think that intensifying advertising efforts alone can contribute to expand company's market? Which are other aspects that company must concentrate to expand its market successfully?

Case 17: (Introductory Marketing Strategy)

Recently, Puja Chemicals, Ahmedabad-based sole propriety unit, has developed new hair oil. The product is based on Ayurvedic concept. All formalities including packing and packaging, labeling, and brand name have been just completed. Mr. Mohanlas, the promoter of firm, is not professionally qualified and so he wants to take help of management consultant to introduce the product successfully in the local market. He is planning to introduce the same within the city first to know reactions of consumers and dealers. Mr. Mohanlas requests you to help him.

Exercise

1. What is the first step you initiate in launching a new product in market?
2. What types of advertising programme would you suggest to Mr. Mohanlas?
3. Give your comment on pricing strategies for introductory stage.
4. Do you recommend personal selling? Why?
5. Suggest him suitable sales promotion tools.
6. Do you think that Mr. Mohanlas should appoint professionally qualified and experienced manager to handle marketing activities?

CHAPTER

17

PROJECT REPORT IN MARKETING – PRACTICAL STUDY

- Introduction and Meaning of Project Work
- Purpose of Practical Study
- List of Topics for Project Work
- Contents of Each of the Topics
- Guidelines for Preparing Project Report
- Format of Project Report

INTRODUCTION

In most of undergraduate and postgraduate courses in management discipline, students have to prepare a project report for 100 marks or more. This is a practical study paper. It is a separate paper, and is considered as the formal part of the syllabus. At postgraduate level, the paper is known as Dissertation (Minor Thesis). The said paper is divided into two parts – Report and Viva (oral test). Marks may be evenly distributed between report and viva. In some universities, students are deputed to business enterprises (mostly public companies) for training purpose for not less than 10 days. They have to stay as full-time trainees and study activities of different departments. They have to collect necessary detail relevant to the subject/topic assigned. And, the details collected are presented in form of training/project report. Mostly, the report is submitted in hard copy form. Some institutes insist students to conduct market survey on the assigned topics.

Even, some companies undertake survey in marketing field to know views and response of the target market. The list of topics and contents of each of the topics, and guidelines given in this chapter can be used by academic institutes for academic purpose and corporate sectors for survey purpose as well. However, the chapter is more relevant to management students to conduct practical study.

PURPOSE OF TRAINING/PRACTICAL STUDY

Practical training in marketing field is multipurpose tool. The basic purpose of industrial training is to expose commence and management students the actual functioning of industrial unit. Students can learn practical aspects of management. Additionally, they can assess their theoretical knowledge with actual practice of management. They can be made aware of overall business environment. Students can easily judge the key difference between theory and practice, classroom work and practical study.

Practical study can also help develop and improve decision-making skills. Students can learn how to prepare reports. It helps develop writing skills. This paper contributes positively to their personality.

Particularly, undergraduate students can learn how to adjust in different situations, away from homely environment. Problems and difficulties faced by students can improve confidence and overall personality. They can prepare themselves for actual/practical life in advance. Due to trading, they can easily adjust with work as and when they join any job after the study.

The present chapter covers **three parts:**

1. A list of topics for practical study,
2. Contents (points to be studied) in each of the topics, and
3. The guidelines for preparing a report of practical training/study and report format.

PART I
LIST OF TOPICS

A list of some topics is given here. Management students and trainees have to study the topic in relation to the business enterprises. Students can access theoretical details from the relevant chapters of this book. They can carry their practical work on any one or more of following topics:

1. Applicability of alternative marketing concepts/approaches in the real practice.
2. A study on Organisation of Marketing Department.
3. An overview of Marketing Mix.
4. Product Decisions.
5. Product Related Strategies
6. Pricing Decisions
7. Market Promotion Decisions.
8. Physical Distribution and Channel decisions.
9. Product and Pricing Related Strategies.
10. Product and Promotion Related Strategies.
11. Product and Distribution Related Decisions.
12. Price and Promotion Related Decisions.
13. Price and Distribution Related Decisions.
14. Promotion and Distribution Related Decisions.
15. A Detailed Study on Advertising Activities of Company.
16. Relevance of Sales Promotion Efforts in the Company.
17. Sales Management including Sales Force Management.
18. Sales Force (Personal Selling) Management in the Company.
19. A Study on Advertising and Sales Promotion Efforts in the Company.
20. Advertising and Personal Selling Efforts.
21. Analysis of Advertising and Publicity Practices in the Company.
22. Role of Public Relations and Publicity in today's Marketing Practices.
23. A study on Marketing Research Practices in the Company.
24. An Analysis of MIS with Special Reference to Marketing Research.
25. Issues Related to New Product Development and Product Related Strategies.
26. An analytical Study of Product Life Cycle with Relevant Strategies.
27. Relevance of Product Life Cycle and Consumer Adoption Process.

28. A Systematic Study on Branding, Packaging, Labeling, and Trade Marking.
29. Issues Related to New Product Development, Product Life Cycle, and Consumer Adoption.
30. International Marketing
31. Modern Marketing and Social Responsibility.
32. A Survey on Consumer Trend (behaviour) in Specific Region.
33. Study and Analysis of Public Relations, Customer Orientation, and Integrated Marketing with Reference to the Company.
34. Functioning of the District Consumer Forum
35. Constitution (key provisions) and Effects of Consumer Protection Act on Company's Marketing Decisions.
36. Prospects, problems, and remedies of Cyber Marketing (e-marketing)
37. Impact of legal provisions of a few Acts closely related to consumer protection.
38. Green Marketing
39. Marketing Services
40. Retailing
41. Study on Competitive Strategy of the Company
42. Marketing Control Practices

PART II
CONTENT OF EACH OF THE TOPICS

This part provides a detail for each of the topic listed in the former part. It shows the points to be covered under the specific topic/title.

1. Applicability of alternative marketing concepts/approaches in the real practice.

Students have to study and apply five Marketing Concepts. For detail, refer Marketing Concepts, chapter 1. The topic may include following points:

- Introduction
- Modern marketing theories and its applicability.
- Detailed discussion of modern marketing approaches/concepts – meaning, characteristics, role, key elements, parties considered, and relevant aspects related to each of the concepts (theoretical aspects).
- Recent trend in the industry and country.
- Names and features of approach practiced by concerned business unit.
- Reasons to practice particular concept.
- Benefits of such approach/concept.
- Students' overall observation, suggestions and conclusion.

2. A study on Organisation of Marketing Department.

The topic is related to study marketing organisation of a particular company. For detail, refer chapter 1.

- Introduction – critical decision, affects current and future performance, employees' productivity, morale and satisfaction, conflict and appropriate structure, etc.
- Brief idea of organisation structure and its types – theoretical aspects.
- Various alternative organisation structures.
- Organisation structure of the concerned enterprise – type, reasons for particular type(s) of structure and characteristics.

- Factors/key aspects considered by the company while deciding on the organisation structure.
- Who decides about organisation structures, and modification thereof and need of external experts?
- Organisational chart – Master chart and functional chart (for marketing department).
- Levels, key position holders, their duties/functions and other relevant details.
- Details regarding organisational manuals, if available, and its uses.
- Organizing process – relevant steps followed to formulate the structure of organisation.
- Characteristics of ideal organisation structure (company views)
- Recent changes in the chart, if any.
- Benefits of the suitable organisation – Company's views.
- Students' overall observation, suggestions and conclusion.

3. An overview of Marketing Mix.

Here, the students have to study all elements of marketing mix – products, price, promotion, and place. For conceptual detail, refer chapter 1. The topic includes:

- Introduction – Consumer satisfaction and marketing decision, marketing mix as a tool for serving consumer needs and facing competition, and other related issues can be discussed.
- Meaning, definitions, and elements of marketing mix (theory portion)
- Elements of marketing mix in brief (practical aspects):
  - ❖ Product mix/decision: (Note: See product decisions)
  - ❖ Price mix: (Note: See price decisions)
  - ❖ Promotion mix: (Note: See promotion decisions)
  - ❖ Place mix: (Note: See place decisions)
  - ❖ Factors affecting marketing mix – internal and external and opinion of the manager
- Students' overall observation, suggestions and conclusion.

4. Product Decisions.

Product decisions include all relevant issue related to product(s) of a company concern. For detail, refer chapter 5. It mainly covers following points:

§Introduction – Product as basic decision in marketing mix, its significance.

- Definition of product. Its dimensions and product elements – core product, product related strategies, and product related services.
- Brief idea of company's product – core product, product related strategies and product related services. Explanation of total product/offer.
- Product mix of company – Range, depth, width, and consistency related to existing products of the company.
- Who decides on the products?
- Product life cycle – Meaning and brief idea of the PLC, Different strategies practiced by the company during different stages of the PLC. Stage the PLC in which the product of the company is passing through and relevant strategies.
- New product, if company wants to develop or has developed recently.
- Reasons to develop a new product – as applicable to company.
- Important issues/factors the company considers while developing a new product.
- New product development process practiced by the company in comparison with the systematic process studied in the classroom.

- Relevance of consumer adoption process. (How is it useful to manager?)
- Brief study of branding, packaging, labeling and after sales services related to the company's products.
- Students' overall observation, suggestions and conclusion.

5. Product Related Strategies

Product related strategies packaging, branding, labeling, and after-sales services. Refer chapter 5.1 for more detail. Students have to collect following details for this topic during industrial training:

- **Introduction** – Product and relevant decisions, product is the key decision.
- Meaning and definition of product related strategies and its impact on product personality.
- Importance of product in marketing and role of product related strategies.
- **Product concept** – core product, product related strategies, product related services.
- Scope of product related strategies:
- **BRAIDING:** Meaning, importance/role, various brand names used by the company, explanation of them with special features, reasons to select that brand name, benefits of brand names (company's views), factors to be considered with special reference to consumer behaviour and legal restrictions or relevant legal provisions, Trade Mark of company, limitations of branding the product.
- **PACKAGING:** Packaging – an important decision, concept of packing and packaging, its role in modern marketing, company's packaging decisions – special characteristics of package, type of package, materials used, benefits, and comparison with competitors. Who decides on packaging? Brief outline of factors relevant of packaging decisions. Price and packaging, and limitations of packaging.
- **LABELING:** Concept, labeling decision maker, important decisions, characteristics/elements of company's label, , contents of company's label, usefulness of label – company's views
- **AFTER SALES SERVICES:** Meaning, characteristics and significance of after sales services (theory portion), types and number of after sales services offered by the company, special features of company's services, impact of services on price, consumer satisfaction, competitive strengths, and consumer loyalty, problems related to after sales services and other relevant issues.
- Students' overall observation, suggestions and conclusion.

6. Pricing Decisions

The topic concerns with price related issues. Students have to study pricing policies and practices with reference to the industrial unit and have to collect relevant detail from concerned executive. For detail, refer chapter 6. Normally below listed points must be studied:

- Pricing – a critical decision in marketing.
- Concept of price and pricing.
- Who takes pricing decisions?
- Company's pricing objectives.
- Company's general pricing policies.
- Product life cycle and pricing strategies.
- Price setting methods practiced by the company.
- Factors affecting company's pricing decisions.
- Detail related to discounts, rebates, money back guarantee, cash or credit sales, seasonal pricing, discriminative/uniform pricing, level of profit margin, etc.

- Any other special feature of company's pricing policies.
- Students' overall observation, suggestions and conclusion.

7. Market Promotion Decisions.

The topic deals with all promotional efforts of business unit. Students are required to study basic aspects of market promotion and all elements of promotional mix, i.e., advertising, personal selling, sales promotion, publicly and public relations. For detail, refer chapter 7 to chapter 7.4. Following are the contents of the topic:

Market Promotion: Meaning of market promotion, market promoting is market communication, its role of promotion efforts as perceived by the company, Promotion mix – concept, elements and its role in modern marketing practices.

Advertising: All relevant aspects of advertising activities of the company. The topic deals with only advertising related issues. Students have to study all advertising activities of the concerned business enterprise. The topic includes:

- Meaning of market promotion, market promoting is market communication, its role of promotion efforts as perceived by the company.
- Elements of market promotion and advertising
- Role of advertising in relation to nature of contemporary marketing environment.
- Advertising objectives of company
- Organisation of advertising department – organisation chart, manager, staff, faculties, duties and functions of manager.
- Detail of company's advertising message and advertising copy.
- Advertising media used by the company – type and number of media used, factors affecting media selection, special features of advertising media used by company.
- Media scheduling
- Advertising budget of company – decision-maker, methods used and factors considered, amount spent for advertising during past years.
- Advertising agencies – concept and functions, whether it is used, reasons for using/not using professional services of ad agencies and student's opinions.
- Manager's views on advertising efforts and positive impact on sales, profits, consumer satisfaction and competitive edge.
- Measuring advertising effectiveness – methods used and results.
- Social aspects of advertising – manager's views positive and negative impact of advertising on society.
- Any special issue relevant to topic.

Personal Selling: All relevant aspects of personal selling activities of the company. It includes:

- Concept, nature and significance
- Whether personal selling used and reasons for using/not using it.
- Management of personal selling activities (sales force management of Company)
- Sales force department, chart, manager and staff, facilities, etc.
- Sales force objectives of company
- Sales force size of company methods used and factors considered.
- Manpower planning, recruitment, selection, and induction practices adopted by the company
- Company's sales force remuneration plan
- Sales force training practices

- Supervising and Controlling sales force activities
- Any other related issue.

Sales Promotion: All relevant aspects of sales promotion activities of the company. The point includes:

- Introduction – increasing role of sales promotion activities.
- Meaning and definitions.
- Its role and objectives – company's views (reasons to use it)
- Costs of sales promotion efforts.
- Who decides on sales promotion?
- Amount spent during last a few years for market promotion.
- Types of sales promotion: **Consumer level sales promotion** – Discuss techniques/ methods used by the company. **Dealer level sales promotion** – Discuss techniques/ methods used by the company. **Sales force level sales promotion** – Discuss techniques/ methods used by the company.
- Time of sales promotion: When does company direct sales promotion efforts – regularly, seasonally, or as and when necessary
- Actual positive impacts of sales promotion efforts as experienced by the company

Publicity: This point covers all relevant issues and company's efforts in this regard.

- Concept and characteristics and its role.
- Who decides on this matter?
- Special efforts made by the company in this regard.
- Costs incurred for this purpose.
- Detail related to past events/occasions for getting publicity.
- Future plan.

Public Relations: This point concerns with public relation efforts of the company. All relevant issues are to be discussed including:

- Introduction
- Meaning and definitions
- Its role, benefits or significance in today's marketing
- Information about public relation department, head of that departments with qualifications and experience, sporting staff, and facilities
- Special efforts made, and methods used by the company to establish and maintain public relations
- According to company, the effects of public relations on sales volume, profitability, reputation, competitiveness, etc.
- Past year data on money spent for the purpose
- Cost effectiveness: The actual contribution of money spent for the above effort

Students' overall observation, suggestions and conclusion.

8. Physical Distribution and Channel decisions.

The topic includes two aspects – physical distribution and channel of distribution. Chapter 8 describes relevant aspects. Students who want to prepare report/project on this topic have to collect detail on following points:

Physical Distribution: It covers following points:

- Introduction
- Concept, features and its role.
- Company's physical distribution objectives
- Who decides on physical activities?
- Detail about company's physical distribution activities including transportation, warehousing, communication, banking, insurance, inventory, order processing, middlemen (marketing channel) and other relevant issues for firm's national and international marketing activities.
- Organisation structure of physical distribution department – chart, staff and facilities.

Channel of Distribution: It includes:

- Introduction
- Concept, features, types and its role (theory)
- Type of company's marketing channel(s).
- Functions and services of marketing channel(s).
- Who decides on marketing channel?
- Factors affecting channel decisions
- Relationship between selling price and cost of marketing channel.
- Salient features of company's channel of distribution
- Performance of company's marketing channel in relation to sales/profits objectives, consumer satisfaction and competitiveness.
- Students' overall observation, suggestions and conclusion.

9. Product and Pricing Related Strategies.

The topic consists of two marketing mix decisions – product decisions and pricing decisions. Students have to study all relevant aspects these decisions.

Product Related Strategies

(**Note:** Refer Product Related Strategies, point 5)

Pricing Related Strategies

(**Note:** Refer Pricing Decisions in the former part)

10. Product and Promotion Related Strategies.

The topic consists of two marketing mix decisions – product decision and promotion decision. Students have to study all relevant aspects these decisions.

Product Related Strategies

(**Note:** For detail, refer product decisions)

Promotion Related Strategies

(**Note:** For detail, refer promotion decisions)

11. Product and Distribution Related Decisions.

The topic consists of two marketing mix decisions – product decision and promotion decision. Students have to study all relevant aspects these decisions.

Product Decisions

(**Note:** Refer Product Decisions)

Distribution Decisions

(**Note:** Refer Distribution Decisions)

12. Price and Promotion Related Decisions.

The topic consists of two marketing mix decisions – product decision and promotion decision. Students have to study all relevant aspects these decisions.

Price Related Decisions

(Note: Refer Pricing Decisions)

Promotion Related Decisions

(**Note:** Refer promotion decisions)

13. Price and Distribution Related Decisions.

The topic consists of two marketing mix decisions – product decision and promotion decision. Students have to study all relevant aspects these decisions.

Price Related Decisions

(Note: Refer Pricing Decisions)

Distribution Related Decisions

(**Note:** Refer Distribution Decisions)

14. Promotion and Distribution Related Decisions.

The topic consists of two marketing mix decisions – product decision and promotion decision. Students have to study all relevant aspects these decisions.

Promotion Related Decisions

(**Note:** Refer Promotion Decisions)

Distribution Related Decisions

(**Note:** Refer Distribution Decisions)

15. A Detailed Study on Advertising Activities of Company.

In this topic, students have to study advertising practices of the concerned business unit and have to collect necessary information about all the issues related to advertising efforts of the unit.

(**Note:** For detail, refer Promotion Decisions, particularly, Advertising)

16. Relevance of Sales Promotion Efforts in the Company.

This topic relates with only sales promotion efforts of the firm.

(**Note:** For detail, refer Promotion Decisions, particularly, Sales Promotion)

17. Sales Management including Sales Force Management.

This topic covers all relevant issues of sales management. Students are required to study activities of sales department of company. Under the topic, following points can be included:

- Concept of sales management and sales force management
- Organisation firm's of sales department, charts and brief explanation
- Objectives of sales management
- Duties and functions of sales managers and officers including storage, inventory control, order processing, dispatching, transportation, billing and other relevant activities.
- Sales force management. (**Note:** For detail, refer Promotion Decisions, particularly, Personal Selling)

18. Sales Force (Personal Selling) Management in the Company.

The topic only concern with personal selling activities of the firm. Students have to study all important decisions related to personal selling efforts of company.

(**Note:** For detail, refer Promotion Decisions, particularly, Personal Selling)

19. A Study on Advertising and Sales Promotion Efforts in the Company.

Under this topic, students have to study company's advertising and sales promotion efforts.

Company's Advertising Efforts

(**Note:** For detail, refer Promotion Decisions, particularly, Advertising)

Company's Sales Promotion Efforts

(**Note:** For detail, refer Promotion Decisions, particularly Sales Promotion)

20. Advertising and Personal Selling Efforts.

The topic contains are two major points – advertising and personal selling. Students are required to collect details on advertising and personal selling from executives of the business unit.

Company's Advertising Efforts

(**Note:** For detail, refer Promotion Decisions, particularly, Advertising)

Company's Personal Selling Efforts

(**Note:** For detail, refer Promotion Decisions, particularly, Personal Selling)

21. Analysis of Advertising and Publicity Practices in the Company.

Students, under the topic, have to study two aspects of market promotion – advertising and publicity in relation to the concerned firm.

Advertising Practices

(**Note:** For detail, refer Promotion Decisions, particularly, advertising)

Publicity Practices

(**Note:** For detail, refer Promotion Decisions, particularly, Publicity)

22. Role of Public Relations and Publicity in today's Marketing Practices.

Students have to study publicity and public relations practices of particular company.

(**Note:** For detail, refer Promotion Decisions, particularly, Publicity and Public Relations).

23. A study on Marketing Research Practices in the Company.

This topic concerns with marketing research practices of the company. Students can study following aspects under this tile:

- Introduction
- Concept and nature (theory portion)
- Organisation firm's marketing research department – chart and brief description.
- Who performs marketing research activities?
- Marketing research objectives (manager's views)
- Significance of marketing research in today's marketing practices (manager's views)
- Types data used by the company
- Company's research design
- Population and sampling decisions
- Sources used by the company to collect data
- Tools used for data collection (with special reference to questionnaire
- Methods practiced by the company to collect data
- Field work
- Costs of marketing research activities – costs incurred during past few years
- Data analysis – who performs this task and methods used?
- Marketing research process practiced by the firm

- Research report – format, important consideration, parts and chapters, and who prepares it.
- Practical utility of marketing research as perceived by the manager.
- Student's overall observation and suggestions

24. An Analysis of MIS with Special Reference to Marketing Research.

This topic relates with management information. It contains two aspects – Marketing Information System (MIS) and Marketing Research.

Marketing Information System

- Concept and nature (theory portion)
- Objectives of MIS (manager's views)
- Its usefulness in planning and controlling
- Company's MIS – organisation, staff, structure, facilities, components and special features

Marketing Research

(**Note:** For detail, refer Marketing Research, topic number 23)

25. Issues Related to New Product Development and Product Related Strategies.

The topic concerns with key issues related to new product development practices of the firm. The topic can be divided into two parts – new product development practices and product related strategies.

New Product Development Practices

- Concept of new product
- Who deals with new product development decisions?
- Company's Objective(s) to develop a new product
- Important issues that company considers while developing a new product
- New product development option(s) adopted by the firm
- Detailed study of new product development process of the company.
- Relevance of consumer adoption process. (How is it useful to manager?)
- Comparison of company's new product development process with theory and relevant comment of the students.
- Past experience related to new product development.
- Costs incurred by the firm for developing a new product.

Product Related Strategies

This sub-topic involves product related strategies of company including branding, packaging, labeling and after sales services

(**Note:** For detail, refer Product Related Strategies, topic number 5).

26. An analytical Study of Product Life Cycle with Relevant Strategies.

The topic is, in fact, a part of new product development decisions. But it only concerns with launching a new product in the market. Product life cycle starts when new product development process ends. Students have to study only product life cycle related aspects. The topic involves:

- Introduction
- Concept of product life cycle with stages and figure, conditions for ideal 'S' shaped cured, its usefulness and limitations (theoretical portion).

- Life cycle of company's product – stages, current stages and diagram. (Students can prepare life cycle diagram with the help of past few years' information on sales and profits).
- Systematic study of all stages in terms of sales, profits, competition, etc.
- Detailed study of company's marketing strategies for each of the stages of product life cycle and students' relevant comment.
- Manager's views on product life cycle – usefulness and practical problems.
- Relevance of product diffusion and consumer adoption

27. Relevance of Product Life Cycle and Consumer Adoption Process.

In this topic, students have to assess practical utility of product life cycle concept and consumer adoption process with reference to the business firm under study. The topic can be divided into two parts:

Product Life Cycle

(**Note:** For detail, refer topic number 26).

Consumer Adoption

The subtopic concerns with practical study of consumer adoption process. It may involve:

- Concept, process, and significance (theoretical portion).
- Manager's views on usefulness of the concept.
- Does manager take clues from implications of consumer adoption process?
- Implications consumer adoption process for formulating marketing strategies.
- Students' overall observation, suggestions and conclusion.

28. A systematic Study on Branding, Packaging, Labeling, and Trade marking.

(**Note:** For detail, refer Product Related Strategies, topic number 5).

29. Issues Related to New Product Development, Product Life Cycle, and Consumer Adoption.

The topic covers the study of various issues related to new product development, product life cycle and consumer adoption process with reference to particular business unit.

(**Note:** For detail, refer topic number 25, 26 and 27)

30. International Marketing

Students have study international marketing operations of the concerned enterprise. It covers a study of all elements (4Ps) in relations to international business of the unit. For conceptual detail, refer chapter 13. The topic covers following points:

- Introduction
- Concept, features, and role of international marketing (theoretical aspects).
- Company's objectives of international marketing.
- Introduction to company's international business – names of nations, proportion of domestic and international business, historical background of company's international trade and forces, objectives of international marketing, special problems facing company, etc.
- Brief explanation of organisation structure for international marketing including type of organisation, whether separate department or part of the main organisation, functions manager dealing with interlamination marketing activities, his subordinates and superiors, etc.

- Company's international marketing environment – opportunities, threats and factors of international environment; role and assistance of domestic and international agencies (organisations) – names and activities of such organisations.
- Brief outline marketing mix for international marketing. Students are required to discuss all these elements of marketing mix for international business. This is the main point in this topic and must be discussed in detail. (Note: For detail, refer topic number 3)
- Marketing research activities in regard to international marketing.
- Company's future plan for international trade.
- Students' overall observation, conclusions, and suggestions.

31. Modern Marketing and Social Responsibility.

This can be a theoretical topic. Students can work on the topic purely on secondary data. However, the topic can also be studied by primary data. When primary data are to be used, students have to undertake survey of a few companies to find out the way they operate and discharge social responsibilities. The topic may include following points:

- Introduction
- Theoretical background of social responsibilities – concept, key elements, scope
- A detail study of modern marketing including definitions, central theme, key features of modern marketing, illustrations of companies, management philosophies, international trend concepts, priorities, etc
- Students should study the corporate practices in relation to social responsibilities including activities, policies, contribution, budget, etc.
- Evaluation of past year efforts and contribution for social responsibilities including comparison with leading national and international business enterprises.
- Students' overall observation, conclusions, and suggestions.

32. A Survey on Consumer Trend (behaviour) in Specific Region.

Students are required to carry out market survey in particular region. The survey can be conducted in relation to any company or consumer trend in general. Questionnaire can be prepared in relation to consumers' response/priority to quality, availability, value, brand image, etc.

Criteria to be Included in Survey

Normally survey consists of the study consumers' behaviour (response) to following criteria:

- Product quality
- Product availability
- Price
- Product features
- Company reputation and brand image, packaging and labeling
- After sales services. (All services must be included. Refer topic number 5).

Market Survey Report

- Introduction
- Objectives
- Methodology – research design including population of the study, sampling, types of data, sources, tools, field work, etc. must be stated.

- Findings and interpretation with charts and figures (how much emphasis is given to every aspects while taking buying decision).
- Problems faced by the students and limitation of study

Students' overall observation, conclusions, and suggestions

33. Study and Analysis of Public Relations, Customer Orientation, and Integrated Marketing with Reference to the Company.

Students have to study these aspects in relations to the company. They have to verify application of marketing theory/philosophy in actual marketing practices.

Public Relations

- Introduction
- Meaning and definitions
- Its role, benefits or significance in today's marketing
- Information about public relation department, head of that departments with qualifications and experience, sporting staff, and facilities
- Special efforts made, and methods used by the company to establish and maintain public relations
- According to company, the effects of public relations on sales volume, profitability, reputation, competitiveness, etc.
- Past year data on money spent for the purpose

Customer Orientation

- Introduction
- Meaning and definition
- Points or contents involved in customer orientation – marketer's perception of customers (how does the company perceive customer orientation?), customer satisfaction, long-term welfare, way to treating customer, response of trader, relation building, offerings, etc.
- Its role, benefits or significance in today's marketing.
- Company's efforts: How does company actualize customer orientations in the real practice? Or efforts made by the company to practice the concept.
- Conclusion: According to you, does company practice customer orientation?
- Suggestions: What do think the company should do in this regard?

Integrated Marketing

- Introduction
- Meaning and definitions
- What aspects are involved in integrated marketing
- Its role, benefits or significance of it in today's marketing.
- Does the company follow this concept? How?
- According to you, what should the company do to practice this philosophy?
- How does integrated marketing reflect in sales, profits, customer satisfaction, etc.?

Students' overall observation, conclusions, and suggestions

34. Functioning of the (ANY DISTRICT) District Consumer Forum

Students can work on functioning of the District forum of any district. They have to visit the District Forum, discuss with presidents and members to get necessary details. The topic may include:

- Introduction – consumers' plight in India, need of legal protection, list of various Acts with special reference to the Consumer Protection Act.
- Consumer Protection Act and various authorities.
- Consumer Dispute Redressal Agencies – brief idea of the National Commission, the State Commission and the District Forum
- A detail study of various provisions of District Forum along with recent amendments
- Study of particular district forum – establishment, address of office, timing, facilities, authorities (president and members), qualifications of members, etc.
- Functioning of district forum – Procedure to file complaints, costs, evidences, etc.
- Complaints received by the forum in last two to five years, and settlement of disputes.
- Special efforts and activities for consumer awareness and protection of their rights.
- Other relevant aspects can be included in the topic
- Students' overall observation, conclusions, and suggestions.

35. Constitution (key provisions) and Effects of Consumer Protection Act on Company's Marketing Decisions.

The topic concerns with a detailed study and application of Consumer Protection Act, 1986. Students have to discuss main provisions, recent amendments made by the Government, and objectives of the Act. This topic depends on primary as well as secondary data. For collection of primary data, students can select a few business units as a sample to study impacts of the provisions of the Act on their functioning and decisions-making. Those students who want to work on the topic are required to study the Act in detailed and have to find our relevant aspects. On the basis of key provisions, students can prepare questionnaire. In short, this is survey-based topic and it may contain following points:

- Introduction – Needs of providing the legal protection to consumers, social responsibility of businessmen, consumerism, practices adopted by other countries, and relevant aspects can be mentioned in introductory part.
- Objectives of the study
- Methodology – nature, scope, type of data, sources data, population, sample, data collection tools including questionnaire, data collection methods, fieldwork, analysis of data, etc. points can be discussed in methodology.
- Brief study of various Acts formulated by Indian Government to protect consumer rights and interests.
- A detailed study of Consumer Protection Act, 1986.
- Data collection and analysis
- Findings and limitations
- Students' observation, conclusions and suggestions.

36. Prospects, problems, and remedies of Cyber Marketing (e-marketing)

The topic concerns with cyber or online marketing practices. For theoretical detail, refer chapter 2 on emerging issues. Students are required to assess this option of promoting and distributing products. With reference to those companies practicing cyber marketing, the students have to collect data, analyse the same and have to put their comment in the report.

Important points to address include:

- Concept and features
- Applicability of cyber marketing (in term of different fields)
- Marketing Activities via cyber marketing

- Cyber marketing process
- Benefits offered by cyber marketing
- The future prospects of cyber marketing
- Infrastructure and mentality of customers
- Limitations
- Issues Cyber Crime
- Practical experience of some companies
- A few suggestions

37. Impact of legal provisions of a few Acts closely related to consumer protection.

Particular topic involves study, application and impact of legal provision meant for consumer protection. Students can study and assess important provisions of four to five Acts. Acts may include Consumer Protection Act, Food and Adulteration Act, Essential Commodity Act, Brand Name and Trade Mark Act, or any other.

38. Green Marketing

The topic concern with green marketing practices. It involves all issues related to company's green marketing philosophy and efforts. For detail, refer chapter 2. The topic may include:

- Introduction and concept
- Need and importance
- Factors necessitating Green Marketing
- Global efforts to promote green marketing and Green Marketing practices across the world
- Green marketing efforts in India – various methods or ways practiced in India.
- Prospects and constraints related to Green Marketing
- Role of citizens in green marketing

Students can prepare report on green marketing practices and/efforts in particular region or by particular company.

39. Marketing Services

Students can undertake project on service marketing. For theoretical detail, refer chapter 11. The topic may contain:

- Introduction
- Meaning and key features of services.
- Key services of relevant service sector unit.
- Marketing mix for service
- Importance of personal dealing with customers
- Students' observation, conclusions and suggestions

40. Retailing

Students can prepare their practical reports on retailing practices in India. They can also prepare their project on functioning of particular retail chain, departmental store, or shopping malls. They are required to study every aspect related to retail trade. For detail, refer chapter 12.

41. Study on Competitive Strategy of the Company

Students, under the topics, are required to analyse company's competitive strategy. For detail refer 15. The topic may include:

- Competition – a key influencer in marketing decisions
- Company's competitive position in market

- Main competitors of the company and their brief profile
- Process followed by the company for analysing competitors
- Who decides on competition strategy and how?
- Company's marketing strategy for competitors – as a leader, challenger, follower, or as a nicher
- Students' observation, conclusions and suggestions

42. Marketing Control Practices

The topic is associated with company's controlling system for marketing operations. For detail, refer chapter 14. The topic may covers following points:

- Concepts, meaning, and process
- Role of marketing control system (company's views)
- Who performs controlling task and how?
- MIS and controlling system
- Tools and methods used for controlling marketing operations
- Qualities of good controlling system with reference to company concern
- Students' observation, conclusions and suggestions

PART III
GUIDELINE FOR REPORT PREPARATION

Practical training report at graduate level (for example, for the second and the third year BBA) can be divided into two parts – General Information and Main Report.

GENERAL INFORMATION

This part consists of general information about the industrial unit. Students have to collect brief information about the unit irrespective of the area of study or the topic. Normally, following points are included:

1. Full name of company and relevant details
2. Registered office.
3. Location aspects
4. Form of organisation (ownership) and size of business unit.
5. Names of promoters and present body of management.
6. Brief history and development the unit.
7. Manufacturing process and products, and other product related aspects.
8. Organisational structure – organisation chart, type and explanation.
9. Time keeping system.
10. Number of employees and services offered to them.
11. Contribution of the unit to the industry.
12. Special achievements (awards, prizes and certificates) received by the company.
13. Future prospects and plan
14. Other relevant information, if any.

MAIN REPORT

This part contains subject or topic-related details. The second year BBA/BBM students have to explain activities and operations of three departments i.e. marketing departments, financial department, and personnel department. Whereas the third year students have to state practical aspects related to the topic assigned by concerned teacher or selected by the students. Main report contains:

1. Name of topic or title.
2. Brief explanation of the selected topic.
3. Definitions, importance, and contents of the topic to be studied.
4. Study of the topic/subject areas with company. This is the main part of the report. Here, student has to collect information about every aspect of the topic or specific area of management from the relevant officials of the company concern. The student is required to prepare questionnaire to collect information. He is has to undergo theoretical study prior to the training.
5. Conclusion: Students must mention following issues in the conclusion:
   i. Management qualities
   ii. Market performance
   iii. Future plan of the company
   iv. Future prospect, according to the student, in relation to current marketing environment
   v. Special suggestions of the students to improve marketing performance
   vi. Problems faced by the students during training
   vii. Value of industrial training (Utility of such training practical)

GUIDELINE TO CONDUCT PROJECT REPORT IN MARKETING

Students have to follow certain guideline during training, and also while preparing practical reports. They have to observe a number of provisions. Some important issues have been discussed here.

GENERAL PROVISIONS (As per some Universities of Gujarat)

1. The Second Year B.B.A., the Third Year B.B.A. and other management students attending the industrial unit for the Practical Training shall abide by all rules, regulations and conditions prescribed for them. They shall observe general discipline expected by the industrial unit.
2. They will remain present in the office every day and for the full working day and will not leave office even for some time in a day or for a whole day without obtaining the prior permission of the executive concerned.
3. In cash of practical training of SY BBA students, every student will generally be placed under an executive of the industrial unit who will make arrangement for his/her training in various departments.
4. The executive in charge of the training for SY BBA & TY BBA students will observe the working as well as behaviour of the students during the period of training.
5. Every student will obtain prior sanction of the proper executive for all the data relating to the unit to be included in the report it would be better if a "No Objection" certificate from the executive concerned is obtained so as to avoid complication in future.
6. The students are expected to meet all their expenses of their practical training. The colleges as well as the industrial unit are not expected to pay them stipend, honorarium or any kind of financial aid. However, the college will have no objection if, in some special cases, the industrial unit pays the student some amount in order to meet the expenses on practical training. In such circumstances, it would be better if the college is informed thereof.

CERTIFICATE NORMS

Each student shall obtain an attendance certificate from the appropriate executive of the business unit. It must contain needed particulars. This certificate will be attached to the report to be submitted to the University for the Assessment, and a copy of such certificate will be submitted to the college for record. The certificate must contain following detail:

i. Name of student in full, Roll Number and Class.
ii. Name of the Academic Institute.
iii. Date from which the training was started and the same was ended.
iv. General behaviour of students during their stay in industrial unit.
v. Reference Number and the date of the certificate, name and designation of the executive signing the certificate.

STRUCTURE (OUTLINE OR FORMAT) OF PROJECT REPORT

The students should observe certain norms while drafting the final training reports. Some colleges have set their common provisions. For example, N. R. Vekaria Institute of Business Management Studies, affiliated with Saurashtra University, Rajkot underlines following provisions for Practical Training Report for the Second Year BBA and the Third Year BBA:

1. **Font Type:** Time New Roman
2. **Paper Size:** A4 (8.27" X 11.69")
3. **Paper Type:** Medium quality white paper without boarder design or boarder line.
4. **Font Size:** 14pt.
5. **Line Spacing:** Double Spacing
6. **Colour of Cover page:** Blank Colour or Blue Colour (as specified by the concerned college and/or university.
7. **Chapter Plan or Structure of Report:** Students can prepare their report in different parts as per the provisions of the concerned universities and instructions of subject teachers. Normally, following format is used.
   a. **Cover Page:** Full name of student, roll number, name of topic and the name of industrial unit.
   b. **Title Page:** Full name of students, standard, roll/seat number, class, area of study and name of topic, name and address of industrial unit, name and address of college/institute, month and year, etc.
   c. **Company Detail:** Name, address, phones, fax, website, e-mail address, etc.
   d. **A Copy of the Certificate:** One has to attach the (copy of) certificate issued by the company concerned.
   e. **Certificate Issued by the College (Optional):** students can attach the certificate if the same has been issued by the college authority or the guiding teacher.
   f. **Acknowledge:** Students should acknowledge the cooperation or contribution of those who contributed directly or indirectly before, during, and after the training. It may contain expressing sincere thanks to teachers (the guide), principals (head, or director), and trainer executive and other employees of the concerned unit, typist, friends, relatives, parents, and so forth. In short, the students have to accept obligation of all those who assisted in collection of information, analysis and preparation of report.
   g. **Preface:** In this part, provisions of the university, need of practical training, name and brief detail of company, brief idea of topic and field of training, training time,

brief contents/chapter of the report, and other relevant issues can be discussed. It is just like introduction.

h. **Index with Contents and Page Number:** serial number, name of topic and the page number should be stated.

i. **Methodology (Optional):** Students may brief up the methodology they followed to collect, analyse, and interpreter the data. They can mention methods they have followed and tool used.

j. **General Information:** (As stated earlier in the same chapter)

k. **Main report:** It contains the topic-related information. It is the unique part of the report and includes theoretical explanation of the topic – definitions, feature, and (contents) scope. Students have to explain the topic in relation to the company. The part concerns with practical study and all relevant details must be furnished. (For more detail, refer Contents of Report, in the former part of the chapter

l. **Conclusion:** students have to conclude their entire work in one or two pages. Final outcomes of training should be highlighted. They have to explain their overall observation including problems they faced, companies current performance and the future plan, drawbacks they detected in management of company, their suggestions to improve performance, and other related aspects. In case of analytical work, final results or outcomes can be summarized.

m. **Bibliography:** In this part, names of books, magazines, reports, other references used must be written. Names of publisher, edition, and year of publication can be mentioned. Students may write separately books, magazines, reports, etc.

n. **Appendix (if necessary):** Here, additional details can be attached. The part may contain a copy of questionnaire, printed forms used for collection of data and/or recording response of respondents, statement of expenses, tables and charts not used in the main report, pictures, pamphlets, or any other information seem relevant.

8. **Other Rules:** Apart from above provisions, there are some minor provisions that students have to observe while drafting the report. They include:

   i. Reports should be written on one side of a paper in a clear and legible handwriting or be typed. Page Number must be given on the right side of page at top.

   ii. Each student will write his/her name, roll number, class, academic year and the name of the institute on the first page. The Third Year B. B. A. students have to state the area of study as well as the topic/title of the area. Students have to attach paper sticker on the cover with needed details.

   iii. In the title page, students must write name & the address of the organisation where training was taken along with the date of beginning and completing the training.

   iv. Each student shall prepare four copies of the report. He/she should send one copy to the industrial unit concerned and obtain a receipt thereof, and submit the same to the college for the record. He/she will submit two copies to the college office on or before the date fixed by the college authority. One of the copies will be sent to the University for Assessment, while another will be retained by the college for the future reference. The last copy will be retained by the student for his/her personal record. The student can retained any of the copies. The college may withdraw the examination forms of such students who do not submit their reports in time as notified. (Actions depend on the contemporary norms of institute and/or university)

v. Each student will draft his/her report independently. Joint report by more than one student even if they worked in the same industrial unit on the same project is not permissible. No. student shall copy from another report.

vi. All B. B. A. students are required to appear at viva arranged by the university as a part of the university assessment on the date(s) to be notified by the university.

vii. The reports shall be assessed by the panel of examiners appointed by the university. Two criteria shall be considered while assessing the training report, (1) Training Report (2) Performance in the Viva-Voce. Marks allocation between Report and Viva-voce depends on the contemporary provisions of the university.

BIBLIOGRAPHY

Books:

1. **Chunawalla, S. A. & Sethia, K. C,** Foundation of Advertising, (2002), 5th ed., Himalaya Publishing House, New Delhi.
2. **Green, Paul E., & Tull, Donald, S.,** Research for Marketing Decisions, (1996), Prentice-Hall of India Pvt. Limited, New Delhi.
3. **Kapoor, V. K.,** Operation Research Techniques for Management,(2006), 7th ed., Sultan Chand & Sons Publication, New Delhi.
4. **Kotler, Philip & Armstrong, Gary,** Principles of Marketing (2000), Prentice-Hall of India Pvt. Limited, New Delhi.
5. **Kotler, Philip, Marketing Management,** (1998), Prentice-Hall of India Pvt. Ltd., Hew Delhi.
6. **Kothari, C. R.,** Research Methodology, (1990), 3rd ed., Wishwa prakashan,. New Delhi.
7. **Kundiff, Still & Govoni,** Fundamentals of Modern Marketing,(1980)
8. **Mamoria, C. B. & Mamoria, S.** Marketing Management, (1991), Kitab Mahal, New Delhi
9. **Onkvisit, Sak and Shaw John,** International Marketing, 3rd ed., Prentice-Hall of India Pvt. Limited, New Delhi.
10. **Pathan, Swapna,** Retailing Management, Tata McGraw-Hill Publishing Company, Ltd, New Delhi, 2008.
11. **Pane, Adrian,** The Essence of Services Marketing, (1998), Prentice-Hall of India Pvt. Limited, New Delhi.
12. **Rao, K. Rama Mohan,** Services Marketing, Person Education, New Delhi, 2005.
13. **Saxena, Rajan,** Marketing Management, Tata McGraw-Hill Publishing Company Ltd., New Delhi.
14. **Schiftman, Leon,** Consumer Behavior, 7th ed., (2002), Prentice-Hall of India Pvt. Limited, New Delhi.
15. **Sharlekar, S. A.,** Marketing Management, (2007) Himalaya Publishing House, New Delhi.
16. **Singh, Awadhesh Kumar& Pandey, Satyaprakash** Rural Marketing – Indian Perspective, (2005), New Age International Pvt. Limited, New Delhi.
17. **Vora, N. D.,** Quantitative Techniques in Management, (1992), Tata McGraw-Hill Publishing House Co., Ltd., New Delhi.